SCOTLAND GUIDE

BE A TRAVELER - NOT A TOURIST!

Dan McQuillan

OPEN ROAD PUBLISHING

This guide is dedicated to my parents, Bill and Versie, who are after all, the real inspiration behind my writing.

1st Edition

Front cover photo and top back cover photo©Douglas Corrance. Lower back cover photo courtesy of British Tourist Authority.

Maps by James Ramage.

All information, including prices, is subject to change. The author has made every effort to be as accurate as possible, but neither he nor the publisher assumes responsibility for the services provided by any business listed in this guide; for any errors or omissions; or any loss, damage, or disruptions in your travel for any reason.

TABLE OF CONTENTS

1. INTRODUCTION 13

2. OVERVIEW 14

3. SUGGESTED ITINERARIES 24

4. LAND & PEOPLE 35
Land 35
People 39

5. A SHORT HISTORY 43

6. PLANNING YOUR TRIP 62
Before You Go 62
   When to Visit – Climate & Weather 62
   What to Pack 63
   Entry Requirements 64
   Customs Regulations 65
   Scottish Representatives Abroad 66
Getting to Scotland 67
Hotel & Inn Terms 68
Getting Around Scotland 71
   By Bicycle 71
   By Bus 71
   By Car 72
   By Hitchhiking 79
   By Train 79
The Scottish Tourist Board 79
Cost of Travel 80

7. BASIC INFORMATION   83

Business Hours   83
Electricity   83
Embassies & Consulates   83
Health   83
Laundry   84
Money & Banking   84
Newspapers   85
Postal Service   85
Radio   86
Safety & Avoiding Trouble   86
Taxes   87
Television   87
Tipping   87
Telephones   88
Time   91
Weights & Measures   91

8. SPORTS & RECREATION   92

Professional Sports   92
   Rugby   92
   Soccer   92
Recreation   93
   Angling   94
   Bird Watching   95
   Cycling   95
   Golf   96
   Hillwalking   98
   Horseback Riding   99
   Highland Games   101
   Nessie Hunting   102
   Sailing & Windsurfing   102
   Scuba Diving   103
   Surfing   104

9. SHOPPING   105

10. TAKING THE KIDS   108

Suggested Kid's Itinerary for Edinburgh   108
Other Fun Activities   109

SCOTLAND

GUIDE

BE A TRAVELER ~ NOT A TOURIST!

OPEN ROAD TRAVEL GUIDES SHOW YOU
HOW TO BE A TRAVELER – NOT A TOURIST!

*Whether you're going abroad or planning a trip in the United States, take Open Road along on your journey. Our books have been praised by **Travel & Leisure, The Los Angeles Times, Newsday, Booklist, US News & World Report, Endless Vacation, American Bookseller, Coast to Coast,** and many other magazines and newspapers!*

Don't just see the world – experience it with Open Road!

ABOUT THE AUTHOR

Dan McQuillan is a professional writer specializing in travel and technical subjects. He is also the author of Open Road's *Ireland Guide*. Dan lives in Denver, Colorado, with his wife and six children. If you'd like to contact Dan directly about anything in this book, his e-mail address is: *danielmcq@juno.com*.

BE A TRAVELER, NOT A TOURIST - WITH OPEN ROAD TRAVEL GUIDES!

Open Road Publishing has guide books to exciting, fun destinations on four continents. As veteran travelers, our goal is to bring you the best travel guides available anywhere!

No small task, but here's what we offer:

• All Open Road travel guides are written by authors with a distinct, opinionated point of view – not some sterile committee or team of writers. Our authors are experts in the areas covered and are polished writers.

• Our guides are geared to people who want to make their own travel choices. We'll show you how to discover the real destination – not just see some place from a tour bus window.

• We're strong on the basics, but we also provide terrific choices for those looking to get off the beaten path and experience the country or city – not just see it or pass through it.

• We give you the best, but we also tell you about the worst and what to avoid. Nobody should waste their time and money on their hard-earned vacation because of bad or inadequate travel advice.

• Our guides assume nothing. We tell you everything you need to know to have the trip of a lifetime – presented in a fun, literate, no-nonsense style.

• And, above all, we welcome your input, ideas, and suggestions to help us put out the best travel guides possible.

11. FOOD & DRINK   111

Food   111
Scotland's Best Restaurants   113

12. SCOTLAND'S BEST PLACES TO STAY   120

13. EDINBURGH   134

Arrivals & Departures   136
Orientation   138
Getting Around Town   138
Where to Stay   140
Where to Eat   161
Seeing the Sights   178
Nightlife & Entertainment   191
Sports & Recreation   194
Excursions & Day Trips   195
    St. Andrews   196
    Dundee   202
    Near Dundee   204
    Linlithgow   206
Practical Information   207

14. GLASGOW   210

Arrivals & Departures   211
Orientation   213
Getting Around Town   213
Where to Stay   215
Where to Eat   232
Seeing the Sights   247
Nightlife & Entertainment   257
Sports & Recreation   260
Shopping   261
Excursions & Day Trips   262
    Loch Lomond   262
    Stirling   267
    Doune   273
    Callander   274
    Killin   276
    Ayr & Alloway   281
    Maybole   287
    Troon   288
Practical Information   289

15. THE HIGHLANDS   292

Inverness   294
Tongue   318
Durness   320
Ullapool   324
Loch Ness   328
John O'Groats   335
Southern Highlands   335
Fort William   337
Oban   345

16. THE GRAMPIAN HIGHLANDS   347

Aberdeen   348
    The Castle Trail   358
    The Malt Whisky Trail   362
        Near Stonehaven   366
        Royal Deeside   366
        Banchory   367
Ballater & Balmoral Castle   368
Braemar   373
Dufftown   377
Elgin   378
Perth   380
Pitlochry   385

17. THE BORDERS & THE SOUTHWEST   388

Melrose   390
Dryburgh   396
Jedburgh   398
Selkirk   402
Kelso   405
Peebles   409
Dumfries   412
Kirkcudbright   419
Wigtown   422

18. THE ISLANDS   424

Isle of Skye   426
Isle of Mull   434
Iona & Staffa   438
Isle of Arran   441

The Outer Hebrides – Lewis & Harris   445
   Lewis   446
   Harris   449
Orkney   451
The Shetland Islands   464

INDEX   478

MAPS
Scotland   15
Edinburgh Hotels   142-143
Edinburgh Restaurants   164-165
Edinburgh Sights   180-181
Glasgow Hotels   216-217
Glasgow Restaurants   234-235
Glasgow Sights   248-249
The Highlands   293
The Grampian Highlands   349
The Boders & The Southwest   389
The Hebrides   425
Orkney & Shetland   455

SIDEBARS

Great Scots!   36-37
Facts on Scotland   38
The Thistle – National Emblem of Scotland   39
Scotland – More or Less!   42
The Tomboy Queen   55
Average Daytime High Temperatures
in Edinburgh (Fahrenheit)   63
What's Happening When?   70
Round-Abouts   73
Scottish Driving Terms   77
Scottish Mileage Chart   78
Exchange Rates   85
Telephone Codes   88
Watching the Costs Calling Home   89
Useful Telephone Numbers   90
Cycling Tour Operators   96
Walking Tour Operators   99
So You Want to be a Bagpiper?   106
Some Scottish Dining Terms   113
Scotland's Top Scotch Whiskies   119
Edinburgh's Must-See Sights   135
Edinburgh's Best Places to Stay   146
Edinburgh's Top Restaurants   166
The Edinburgh Festival – Party Time!   182
The Strange Case of Deacon William Brodie   185
Glasgow's Must-See Sights   211
Glasgow's Best Places to Stay   221
Glasgow's Top Restaurants   237
The Glasgow Coat of Arms   251
Tour the Trossachs   267
A Recipe Worth Trying   279
The Highland's Must-See Sights   294
Best Places to Stay in the Highlands   296
The Massacre of Glencoe   344
The Grampian Highland's Must-See Sights   348
Best Places to Stay in the Grampian Highlands   351
Hitting the Malt Whisky Trail   364
The Murder of a King   383
The Borders & the Southwest's Must-See Sights   390
Best Places to Stay in the the Borders & the Southwest   392
Melrose Abbey in Poem   395
Flodden Field   404
The Killing Times   423
The Islands' Must-See Sights   426
Best Places to Stay in the Islands   427
Quarreling Saints   440
Up Helly AA Festival   466

1. INTRODUCTION

Scotland. The very mention of the name conjures up visions of swirling kilts and skirling bagpipes, Highland heather and lowland bogs, Loch Ness and her fabled monster Nessie. But Scotland is so much more – and so much more is what you'll experience in *Scotland Guide*.

Simply stated, Scotland is an extraordinary place. I will help you experience every aspect of Scotland, from her heather-clad Highlands to her daisy- and bluebell-carpeted Borders area, from her western isles to the castles and dungeons of scores of monarchs. In between, you'll comb through the ruins of an ancient civilization and discover such popular tourist sights as Edinburgh Castle and the Palace of Holyroodhouse. You'll explore Urquhart Castle and sit in her shadow as you peer through the Highland fog for a glimpse of Nessie, the monster that put Scotland on the map. You'll enjoy exploring Edinburgh and love the striking architecture of Glasgow, proud owner of the title, "United Kingdom City of Architecture and Design." You'll cheer Scottish victories over the English at Stirling and Bannockburn, and then you'll weep with them over their crushing defeat at Culloden.

You will learn the dark secrets of the beautiful and flamboyant Mary Queen of Scots and her ambition to unite the thrones of England and Scotland – under her. You'll thrill at the exploits of William Wallace, Bonnie Prince Charlie and Robert the Bruce, and learn to curse the very names of Oliver Cromwell, Henry VIII and the Earl of Hertford.

Open Road's travel guides are acclaimed for their extensive hotel and restaurant sections, and this book is no exception. I have included an abundance of hotel reviews – spanning the range from low-cost cottages to the lavish luxury of castles and keeps. In the event you were hoping to eat during your holiday in Scotland, you will appreciate the many thoughtful, complete and accurate restaurant reviews.

So come along and prowl through the ruins of an ancient race. Come to know their heroes and cheer their deeds. Discover Scotland's past and appreciate her future.

2. OVERVIEW

Scotland is, in a word, magnificent. If you have never been here, you are in for a treat. (Actually, even if you *have* been here before, you'll still be in for a treat!) Scotland has so much to offer visitors that you will be assured of finding something that will be of interest to you. This book will help you experience some of the most popular tourist attractions Scotland has to offer, such as Edinburgh and Stirling Castles, the Palace of Holyroodhouse, Loch Ness, and the delightful Highland berg of Inverness. But through the pages of this guide, you'll find so much more.

If you have always wanted to see a vase from the Ming dynasty, paintings by Cezanne and sculptures by Rodin, then you'll definitely want to spend some time in the **Burrell Collection**, a fabulous museum on the outskirts of Glasgow. If you like castles furnished as they were in days gone by, then I'll take you inside the massive stone walls of Cawdor, Braemar, and Culzean castles. You say ruins are what really turn you on? Then be sure and stop by the extraordinary ruins of Kildrummy, Threave, or Urquhart castles (there are hundreds more, but these are among the grandest). These and many other fabulous sights are yours in Scotland.

For the purposes of this book, I have divided the country into four areas: **The Highlands**, **The Grampian Highlands**, **The Borders and the Southwest**, and **The Islands**. In addition, I have separate chapters for Scotland's two major cities: **Edinburgh** and **Glasgow**. Following is a short synopsis of the high points of each of the destination chapters:

EDINBURGH

Edinburgh is Scotland's capital city, and has a wonderful medieval feel and youthful buoyancy. It offers a wide variety of hotels, guesthouses and B&Bs, and some of the finest restaurants in Scotland call Edinburgh home. Depending on what you like to see and do, I believe you could easily spend a week exploring Edinburgh, and still leave more than a few stones unturned. Medieval castles and art galleries, museums and gardens, theaters and zoos all beckon you.

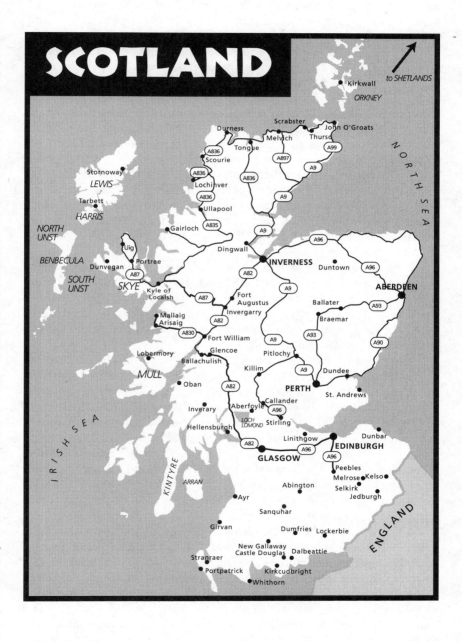

The central street in Edinburgh is called **The Royal Mile**, and it extends from **Edinburgh Castle** to the **Palace of Holyroodhouse**, with scores of interesting shops, restaurants and sites to explore in between. Edinburgh Castle has been the seat of Scottish monarchs since the 11th century, and has been renovated and furnished with period furnishings, tapestries, and artwork. As impressive as it is inside, it is exceptionally so from the outside. Perched atop an ancient volcanic mount, it has a commanding view of the surrounding city. Unfortunately, it also had commanding views of surrounding armies, and fell many times to the clutches of marauding English armies. At night it is floodlit and provides a surreal scene above the city. As you descend the Royal Mile from Edinburgh Castle toward the Palace of Holyroodhouse, you'll pass a number of historically significant sites. You'll be intrigued by the witch hunts that occurred in the very shadow of Edinburgh Castle, and if you look closely, you'll see Brodie's Close, the narrow alley down which **Deacon Brodie** lived. You'll learn a little about the good deacon, a former resident of Edinburgh and the real-life model for Robert Louis Stevenson's *Dr. Jekyll and Mr. Hyde.*

If you enjoy art galleries, Edinburgh has a number of excellent options for you to consider. My personal favorite is the **National Gallery of Scotland**. Located in the heart of the city, this wonderful gallery houses a number of fine art works by some of the world's most recognized artists, including such luminaries as Degas, Goya, Raphael, Rembrandt, Renoir, Rubens and Van Gogh.

The **Scottish National Portrait Gallery** is a wonderful place to acquaint yourself with the major historical figures of Scotland. Portraits of the highest echelon of Scottish society through the years are featured. Gaze upon the lovely Mary Queen of Scots and the heroic Flora MacDonald. Look into Bonnie Prince Charlie's eyes, or check out the countenance of the man who united the thrones of England and Scotland: James I.

If your tastes run more to modern art, then never fear – the **Scottish National Gallery of Modern Art** is for you. Picasso and Matisse, Kirchner and Koschka, and a host of other artists have their works displayed in this intriguing gallery. Sculptures and cubes, paintings and doodads provide a wonderful sensory adventure.

There are a number of fine museums in Edinburgh, and one of the best is the **Royal Museum of Scotland**. It houses a fascinating array of splendid objects that capture the imagination and might even send a shiver down your spine (note the *Maiden*, nickname for the guillotine that formerly dispensed justice in Edinburgh). The **Huntly House Museum** is often overlooked by visitors to Scotland, and it should not be. It is a restored 16th-century mansion decorated with period furnishings and works of art. It is an interesting peek into the way at least a few folks lived four hundred years ago. The **Museum of Childhood** on the Royal Mile is a fun and interesting museum for adults as well as children. Exhibits include a wide array of toys and games alongside sections on children's health and education. Four stories worth of things to see, it is well worth a nostalgic trip down memory lane.

Since we're discussing things for children to do, this is a good place to mention the **Edinburgh Zoo**. It is located about 10 minutes from the center of the city, and like zoos all over the world, it is a nice place for the kids to visit. They are proud to tell you that they have the world's largest penguin pool. Just north of the city center is a 70-acre park called the **Royal Botanic Garden**. Thousands of plants vie for your attention, and it is a pleasant respite from your normal hectic sightseeing pace.

As mentioned earlier, some of the best restaurants in the country are located in Edinburgh. They have combined a continental flair to their cooking with exceptionally fresh ingredients from the surrounding hills and valleys. The results are marvelous, and if you enjoy making elegant dining a part of your visit to Scotland, you'll not be disappointed.

Edinburgh's location in central Scotland makes it an ideal place from which to tour the surrounding countryside. There are many beautiful sites within a short drive from Edinburgh. For those of you who have traveled to Scotland to pay homage to **St. Andrews**, the fabled mecca of golf, you'll find it a short and pleasant drive from Edinburgh. Here you'll find the incredible Old Course, along with the six other courses that make up the St. Andrews golf complex.

Only slightly behind St. Andrews in the religious worship of the Golf Gods are the impressive courses of **Carnoustie** and **Gleneagles**. Carnoustie is just a hop, skip, and a jump north of St. Andrews, and Gleneagles is about an hour north of Edinburgh (depending on how many wrong turns you take!).

You'll find Scotland's national aquarium on the outskirts of Edinburgh in North Queensferry. **Deep Sea World** makes for a fascinating and delightful place to visit, especially if you've brought the kids and they are getting a little restless looking at castles, art galleries and museums. The trip is especially fun because you can get up-close and personal with 5,000 fish – visitors to the aquarium enter the fishy world via a clear acrylic tunnel that provides marvelous views.

If you've been captivated by Mary Queen of Scots (as this travel guide writer has been captivated), then you'll want to drive a short distance northwest of Edinburgh to visit the market town of Linlithgow. In addition to having great shops to explore, Linlithgow features Linlithgow Castle, Mary's birthplace.

GLASGOW

Glasgow is still basking in the glow of being named the "1999 UK City of Architecture and Design." They received that honor on the strength of their rich Victorian heritage and the lasting impression famed turn-of-the-century architect **Charles Rennie Mackintosh** left on the city.

When I think of Glasgow, I think of wonderful museums. And when I think of wonderful museums, I think of the **Burrell Collection**. I have been to museums all over the world, and square foot for square foot, I believe the Burrell Collection is the finest museum I have ever visited. Have you ever wanted to see a vase from the Ming Dynasty? How about some fine Egyptian artifacts? Or perhaps you're more interested in French impressionist artwork, or maybe even sculptures by Rodin. Regardless, I guarantee you'll find something to interest you here. It has been the most popular tourist attraction in Scotland for years.

The **Hunterian Art Gallery** is associated with the University of Glasgow. If you've ever wanted to see some of **James MacNeill Whistler**'s work (yes – he of *Whistler's Mother* fame), then this is a great place to stop. Many of his paintings are on display, and you'll see that he was truly a gifted artist. Unfortunately the portrait of his mother isn't located here – you'll have to journey to Paris to see her. In addition, there is an interesting exhibit on Charles Rennie Mackintosh. The museum has recreated his home and furnishings.

Another fine museum in Glasgow is the **Glasgow Art Gallery and Museum**. It is well designed and has a number of interesting displays. I particularly liked the collection of armor, including a life-size set of armor worn by the Imperial storm troopers from *Star Wars*! If your kids are getting tired of traditional museums, a fun place to visit is the **Museum of Transport**. A fascinating tour of locomotives, old automobiles and horseless carriages await your perusal. There is also a small exhibit on bicycles and their evolution that might interest your kids (you too!).

Another fun place to visit is the **Glasgow Gallery of Modern Art**, just south of George Square. This eclectic and avant-garde museum is chock-full of eccentricities. The basement, in particular, has a number of exhibits that are extraordinarily interesting for children (of all ages).

You'll certainly want to stop by the 12th-century **Glasgow Cathedral**. Featured briefly in **Sir Walter Scott's** *Rob Roy*, the cathedral is a cavernous monument to the faith and ability of ancient stonemasons. There are a number of interesting tombstones and memorials within the cathedral. Just outside the cathedral is the **Necropolis**, a cemetery with a plethora of interesting and elaborate tombs, crosses and statues. **Glasgow Green** is a large park that rests along the River Clyde. It is a pleasant place to stroll and people-watch during the spring and summer months. If you're lucky, you'll catch a street performer or two, but mostly you'll just see folks out and about and enjoying the green luxury of the park. Glasgow is an excellent base for exploring much of the central lowlands region of Scotland. Within an hour or so of Glasgow are the southern shores of famed **Loch Lomond**, famous because of a wonderful old Scottish ballad, but it is well worth the visit on the merits of its beauty alone. Picturesque and inviting, it is certainly worth a couple hours' exploration. Next to Loch Lomond is one of the most spectacular sections of the country. Known simply as **The Trossachs**, it is a region renowned for its beauty in a country renowned for its beauty. The rolling hills and tall peaks of the Trossachs are interspersed with lovely lochs here and there. Along with Loch Lomond, **Loch Katrine** also draws its fair share of visitors due to its beauty.

North of Glasgow about an hour is the market town of **Stirling**, which is to Scotland what Lexington is to the United States. It was here that Scottish rebels marshaled under **William Wallace** won a great victory for the Scots against a superior English army. A neo-Gothic monument exists to honor Sir Wallace's life and accomplishments, and **Stirling Castle** overlooks the site from a craggy mount nearby. Both are worth the time it takes to tour them.

Robert Burns is Scotland's national poet, and his stomping grounds were **Ayr** and **Alloway**, about 40 minutes south of Glasgow. His home and a small museum honor the poet and draw visitors from all over the world each year. You may not have heard much of Mr. Burns before now, but it is certain you are familiar with at least one of his works: *Auld Lang Syne*.

THE HIGHLANDS

If you're like me, the mere mention of the Highlands conjures up visions of misty mountains and marshy moors, Scotch whisky and lengthy lochs, whirling kilts and skirling bagpipes. Names such as Flora MacDonald, Bonnie Prince Charlie and Robert the Bruce are also indelibly linked to the Highlands. And I'm here to tell you that you won't be disappointed when you venture into this relatively wild area of Scotland.

Inverness is the best-known city in the Highlands. You'll find this fascinating berg resting peacefully along the verdant banks of the River Ness as it wends its way out to the North Sea. Originally a convenient gathering point for the Highland clans, Inverness has grown to a lovely and lively medium-sized city. Today it serves as an excellent base for exploring the northern and western stretches of the Highlands.

On the outskirts of Inverness is **Culloden Battlefield**, the site of a crushing defeat of Bonnie Prince Charlie's forces that essentially ended the Jacobite threat in Scotland. Nearby is the immensely interesting

Cawdor Castle, a castle immortalized in a little play by Shakespeare called *Macbeth*.

Inverness sits at the northern end of the **Great Glen**, a mammoth valley that very nearly slices off the Highlands from the rest of Scotland. Along the bottom of this Great Glen you'll find several long and slender lochs. The most famous of these lochs is **Loch Ness**, that great loch which boasts a monstrous fame. A short drive from Inverness, I guarantee you will crane your neck and search the rolling gray waters for a glimpse of Nessie, the famous yet elusive resident of the loch's depths.

Heading north out of Inverness takes you to one of the loneliest areas in all of Scotland. Lochs and tall heather-covered mounds dot the windswept landscape. Single-track roads are the standard here, but they seem ample to carry the traffic through this lonely area. I believe the drive between Inverness and the small but precise fishing village of **Ullapool** is one of the prettiest in Scotland. You'll wend among tree-lined roads, through velvet green hills and dales, and along sweeping lochs. If you decide to drive to the Isle of Skye, keep an eye out for picturesque **Eilean Donan Castle**, a marvelous 13th-century castle perched majestically along the shores of Loch Duich.

If you happen to be in the Highlands between mid-August and mid-September, lucky you! You needn't have me describe the fabulous scene you see everywhere you look. The heather is a glorious sight to see, dressed in violet, fuchsia, purple and a dozen other similar shades. It is fascinating and stunning all at the same time. Keep your eyes on the road – or better yet, find a place to pull off and admire the incredible panoramas unsurpassed on this beautiful planet of ours.

THE GRAMPIAN HIGHLANDS

The term the **Grampian Highlands** is a bit of a misnomer, in my opinion. This is an area of intense beauty and many fine castles and ruins, but it is not the Highlands, as you and I envision the Highlands. Nevertheless, it is certainly an area you should visit if you have the time.

Aberdeen is the principal city of the Grampian Highlands. It is called the "Granite City," because many of its buildings are constructed of the blue-gray stone. Aberdeen makes an excellent base from which to see the surrounding countryside and to see the marvelous ruins that are scattered about in this part of the country. And speaking of ruins, one of the best places to visit in this part of Scotland is **Kildrummy Castle**. These photogenic ruins will capture your imagination. Or perhaps you prefer your castles a little more intact; then you should try **Balmoral** (the Queen's residence) or **Braemar Castle**.

If you are a connoisseur of whisky, then you'll certainly want to snoop around the **Malt Whisky Trail** and visit a distillery or two. The one I most enjoyed was the distillery at **Glenlivet**.

THE BORDERS & THE SOUTHWEST

The **Borders and the Southwest** comprises the part of Scotland that lies south of the line between Glasgow and Edinburgh and north of Scotland's border with England. This area is littered with the ruins of monasteries and abbeys, castles and hill forts. Many have disappeared, casualties of centuries of the wind and rain that frequent the area. Most of the remaining ruins are mere shells of their former selves, mute witnesses to the workmanship and faith of their builders (not to mention the ferocity of their foes!).

Four of the finest ruins in Scotland are located within a short distance from one another. These sister abbeys were built in **Jedburgh**, **Kelso**, **Melrose**, and **Dryburgh** in the 12th century, and each weathered centuries of seizures, burnings, raids and razings. Today, they stand boldly but silently in the face of charging tourists and pilgrims. Jedburgh Abbey is located in the town of the same name, and is a phenomenal ruin to visit. Its walls are straight, tall and proud, and complemented by large Gothic window openings. Nearby are Jedburgh's sister abbeys that also possess the names of their towns (or is it the other way around?): Melrose and Kelso. Each is a distinctive ruin, and well worth the time it takes to drive through the undulating countryside to view them. When in Kelso, don't drive past **Floors Castle** without stopping. This stunning castle is still the home of the Duke and Duchess of Roxburghe. Chock-full of antiques, it is an incredible place to visit.

But Dryburgh Abbey is different from her sisters. While her three siblings rest comfortably amid the towns that grew up around them, Dryburgh Abbey is a jewel amid the lovely verdant countryside of the Borders. A treat at Dryburgh is the tomb of Sir Walter Scott, one of the most famous members of Scotland's writing fraternity. His modest marble tomb rests serenely amid the scant ruins of Dryburgh Abbey in the peaceful Scottish countryside.

If you have come to Scotland to see the ruins of ancient castles, then you won't be disappointed here either. Once of the finest examples of a medieval castle is the moat-surrounded **Caerlaverock Castle** near Castle Douglas, and nearby **Threave Castle** figures in some of the most treasonous and sinister acts to have occurred in Scotland.

THE ISLANDS

There are 800 islands peeking stonily out of the waters that surround Scotland, and 130 of them are inhabited. The best-known islands are the **Inner and Outer Hebrides, Orkney,** and the **Shetland Islands.** All are a throw-back to an earlier day, and thus far they all provide a visit relatively unsullied by touristy sites. Rather, ancient dwellings, abandoned religious sites and marvelous seascapes await visitors.

The Hebrides lay off the west coast of Scotland. The three best known islands that comprise the Inner Hebrides are the **Isle of Mull, Iona,** and the **Isle of Skye.** Mull is accessible via ferry from Oban, and boasts rugged and romantic scenery, including impressive Ben More that juts suddenly out of the island's core to over 3,100 feet. It is accompanied by about a dozen smaller peaks that range from 1,000 to 2,500 feet above the island. In addition, a number of fine ruins are available to visit, including Duart and Moy Castles.

A short ferry ride from the Isle of Mull is the pretty little island of Iona. Known primarily for the monastic settlement founded here in the 13th century, it is also the site of a 6th century monastery founded by St. Columba, and it was from here that he launched his missionary efforts into Scotland. Don't miss the **Graves of the Kings** – the burial place for dozens of ancient Scottish kings, including **Macbeth** and his predecessor and victim, **Duncan.** Further north you come to the Isle of Skye. This beautiful island provides visitors a plethora of seascapes and fascinating flora and fauna. Popular with hillwalkers, the Isle of Skye is easily reached either by bridge at the Kyle of Lochalsh or via ferry from Mallaig.

Further west from the Isle of Skye are the remote and rocky **Outer Hebrides,** a chain of islands that stretches over 130 miles along the northwest coast of Scotland. They are for the most part barren and windswept, and the main draws to these islands are the craggy seascapes and remote reaches. Walkers and bird watchers seem to be the most prevalent tourists to these rugged places.

About six miles north of the Scottish mainland you'll find the island chain known as **Orkney.** This large set of islands, 29 of which are inhabited (at last count), provides a wonderful opportunity to see stunning scenery, do some serious fishing, and even do some wreck diving. Besides these activities, one of the highlights of your Scottish holiday may well be a visit to the Stone Age burial site called **Maes Howe.** Another incredible archaeological find not far from Maes Howe is the ancient village of **Skara Brae.** This small Stone Age village was covered by a massive sandstorm 4,500 years ago. Uncovered by another storm in 1850, it presented archaeologists with a nearly perfect and intact village to study. Today it provides 21st century tourists with a glimpse into the lives of the ancient inhabitants of these lonely islands. Further north from Orkney you'll find the Shetland Islands. Rocky and rugged, windswept and wild, you'll find plenty of solitude in the Shetlands.

Whether you are looking for remote and rugged adventure, the comparatively civilized life of a medieval lord, or lively towns, fascinating museums and art galleries, and world-class dining, you will be delighted with Scotland. There is something here for everyone. What will it be for you?

3. SUGGESTED ITINERARIES

Here are a few suggested itineraries for varying interests and lengths of stay in Scotland. I've outlined itineraries of three, seven, ten and fourteen days. Remember, these are just suggestions. If you are enjoying prowling around an old ruin longer than I suggest, by all means stay there. Remember: this is your vacation; go at your own speed. Conversely, if you find yourself a little ahead of schedule, stop at a tourist office and ask for suggestions of things to see and do in the surrounding area. Or better yet, just follow your nose.

Whether you're in the city, the country, or somewhere in between, you should find something that will interest you, and it might even prove to be the highlight of your trip. Several of my most interesting pictures and best memories are of abandoned ruins on back roads I took on a whim.

Most sights are open until about 5:30pm or 6:30pm during the summer months, and some stay open as late as 7:00pm. During other times of the year, most sights close by 4:30pm or 5:00pm. One way to maximize your touring is to see all you can in an area during the day, and use the evening to drive to your next destination.

Many – too many – tourists try and "do Scotland" in anywhere from two to four days as part of a longer trip to England. Personally, I think you should spend the majority of your vacation in Scotland and "do England" in just a few days! However, if you are limited – for whatever reason – to just a few days in Scotland, I have provided a couple of three-day itineraries with the "must-sees" during your short jaunt here. But I'm confident that they will merely whet your appetite, and there is a good chance you'll come back for an extended stay!

THREE DAYS IN EDINBURGH
Day 1
Visit Edinburgh Castle
Stroll down the Royal Mile, visiting the shops along the way

Stop at the John Knox House
Check out the Museum of Childhood
Eat lunch at Dubh Prais restaurant
Visit the Palace of Holyroodhouse
Walk up to Arthur's Seat for fine views and photo ops
Stroll through the Princes Street Gardens
Dine at The Witchery Restaurant (make reservations!)
After dark, return to Edinburgh Castle; enjoy the views
Spend the night at Kildonan Lodge

Day 2
(This is a day of culture...)
Start your morning at the Royal Museum of Scotland
Visit the Huntly House Museum
Grab a quick lunch at Café Rouge
Visit the Scottish National Gallery
Stop by the Royal Scottish Academy
Tour the Scottish National Portrait Gallery
Visit the Scottish National Gallery of Modern Art
Dine at the Cosmo Restaurant
Spend the night at Balmoral Hotel or Cameron Toll Guest House

Day 3
Start at Camera Obscura at the top of the Royal Mile
Visit the Scotch Whisky Heritage Centre
Stop by the Writer's Museum in Lady Stair's House
Visit the Royal Botanic Garden; stop and smell the roses
Take lunch at Le Sept
Spend the afternoon at the Edinburgh Zoo and/or Deep Sea World
Dine at The Grain Store Restaurant
Spend the night at 24 Northumberland

THREE DAYS IN EDINBURGH, THE BORDERS & SURROUNDING AREAS

You'll get a mixture of city sights, royal ruins, and beautiful scenery on this itinerary. Some of the most important and renowned ruins in Scotland are included in this itinerary.

Day 1
Visit Edinburgh Castle
Stroll down the Royal Mile, and stop at the John Knox House

Visit the Huntly House Museum
Eat lunch at Dubh Prais restaurant
Visit the Palace of Holyroodhouse
Stroll through the Princes Street Gardens
Stop by the Royal Scottish Academy
Tour the Scottish National Portrait Gallery
Dine at The Witchery (make reservations!)
After dark, return to Edinburgh Castle; enjoy the views
Spend the night at Kildonan Lodge

Day 2
Drive to and tour Linlithgow Castle, birthplace of Mary Queen of Scots
Drive on to Stirling, visit Stirling Castle and the Wallace Monument
Enjoy the scenery by driving from Stirling to St. Andrews
Visit Castle of St. Andrews and St. Andrews Cathedral and Priory
Stay and dine at Rufflets Country House Hotel or drive back to Edinburgh,
    and spend the night at Lauderville House

Day 3
Head south and enjoy the rolling hills, castles and ruins of the Borders
    region
Visit Melrose town and abbey
Visit Dryburgh Abbey, see Sir Walter Scott's tomb
Drive and hike to the William Wallace statue
Visit Jedburgh Abbey
Stop by the Mary Queen of Scots House
On to Kelso and Kelso Abbey
Tour Floors Castle in Kelso
Head east to the coast, then follow the coast road back to Edinburgh
Dine at Pierre Victoire Restaurant
Spend the night at 24 Northumberland

SEVEN DAYS IN SCOTLAND

Edinburgh and Glasgow are two of the most recognizable city names
in Scotland, and I have included both in this itinerary. In addition, I've
suggested some side trips into the surrounding countryside to explore
and enjoy the sights that can be found there. Golfers will like this itinerary,
as I've included that golfing mecca of St. Andrews.

Day 1
We'll be in Glasgow today...
Start off with the Kelvingrove Art Gallery and Museum

Visit the Museum of Transport
Visit the Hunterian Art Gallery and Museum
Stop by the Charles Rennie Mackintosh House
Lunch at the Cul-de-Sac Restaurant
Visit the Cathedral of St. Kentigern (also known as Glasgow Cathedral)
Visit George Square in downtown Glasgow
Spend the afternoon in the Burrell Collection on the outskirts of Glasgow
Spend the night at One Devonshire Gardens or the Argyll Hotel

Day 2
Travel from Glasgow toward Loch Lomond
Stop in Balloch and purchase goodies for a picnic
Take a cruise on Loch Lomond aboard the *Silver Marlin*
When the *Silver Marlin* docks at the island of Inchmurrin, get off and
    explore, then enjoy the picnic lunch you've packed
Back in Balloch, visit Balloch Castle Country Park
Drive along the eastern shores of Loch Lomond to Rowardennan. Stop
    in the car park and stroll along the wooded footpaths that follow the
    shore of the loch
Spend the evening in Balloch at Gowanlea Bed and Breakfast

Day 3
From Balloch, head east toward Stirling
Swing by Doune and visit Doune Castle
Visit Stirling Castle
Visit the William Wallace Monument
Visit Bannockburn Battlefield and Heritage Centre
Head to Callander and spend the night at the Roman Camp Hotel

Day 4
Spend some time visiting the shops in Callander
Head for St. Andrews, enjoying the countryside along the way
Once in St. Andrews, visit St. Andrews Cathedral and the Castle of St.
    Andrews
Spend the night at Rufflets House outside of St. Andrews, or drive to
    Edinburgh and stay at Kildonan Lodge

Day 5
Once in Edinburgh...
Visit Edinburgh Castle
Stroll down the Royal Mile, visiting the shops along the way
Stop at the John Knox House
Check out the Museum of Childhood

Eat lunch at Dubh Prais restaurant
Visit the Palace of Holyroodhouse
Walk up to Arthur's Seat for fine views and photo ops
Stroll through the Princes Street Gardens
Visit the Royal Botanic Garden; stop and smell the roses
Dine at The Witchery (make reservations!)
After dark, return to Edinburgh Castle; enjoy the views
Spend the night at Kildonan Lodge

Day 6
(This is a full day of culture...)
Start your morning at the Royal Museum of Scotland
Visit the Huntly House Museum
Grab a quick lunch at Café Rouge
Visit the Scottish National Gallery
Stop by the Royal Scottish Academy
Tour the Scottish National Portrait Gallery
Visit the Scottish National Gallery of Modern Art
Dine at the Cosmo Restaurant
Spend the night at Balmoral Hotel or Cameron Toll Guest House

Day 7
Start at Camera Obscura at the top of the Royal Mile
Visit the Scotch Whisky Heritage Centre
Stop by the Writer's Museum in Lady Stair's House
Take lunch at Le Sept
Spend the afternoon at the Edinburgh Zoo and/or Deep Sea World
Dine at The Grain Store Restaurant
Spend the night at 24 Northumberland, or if you have an early morning
    flight out of Glasgow, drive there and spend the night at East
    Lochhead B&B or Glynhill Leisure Hotel

TEN DAYS IN SCOTLAND

Ten days is a nice amount of time to spend in Scotland. It's not enough to see the entire country, but it is enough to see many of the major sights without feeling stressed. You'll visit two of my favorite cities – Inverness and Edinburgh. But along the way you'll experience the beauty and rusticity of Scotland.

Day 1
We'll be in Glasgow today...
Start off with the Kelvingrove Art Gallery and Museum

Visit the Museum of Transport
Visit the Hunterian Art Gallery and Museum
Stop by the Charles Rennie Mackintosh House
Lunch at the Cul-de-Sac Restaurant
Visit the Cathedral of St. Kentigern (also known as Glasgow Cathedral)
Visit George Square in downtown Glasgow
Spend the afternoon in the Burrell Collection on the outskirts of Glasgow
Spend the night at One Devonshire Gardens or the Argyll Hotel

Day 2
Travel from Glasgow toward Loch Lomond
Stop in Balloch and purchase goodies for a picnic
Take a cruise on Loch Lomond aboard the *Silver Marlin*
When the *Silver Marlin* docks at the island of Inchmurrin, get off and
    explore. then enjoy the picnic lunch you've packed
Back in Balloch, visit Balloch Castle Country Park
Drive along the eastern shores of Loch Lomond to Rowardennan. Stop
    in the car park and stroll along the wooded footpaths that follow the
    shore of the loch
Spend the evening in Balloch at Gowanlea Bed and Breakfast

Day 3
From Balloch, head east toward Stirling
Take a side trip to Doune and visit Doune Castle
Back to Stirling, and visit Stirling Castle
Visit the William Wallace Monument
Visit Bannockburn Battlefield and Heritage Centre
Head to Callander and spend the night at the Roman Camp Hotel

Day 4
Head toward Ballachulish on the west coast
Visit Glencoe, site of the Massacre of Glencoe
Drive north along the Great Glen to Loch Ness
Visit the Loch Ness Exhibit in Drumnadrochit
Take a boat tour of the loch with Loch Ness Tours
See and photograph Nessie, become world famous
Visit Urquhart Castle
Spend the night at Inchnacardoch Lodge or Court Green B&B

Day 5
On to Inverness...
Visit the shops in Inverness, walk along the peaceful banks of the River
    Ness

Visit Culloden Battlefield
Visit Cawdor Castle between Inverness and Nairn
Head southeast out of Inverness to the Malt Whisky Trail
Visit the Glenlivet Reception Centre
Visit Castle Country, and Kildrummy, Fraser and Fyvie Castles
Spend the night at Callater Lodge Hotel in Braemar

Day 6
Head for Edinburgh, enjoying the scenery along the way
Eat lunch at Dubh Prais restaurant
Visit Edinburgh Castle
Stroll down the Royal Mile, visiting the shops along the way
Stop at the John Knox House
Check out the Museum of Childhood
Visit the Palace of Holyroodhouse
Dine at The Witchery Restaurant (make reservations!)
After dark, return to Edinburgh Castle; enjoy the views
Spend the night at Kildonan Lodge

Day 7
(This is a day of culture...)
Start your morning at the Royal Museum of Scotland
Visit the Huntly House Museum
Grab a quick lunch at Café Rouge
Visit the Scottish National Gallery
Stop by the Royal Scottish Academy
Tour the Scottish National Portrait Gallery
Dine at the Cosmo Restaurant
Spend the night at Balmoral Hotel or Cameron Toll Guest House

Day 8
Start at Camera Obscura at the top of the Royal Mile
Visit the Scotch Whisky Heritage Centre
Stop by the Writer's Museum in Lady Stair's House
Visit the Scottish National Gallery of Modern Art
Take lunch at Le Sept

Day 10
Head south and enjoy the rolling hills, castles and ruins of the Borders
    region
Visit Melrose town and abbey
Visit Dryburgh Abbey, see Sir Walter Scott's tomb
Drive and hike to the William Wallace statue, enjoy the views

Visit Jedburgh Abbey
Stop by the Mary Queen of Scots House
On to Kelso and Kelso Abbey
Tour Floors Castle in Kelso
Drive to Glasgow
Spend the night at the Malmaison Glasgow or East Lochhead B&B

FOURTEEN DAYS IN SCOTLAND

Fourteen days gives you plenty of time to visit Scotland. You won't see everything, but you'll see many of the major sights and have time for quite a few of the minor ones, too. This itinerary begins in Glasgow and encircles the country in a clockwise manner.

Day 1
We'll be in Glasgow today...
Start off with the Kelvingrove Art Gallery and Museum
Visit the Museum of Transport
Visit the Hunterian Art Gallery and Museum
Stop by the Charles Rennie Mackintosh House
Lunch at the Cul-de-Sac Restaurant
Visit the Cathedral of St. Kentigern (also known as Glasgow Cathedral)
Visit George Square in downtown Glasgow
Spend the afternoon in the Burrell Collection on the outskirts of Glasgow
Spend the night at One Devonshire Gardens or the Argyll Hotel

Day 2
Travel from Glasgow toward Loch Lomond
Stop in Balloch and purchase goodies for a picnic
Take a cruise on Loch Lomond aboard the *Silver Marlin*
When the *Silver Marlin* docks at the island of Inchmurrin, get off and
    explore, then enjoy the picnic lunch you've packed
Back in Balloch, visit Balloch Castle Country Park
Drive along the eastern shores of Loch Lomond to Rowardennan. Stop
    in the car park and stroll along the wooded footpaths that follow the
    shore of the loch
Spend the evening in Balloch at Gowanlea Bed and Breakfast

Day 3
From Balloch, head east toward Stirling
Take a side trip to Doune and visit Doune Castle
Back to Stirling, and visit Stirling Castle
Visit the William Wallace Monument

Visit Bannockburn Battlefield and Heritage Centre
Head to Callander and spend the night at the Roman Camp Hotel

Day 4
Spend some time visiting the shops in Callander
Head to Killin and walk along the banks of Loch Tay or check out the views
    from the slopes of Ben Lawer
On to Oban...
Catch the ferry from Oban to the Isle of Mull
Spend the rest of the day seeing the sights on the Isle of Mull

Day 5
Spend this day seeing the sights on the Isles of Iona and Staffa. Take your
    time – it may be the highlight of your trip!

Day 6
Back to Oban, then north along the coast road to Glencoe
Visit the Glencoe, site of the Massacre of Glencoe
Head toward the Kyle of Lochalsh – watch for Eilean Donan Castle
On to the Isle of Skye
Try your hand at hillwalking
Visit Dunvegan Castle
Spend the night at Roskhill House

Day 7
Head east toward Loch Ness
Visit the Loch Ness Exhibit in Drumnadrochit
Take a boat tour of the loch with Loch Ness Tours
See and photograph Nessie, become world famous
Visit Urquhart Castle
On to Inverness
Visit the shops in Inverness, walk along the peaceful banks of the River
    Ness
Visit Culloden Battlefield
Spend the night at Clach Mhuilinn

Day 8
See the western Highlands today. Lots of driving and marvelous scenery...
Drive north out of Inverness to Tongue
Follow the coastline from Tongue to Ullapool
(Stop often to take photographs!)
Along the way, visit Smoo Cave and sandy beaches in Durness

Spend the night at Ardvreck House in Ullapool, or Boath House in
   Inverness

Day 9
Head southeast out of Inverness to the Malt Whisky Trail
Visit the Glenlivet Reception Centre
Visit Castle Country, and Kildrummy, Fraser and Fyvie Castles
Visit Balmoral Castle
On to Braemar and a visit to Braemar Castle
Drive west out of Braemar to the Linn of Dee and the Devil's Punchbowl
Spend the night at Callater Lodge Hotel

Day 10
Head for St. Andrews, enjoying the countryside along the way
Once in St. Andrews, visit Holy Trinity Church and Castle of St. Andrews
On to Edinburgh
Visit Edinburgh Castle
Stroll down the Royal Mile, visiting the shops along the way
Stop at the John Knox House
Check out the Museum of Childhood
After dark, return to Edinburgh Castle; enjoy the views
Spend the night at Kildonan Lodge Hotel

Day 11
Visit the Palace of Holyroodhouse
Walk up to Arthur's Seat for fine views and photo ops
Stroll through the Princes Street Gardens
Eat lunch at Dubh Prais restaurant
Visit the Royal Museum of Scotland
Visit the Huntly House Museum
Dine at The Witchery Restaurant (make reservations!)
Spend the night at Cameron Toll House

Day 12
More culture today...
Visit the Scottish National Gallery
Stop by the Royal Scottish Academy
Tour the Scottish National Portrait Gallery
Visit the Scottish National Gallery of Modern Art
Grab a quick lunch at Café Rouge
Visit the Scotch Whisky Heritage Centre
Stop by the Writer's Museum in Lady Stair's House

Dine at The Grain Store Restaurant
Spend the night at 24 Northumberland

Day 13
Head south and enjoy the rolling hills, castles and ruins of the Borders
    region
Visit Melrose town and abbey
Visit Dryburgh Abbey, see Sir Walter Scott's tomb
Drive and hike to the William Wallace statue, enjoy the views
Visit Jedburgh Abbey
Stop by the Mary Queen of Scots House
On to Kelso and Kelso Abbey
Tour Floors Castle in Kelso
Drive to Glasgow
Spend the night at the Malmaison Glasgow

Day 14
A relaxing day today...
Stroll through Glasgow Green
Visit the Botanic Gardens
Stop by the St. Mungo Museum of Religious Life and Art and Glasgow
    Cathedral
Visit the Provand's Lordship House
Tour the City Chambers building
Dine at the Cul-de-Sac restaurant
Spend the night at East Lochhead B&B or Glynhill Leisure Hotel

4. LAND & PEOPLE

LAND

Scotland is just a little smaller than the states of Maine and South Carolina. In other words, it's not very large. The country is about 260 miles long from its northern beaches to its southern border with England, and about 160 miles wide at its widest, 35 miles at its narrowest. No matter where you travel in Scotland, you are never more than about 45 miles from the sea.

Scotland is a land of contrasts, with the rolling plains of the Borders giving way to the craggy peaks, marshy moors and heather-laden hillsides of the Highlands. Wildflowers and brilliant gorse blend with rich green grasses to provide a picturesque palate of colors. Pity those who are truly color blind and cannot appreciate the riot of colors and hues that greet most of us!

At the southern end of the country, a 60-mile border separates Scotland from England. In fact, this area of southeastern Scotland is known as **The Borders**. For the purposes of this guide, I have used the term **The Borders and the Southwest** to describe all of the country that lies north of the border with England and south of a line that runs between Dunbar on the east coast and Girvan on the west coast. To be blunt, much of this area along the border with England caught hell through the centuries of battles with that contentious neighbor. Abbeys, castles and strongholds were built, razed and rebuilt too many times to count. Some of the most intriguing ruins in Scotland are located in this area.

The eastern portion of this region of Scotland is gentle and lovely. Verdant pastures nestle comfortably amid softly rolling hills. The western side features more aggressive hills, and even boasts a few peaks that exceed 2,000 feet. The Borders is largely an agricultural section of Scotland.

Across the midsection of Scotland is the area called the **Central Lowlands**. This narrow 45-mile-wide band is where the majority of Scots live. Some 3.5 million Scots call this section of Scotland home. It hosts

GREAT SCOTS!

You'll see their names on street signs, parks, bridges, and railway stations (maybe even in Hollywood movies). These are important men and women in Scottish history:

Alexander Graham Bell *(1847–1922). Born in Edinburgh, Bell was an inventor who immigrated to the US to improve his health. His efforts to invent a machine to help the deaf hear resulted in the invention of the telephone.*

Robert Burns *(1759–1796). Scottish writer and satirist, born in Dumfries. Scots celebrate his birth every January 25 with Robbie Burns Day. He is considered the National Poet of Scotland.*

Bonnie Prince Charlie *(1720–1788). The grandson of James VII of Scotland (also known as James II of England). He led the short-lived Jacobite Rebellion in 1745 in an attempt to reclaim the throne, but lost at the Battle of Culloden.*

Sir Arthur Conan Doyle *(1859–1930). Edinburgh novelist famous for writing the novels that chronicled the adventures of Sherlock Holmes.*

Flora MacDonald *(1722–1790). Flora gained fame and a page in Scottish history by providing protection for Bonnie Prince Charlie as he fled from his defeat at Culloden.*

James VI *(1566–1625). The only son of Mary Queen of Scots, he was the first to unite the thrones of Scotland and England. James VI of Scotland became James I of England. Unfortunately, he turned his back on his fellow Scots. He commissioned a translation of the Bible, and insisted on the term Great Britain. He reigned over two decades before he was murdered.*

John Paul Jones *(1747–1792). John was the Scottish-born founder of the American Navy during the American War for Independence.*

John Knox *(1505–1572). John was one of the catalysts of the Reformation in Scotland. Through his efforts, Presbyterianism became the national religion of Scotland. He was probably not on Mary Queen of Scots' Christmas card list.*

Eric Liddell *(1902–1945). Famed Scottish athlete who was portrayed in the movie "Chariots of Fire."*

GREAT SCOTS!

Macbeth *(1005–1057). Yes, this is the king made famous by the bard from Stratford-on-Avon. He was indeed a real king, and apparently a wee bit better than portrayed by Mr. Shakespeare. He ruled Scotland from 1040 to 1057.*

Mary Queen of Scots *(1542–1587). Mary was one of the most beautiful and flamboyant rulers Scotland ever had. Unfortunately, her religion (Catholic), timing (she came to power during the Reformation), and poor luck all worked against her, and she was eventually executed by her cousin, Queen Elizabeth I.*

Robert the Bruce *(1274–1329). A significant player in the wars for independence with England. He was crowned king of Scotland in 1306 and ruled for over two decades.*

St. Columba *(521–598). The most famous of the early Christian missionaries to Scotland. He was a tireless advocate for his Lord and was successful in establishing a significant Christian foothold in Scotland (St. Columba was Irish).*

Robert Louis Stevenson *(1850–1894). Novelist born in Edinburgh. Author of such classics as "Treasure Island" and "Kidnapped."*

Adam Smith *(1723–1790). Born in Kirkaldy, Adam Smith has been called the "Father of Classical Economics." Author of the book "Wealth of Nations."*

William Wallace *(1274–1305). Thanks to Hollywood, many outside of Ireland now know of Sir William Wallace's exploits and efforts to free Scotland from English tyranny. Wallace was never crowned king of Scotland, nor did he seek that (so they say). Rather, he chose the title Guardian of Scotland for himself.*

James Watt *(1736–1819). Inventor of the steam engine. The unit of electrical power is also named after him (watt), and he coined the term "horsepower."*

three of the four largest cities in Scotland: **Glasgow** (700,000), **Edinburgh** (725,000), and **Dundee** (190,000).

The Central Lowlands and its major cities lay at roughly the same latitude as Moscow. However, because of the Gulf Stream the area does not suffer the same nasty winters its eastern neighbor does. And spring and summer in this region of Scotland are downright pleasant. This region of Scotland may be populous, but it is beautiful, too. Once you get out of the cities, you see for yourself what drew the earliest inhabitants here. Just beyond the hubbub of Edinburgh and Glasgow you find the lovely countryside called the Lothians and the **Trossachs**. This fertile land must have seemed like a paradise to the early inhabitants of Scotland, and as you can see, many people migrated here.

As you move north, you come to the beginnings of the **Highlands**. The hills get a little steeper and more massive, and the heather seems to be far more plentiful here. Scattered hither and thither throughout the Highlands is water – lochs, rivers and firths (inlets). The views are stunning and are a huge draw to people from all over the world. In many parts of the Highlands you'll find heavily wooded areas; in other parts you find heather-clad mounts, and in still other parts, you find marshy and mysterious moors.

Scotland is host to hundreds of islands. Off the west coast you'll find the Inner and Outer Hebrides. To the north are the group of islands known as Orkney, and still farther north are the remote Shetland Islands.

FACTS ON SCOTLAND

Highest mountain: Ben Nevis, 4406 feet
Number of Mountains over 3,000 feet: 284 (called Munros)
Highest waterfall: Eas Coul Aulin, 692 feet
National Emblem of Scotland – the thistle
Longest River: Tay, 117 miles
Largest city: Edinburgh, population 725,000
Deepest lake: Loch Morar
Largest lake: Loch Lomond
Lake with most famous monster: Loch Ness
Total population: 5.1 million (1997)
Religious affiliation: predominantly Presbyterian
Number of universities – 13
Number of colleges – 45
Unemployment: 5.6%
Land mass: consists of about 30% of the island of Great Britain
Total Area: 30,405 square miles (slightly smaller than South Carolina)

PEOPLE

Over five million people call Scotland home, and twenty million people around the world claim Scottish ancestry. As you travel about Scotland, you will be overwhelmed by its beauty. And yet, some of my favorite memories are of the times I spent with the people of Scotland.

It is said that the Scottish people have a tendency toward dourness and can be difficult to get along with. While I am sure some Scots fit that description, my personal experience with the Scottish people has shown me that the Scots are a pleasant and friendly people. It is true that they can be blunt, but they are always quick to smile and laugh, and always seem more than willing to visit for a wee minute with you.

THE THISTLE - NATIONAL EMBLEM OF SCOTLAND

As you browse tourist brochures and tour around the country, you will continually see images of the thistle, and that is because the thistle is Scotland's national emblem. Legend has it that during an ancient military campaign, the English army was sneaking up on a group of Scots under cover of night. One barefooted soldier stepped on a thistle unexpectedly and let out a yelp, warning the Scots of the impending attack. The Scots promptly adopted the thistle as their national emblem, along with the Latin motto **Nemo me impune lacessit** *(No one attacks me with impunity!). Both the weed and the saying seemed to capture the Scottish outlook on life, especially as it pertained to the English.*

Here are a few interesting tidbits about the Scottish:
- Something about Scotland encourages creativity and free thinking, as evidenced by the number of world-famous inventors, philosophers and academics that have called Scotland home. Some of the more well-known individuals are such giants as Alexander Graham Bell (telephone), James Watt (prototyped the steam engine and the electrical term watt was named after him), John Napier (mathematician that invented logarithms), Adam Smith (one of the leading economists of all time, wrote *The Wealth of Nations*), and authors Robert Louis Stevenson, Sir Walter Scott, and Sir Arthur Conan Doyle.
- Christianity first came to Scotland in about 400 AD. **St. Ninian** was one of the earliest Christian missionaries to bring the news of the gospel to the pagan tribes of Scotland. However, one of the most successful missionaries to serve Scotland was St. Columba. St. Columba was a refugee from some troubles in Ireland, and came to Scotland to seek

souls for Christ as penance for his misdeeds. Most historians would acknowledge his penance was successful: the work he did helped establish a strong foothold for Christianity to truly gain acceptance in Scotland.

• Through the centuries, Scotland has hosted numerous peoples. Ireland has been a major contributor, and one group which came to Scotland from Ireland were the Scoti, a race who left their permanent impression on the country.

Thanks to the Hollywood megahit *Braveheart*, Scotland has become associated with a fighting spirit and a love of independence. And much of her history betrays a real-life affinity to **William Wallace**, the hero in that Hollywood epic. The Scots can indeed be a quarrelsome people when provoked, as their history attests. But they are also a pleasant people, quick to laugh and see the humor in any situation. Their wit is legendary, and you will enjoy sampling it for yourself.

Language

English is the official language of Scotland. **Gaelic** is the language that has been spoken in Scotland for over a thousand years, for it was the language of the Celts, early inhabitants of Scotland. Today, linguists estimate that only about 2% of the Scottish population speak Gaelic.

Below are some of the more common Scottish words you are certain to encounter during your visit. Many of them are anglicized versions of Gaelic words – for example, *dun* is the Gaelic word for fortress or castle. Many towns in Scotland begin with dun, signifying the presence (at least at one time) of a castle or fortress. A few examples include Dunbar, Dunbeath, Dunblane, Dundonald, etc. In your travels, see how many names of Gaelic origin you can identify and translate.

Scottish	English
aber	mouth of a river
ard	a high place
alt	stream
ath	ford
bally	town
ben	large hill or mountain peak
brae	hillside
ceilidh	party, gathering with music (pronounced *kay-lay*)
clach	stone
clachan	small town, hamlet
craig	rock
drum	low ridge or mound

dun	fortress, castle
ennis	island
gal	river
kil, kirk	church
mac	son
mon	hill
mor	great
skerry	sea rocks
strath	valley
tully	small hill

The Scots use the English language a little differently than those of us from across the big pond (or is it vice versa?) At any rate, here are a few words you may think you know, but the meanings may not be quite what you expect:

Scottish	**American**
aye	yes
bonnie	attractive, pleasant, cheerful
call	visit
chips	French fries
crisps	potato chips
gob-smacked	amazed, struck speechless
hire	rent
homely	homey, down-to-earth
kirk	church
lemonade	lemon-lime drink (like Sprite or 7-Up)
lift	elevator
loo	restroom
lorrie	truck
on holiday	on vacation
pram	baby stroller
queue	line
return	round-trip (as in a round-trip ticket)
ring	call on the phone
single	one-way (as in a one-way ticket)
ta	thanks
tariff	rate (as in the rate for a hotel room or rental car)
tatties	potatoes
toilet	restroom

Scots or Brits?

Now, here is a touchy subject: *Do Scots consider themselves British?* I asked a number of Scots to get an answer to this question, and the consensus seemed to be that, yes, formally and politically they were British. But each hastened to add that they preferred to think of themselves as Scots or Scottish, and preferred being referred to as Scots or as being Scottish.

One last lesson: *Celtic* is generally pronounced differently than the way we pronounce the name of the NBA team from Boston. The Celtic you see in Scotland is pronounced Keltic, with a hard K, and it was spoken by Kelts – not *Seltic* spoken by *Selts*. There is one notable exception to this rule: one of the football (soccer) teams in Glasgow is called the Celtics, and the name is pronounced the same as that of the NBA team of the same name – the *Seltics*. Go figure!

SCOTLAND – MORE OR LESS!

As you travel about Scotland, you'll be struck by the differences between Scotland and the United States or Canada. There are the obvious differences: accents, castles, driving on the other side of the road. But here are a few more subtle differences. Can you think of any others?

In Scotland there are more......	*In Scotland there is less.....*
Women walking arm-in-arm	*Make-up*
Dresses	*Joggers*
Kilts	*Large luxury cars*
Body piercings	*Interstate highways*
Ancient buildings	*4X4s*
Baby carriages	*Pick-up trucks*
Double-decker buses	*Stop signs*
Germans	*Traffic lights*
People smoking	*Baseball caps*

5. A SHORT HISTORY

Scotland is one of the most tranquil places you will ever visit. Unfortunately, her peaceful repose belies her bloody history. Sinister and malevolent activities, tinged with intrigue and deceit are woven throughout Scotland's history. From subtle politics to bloody uprisings, Scotland's past is checkered with machinations, drama, and pathos that rivals today's fictional best sellers.

And yet natives of this incredible land are resilient. Time and again they have fought to be recognized. Sometimes they won, sometimes they lost. But they always kept trying.

ANCIENT HISTORY

The earliest Scottish residents were probably Mesolithic hunters. It is widely believed that these ancient nomads arrived in Scotland near the beginning of the Stone Age, as people on the European continent expanded their fishing and hunting grounds to the western edge of the continent and on to what is now Scotland. Little of substance is known of these Mesolithic people, as they left few traces of their passing. Ancient sites in the central section of Scotland and on her outlying islands have yielded such archaeological finds as ancient stone implements, the remains of shellfish, and hazelnuts. Carbon dating on these last items indicates they date from 6500 BC!

The beginning of the New Stone Age (4000 BC) was the first of many renaissances in Scotland, when Neolithic man appeared here. It was during this period that these early men and women began settling down and tilling the earth, and crude stone farm implements attest to their new occupation as farmers. As time went on, the crudeness of their tools softened to a unique sophistication. Stone axes were sharp and plentiful enough to make massive timbering projects possible on the island – the beginning of the deforestation of Scotland. When needed, these implements of harvest also provided protection for these early Scots.

Some of the most extraordinary evidences we have of these Neolithic men in Scotland are the signs of their death. These advanced Stone Age men began the practice of building massive tombs for their dead. Thousands of these tombs can be found dotting the fields and hills of Scotland to this day, and most especially on the outlying islands off Scotland's shores. They include **passage graves** (so-called because of the presence of a central passage into the tomb), stone circles along the same lines as Stonehenge, and a variety of other monuments, all apparently to honor their dead. Many of them also reflect knowledge of astronomy, as they show some solar orientation. One of the finest of these is **Maes Howe**, an extraordinary example of a Stone Age burial cairn found on Orkney. Like similar cairns in Ireland, Maes Howe has a passageway that is lighted by sunlight only at the winter solstice. Archaeologists estimate that Maes Howe has been around for 4,500 to 5,500 years.

The Bronze Age in Scotland lasted from about 2,000 BC to 700 BC. While these people are long gone, they left behind telltale evidences of their passing: fine jewelry, weapons, and tools that have been unearthed in recent years. Many of the finer examples are on display in museums such as the **Hunterian Museum** in Glasgow.

Around 700 BC, the Bronze Age gave way slowly to the Iron Age as wandering bands of iron-users made their way to Scotland. These new settlers came to be known by today's historians as **Celts**, although it's doubtful that's what they called themselves. Whatever they called themselves, they were preoccupied with safety, as the ancient ruins left behind so eloquently attest. Southern Scotland in particular is speckled with some 1,500 **stone hill forts** as rival families played their version of king of the hill. These hilltop fortifications provided some semblance of safety in a time when the clan-to-clan fighting that typifies Scotland's history began. The largest of these, **Eildon Hill North**, is thought to have been home and a safe haven to perhaps as many as 2,000 people at one time.

The Celts had a long and event-filled history in Scotland. Like their cousins in Ireland, their distrust for one another never allowed them to band together and stand effectively against warring nations like the Romans. The Greek geographer Strabo said of these Celts, "...the whole race which is now called Celtic is madly fond of war, high spirited and quick to battle, but otherwise straightforward and not of a devious nature."

Celtic religious leaders were called **Druids**, and their gods became the gods of the Scottish people for many hundreds of years. The Druids worshipped a number of deities, and presided over the human sacrifices that were often an important part of some of their ceremonies.

ANGLES & SCOTS & PICTS, OH MY!

The history of Scotland in the first thousand years AD is mostly a combination of supposition based on a few facts and limited journals kept by Roman historians of the time. During this period, four major groups found their way to Scotland: the Picts, Angles, Scots and Britons.

The first two hundred years AD saw an increasing number of military encounters between the Celts and the Roman army. When Hadrian became emperor of Rome, he decided that rather than continue expending soldiers in these skirmishes, the Romans would settle for containing the troublemakers in northern Scotland. (His directive came shortly after Celtic warriors annihilated an entire Roman legion in York. Coincidence? I think not!) In 122 AD he directed the building of a wall across the girth of southern Scotland to hem the Celts in. The edifice, called **Hadrian's Wall**, stands 12 to 15 feet high and stretches 73 miles across southern Scotland, and can still be clearly seen.

Around 300 AD we find the first reference to the people known as the **Picts**. The Roman name is *Picti*, which means "painted ones," a reference to their tradition of dying their skin purple for battle. Little is known of these people except that they were fierce warriors, expert horsemen, and most probably a mixture of the now native Celts and some other group.

In about 500 AD, a Celtic tribe known as the *Scoti* immigrated to Scotland from the northern shores of Ireland. **Fergus Mor** brought a small contingent of Irish fighters with him from Dunseverick Castle in County Antrim (now in Northern Ireland). Representatives of the ancient Irish kingdom of Dalriada, over the years these **Scots** proved to be menacing and successful foes of the Picts. They staked their initial claim to Scotland along the western shores of Argyll. As you have surmised by now, it is from these erstwhile Irishmen that Scotland takes its name.

The **Britons** were related to the Scots and Picts, in that they too were a Celtic tribe. They had settled the southern regions of Scotland. Despite their shared ancestry with their northern cousins, the Britons did not fare well at their hands. This little family feud resulted in the immigration of another people to Scotland, the **Angles**. Like bullies picking on their favorite 98-pound weakling, these northern warriors thought it great sport to ride into the land of the Britons, pillage and plunder, and return with their treasures. This happened so often that the victims began howling loudly for help from Mother Rome. But their timing was bad: Rome had her hands full with Attila and his friendly Huns who were sweeping rapidly across Europe toward Rome. Desperate, the Britons sought mercenaries and offered land as a reward to all that survived. The offer was enough to attract numerous soldiers, including large contingents of Angles from Denmark.

Upon their arrival, the Angles had a measure of success in driving the Picts and Scots back north where they belonged. True to their word, the Britons awarded lands to these soldiers of fortune in the southeastern part of Scotland. Their families from Denmark and northern Germany soon joined the Angles. The Britons remained in the southern reaches of Scotland in an area that came to be known as Strathclyde.

CHRISTIANITY COMES TO SCOTLAND

The honor of bringing Christianity to Scotland is generally given to **St. Ninian.** Ninian was a Briton, and he began his missionary service to Scotland around 400 AD. Prior to his missionary service, Ninian spent a number of years in Rome receiving religious instruction. He seems to have been a tireless emissary, and personally declared the word of God to the Picts as well as sent many missionaries to the northern extremes of Scotland. But after his death the work waned, and the Picts returned to their Druidic religion.

About 150 years after St. Ninian's death, another missionary arrived on the shores of Scotland. **St. Columba** was also a tireless emissary for his Lord. He established a monastery on the tiny island of Iona, and with it a significant Christian foothold in this land that was still staunchly pagan. Columba is credited with giving Christianity the firm foundation it needed to grow and expand in Scotland.

After his arrival in Scotland, St. Columba busied himself with both the work of the ministry as well as the work of the state. It is said he began to have success with the sun-worshipping Picts when he presented the Son of God as the *Sun* Incarnate. At the same time, he labored among the Scots to convince them to select his cousin as their king. This combination of church and state was to serve St. Columba and the cause of Christianity well throughout the ensuing years.

VIKINGS & SHAKESPEARE

For several hundred years, the Scots and the Picts waged war on the Britons, the Angles, the Romans, and each other. Sometimes they were allies, but usually they fought each other. They were clearly the strongest of the tribes in Scotland.

In the late 700s, the beginning of the end came for the Picts. A new enemy began depredations on the northern holdings of the Picts. Viking longships completed their short two-day voyage from Norway and landed on Orkney and Shetland, both Pict holdings. Their appearance swung the balance of power in favor of the Scots. The Picts fought and bled much trying to protect their lands and people from these fierce Norsemen. But the fighting took its toll. The strength of the people was their young men, and those young men were giving their lives in increasing numbers in battle with the Vikings.

In the early 800s, a new king emerged among the Scots. **Kenneth MacAlpin** was a cunning warrior and a charismatic leader. He was king of the Kingdom of Alba (the Irish name for Scotland), and some feel he may have laid claim to the throne of the Picts. The Picts followed a tradition of matriarchal succession, and Kenneth's father had married the daughter of a Pictish queen. While the records are vague as to whether Kenneth ascended to the throne of both kingdoms as a result of his exploits on the battlefield or in the bedroom, it is clear that he was crowned and accepted as king of both peoples. In 843 we find a united Scot and Pict kingdom under Kenneth MacAlpin.

In 1040 the last Pictish king rose to the head of the Scots/Picts people. Immortalized by William Shakespeare, **Macbeth** reigned from 1040 to 1057 (yes, Macbeth was a real person). He rose to the monarchy by killing his predecessor, King Duncan. Rather than kill Duncan's young sons, Macbeth banished them in an effort to keep them from coming after him and the throne. The young lads were sent to the court of the English King **Edward the Confessor**. As it turns out, it would have been better for Macbeth's health to have slain them.

Macbeth seems to have been a good king, and his reign resulted in the first real uniting of Scotland under one king. Notwithstanding the murder that gained him the throne (situational ethics?), he was a devout Christian, and even made a pilgrimage to Rome in 1050. He reigned for 17 years before his luck ran out. Supported by Edward the Confessor, Malcolm Canmore, son of Duncan, returned to Scotland with an army and killed Macbeth. Malcolm did not repeat Macbeth's mistake of charity: he killed all of Macbeth's family and close kin to ensure that no son, nephew or grandson would be coming for him in a few years. He in turn married an English woman of the royal family, thus setting in motion a chain of events that would ensure Scotland's rule by English monarchs for many years to come.

WAR OF INDEPENDENCE

In 1286 a crisis of royal proportions arose in Scotland. The heir to the throne of Scotland was a three-year-old lass named Margaret, daughter of Eric of Norway and granddaughter of Scottish King Alexander III. Alexander III, the second great-grandson of Malcolm, had died when his horse rode over a cliff on a dark and stormy night. He left no heirs, and his brothers and sisters were all dead. The only one having legal title to the throne was young Margaret. Margaret's father feared for his young daughter's life, and went to England to arrange a marriage that would help her retain the throne and that would also help her survive. The groundwork was laid for Margaret to wed the son of Edward I. Such a marriage would have united the throne under Edward II.

Alas, destiny took a hand and the union did not take place. In 1290, it was agreed that Margaret should leave Norway for England and be reared there in the royal courts of Edward I. But she became ill during the voyage and died. The royal crisis had just worsened.

Scotland now found herself with no legal heir to the throne. Thirteen individuals stepped forward and claimed their right to the throne. Eventually, the competition devolved to two men: **Robert Bruce** and **John Balliol**. Both were powerful nobles who were descendants of Malcolm Canmore and each had well-equipped armies, which they were ready to press into service to support their claims to the crown. There seemed to be no clear way to avoid a civil war between these two contenders for the throne, so the bishop of St. Andrews suggested an arbitrator. Both sides agreed, and Edward I, King of England, was chosen. He was hardly an unbiased choice, but all parties agreed to abide by his decision.

Edward chose John Balliol as the servant King of Scotland. But John's joy must have been short-lived, as almost immediately Edward began a series of humiliating demands. First, he removed from the Scottish king the right to hear appeals in matters of law, demanded compensation for military conquests, and on the petty side, demanded payment of a wine bill left unpaid by a former Scottish king.

Continually pushed and humiliated, John finally decided to take a stand against the arrogant king. When Edward demanded Scottish support in the form of armies and weapons for his struggle with France, John balked. He refused to go, renounced his allegiance to England, and sent emissaries to France to negotiate an alliance with them.

Robert Bruce threw his support to Edward, and in fact supplied soldiers to Edward's army as it took on and defeated John Balliol's army. Edward wanted the Scots to know who was their lord and master, and he drove his point home with a vengeance. John Balliol was imprisoned in the Tower of London for his insubordination. (After three years he was released, retreated to France, and died in obscurity in 1313.) Over 2,000 Scottish nobles were required to sign an oath of allegiance to Edward, and many were called to go to foreign battlefields with their armies to support Edward's wars. Those permitted to stay behind could not leave Scotland without Edward's express permission. Every important castle in Scotland had new house guests: regiments of English soldiers.

Finally, the governance of Scotland was taken from Scots and handed to two Englishmen, John de Warenne (the Earl of Surrey), and Hugh Cressingham. As a final insult, upon his return to England, Edward took with him the Stone of Destiny, the stone upon which Scottish kings were crowned. It was brought to Westminster Abbey and placed below the throne of England. (The Scots may have pulled a fast one here: legend has it that an official-looking but rather ordinary stone was substituted for the Stone of Destiny just before its kidnap!)

WILLIAM WALLACE & ROBERT BRUCE

The stage was set for some dramatic heroics and Scotland was primed for a hero to step forward and save her from the clutches of the evil empire. And **William Wallace** didn't disappoint them. Born in 1270 near Elderslie, William represented the rebel in all Scotsmen. From the Central Lowlands (just outside present-day Glasgow), William refused to accept English rule. He gathered an army and vowed to win independence from the hated English. His first act of note was to assassinate the sheriff of Lanark and chop him into little pieces in reprisal for the murder of William's wife by English soldiers. Wallace became an expert in guerilla warfare, and used those tactics to harass much larger English forces and make life generally miserable for them.

Wallace joined ranks with **Andrew of Moray**, a Highland nobleman. Like the Minutemen of the American Revolution, they were passionate about their freedom, and they were generally outnumbered by professional soldiery on the other side of the field of battle. Many of their weapons were of the homemade variety, and there was little armor to protect them. But what they lacked in armaments, they made up for in courage and a savage quest for liberty. Against the mercenaries of England, they generally fared well when they chose their ground and moments prudently.

Their fight and passion was not shared by a majority of the Scot noblemen. Cognizant of the fact that they had signed an oath of allegiance to Edward, most of these noblemen stood idly by while these two warriors and their ragged band of patriots marched into the annals of history (and Hollywood). However, while they generally didn't join the freedom fighters, they also didn't support the English. It was William's and Andrew's war to win or lose.

Stirling Bridge and September 11, 1297 are to Scotland what Lexington Green and April 19, 1775 are to the United States. It was at Stirling Bridge that the armies of William Wallace and Andrew of Moray clashed with a vastly superior English army led by the Earl of Surrey (John de Warenne) and Hugh Cressingham.

But tactics and courage carried the day for the rebels. The two armies were separated by a river, which could only be crossed by a narrow bridge. Wallace and Moray waited until a significant number of soldiers and cavalry had crossed, then launched a vicious attack. The cavalry who had cleared the bridge found their steeds mired in swampy ground and found themselves immersed in thousands of fanatic rebels. Those who had made it across the bridge fought valiantly, but the majority of their army was forced to stay on the other side of the river and watch helplessly as their compatriots-in-arms were annihilated. The battle lasted an hour, and at the end of it the remaining English army had fled. When the smoke cleared, the Scots had won a decisive victory. Among the dead was Hugh Cressingham, whom the Scots hated almost as much as Edward. Wallace reportedly flayed Cressingham and some say he even made a sheath for his sword out of Cressingham's skin. Whether this is true is a matter of some conjecture; so many legends swirl around the robust warrior that from 700 years distance it is difficult to determine which stories are true and which are not.

But the Battle of Stirling Bridge cost the patriots dearly. Andrew of Moray received a mortal wound from which he died about six weeks later.

For his exploits, Wallace was knighted. Many of the commoners and middle class wanted him to claim the kingdom for his own. Wallace, however, was a supporter of John Balliol, and refused, taking for himself instead the title *Guardian of Scotland*.

The following seven years were difficult ones for Scotland. The reticent nobles were still torn between fear of Edward's reprisals and the desire to support a free Scotland. In the end, Edward won out. Edward waged no fewer than six military campaigns in Scotland between 1297 and 1305. Notwithstanding Wallace's guerilla tactics, Edward slowly regained all the castles he had lost to Wallace. Yet Wallace remained elusive, and time and again slipped through the grasp of the mighty King of England.

That all changed in August 1305, when Wallace was betrayed into the king's hands by a Scottish nobleman, Sir John Menteith (Benedict Arnold?). Wallace was tried and convicted of treason (an interesting verdict, since Wallace never pledged his allegiance to Edward – a small matter). He was hung until almost dead, then drawn and quartered. To top it all off, he was beheaded, and his head was stuck on a pike on London Bridge. His quarters were sent to the Scottish towns of Aberdeen, Berwick, Newcastle and Tweed as a warning to all who would rise against Edward. An English poet penned the following epitaph for William Wallace, Guardian of Scotland:

Butcher of thousands, threefold death be thine.
So shall the English from thee gain relief,
Scotland be wise and choose a nobler chief.

Following Wallace's capture and gruesome death, **Robert Bruce** (also called Robert *the* Bruce) formally entered the stage of Scotland's history.

Prior to entering the spotlight, he had stayed in the wings as the drama played out. Robert was the eighth Bruce in succession to bear the name, and he was the son of the man who competed with John Balliol for the kingship of Scotland. During the years of war with England, Robert flip-flopped sides time and again. At times he signed oaths of allegiance to Edward. At other times, he fought alongside Wallace. And at still other times he plotted against Edward on one hand and against his principal rivals for the Scottish throne on the other.

In February 1306 Robert killed Red John Cromyn, his strongest rival for the throne. This act paved the way for his ascension to the throne. One month later, Robert Bruce was crowned King of Scotland. It was not an elaborate ceremony: the only ones in attendance were Bruce and his four brothers, his wife, John Menteith (the Betrayer), two abbots and two nobles. Isabella, Countess of Buchan, crowned Robert Bruce King of Scotland.

Upon receipt of the news, Edward went into a frenzy. He executed three of Robert's brothers in gruesome fashion. Thomas Bruce, for example, was tied to horses and dragged pell-mell through the town of Carlisle until he was very dead. He was then hanged, and as a final insult, beheaded! In addition, Edward imprisoned Robert's wife and five-year-old daughter, as well as the Countess of Buchan (not bad punishment when considered in the light of the sentences their brothers-in-law received). He convinced the Pope to excommunicate Robert for his murder of Red John Cromyn. He sent fresh armies to the north to squelch the upstart.

But it seems fate had finally turned in Scotland's favor, and Robert Bruce was in the right place at the right time. Edward died on July 7, 1309, and his son, **Edward II**, succeeded him. Edward II was not nearly the military man his father was and in fact took little interest in the activities occurring in the northern stretches of the realm. Bruce went from one victory to another, gaining courage and increasing morale for his troops. The ranks of the Scottish army burgeoned as Scots from all four quarters of Scotland came to be part of the rout. That is, Scots from all over Scotland, except many of the nobles, who were still trying to stay uninvolved. Bruce was not the least bit patient with them. Seemingly forgetting his former ambivalence (flexibility?), he ruthlessly pulled down these nobles at the same time he was defeating the English.

The battle that broke the will of the English was at **Bannockburn**. Bruce had besieged Stirling Castle, held by the English. Edward II arrived (finally) with an army of 23,000 men. But Edward II was not a cunning warrior and made several tactical errors. He led his army onto low, marshy ground, and they were forced to fight from that position a smaller though better positioned army. The Scots, hardened by years of fighting and seasoned much more than the English troops, pushed the battle at just the right times and places. Soon the English were in rapid retreat and the battle – and Scotland – was lost.

King Robert I formed a **Scottish parliament** and began enacting laws. At Arbroath in 1320, a **Declaration of Independence** was drafted and sent to Pope John XXII, along with a request for his reinstatement to the Church. There was also a request that the Pope tell Edward II to keep his hands off of Scotland. The Pope concurred, and dubbed the new monarch King Robert I.

Edward II was not so quick to recognize Robert's kingship; in fact, he never did. Recognition of Robert as King of Scotland did not come until Edward II died and his son, Edward III, finally recognized Robert's claim in 1328. Not only did he recognize Robert's claim, but he agreed to the betrothal of his infant sister to Bruce's infant son David.

THE STEWARTS

A crucial event occurred at this juncture in Scottish – and English – history. In 1326, Robert I persuaded the Scottish parliament to support his son David for succession, as well as his daughter Marjory's son. Marjory was married to James fitz Alan, the hereditary Steward of Scotland. The fitz Alan family went by the name of their title – the Stewarts. When he was 54 years old, Robert Bruce sensed that his life was slipping from him and sought parliament's support for the succession of his son and grandson. He succeeded in rallying their support, and ruled three more years before his death. The great Robert Bruce, King and Liberator of Scotland, was dead.

The throne passed to his son David, known to history as David II. Even though he was only five years old upon his ascension, both England and Rome recognized his sovereignty. When he was seventeen years old, David assumed active leadership of Scotland, along with the help of capable advisors. He reigned for four years before being captured and imprisoned in the infamous Tower of London. He was to languish there for eleven long years. During David's imprisonment, **Robert the Steward** assumed the reigns of government in Scotland as the Regent of Scotland. He was to be the first Stewart to govern Scotland. He would not be the last.

David finally convinced Edward to release him, and upon his release unpatriotically agreed to allow the succession of the throne of Scotland to pass from him to either Edward or one of his sons upon his (David's) death.

This capitulation was met with disgust and outrage in Scotland. Several nobles, including Robert Stewart, rebelled. The Scottish parliament also refused this agreement and set about to see that it did not happen. When Edward needed cash a few years later for his war with France, he agreed to set aside the agreement for payment of £4,000 per year. The Scottish parliament readily agreed, and Scotland was once again free of English rule.

Upon David II's death in 1371, Scotland was plunged into a murky period of monarchical history. With no clear successors to the throne (David died without producing an heir), chaos reigned. For the next 75 years Scotland was ruled by a procession of ill-supported kings, rapacious regents and greedy governors. One of the kings who ruled during this time penned his own lamentable epitaph just days before his death: "Here lies the worst of kings and the most miserable of men." Because of a lack of leadership, heavy taxes, and difficult times, Scotland devolved into a lawless, clan-led region, and it is perhaps this time that most keenly honed the clan tradition in Scotland.

In May 1424, **James I** was crowned King of Scotland at the age of thirty. James was the second great-grandson of Walter Stewart, the first of the Stewarts of Scotland. His reign was to be the beginning of the Stewart dynasty in Scotland and, eventually, England. It also began a string of kingships typified by early deaths and child kings.

MARY QUEEN OF SCOTS

On December 8, 1542, at Linlithgow Castle, Mary Guise bore James V a daughter, christened Mary. James was the second great-grandson of the first Stewart king. Less than a week after Mary's birth James died at the age of thirty, leaving an infant Stewart to rule Scotland. Once again regents would rule Scotland until the royal heir was old enough to assume the reins of control. And once again, nobles would divide among themselves as they jockeyed for more power and position within the leaderless kingdom.

Henry VIII, the irritable King of England, immediately seized the opportunity to bring the troublesome Scotland under his control. He proposed that the infant Mary be betrothed to his 5-year-old son Edward. The proposal was a fearsome thing to most Scots, and they rebelled at the idea. In response, Henry sent the **Earl of Hertford** to enforce his proposal with military might. The earl carried out his orders with supreme efficiency. According the earl's own account, he and his forces destroyed sixteen fortified castles, 243 villages, and a number of monasteries. His acts were dubbed the "**Rough Wooing**" of Henry. The attacks were so fierce and so complete that many Scots demanded a renewal of Scotland's alliance with France.

Mary's mother feared for her daughter's life, and the two of them fled to France. Mary was raised in the royal courts of the French King Henry

II. While there, she fell in love and when she was 15 and married Francois, the king's son in Notre Dame Cathedral. Shortly thereafter, Mary's father-in-law Henry II died, and Francois became the King of France. His wife Mary became the consort Queen of France, and also became the undisputed Queen of Scotland.

JOHN KNOX & THE REFORMATION

In 1517, Martin Luther tacked his 95 Theses to the Wittenberg Cathedral in Germany, and thus began the **Protestant Reformation**. During the years Mary was in France, the Protestant Reformation, now a significant movement, had carved a firm foothold in Scotland. Many reasons are given for its success, but who is to say just what it is that moves men to make decisions on religion? Many have speculated that the rebelliousness of the Reformation was enough to speak to the hearts and souls of the Scottish nobles and clans, no strangers to rebellion themselves. Others have laid the success of the Reformation at the feet of the Catholic Church. Centuries before (some claim), the clerics had left their ministries in search of the vain things of the world. Regardless of the reasons, Scotland was fertile ground for the reformationists of the 16th century, and the foremost sower of the seeds of religious discord in Scotland was **John Knox**.

A former Catholic priest, John Knox was heavily influenced by the teachings of **John Calvin**, and he left the Catholic Church to become involved in the Reformation. He became an indefatigable champion of Calvinism and the Reformation, as well as an inexhaustible foe of Catholicism in Scotland. He found a sympathetic ear among many of the most powerful nobles in Scotland. Already Scotland was moving away from the Catholicism with which St. Columba had conquered paganism and moving toward the Protestant beliefs of Calvinism.

It was to this new religious environment that Mary Queen of Scots returned from her long stay in France.

Mary's husband Francois died in the winter of 1560, just two and a half years after their marriage. All accounts say that Mary truly loved the young French king, and when he died less than a year after their marriage of an ear infection, it is said she mourned sincerely for forty days. (John Knox, on the other hand, reportedly had this to say about the young king's demise: "The King of France suddenly perisheth of a rotten ear – that deaf ear that would never hear the word of God!")

Mary decided it was time to assume her role as the Queen of Scotland. Mary's arrival in Scotland was an enchanting affair. By all accounts, Mary was incredibly beautiful. She was nearly six feet tall and had striking auburn hair. Large eyes with long, thick lashes accentuated her milky-white complexion. As she rode slowly through Edinburgh, the streets were lined with curious Scots – curious to see this strikingly beautiful woman, the one who was already being called Mary Queen of Scots.

THE TOMBOY QUEEN

Today she would be called a "tomboy." Mary Queen of Scots loved to ride about the countryside in men's clothes, loved to hunt and hawk, was considered a better-than-average archer, and loved to dance. On one occasion she donned a coat of mail and helmet, and with a pistol strapped to her saddle joined her army to put down a rebellion in western Scotland. This was not a quiet, submissive woman! Mary was nearly six feet tall, and her striking auburn hair and beautiful eyes were the subjects of many a poet's pen in Scotland. Sometimes her beauty got in the way – of particular bother was the fact that at least a few of the men of her court fell in love with her and made nuisances of themselves. One, Sir John Gordon, became so insistent that he was eventually executed (not so much for his love, but for his plot to kidnap her).

Upon her arrival, she was presented with a lovely velvet-covered Protestant Bible. The gesture was lovely; the handwritten note on the inside cover was not: "A gift more precious could we none present, Nor yet more needful to your Excellence."

Mary's Catholic upbringing and devotion to that religion put her on a collision course with John Knox. To say that Mary and John Knox didn't get along is an understatement. Neither trusted the other, and each saw much in the other to dislike. The Sunday following Mary's attendance at her first mass in Scotland, John Knox thundered from a nearby pulpit, "One mass is more fearful to me than 10,000 armed men." Mary continued the religion/army comparison when she commented, "I fear the prayers of John Knox more than all the assembled armies of Europe!"

The Scottish parliament decided it would be advantageous to Scotland's future if their queen remarried. They saw some positive possibilities in aligning with one of the major European powers. Mary was what might be called a very eligible lady. Not only was she gorgeous, but she was the Queen of Scotland with a legitimate claim to the throne of England (her grandmother was Henry VIII's sister). As Queen of Scotland, Mary considered serious marriage proposals from most of the major European countries, including France, Spain, Austria, Denmark, and Sweden. In addition to these royal proposals there were many others of lesser stature (from assorted dukes and earls). Her beauty and power were intoxicating possibilities, and the royal courts of Europe hummed with speculation.

Mary rejected them all. Instead, she chose a handsome cousin, **Lord Darnley**. They were secretly married early in 1565, publicly on July 29, 1565. The wedding was Catholic, and did not endear the new couple to the Protestant faithful. The married bliss of the royal couple, however, was not to last. Within weeks of the wedding, Mary reportedly caught Lord Darnley in bed with one of his male servants. She was incensed, and it was the beginning of the end for the marriage. After Mary's discovery, Lord Darnley showed a dark, angry side that Mary had not seen before. He was envious of Mary's power and position, and indignant that she had not elevated him to the full kingship of Scotland. He became abusive, and began to drink excessively. The honeymoon was over.

Mary turned to her personal secretary for comfort and friendship. David Riccio was an Italian who had come to Mary's court as a singer and risen rapidly and dramatically to the position of personal secretary. His friendship with Mary incensed Lord Darnley, even though the two had formerly been good friends.

In December 1565, Mary announced her pregnancy. But Darnley began to suspect that the child was Riccio's, not his. This is highly unlikely, since even though this was an age of accepted promiscuity (especially among royals), Mary seems to have studiously kept herself above such tawdry liaisons. Nevertheless, Darnley was furious. It may be that he felt threatened by the birth of this child. This child, whether his or Riccio's, would be heir to the throne of Scotland – thus quenching any possibility that Lord Darnley could claim the throne for himself. Darnley formed a diabolical plan to rid himself of the hated Riccio, and possibly to secure the throne for himself.

March 9, 1566 was a fateful day for David Riccio. He attended a quiet dinner with Mary and as was his custom, sang a song for her. Shortly after the song, Lord Darnley and a group of his followers burst into the room and attacked Riccio. Clinging to Mary for protection, he was ripped from her and brutally stabbed to death in her presence. Darnley's knife was left in Riccio's chest – a sign that he was the one who engineered the assassination. Darnley hoped the brutal episode would rid him of Riccio (it did), and at the same time cause such trauma to Mary that she would miscarry the child she was carrying (it did not).

Mary survived the traumatic ordeal, and three months later in June 1566 she gave birth to a baby boy. He was christened **James VI** of Scotland, and he was destined to do something many a Scotsman had dreamed of for generations: he would unite the thrones of England and Scotland.

Shortly after Riccio's death, Darnley died in a gunpowder mishap. Plotters saw Mary's hand in his death although most historians feel Darnley may have died in an explosion meant for his wife. Regardless, Mary found herself a widow again. Another ill-timed marriage to a southern Scottish noble named **Lord Bothwell** caused Mary's downfall. Along with Mary, Lord Bothwell was suspected as one of Darnley's assassins; their marriage within three months of Darnley's death was too much for many of the Scottish nobles. They rejected Mary as their queen, and crowned her 13-month-old son James King of Scotland. Mary was imprisoned and Bothwell fled to Norway, where he was immediately imprisoned.

This was the beginning of the end for Mary Queen of Scots. She sent a request for asylum to her cousin, Queen Elizabeth, and before she received a response she fled to England. Elizabeth was in a difficult spot – what to do with this fellow queen who had once proclaimed herself the rightful monarch of England, and who many felt had a more legitimate claim to the throne than Elizabeth? Elizabeth decided a life of seclusion for Mary would solve the problem.

Mary became a prisoner of the state, although it was a very amicable captivity – quite frankly, she lived like a queen. For the next 18 years she was shuttled between various castles around England. When world affairs made Mary a dangerous political liability and a threat to the throne of England, Elizabeth issued a warrant for Mary's execution. The life of one of the most intriguing and beautiful Scots came to an ignominious end on the chopping block on February 8, 1587.

Mary's son James, who was crowned King of Scotland at the tender age of 13 months, proved to be at the right place at the right time. When his second cousin Elizabeth died without heir or spouse in March of 1603, the throne of Scotland was united with the throne of England, and a Scotsman sat upon it. James VI of Scotland became **James I** of England. The hope of Scotland was quickly extinguished, however, as James decided to rule both countries from London, not Edinburgh. Almost immediately he left Scotland for London, and returned to Scotland only once in the ensuing years.

Besides uniting the thrones of the two countries, James is most remembered for two things. First, his is the name that graces the version of the Bible used by millions of Christians worldwide. James commissioned a committee of scholars to translate the Bible from the original languages into English. They accomplished the task and gave the world the **King James Version of the Bible**. In addition, James introduced the term **Great Britain** and insisted that the term be used by Parliament. Initially they refused, but James was forceful enough to force the issue.

When James was murdered in 1625 by a close associate (some claim he was a former lover), James' son Charles ascended to the throne of Great Britain. Charles decided it was high time the religions of England and Scotland should be united. The only problem was that neither the English nor the Scots were willing to change.

THE COVENANTERS

After John Knox's death in 1572, the Reformation he had championed continued to grow in Scotland. Presbyterianism became entrenched and for all intents and purposes replaced Catholicism as the religion of the Scots. Among other things, it featured a vehement intolerance for Catholicism and its trappings, and it stood for a fierce independence from the rule of kings. So it was only natural that when Charles sought to make changes in the worship of the Scots, those changes were violently opposed.

Riots in the streets of Edinburgh and Glasgow erupted when some of the changes were introduced in churches there. Chairs were thrown, fights took place, and general mayhem reigned. A radical arm of the Presbyterian faithful drafted the **National Covenant**, which pledged faith to the true religion (Presbyterianism), and proclaimed the preeminent authority of the General Assembly of the Church of Scotland.

Meanwhile, Charles was having troubles enough in England. A civil war had erupted, Parliament had rebelled against Charles, and he was fighting for his crown and his head. In the end, he lost both. The main thorn in Charles' side, besides Parliament, was **Oliver Cromwell**. Cromwell was a religious fanatic who was intolerant of any beliefs but his own. He and his followers believed that no king could further God's causes, and fought to bring an end to the monarchy in England. With the support of Parliament, he was successful in his quest. After a disastrous military campaign, Charles was tried for treason and found guilty. He was beheaded on January 30, 1649.

The Scots were astounded and horrified. How dare those arrogant English behead their king, a Scotsman! They seemed to be of the opinion that it was okay for Scotsmen to fight against their king, but let an Englishman do so, and real trouble was brewing. They responded by crowning the king's 18-year-old son **Charles II** King of Scotland and England. Oliver Cromwell and his **Roundheads** (so named because of their exceptionally close-cropped hair) invaded and occupied Scotland. The scenario was all too familiar to the Scots: English troops infested their castles and demanded taxes for support.

In 1660 troops loyal to Charles II were successful in restoring Charles to the united throne of Scotland and England. After ten years under Cromwell, the Scots welcomed the return of the monarchy and once again rejoiced that they were being led by a Scotsman. Their joy, however, was short-lived. Charles preferred the royal courts of London to the rolling hills of Scotland, and after his restoration to the throne never again graced Scotland with his presence. The years of his reign were intense and bloody. Like his father and grandfather, Charles insisted that Scotland

and England needed to be united religiously as well as politically. He once again tried to introduce changes to the structure and worship of the Scottish Church; once again the Covenanters rebelled. Initially, the rebellion was (somewhat) peaceful. Three hundred stood down from their officially sanctioned ministerial posts and took their flocks to the fields, where open-air meetings, called **Conventicles**, were held. Armed guards protected these services, as the ministers feared attacks from Charles' armies.

Their fears were well founded. Charles took a strong stance with these religious rebels, and demanded adherence to the new religion. These demands seemed to fortify the Covenanters, and the number and frequency of the Conventicles increased. Scarcely had the Conventicles begun than Charles' armies found and attacked them mercilessly.

Years of killing and persecution followed. As the years progressed, the rebels became more rebellious and the armies of Charles became more hardened and focused. Many on both sides of the cause lost their lives in the name of religion.

To the relief of the Scots, Charles died unexpectedly of apoplexy in 1685. His brother James (briefly) succeeded him. But in an age of religious intolerance, James had a fatal flaw: he was Catholic. As much as the Covenanters hated the Episcopalians of England, and as much as the Episcopalians of England hated the Presbyterians of Scotland, both groups had a common enemy in Catholicism. James was doomed to fail quickly. Officially, his reign lasted less than five years. Unofficially he was probably never really in charge. He was briefly supported by a group of Highland clans called the **Jacobites** (*Jacobus* is the Latin name for James). Their resistance was brief and ineffective, and James was replaced by his Protestant daughter Mary and her husband (James' nephew) William of Orange. James fled to Ireland for support, and then retired to France, where he died in relative anonymity several years later. William resumed the religious purge of Scotland, and his popularity and support, already low, plummeted. His armies were given a free hand in Scotland, and they burned, pillaged and raped with impunity.

Scotland of the 1700s was a Scotland of rebellion and dissension. (Why should the 1700s be any different from any of the preceding centuries?!) During most of the century the Jacobites were busy fomenting discord among the Highlanders. In the mid-1700s, Charles Edward Stewart, called **Bonnie Prince Charlie**, sought to reclaim the throne for the Stewart line. A brilliant and charismatic young man, he was successful in uniting many of the major clans against the crown. A series of decisive battles ensued, and it looked as though Bonnie Prince Charlie was well on his way to restoring the throne to his family.

However, the battles had taken their toll: some of Charlie's best generals were lost. On April 16, 1746 he met English troops in the **Battle of Culloden**. Superior positioning and a deadly artillery barrage helped the English rout Bonnie Prince Charlie's army and dash his hopes for the throne. Charles fled Scotland and went into exile in France.

Because most of his military support had come from the Highland clans, the English government passed the **Disbanding Act** that forbade the wearing of tartans and the playing of bagpipes. That is all the Scots needed to establish those two symbols as indelibly Scottish! Their naturally rebellious nature caused these martyrs of fashion and music to become synonymous with Scotland.

The 1800s were less bloody than preceding centuries and can be considered a fairly quiet time. The industrial revolution that began in the 18th century and continued into the 19th century may have been the primary cause for this. From the mid-18th century to the end of the 19th century, the little berg of Glasgow blossomed from a population of 17,000 to nearly 500,000. Textile mills were the heart of industrial Glasgow, although they were joined by a host of other economic enterprises: ironworks, coal mines, distilleries and shipyards. The **Great Potato Famine** in Ireland caused a surge of immigrants from that fair but troubled island, and many found homes in the factories and shipyards of Glasgow and Edinburgh.

From both the English and Scottish point of view, anarchy and rebellion were bad for business. Dead workers couldn't produce or purchase products, and no products meant no taxes. Scotland and England settled into an uneasy, relatively peaceful period that benefited both.

As the 20th century dawned on Bonnie Scotland, most Scots were urban dwellers, living in the cramped and (at the time) crime-ridden bergs of Glasgow and Edinburgh. When World War I began, and again during World War II, many Scottish youth enlisted in the British army to escape the squalor of the cities. They channeled their native aggression toward a common enemy, and provided great strength to the British army.

SCOTLAND TODAY

From a political standpoint, Scotland has entered an important time in her history. From time to time, nationalistic fervor strikes Scotland, and Scots demand freedom from England's rule, and we seem to be in one of those times at the present. Referred to as **Home Rule** or **Devolution**, these efforts have always seemed to run out of steam in the past. But Scotland may be closer now than ever before to this reality. In 1987 Scottish voters were asked to decide whether they wanted their own parliament. They responded with a resounding "Yes!" and the vote carried by more than a 2-to-1 margin. In 1999 elections were held to determine who would represent Scotland in their own parliament, and the **Scottish Parliament** became a reality in 2000. Time will tell whether this giant step will move Scotland closer to freedom from British rule, or whether it will merely mollify her for many years to come.

Religiously, Scotland has settled into a staunch Presbyterian mode. Religious tolerance abounds more than any other time in Scottish history, and there are plenty of other denominations that have found their home in Scotland, including Catholic, Mormon, Methodist, and Baptist congregations.

Following World War II, the Scots introduced the **Edinburgh Festival** to help combat the new enemy they faced: economic doldrums. While the first years were lean, they slowly got better and now the Edinburgh Festival is a tremendously successful economic venture not only for Edinburgh, but for all of Scotland. (Try and get a flight to Scotland on short notice or a B&B room anywhere in central Scotland during festival time, and you'll see what I mean.) Those meager beginnings have turned into a booming tourism industry that just seems to grow by leaps and bounds.

Today Scotland is a thriving nation with an eye firmly and optimistically fixed on the 21st century. Many of the smokestack industries of the late 1800s and early 1900s have been replaced by the software and electronics industries. Indeed, near Glasgow is an area referred to as the "Silicon Glen." While it certainly won't rival California's Silicon Valley anytime soon, it has taken an important role in the Scottish economy, a role that is certain to expand during the 21st century.

In addition, in 1970 oil was discovered in the North Sea off the coast of Scotland, and that has proven an important and lasting boon to the Scottish economy. And while these high-volume industries have come to Scotland, there is still a significant woolen and agricultural industry here.

Scotland is enjoying this economic renaissance, and they have one of the lowest unemployment rates in western Europe at just under 6%. Over the past two decades Scotland has had an aggressive plan for economic development, and they are beginning to see the fruits of their labors. Economically, things are going well, and the future looks very bright indeed.

6. PLANNING YOUR TRIP

WHEN TO GO - CLIMATE & WEATHER

Scotland enjoys a temperate climate most of the year, thanks to the warm waters of the Gulf Stream. Most tourists find the weather pleasant and more than acceptable for vacationing from April through October, although I have been there in the winter months and found it to be delightful as well (though a wee bit chilly). During April and May, the temperatures are generally in the mid-50s during the days. During the summer months, you can expect the temperatures to be in the 60s, with even an occasional day or two in the 70s (very occasional).

Fall temperatures are generally a little cooler than the summer months, but warmer than April and May. Daytime temperatures usually range from the mid-50s to the low 60s. For the most part, winters in Scotland are also mild, with average temperatures in the mid-30s to low 40s, although the wind will makes it seem much colder. Prepare to bundle up during those winter months!

Scotland has plenty of "**dull days**" – the term in this part of the world for overcast or cloudy days. But other than providing an opaque backdrop for most of your photographs (use ASE 100 or 200 film), there's really no harm done by the dull days. During most months of the year, there is an omnipresent breeze. A light sweater or sweatshirt is usually enough to combat its effects. As you visit some of the coastal sights you'll experience more wind – so hold on to your hat.

Scotland has Daylight Savings Time – called **Summer Time**. It begins the last Sunday of March, and reverts to Standard Time the last Sunday in October. This is a complimentary bonus of extra daylight hours with which to continue your walks on the beach, or an extra hour or two to prowl around deserted ruins.

AVERAGE DAYTIME HIGH TEMPERATURES IN EDINBURGH (FAHRENHEIT)

Month	Temp	Month	Temp
January	43	July	65
February	43	August	66
March	48	September	60
April	50	October	55
May	52	November	49
June	59	December	44

WHAT TO PACK

I have had a tendency in my travel life to pack for every possible social contingency and every conceivable weather condition. Years of international travel have taught me the importance of one word: versatility. For example, I bring a shirt and slacks that are comfortable, yet if necessary would work for a more formal setting with the addition of a jacket and tie.

Here are the necessities for a week's trip: sweater (remember the wind!), three or four shirts (usually long sleeve), a couple of pairs of casual-style pants, and one or two skirts for women, comfortable shoes, several pair of underwear and socks. If you plan on eating in the finest restaurants in Scotland, of course you'll want to bring a suitable pair of slacks, a suit or sports jacket, and a tie for men. Women should bring a nice dress, skirt and blouse, or pants suit and nylons and shoes. Children tend to go through their clothes faster, but I recommend you pack clothes comparable to what you pack for yourself, although they may need a few extra changes of clothes.

You should be prepared for rain. I prefer not to carry an umbrella, choosing instead to fend off the rain with a cap: on all of my trips to Scotland it has rarely rained hard enough to make me wish for an umbrella. But don't let me steer you wrong – it can rain hard here. But I've found that at those times it is best to stay in your B&B and enjoy the company of your hostess, or search out a good museum or art gallery to pass the time. I suggest taking one of those small retractable umbrellas, if a cap won't do the job for you. A lightweight raincoat combined with a heavy wool sweater is usually all I need (except in winter – bring a heavy coat and a pair of longjohns).

You can get just about any toiletry you might need in Scotland: toothpaste, deodorant, shampoo, lotion, make-up and feminine care products. You'll have to decide how important your particular brand is to you, because it may not be sold in Scotland. If you require prescription drugs, bring enough for your trip, but be sure you know exactly what you take, how often, and in what dose in case you lose your medication. Hairdryers are generally available in most hotels and many B&Bs and guesthouses. If you have to have a hairdryer, you should bring your own, but make sure you also bring a converter and plug adapter. Finally, there are places to have your clothes pressed; alternatively, you may want to purchase a small travel iron (with converter and adapter).

If you are traveling with kids, don't forget to bring books, crossword puzzles, magnetic games like chess, checkers, or backgammon, or a Gameboy (or whatever they like), to keep them entertained as you drive from town to town and in the evenings. Also, depending on their age, you should consider purchasing them their own disposable cameras so they can take pictures (it's their vacation too, after all), and they won't bug you to use your camera.

You will need good maps. If you are renting a car, the rental agency will give you one that is fairly general, but not too bad. Some of the smaller towns and more rural roads won't be on the maps you receive from them. You may want to pick up regional maps in the areas you are traveling to; they are usually available at the tourist offices.

You may want to supplement this guide with another B&B or hotel guide. The Scottish Tourist Board publishes two books annually on Bed and Breakfasts and hotels. Each lists about 1,500 STB-approved B&Bs, guesthouses, and hotels throughout the country. *Where to Stay: Bed and Breakfasts* and *Where to Stay: Hotels and Guest Houses* will cost you £6 and £9 respectively, but they'll give you a good selection of additional places to stay. The descriptions are quite brief, far briefer than those you'll find in this travel guide, but the selection is much broader. You can find them at Tourist Information Centres. Use this guide for personal insights into each accommodation; use these other two if you find you are out in the middle of nowhere and it's getting late, or if all the accommodations I have suggested are full.

ENTRY REQUIREMENTS

First and foremost, you must have a **current passport** to enter Scotland. If you have traveled internationally, you probably already have one; it's a good idea to check the expiration date well before you plan to travel. American passports are valid for five years for children and 10 years for adults. Canadian passports are valid for five years. All US citizens traveling to Scotland must have a valid passport. For Canadian citizens, children under 16 can be included on their parents' passports, but they must have their own passport if they are traveling alone.

If you are getting a new passport, you should apply six weeks before you plan to depart (four weeks in Canada). That should give you plenty of time to receive your passport. If you are inside the six-week window, don't fear – you can still get a passport, but it will be more expensive, as you will have to pay for overnight mail charges. About five days is the quickest you can get a passport, but I wouldn't cut it that short! Applications are available at US or Canadian passport offices as well as at some post offices. Some Canadian travel agencies also have passport applications.

Scotland requires only a passport for entry into their country, but it must be good for six months after your intended length of stay. No visa is necessary if you are a citizen of a European Union member country, or a citizen of Australia, Japan, Canada or the United States, and if your stay is less than 90 days. If you plan an extended stay that lasts longer than that, you must demonstrate that you have adequate funds to stay and already possess a return airline ticket.

If you are getting a new passport, here is what will be required:
• a notarized copy of your birth certificate. A hospital copy won't work. Naturalization papers or an old passport are acceptable.
• two identical passport photos taken within the last six months. I've found my local AAA agency to be the best place to get these.
• you'll need to bring a picture ID, such as a driver's license.
• if this is your first passport, you must apply in person.
• the cost is (currently) $60 if you are 16 or over, and $40 if you are younger than 16.
• if you are renewing a passport, and it has expired within the last two years, the cost is $40 (if you are over 18 and your last name is still the same.)

CUSTOMS REGULATIONS
American Citizens
Americans who have been out of the country for more than 48 hours may return to the US with up to $400 worth of goods without paying duty. In addition, you may return with up to 200 cigarettes and one liter of alcohol (you must be at least 21 years old to bring liquor back). If you are traveling as a family, the exemptions apply to each person, but can be pooled as a group.

If the total value of your purchases is greater than $400, you will be expected to pay additional duty. Currently, you must pay 10% duty on the next $1,000 worth of items you are returning with. Beyond the $1,400 threshold (the $400 duty free and the next $1,000 worth of goods), you will be assessed a fee based on the category your purchases fall into. If you need to pay additional duty, cash, checks, travelers' checks, and (in some places) credit cards are acceptable.

If you are an antique aficionado, you are in luck. US customs allows you to bring back antiques duty-free. They define antiques as anything over 100 years old. Original artwork (paintings, drawings, and sculptures) can also be brought into the US duty free.

Canadian Citizens

Once a year, Canadian citizens are allowed to bring C$300 worth of foreign goods back home without paying duty. That applies if you have been out of the country for at least seven days. If you have been gone less than seven days, but more than 48 hours, you can bring back C$100 duty-free each trip, and there is no limit to the number of times you can do this. Exemptions apply to all members of a family traveling with you, but the exemptions cannot be combined as a group.

You may also bring home, duty-free, 1.14 liters of wine or liquor or twenty-four 12-oz. bottles of beer or ale. If you are 16 years of age or older, you may bring home, also duty-free, 200 cigarettes, 50 cigars or cigarillos, and 400 tobacco sticks or 400 grams of manufactured tobacco.

Both American and Canadian citizens can mail gifts home duty-free if the gifts are valued at less than US$50 and C$60. You can only mail one package per day per addressee. Packages should be marked "Unsolicited gift." Packages should also be marked on the outside with the retail value. The value of these gifts is not part of your exemption, and they are duty-free.

During your return flight home, flight attendants will hand out Customs forms for you to complete. You are expected to declare the total value of all products you bring in with you.

SCOTTISH REPRESENTATIVES ABROAD

Before you leave for Scotland, you may wish to contact some of the following organizations. They can be of great help in planning your vacation. Whether you are looking for brochures, travel information, or travel advice, they should be able to meet your needs.

In the United States
- **British Tourist Authority,** *551 Fifth Avenue, Suite 702, New York City, New York 10176. Tel. 800/462-2748; E-mail: 74443.1520@compuserve.com; Website: www.bta.org.uk or www.visitbritain.com*
- **British Tourist Authority,** *625 North Michigan Avenue, Suite 1510, Chicago, Illinois 60611. Tel. 800/462-2748*
- **Consulate General of Scotland,** *345 Park Avenue, New York, NY 10154. Tel. 212/319-2555*

In Canada
• **British Tourist Authority**, *111 Avenue Road, Toronto, Ontario, Canada M5R 3J8. Tel. 416/925-6326, Fax 416/961-2175*

GETTING TO SCOTLAND

You have several options for arranging your trip. If you are an experienced traveler, you may feel comfortable scouting for the best airfares around. Most of us, however, will benefit from the expertise of a qualified international travel agent.

Find an agent that specializes in international travel. Check with friends and relatives who have traveled abroad and get their recommendations. Interview several travel agencies until you find one with which you are comfortable. After you have decided on a travel agent, provide him or her with all the organizations you are affiliated with – AAA, AARP, your credit union, your company, etc. Sometimes these entities have negotiated special rates with the airlines, and your travel agent can find those rates for you. Also keep in mind that airlines sometimes run discount fares that beat any affiliation-negotiated rates.

At the time of this writing, the following airlines fly directly to Glasgow from the US: **American** (from Chicago), **British Airways** (from New York's JFK), **Continental** (from Newark), **Northwest** (from Boston during the summer and occasionally during the rest of the year), and **United** (from Dulles in Washington, D.C.). There are no direct flights from Canada.

Most of the major airlines that don't fly directly to Glasgow fly into London and then connect with local airlines to get to Scotland. The following airlines fly to Scotland from London from the indicated airports:

From Heathrow
• **British Airways**, *Tel. 0181/754-7321,* to Aberdeen, Edinburgh, Glasgow
• **British Midland**, *Tel. 0345/554-554,* to Aberdeen, Edinburgh, Glasgow

From Gatwick
• **British Regional Airlines**, *Tel. 0345/256-256,* to Inverness
• **British Airways**, *Tel. 0181/754-7321,* to Aberdeen, Edinburgh, and Glasgow

From London City
• **Air UK**, *Tel. 0345/666-777*, to Edinburgh

From London Luton
• **Easyjet Airlines**, *Tel. 0870/600-0000*, to Aberdeen, Edinburgh, Glasgow

From London Stansted
• **Air UK**, *Tel. 0345/666-777*, to Edinburgh
• **KLM UK**, *Tel. 0181/750-9820*, to Aberdeen, Edinburgh, Glasgow
• **Ryanair**, *Tel. 1279/681-300*, to Prestwick

The London-Scotland route is extremely competitive, which works to your advantage. Watch for price wars, and you may be able to find fares as low as £55 to £70; normal fares run between £100 and £150.

HOTEL & INN TERMS

Most accommodations in Scotland fall into one of five categories: youth hostels, B&Bs, guest houses, hotels, and self-catering facilities. In most European countries, **youth hostels** are typically spartan places to lay your head, get a shower, eat some basic food, and that's about it. While that is often the case in Scotland, there are a number of Scottish youth hostels that are housed in gorgeous mansions and townhouses.

While they are still inexpensive, you may be somewhat surprised at the quality of some of the Scottish youth hostels. Hostel accommodations range from single rooms to dormitory-style (10 to 18 beds). Costs are low, ranging from £5 to £13 for the dormitories to the equivalent of B&B rates for a single room (£20+). These days, you'll see "youth" from ages 18 to 70 and beyond (literally), so don't let the label "youth hostel" stop you from considering it if you are looking for inexpensive lodging. Most hostels provide a self-catering kitchen for cooking your own food. Some charge a nominal fee for sheets and towels, while others include them in the price. Most take credit cards, some do not. Hostels do not include breakfast in their prices. All in all, hostels are an excellent way to lower your costs while traveling in Scotland.

There are two categories of youth hostels in Scotland. The first are those that are members of the **Scottish Youth Hostel Association** (SYHA). You can count on these to meet minimum standards of cleanliness, condition, and safety. Other hostels are considered "independents," and run the gamut from pretty grim to extremely nice. To stay in a SYHA youth hostel, you must obtain a hosteling card. This card is free, but you must purchase a £1 stamp to put on it the first six times you stay in a hostel. After that, there is no additional charge.

Bed and Breakfasts, more commonly known as **B&Bs**, mean you will probably be staying with a family in one of the rooms in their home. By Scottish regulation, B&Bs cannot accommodate more than six individuals at a time. By definition, breakfast is included in the rate. B&Bs will generally range from £16 to £25 per person.

Guest Houses are very similar to B&Bs, although owners are allowed to offer rooms to more than six individuals. Hence, most guest houses have more rooms than B&Bs have to offer. Most (if not all) guest houses operate on the same pricing format as B&Bs – the rate includes breakfast. Many guest house owners will also provide dinner for a reasonable price (£10 to £15) if arranged in advance. Rates at guest houses will generally range from £25 to £35 per person.

Most B&Bs and guest houses charge a slight premium for renting a double room to a single traveler, since their rates usually are **per person sharing**. The "norm" and expectation is that two people will share a room. If a B&B lists its rate as £16 per person, then the cost for the room is £32 for two people. If only one person rents the room, instead of charging the full £32 for the double room, singles are usually charged a little more than the per person rate for doubles. For instance, in the above example, a person traveling alone might have to pay £21 or £22 to stay in the double room. I have included the rate for singles in all the hotel and B&B listings. Given the above rates, if three people want to share that double room, the cost would be £48 (£16 per person sharing).

Hotels generally have more than six rooms available for renting and will normally have a liquor license, pub and/or restaurant on-site for guests and non-residents. Rates at hotels are sometimes listed as per person, and sometimes one rate for the room itself, regardless of how many people are staying. Be sure and clarify this point when you make a reservation. I have tried to be clear in my hotel write-ups which pricing scheme they are using (per person or per room), but please verify this with whomever you are making your reservations. Rates at hotels start as low as £40 per room and go up from there.

Self-catering facilities are those places of accommodation that provide a kitchen and (often) laundry facilities for their guests. No meals are included in the rates; guests are expected to prepare their own meals in the self-catering kitchen. Rates are charged by the week regardless of how many people are staying. This is an excellent option if you are going to be staying in one place and exploring those parts of Scotland that are within easy driving distance.

WHAT'S HAPPENING WHEN?

There is a difference in the seasons between the southern and northern parts of Scotland, but here are some generalizations you should find reasonably accurate:

April – Daffodils, tulips, and yellow gorse are in bloom. The trees are beginning to leaf out in spring-green. Baby lambs gambol everywhere.

May – Rhododendrons begin blooming (their peak is late May), and the trees are leafed out.

*June/July – Summer flowers are everywhere, and the deep green of the leaves is unbelievable. The **Glasgow Folk Festival** features wonderful Scottish folk music.*

*August – August 12th is called the "Glorious 12th" when the heather is at its zenith. Most of the **Highland Games** are in August, and the **Edinburgh Festival** runs for three weeks in August.*

September – Early in the month the heather is still in bloom, leaves are beginning to put on their fall colors. The granddaddy of the Highland Games are in Braemar in September.

October – The leaves are still turning at the beginning of the month. The weather is still generally warm enough to tour and enjoy out-of-doors activities.

November to February – The weather can be brisk and breezy. These are great months to concentrate on museums and indoor activities.

*March – Spring begins to come. The **Edinburgh Folk Festival** is held (not 'the' Edinburgh Festival), but a great opportunity to hear Scottish folk music.*

In the *Where to Stay* sections in this book, "All major credit cards accepted" means the facility will accept American Express, Diner's Club, MasterCard, and Visa. If any one of these is not accepted, I have listed those credit cards that are accepted. I have listed a range of rates if the rates vary throughout the year. The lower rates are typically only valid during the off or low seasons, and the higher rates are valid from about June through September.

You'll also run across the term **ensuite**, which I use in this guide as well. If you get a room ensuite, this means you have a bathroom in your room or suite; otherwise, you'll have to use a bathroom out in the hall. Most places offer ensuite rooms, and the few that do not generally have a private bath in the hall for the one room that isn't ensuite.

But beware – guaranteeing a reservation at a hotel in Scotland with a credit card may mean just that – *guaranteeing* a reservation. At some of the upscale hotels in Scotland, if you cancel a reservation *within seven days* of your intended day of arrival, and you guaranteed the reservation with a credit card, you will still pay for one night's lodging whether you stay or not. With the rates at luxury hotels ranging from $200 per night to over $750 per night, that's a pretty expensive cancellation! So, when you make your reservation, be sure and ask about the hotel's cancellation policy.

As you might expect, rates in hotels and B&Bs are seasonal, and you'll pay slightly more during the high season (from May through August) than you will the rest of the year. Some hotels have another rate from March to April and during September and October that is less than the high season, but higher than the rate they charge from November to February.

GETTING AROUND SCOTLAND

There are many ways to get around Scotland, and the mode depends entirely on your purpose, destinations, adventuresome spirit and desires. Bicycle, bus, rental car, hitchhiking, and train – or a combination of any of them – are the major options.

BY BICYCLE

If you choose to see Scotland on two wheels, congratulations. This is one of the most popular modes of transportation for tourists from May through October. Most cities of any size have bicycle rental shops with bicycles for hire on a daily, weekly, and monthly basis. Expect to pay about £7 per day, £30 per week, or £115 per month. Most bicycles for hire are the currently popular 18- or 21-speed mountain bikes.

Many of the bicycle shops close down during the off-season. So if you're going to Scotland from about November through March or April, you may want to call the Tourist Information Centre in the city where you want to begin your cycling and get the names of companies that are open that time of year.

BY BUS

Buses are a popular means of travel in Scotland for tourists as well as Scots. There are two primary bus companies in Scotland: **National Express**, *Tel. 0990/808-808; Website: www.nationalexpress.co.uk;* and **Scottish Citylink**, *Tel. 0990/505-505; Email: info@citylink.demon.co.uk; Website: www.citylink.co.uk.timetable*. Both offer discount cards that are good for one year and provide a 30% discount off regular fares. The **National Express Discount Coachcard** costs £8, and the **Scottish Citylink Smart**

Card costs £5. Both discount cards are for people under 25 years old or 50 years old or older. If you are in that hazy period called "middle age" (at least as defined by the bus company) you can get a discount card if you can prove that you are a full-time student, so bring that college ID card with you. Discounts are available for children younger than 16 years old, and children under 5 years old travel free.

In addition to these discount cards, you can buy a **Tourist Trail Pass**, which allows unlimited travel on all National Express and Scottish Citylink services throughout Scotland (as well as the rest of Britain). Adult fares range from £49 for three days to £187 for two weeks. Those who fall into the magical age groups (children 5 to 15, young person from 16 to 25, or senior citizens 50 or older), then your Tourist Trail Pass will range between £39 for three days to £143 for two weeks.

There is a combination rail/bus card available if you intend on traveling throughout the Highlands. It is called the **Highland Rover** and it is available for £42. This allows you to travel any four out of eight consecutive days. Train service is available on this card between Glasgow and Oban, Fort William and Mallaig. Then from there you can take advantage of the Scottish Citylink bus system to travel between Oban, Fort William and Inverness. You can also catch a train between Inverness and Wick, Thurso, Aberdeen, and a host of towns along the way.

BY CAR

"Left is right and right is wrong" when it comes to driving in Scotland. That's right – the Scottish drive on the left, as do the English.

Surprisingly, driving on the left is not difficult to get used to. However, if you rent a car with a manual transmission, you should have reasonable coordination since you'll be shifting with your left hand instead of your right. If you can't pat your head and rub your stomach at the same time, you may want to consider paying extra for an automatic transmission. But it will cost you from £8 to £15 extra per day, depending on the time of year, the agency, and the class of car you rent. That's a little pricey, and you have to make the decision, but it will be just one less thing to worry about. And one less thing to worry about is exactly what you'll need as you encounter your first "round-about."

If you live in the eastern United States, you are probably familiar with traffic circles – the US name for round-abouts. But if you are from west of the original 13 colonies, they may be a mystery. Round-abouts are a traffic control system found at the intersection of two or more roads. Generally, no stop signs or traffic lights are employed – drivers merely enter the circle continuing on their journey until they reach the outlet that takes them in the direction they want to go (got that?). Initially a skeptic, I came to admire the smooth and efficient way they manage traffic.

ROUND-ABOUTS

Round-abouts can be intimidating the first few times you enter one. The following will help you navigate your way in and out:
- *traffic in round-abouts moves clock-wise;*
- *traffic already in the round-about has the right-of-way and cars in the round-about and those behind you will expect you to stop if the road is not clear;*
- *round-abouts are generally well-signed going into and within them;*
- *round-abouts that handle lots of traffic are often augmented by traffic signals.*

There are several types of roads in Scotland. Roads are categorized as M-, A- or B-roads. M-roads are the main arteries that run between major cities. A-roads are the main roads, and B-roads are the local roads.

M-roads are about the same as interstate highways in the United States. The speed limit on these roads is 70 mph. There are not many of these roads in Scotland.

A-roads are similar to two-lane highways in the United States. The speed limit on A-roads is 60 mph. Occasionally you'll see signs for a "dual carriageway" and you'll come to love them. They are similar to divided highways and are a welcome sight after the narrow roads you primarily drive in Scotland.

B-roads make up the majority of the roads in Scotland and are extremely narrow. They are well maintained and the speed limit on these roads is also 60 mph, unless otherwise posted. However, as a practical matter, I found 40 mph to be the speed I was most comfortable with.

In addition to these roads, there are myriad other smaller, more rural roads throughout Scotland. These roads are neither lettered nor numbered, and they may or may not be on the map you have with you. They are the paved ancient carriage roads of medieval Scotland. Often referred to as **single-track roads**, they are painfully narrow. Extreme caution is needed as you drive these roads, because of their slimness and because you will probably be driving through lovely countrysides that you want to look at. You'll find many of these roads primarily in the north and west of Scotland.

Bear in Mind...
- Drivers and front seat passengers are required to wear seat belts.
- Small children and babies must be in a car seat.
- Motorcyclists and their passengers are required to wear helmets.

- Scotland has very aggressive laws when it comes to driving under the influence of alcohol.
- A solid white line serves the same purpose in Scotland as the solid yellow line does here – it means no passing.
- Gasoline is more expensive in Scotland than in the US, but on a par with the rest of Europe. The last time I was there, the cost averaged about 60 pence per liter. That works out to about £2.25, or roughly $3.60 per gallon. The cost will vary, of course, depending on the exchange rate when you are traveling.
- Unless you are traveling on M-roads, remember travel times will be much slower than in the states due to narrow winding roads, frequent villages, tractors, sheep, cattle, etc. I found 40 miles an hour is a fairly aggressive estimate for most roads.
- In general, locals tend to drive at much higher speeds than I am comfortable with. In those cases, I simply look for an opportunity to pull over and let them pass, then continue my driving and sightseeing at a leisurely pace.

Driving in Cities

Driving in the cities requires special attention. Bicyclists, motorcyclists, and pedestrians are more plentiful and far more aggressive than in most American cities. Motorcyclists in particular can be maddening: passing on your left or right, darting in and out of traffic, and making a general nuisance of themselves! Traffic lights are on the corners – not hanging in the air over the intersections. I never did get accustomed to this, and had to consciously remind myself to watch closely. In the larger cities like Glasgow and Edinburgh it is virtually impossible, and dangerous, to sightsee while you are driving. Find a place to park, and walk around the cities, seeing all that you wish in relative safety.

I say relative safety, because as a pedestrian in Scotland you need to concern yourself with the different traffic patterns. Rather than looking left for traffic before stepping off the curb, as you would in the US, you must look to the right! During World War II, Winston Churchill had an accident that underscores the importance of this. On a trip to New York City, he looked to the right for traffic – as he would in London – and stepped into the path of an oncoming taxi – coming from his left. Fortunately, he sustained only minor injuries. So remember: look to the right!

Parking

If you are driving in Scotland, you will assuredly be parking. Parking rules are a little different than in the United States, and sometimes the rules are not intuitively obvious. Here are a few pointers.

It is illegal to park:
• within five meters of an intersection
• at a taxi stand or bus stop
• where there is a continuous white line, unless the roadway has at least three traffic lanes
• in such a manner as to cause an obstruction
• within 15 meters of the approach side of a cross-walk, or within five meters on the other side of a cross walk
• when double yellow lines are present. If a single yellow line is present, it is illegal to park from 8:30am to 6:30pm, Monday through Friday.

Just when it appears that you have found a parking space in an area free of restrictions, look carefully for a **parking meter box**. In many Scottish cities, there are no individual parking meters for each parking space. Rather, about every half block or so, there is a parking meter box that dispenses a little piece of paper that you put either on your dashboard, or on the window closest to the curb. Don't overlook these little boxes, or you may find yourself with a £20 souvenir you hadn't planned on! While Scotland is very tuned into tourists and tourism, there seems to be no hesitation to ticket rental cars for failing to follow the parking rules of the city! I can think of better ways to spend £20 than for a parking ticket; how about you!?

Rental Cars
While airfares are usually fairly price-competitive, you will need to shop around for the best car rental rates. You can do this through your travel agent, or you can do it yourself. Rates on rental cars seem to change on a daily basis, and car rental agencies also have a series of discounts based on negotiated rates with affiliated companies and organizations. I recently checked the major rental car agencies – Hertz, Avis, National (which is Europcar in Scotland) – and found a surprisingly wide range of prices. For a two-week rental, I was quoted prices from $425 to over $975 for the same class of car and the same coverages!

When comparing rental car rates, be certain you are shopping "apples to apples," such as length of time, type of insurance, size of car, mileage charges, service charges and taxes. When I checked, I asked the companies to include Collision Damage Waiver (CDW – see below), theft insurance, and Value Added Tax. All the agencies I checked with included unlimited mileage in their rates, but ask just to make sure. Also, be sure you compare dollars to dollars, or pounds to pounds. Most agencies will quote their rates in dollars as well as pounds.

Regarding gasoline, some rental agencies give you a full tank of gas and require you to leave a £25 or £30 deposit. If you return the car with a full tank, they refund the deposit. Other agencies give you a full tank of gas and expect you to return it empty; they do not give you credit for any gas left in the tank, even if you filled it at the airport. Be sure and check which policy is in effect when you rent your car.

You'll need a valid US or Canadian driver's license and a major credit card to drive in Scotland, but you do not need an International Drivers license unless you are staying for more than one year.

Most car rental agencies in Scotland will only rent to drivers who are at least 23 years old and younger than 75 years old. Some rental agencies require you to be at least 25.

Car Insurance

If you are accustomed to renting cars in the United States, you know your own car insurance usually covers you while you are driving a rental car in the US. *Such is not the case in Scotland.* Your domestic car insurance will *not* cover you while you are driving a rental car in Scotland. However, some credit card companies will cover your car rental insurance, so you can forgo the **Collision Damage Waiver** (CDW) charge. That amounts to about £8 or more per day.

Before you accept or forego the CDW, check with your credit card company to determine whether or not you are covered if you rent a car with your credit card. For example, my credit card company covers collisions, rollovers, vandalism, theft, tire blowout or damage, and windshield damage. Also check what restrictions, deductibles, or requirements apply. My credit card company has the following policies:
• they cover your rental car for a maximum of 31 days
• all drivers must be listed on the rental agreement
• all claims must be submitted to the credit card company within 20 days
• the entire car rental must be charged to the credit card

In addition, among other things, they do *not* cover:
• injury of anyone or anything inside or outside the rental car
• loss due to off-road operation of the rental car
• loss due to intentional acts, or due to driver(s) being under the influence of alcohol or drugs
• expensive, exotic, and antique vehicles (e.g., Bentley, Daimler, Ferrari,
• Lamborghini, Lotus, Maserati, Rolls-Royce, etc.)
• loss due to hostility of any kind (including war, invasion, rebellion, or insurrection)

I asked for and received a copy of the coverage and restrictions my credit card company offered. Be sure and read the fine print, because whether it is in 6-point font or 18-point font, you will still be required to adhere to their policies. Many major credit card companies offer a similar service, but please don't assume yours does. Even if you have checked in the past, check again before you leave: programs change, services expire, or new stipulations may be put in place. It would be a shame to have a lasting and unpleasant monetary memory from your trip to Scotland because you didn't make a 5-minute phone call.

Here is a **rental car caution**: Do not take your rental car on any of the inter-island ferries unless you have told your rental car company (and paid a substantially higher rate). If you choose not to tell them and you have a ferry mishap, you may find yourself making car payments on a car that is resting on the bottom of the North Sea.

SCOTTISH DRIVING TERMS	
bonnet	*hood*
boot	*trunk*
caravan	*trailer (like a travel trailer)*
car park	*parking lot*
coach	*bus*
dip	*dim (as in: dim your lights)*
diversion	*detour*
dual carriageway	*divided highway*
give way	*yield*
lay by	*rest area*
lorrie	*truck*
margin	*shoulder*
M__, Motorway	*interstate highway*
overtaking	*passing*
petrol	*gasoline*
way out	*exit*

As you might expect, there are several dozen car rental agencies in Scotland. Following are a few of the more notable agencies:

Car Rentals in Glasgow
- **Arnold Clark Car Rental**, *Phoenix Retail Park, Paisley, PA1 2BH, Tel. 0141/889-6512*
- **Avis Rent-a-Car**, *161 North Street. Tel. 0141/221-2827*
- **Avis Rent-a-Car**, *Glasgow Airport. Tel. 0141/887-2261*
- **Budget Rent-a-Car**, *101 Waterloo Street. Tel. 0141/225-4141*
- **EuroDollar Rent-a-Car**, *76 Lancefield Quay. Tel. 0141/204-1051*

• **Hertz Rent-a-Car**, *106 Waterloo Street. Tel. 0141/248-7736*
• **Hertz Rent-a-Car**, *St. Andrews Drive, Glasgow Airport. Tel. 0141/887-2451*
• **Mitchell's Self Drive**, *47 McAlpine Street. Tel. 0141/221-8461*

Car Rentals in Edinburgh
• **Arnold Clark Car Rental**, *Lochrin Place, Tollcross. Tel. 0131/228-4747*
• **Avis Rent-a-Car**, *100 Dairy Road. Tel. 0131/337-6363*
• **Budget Rent-a-Car**, *The Royal Scot Hotel, 111 Glasgow Road. Tel. 0131/ 334-7739*
• **Europcar UK Ltd.**, *24 East London Street. Tel. 0131/557-3456*
• **Hertz Rent-a-Car**, *10 Picardy Place. Tel. 0131/556-8311*
• **Mitchell's Self Drive**, *32 Torphichen Street. Tel. 0131/229-5384*
• **Woods Care Rental**, *Edinburgh Airport. Tel. 01506/858-660*

Car Rentals in Aberdeen
• **Arnold Clark Car Rental**, *Girdleness Road. Tel. 01224/249-159*
• **Avis Rent-a-Car**, *16 Broomhill Road. Tel. 01224/574-252*
• **Hertz Rent-a-Car**, *Railway Station. Tel. 01224/210-748*
• **Mitchell's Self Drive**, *35 Chapel Street. Tel. 01224/642-642*

Car Rentals in Inverness
• **Arnold Clark Car Rental**, *47 Harbour Road. Tel. 01463/236-684*
• **Budget Rent-a-Car**, *Railway Terrace. Tel. 01463/713-333*
• **EuroDollar Rent-a-Car**, *Shore Street. Tel. 01463/238-084*
• **Hertz Rent-a-Car**, *Inverness Airport, Terminal Building. Tel. 01667/462- 652*

SCOTTISH MILEAGE CHART

Here is a driving chart that gives you the mileage between various cities and towns in Scotland:

Aberdeen							
131	*Edinburgh*						
161	*138*	*Fort William*					
152	*45*	*108*	*Glasgow*				
109	*162*	*69*	*178*	*Inverness*			
201	*182*	*44*	*152*	*109*	*Mallaig*		
190	*125*	*50*	*96*	*118*	*94*	*Oban*	
171	*222*	*119*	*238*	*63*	*114*		*Ullapool*

BY HITCHHIKING

Hitchhiking is legal in Scotland, and is a wonderful way to see the country and meet a host of Scots from all walks of life. It is especially effective if you don't really care where you are going or when you will get there. You'll see far more people hitchhiking in Scotland than you do in the US. If you're going to hitchhike, use caution, go in pairs whenever possible, and if you feel the least bit uncomfortable about a car or truck that stops to pick you up, wait for the next one.

BY TRAIN

The railway system in Scotland isn't as omnipresent as it is in many European countries, but it does get you to most sections of the country. Service connects the major cities across the middle of Scotland like Edinburgh, Glasgow, Perth, Stirling and Dundee. Trains reach the northern towns of Aberdeen, Inverness, Wick and Thurso. But heading into the hinterlands of the Highlands you are pretty limited as far as train service goes. There is spotty train service to the Borders and the Southwest, so to see these areas effectively you either need to rent a car or take buses.

THE SCOTTISH TOURIST BOARD

The reception you receive as a tourist in Scotland will be warm and cheerful. The Scots take tourism in their country very seriously. Approximately one out of every fourteen Scottish workers is employed in the tourism industry. Tourism in Scotland accounts for over about 5% of the Scottish Gross Domestic Product (GDP).

With that kind of impact on the Scottish economy, you can be sure the **Scottish Tourist Board** (STB) is anxious to see that you have a pleasant and enjoyable trip to their country. Several months prior to your trip, call or write to any of several STB locations in the part of the country you wish to visit, and they will provide you with an abundance of tourism material. You should request the specific types of information you are interested in: tourist attractions, Bed and Breakfasts, hotels, etc. Some of the material they send you is free, and they will also send you a price list for other materials you can purchase.

The main office of the STB is in Edinburgh (see below for address and telephone numbers). The STB also has an office in London, *19 Cockspur Street, London SW1Y 5BL, Tel. 0171/930-8661.* There is no STB office in the United States, but the **British Tourism Office**, *551 Fifth Avenue, Suite 702, New York, NY 10176, Tel. 212/986-1188, 800/462-2748* can help you. There is also an office in Toronto, *111 Avenue Road, Toronto, Ontario, Canada M5R 3J8, Tel. 416/925-6326, Fax 416/961-2175.*

The STB has a network of tourist offices throughout the width and breadth of Scotland. These local offices are a great source of information for points of interest in their respective areas. Following are the regional offices of the STB:

- **Scottish Tourist Board Central Information Department**, *23 Ravelston Terrace, Edinburgh EH4 3EU. Tel. 0131/332-2433, Fax 0131/315-4545*
- **Ayrshire and Arran Tourist Board**, *Burns House, Burns Statue Square, Ayr, KA7 1UP. Tel. 01292/262-555, Fax 01292/269-555*
- **Dumfries & Galloway Tourist Board**, *64 Whitesands, Dumfries DG1 2RS. Tel. 01387/245-550, Fax 01387/245-551*
- **Scottish Borders Tourist Board**, *Murray's Green, Jedburgh TD8 6BE. Tel. 01835/863-435, Fax 01835/864-099*
- **Edinburgh and Lothians Tourist Board**, *3 Princes Street, Edinburgh EH2 2QP. Tel. 0131/473-3800, Fax 0131/473-3881*
- **Greater Glasgow and Clyde Valley Tourist Board**, *11 George Square, Glasgow G2 1DY. Tel. 0141/204-4400, Fax 0141/221-3524.*
- **Argyll, The Isles, Loch Lomond, Stirling and the Trossachs Tourist Board**, *7 Alexandra Place, Dunoon, Argyll PA23 8AB. Tel. 01369/701-000, Fax 01369/706-085.*
- **Angus and City of Dundee Tourist Board**, *7-21 Castle Street, Dundee DD1 3AA. Tel. 01382/527-527, Fax 01382/527-550*
- **Kingdom of Fife Tourist Board**, *St. Andrews Tourist Information Centre, 70 Market Street, St. Andrews KY16 9NU. Tel. 01334/472-021, Fax 01334/478-422*
- **Perthshire Tourist Board**, *Administrative Headquarters, Lower City Hills, West Mill Street, Perth PH1 5QP. Tel. 01738/627-958, Fax 01738/630-416*
- **Aberdeen and Grampian Tourist Board**, *27 Albyn Place, Aberdeen AB10 1YL. Tel. 01224/632-727, Fax 01224/581-367*
- **The Highlands of Scotland Tourist Board**, *Peffery House, Strathpeffer, Ross-shire IV14 9HA. Tel. 0870/514-307, Fax 01997/421-168*
- **Orkney Tourist Board**, *6 Broad Street, Kirkwall, Orkney KW15 1NX. Tel. 01856/872-856, Fax 01856/875-056*
- **Shetland Islands Tourism**, *Market Cross, Lerwick, Shetland ZE1 0LU. Tel. 01595/872-856, Fax 01595/695-807*
- **Western Isles Tourist Board**, *4 South Beach Street, Stornoway, Isle of Lewis HS1 2XY. Tel. 01851/701-818, Fax 01851/701-828*

COST OF TRAVEL

Obviously, the mode of transportation you choose for your travels and the lifestyle you lead while in Scotland will have great bearing on your travel costs. Having said that, here's some general information about travel costs in Scotland.

Generally speaking, costs in Scotland are about what you'd expect to pay for things in the United States, if you ignore the dollar/pound conversion rate. In other words, if you'd expect to pay $4 for a sandwich, it will generally cost around £4 (which is really about $6.60). Or if you'd expect to pay $50 for a room, it will probably cost around £50 (which is really about $82.50). One notable exception is the cost of gasoline. For years, gasoline in Europe has been far more expensive than it is in the US. On my most recent trips, petrol was running about $4.35 per gallon.

Rates for Bed and Breakfasts (B&Bs) around the country generally range from about £16 to £25 per person sharing, guesthouses run from £25 to £35 per person sharing, and hotels run from £40 to £100 per room, and luxury hotels run much higher. If you choose to stay in youth hostels, where the accommodations are usually clean but very basic, expect to pay from £5 to £9. Rooms in Glasgow and Edinburgh will generally be at the higher end of the spectrum and rooms in rural areas at the lower end.

The rate for rental cars varies widely, so it pays to shop diligently. A weekly rental in Glasgow should run you in the neighborhood of $200, depending on the car size, time of the year, etc.

Trains crisscross Scotland and are a viable transportation option. There are a number of different fares for travel throughout Scotland. In addition, there are several discounts available to travelers. If you are under 25 or over 50 you can purchase one of several discount cards that provide 33% discounts off regular fares. (Sorry – those of us in that "middle-age" range pay full fare) The discount cards cost £18 and are good for one year. They are pretty good deal if you intend on traveling a lot by train. The cards are called the **Young Person's Railcard** (for travelers 16-25 years old), and the **Senior Citizen's Railcard** (for those 50 years of age and older). Discounts are available for children younger than 16 years old, and children under 5 years old travel free.

Bus service in Scotland is very good, and reaches most any place you might want to go within the country. There are two main bus companies in Scotland: National Express and Scottish CityLink. Both have routes that cover significant portions of the country, and can get you just about any place you want to go, or at least in the general vicinity. Fares are reasonable, and you can leave an unlimited amount of driving to them for as little as £49 for three days up to £187 pounds for two weeks.

Bicycling across Scotland has become fashionable in recent years. The mild climate and beautiful country lends itself to this mode of transportation, even though the narrow roads do not. Bicycle shops are plentiful around the country, especially in areas such as Edinburgh, Glasgow, Aberdeen and Inverness. Expect to pay around £7 per day, £30 per week, or £115 per month for a bicycle.

Shop owners usually require something of value to be left behind as a deposit. Generally speaking, your passport or a major credit card will do. Bicycling is an excellent way to augment motorized travel in Scotland, whether you've chosen car, bus, train, or hitchhiking. If you do rent a bicycle, please be careful. The roads are painfully narrow, with lots of curves. Bicycle riders are expected to ride with traffic, not against it.

If you are planning to mix bike riding with bus and train riding, plan ahead. Buses will allow bicycles sometimes, but are hesitant to do so during the peak tourist months. The train lines require reservations to be made a month in advance.

It is estimated that there are nearly 800 islands off the coast of Scotland, about 130 of which are inhabited. Many of these islands have ferries that will whisk you to their shores. There are a host of fares for ferries available to travelers. One of the most attractive is the **Island Hopscotch fare** available from **Caledonian MacBrayne** (normally referred to as **CalMac**). It offers travelers with or without cars a series of pre-planned itineraries to several islands. The fare is good for one month from the first day of travel. Fares range from £6.85 per person to £20.30 per person, depending on the islands you wish to visit. Rates for your rental car range from £40 to £96, again depending on where you want to go.

Another popular fare for ferries is the **Island Rover fare**. It allows unlimited travel on CalMac ferries to any of the islands they serve. The cost for an 8-day pass is £39 per person, or £199 per person for a 15-day pass. If you want to take your car, it will cost an additional £56 (8-day pass) or £299 (15-day pass). (Remember – most of the rental car companies do not cover your car while on a ferry unless you have informed them and paid a higher rate.)

7. BASIC INFORMATION

BUSINESS HOURS

Businesses are generally open Monday through Saturday from 9:00am to 5:30pm or 6:00pm, although in practice many stores open at 9:30am or 10:00am. Outside of the major cities, many businesses still close for an hour at lunchtime. In the more rural areas, some shops also close early on Tuesday or Wednesday afternoons.

ELECTRICITY

Electricity in Scotland is 240 volts (50 cycles) and an adapter is required. Most discount stores like Target, K-Mart, and Wal-Mart, as well as Sears and J.C. Penny carry inexpensive adapters that will do the job nicely. Remember, if you expect to use your hairdryer, curling iron, or electric razor, you'll need an adapter. Oh yes – unless you're going to bring lots of very expensive (and heavy) batteries, you'll want that adapter to recharge the batteries for your camcorder (common oversight).

EMBASSIES & CONSULATES IN SCOTLAND

• **American Consulate**, *3 Regent Terrace, Edinburgh. Tel. 0131/344-3250*
• **Canadian Embassy**, *3 George Street, Edinburgh. Tel. 0131/220-4333*

HEALTH

Before you leave for your holiday in Scotland, check with your health insurance company to see if you are covered in the event of an emergency, illness, or injury during your travels in Scotland. If you are covered, find out the procedure that they require you to follow before seeking treatment. As you may know, Scotland has a national health care system, and unless you have insurance, you will only be treated in the event of an emergency. If, however, it is necessary to be admitted as a patient, you may find yourself responsible for the bill. As of this writing, Medicare doesn't cover overseas medical expenses, but some of their supplemental plans do. Check before going.

LAUNDRY

If you are staying for more than a week, you probably will need to do your wash. That is easier said than done. But, if you are diligent (and in a city) you should be able to find a place.

You have several options. Most major hotels have valet laundry services. If you are staying in a B&B, many of the hostesses will allow you to use their washing facilities. The cost is usually minimal, roughly equivalent to what you'd expect to pay in a laundromat. But don't assume the B&B will allow you to use its facilities. When you call to make or confirm your reservation, ask about the policy.

You can also ask your host to direct you to the laundromat, or you can use the local "yellow" pages or inquire at the local tourist office. Laundromats are called *washeterias* or *launderettes*, and are self-serve. The cost to use a launderette is usually around £3.00 for a load of wash. You'll need exact change, and the machines usually take £1, 50p, and 20p coins.

MONEY & BANKING

The currency used in Scotland is the British pound sterling. As with all foreign currencies, the exchange rate fluctuates. The past several years the conversion rate has been in the neighborhood of US$1.60 to $1.68 and CD $2.25 to $2.45 for each pound (£1). To find out what the conversion rate is just before you leave, call any sizable bank, AAA, currency exchange office or check the Foreign Exchange box in the business section of your local newspaper.

If you forget or can't get to a bank or currency exchange office to exchange your money before you leave, don't worry. There are currency exchange kiosks in most gateway city airports (Newark, New York, Atlanta, Chicago, and London), as well as at the Glasgow and Edinburgh airports. You'll have to pay a minimal service charge, usually around $5.

Banks in Scotland are open...well...they're open banker's hours. Traditionally, banks in Scotland are open Monday through Friday from 9:00am or 10:00am to 12:30pm, and from 1:30pm to 4:00pm or 5:00pm. In the larger cities like Glasgow, Edinburgh and Aberdeen, the banks don't close for lunch.

Several of the largest banks in Scotland issue their own bank notes. These bank notes are still considered British pounds, and are accepted throughout the United Kingdom. It is suggested, however, that you exchange your £1 notes for £1 coins before you leave Scotland.

For exchanging money, the banks usually provide the best rates. Post offices in the main cities in Scotland will also exchange money for you. Be aware, however, that many post offices will not accept $100 bills (I tried). Some larger hotels will also change money for you, but as often as not you must be staying there to take advantage of this service.

Automatic Teller Machines (ATMs) have started making their appearance in Scotland. Although they are nowhere near as ubiquitous as in America, they can usually be found on the outside wall of banks. **Cirrus** and **Plus** are the international networks most of these ATMs are part of. Most of the banks that provide ATMs charge a small transaction fee for withdrawals (about $1.50). Check with the bank that issued your ATM card to see if your current Personal Identification Number (PIN) will work overseas. Many of the ATMs overseas only accept four-digit PINs.

EXCHANGE RATES

US$1 = 1.65 pounds

Pound	1	10	100	500	1,000
US Dollars	$1.65	$16.50	$165	$825	$1,650

C$1 = 2.39 pounds

Pound	1	10	100	500	1,000
Canadian Dollars	$2.39	$23.90	$239	$1,195	$2,390

Note: The currency situation vis-à-vis the US and Canadian dollar is constantly floating. Please check the paper or a bank for the current rates of exchange.

NEWSPAPERS

In addition to a score of local newspapers, there are three primary newspapers in Scotland. The *Glasgow Herald* is the organ of the liberal Labor party, and the *Scotsman* out of Edinburgh is the more conservative newspaper. Also popular is the *Daily Telegraph* from London.

POSTAL SERVICE

Letters sent from Scotland to the United States and Canada cost 39 pence (written as "39p") and postcards cost 35p.

Most post offices in the country are open Monday through Friday from 9:00am to 5:30pm, and Saturday from 9:00am to 12:30pm. In the rural areas, the post offices may close for lunch. If you're going to be in one place for a time, you can arrange to have your mail sent to a post office in your area. They will hold the mail for you free of charge for up to one month. Mail should be marked *Poste Restante* in the top left-hand corner of the envelope or package, and your name should be on the first line above the address of the post office. Be sure and take identification when you go to pick up your mail.

RADIO

You are almost always within distance of radio stations, the most common being several BBC stations out of England. There are a number of excellent radio stations in Scotland, and you are sure to find something that will interest you as you tour around the country. **Radio 1** (FM 97.6 to FM 99.5) is a good source of music as well as frequent news updates. **Radio 2** (FM 89 to FM 90) has a variety of offerings, including some talk shows, entertainment, and sports updates. For classical music, look for **Radio 3** between FM 90 and FM 92. **Radio 4** (FM 92.2 to FM 94.2) provides a mix of entertainment, news, and talk shows. If you are a sports fan, **Radio 5** should be your choice (MW 693).

In recent years, regional radio stations have emerged and become immensely popular, as have stations in Edinburgh, Glasgow, Aberdeen and Perth. These smaller stations focus on local and regional news, covering regional athletic teams, political wrangling, and obituaries for the area.

SAFETY & AVOIDING TROUBLE

Safety? If you use common sense in your travels you will be fine. Scotland is far from crime-free, although it is still a very safe place to travel.

I think the biggest concern I have in the area of safety is driving. Roads are narrow, speeds are fast, and there are a lot of Americans on the roads! Don't try to keep up with the Scots until you have logged a few miles on these narrow roads. And on the exceptionally narrow roads of rural Scotland (especially the Highlands!), give way to those who are driving faster than you, and enjoy the scenery. And Scotland has very aggressive laws when it comes to driving under the influence of alcohol, so be sure and use a designated driver if you plan to imbibe at one of those delightful Scottish pubs.

Crime in Scotland is far from non-existent, but if you exercise a dose of common sense and use normal prudence, you should be just fine. Crime is higher in the cities, so be careful where you walk at night. As long as you stay in the predominantly tourist areas and the quiet neighborhoods, all should be well for you.

Of course, when traveling on your own you should take some precautions. Let someone back home know your tentative schedule and when you expect to be back, for example. Lone travelers tend to be more of a target than two or more people traveling together. When I travel on my research trips, I am generally alone. I leave an itinerary with my wife that has the list of hotels and B&Bs where I plan on staying, along with their respective telephone numbers. Just be cautious, and use common sense.

If you do have trouble, remember that the Scottish equivalent of 911 is **999**.

TAXES

As with all of Europe, Scotland has a **Value-Added Tax (VAT)** that is applied to all goods and services. It is added at the rate of **17.5%**. About the nicest thing you can say about VAT is that all prices quoted and posted in stores include VAT.

The good news is, if you are not from a country that is a member of the European Community (EC), you can get a refund on the VAT you pay on goods and services. Whenever you make a purchase, ask the proprietor for a **Tax-Free shopping form**. Take the time to fill out all the forms you collect. You present the completed forms to HM Customs and Excise at the end of your holiday. It only takes a few minutes to do this, so be sure you leave time to do this at the airport. VAT also applies to food, but you do not get a rebate on the VAT paid for food, nor for VAT paid on rental cars, hotel rooms, etc.

If you made your purchases with a credit card, your VAT refund will either be mailed to you, or credited to your credit card. A small handling fee is charged, but it's still worth your time to fill out the forms.

TELEVISION

Cable and satellite TV are becoming pretty widespread in Scotland, so you might even be able to pick up some of your favorite shows from the US during your visit – at least their reruns. The main BBC stations are BBC1 and BBC2. These stations carry English television shows and news shows, as well as American and Australian entertainment. *Coronation Street* (Monday, Wednesday and Friday evenings at 7:30pm) is a popular English soap opera about the people who live on a street in Manchester, England. *They Think It's All Over* is very popular, as are cop shows *Macbeth* and *The Bill*. The two most popular sitcoms are *Eastenders* and *Brookside Close*. American shows that are popular in Scotland include *Ally McBeal*, *Dr. Quinn Medicine Woman*, and *Seinfeld*.

TIPPING

Tipping is acceptable and expected in Scotland. But be warned that if you give your customary 15% to 20% tip for outstanding service, you may in reality be giving up to 30%. Many restaurants in Scotland automatically tack on a service charge of 10% to 15% to your meal. If a gratuity has been added to the bill, the bill will reflect that. Just review the check to see whether or not you should pay a tip. Most waiters and waitresses expect an additional 3% to 5% if the service provided warrants it.

It's customary to tip cab drivers around 10% (they don't automatically add it to the fare), more if the driver acts as a tour guide, filling you in on interesting tidbits of trivia about the sites you're passing. Porters should be tipped £1 per bag.

TELEPHONE

Unless you are a hermit, in trouble with the law, or trying to lose yourself from the world, you will need to use Scotsman Alexander Graham Bell's grand invention – the telephone. Be warned: you will not find the same consistent, user-friendly interface you are accustomed to in North America. Without a doubt you will experience uncooperative phones, occasional poor reception, and just plain frustration. It may take you two or three times dialing exactly the same numbers to get a call through, or you may need to deposit your coins two or three times before they'll register. But, with a little patience, you will be able to get your calls placed.

Phone cards are an efficient way to call within Scotland, and they can be purchased at post offices, Newsagents, and some Tourist Information Centres.

TELEPHONE CODES
Emergency 999
International Direct Dialing 00
International Credit Card 01
Operator 100
International operator 155
International directory inquiries 153
Directory inquiries (information) 192
Scotland country code 44
Glasgow city code 0141
Edinburgh city code 0131
Aberdeen city code 01224

In Scotland, there is no set way to list telephone numbers. They used to be listed as a five- or six-digit string of numbers. However, several years ago it became necessary to add a seventh digit to phone numbers in Glasgow and Edinburgh. Rather than list a string of six or seven numbers (which is often done in Scotland), I have Americanized all the telephone numbers to make it easier for you to deal with them.

WATCHING THE COSTS CALLING HOME

You'd be surprised at how many options you have to call home. You would also be surprised at the variation in costs to place that call home. I priced a ten-minute call from Glasgow to the United States using the following four options, and I think you'll find the information surprising. As you can see, it will pay you to establish an international calling card account before you leave, rather than use the international operator once you arrive in Scotland. Here is what I found (in US dollars):

	First Minute	Each extra Minute	Total for 10-minute call
AT&T Card	*1.01*	*.12*	*$2.09*
MCI Card	*.99*	*.10*	*$1.89*
Sprint Card	*1.85*	*.85*	*$9.50*
International Operator	*4.67*	*4.76*	*$42.86*

AT&T and MCI charge a $3 monthly surcharge for the plans quoted above.

A word of caution: Even though you already have an international calling card from your long distance service provider, be sure and check the specific plan you are signed up for. Each provider has a variety of programs, and with very little difference in the plans, you might end up paying up to 10 times as much as you would if you use another program that your long distance carrier provides.

These rates were in effect at the time I called. They are surely different now, especially with the fierce competition between the long distance heavyweights. Be sure and check with the carriers to determine which is the best deal for you.

Calling Scotland

If you're going to call Scotland from the United States to make hotel reservations, you must dial the international dialing code, (011), the country code (44), then the city code, then the telephone number. *Sort of.* In the case of Glasgow telephone numbers, the city code is 0141, but you drop the 0 when dialing from outside Scotland (but leave it on if you are dialing from inside Scotland). Therefore, if you were calling the Glasgow Hilton from the United States, you should dial 011/44/141/203-5555. Remember: 011 is the international long distance direct dialing code; 01 is the international code for credit card calls.

Calling from Scotland

When calling home from Scotland, dial *0500/890-011* if you're using AT&T, or *0800/890-222* if you're using MCI. You will be connected to an AT&T or MCI operator in the United States who will help you complete your calling card or collect call. See the following sidebar for rate information.

Some hotels only allow you to place international calls through the international operator (*155*) from their rooms. If that's the case in your hotel, you may want to use the pay phone in the lobby or on the street. While not as convenient, it's a lot more reasonable. Also, some hotels levy a surcharge for in-room international calls that can equal what the long distance carriers charge, effectively doubling the cost of your call. If this matters to you, check with the front desk before you make calls from your room.

Calling within Scotland

Most of your calls within Scotland will be made from one of two types of public telephones: coin phones or phonecard phones.

Most **coin phones** are being updated and will accept only 20p and 50p coins. All calls are metered. A digital screen on the phone registers the amount of money you enter, and counts down to 0 as you talk. At 0, you receive three warning tones, and if you do not add additional coins within 10 seconds, your call will be cut off. If you have credits remaining at the

---

USEFUL TELEPHONE NUMBERS

Emergency – 999
International Operator – 155
Operator Assistance – National – 100
Glasgow Airport – 0141/887-1111
Edinburgh Airport – 0131/333-1000
British Airways – 0345/222-111
British Midland – 0181/754-7321, 844-4170
ScotRail (passenger info) – 0191/269-0203
Scottish Citylink Coaches – 0990/505-050, or 0141/332-9644
National Express Coaches – 0990/808-080
Caledonian MacBrayne Ferries – 01475/650-100
P&O Scottish Ferries – 01224/572-615
John O'Groats Ferries – 01955/611-353
Orkney Ferries – 01856/872-044
Scottish Tourist Board – 0141/602-4000

end of your call, you can push a button that allows you to make another call without adding additional coins. Unused, whole amounts will be returned to you.

Phonecard phones are becoming increasingly popular in Scotland. Post Offices, Newsagents and some of the larger Tourist Information Centres sell phonecards of varying denominations: £1, £2, £4, and £10. Like the coin phones, once the card is inserted, a digital readout on the phone displays remaining units. On local calls, one unit is roughly equal to three minutes; slightly less for long distance calls, depending on the distance involved.

Emergency Telephoning

In Scotland, it is important to remember that **911 = 999**. If you have an emergency requiring police, an ambulance, or a fireman, dial 999.

TIME

Scotland is on **Greenwich Mean Time**, and for most of the year that means they are five hours ahead of New York and Montreal, and eight hours ahead of Los Angeles and Vancouver.

Scotland has Daylight Savings Time (called **Summer Time**), but it doesn't coincide exactly with the beginning and ending of Daylight Savings Time in North America. Summer Time begins one week earlier than Daylight Savings Time – the last Sunday of March. It reverts to Standard Time the last Sunday in October as it does here.

During the summer, the sun sets very late in Scotland. Remember, Scotland is at the same latitude as Moscow, so you are pretty far north. During the summer months, Scotland has what they call the *simmer dim*, a term used to describe the daylight that seems to refuse to leave in the evenings.

WEIGHTS & MEASURES

For the most part, Scotland uses the metric system. Your main concern here is that the petrol you purchase for your rental car will be measured in liters. If you're like me and have this fetish for knowing how many miles to the gallon your car is getting, there are 3.7854 liters in a gallon.

8. SPORTS & RECREATION

When it comes to sports and recreation, there is a lot to do in Scotland, both as a spectator and as a participant. For the purposes of this chapter, activities under **Sports** involve professional athletes and your role as the spectator. Those activities under **Recreation** involve your participation.

Scots are sports fanatics. They love a good contest, and they are as avid as fans anywhere in the world. They are fiercely proud of their national teams, especially those competing in international competition. Front-page headlines carry the result of their games, and the games are often the lead stories on the evening news.

PROFESSIONAL SPORTS

RUGBY

Rugby is a wildly exciting game played in Scotland, and its followers are as avid here as they are any place else. If you've never seen rugby, it's sort of a non-stop football game where husky men try and ram an over-inflated football through the defense of their opponent. The National Rugby Team of Scotland is headquartered in Edinburgh. They play their home games at **Murrayfield Stadium**, *Murrayfield, Tel. 0131/337-8993*.

The rugby season runs from September through April, and games are generally played on Saturdays. For ticket information and schedules, contact the stadium. Tickets range between £20 and £25.

SOCCER

Since Scotland is a European nation, of course they play soccer. (I think this must be required to become a member of the European

Economic Community!) Soccer (football) is rabidly followed in Scotland and fans are passionate. Add to the natural European passion for soccer the additional ingredient of religion – many of the clubs are either predominantly Protestant or Catholic, and you get avid fan support. The two main Protestant teams in the country are the Rangers of Glasgow and the Midlothian Hearts (Hearts) of Edinburgh. The main Catholic teams are the Celtics of Glasgow and the Hibernians (Hibs) of Edinburgh. As you can imagine, competition between these teams (and their fans, of course) is intense, and you can bet their games are followed very closely in the homes and pubs of Glasgow and Edinburgh. There are of course other professional soccer teams from all over the country, including Stirling, Dumbarton, Ayr, and Falkirk.

Like Rugby, games are played on Saturdays, and tickets range between £14 and £25. The home stadiums for some of these teams are:
- The Hearts play at **Tynecastle Park**, *Gorgie Road, Edinburgh, Tel. 0131/ 337-6132.*
- The Hibs play their home games at **Easter Road Park**, *Easter Road, Edinburgh, Tel. 0131/661-2159.*
- The Rangers play at **Ibrox Stadium**, *Glasgow, Tel. 0141/427-8500*
- The Celtics play at **Parkhead**, *Glasgow, Tel. 0141/556-2611*

If you wish to learn a little more about the teams before arriving, several of them have official team websites, complete with schedules, information about upcoming opponents, the latest trades and injury reports, etc. Check them out:
- **Glasgow Rangers**: *www.rangers.co.uk*
- **Midlothian Hearts**: *www.heartsfc.co.uk*
- **Glasgow Celtics**: *www.celticfc.co.uk*
- **Edinburgh Hibernians**: *www.erinweb.co.uk*

RECREATION

There are many recreational activities you can involve yourself in while on holiday in Scotland. One of the most common is **hillwalking**. With 284 peaks over 3,000 feet (called *Munros* after an intrepid hiker who climbed all 284), Scotland is ideal for walking and hiking.

If you prefer to do your walking on sculpted fairways and manicured greens, then Scotland is the place for you. Nearly 500 **golf courses**, including such legendary courses as St. Andrews, Carnoustie, Prestwick, Royal Troon, Royal Dornoch, and Turnberry beckon to golfers from all over the world. With all that water in and around Scotland, you would imagine that **fishing** is popular, and you'd be right. But don't overlook these recreational opportunities: bicycling, horseback riding and believe it or not, surfing, scuba diving and skiing (yes – as in *snow* skiing!).

ANGLING

Scotland has a lot to offer in the way of **fishing**, called **angling** here. Salmon, sea trout, brown trout, pike, and a variety of other fish are plentiful in Scotland's lakes and streams, not to mention those available off the coast.

You are required to have a license (called a permit), if you wish to fish in Scotland. Permits are available on an annual, weekly, or daily basis, and are relatively inexpensive. There are many fishing clubs in Scotland that own the rights to fishing in the lochs and rivers in their part of the country. Ask at the local post office, Newsagent, or Tourist Information Centre for information on who to contact locally for fishing permits. The permits are not too expensive, usually in the £5 to £20 range for a week's worth of fishing.

Those in the know say that the best game fishing in Scotland is from May through July and September. Some of the hottest fishing for trout is on the rivers Don, Spey, Tay and Tweed, and many of the lochs in northwest Scotland offer fine trout fishing. If it's salmon you're angling for, try those same rivers, as well as the Esk and Islay rivers.

In addition to getting a permit, another good place to learn about the local hot spots is in the local angling shop. They are all over the country, especially in towns near lakes and streams. Here is an angling shop that can give you tips about where to go and what tackle to use: **The Glasgow Angling Centre**, *6 Claythorn Street, Gallowgate, Glasgow, Tel. 0141/552-4737; Website: www.dholt.demon.co.uk/gac.g.*

You can get more information on angling in Scotland by writing to or calling one of the following agencies:
• **Salmon and Trout Association**, *10 Great Stuart Street, Edinburgh EH3 7TN. Tel. 0131/225-2417*
• **Scottish Anglers' National Association**, *Caledonia House, South Gyle, Edinburgh EH3 9DQ. Tel. 0131/339-8808*
• **Scottish Federation for Coarse Angling**, *17 Barhill Court, Rosebank, Kirkintilloch G663PL. Tel. 0141/776-6741; E-mail: sfca@cableinet.co.uk; Website: www.sfca.freeserve.co.uk*
• **Scottish Federation of Sea Anglers**, *Caledonia House, South Gyle, Edinburgh EH3 9DQ. Tel. 0131/317-7192*

One last word about fishing in Scotland. If you are fishing in the summer, you may have to put up with a nasty little biting insect called a *midge*. These tiny flying insects can deliver a monster of a bite, and they frequent areas that have lots of water (like lochs and streams). Be prepared to use a stiff insect repellant. Local store owners will be able to sell you the most effective brands.

BIRD WATCHING

Amateur and professional ornithologists from around the world come to Scotland for a peek at their feathered friends. Nearly 500 species of birds have been found in and around Scotland and her islands. Orkney and the Shetland Islands in particular provide a treasure trove of wonderful viewing opportunities for bird watchers. The area around St. Abbs on the southeast coast is famed for its sightings of multiple varieties of nesting birds.

If you'd like information on the best places to go, contact the **RSPB Scottish Office**, *17 Regent Terrace, Edinburgh EH7 5BN, Tel. 0131/ 556-6042.*

CYCLING

If you have the time, desire, and endurance, cycling is probably the all-around best way to see Scotland (if the roads just weren't so darned narrow). When it comes to cycling around this beautiful country, you have several options. First, you can rent a bike at one of the many bicycle shops in Scotland, and roll out of the shop on your way to great adventures. Expect to pay somewhere in the neighborhood of £7 to £10 per day, or £30 to £40 per week. Or, you can engage a company that provides excursions for bikers. You'll see the vans and buses of these companies all over Scotland. For a reasonable fee, they'll rent you a bicycle and helmet, shuttle your personal belongings to the location where you'll be spending the night, and they'll even pack lunch for you if you wish. They also provide maps and details about the routes you'll be taking.

If you choose to use a bicycle company, these companies usually provide package deals that include meals, bike rental, maps, itinerary, luggage transport, roadside maintenance, and accommodations (usually at B&Bs) for a set price. The prices vary according to your requirements, but figure on paying around £300 for a week and £575 for two weeks. When you figure what a week's bicycle rental (about £40) and one week's B&B accommodations (from about £100 to £140) would run you, that's not really too bad a deal. Many of the companies listed here will also arrange to pick you up at the airport and return you there at the end of your journey as part of the package.

There is a nonprofit organization in England charged with working to get the best possible cycling facilities for cyclists in the United Kingdom. Contact the **Cyclists' Touring Club**, *69 Meadrow, Godalming, Surrey, GU7 3HS, England. Tel. 01483/417-217.*

CYCLING TOUR OPERATORS

Bespoke Highland Tours	*Tel. 01687/450-272*
Fairburn Activity Centre	*Tel. 01997/433-397*
Highland Adventure Centre,	*Tel. 01687/462-274*
Huntley Nordic ski Centre	*Tel. 01466/794-428*
Scottish Border Trails	*Tel. 01721/723-336*
Tullichewan Holiday Park	*Tel. 01389/759-475*
Wheels	*Tel. 01877/331-100*
Wildcat Mountain Bikes	*Tel. 01786/832-321*
Wild Explorer Holidays	*Tel. 01471/872-487*

GOLF

If you know nothing else about Scotland, you know that it is quite simply *the* golfing mecca. Some of the most famous courses in the world are located here, including **St. Andrews, Gleneagles, Old Prestwick, Royal Troon** and **Royal Dornoch**. But there are more – oh so many more golf courses to see in Scotland. By some counts, there are nearly 500 golf courses in Scotland. That means there is one golf course about every 60 square miles in Scotland, so theoretically, you should never have to travel more than 7 or 8 miles to find a golf course. You will have no excuse whatsoever for not golfing while on holiday in Scotland.

Golf courses in Scotland are among some of the most beautiful and challenging in the world. Some are verdant, lush, and about everything you've ever dreamed of for a game of golf. Others are links courses, with their dunes and deep bunkers, and fairways that are windblown and deceptive.

Greens fees vary, of course, but you can expect to pay between £15 and £55 for 18 holes. Greens fees are slightly more on the weekends. Most courses have clubs available for rent from £8 to £20 (the term in Scotland is "club hire"), as well as golf carts and caddies (about £20 per 18 holes).

Many of Scotland's golf courses are actually part of a golf club. But unlike America and other countries around the world, these courses welcome players who do not belong to their club – even the legendary courses like St. Andrews, Old Prestwick, and Royal Troon. However, at some of these elite courses, you may be asked to produce a handicap card that reflects an under-20 handicap before you'll be allowed to play. And several courses have a gnawing restriction: either women must be accompanied by men to play (Muirfield), or they are not allowed at all (Royal Troon). While it's not practical to list all 500 golf courses in Scotland, here's a sampling of some of the better courses, with a bit of information about each. I have sprinkled more information about these and other courses throughout the various chapters in the book.

The Highlands
- **Golspie Golf Club**, *Golspie, Sutherland. Tel. 01408/633-266.* Par 68, 5,836 yards.
- **Royal Dornoch Golf Club**, *Golf Road, Dornoch, Sutherland. Tel. 01862/ 810-219.* Greens fees are £40 during the week, £50 weekends, Par 70, 6,576 yards.
- **Tain Golf Club**, *Chapel Road, Tain, Ross-shire. Tel. 01862/892-314.* Par 70, 6,207 yards.

The Central Lowlands
- **St. Andrews**, *St. Andrews, Kingdom of Fife. Tel. 01334/475-757.* Weekends are *extremely* busy from May through September. There are seven courses in all:
     The Old Course, greens fees are £55. Par 72, 6,566 yards, handicap certificate required. Tee times are by ballot the day before. **Balgove**, par 30, 9-hole course for beginners and youth. **Eden**, green fees £20, par 70, 6,112 yards. **Jubilee**, green fees £25, par 72, 6,805 yards. **New Course**, green fees £25, par 71, 6,604 yards. **Strathtyrum**, green fees £15, par 69, 5,094 yards. **Dukes Course**, *Craigtoun Park, Fife. Tel. 01334/474-371.* Par 72, 7,110 yards. Considered part of St. Andrews, it is about two miles from the rest of the courses.
- **Carnoustie Golf Links**, *Carnoustie, Angus. Tel. 01241/853-789.* £50, visitors welcome any day, but after 2:00pm on Saturday and after 11:30am on Sunday. Par 72, 6,700 yards. There are two other 18-hole courses at Carnoustie that are also worth looking into.
- **Gleneagles**, *Auchterarder, Perthshire. Tel. 01764/663-543.* Monarch Course: par 72, 7,100 yards. King's Course: par 70, 6,471 yards. Queen's Course: par 68, 5,965 yards.

The Borders & Southwest
- **Prestwick Golf Club**, *Prestwick, Ayrshire. Tel. 01292/774-044.*
- **Royal Troon**, *Craigend Road, Troon, Ayrshire. Tel. 01292/311-555.* Greens fees are £85 for 36 holes and a luncheon is included. Par 70, 6,211 yards.

• **Turnberry Golf Club**, *Turnberry, Ayrshire. Tel. 01655/331-000.* Greens fees are £55. Arran Course: par 69, 6,310 yards. Ailsa Course: par 72, 6.668 yards.

HILLWALKING

Scotland draws walkers from all over the world. The terrain and climate lend themselves to walking. The terrain provides such a varied experience for walkers that it can suit the needs of the most aggressive adventurer or the Sunday stroller. You want steep and arduous climbs? The Highlands is proud to provide you more than a few of those. If you prefer flat lands or rolling hills for your adventuring, then the southeastern area called The Borders is the place to head. During most months of the year, the weather is almost always pleasant, and seldom too cold. With summer hiking temperatures rarely above the low- to mid-60s, it's ideal weather for walking. Rain, of course, is a threat at any time, but is seldom of the heavy downpour variety. Winter hikes can be accompanied by cold weather, but crisp and quiet solitude will no doubt offset that minor inconvenience.

Hiking trails crisscross the country. Some are very popular and well marked; others are more obscure, and not signposted well, if at all. The Tourist Information Centres are an excellent source for recommendations. Some of the more popular easy trails are in the **Queen Elizabeth Forest Park** east of Loch Lomond and the **Galloway Forest Park** in southern Scotland. The most popular long-distance walk is the **West Highland Way**. This 95-mile jaunt starts (or ends) at the edge of the Glasgow city limits and runs to Fort William.

There is no charge for walking these paths, of course, unless you employ a guide to take you to show the way, comment on the topography, flora, and fauna, etc. But these trails were generally designed for freelance walkers. Walkers are kindly asked to only take pictures and leave only footprints.

If you think this sounds like an ideal activity, there are several publications that will be helpful to you. The Scottish Natural Heritage organization publishes a small pamphlet on some of the more popular Scottish walking trails. You can also contact any of the Tourist Information Centres and they can provide leaflets that pertain to walking in their areas.

If you decide to use a walking tour coordinator, expect to pay around £100 per person for a 5-day trek, with discounts for groups of four or more. That price does not include accommodations or meals. For a full guided walking experience including accommodations, meals, transportation, etc., expect to pay between £200 and £400 for 5-days.

WALKING TOUR OPERATORS

You can certainly strike out on your own on many of these walking trails, or you can engage a tour operator that will point the way, guide your walks and regale you with local history, arrange for lodging along the way, and even pack lunches and/or haul luggage for you. Here are a few:

C-N-Do Scotland Ltd., 32 Stirling Enterprise Park, Stirling. Tel. 01786/445-703; E-mail: cndo.Scotland@btinternet.com; Website: www.members.aol.com.mmgwalks/middle

Croft-na-Caber, Loch Tay, Kenmore. Tel. 01887/830-236, Fax 01887/830-649

East Neuk Outdoors, Cellardyke Park, Anstruther, Fife. Tel. 01333/311-929

Highland Adventure Centre, Ardintigh, Loch Nevis, Mallaig. Tel. 01687/462-274, Fax 01687/462-274

Middle Marches Guided Walks, Riversdale, Slitrig Crescent, Hawig. Tel. 01450/377-383; E-mail: lknox46426@aol.com

Rob Roy Tours, 27 Wardie Square, Edinburgh. Tel. 0131/477-4566, Fax 0131/477-4566; E-mail: RobRoyTour@aol.com; Website: members.aol.com/RobRoyTour

Scottish Border Trails, Drummore, Venlaw High Road, Peebles. Tel. 01721/720-336, Fax 01721/723-004; E-mail: arthur@trails.scotborders.co.uk

Tamerlaine, Loaningbank, Menstrie, Clackmannanshire. Tel. 01259/763-107, Fax 01259/763-093; E-mail: Tamerlaine@msn.com

Thistle Activities, 87 Perth Street, Blairgowrie, Perthshire. Tel. 01250/876-100, Fax 01250/873-383

Wild Explorer Holidays, Skye Environmental Centre, Bradford. Tel. 01471/872-487

HORSEBACK RIDING

There is probably no more peaceful way of seeing this beautiful country than by horseback. Across the width and breadth of Scotland you can find stables that will help you enjoy Scotland from atop one of their steeds. Expect to pay anywhere from £8 to £25 per hour, depending on where you are and the extent of the experience you want. Whether you are looking for a brisk gallop along a sandy beach or a long quiet ride through the remote Highlands, you'll be able to find it in Scotland. Here are a few riding stable:

The Highlands

• **Castle Riding Centre**, *Ardrishaig, Argyll. Tel. 01546/603-274, Fax 01546/603-225; E-mail: 106.410337@compuserve.com*

- **Brenfield Estate and Farm**, *Brenfield. Tel. 01546/603-274*
- **Coul House Hotel**, *near Strathpeffer, Ross-shire. Tel. 01997/421-487, Fax 01997/421-945*
- **Glen Tanner Equestrian Centre**, *Aboyne, Aberdeenshire. Tel. 01339/886-448, Fax 01339/887-042*
- **Hayfield Riding Centre**, *Hazelhead Park. Tel. 01224/315-703, Fax 01224/313-834; E-mail: hayfieldhols@equi.net; Website: www.equi.net/hayfield/international*

The Central Lowlands
- **Boreland Park Farm and Holiday Riding**, *Fearnan, near Aberfeldy. Tel. 01887/830-212, Fax 01887/830-606*
- **Glenmarkie Farm Riding Center**, *Glenisla, Perthshire. Tel. 01575/582-341, Fax 01575/582-341*
- **Lochore Meadows Riding Stables**, *Chapel Farm Road, Lochore, near Lochgelly. Tel. 01552/861-596, Fax 01552/861-899*
- **Scottish Equi Complex**, *Lanark Moor Country Park, Lanark. Tel. 01555/661-853; Email: scotequicomplex@btinternet.com*
- **Tamerlaine**, *Loaningbank, Back Road, Menstrie, Clackmannanshire. Tel. 01259/763-107, Fax 01259/763-093; E-mail: Tamerlaine@msn.com*
- **Thistle Activities**, *87 Perth Street, Blairgowrie, Perthshire. Tel. 01250/876-100, Fax 01250/873-383; E-mail: ThistleActivities@compuserve.com*

The Grampian Highlands
- **Balmoral Pony Trekking**, *Balmoral Castle Estates, Ballater. Tel. 01339/742-334*
- **Glen Tanar Equestrian Centre**, *Aboyne. Tel. 01339/886-448*

The Borders & Southwest
- **Barend Properties Riding School and Trekking Centre**, *Sandyhills, Dalbeattie, Kirkcudbrightshire. Tel. 01387/780-663*
- **Brighouse Bay Leisure Club**, *Borgue, near Kirkcudbright. Tel. 01557/870-409*
- **Brighouse Bay Trekking Ponies**, *Borgue, near Kirkcudbright. Tel. 01557/870-222*

The Islands
- **Cairnhouse Riding Centre**, *Blackwaterfoot, Isle of Arran. Tel. 01770/860-466*
- **Cloyburn Equestrian Centre**, *Brodrick, Isle of Arran. Tel. 01770/302-800*
- **Portree Riding Stables**, *Garalapin, Portree, Isle of Skye. Tel. 01478/612-945*

• **Skye Riding Centre**, *Borve, near Portree, Isle of Skye. Tel. 01470/532-233*
• **Skye Riding Stables**, *Portree, Isle of Skye. Tel. 01470/582-419*
• **Uig Hotel Pony Trekking**, *Uig, Isle of Skye. Tel. 01470/542-205*

HIGHLAND GAMES

If you come to Scotland, you have to sample that oh-so-Scottish event known as the **Highland Games**. These events, which take place in numerous locations in July, August and September, climax with the Braemar Highland Games, held the first Saturday of each September. I suppose the closest relative to the Highland Games in the US would be the Mountain Man Rendezvous of the Rocky Mountain west, where rough-and-tumble men gathered to socialize, do some trading and storytelling, and see who was the better shooter, thrower, runner, etc.

The Highland Games include fierce competition in such activities as Highland dancing, bagpiping, caber toss, putting the stone, hammer toss, sprinting, long jump, tug-of-war and relay races. Winners of the various events from all the Highland Games around Scotland are invited to come to Braemar and compete against the "local lads" for all the marbles.

The events are so varied that there will be something for everyone to enjoy. The **Highland Dancing** features competition among all age classes, from teeny tiny on up. Dancers dressed in traditional Scottish attire (tartans and kilts) dance in a controlled frenzy to skirling bagpipes, pipes and drums. Many of the other events feature men – big men. The most impressive to me is the **caber toss**. A caber is a long wooden pole, roughly the height and dimensions of a telephone pole (really). These stout men pick up one end of the caber, balance it momentarily, and then toss it, striving for the greatest distance.

The **bagpiping competition** pits the best pipers in the country against one another. As you listen to this competition, you'll be amazed at the skill and capability of some of these pipers, as they coax the most splendid sounds out of these bags of pipes. Like musical competition for instruments the world over, the winner is chosen for his or her ability to touch the hearts and souls of the judges, whether it be through a mournful tune of lament or an upbeat, peppy presentation. A rich dollop of showmanship is also often the difference between the good and the very good.

If you have never attended any Highland Games before, then you should really try to arrange your schedule to do so. It is good fun. While the Braemar Games are the largest and most televised, other towns that offer games in July and August include Aberdeen, Ballater, Elgin, Inverness, Newtonmore and Oban.

NESSIE HUNTING

Many of Scotland's sons and daughters are known worldwide. Names like Alexander Graham Bell and Sean Connery may be easily recognizable, but perhaps Scotland's most famous celebrity is none other than an elusive, shy, unphotogenic plesiosaurus named **Nessie** (you may know it as the Loch Ness Monster).

Notwithstanding an impressive number of "Nessie sightings" that span several centuries, and a number of grainy, out-of-focus photographs, there is no evidence that the creature exists. But that doesn't stop thousands of tourists from descending upon the mysterious waters of Loch Ness each season to try and catch a glimpse of this anachronism that has boosted Scotland's tourist industry for years.

Scientists have of course pooh-poohed the possibility of the creature's existence. Extensive (and expensive) searches of the loch have proven unproductive. The loch's sheer size (21 miles long) and depth (800 feet) have made effective searches impossible. The presence of underwater caves also keeps the possibilities alive in the minds and imaginations of Nessie believers worldwide.

Nessie boasts a cyber-fan-club, and if you are interested in visiting Nessie from the comforts of your own home, then click on *www.lochness.co.uk/fan_club*.

SAILING & WINDSURFING

There are two things Scotland has plenty of: water and wind. With such a combination, it is only natural that **windsurfing** and **sailing** are popular sports. (Sailing was a popular sport in Scotland before sailing was even considered a sport.) The ocean surrounding Scotland and the many lochs across Scotland provide outstanding venues for these water sports. There are a number of sailing and windsurfing centers around Scotland. Here are a few:

The Highlands
• **Great Glen Water Park**, *near Invergarry*. *Tel. 01809/501-381*
• **Linhe Marine**, *Lettershuna*. *Tel. 01631/730-227*
• **Loch Insh Watersports Centre**, *Kincraig*. *Tel. 01540/651-272*

The Central Lowlands
• **Croft-na-Caber**, *Loch Tay, Kenmore*. *Tel. 01887/830-236, Fax 01887/830-649*
• **Strathclyde Park**, *Strathclyde*. *Tel. 01698/266-155*
• **Loch Tay Boating Centre**, *Pier Road, Kenmore*. *Tel. 01887/830-291*

The Borders & Southwest
- **Castle Semple Country Park**, *Lochwinnoch. Tel. 01505/842-882*
- **Kip Marina**, *Inverkip. Tel. 01475/521-485*
- **Wigbay Sailing Centre**, *Stranraer. Tel. 01776/703-535*

SCUBA DIVING

It might surprise you to learn that scuba diving is popular in Scotland. It's not widespread, but it is gaining in popularity. Diving is available all around Scotland, but those in the know say the best diving is off the islands (Hebrides and Orkney), and along the northwest coast. Some of the towns where scuba diving is offered are Oban, Dunbar, Ullapool, Anstruther, Eyemouth, St. Abbs and Stromness. There are also dive companies in Edinburgh and Glasgow.

The waters around Scotland are chock full of wrecks of various vintages, from ancient Spanish galleons to World War I and World War II vessels. Add to those man-made sights the plentiful marine life and you have a wonderful underwater experience awaiting you. Check with the local angling shop or Tourist Information Centre in the city you're going to be in for more information. Conditions in the water are generally good, especially on the west coast of Scotland. The waters are surprisingly warm thanks to the Gulf Stream, and visibility is usually at least 45 feet, and often exceeds 100 feet.

Here are a few places to investigate for more information and/or scheduling dive excursions:

The Highlands
- **Atlantic Diving Services**, *Ullapool. Tel. 01854/622-261*
- **Buchan Divers**, *Peterhead*
- **M&M Diving**, *Findhorn Bay, Forres. Tel. 01309/690-893*

The Islands
- **The Diving Cellar**, *4 Victoria Street, Stromness, Orkney. Tel. 01856/850-055 Fax 01856/850-395; E-mail: leigh@divescapaflow.co.uk; Website: www.divescapaflow.co.uk*
- **Dolphin Scuba**, *Garisle, Burray, Orkney. Tel. 01856/731-269*
- **Hebridean Diving Services**, *Lochbay, Isle of Skye. Tel. 01478/592-219*
- **Houton Diving**, *Heatherlea, Houton, Orphir, Orkney. Tel. 01856/811-251*
- **Scapa Flow Charters**, *5 Church Road, Stromness, Orkney. Tel. 01856/850-879*
- **Scapa Flow Diving Centre**, *Burray, Orkney. Tel. 01856/731-225*
- **Scapa Flow Diving Holidays**, *Lerquoy, Outertown, Stromness, Orkney Tel. 01856/851-110*

• **Scapa Flow Technical Diving**, *Polrudden, Pickaquay Road, Kirkwall, Orkney. Tel. 01856/874-761*
• **Scalpay Diving Services**, *Scalpay. Tel. 01859/540-328*
• **Stormdrift Charters**, *1 Sabiston Crescent, Weyland, Kirkwall, Orkney. Tel. 01856/873-475*
• **Stromness Diving Centre**, *Barkland, Cairston Road, Stromness, Orkney. Tel. 01856/850-624*

The Central Lowlands
• **Argyll Dive Boats**, *Barmore Road, Targart, Argyll. Tel. 01880/820-543; E-mail: calum@argylldiveboats.co.uk; Website: www.argylldiveboats.co.uk*
• **Dive Scotland**, *Edinburgh. Tel. 0131/441-2001*
• **Gaelic Rose**, *Lochaline, Oban, Argyll. Tel. 01967/421-654*
• **Nervous Wrecks**, *Oban. Tel. 01631/566-000*
• **Oban Dive Shop**, *Glenshellach Road, Oban. Tel. 01631/566-618*
• **Scottish Sub-Aqua Club**, *The Cockburn Centre, 40 Bogmoor Place, Glasgow, G51 4TQ. Tel. 0141/425-1021, Fax 0141/445-6192; E-mail: m.maccallum@napier.ac.uk; Website: www.ssac.demon.co.uk/SSAChome*

The Borders & Southwest
• **C&C Marine**, *Largs, Ayrshire. Tel. 01475/687-180, Fax 01475/687-388*
• **Clyde Diving Charters**, *Inverkip. Tel. 01475/522-930, Fax 01475/521-339*
• **Scoutscroft Holiday Centre**, *St. Abbs. Tel. 01890/771-338, Fax 01890/771-746*

In addition to these sites, you can find a pretty complete listing of dive shops at *www.3routes.com/scuba/europe/uk/scot.*

SURFING
You didn't know you could surf in Scotland, did you? There are a several beaches in Scotland that are recognized as respectable surfing beaches. Those in the know say the best are at Thurso and Strathy Bay in the Highlands, Pease Bay and Coldingham Beach in the St. Abbs. Here are a few shops and surfing clubs:

The Highlands
• **Stornoway Surf and Sports**, *Stornoway. Tel. 01851/705-862*

The Central Lowlands
• **Clan Skates**, *Glasgow. Tel. 0141/339-6523*
• **Momentum Surf Shop**, *22 Bruntsfield Place, Edinburgh. Tel. 0131/221-6665, Fax 0131/221-6665; E-mail: theshop@momentum.prestel.co.uk*

9. SHOPPING

Scotland is a wonderful place to purchase all those things that remind you of Scotland: sweaters, Scottish tartans, Scotch whisky, wools and tweeds, and bagpipes (for the adventurous). I was pleasantly surprised to find that merchandise prices varied little across the width and breadth of the country. The cost of items seemed driven more by the variations in their design than by the area of the country where they were purchased. Remember, it is a small country, smaller than the majority of the states in the United States, so it makes sense that there is little variation in price across the country.

The following table will give you an idea of what you can expect to pay for a variety of items:
- Sweaters   £35 – £75
- Sheepskins   £40 – £70
- Wool kilt   £50 – £80
- Tweed hats   £13 – £20
- Tweed skirts   £35 – £75
- Tartan ties   £10 – £30
- Malt whisky
  (per shot)   £1.25 – £1.50
- Bagpipes   £100 – £2000+

Typically, stores in Scotland are open from 9:00am to 5:30pm or 6:00pm Monday through Saturday, and closed on Sunday. Some Glasgow and Edinburgh stores are open late on Thursday evenings (7:00pm or 8:00pm), and some are even beginning to stay open on Sunday. But this latest venture is the exception rather than the rule. When you're in the rural parts of Scotland, expect Sunday to be a very slow day for shopping (since most of the stores will be closed!). Also, some stores in rural Scotland close early on Tuesday or Wednesday afternoons.

Newsagents in the towns tend to open a little earlier than most stores – around 7:00am, as do bakeries. Newsagents have sort of a country-store feel, even in the city. They are typically small, with cribs full of fresh produce, and a little bit of everything.

If you have Scottish ancestry someplace in your family tree, then my suggestion is that no trip to Scotland is complete without finding and purchasing a garment or item that is made from the tartan of your family. There are many (many!) shops in Scotland that feature **tartan kilts**, **ties**, **hats**, **bonnets**, etc. And each has a book or books that should be able to identify the tartan of even the smallest Scottish clan. If your budget is tight, then purchase a tie, hat or small scarf – they'll run you no more than £10 to £15. If you are able to spend a little more, then a kilt might meet your fancy. Off-the-rack kilts will run you anywhere from £50 to £80, although if you wish to have one custom-made, the cost can sometimes soar to £250 or £300. But whether you spend £10 or £300, I'd recommend that you not go home without some item made of your family tartan. I found that it was a much-appreciated and enjoyed gift for friends and family members at home, too.

There are also numerous **antique shops**, with excellent variety and relatively low prices from days gone by. As with antique shopping in the US, once something is identified as an antique, the cost goes up. However, you will generally find very reasonable prices on antiques, whether antique mantles, glassware, curios or books. The shops in the major cities are more expensive (as you would expect), while their country cousins have much more reasonable deals. Of course, depending on what you purchase, you may be looking at rather expensive shipping costs, so don't get carried away. Remember, you are on another continent, and a long way from home.

SO YOU WANT TO BE A BAGPIPER?

Okay, so you went to the Military Tattoo at Edinburgh Castle and you think you'd like to learn how to be a bagpiper. According to Andrew Deans (who, with his wife Mary, own Cameron Toll Guest House in Edinburgh), here's what to look for and what you can expect to pay:

Most people begin with an inexpensive "practice chanter" and instruction book that costs £40. Once you master that, you can purchase bagpipes for anywhere from £100 (although these are most suitable for hanging over your fireplace than for musical quality) on up. A decent set of acceptable quality starts at around £500 and goes up from there to around £2000 (for one with silver mounts), or £2000-plus for one with gold mounts. The good pipes tend to be made of ebony or African blackwood. Both woods are close-grained so the moisture from your breath does not split the wood.

CLOTHING SIZES IN SCOTLAND

Clothing sizes in Scotland do not follow the American or Canadian sizing formats. Below is a chart comparing Scottish sizes to sizes in the United States and Canada. Your best bet, however, is to try on any article before buying it.

Men's suits

US/Can.	36	38	40	42	44	46
Scottish	46	48	50	52	54	56

Shirts

US/Can.	14	15	16	17	18
Scottish	36	38	41	43	46

Women's dresses

US	8	10	12	14	16	18	20
Canadian	10	12	14	16	18	20	22
Scottish	38	40	42	44	46	48	50

Men's shoes

US/Can.	6 1/2	7 1/2	8 1/2	9 1/2	10 1/2	11 1/2
Scottish	40	41	42	43	44	45

Women's shoes

US	3 1/2	4 1/2	5 1/2	6 1/2	7 1/2	8 1/2
Canadian	4	5	6	7	8	9
Scottish	34 1/2	35 1/2	36 1/2	37 1/2	38 1/2	39 1/2

10. TAKING THE KIDS

Scotland is a great place to visit with kids. Most tourist attractions have discounted fares for children, as do many of the B&Bs and hotels in the country. The discount for attractions and activities is generally about 50% off the adult fare, and many attractions offer family fares, typically discounted rates covering the admission charge for two adults and from two to four children. There are a number of activities around the country targeted specifically for families with children. As the father of six children, I know well how quickly children tire of a steady diet of museums, cathedrals, and art galleries. The key is to find diversions to break up the day for your children.

Don't forget to bring books, crossword puzzles, magnetic games like chess, checkers or backgammon, or a Gameboy (or whatever your children like), to keep them entertained as you drive from town to town and in the evenings. Also, depending on their age, you should consider purchasing them their own disposable cameras so they can take pictures (it's their vacation too, after all), and they won't bug you to use your camera.

SUGGESTED KID'S ITINERARY FOR EDINBURGH

To have a successful family vacation in Scotland, you should intersperse "kid activities" with those things you want to see. For example, following is a sample itinerary for a day in Edinburgh with children.

I recommend beginning the day at Edinburgh Castle while the kids are still fresh. After leaving the castle, head down the Royal Mile a few steps to Camera Obscura for a wonderful and intriguing look at Edinburgh through a Victorian-era camera. After Camera Obscura, your kids should be okay while you stop in at either Gladstone's Land or Lady Stair's House. That should pretty well take you to lunchtime. Stop in at the Filling Station Restaurant for a bite to eat – both you and your kids will be intrigued by the many things to look at.

Back on the Royal Mile, make a beeline for the Palace of Holyroodhouse at the bottom of the Royal Mile. After your tour there, walk back up the

Royal Mile to the Museum of Childhood. Between these two activities, you might very well spend the entire afternoon. You could hit the Museum of Childhood on your way down the Royal Mile, but that means you have left the Palace of Holyroodhouse to the end of the day, a dangerous proposition with tired children. If there are a few minutes of sightseeing left after the Museum of Childhood, you could bribe your children with a piece of fudge from Garrahy's Fudge Kitchen. Then head across the street to the John Knox House to round out your first day of sightseeing.

For dinner, depending on your budget, you might consider going to The Witchery, a restaurant that will provide sensory stimulation for your tired children. If that's not in your budget, there are restaurants in Edinburgh that range from Burger King (just off Princes Street) on up.

Your next day in Edinburgh could include such adult activities as the Royal Museum of Scotland, Huntly House Museum, or the Scottish National Portrait Gallery. You can intersperse these with a bus ride (depending on the age of your children, this may be one of the highlights of their trip!), a stroll through Princes Street Gardens or a visit to either the Edinburgh Zoo or Deep Sea World. Once again, depending on the age of your children, perhaps you can convince them not to be too wiggly while you visit museums in the morning if you'll promise to treat them to the zoo or Deep Sea World in the afternoon.

OTHER FUN ACTIVITIES

There are a number of other things to do in addition to those mentioned in the suggested itinerary. Scotland is made for outdoor activities, and since the weather rarely runs to extremes, outdoor activities are especially enjoyable in Scotland.

Take a boat ride out to a castle in the Borders. Go "pony trekking" (horseback riding), available virtually everywhere you drive outside of the cities. There are thousands of miles of walking trails around the width and breadth of Scotland, some quite arduous as well as those that are gentle and easy. Try your hand at seal watching from Dunvegan Castle, or dolphin watching in Inverness.

These are just a few of the many activities that await you and your children. Put yourself in their shoes and look for activities that will enrich as well as entertain your children. But above all, have a good time with them in Scotland. Following are a few other thoughts on seeing Scotland with your children.

Hiking

Hiking is one of the most popular tourist activities in Scotland. And kids love to hike (run, skip, jump). Whether you are a family that's into serious hiking and want to hike 20 miles a day, or whether you just need a mile or two of trail to work off some energy, Scotland has it all. There are thousands of miles of walking trails throughout Scotland and you'll easily find a few trails to suit your family.

Lakes & Rivers

Scotland is blessed with a considerable number of lakes and rivers. There are thousands of lochs and inlets and firths in this small country. The lakes are all beautiful, and perfect places for shoreline picnics, inexpensive boat rides out to islands lush with greenery and guarded by ancient ruins, and fishing (angling equipment can be rented). Loch Lomond is one of my favorite lakes for this pastime. Boat trips out onto the loch stop at an island and allow you to disembark and stay for awhile, returning on a later boat.

Ocean & Sea

There is no place in Scotland that is more than 45 miles from the ocean, and there are many shores that children in particular would enjoy. Whether they want to swim, skip along the shore, build sand castles, or just throw rocks in the water, the ocean is always near-by. Scots *do* swim in the Atlantic Ocean and the North Sea, although their swimming season usually doesn't begin until around mid- to late-June, and extends into September. The water never gets really warm, but (apparently) warm enough for hardy swimmers.

If you are in Scotland when the water is too cold to swim, don't automatically discount the beaches. If your kids are like mine, they will still enjoy the sand between their toes, the jetsam and flotsam that washes up on the shores, and the thrill of being at the ocean. Some great beaches include those in Durness (in the Highlands), in Aberdeen, and in the Borders town of Ayr.

Ruins

I was surprised to learn that some of my children's favorite things were prowling around the ruins of ancient and medieval Scotland. Ruins that are particularly intriguing include Kildrummy and Dunnottar Castles in the Grampian Highlands, Threave and Caerlaverock Castles in the Borders, and about 10,000 unnamed ruins across the countryside.

There are ruins all over Scotland: castles, abbeys, friarys, houses, stables, and burial grounds. If your kids need to burn off some energy, look for a deserted ruin, (you'll only have to look a short time), and let the kids explore them and give flight to their fantasies. Let them pretend they are defending or attacking a castle, or let them imagine what it would have been like to be a monk looking desperately for a place to hide the monastery's gold and silver chalices from an approaching army.

11. FOOD & DRINK

FOOD

I have found the food in Scotland to be deliciously **continental**. By that I mean that first of all you can find just about any kind of European food your heart desires, from baklava to cannelloni, wienerschnitzel to escargot, and from crepes to ravioli. But I also mean continental because many of the chefs in Scotland have honed their cooking skills at the fine cooking schools that are found throughout Europe, and/or have gained experience in some of the finest restaurants in the world. Many have returned to their native land to practice their craft, and for that you and I can be gastronomically grateful.

If you know anything about Scottish cooking or meals, two words probably come to mind: oats and haggis. **Oats**, because the Scots have used them as a primary staple of their diet for generations. **Haggis**, because it is considered the national dish of Scotland. It is a combination of portions of the lungs, liver and heart of a sheep, accented with herbs, onions, spices and oatmeal. Traditionally this interesting concoction is cooked in the stomach of a sheep. Mmmm. Now having said that, do try it at least once while you are in Scotland. I decided to try it just once, and ended up ordering it with most of my meals. It really is quite delicious, especially when seasoned just right.

However, for those who prefer a little less exotic fare, never fear. Fish, lamb, wild game and beef are all plentiful. As a nation surrounded on three sides by water as well as having a plenitude of freshwater lochs and rivers, Scotland offers up a wonderful variety of dishes from the sea and lake. **Aberdeen Angus beef** is a favorite Scottish dish, and the variety of ways to prepare and present it are seemingly endless.

In your travels about Scotland, you will often encounter the dining term *Full Scottish Breakfast*. Most Bed and Breakfasts and guest houses offer a full Scottish breakfast, and some hotels include it in their rate. Inasmuch as this term seems to have varying meanings across the country, let me define it here for you. Generally speaking, a full Scottish breakfast consists of one egg, two thick slices of bacon (now that's bacon!), link sausage, white or wheat toast, coffee, tea and orange juice. Also, there is generally a selection of cold cereals: corn flakes, Wheat-a-Bix, muesli, and all-bran (that will be the one in the full container). Sometimes fresh fruit and yogurt are available. Some places also offer such additional items as kippers, waffles, haggis (remember – you're going to try this at least once), black pudding, or porridge. Some of the less expensive B&Bs offer only a continental breakfast: rolls, yogurt and fruit, tea or coffee. By the way, here's something for you to watch for: while all the breakfasts I've had in Scotland were wonderful, I think every one came with toast that was about four shades darker than the golden brown shade I like. I would call it burnt; my wife would say it was well done. Just watch for yourself.

Let me say a word about Scottish **porridge**: it's delicious. I was surprised that it was more than just plain old oatmeal. After having a steaming bowl of porridge one cool and damp morning, I immediately saw why porridge has been a staple of the Scottish diet for centuries: it warms the body as well as the soul, and it sticks with you. The porridge in Scotland is as creamy as can be; some say it is because it is cooked in milk, not water. At any rate, I highly recommend it to you.

Scots are a lively people, insisting on good friends, good pubs, and good food – not necessarily in that order. Fortunately they are all easy to come by in Scotland, and in the larger cities in particular. From small bistros to hotel dining rooms to top-notch restaurants, Scotland offers a wide selection of eating establishments. Over the past few years, Scotland has seen the introduction of a number of fine restaurants, the renovation of a number of older restaurants, and the rapid growth of good ethnic restaurants.

There's an organization in Scotland that evaluates restaurants here. *A Taste of Scotland* evaluates the restaurants based on quality of food, presentation, ambience and flavor. Their stamp of approval is highly regarded and much sought-after by Scottish restaurateurs. Look for their distinctive seal in the window of the restaurants you patronize. I've also included their recognition in my write-ups on those restaurants.

For most of the restaurants listed in the *Where to Eat* sections in this guide, I've included samples of what's on the menu and their price. Remember, however, that prices are subject to change, and restaurants tend to change their menus daily or seasonally. Unless specifically noted, all the prices listed are for dinner (salad, entrée, dessert, and coffee). Often the lunch menus are merely scaled-down versions of the dinner menus, at about half to two-thirds the cost of dinner.

I have also provided their hours of business. In most cases, the closing times listed are the last time they will accept orders, although for many it also depends on business. If business is really slow due to weather or some other reason, they might close a little early; if business is brisk at closing time, they might stay open longer. Most if not all of these restaurants are closed on Christmas and Easter.

Most things in Scotland are very casual, and restaurants are no exception. Every restaurant I've been to in Scotland says casual dress is fine, although a number of the more upscale restaurants request no blue jeans or grubbies. In practice, however, most of the clientele in the nicer restaurants wear suits and ties or dresses.

Some restaurants in Scotland automatically tack a 10% to 15% gratuity onto your bill. If you feel the service was exceptional beyond that level, feel free to leave an additional tip. Most waiters and waitresses expect an additional 3% to 5% from their guests. The legal drinking age is 18, although many restaurants (especially) and some pubs enforce a house minimum of 21 years.

SOME SCOTTISH DINING TERMS

cock-a leekie	soup made from boiled fowl and leeks
creamed potatoes	mashed potatoes
gammon	thickly cut grilled ham
haggis	Scottish national dish
jacket potatoes	baked potatoes
neeps	turnips
skirlie	browned and seasoned oatmeal
stoved howtowdie	roasted chicken
take away	take-out (as in: take-out food)
tatties	potatoes
top-ups	refills

SCOTLAND'S BEST RESTAURANTS

My criteria for the best restaurants in Scotland include quality, presentation, selection, service and ambiance.

ONE DEVONSHIRE GARDENS RESTAURANT, *One Devonshire Gardens, Glasgow. Tel. 0141/339-2001. £35-50. Open daily from noon to 1:45pm, and from 7:15pm to 9:45pm. All major credit cards accepted.*

This is the restaurant for One Devonshire Gardens hotel, and it is as exquisite as you would expect it to be. This award-winning restaurant achieves excellence in food, wine and ambience. The dining room itself is exquisite: 14' ceilings, rich oak trim along the walls and modern art on the walls. Crystal and china, linen and silver are also part of the setting.

A smaller overflow dining room with half a dozen tables is available for small dinner parties if you wish. Prior to your meal, you'll have the luxury of relaxing with a glass wine in the marvelous Drawing Room in front of a crackling fire.

The menu changes frequently, but you'll find such offerings as herb-roasted chicken, fondant potatoes and Caesar salad, or you might also like to try the pavé of potato, roasted peppers and goat's cheese with parmesan. Whatever your choice of entrée, you'll be delighted with your selection. The meals prepared here are wonderful, and the presentation is nothing short of works of art. Dress ranges from nice casual to pretty formal. Personally, I would err on the side of dressing more formally for this restaurant. Reservations are a must during the summer months.

UBIQUITOUS CHIP, *12 Ashland Lane, Glasgow. Tel. 0141/334-5007. £16-32. Open Monday through Saturday from noon to 2:30pm, and 5:30pm to 11:00pm, and Sunday from 12:30pm to 2:30pm, and from 6:30pm to 11:00pm. MasterCard and Visa accepted.*

The Ubiquitous Chip is a little tough to find as it is tucked back in an L-shaped alley behind Byre Street, but it is well worth the effort you make to locate it. This little place has been going strong since its establishment in the early 1970s, and in fact has a bit of a cult following. Ronnie Clydesdale is the owner, and he has been highly successful in providing excellent food in a wonderful setting. You'll find plain pine tables, flickering candles and white-painted brick walls. But the thing that will leave the greatest impression is the profusion of plants in the restaurant – they are everywhere! You will feel as though you are dining in the middle of a rain forest. There are so many that they threaten to block the massive skylight (actually, the ceiling is simply a series of windows). The atmosphere is one of pleasant chatter all around the room, from college-age kids to silver-haired businessmen to talkative tourists.

The menu changes frequently, but selections might include howtowdie breast of free-range chicken, skirlie, glazed shallots and quail's egg, Scottish salmon smoked in darjeeling tea, cured cabbage washed in riesling and potatoes in truffle oil. The Ubiquitous Chip has earned recognition by the *Taste of Scotland*. A set two-course meal and coffee runs £27, and a three-course meal is £32.

BOATH HOUSE RESTAURANT, *Aberdeen Road, Auldearn, Nairn. Tel. 01667/454-896, 01667/455-469. £21-32. Open Thursday through Sunday from 12:30pm to 2:00pm, and Wednesday through Sunday from 7:00pm to 9:00pm. All major credit cards accepted.*

The Boath House Restaurant is one of the finest restaurants in northern Scotland. Within their first 18 months of business they had garnered two AA rosettes and when I last visited, they had just been tested for a third rosette. Need I say more?

Charles Lochley is the gifted chef who has put Boath House Restaurant on the culinary map. The artful interpretation he brings to the traditional Scottish fare he prepares results in extraordinary meals. The menu changes frequently, but you might expect something along the lines of roast breast of pheasant with a confit of leg, celariac and Savoy cabbage topped with sautéed foie gras and Bayonne ham in a port wine and rosemary essence. As you'd imagine, the dessert offerings are also scrumptious, and you might find something like a banana toffee crumble or a nougat glace served with a dark chocolate sorbet and mascerated berries. Dress is definitely suit and tie, and reservations are required.

WITCHERY BY THE CASTLE, *Castlehill, Edinburgh. Tel. 0131/225-5613, Fax 0131/220-4392. £20-35. Open daily from noon to 4:00pm and from 5:30pm to 11:30pm. All major credit cards accepted.*

You'll find Witchery by the Castle just below Edinburgh Castle on Castlehill/Hill Street. What a marvelous restaurant. Management plays the witchery theme to the max, and while sinister surroundings usually give me the creeps, it works very well for this restaurant. Dark wood, a dark room and eerie dark shadows cast by flickering candles are the norm here. The Witchery by the Castle was an alehouse in the 1500s, and individuals thought to be witches were burned at the stake right outside the door.

While the Witchery draws a big crowd because of the eerie ambience, they also serve award-winning meals. The menu offers a good selection, including grilled filet of seabream with poached leeks in a warm oyster and vanilla sauce (to die for!), or for a traditional Scottish meal with a twist, try the roasted Aberdeen angus beef with a brioche crust and winter chanterelles. The dessert menu is enough to tempt even the most strident dieter to succumb; try the warmed chocolate torte with white chocolate sorbet for a treat. The wine list is not only one of the finest in the *country*, it has won awards as one of the best wine lists in the world, with between 850 and 1,000 wines available.

This *Taste of Scotland* restaurant is perhaps one of the most famous restaurants in the country. I promise that you will definitely remember your dining experience here. As you enter the restaurant, there is a quote from Dante's *Inferno* on the ceiling: *Que altro que ne fianche, Michele Scotto Fu, che veramente, Delle magiche frode seppe il gioco.* Translation: "Nobody else is quite like Michael Scott and his magical ways and his small stature." Michael Scott was one of the most powerful and feared men in Scotland during the beginning of the 13th century. Very intelligent and well-educated (that was scary enough for some folks), he was considered a prophet and powerful sorcerer. The painting above your head as you enter the restaurant is a fanciful view of Michael Scott the Magician.

THE SECRET GARDEN, *Castlehill, Edinburgh. Tel. 0131/225-5613, Fax 0131/220-4392. £20-35. Open daily from noon to 4:00pm and from 5:30pm to 11:30pm. All major credit cards accepted.*

You'll get a much different dining experience here than at the Secret Garden's sister restaurant, the Witchery by the Castle. Whereas the Witchery has an eerie atmosphere, the Secret Garden gets my vote as one of the most romantic restaurants in Scotland. You'll descend stairs into a large candlelit room with tall, open-beam ceilings enhance the setting. You'll find a pleasant chatty atmosphere here.

Here's an interesting historical note about the restaurant: it is located on the site of the 16th-century Lord Mayor's house. The house was the end of a secret passage from the castle, several hundred yards up the hill (just in case of trouble!).

The Secret Garden shares the menu and wine list with its sister restaurant the Witchery, so you'll enjoy the same wonderful cuisine available there. The Secret Garden's guest book reads like a Who's Who of world-renowned celebrities. Here are a few who have enjoyed meals here: Jack Nicholson, Michael Douglas, Jane Russell, Neil Sedaka, Gloria Estefan, Christopher Lloyd and Andrew Lloyd Webber. While you're waiting to be seated, check out the hand-carved oak reception desk – it is extraordinary.

FOWLER'S RESTAURANT, *Scotsburn Road, Tain. Tel. 01862/892-052, Fax 01862/892-260. £20-30. Open daily from noon to 2:00pm and from 7:00pm to 9:00pm. Amex, MasterCard and Visa accepted.*

I have eaten in a lot of restaurants around the world, and Fowler's would definitely rank in the top echelon of those restaurants. Chef David Lauritsen is the proud owner of 2 AA rosettes, and in my opinion, a third cannot be far behind. Not only is the food marvelous, but David has mastered the art of presentation – the meals are almost too pretty to eat (almost).

The menu changes, but my last meal here began with seared west coast scallops, with a tempura of squid with tomato and lemon dressing. That was polished off quickly to make room for the filet of Highland beef topped with langostine and coriander bake, served with a sloe gin glaze. Dessert was a mille feuille of meringue and fresh local berries, latticed with two chocolate sauces. It was delicious, and so pretty. If those dishes don't start your mouth watering, how about the breast of duck nestled in a bed of apricots and served with a cointreau sauce, topped with crispy leeks, or the wild Scottish salmon filled with hot smoked trout mousseline and a shellfish and lemongrass bouillabaise?

As good as your meal will be (and it will be good), the dining room adds a nice touch to the meal. It is a wonderful long room, with the original plasterwork around the ceiling. Large windows look out onto the sculpted lawns, and provide a wonderful setting in which to enjoy your meal. Dress is suit and tie, and reservations are a must on weekends and nightly during the tourist season.

THE GRAIN STORE RESTAURANT, *30 Victoria Street, Edinburgh. Tel. 0131/225-7635, 0131/225-7125. £10-15 lunch, £15-20 dinner. Open daily from noon to 2:00pm and 6:00pm to 11:00pm (until midnight on Saturday). Amex, MasterCard and Visa accepted.*

All things considered, this is my favorite restaurant in Edinburgh. I was alerted to it by Maggie Urquhart, owner of Kildonan Lodge Guest House, as one of her favorites. I can see why. From the moment you enter the restaurant, you're swept up by the atmosphere; stick around a bit and your meal will create another pleasant memory. (The *Taste of Scotland* judges must have agreed, as they have recognized The Grain Store Restaurant for their excellence also.)

The restaurant is on the second story above street level, and you ascend a wide avant-garde staircase (blue stairs amid pink walls) to reach the entrance to the restaurant. The moment you walk in, you will be enchanted by the surroundings: rough-hewn stone walls, plank floors that match the plank tables, and flickering candles that cast a warmth upon your dining experience. Large floral arrangements strategically situated throughout the restaurant add an additional touch of class and beauty to the setting. The moment you walk in the door look to your right; at the far end of the restaurant you'll see an enormous old oak clock, with a ponderous pendulum swaying slowly and methodically.

The manager describes their cuisine as "imaginative modern Scottish," and it is truly exceptional. The menu changes seasonally, but you might find such delicacies as roasted saddle of hare in juniper jus or a more traditional offering of filet of Aberdeen beef or cured pork and button mushrooms. Vegetarian dishes are also available. A fine wine list with about five dozen selections provides a wide range of choices and prices.

You'll have a pleasant, quiet dining experience at the Grain Store, and you'll find everything from very casual dress to very formal. The restaurant has a broad appeal. You'll see university students to folks who probably graduated from the university 50 years ago. But they all have one thing in common – they enjoy the excellent food and atmosphere immensely. And I believe you will too.

DRINK

Liquor, especially **whisky**, is big business in Scotland. Each year over 100 Scottish distilleries produce and ship enough whisky to account for about £2.5 billion in Scottish exports – about 5% of their GDP. There is some debate as to whether Scotland brought the world whisky or merely perfected it. Most of the information I have read indicates the brew was developed across the North Channel in Ireland. Irish monks introduced whisky to the world in the sixth century. The word whisky comes from the anglicized Gaelic words *uisce beatha* (pronounced ISK-kee-BAH-hah), which means the "water of life." By the time Anglo-Norman invaders hit the shores of Ireland, whisky was well established in the Irish culture. Unable to pronounce *uisce beatha*, the English soldiers shortened it to *uisce,* which they eventually anglicized to whisky.

Connoisseurs of whisky will immediately notice the difference between Irish whiskey and Scotch whisky (other than the fact that one uses an "e" in its spelling, and the other does not). The difference is attributed to the malt: Scotch malt is dried over open peat fires, whereas Irish malt is dried in a closed kiln. The former method imparts a distinct smoky flavor to Scotch whisky that is absent in Irish whiskey. Another difference is that Scotch whisky is distilled twice, while Irish whiskey is distilled thrice.

There are two primary types of Scotch: **single-malt** and **blended**. Single-malt whiskies, as the name implies, are distilled using a single malt. Blended whiskies mix the distilled malt with other grains, including American corn or Finnish barley. Blended Scotch is considered the smoother of the two, although single-malt fans will tell you that there are plenty of smooth single-malt whiskies in Scotland.

While Scotch whisky is the banner liquor product in Scotland, there are of course other liquors that are brewed and distilled here. **Scottish beer,** also known as **Scotch ale**, is brewed here, as well as a variety of fruit wines. But the real attention-getter is Scotch.

One final comment on Scotch whisky. I'd like all readers of this guide to be politically correct when ordering their first Scotch in the country of its origin. Do not order *Scotch* – all the whiskies distilled in Scotland are Scotch by definition. Ask for a specific brand name (such as those suggested by Andrew Deans in the sidebar on the next page), or, if you're still uncertain, ask the bartender for his or her suggestion.

SCOTLAND'S TOP SCOTCH WHISKIES

Along with his wife Mary, Andrew Deans owns and operates Cameron Toll Guest House in Edinburgh. When I found Andrew was a connoisseur of malt whiskies, I asked him to recommend the top single-malt Scotch whiskies for my readers. Following are his top choices, along with a comment about each:

Glenkinchie: *our local whisky, only 15 miles from Edinburgh. Good for beginners, gentle.*

Talisker: *from the Isle of Skye, called Lava of the Cuillins, for the adventurous smell of seaweed. Very powerful.*

Oban: *from the west coast port town of Oban. Smooth, fresh air and peat flavours.*

The Macallan: *From Craigellachie on Strath Spey. Said to be the Rolls Royce of single-malt whiskies. Smell the sherry.*

Lagavulin: *from the Isle of Islay. Dry and smoky, with a complex taste, but well worth persevering with, especially late at night!*

Glenmorangie: *The best-selling malt in Scotland. Selection of different finishes now available. Light and smooth.*

Glenfarclas: *from Strathspey, the tall dark handsome whisky, with sherry and oak flavors, from this truly independent distillery.*

12. SCOTLAND'S BEST PLACES TO STAY

While most of the accommodations I've stayed in over the many years I've been going to Scotland were quite good, there are a few that still linger in my memory. These were the ones I couldn't wait to tell my family and friends about when I got home. Some of these hotels and B&Bs you'll remember for their history and beauty; others for their genuine warmth and the people you meet there. And I guarantee that there will be some that you return to year after year.

AUCHTERARDER HOUSE, *Auchterarder. Tel. 0764/636-646, Fax 0764/662-939; Website: www.wrensgroup.com. 15 Rooms. Rates: £120-140 single; £160-350 double. All major credit cards accepted.*

There are many hotels in Scotland that strive to look and feel like an ancient Scottish hunting lodge, but few succeed. But some do, and one of the best is Auchterarder House in the Perthshire countryside.

From the moment you enter Auchterarder House you will be enthralled (anyway, I was). A photograph of Ronald and Nancy Reagan greet you in the entryway: their beaming smiles seem to assure you that if Auchterarder House was good enough for them, you are simply going to love it. The home was originally built in 1832 for an army officer, but it wasn't until James Reid purchased it in 1882 that it became the lavish home you see today. Mr. Reid owned a company that manufactured steam engines, and you can see from the house that business was very, very good. Mr. Reid spent significant sums of money decorating this country getaway; many of the antiques and all of the tapestries and silk wallpaper in the house are those selected by Mr. Reid himself. Every public room has an ornate fireplace and most have exquisite Waterford crystal chandeliers. You'll marvel at the choice wood carvings that add to the elegance here.

Auchterarder House is run like the country home it was, and not merely as a hotel. For example, you'll not find a bar here, but rather a well-stocked cabinet with an array of fine malt whiskies and cognac – in the manner of a Victorian-era country house.

Since you might plan on sleeping here, you may wish to know a little about the rooms. No surprises here, unless you were expecting run-of-the-mill, boring sleeping quarters. Each room is exceptionally large and furnished with some of the finest bedroom furnishings in the country. All the rooms are generously endowed with antiques, most of which have been in the house for well over 100 years. Each room is named after an ancient Scottish clan.

But wait, that's not all! Each of the bathrooms in the house are stunning in and of themselves. Each is nearly as large (or so it seems) as some entire hotel rooms, and they are exquisitely furnished. As with most hotels and guest houses in Scotland, each room is equipped with a phone and TV. But taking their service a step beyond most, you'll enjoy complimentary malt whisky, along with an accompanying history of that particular brand. Fluffy bathrobes and a complimentary fruit tray help you feel at home. There are tea- and coffee-making facilities, but here you'll find them served with silver teapots.

The dining room is nothing less than exquisite. Again, superb silk wallpaper and ancient oil paintings grace the walls. Your meals will be served amid china, crystal and candlelight in a manner befitting the royal guests that have dined here through the years. You'll either take your breakfast in the dining room or the conservatory (your choice). The conservatory is a former breezeway between the house and the family chapel. Encased in windows, the conservatory looks out onto the gorgeous grounds and gardens and a lovely Victorian fountain. Soft music provides just the right touch to your dining experience here.

The grounds are certainly worth more than a brief mention. They are, in a word, extraordinary. Seventeen acres of beautifully sculpted lawns punctuated with magnificent gardens. You'll find over 400 varieties of rhododendrons, firs, oaks, and azaleas pleasantly placed for your viewing and strolling pleasure.

Can you tell I fell in love with Auchterarder House? If you stay here, you will too. As you leave, tip your hat to Mr. Reid, whose portrait, with a stern but not unfriendly visage, gazes down on you during your stay here. His lavish taste and lifestyle makes for a most enjoyable experience for you.

MANSFIELD HOUSE HOTEL, *Scotsburn Road, Tain. Tel. 01862/892-052, Fax 01862/892-260; E-mail: info@mansfield-house.co.uk; Website: www.mansfield-house.co.uk. 18 Rooms. Rates: £45-75 single; £70-130 per person double. Rates include breakfast. Amex, MasterCard and Visa accepted.*

My oh my – you are going to like Mansfield House Hotel. This splendid and elegant Georgian house was built in 1875 as the landowner's home. It was a private home until World War II, when it was converted into a hotel. In 1995 Norman and Norma Lauritsen purchased it and have renovated it to its former luxurious stature. Everywhere you look you see splendid pine paneling, ornate ceilings, quality furnishings and art. The tartan carpet on the stairs is that of the MacKenzie Clan. For years, Mr. Lauritsen was an international businessman used to seeing hotels from the traveler's point of view. He has brought that perspective to Mansfield House and the results are marvelous.

This stunning four-star country house sits in the midst of 3.5 acres of spectacular grounds. Among many other trees, there are two 140-year-old Canadian redwoods on the property. In addition, lots of well-manicured lawns give the grounds a park-like feeling. There are eight bedrooms in the main house, and another ten are located in a new wing of the house that was completed in 1980. The rooms in the main house are spacious and most have large, well-appointed bathrooms. Four of the bathrooms include Jacuzzi baths. The best rooms in the main house are the Haakon, Ankerville, Rose, Ross and Croftmary rooms. The rooms in the new wing are generally a little smaller, but they are also furnished with top-quality furnishings and are very comfortable. These rooms feel more like traditional hotel rooms in a very nice hotel. Regardless of which room you stay in, you'll find a TV and radio, hairdryer, trouser press, tea- and coffee-making facilities and a complimentary decanter of sherry.

As you would expect, the dining room at the Mansfield House Hotel is marvelous. Keeping things in the family, the head chef is David Lauritsen. He has shown he earned this role by being more than merely the owners' son; he already has two AA rosettes to his credit, and I believe a third cannot be far behind.

Mansfield House has recently added a Beauty Salon to the amenities they offer their guests. Why not try an aromatherapy treatment, or possibly a massage at the hands of a skilled masseuse? As pleased as the Lauritsen's are about their hotel and the food that is served here, there is another area of which they are especially proud. They and their staff have a focus on customer service that is truly above and beyond what most hotels expect. The Lauritsen's are experts in finding and retaining the best and the brightest individuals to serve their guests. A quick scan of their guest book will assure you that the service provided here is far more than lip service. It seems that a vast majority of the comments mention the staff (as well as the food).

If you stay at Mansfield House, you will be joining politicians and movie stars that have called Mansfield House Hotel home, if only for a little while. I guarantee you will really enjoy it here.

PRESTONFIELD HOUSE, *Priestfield Road, Edinburgh. Tel. 0131/ 668-3346, Fax 0131/668-3976. 31 Rooms. Rates: £125–225 single; £125-225 per room double; £325-500 per room suite. All major credit cards accepted.*

If you've always wanted to stay someplace where one of the US founding fathers stayed, then Prestonfield House is for you. In 1759 Benjamin Franklin stayed at Prestonfield House. His stay was so memorable that he penned the following poem upon his return to the US:

Joys of Prestonfield, adieu
Late found, soon lost but still we'll view
The engaging scene oft to these eyes
Shall the pleasing vision rise.
Hearts that warm towards a friend:
Kindness and kindness without end.
Easy converse, sprightly wit;
These we found in Dame and Knight.
Cheerful meals, balmy rest
Beds that never bugs molest.
Neatness and sweetness all around
These, at Prestonfield, we found.

To be honest, I was unprepared for the adventure Prestonfield House presented. But as I drove up the driveway and saw the colonnaded front of the mansion, I began to suspect I had found someplace special.

To enter Prestonfield House, you walk up a half dozen ancient steps into an entry hall endowed with large impressive (and old) oil paintings. As you walk throughout the house, notice the art on the walls – it is stunning. Richard Scott, the directing manager at Prestonfield, commented on the art: "We're fortunate that the family members were hoarders – they kept everything." The term "everything" applies especially to the artwork and many of the furnishings in the hotel. Resident in the house are the portraits of all the Lords and Ladies of Prestonfield House, dating back to the 1600s. A goodly number of them will smile down on you from their lofty perches in the dining room if you eat dinner here.

Prestonfield House was built in several stages. The first part – the front – was built in 1689. Sir William Bruce, the same architect who designed the Palace of Holyroodhouse, designed Prestonfield House. A section was added in 1822 (referred to by the staff as the "new" section), and 26 rooms (the "newest" section) were added at the back in 1997. As you go from the new part of the house to the newest part of the house, check out the scores of ink drawings of Edinburgh in her medieval years. These prints, some of which are over 150 years old, are exquisite and in splendid condition.

Now that you know a little of the history, let me share a bit about the rooms you'll find here. The rooms are large and decorated in soft colors, and each is furnished with reproduction antiques and top quality furnishings. All the rooms are large and comfortable. And almost all of them have large windows that look out on the fabulous grounds. The public rooms are full of antique furnishings, many of which are original to the house. As mentioned previously, you can scarcely venture any place in the house without seeing the portraits of the former inhabitants of Prestonfield.

Breakfast is served in an atrium that looks out on the relaxing and well-sculpted grounds. If you eat dinner here, it is taken in the marvelous dining room. All in all, Prestonfield House is a wonderful, captivating place to stay, and I highly recommend a stay here if it fits your budget.

THE WITCHERY SUITES, *Castlehill, Edinburgh. Tel. 0131/225-5613, Fax 0131/220-4392. 2 Rooms. Rates: £195 per room. All major credit cards accepted.*

If you want a different kind of accommodation experience, one that will stay in your mind for years to come and one that you will definitely share with friends and family when you return home, then spend a night in one of the Witchery Suites. If you're not interested in that kind of experience, then skip this entry and go on to some of the others.

What a find! Frankly, I stumbled across these two suites quite by accident, but what an accident. Associated with the Witchery Restaurant, these two suites at the top of Castle Hill on the Royal Mile are appealing to those with eclectic and (perhaps) eccentric tastes. They are Edwardian. They are Victorian. They are Louis XIV. Full of antiques, they are anything but understated. There are two suites; one is called the Inner Sanctum, and the other is the Old Rectory. The decorating theme is probably best termed Excessive.

The Old Rectory is chock full of antiques. The hand-painted ceiling, the green plants, the crystal and the fireplace all vie for your attention at the same time. The bed is a hand-carved French beauty, the likes of which will make you wonder where all the world's craftsmen have gone. Perhaps the most intriguing aspect of the Old Rectory is the bathroom. In the center sits an old porcelain claw-foot bathtub. Surrounding the tub are mirrors – on all sides. Subdued lighting adds to the atmosphere. Now that's a bathroom.

As wonderful as the Old Rectory is, the Inner Sanctum is my personal favorite. Cosmopolitan magazine went on a search of the best hotel rooms in the world. They were bowled over by the Inner Sanctum, and labeled it the *Sixth Wonder of the World* among hotel rooms. As you enter the Inner Sanctum you are immediately aware of scores of antiques, live plants, candles, and a crackling fireplace. A large four-poster bed presides over the bedroom, complete with a leopard-skin across its bedding. The bathroom features an ancient porcelain tub with what purports to be one of the world's first attempts at a shower. A semi-circular wall rests atop the back half of the tub, with hundreds (thousands?) of tiny holes in it. These holes are for the shower, which shoots water out horizontally instead of from above.

Both the Inner Sanctum and the Old Rectory are incredibly popular, and both are often booked as much as a year in advance, especially on the weekends. They are used for romantic getaways, honeymoons, and wedding anniversary celebrations. In my estimation, the £195 per night for the rooms is a bargain. They would probably be just as full at £500 or £1,000 per night. But the owner is anxious for everyone to be able to experience these suites. Both suites have TVs, CD players, fireplaces and complimentary champagne.

So, even if you are trying to do Scotland on a shoestring, it might pay you to save your pennies and splurge for one night at either the Inner Sanctum or the Old Rectory. I guarantee you'll be glad you did. One caution, though: be careful when you enter either room, as you may experience sensory overload.

RUFFLETS COUNTRY HOUSE HOTEL, *Strathkinness Low Road, St. Andrews. Tel. 01334/472-594, Fax 01334/478-703; E-mail: rufflets@standrews.co.uk; Website: www.standrews.co.uk/hotels/rufflets. 25 Rooms. Rates: £70-90 single; £60-95 per person double; £85-90 per person Rose Cottages. All major credit cards accepted.*

I fell in love with Rufflets Country House Hotel. This 1920s-era country house is a delightful and pleasant place to stay. It is one of those hotels that stands out in your memory because of the facility, the staff, and the grounds.

Elegance is the one word that comes to mind when I consider Rufflets. Whether you are nestled into the depths of a comfy leather chair in the drawing room or sitting on the patio taking in the lovely gardens, you'll feel a touch of class. You'll enjoy resting for a spell in the Old Library, a quirky room for visiting, card playing, or golf review sessions. And it is really a disservice to call the gardener's handiwork mere *gardens*. They are breathtaking, awe-inspiring works of art! And set amidst the ten acres of the estate, they are beautiful indeed.

The bedrooms are wonderful. Large and well-lit, each room is individually decorated and features antiques and designer wallpaper. The rooms are decorated in spring-time colors: lilacs, greens, yellows and roses. The rooms at the back of the property are the best, as they get the full effect of the gardens and grounds. Each room has a nice large tile bathroom with the latest fixtures. There are other rooms separate from the main house called the Rose Cottages. The rooms in these apartments are not quite as large as those in the main house, but the additional privacy is nice. There are no elevators in the main house, but there is wheelchair access in the one-story Rose Cottages.

There is one restaurant and one bar on-site. The restaurant is renowned for its fine cuisine. The bar features over 100 varieties of malt whisky and a bartender who will be delighted to pick just the right one for you.

Rufflets Country House is not in downtown St. Andrews, but rather a 15-minute or so drive out into the country. Be sure and call for directions, as it is a bit difficult to find without them. All but two of the bedrooms are non-smoking, although smoking is allowed in certain parts of the public rooms.

BOATH HOUSE, *Aberdeen Road, Auldearn, Nairn. Tel. 01667/454-896, 01667/455-469; E-mail: wendy@boath-house.demon.co.uk; Website: boath-house.demon.co.uk. 7 Rooms. Rates: £80-100 single; £55-88 per person double. All major credit cards accepted.*

As you enter the spectacular grounds of Boath House, your anticipation will mount with each curve of the driveway. As you round the last bend, your anticipation will be rewarded with your first view of the palatial Georgian mansion you will be staying at. Built in 1820, the Boath House of today must look very much like it did 180 years ago.

Your hosts at Boath House are Don and Wendy Matheson, and you will be hard pressed to find a more pleasant and congenial couple in Scotland. Don is charming and an exceptional conversationalist; Wendy is an elegant and gracious hostess and you will enjoy her attention as well as her home. Don and Wendy have worked very hard to restore this splendid mansion to its former elegant and royal condition. In doing so, they have been painstakingly faithful to many details, including selecting paint from the "Georgian paint palate" that would have been in use during its construction.

While Boath House is non-smoking, the Mathesons have provided a lounge especially for their guests who do wish to smoke. Another lounge and library are available for guests to relax, read, chat, or just enjoy the warmth of the open fire. Both the lounges and the library have been furnished with exquisite furniture and impressive artwork. The dining room is another delightful public room. It overlooks the Matheson's own private lake and part of the 20-acre estate. The meals here are superb, and they have been recognized with two AA rosettes.

As you move from the public areas of the restaurant to the bedrooms, you won't be disappointed, as the richness of your experience will be continued. First of all, you'll likely ascend to your room via a magnificent spiral staircase. When you reach the rooms, you'll find spacious, comfortable and eye-catching places. Each bedroom has been individually and expensively decorated. You'll find antique French beds, claw-foot porcelain bathtubs and scads of antiques everywhere. My favorite bedrooms were Rooms 3 and 4. Each is huge, and they overlook the sumptuous grounds. Room 3 has a huge bathroom with a large porcelain tub in the center of the room; three other rooms have similar bathtubs.

Boath House also offers its residents an on-site beauty and well-being salon, including aromatherapy, massages, and reflexology. A small exercise room, sauna and Jacuzzi are available to help you relax and unwind. The estate itself deserves a word or two. Boath House nestles serenely amid 20 acres of stunning scenery. The grounds were planned and laid out in the early 1700s, prior to the home being built. Many of the trees on the estate are over 400 years old, and include a wide variety of flora, including trees and shrubs from many countries.

All things considered, Boath House is one of the best places to stay in Scotland. I guarantee that if you do stay here, you will thoroughly enjoy the experience.

MARCLIFFE AT PITFODELS, *North Deeside Road, Aberdeen. Tel. 01224/861-000, Fax 01224/868-860; E-mail: reservations@marcliffe.com; Website: www.nettrak.co.uk/marcliffe. 42 Rooms. Rates: £105-155 single; £115-165 per room double. All major credit cards accepted.*

What do Mikhail Gorbachev and Charlton Heston have in common? How about Prince Charles and Rod Stewart? Okay, those were sort of tough – how about Tony Blair and Margaret Thatcher? That's right – each of them has stayed at this incredible hotel (along with a host of other world-renowned luminaries). The Marcliffe at Pitfodels in Aberdeen is one of the nicest hotels in Scotland, and is also one of the best buys for the money. It is a grand hotel – a member of the *Small Luxury Hotels of the World*. And rightly so – it is truly a magnificent place to stay. Everything about the Marcliffe is first class, and a stay here will be one of your most pleasant memories. Top-of-the-line furnishings, designer wallpaper and window coverings, and a vast array of antiques sprinkled liberally throughout the hotel assures you of a comfortable and delightful stay. And yet, the Marcliffe is anything but stuffy. It is a truly welcoming and warm reception you'll receive here.

As you would expect, the bedrooms are all large and well-appointed. Top-quality furniture, bright colors and creature comforts like fluffy bathrobes, mini-bars, and fresh fruit are all standard offerings for those who stay here. The bathrooms are all ultra-modern and furnished nicely. You'll take your breakfast in a cobblestoned, glass-enclosed Conservatory. Views onto an inviting patio (where you can also dine, weather-permitting) and the woods beyond enhance the delicious fare served in the Conservatory. For more formal dining, the Invery Restaurant also serves residents of the Marcliffe. This award-winning restaurant provides a marvelous atmosphere and delicious meals.

The Marcliffe sits regally amid 20 acres of sculpted lawns, brilliant gardens and tremendous trees. You may choose to go for a walk among the verdant greenery, or perhaps you'll have a spot of tea on one of the many benches provided for your benefit. If your travels bring you to Aberdeen, then the Marcliffe should be at the top of your list of places to stay. I know it is at the top of mine.

ROMAN CAMP COUNTRY HOUSE HOTEL, *Main Street, Callander. Tel. 01877/330-003, Fax 01877/301-533; E-mail: mail@roman-camp-hotel.co.uk. 14 Rooms. Rates: £70-85 single; £95-115 double per room; £140-165 superior double per room; £160-186 suite per room. All major credit cards accepted.*

Unbelievable – that's the only word I can think of to describe Roman Camp Country House Hotel. Well, maybe that and elegant...and lavish. And, well, unbelievable. In my humble opinion, this is one of the loveliest hotels in the United Kingdom.

Eric and Marion Brown are your host and hostess, and they are rightfully proud of their hotel. They have accentuated your stay here with freshly cut flowers, welcoming fires in ancient fireplaces, and a staff that is attentive and friendly. The flowers are cut from those that grow throughout the 20-acre estate within which the hotel nestles. Roman Camp was built in 1625 on the site of an old Roman army camp as a hunting lodge for the Dukes of Perth. It has attracted dukes and duchesses, kings and queens, and presidents and their first ladies ever since. Converted into a hotel in 1939, you may now enjoy what was once the domain of royalty.

It has the grace of a French chateau, yet the comfort and welcome of a home in the country. Each bedroom is individually decorated with top-of-the-line furnishings, and complemented by a host of antique furniture and accoutrements (my room had an antique silver hand mirror, comb and brush). Most of the rooms are large and tastefully decorated, and each has views of the lovely gardens and grounds. Each room comes with complimentary sherry and bottles of mineral water. Each also offers hairdryers, tea- and coffee-making facilities, TV and a radio. Several rooms have been recently added, and though they are quite nice, they lack the antiquity of the others.

The public rooms are an absolute delight. Each is exquisitely adorned with fine and comfortable furniture, tasteful art and marvelous window coverings. Choose from the drawing room, library or conservatory to rest and relax, take afternoon tea or a wee dram in the evening. My favorite of the public rooms is the library. If you know where to look, you'll even find a small personal chapel behind those book-lined and paneled walls. You'll enjoy dinner and breakfast at Roman Camp Country House Hotel. Each is served in the tapestry-lined round dining room. The room is painted in bright colors and provides elegant dining in a restful and alluring atmosphere. The meals are superb, having been prepared with only the freshest ingredients, including fresh herbs and seasonings from the walled garden on the estate.

The hotel is in the middle of downtown Callander and can be a bit difficult to locate at first. The entrance is unobtrusively marked (on your left if you're coming from the south on the A84) between two cottages. But once you pass through the small entrance, the estate opens up before your eyes, and you will be delighted with all you find here. Flowerbeds and gardens, lush sculpted lawns, and the meandering River Treith all invite your explorer's spirit. Roman Camp is definitely a place you'll want to asterisk for a stay.

KILDONAN LODGE, *27 Craigmillar Road, Edinburgh. Tel. 0131/667-2793, Fax 0131/667-9777; E-mail: kildonanlodge@compuserve.com; Website: www.smoothhound.co.uk/hotels/kildonan. 12 Rooms. Rates: £45-64 single; £30-54 per person double; £45-60 per person four-poster bedroom; £80-125 family room. MasterCard and Visa accepted.*

Kildonan Lodge looks like so many of the old Victorian homes in Edinburgh: neat and tidy, stately and inviting. But once you walk through the front doors, you'll know that you have come to stay at a very special place. This Victorian beauty was built in 1874, and has been carefully and lovingly restored to its former elegance. Throughout the home the stunning plasterwork and cornices on the ceilings have been maintained, and the effects are extraordinary.

Each of the rooms is large and spacious, and seems especially so because of the tall ceilings that are the trademark of these Victorian homes. Each is tastefully appointed with quality furnishings, soft colors (yellows and creams), and all are highlighted with tartan. Several of the rooms have marvelous four-poster beds that are a favorite of honeymooners. The decanter of complimentary sherry in each room is a way of welcoming you and making sure your stay is pleasant.

The tile bathrooms are all upgraded and top quality. Six of them have Jacuzzis for helping you relax at the end of a long day of sightseeing. One of my favorite rooms is the lounge on the first floor. It is large and pleasantly appointed with over-stuffed furnishings, prints of medieval Scotland, and an honesty bar. If you choose to dine at Kildonan Lodge (I strongly suggest it!), you will wait here while your dinner is being prepared. You are welcome to sample any of the wide variety of alcoholic beverages or sodas available, and you merely write your name on a pad, indicating what you had. The charge is nominal, the trust is refreshing.

Breakfast and dinner are available in the dining room at the front of the guest house. It overlooks the lovely front yard, and is large and spacious. I was particularly interested in the dinner – it was wonderful! I was surprised to learn that the Urquharts don't open this aspect of Kildonan Lodge to the public – the meals were every bit as good as some of the top restaurants I sampled in Scotland. Maggie patiently explained that her reasoning was that she did not want to take away from the experience of her guests, and she was afraid the additional traffic would harm the experience for those who were staying here.

As wonderful as Kildonan Lodge is, the best part of your stay here will probably be the reception and care you receive from your hosts, Bruce and Maggie Urquhart. No matter which greets you upon your arrival, you will feel warmed like a member of the family coming for a visit. They are delightful and most interested in seeing that you are comfortable and enjoying your stay in Scotland. The guest book is liberally sprinkled with comments such as, "lovely," "beautiful," and "marvelous," But the one that is repeated most often is, "Glad we came back!" I guarantee you will add your name to this guest book, and you will say some of the same things. All things considered, Kildonan Lodge is one of my favorite places to stay in Scotland.

24 NORTHUMBERLAND, *24 Northumberland Street, Edinburgh. Tel. 0131/556-8140, Fax 0131/556-4423; E-mail: ingram@ednet.co.uk; Website: www.ingrams.co.uk. 3 Rooms. Rates: £50 single; £40 per person double. MasterCard and Visa accepted.*

What a gem! 24 Northumberland is elegance and eccentricity, excellence and enthusiasm. I am not sure which is the best to highlight here: your hosts or the house. Let's start with the house.

24 Northumberland is a stately mansion a couple of blocks north of Princes Street – close enough to the action of downtown Edinburgh, but away from the hustle and bustle of the city. Here's a test for you history majors out there: In what year did the War of 1812 begin? Right – 1812, the very year 24 Northumberland was built. This beautiful mansion has

been converted into four floors of the loveliest guest house you are likely to find in Scotland.

Each room is large, has tall ceilings, and has been tastefully decorated in bright, warm colors: green, yellow and cream. The furnishings throughout are exquisite and top quality – and complemented by a rich assortment of fine antiques sprinkled throughout the house and bedrooms. Breakfast is taken in the exquisite dining room, and is an event in and of itself. You begin with a bowl of fresh fruit salad, which is followed by David's hand-stuffed link sausage and silky smooth scrambled eggs.

Your hosts are David and Theresa Ingram, and they are two of the warmest, most genuine people you will meet in Scotland. David is a delightful conversationalist who will enhance your stay at 24 Northumberland. He is also an antique dealer by profession, and has used his eye for antiques to furnish 24 Northumberland with scores of period antiques and ancient knick-knacks.

David is a specialist in the history of Edinburgh, and is a great source for history and places to go. He is an excellent conversationalist who has been referred to as "mildly eccentric," and I have to agree (in addition to bearing an uncanny resemblance to a younger David Niven)! His humor is warm and delightful, but he is also very serious about the experience he wants for his guests. David says he has purposely kept 24 Northumberland small because, "I love to see people happy and enjoying themselves, and know that I have in some way been responsible for it."

Need I say that I heartily recommend 24 Northumberland as one of the best places to stay in Scotland?

ROSKHILL GUEST HOUSE, *Roskhill, near Dunvegan, Isle of Skye. Tel. 01470/521-317, Fax 01470/521-761; E-mail: stay@roskhill.demon.co.uk; Website: www.roskhill.demon.co.uk. 5 Rooms. Rates: £32-40 single; £27-35 per person double. Rates include breakfast. Amex, MasterCard and Visa accepted.*

What a delightful find – Roskhill House is an exceptional B&B sitting just off the A863 as you come into (or as you are leaving) Dunvegan. Your hostess here is Gillian Griffith, and she will provide you a warm welcome, a warm meal, and marvelous memories of a great place to stay. The home was built in 1890, and it has been renovated tastefully, resulting in a warm, comfortable B&B. Gillian's hostessing philosophy is summed up in these words, "The whole idea of Roskhill is home, not hotel," and she has successfully implemented her philosophy at Roskhill House.

There are five bedrooms, and all of them are good sized and decorated with light paint and floral accents. The furnishings are new and very comfortable. Four of the rooms are ensuite, and the fifth has its own private bath in the hallway. The bathrooms have showers that I would suggest might be among the best in Scotland, if not all of Europe. They are exceptionally powerful, an unusual find in a Scottish B&B. In addition to her significant abilities as a hostess, Gillian is a fabulous cook. Her efforts have gained her recognition by *A Taste of Scotland*, an unusual feat for a B&B owner. You'll of course have breakfast here, and that will be a treat. But if you choose to eat dinner here (you should!) you'll be thrilled. Just let Gillian know before noon what you wish to have for dinner, and she will procure the necessary ingredients – all fresh from the local countryside or sea. The night I stayed, she made chicken in a sage sauce that was nothing short of exquisite. It was followed by a delectable banana mousse that was spectacular. Both were of the quality and presentation you would expect to find in some of the finest restaurants in the country. Dinner is a reasonable £14.50 per person for two courses and £17.50 per person for three courses. Gillian also tends a small bar that offers about 20 malt whiskies, wines from all over the world, and a fine selection of beers and ales.

When you arrive, in addition to Gillian you will probably be greeted by Minnie the Mouser, the feline part-owner of the B&B. She makes her home in the lounge area. If you are allergic to cats, Gillian and Minnie will vote on whether Minnie will leave. So far, all votes have been ties, so Minnie stays.

Roskhill House takes its name from Gaelic words meaning "white water," and in this case, those Gaelic words refer to a nearby waterfall. Before you come, you might wish to check out Gillian's website: it is excellent, listing not only information about Roskhill House, but also about the things to see and do around the Isle of Skye. It is an impressive website, and doubly so once you learn that Gillian developed it herself.

If you venture to the Isle of Skye, I strongly suggest that you stay and dine with Gillian. Both experiences may be some of your finest while touring Scotland.

EAST LOCHHEAD COUNTRY HOUSE, *Larg's Road, Loch Winnoch. Tel. 01505/842-610, Fax 01505/842-610; E-mail: winnoch@aol.com; Website: www.selfcatering-accommodation.co.uk. 2 Rooms. Rates: £33 single; £33 per person double. MasterCard and Visa accepted.*

East Lochhead Country House is undoubtedly one of my favorite places to stay in Scotland. It combines a wonderful home, gracious hosts, and an idyllic setting to create one of the most memorable lodgings you are likely to have in Scotland. This four-star Bed and Breakfast is located about 30 minutes outside Glasgow and sits in the rolling countryside east (and a little south) of Glasgow. It is also about 15 minutes from the Glasgow airport, so you might consider this for your last night's stay in Scotland.

Mrs. Janet Anderson is your hostess, and you will be hard-pressed to find a more gracious and elegant hostess in all of Scotland. She adds a touch of elegance to this oasis of hospitality. You will feel truly welcomed into her home when you arrive. The Andersons have lovingly and beautifully renovated this 100-year-old stone farmhouse. To put their efforts in perspective, their daughter Heather says the house was "horrific" prior to the renovations. You'd never know it now.

You'll take your breakfast (and dinner if you have arranged it previously) in an alcove off the sitting room. Enclosed by floor-to-ceiling windows, the alcove looks out onto the well-landscaped lawn and stunning gardens. A nearby bird feeder attracts scores of songbirds to complement your meal. Lift your eyes a little higher and you can see tranquil Barr Loch and beyond that the dappled hills of Renfrewshire. Not only is the dining experience wonderful because of the setting, but the meal itself is marvelous. Mrs. Anderson is an award-winning chef recognized for her expertise by *A Taste of Scotland*. The breakfast she prepares will be filling and delicious, and includes eggs, bacon, sausage, and porridge. If you prefer a lighter meal, cereal, yogurt and fresh fruit are also available. Be sure and sample the honey – it's from Mrs. Anderson's own beehives.

After breakfast or dinner, stroll among the amazing variety of flowers and plants in the Anderson's gardens. Just a stone's throw from the gardens you'll see several Highland cattle and Jacob's sheep gazing nearby. It is truly a peaceful setting.

There are two bedrooms in the main house at East Lochhead. Both are large and spacious, and feature tasteful decorations and exceptionally comfortable furniture. One room is ensuite, and while the other isn't ensuite, it has its own private bath in the hallway. Check out the view from the private bathroom. It has been said that it is the best in Scotland. In addition to the rooms in the main house, there are four self-catering apartments adjacent to the house.

I'm telling you East Lochhead is wonderful, but don't just take my word for it. Following are some comments from the guest book: "A superb place in all aspects – a little jewel." "I count myself lucky to have found you." Perhaps the most telling is "We found you be accident, but next time we'll come by design." With that said, I think your designs for Scotland should include at least one night at East Lochhead. The Andersons request that their guests not smoke at East Lochhead.

13. EDINBURGH

Edinburgh is one my favorite European cities, and certainly one of my favorite places to visit in Scotland. I find a vibrancy and excitement about life here that is invigorating and contagious. Others apparently feel this way, too, as Edinburgh has been dubbed the "Athens of the North." Edinburgh is ancient and medieval, but at the same time it is fresh and new, modern and stylish. It just feels like a city you want to spend time in.

There has been a settlement on the site Edinburgh now occupies for many hundreds of years. By the end of the 11th century, it was a walled city, and **Edinburgh Castle** had its beginnings here in the late 11th century or early 12th century. Edinburgh became the seat of government in Scotland, and as such it swirled with intrigue and plots within plots. It also became the seat of learning, as dozens of institutions of higher education were founded here.

Today, Edinburgh is a delightful city to visit. Most of the sights to see are centered around Edinburgh Castle and the **Royal Mile**. Edinburgh Castle is many people's favorite castle because there is so much to see.

As you walk downhill from Edinburgh Castle along the Royal Mile, you'll encounter a host of tartan shops, restaurants and hotels. There will be a number of sights to see along the way, including the home of **John Knox**, the petulant reformer that caused so much misery for anyone who dared to believe differently than he – especially Mary Queen of Scots. As you reach the end of the Royal Mile, you'll find yourself at the **Palace of Holyroodhouse**. Currently the official residence of Her Majesty the Queen of England when she visits Edinburgh, it was originally built as an abbey in the 12th century. It has been added to many times in the ensuing years, with the most significant additions taking place in the 16th and 17th centuries. It served as the residence of a number of Scottish monarchs, including its most famous resident, Mary Queen of Scots. It is magnificent and it's fun to imagine what it would have been like to have lived here. But it wasn't all fun and games: plots within plots within plots were conceived here, and some were actually enacted within its stony walls.

If you are an art devotee, then you'll be most pleased with the offerings you'll find in Edinburgh. Between the **National Gallery of Scotland**, the **Dean Gallery**, the **Scottish Gallery** and the **Scottish National Portrait Gallery** you'll encounter works by some of the most gifted artists in history: Degas, Gauguin, Goya, Monet, Picasso, Raphael, Rembrandt, Renoir, Rubens, Van Dyck and Van Gogh. In addition, you'll get to consider the works of some of Scotland's brightest and most talented artists, such as Gillies, MacTaggart, Peploe, Raeburn, Ramsay, Redpath and Wilkie.

If modern art is more to your liking, then the **Scottish National Gallery of Modern Art** will draw your attention. Paintings and sculptures, special exhibits and wondrous sights await you here, including works by Dada, Matisse and Picasso.

Edinburgh is divided into several sections. **Old Town** is the area that surrounds the Royal Mile. From Edinburgh Castle east to the Palace of Holyroodhouse and just south of that line is the area that constitutes Old Town. As in so many medieval cities, the town grew up around the central building there – in this case Edinburgh Castle. If you venture north of Old Town below the castle, you'll find **New Town**. Princes and George Streets are the principal streets in New Town, and this section of town evolved during the last half of the 18th century (it gives you some idea of the age of the city when *New Town* is over 200 years old). Princes Street is known for its shopping and it is always a hubbub of activity.

Edinburgh offers just about anything tourists would like: history and art, antiquity and modernity. To repeat an old advertising phrase, "Try it, you'll like it!" I did, and I do.

EDINBURGH'S MUST-SEE SIGHTS

Edinburgh Castle – *If you see nothing else in Edinburgh, this is the place to visit.*

Palace of Holyroodhouse – *Former home of Mary Queen of Scots and other Scottish monarchs, this is a great place to visit.*

National Gallery of Scotland – *The National Gallery features a fine selection of masterpieces.*

Royal Museum of Scotland – *This spectacular Victorian building is home to a wonderful museum full of interesting and intriguing things to see. The building itself is worth a visit, with its vaulted and ribbed ceiling.*

Royal Botanic Gardens – *Seventy-two acres of splendid and spectacular gardens offer a quiet place to stop and smell the roses (literally as well as figuratively) and the rhododendrons.*

ARRIVALS & DEPARTURES

Edinburgh can be reached by air, train, bus or car. As one of the principal cities in Scotland, access is plentiful and easy.

BY AIR

Edinburgh Airport, *Tel. 0131/333-1000*, lies about eight miles north-west of the city center. There are no direct flights to Edinburgh from the US or Canada – you'll need to connect in either London or Glasgow. There are a number of airlines that fly to Edinburgh Airport from London, and the route is extremely competitive. Watch for price wars, and you may be able to find fares as low as £55 to £70; normal fares run between £100 and £150.

The following airlines fly to Edinburgh from the indicated London airports:

From Heathrow
• **British Airways**, *Tel. 0181/754-7321*
• **British Midland**, *Tel. 0345/554-554*

From Gatwick
• **British Airways**, *Tel. 0181/754-7321*

From London Luton
• **Easyjet Airlines**, *Tel. 0870/600-0000*

From London Stansted
• **KLM UK**, *Tel. 0181/750-9820*

Getting to Town by Taxi

It is a short taxi ride from the airport to Edinburgh's town center. It will cost you £11 to £15 for the ride, depending on traffic conditions and how generous a tipper you are. You can catch a cab outside the main terminal.

Getting to Town by Bus

Once you arrive at Edinburgh Airport, you can get into the city center by catching a bus outside the terminal. Buses into the city are run by either **Lothian Regional Transport** (LTR) or **Guide Friday**. The half-hour ride costs £3.20 (LTR) or £3.50 (Guide Friday). Buses leave every 15 minutes throughout the day, every half hour in the evenings. Buses will drop you at Waverley Bridge in New Town, right at Princes Street.

Renting a Car at the Airport

There are a number of car rental agencies at Edinburgh Airport, and they are located in the main terminal. You'll find Avis, Budget, Europcar, and Hertz there. Occasionally, you can get better rental deals by going with agencies that are not at the airport. Here are a few you might try:

- **Arnold Clark Car Rental**, *Lochrin Place, Tollcross. Tel. 0131/228-4747*
- **Avis Rent-a-Car**, *100 Dairy Road, Edinburgh. Tel. 0131/337-6363*
- **Budget Rent-a-Car**, *The Royal Scot Hotel, 111 Glasgow Road, Edinburgh. Tel. 0131/334-7739*
- **Europcar UK Ltd.**, *24 East London Street, Edinburgh. Tel. 0131/557-3456*
- **Hertz Rent-a-Car**, *10 Picardy Place, Edinburgh. Tel. 0131/556-8311*
- **Mitchell's Self Drive**, *32 Torphichen Street, Edinburgh. Tel. 0131/229-5384*
- **Woods Care Rental**, *Edinburgh Airport, Edinburgh. Tel. 01506/858-6600*

Sample trip lengths from Edinburgh around the country (on the main roads without stopping to take pictures, visit sights or take detours):
- Aberdeen: 3 hours
- Glasgow: 1 hour
- Inverness: 4 hours
- Fort William: 3 hours
- London: 8 hours
- Oban: 3 hours

BY BUS

Edinburgh is accessible via bus from most major cities in Scotland. **Scottish Citylink**, *Tel. 0990/505050*, and **National Express**, *Tel. 0990/808080*, both arrive at and leave from **St. Andrew Bus Station**, *Clyde Street*, which is about a three-minute walk from Princes Street.

If you are arriving here via bus from London, as so many tourists do, expect to arrive a little stiff after your eight-hour journey. Also expect to pay about £25-30 for a round-trip ticket.

BY CAR

All roads in Scotland lead to Edinburgh. Well, not really, but there are a goodly number that will get you here. If you are driving up from England, take the M6/A74 north to either the A7 or the A702. (If you take the A7, you'll connect with the A68 about 25 miles south of Edinburgh.) If you are coming from Glasgow, take the M8. From Inverness, take the A9 and connect with the M90.

Routes to Edinburgh and Glasgow are both exceptionally well-marked throughout the country – you should have no trouble finding the correct roads – a good map, however, is essential.

BY TRAIN
Trains arrive throughout the day at **Waverley Station** *at the east end of Princes Street, Tel. 0131/556-2451.* If you intend to use this method of travel to come here from London, expect about a 5-hour ride.

ORIENTATION

The downtown area of Edinburgh is laid out in a nearly north-south, east-west fashion, so it is very easy to get and keep your bearings. **Edinburgh Castle** is pretty much the center of everything in the downtown area, and you should always have a good feel about where you are when you are downtown.

The area called the **Royal Mile** is a slightly inclined street that leads from Edinburgh Castle at one end down to the **Palace of Holyroodhouse** at the other. **Princes Street** is at the bottom of a pretty steep hill below the castle, but once you are there, getting around is pretty easy, as the area is quite flat.

Outstanding and frequent bus service runs between the downtown area and the suburbs where many excellent hotels, guest houses and bed and breakfasts are located. While parking in Edinburgh is more plentiful than in Glasgow, it is still difficult during the tourist season, so I would suggest you leave your car at your accommodations and take the bus into town.

GETTING AROUND TOWN

By Bicycle
Edinburgh features relatively wide streets as European cities go, but the traffic is always a consideration for bicyclists. But it wouldn't be too bad to bike from your B&B or guest house in the suburbs, then lock up your bike and see the sights along the Royal Mile. Then you can coast down the steep hill to Princes Street and check out all there is to see there. The hardest part is getting back up the 200-yard hill that leads from Princes Street to the Royal Mile.

You can rent (hire) bicycles in the following shops in Edinburgh:
• **Central Cycle Hire**, *11 Lochrin Place, Edinburgh. Tel. 0131/228-6333*
• **Edinburgh Cycle Hire**, *Blackfriar Street, Edinburgh. Tel. 0131/556-5560*
• **Sandy Gilchrist Cycles**, *1 Cadzow Place, Abbeyhill, Edinburgh. Tel. 0131/652-1760*

By Bus
As mentioned earlier, there is excellent bus service along the main arteries that feed downtown Edinburgh, and this is an excellent transportation option. Once in the downtown area, everything is pretty much

within easy walking distance. Bus fares run from 50p to 65p, depending on how far you are going in the city. Be sure to have exact change before you get on the bus.

By Car

If you have a car, my recommendation is to either leave it parked at your hotel or guest house and catch one of the many buses that travel into the downtown area. However, if you do wish to drive, you should be aware of a number of parking garages that are in the downtown area. Each of these car parks is open 24 hours a day.

- **Greenside Car Park**, *Greenside Row. Rates: £1.10 for two hours, £8 for 24 hours*
- **National Car Parks**, *Castle Terrace. Rates: £1.40 for two hours, £8 for 24 hours*
- **St. James Centre**, *St. James Shopping Centre. Rates: £1 for two hours, £16 for 24 hours*
- **Festival Square Car Park**, *1 Festival Square. Rates: £1.50 for two hours, £12 for 24 hours*
- **Waverley Car Park**, *New Street. Rates: £2.50 for two hours, £10 for 24 hours*

Watch out for parking tickets: while Edinburgh is tourist-oriented, rental cars are notorious for having parking tickets on them. I can think of better ways of spending £20; how about you?

By Foot

This is certainly the best way to see downtown Edinburgh. The sights to see are all clustered along the Royal Mile and below along Princes Street. For locations on the outskirts, like Deep Sea World, Linlithgow Castle, etc., you'll need to take a car.

By Taxi

Edinburgh has a number of taxi companies that will be happy to cart you where you need to go. Here are a few:

- **Cabs Direct**, *Tel. 0131/444-1313*
- **Capital Castle Cabs**, *Tel. 0131/228-2555*
- **Central Radio Taxis**, *Tel. 0131/229-2468*
- **City Cabs**, *Tel. 0131/228-1211*

WHERE TO STAY

The Royal Mile

1. CROWNE PLAZA, *80 High Street, Edinburgh. Tel. 0131/557-9797, Fax 0131/557-9789; Website: www.crownplazaed.co.ed. 283 Rooms. Rates: £125-185 single; £150-210 double; £ 250-300 suite. All major credit cards accepted.*

This is a lovely hotel in the heart of the Royal Mile. From the black and white checkerboard marble tile in the reception area to the marvelous rooms everything is top quality. If you want to stay right where all the action is in Edinburgh, this would definitely be a place to consider.

I often find that the hallways in these large hotels are narrow, dark and claustrophobic. But not so at the Crowne Plaza. The hallways are all wide and decorated in soft colors: cream or rose and gold. The walls are adorned with quality paintings and drawings. The rooms are all nice sized and tastefully decorated in blues with dark oak trim. Each room has satellite TV, phone, modem port, mini-bar with soft drinks and alcoholic beverages, trouser press and tea- and coffee-making equipment. Sixty percent of the rooms are non-smoking. All the rooms have double glazed windows, so there are no worries about noise from the outside disturbing your stay. Quality tile bathrooms enhance each room.

There are 10 luxury suites, and they are exceptionally nice. They are very large, some of them approaching the size of small apartments. Comfortable overstuffed furniture, several TVs, and quality artwork enhance the experience here. The Crown Plaza offers a host of amenities to those who stay here. A restaurant, fitness room and solarium are available, along with a pool and sauna.

2. CARLTON HIGHLAND HOTEL, *North Bridge, Edinburgh. Tel. 0131/472-3000, Fax 0131/556-2691; E-mail: chh@scottishhighlandhotels.co.uk. 200 Rooms. Rates: £119-125 single; £140-210 double; £250 suite. All major credit cards accepted.*

The Carlton Highland Hotel sits in an ideal location to see all the sights in Edinburgh. Just a half block off the Royal Mile, it makes for an excellent base for exploration. It is, however, a little pricey for what you get. Once a grand hotel, it is now showing the effects of its age, and unlike some of the other top-tier hotels in Edinburgh, it doesn't appear to have expended the funds on renovation. There's not a lot required, but fresh paint, new carpets and new bedspreads would do wonders for this hotel.

There is a mixture of large and small rooms. They are furnished functionally with standard furnishings, including TV, hairdryer, trouser press and tea- and coffee-making facilities. Some of the rooms have lovely views of the city. If you are looking for location, this isn't a bad place to stay; however, there are better values for your money close by.

3. THE WITCHERY SUITES, *Castlehill, Edinburgh. Tel. 0131/225-5613, Fax 0131/220-4392. 2 Rooms. Rates: £195 per room. All major credit cards accepted.*

If you want a different kind of accommodation experience, one that will stay in your mind for years to come and one that you will definitely share with friends and family when you return home, then spend a night in one of the Witchery Suites. If you're not interested in that kind of experience, then skip this entry and go on to some of the others.

I would define the theme of the Witchery Suites as *eclectic eccentricity*. I stumbled across these two suites quite by accident, but what an accident. Associated with the Witchery Restaurant, these two suites at the top of Castle Hill on the Royal Mile are appealing to those with eclectic and (perhaps) eccentric tastes. The two suites are Edwardian. They are Victorian. They are Louis XIV. Full of antiques, they are anything but understated. One is called the Inner Sanctum and the other is the Old Rectory. The decorating theme is probably best termed *excessive*. The Old Rectory is chock full of antiques. The hand-painted ceiling, the green plants, the crystal and the fireplace all vie for your attention at the same time. The bed is a hand-carved French beauty, the likes of which will make you wonder where all the world's craftsmen have gone. Perhaps the most intriguing aspect of the Old Rectory is the bathroom. In the center sits an old porcelain claw-foot bathtub. Surrounding the tub are mirrors – on all sides. Subdued lighting adds to the atmosphere. Now that's a bathroom.

But the Inner Sanctum is my personal favorite. *Cosmopolitan* magazine went on a search of the best hotel rooms in the world. They were bowled over by the Inner Sanctum, and labeled it the *Sixth Wonder of the World* among hotel rooms. As you enter the Inner Sanctum you are immediately aware of scores of antiques, live plants, candles and a crackling fireplace. A large four-poster bed presides over the bedroom, complete with a leopard skin across its bedding. The bathroom features an ancient porcelain tub with what purports to be one of the world's first attempts at a shower. A semi-circular wall rests atop the back half of the tub, with hundreds (thousands?) of tiny holes in it. These holes are for the shower, which shoots water out horizontally instead of from above.

Both the Inner Sanctum and the Old Rectory are incredibly popular, and both are often booked as much as a year in advance, especially on the weekends. They are used for romantic getaways, honeymoons and wedding anniversary celebrations. In my estimation, the £195 per night for the rooms is a bargain. They would probably be just as full at £500 or £1,000 per night. But the owner is anxious for everyone to be able to experience these suites. Both suites have TVs, CD players, fireplaces and complimentary champagne.

Selected as one of my Best Places to Stay – see Chapter 12.

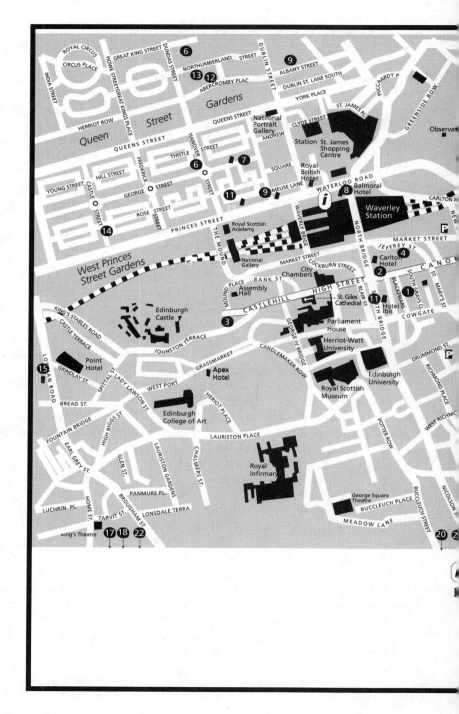

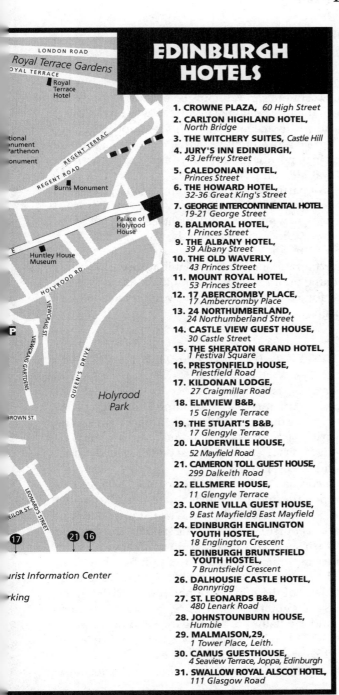

EDINBURGH HOTELS

1. **CROWNE PLAZA**, *60 High Street*
2. **CARLTON HIGHLAND HOTEL**, *North Bridge*
3. **THE WITCHERY SUITES**, *Castle Hill*
4. **JURY'S INN EDINBURGH**, *43 Jeffrey Street*
5. **CALEDONIAN HOTEL**, *Princes Street*
6. **THE HOWARD HOTEL**, *32-36 Great King's Street*
7. **GEORGE INTERCONTINENTAL HOTEL** *19-21 George Street*
8. **BALMORAL HOTEL**, *1 Princes Street*
9. **THE ALBANY HOTEL**, *39 Albany Street*
10. **THE OLD WAVERLY**, *43 Princes Street*
11. **MOUNT ROYAL HOTEL**, *53 Princes Street*
12. **17 ABERCROMBY PLACE**, *17 Ambercromby Place*
13. **24 NORTHUMBERLAND**, *24 Northumberland Street*
14. **CASTLE VIEW GUEST HOUSE**, *30 Castle Street*
15. **THE SHERATON GRAND HOTEL**, *1 Festival Square*
16. **PRESTONFIELD HOUSE**, *Priestfield Road*
17. **KILDONAN LODGE**, *27 Craigmillar Road*
18. **ELMVIEW B&B**, *15 Glengyle Terrace*
19. **THE STUART'S B&B**, *17 Glengyle Terrace*
20. **LAUDERVILLE HOUSE**, *52 Mayfield Road*
21. **CAMERON TOLL GUEST HOUSE**, *299 Dalkeith Road*
22. **ELLSMERE HOUSE**, *11 Glengyle Terrace*
23. **LORNE VILLA GUEST HOUSE**, *9 East Mayfield9 East Mayfield*
24. **EDINBURGH ENGLINGTON YOUTH HOSTEL**, *18 Englington Crescent*
25. **EDINBURGH BRUNTSFIELD YOUTH HOSTEL**, *7 Bruntsfield Crescent*
26. **DALHOUSIE CASTLE HOTEL**, *Bonnyrigg*
27. **ST. LEONARDS B&B**, *480 Lenark Road*
28. **JOHNSTOUNBURN HOUSE**, *Humbie*
29. **MALMAISON,29**, *1 Tower Place, Leith.*
30. **CAMUS GUESTHOUSE**, *4 Seaview Terrace, Joppa, Edinburgh*
31. **SWALLOW ROYAL ALSCOT HOTEL**, *111 Glasgow Road*

4. JURY'S INN EDINBURGH, *43 Jeffrey Street, Edinburgh. Tel. 0131/ 200-3300, Fax 0131/200-0400, US toll-free reservations 800/448-8355; E-mail: enquiry@jurys.com. 186 Rooms. Rates: £45-65 per room. Amex, MasterCard and Visa accepted.*

This is one of the newest hotels in Edinburgh, and it is a good one. First of all, I am a big fan of the Jury's chain of hotels because I have found that they generally give you quality accommodations for a good price. The Jury's Inn Edinburgh is a great representative of that chain. It may not be as elegant as some other Jury's properties, but it is new and nice, and it is located just off the Royal Mile on Jeffrey Street.

The rooms here are not particularly large, but they are large enough to be comfortable, and being a relatively new facility (it opened in April 1999) the furnishings are still new and are good quality. About half of the rooms look out to New Town (Princes Street) over the railway tracks. Each room has a TV, phone with voice mail and tea- and coffee-making facilities. There is one restaurant and a bar available to those who stay here. There are two smoking floors and six non-smoking floors. This is a good quality place to stay for a fair price, and it puts you very near all that is happening in Edinburgh.

Princes Street

5. CALEDONIAN HOTEL, *Princes Street, Edinburgh. Tel. 0131/459-9988, Fax 0131/225-6632. 246 Rooms. Rates: £160-180 single; £225-300 double; £350-875 suite. All major credit cards accepted.*

The Caledonian Hotel rests in the heart of bustling Edinburgh below famous Edinburgh Castle. Once the pride of the Caledonian Railway, the "Caley" has been a favorite of business people and tourists since its construction in 1902. Today it sits regally at the west end of Princes Street inviting its guests to spend the evening.

The rooms at the Caledonian vary in size, from quite spacious to a little small. But all have top-of-the-line furnishings and tasteful decorating touches. The best rooms look up to the castle, which is an impressive sight night or day. The suites are of course a step above the standard rooms, and they are large and nicely furnished. However, as suites go, they are not in the same class as the suites in some of the other top Edinburgh hotels.

The hotel is liberally endowed with marvelous old oil paintings throughout. You'll find many of them in the public rooms of the hotel. The Caledonian is a lovely old hotel (extensively renovated in the early 1990s), but it is step behind the Balmoral for elegance and facilities.

6. THE HOWARD HOTEL, *32-36 Great King Street, Edinburgh. Tel. 0131/557-3500, US toll-free reservations 800/322-2403, Fax 0131/557-6515; E-mail: reserve@thehoward.com; Website: www.thehoward.com. 15 rooms. Rates:*

£125-150 single; £195-260 double; £275-300 suite. Rates include breakfast. All major credit cards accepted.

Oh, you are going to like this place. For starters, take a triplex of stunning Georgian townhouses, furnish them to the hilt with period furnishings, add a healthy dollop of service, and you have the makings of an elegant place from which to base your exploration of Edinburgh. Located in Edinburgh's Georgian New Town within easy walking distance of all there is to see and do in the city, you'll marvel at the luxurious elegance that greets you the moment you walk through the front door.

Each bedroom has been individually decorated with such exceptional taste that they'll make most interior decorators green with envy. You'll experience soft colors, exquisite furnishings and artwork, as well as those wonderful tall ceilings that make these Georgian beauties perfect as hotels and guest houses. Some of the rooms feature four-poster beds, and all have spacious modern bathrooms with wonderful showers (some of the best in Scotland). Each room offers tea- and coffee-making service, hairdryers. And trouser presses.

You'll take your breakfast in the sumptuous paneled and muraled breakfast room, along with silver, linen and crystal. You'll enjoy the views out the window onto the cobblestoned street. Adjacent to The Howard is one of Edinburgh's better restaurants, called simply "36" *(see Where to Eat section).*

7. GEORGE INTER-CONTINENTAL HOTEL, *19-21 George Street. Tel. 0131/225-1251, Fax 0131/226-5644; E-mail: edinburgh@interconti.com; Website: www.interconti.com. 195 Rooms. Rates: £175-195 single; £195-225 double; £445-650 suite. All major credit cards accepted.*

As you walk into the lobby of George Inter-Continental Hotel, you know at once that the George was at one time a magnificent hotel. High-gloss marble floors, massive marble pillars and an elegant Resident's Lounge greet you. But once you venture upstairs, you begin to see the effects of aging on the George. You'll find a hodge-podge of rooms, most basically the same. Since this is an old Victorian mansion, the tall ceilings help to make the rooms feel a little larger than they actually are.

The rooms are nicely decorated, but the furnishings are rather standard and not at all exceptional, as one might expect for the rates charged. Each room has a trouser press, TV, hair dryer and tea- and coffee-making facilities. Two restaurants will provide you with pleasant options for your dining needs (see the *Where to Eat* section). The George provides a relatively central location from which to see Edinburgh, as it rests just a block or so off Princes Street.

EDINBURGH'S BEST PLACES TO STAY

The following hotels, guest houses and B&Bs are listed from most expensive to least expensive. You can get more information on each selection in the reviews that follow. I've left the numbers at the front of each selection for easy reference in the reviews and on the hotel map.

3. THE WITCHERY SUITES, *Castlehill, Edinburgh. Tel. 0131/ 225-5613, Fax 0131/220-4392. 2 Rooms. Rates: £195 per room. All major credit cards accepted. Eclectic eccentricity here! This is one of the most intriguing and interesting accommodation experiences in Scotland.*

8. BALMORAL HOTEL, *1 Princes Street, Edinburgh. Tel. 0131/ 556-2414, Fax 0131/557-8740. US toll-free reservations 800/223-6800. 165 Rooms. Rates: £150-170 single; £170-200 standard double; £160- 205 superior double; £200-270 deluxe double; £220-675 suite. All major credit cards accepted. Plush and posh, you'll feel utterly pampered when you stay in this old railway hotel that has had millions of dollars of renovations in the past decade.*

13. 24 NORTHUMBERLAND, *24 Northumberland Street, Edinburgh. Tel. 0131/556-8140, Fax 0131/556-4423; E-mail: ingram@ednet.co.uk; Website: www.ingrams.co.uk. 3 Rooms. Rates: £50 single; £40 per person double. MasterCard and Visa accepted. It's difficult to determine which is the best aspect of 24 Northumberland: your hosts or the house itself. You'll love both if you choose to stay here.*

16. PRESTONFIELD HOUSE, *Priestfield Road, Edinburgh. Tel. 0131/668-3346, Fax 0131/668-3976. 31 Rooms. Rates: £125–225 single; £125-225 per room double; £325-500 per room suite. All major credit cards accepted. Antique elegance and a wonderful accommodation experience awaits you here. Benjamin Franklin stayed here; if it was good enough for him, perhaps you'd be willing to try it.*

17. KILDONAN LODGE, *27 Craigmillar Road, Edinburgh. Tel. 0131/667-2793, Fax 0131/667-9777; E-mail: kildonanlodge@compuserve.com; Website: www.smoothhound.co.uk/hotels/kildonan. 12 Rooms. Rates: £45-64 single; £30-54 per person double; £45-60 per person four-poster bedroom; £80- 125 family room. MasterCard and Visa accepted. Maggie and Bruce Urquhart are your hosts, and they will see that your stay is pleasant and memorable in this renovated Victorian mansion.*

8. BALMORAL HOTEL, *1 Princes Street, Edinburgh. Tel. 0131/556-2414, Fax 0131/557-8740. US toll-free reservations 800/223-6800. 165 Rooms. Rates: £150-170 single; £170-200 standard double; £160-205 superior double; £200-270 deluxe double; £220-675 suite. All major credit cards accepted.*

If you are looking for an upscale hotel to stay in while visiting Edinburgh, this is my recommendation. Of the top-tier hotels in the city, this is my favorite. Stately and regal, the Balmoral provides Old World elegance. From the kilted-and-capped doorman at the two-story entrance to the spacious rooms, you'll be pleased with your stay here.

Built in 1902 as a railway hotel, the Balmoral Hotel underwent a £23 million renovation in 1990, and in 1998 they did another £7 million refurbishment. The results are extraordinary. Each of the rooms is large and spacious and furnished to perfection. Artwork on the walls complements the feeling of stateliness. The rooms are decorated with soft colors, mostly creams and yellows. The bathrooms are also top quality, with tile, marble vanities and power showers. Each room has air conditioning, a fax machine and printer, data port, phone, voice mail, bathrobes, trouser press and tea- and coffee making facilities,

There are four suites that certainly accentuate the positive. They are large and comfortable, exquisitely furnished to the point of opulence and each has lovely views of the city. The halls are over seven feet wide – wide enough, I am told, to allow two women wearing hoop skirts to pass one another without major mishap!

One of my favorite public rooms in the hotel is the Resident's Lounge. It's plush and pleasant and large murals accentuate the relaxing atmosphere. Afternoon tea is served here to residents and non-residents alike. The staff at the Balmoral Hotel is proud of this room and their award-winning afternoon tea – stop in to sample it yourself. There are two restaurants and two bars associated with the hotel. (See *Where to Eat* section for a report on the two restaurants.) In addition, there is a health club with a fitness room, pool and sauna available to residents.

9. THE ALBANY HOTEL, *39 Albany Street, Edinburgh. Tel. 0131/556-0397, Fax 0131/557-6633; e-mail: 100414.1237@compuserve.com. 21 Rooms. Rates: £75-125 single; £130-200 double. Rates include breakfast. Amex, MasterCard and Visa accepted.*

The Albany is one of those gorgeous Georgian townhouses that has been converted into a sumptuous hotel with all the character and elegance you can imagine. Recent renovations have taken place at The Albany and her manager says that the renovations were completed with "...greater regard for quality than cost." Now that's quite a statement to make; however, once you arrive, you'll know that the statement is true. Quiet elegance and luxury is the word here and you'll feel like you have ventured into the realms of the wealthy when you come to stay here.

Each bedroom has been individually decorated in warm colors and designer wallpaper, with floral accents used in the curtains and bed-spreads. All the rooms are large and their tall ceilings make them seem even spacious. New furnishings are of the highest quality, and each bathroom has been modernized and is exceptional. As impressive as the hotel is, the staff is even more impressive. They pride themselves in providing a warm welcome, and you can count on it when you arrive, and throughout your stay.

10. THE OLD WAVERLY, *43 Princes Street, Edinburgh. Tel. 0131/556-4648, Fax 0131/557-6316. 66 Rooms. Rates: £79-121 single; £79 per person double. Amex, MasterCard and Visa accepted.*

The Old Waverly is aptly named, because it is just that – old. I'm sure it was formerly a lovely hotel, but it is showing its age, despite recent renovations which have spiffed it up a little bit. It is centrally located at about the middle of Princes Street, and that is its most redeeming quality.

The rooms in the Old Waverly are nice sized. They're not huge, but their tall ceilings make them feel larger than they are. The furnishings are pretty much standard and functional. However, the tight, narrow hall-ways will detract from the experience of your stay. Each room has color satellite TV, phone, hairdryer, a trouser press and tea- and coffee-making facilities. The entrance to the Old Waverly is a long and narrow hallway off Princes Street. Walk down the marble hallway to the stairs, and climb up to the hotel. There is no elevator for the entrance, but if you can negotiate the half dozen or so stairs, there is an elevator inside the hotel.

11. MOUNT ROYAL HOTEL, *53 Princes Street, Edinburgh. Tel. 0131/225-7161, Fax 0131/220-4671. 156 Rooms. Rates: £110-120 single; £130-145 per room. Rates include breakfast. All major credit cards accepted.*

The Mount Royal is a functional hotel right in the heart of all that's going on in New Town. While not luxury accommodations, you'll find average-sized rooms and comfortable albeit plain furnishings. Each room offers a television and telephone, hairdryers and tea- and coffee-making facilities. The rooms at the front of the hotel overlook Princes Street Gardens and have fine views of Edinburgh Castle, which are especially memorable at night. For the money, I'd prefer to walk a couple of blocks north and enjoy the splendor and character of any number of old Georgian mansions (e.g., see 24 Northumberland or 17 Abercromby Place below).

12. 17 ABERCROMBY PLACE, *17 Abercromby Place, Edinburgh. Tel. 0131/557-8036, Fax 0131/558-3453. 9 Rooms. Rates: £45 single; £45 per person double. Rates include breakfast. MasterCard and Visa accepted.*

17 Abercromby Place is one of the most stylish of New Town's Georgian townhouses that has been converted into a guest house. But this isn't just any townhouse – it was formerly the home of renowned

neoclassical architect William Playfair, the creative genius who designed scores of buildings in Edinburgh and elsewhere, including the National Gallery of Scotland and the Royal Scottish Academy.

Today you'll find a stunning assortment of antiques, tapestries, old oil paintings and period furnishings in this old mansion. It's a little like staying in a small but interesting museum or antique store. The rooms are large and comfortably furnished. Each room features large windows that look out to cobblestoned streets and Queen Street Gardens. Each room offers a hairdryer, trouser press and tea- and coffee-making facilities.

13. 24 NORTHUMBERLAND, *24 Northumberland Street, Edinburgh. Tel. 0131/556-8140, Fax 0131/556-4423; E-mail: ingram@ednet.co.uk; Website: www.ingrams.co.uk. 3 Rooms. Rates: £50 single; £40 per person double. Rates include breakfast. MasterCard and Visa accepted.*

What a gem! 24 Northumberland is elegance and eccentricity, excellence and enthusiasm. I am not sure which is the best to highlight here: your hosts or the house. Let's start with the house, a stately mansion a couple of blocks north of Princes Street – close enough to the action of downtown Edinburgh, but away from the hustle and bustle of the city. Here's a test for you history majors out there: Built in 1812, this beautiful mansion has been converted into four floors of the loveliest guest house you are likely to find in Scotland.

Each room is large, has tall ceilings and has been tastefully decorated in bright, warm colors: green, yellow and cream. The furnishings throughout are exquisite and top quality – and complemented by a rich assortment of fine antiques sprinkled throughout the house and bedrooms. Breakfast is taken in the exquisite dining room, and is an event in and of itself. You begin with a bowl of fresh fruit salad, which is followed by David's hand-stuffed link sausage and silky smooth scrambled eggs.

Your hosts are David and Theresa Ingram, and they are two of the warmest, most genuine people you will meet in Scotland. David is a delightful conversationalist who will enhance your stay at 24 Northumberland. He is also an antique dealer by profession, and has used his eye for antiques to furnish 24 Northumberland with scores of period antiques and ancient knick-knacks.

David is a specialist in the history of Edinburgh, and is a great source for history and places to go. He is an excellent conversationalist who has been referred to as "mildly eccentric," and I have to agree (in addition to bearing an uncanny resemblance to a younger David Niven)! His humor is warm and delightful, but he is also very serious about the experience he wants for his guests. David says he has purposely kept 24 Northumberland small because, "I love to see people happy and enjoying themselves, and know that I have in some way been responsible for it."

Selected as one of my Best Places to Stay – see Chapter 12.

14. CASTLE VIEW GUEST HOUSE, *30 Castle Street, Edinburgh. Tel. 0131/226-5784, Fax 0131/226-1603; E-mail: coranne@castleviewgh.co.uk; Website: www.castleviewgh.co.uk. 6 Rooms. Rates: £27-42 single; £27-42 per person double; £100-110 family room (four individuals). Rates include breakfast. No credit cards accepted.*

The Castle View Guest House is located just off Princes Street on George Street. Newly renovated, this guest house is a great place to stay if you are visiting Edinburgh on a budget and want to be where all the action is.

This 200-year-old Edwardian building has been tastefully renovated. The rooms are all large and spacious, and are decorated tastefully in pastels. Attractive wallpaper and complementary decorations are found throughout the guest house. For you literature buffs out there, Castle View Guest House is on the top floor of the building where the author of the *Wind in the Willows* (Kenneth Grahame) was born. The main drawback to the Castle View is that it is on the fourth floor and there is no elevator. So if you have trouble negotiating stairs with or without luggage, you may want to pass. However, if that is not an issue, I heartily recommend Castle View Guest House.

Just South Of The Royal Mile

The following hotels, guest houses and B&Bs are located just south of the Royal Mile. If you stay at any of these places, you'll be within at most a mile's walk of the Royal Mile, and most often within a few steps of bus service.

15. THE SHERATON GRAND HOTEL, *1 Festival Square, Edinburgh. Tel. 0131/229-9131, Fax 0131/229-6254, US toll-free reservations 800/325-3535; E-mail: www.sheratongrand.co.uk. 260 Rooms. Rates: £160-225 single; £200-260 per room double; £300-350 suite. All major credit cards accepted.*

You'll find the Sheraton Grand Hotel just south and west of Edinburgh Castle. The Sheraton Grand is...well...grand. It is an elegant five-star luxury hotel within easy walking distance of most of the things there are to see in Edinburgh. When you walk in, you'll find crystal chandeliers, marble floors and a warm reception. It provides a magnificent first impression, although I didn't really get a sense of being in a Scottish hotel here; it was more like being in an international hotel with Scottish flourishes (tartan accents, kilted staff, etc.).

The bedrooms are among some of the largest in Edinburgh, and as you would expect, exceptionally well appointed. Top-of-the-line furnishings are attractively accented with a variety of decorating themes, including a light tartan. Each room offers television, telephone, trouser press, minibar and tea- and coffee-making facilities. A number of the rooms have views of the castle, and these are of course marvelous (check out those night-time views!). Since the Grand caters to business people especially, you'll also find modem jacks in each room. A business center in the hotel also provides business services such as copying and faxing.

The Sheraton offers a small gym and an indoor swimming pool, as well as several award-winning restaurants, The Terrace and The Grill Room (see the *Where to Eat* section). The Lobby Bar also provides a wide variety of malt whiskies from which to choose. If you are looking for five-star luxury in Edinburgh, the Sheraton Grand will provide it.

16. PRESTONFIELD HOUSE, *Priestfield Road, Edinburgh. Tel. 0131/ 668-3346, Fax 0131/668-3976. 31 Rooms. Rates: £125–225 single; £125-225 per room double; £325-500 per room suite. Rates include breakfast. All major credit cards accepted.*

In 1759 Benjamin Franklin stayed at Prestonfield House, and his stay was so memorable that he penned the following salute upon his return to the US:

Joys of Prestonfield, adieu
Late found, soon lost but still we'll view
The engaging scene oft to these eyes
Shall the pleasing vision rise.
Hearts that warm towards a friend:
Kindness and kindness without end.
Easy converse, sprightly wit;
These we found in Dame and Knight.
Cheerful meals, balmy rest
Beds that never bugs molest.
Neatness and sweetness all around
These, at Prestonfield, we found.

Okay, so Benjamin was a better statesman than poet – "Beds that never bugs molest"? But it's the thought that counts.

To be honest, I was unprepared for the adventure Prestonfield House presented. But as I drove up the driveway and saw the colonnaded front of the mansion, I began to suspect I had found someplace special. You walk up a half dozen ancient steps into an entry hall endowed with large impressive (and old) oil paintings. As you move throughout the house, notice the art on the walls – it is stunning. Richard Scott, the directing manager at Prestonfield, commented on the art: "We're fortunate that the family members were hoarders – they kept everything." The term "everything" applies especially to the artwork and many of the furnishings in the hotel. Resident in the house are the portraits of all the Lords and Ladies of Prestonfield House, dating back to the 1600s. A goodly number of them will smile down on you from their lofty perches in the dining room if you eat dinner here.

Prestonfield House was built in several stages. The first part – the front – was built in 1689. Sir William Bruce, the same architect who designed the Palace of Holyroodhouse, designed Prestonfield House. A section was added in 1822 (referred to by the staff as the "new" section), and 26 rooms (the "newest" section) were added at the back in 1997. As you go from the new part of the house to the newest part of the house, check out the scores of ink drawings of Edinburgh in her medieval years. These prints, some of which are over 150 years old, are exquisite and are in such splendid condition that they appear they could have been done yesterday.

Now that you know a little of the history, let me share a bit about the rooms you'll find here. The rooms are large and decorated in soft colors, and each is furnished with reproduction antiques and top quality furnishings. All the rooms are large and comfortable. And almost all of them have large windows that look out on the fabulous grounds. The public rooms are full of antique furnishings, many of which are original to the house. As mentioned previously, you can scarcely venture any place in the house without seeing the portraits of the former inhabitants of Prestonfield. Breakfast is served in an atrium that looks out on the relaxing and well-sculpted grounds. If you eat dinner here, it is taken in the marvelous dining room (see the *Where to Eat* section). All in all, Prestonfield House is a wonderful, captivating place to stay, and I highly recommend it if it fits your budget.

Selected as one of my Best Places to Stay – see Chapter 12.

17. KILDONAN LODGE, *27 Craigmillar Road, Edinburgh. Tel. 0131/ 667-2793, Fax 0131/667-9777; E-mail: kildonanlodge@compuserve.com; Website: www.smoothhound.co.uk/hotels/kildonan. 12 Rooms. Rates: £45-64 single; £30-54 per person double; £45-60 per person four-poster bedroom; £80-125 family room. Rates include breakfast. MasterCard and Visa accepted.*

Kildonan Lodge looks like so many of the old Victorian homes in Edinburgh: neat and tidy, stately and inviting. But once you walk through the front doors, you'll know that you have come to stay at a very special place. This Victorian beauty was built in 1874, and has been carefully and lovingly restored to its former elegance. Throughout the home the stunning plasterwork and cornices on the ceilings have been maintained, and the effects are extraordinary.

Each of the rooms is large and spacious, and seems especially so because of the tall ceilings that are the trademarks of these Victorian homes. Each is tastefully appointed with quality furnishings, soft colors (yellows and creams), and all are highlighted with tartan. Several of the rooms have marvelous four-poster beds that are a favorite of honeymooners. The decanter of complimentary sherry in each room is a way of welcoming you and making sure your stay is pleasant.

The tile bathrooms are all upgraded and top quality. Six of them have Jacuzzis for helping you relax at the end of a long day of sightseeing. One of my favorite rooms is the lounge on the first floor. It is large and pleasantly appointed with over-stuffed furnishings, prints of medieval Scotland and an honesty bar. If you choose to dine at Kildonan Lodge (I strongly suggest it), you will wait here while your dinner is being prepared. You are welcome to sample any of the wide variety of alcoholic beverages or sodas available, and you merely write your name on a pad, indicating what you had. The charge is nominal, the trust is refreshing.

Breakfast and dinner are available in the dining room at the front of the guest house. It overlooks the lovely front yard, and is large and spacious. I was particularly delighted with the dinner – it was wonderful! I was surprised to learn that the Urquharts don't open this aspect of Kildonan Lodge to the public – the meals were every bit as good as some of the top restaurants I sampled in Scotland. One of the owners, Maggie Urquhart, patiently explained that her reasoning was that she did not want to take away from the experience of her guests, and she was afraid the additional traffic would harm the experience for those who were staying here.

As wonderful as Kildonan Lodge is, the best part of your stay here will probably be the reception and care you receive from your hosts, Bruce and Maggie Urquhart. No matter which greets you upon your arrival, you will feel warmed like a member of the family coming for a visit. They are delightful and most interested in seeing that you are comfortable and enjoying your stay in Scotland. The guest book is liberally sprinkled with comments such as, "lovely," "beautiful," and "marvelous," But the one that is repeated most often is, "Glad we came back!" I guarantee you will add your name to this guest book, and you will say some of the same things. All things considered, Kildonan Lodge is one of my favorite places to stay in Scotland.

Selected as one of my Best Places to Stay – see Chapter 12.

18. ELMVIEW B&B, *15 Glengyle Terrace, Edinburgh. Tel. 0131/228-1973, Fax 0131/622-3271; E-mail: marny@elmview.co.uk; Website: www.elmviewco.uk. 3 Rooms. Rates: £25-35 single; £35-50 per person double. Rates include breakfast. MasterCard and Visa accepted.*

The main reason I have included Elmview B&B (besides the fact that it is a fabulous place), is the hearty recommendation from some tourists I ran into in the north of Scotland. They had stayed at several places in Edinburgh, and they couldn't say enough good things about Elmview B&B. They practically made me promise to include it. Once you arrive, you'll see why. Your host and hostess at Elmview B&B are Richard and Marny Hill, and they received as many rave reviews as did the facility. They and their pet Dachshunds really seem to enhance the memory of the stay.

This lovely Victorian home has been beautifully restored to its former glory. The bedrooms are all large and decorated in soft colors with light floral accents. The freshly cut flowers and complimentary decanter of sherry you'll find in your room nicely complement these accents. The beds, desks and other furnishings are new and top' quality. In addition, each room is provided with a telephone, computer jack, television, trouser press, hairdryer, curling irons and refrigerator.

Out back you'll find a lovely walled garden courtyard lovingly cared for by Marny – her pride and joy (next to Richard and the Dachshunds, of course)! All of the bedrooms look out on this peaceful scene, and provide just the right touch. Out front, you're right across the street from one of Scotland's oldest golf courses – Bruntsfield Links. Today it's a pitch and putt course, and Richard is willing to lend you his 8 iron and putter if you want to give it a go.

You'll also find a marvelous host and hostess in Richard and Marny. As exceptional as the facility is, the tourists I spoke with were even more impressed with its owners. I believe you will agree. One comment among many from their guest book might help convince you that this is a great place to stay: "Your hospitality and warmth made our stay unforgettable....It goes without saying that we would not consider staying anywhere besides the Elmview." Elmview is a non-smoking facility, and the Hills regret that they do not cater for children or pets.

19. THE STUARTS B&B, *17 Glengyle Terrace, Edinburgh. Tel. 0131/ 229-9559, Fax 0131/229-2226; E-mail: thestuarts@cableinet.co.uk. 3 Rooms. Rates: £35-45 single; £35-45 per person double. Rates include breakfast. Amex, MasterCard and Visa accepted.*

You are really going to like this bed and breakfast. Located just south of Edinburgh Castle and the Royal Mile, this elegant B&B will be a marvelous place to call home during your stay in Edinburgh. This lovely Victorian home has been renovated to its former glory. Each room in the house has been tastefully and expensively decorated, with the large bedrooms featuring quality, contemporary furnishings. Large windows ensure a bright and cheery atmosphere, and each room features a television, telephone, hairdryer and tea- and coffee-making facilities. You'll have a wonderful breakfast at a common table with other guests in a comfortable and pleasant dining room.

You don't need to take my word for what an elegant place this is to stay: the Scottish Tourism Board has granted The Stuarts B&B a much-sought-after and rare five-star status. So, stop by and see if you agree. I believe you will! The Stuarts B&B is a non-smoking facility.

20. LAUDERVILLE HOUSE, *52 Mayfield Road, Edinburgh. Tel. 0131/ 667-7788, Fax 0131/667-2636; E-mail: lauderville_guest_house@cableinet.co.uk; Website: wkweb5.cableinet.co.uk/lauderville_guest_house. 10 Rooms. Rates: £25-*

48 single; £25-40 per person double. Rates include breakfast. Amex, MasterCard and Visa accepted.

Lauderville House is another of those fabulous old Victorian mansions that lend themselves so nicely to the tourist industry. Your hosts are the Marriotts – Brian and Yvonne. The bedrooms here are nice and large and elegantly decorated. The soft striped wallpaper really enhances the green-and-tartan decorating motif. The furnishings are high quality, and the effect of the rooms is one of peace and serenity. Several of the rooms have lovely plasterwork on the ceilings that just add to the feeling of quality and elegance.

The public rooms are as nice as the bedrooms. The sitting room upstairs is especially pleasant. Be sure and check out the original plasterwork in this room – it is exquisite. The lounge on the main floor is pleasant and looks out onto the patio and lovely gardens of Lauderville House. Brian is the breakfast chef, and his skill in this area will be readily apparent. He serves up a delicious Scottish breakfast complete with sausage, black pudding, scones, and bacon and eggs.

Children under 12 years old are half rate, and children under two years old stay free in their parents' room. Lauderville House kindly asks that their guests do not smoke at all on the premises.

21. CAMERON TOLL GUEST HOUSE, *299 Dalkeith Road, Edinburgh. Tel. 0131/667-2950, Fax 0131/662-1987; E-mail: camerontoll@msn.com; Website: members.edinburgh.org/camerontoll. 11 Rooms. Rates: £26-48 single; £22-42 per person double. Rates include breakfast. MasterCard and Visa accepted.*

Cameron Toll Guest House is one of those places you find and then spend the rest of your trip comparing your other lodgings to. Mary and Andrew Deans are your hosts, and they have worked very hard to see that Cameron Toll will be a pleasant and memorable stay for you. In fact, the Scottish Tourism Board recently recognized their efforts by awarding them 4-Star status, placing them in the top tier of lodging facilities in Scotland. Their location about 1.5 miles from the city center is an added bonus.

One of the first things you'll notice about this lovely old Victorian house is the home-like feeling you'll have here. Throughout the public areas of the house you'll find photographs of Scotland, handmade arts and crafts – all examples of the talents and interests of your hosts. The atmosphere is cordial and comfortable, and it's definitely a place you'll enjoy staying. Most of the rooms have those characteristics that make these Victorian homes so perfect as guest houses: tall ceilings, large rooms and original plaster cornices. Each bedroom is individually decorated and shows off Mary Deans' expertise in this area. Each is also comfortably enhanced with quality furnishings.

A new addition has added three rooms and a nice bright dining room. The dining room is a departure from the traditional Victorian feel of the rest of the house: it features chairs in the Charles Rennie Mackintosh style and modern art on the walls. (The art is the work of Jennie Deans, the talented daughter of your hosts.) Light oak hardwood floors and a vaulted cedar ceiling give the dining room a spacious feeling. The predominant colors are pumpkin and apricot (Pumpricot? Aprikin?) Breakfast here is a treat, as Mary takes her role as chef seriously. The menu is quite complete and offers a wide variety of choices.

The Deans' are rightfully proud of the many awards they and their guest house have won in recent years. They are particularly pleased with their Gold Award for their environmental efforts. They are one of ten businesses in Scotland to receive this level of Eco-Award.

Let me add a few personal notes about Andrew and Mary. Andrew is somewhat of a malt whisky connoisseur and has made a study of the best single malt whiskies in Scotland. He is of course happy to share his knowledge with you. Both Andrew and Mary are avid walkers and bicyclists. If that's not enough Andrew is considered quite an accomplished piper and is often prevailed upon to demonstrate his piping prowess. He is even willing to share a few pointers with guests, and help them try their hand (lips?) at it. So for an all-around pleasant stay, from lodging to meals to hosts, Cameron Toll Guest House is definitely one of the finest.

22. ELLESMERE HOUSE, *11 Glengyle Terrace, Edinburgh. Tel. 0131/ 229-4823, Fax 0131/229-5285; Website: www.smoothhound.co.uk/hotels/ ellesmer. 6 Rooms. Rates: £25-35 single; £25-35 per person twin and double, £25-35 per person family room. Rates include breakfast. Credit cards not accepted.*

Ellesmere House is one of the nicest Victorian homes you'll find offering accommodations in Edinburgh. This lovely four-star guest house is located just a short distance south of Edinburgh Castle and the Royal Mile across from the large grassy park called The Meadows.

Impeccably decorated throughout, Ellesmere House has the feel of a Victorian dollhouse. Throughout, you'll find tall ceilings, exceptional plasterwork and tasteful furnishings. One of my favorite rooms is the guest lounge, a pleasant room with comfortable leather furnishings, a fireplace and large windows looking out onto a verdant golf course (Bruntsfield Links – one of Scotland's oldest courses). The bedrooms are all large and individually decorated. One features a four-poster bed and each has a pleasant floral motif that makes the rooms bright and cheery. Each room offers a television, hairdryer and tea- and coffee-making facilities. The bathrooms are all upgraded and exceptionally clean. Ellesmere House is a non-smoking facility, and children over 10 years old are welcome.

23. LORNE VILLA GUEST HOUSE, *9 East Mayfield, Edinburgh. Tel. 0131/667-7159, Fax 0131/667-7159; E-mail: lornevilla@cableinet.co.uk; Website: www.smoothhound.co.uk/hotels/lornev. 6 Rooms. Rates: £18-35 single; £18-35 per person double. Rates include breakfast. MasterCard and Visa accepted.*

Lorne Villa Guest House is a family-run enterprise in one of the quiet Victorian neighborhoods about a mile south of the Royal Mile. Access is easy to Edinburgh's top sites: you can either take about a 30-minute stroll, or catch a bus within just a few minutes' walk from the guest house.

You'll find pleasant, clean facilities here. The bedrooms aren't exceptionally large, but they are furnished with comfortable, functional furniture. You'll find a television, hospitality tray and tea- and coffee-making facilities in each room. While hairdryers are not provided in each room, one is available for your use. Three of the rooms have bathrooms included (ensuite), while two of the rooms share a bathroom in the hallway, and the last room has its own bathroom in the hallway. Prices vary according to your needs – the ensuite rooms are of course the most expensive, and the least expensive are those rooms that share a public bathroom. If you are bringing your children with you, you'll be pleased to know that children under 12 receive a discount when staying in their parents' room, and children under five stay free.

24. EDINBURGH EGLINGTON YOUTH HOSTEL, *18 Eglington Crescent, Edinburgh. Tel. 0131/337-1120, centralized reservations: 0541/553-255. 17 Rooms. Rates: £9.95-10.95 (under age 18); £11.50-12.50 (over age 18). MasterCard and Visa accepted.*

This nice Scottish Youth Hostel is located just a hop, skip and a jump from Haymarket Station, a little over a half mile due west of Edinburgh Castle. You will be in easy walking distance to the Castle and the Royal Mile, or the museums and art galleries along Princes Street. Alternately, you can catch a bus just down the street from the youth hostel. You'll find nearly 160 beds here, a self-catering kitchen and continental breakfasts (£2) and a laundry. As you can imagine, this hostel is immensely popular, especially so during the summer months. Be sure and call ahead for reservations.

25. EDINBURGH BRUNTSFIELD YOUTH HOSTEL, *7 Bruntsfield Crescent, Edinburgh. Tel. 0131/447-2994, centralized reservations: 0541/553-255. 14 Rooms. Rates: £7.10-8.10 (under age 18); £8.60-9.60 (over age 18). MasterCard and Visa accepted.*

This is another of Scotland's fine offerings in the youth hostel market. You'll find over 150 beds in this Edinburgh youth hostel. You'll also find a clean, quiet environment. Located a little over a mile south of the Royal Mile in a neighborhood setting, you'll be close to bus service and shopping. An on-site laundry allows you to take care of that necessary chore if you need to do so. This hostel is busy year around, but especially so during the summer months. Be sure and call ahead for reservations.

South Suburbs
   26. DALHOUSIE CASTLE HOTEL, *Bonnyrigg. Tel. 01875/820-153, Fax 01875/821-936; E-mail: dalhousiecastle.co.uk; Website: www.dalhousiecastle.co.uk. 34 Rooms. Rates: £95-105 single; £118-170 double; £200-300 suite; £80-120 Lodge rooms; £170 triple; £175 quad. All major credit cards accepted.*

Dalhousie Castle Hotel is located about half an hour from downtown Edinburgh in the southern suburb of Bonnyrigg. Originally the 13th century home of the Ramsay Clan, it has been tastefully renovated into a marvelous 4-star hotel. If it was good enough for the likes of King Edward I, Oliver Cromwell and Queen Victoria, it will certainly meet your accommodation needs for a night or two.

Even though it is a hotel, it might just as well be included in the *Seeing the Sights* section since there are so many interesting things to see here. Antiques and old paintings abound throughout the hotel. Extravagant to the point of opulence, it nonetheless retains a charm that is delightful. My favorite public room is the Old Library. It features leather couches, a large fireplace and immense windows that look out onto the impressive grounds and the peaceful River Eske meandering along. But there's more than books gracing those shelves: there is a hidden bar behind one of the bookcases.

The rooms are all large and comfortably furnished with high-quality furnishings. They are tastefully decorated and are a pleasant place to repose after a hard day's sightseeing. There are several suites that are extraordinary. The Dalhousie Suite is located in one of the turrets of the hotel. It has windows that look out onto the sumptuous grounds, and it is furnished with antiques aplenty, including a spectacular four-poster bed. A fireplace helps chase the chill of the damp weather you may run into during your stay. The Ramseian Suite is another of the suites, and in addition to exquisite furnishings, it features the original well for the castle. Covered for your safety, it is nonetheless intriguing to ponder the presence of countless hands that have drawn water from the well in years gone by.

About 100 yards from the hotel is a Lodge that has been converted into five additional rooms. The rooms lack the antiquity of those in the main part of the castle, but they are quite nice, new, and large, and provide you with a peaceful stay. The dining experience here is also exceptional. Housed in the dungeon, the award-winning restaurant at Dalhousie Castle is a place to be sure and visit. The surroundings are exceptional (swords and armor), and the food is even better (see the *Where to Eat* section). So, if you are willing to stay about a half-hour from the action of downtown Edinburgh, Dalhousie Castle Hotel is an excellent choice.

27. ST. LEONARDS B&B, *480 Lanark Road, Edinburgh. Tel. 0131/ 453-1968, Fax 0131/442-4406; E-mail: ann.r@virgin.net. Rates: £30-35 single; £30-35 per person double. MasterCard and Visa accepted.*

If you're looking for a great B&B experience, consider St. Leonards B&B. St. Leonards is a member of the small but prestigious *Scotland's Best B&Bs* organization, a group of four-star B&Bs that provide exceptional value for the money. You'll find a splendid Georgian home set in lovely gardens about 10 minutes south of the city center. From the B&B, you'll have lovely views of the Pentland Hills south of Edinburgh. Each of the three bedrooms is quite large, and all feature top-quality furnishings. Each room offers a hairdryer and tea- and coffee-making facilities.

Mrs. Russell will wow you with her wonderful breakfasts, and you'll also be able to have your evening meals here too, if you make prior arrangements. St. Leonards B&B is non-smoking throughout.

28. JOHNSTOUNBURN HOUSE, *Humbie. Tel. 01875/833-696, Fax 01875/833-626. 20 Rooms. Rates: £40-80 single; £40-80 per person double. All major credit cards accepted.*

On the outskirts of Edinburgh in the town of Humbie, you'll find this sumptuous 17th-century mansion. Nestled serenely in the undulating Lammermuir hills, Johnstounburn House just looks like the country home of an ancient Scottish laird. It also provides a quiet, serene place to get away from the hustle and bustle of the your busy sightseeing! Depending on traffic, you can make it from Edinburgh's city center to Johnstounburn House within about 30 minutes.

There are 20 comfortable rooms at Johnstounburn House. Most are large and comfortable, and each is individually decorated. All are furnished with quality furnishings, and include a telephone, television, trouser press, hairdryer and tea- and coffee-making facilities. About half of the rooms are in a coach house adjacent to the main house. There is a nice cedar-lined guest lounge with an inviting open fire, perfect for relaxing and reviewing your days' activities. Your meals will be in the pine-paneled dining room, and those meals will be exceptional. It you are interested, you also have access to garden walks and there is even a golf fairway for you to practice your drives, or a range for clay pigeon shooting.

North Suburbs

29. MALMAISON, *1 Tower Place, Leith. Tel. 0131/555-6868, Fax 0131/ 468-5002; E-mail: edinburgh@malmaison.com; Website: www.malmaison.com. 60 Rooms. Rates: £90-135 single; £90-135 per person double; £140-150 suite. All major credit cards accepted.*

Like her sister hotel in Glasgow, you'll find contemporary luxury at the Malmaison. Located a few miles north of downtown Edinburgh in the port city of Leith, the Malmaison occupies a former seaman's Victorian mission.

Each room is individually decorated in a bevy of stripes or an intriguing (large) checkerboard wallpaper. The colors are an eye-catching blend of cream and mocha, deep blue and green, or red and cream. Fluffy down comforters grace the beds and the prints in each room are intriguing (to say the least). The bedrooms are not particularly large, but you're so busy taking it all in that this seems secondary to the experience. The bedrooms offer TV, CD players (you can bring your own CDs or borrow them at the front desk), hairdryer, trouser press, robes and tea- and coffee-making facilities. Room service is available 24 hours a day from the small bistro that is adjacent to the hotel.

30. CAMUS GUEST HOUSE, *4 Seaview Terrace, Joppa, Edinburgh. Tel. 0131/657-2003, Fax 0131/657-2003; E-mail: rowan@camus.ndo. co.uk; Website: www.smoothhound.co.uk/hotels/camus. 5 Rooms. Rates: £16-25 single; £16-25 per person double. Rates include breakfast. MasterCard and Visa accepted.*

If you are looking for a bit more of a seaside experience when visiting Edinburgh, you might try four-star Camus Guest House. Located a few miles north of downtown Edinburgh in the seaside town of Joppa, this guest house provides a pleasant place to stay with some marvelous views of the Firth of Forth.

The facility itself is pleasant and inviting. When you stay here, you'll find a turn-of-the-century red sandstone Victorian home furnished comfortably, if not exquisitely. The bedrooms are average sized, and the furnishings are functional and comfortable. Each room includes a television, hairdryer and tea- and coffee-making facilities. Two of the rooms have bathrooms in the rooms (ensuite), and two have public bathrooms. Prices vary according to your needs (and willingness to put up with a little inconvenience) – the ensuite rooms are of course the most expensive, and the least expensive are those rooms that share a public bathroom. If you are traveling with your children and/or a small pet, you'll find that they are welcome here.

Near the Airport
31. SWALLOW ROYAL SCOT HOTEL, *111 Glasgow Road, Edinburgh. Tel. 0131/334-9191, Fax 0131/316-4507. 259 Rooms. Rates: £115 single; £145 per room double. Rates include breakfast. All major credit cards accepted.*

If you are looking for a hotel close to the airport, then you might consider the Swallow Royal Scot Hotel. Located within two miles of the airport, it still gives you relatively easy access to Edinburgh, as you'll be a mere six miles from the center of town.

Their brochures claim they are a "smart, modern hotel," and I agree. You'll find lots of light, well-lit rooms, and pleasant light colors. The bedrooms are pretty much the same throughout, and each is attractively decorated with good-quality furnishings. Each room includes a telephone, satellite television, trouser press, minibar, iron and ironing board, hairdryer and tea- and coffee-making facilities. There is a small fitness room, spa and solarium, as well as a nice-sized swimming pool if you need a relaxing swim. You'll also find a small restaurant and several bars here. All in all, the Swallow Royal Scot Hotel provides pleasant and comfortable lodging right near the airport (in case you are a nervous traveler).

WHERE TO EAT
The Royal Mile
1. WITCHERY BY THE CASTLE, *Castlehill, Edinburgh. Tel. 0131/ 225-5613, Fax 0131/220-4392. £20-35. Open daily from noon to 4:00pm and from 5:30pm to 11:30pm. All major credit cards accepted.*

You'll find Witchery by the Castle just below Edinburgh Castle on Castlehill/Hill Street. What a marvelous restaurant. Management plays the witchery theme to the max, and while sinister surroundings usually give me the creeps, it works very well for this restaurant. Dark wood, a dark room and eerie dark shadows cast by flickering candles are the norm here. The Witchery by the Castle was an alehouse in the 1500s, and individuals thought to be witches were burned at the stake right outside the door.

While the Witchery draws a big crowd because of the eerie ambience, they also serve award-winning meals. The menu offers a good selection, including grilled filet of seabream with poached leeks in a warm oyster and vanilla sauce (to die for!), or for a traditional Scottish meal with a twist, try the roasted Aberdeen angus beef with a brioche crust and winter chanterelles. The dessert menu is enough to tempt even the most strident dieter to succumb; try the warmed chocolate torte with white chocolate sorbet for a treat. The wine list is not only one of the finest in the *country*, it has won awards as one of the best wine lists in the world, with between 850 and 1,000 wines available.

This *Taste of Scotland* restaurant is perhaps one of the most famous restaurants in the country. I promise that you will definitely remember your dining experience here. As you enter the restaurant, there is a quote from Dante's *Inferno* on the ceiling: *Que altro que ne fianche, Michele Scotto Fu, che veramente, Delle magiche frode seppe il gioco.* Translation: "Nobody else is quite like Michael Scott and his magical ways and his small stature." Michael Scott was one of the most powerful and feared men in Scotland during the beginning of the 13th century. Very intelligent and well-educated (that was scary enough for some folks), he was considered a prophet and powerful sorcerer. The painting above your head as you enter the restaurant is a fanciful view of Michael Scott the Magician. All in all, you'll really enjoy your dining experience here.

Selected as one of my picks for Scotland's Best Restaurants – see Chapter 11.

2. THE SECRET GARDEN, *Castlehill, Edinburgh. Tel. 0131/225-5613, Fax 0131/220-4392. £20-35. Open daily from noon to 4:00pm and from 5:30pm to 11:30pm. All major credit cards accepted.*

You'll get a much different dining experience here than at the Secret Garden's sister restaurant, the Witchery by the Castle. Whereas the Witchery is an eerie atmosphere, the Secret Garden gets my vote as the most romantic restaurant in Scotland. You'll descend stairs into a large candlelit room with tall, open-beam ceilings enhancing the setting. You'll find a pleasant and chatty atmosphere here.

Here's an interesting historical note about the restaurant: it is located on the site of the 16th-century Lord Mayor's house. The house was the end of a secret passage from the castle, several hundred yards up the hill (just in case of trouble).

The Secret Garden shares the menu and wine list with its sister restaurant the Witchery, so you'll enjoy the same wonderful cuisine available there. The Secret Garden's guest book reads like a Who's Who of world-renowned celebrities. Here are a few who have enjoyed meals here: Jack Nicholson, Michael Douglas, Jane Russell, Neil Sedaka, Gloria Estefan, Christopher Lloyd and Andrew Lloyd Webber. While you're waiting to be seated, check out the hand-carved oak reception desk – it is extraordinary.

Selected as one of my picks for Scotland's Best Restaurants – see Chapter 11.

3. IGG'S RESTAURANT, *15 Jeffrey Street, Edinburgh. Tel. 0131/557-8184, Fax 0131/441-7111. £5-16 lunch and £20-30 for dinner. Open Monday through Saturday from noon to 2:00pm and 6:00pm to 10:00pm. All major credit cards accepted.*

This wonderful restaurant is located about 100 paces off the Royal Mile on Jeffrey Street. Ignacious Campos (Iggy) is your host, and he has developed a spectacular, award-winning restaurant – Igg's has earned two AA rosettes and has been recognized by *A Taste of Scotland*.

Igg's features Spanish cuisine and ambience, and you'll enjoy both immensely. You'll find soft candlelight, silver, crystal and linen to accent the fine meals that are served here. Soft classical Spanish music adds just the right touch to your dining experience. As pleasant and elegant as the atmosphere is, the meals here have repeatedly received recognition and awards for their flavor, presentation and variety. The menu changes monthly, but whatever month you come you'll find delicious Spanish fare with Scottish influences (or is it the other way around?). The menu might include such delicacies as filet of ostrich on a bed of apple and watercress with pomme anna together with beetroot and juniper berry jus. If you're interested in seafood, try the duo of black tappia and sea bream set on pan-fried samphire with Parisienne potato and a beurre noisette. There are also a number of vegetarian selections to choose from.

Dress is suit and tie, especially at night, although you'll see dress range from nice casual to suit and tie. Reservations are important during the tourist season and on the weekends.

4. DUBH PRAIS RESTAURANT, *123b High Street, Edinburgh. Tel. 0131/557-5732, Fax 0131/5263. £13-15 for lunch, £20-30 dinner. Open Tuesday through Friday from noon to 2:00pm and from 6:30pm to 10:30pm, and Saturday from 6:30pm to 10:30pm. Closed Sunday and Monday. Amex, MasterCard and Visa accepted.*

If you are looking for a true Scottish restaurant from top to bottom, this is the place! The Dubh Prais is Scottish through-and-through, from its name (dubh prais means "Black Pot" in Gaelic) to the décor to the fare to the Scottish chef and proprietors. You'll descend a steep stairway from street level into this cozy den of a restaurant. When you arrive, you'll find blue carpets, lots of thistle and pine, and a wonderful menu. The restaurant is a perennial *A Taste of Scotland* award winner, and the food served here is exceptional. James McWilliams, who together with his wife Heather owns Dubh Prais, is also your chef. He has earned accolades for the simple yet exquisite Scottish fare he produces. The secret? James' insistence on only the freshest ingredients, his flair for presentation, and a real talent for cooking. Try the lamb cutlets: best of Border lamb served on a light rosemary sauce and garnished with a skirlie tomato. If you'd like to try a little wild game, then you'll want to try the saddle of venison, with medallions of venison pan-fried and garnished with chestnut pavé and served in a juniper sauce. If you are vegetarian, never fear; Dubh Prais has several vegetarian dishes that will more than meet your needs.

Dress for Dubh Prais is nice casual, and while here you'll enjoy a nice quiet dining experience. The restaurant is small, with fewer that 10 tables, so be sure and call ahead for reservations on weekends and especially during the tourist season. It can be a little hard to find; look for the white doorway across the street from the Crowne Plaza hotel.

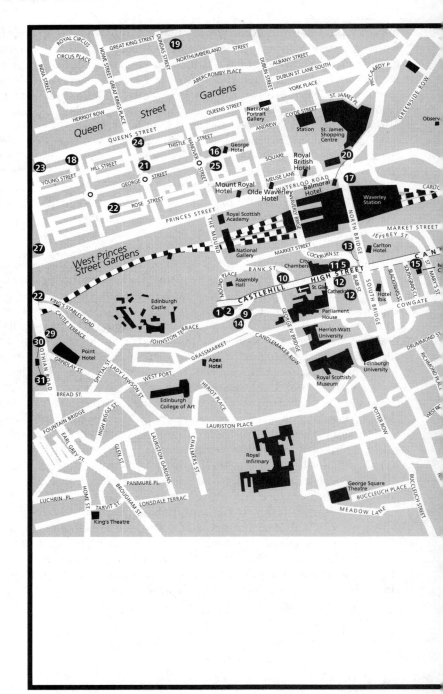

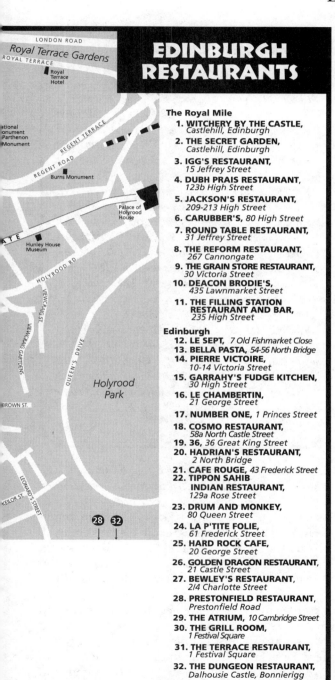

EDINBURGH RESTAURANTS

The Royal Mile

1. **WITCHERY BY THE CASTLE,** Castlehill, Edinburgh
2. **THE SECRET GARDEN,** Castlehill, Edinburgh
3. **IGG'S RESTAURANT,** 15 Jeffrey Street
4. **DUBH PRAIS RESTAURANT,** 123b High Street
5. **JACKSON'S RESTAURANT,** 209-213 High Street
6. **CARUBBER'S,** 80 High Street
7. **ROUND TABLE RESTAURANT,** 31 Jeffrey Street
8. **THE REFORM RESTAURANT,** 267 Cannongate
9. **THE GRAIN STORE RESTAURANT,** 30 Victoria Street
10. **DEACON BRODIE'S,** 435 Lawnmarket Street
11. **THE FILLING STATION RESTAURANT AND BAR,** 235 High Street

Edinburgh

12. **LE SEPT,** 7 Old Fishmarket Close
13. **BELLA PASTA,** 54-56 North Bridge
14. **PIERRE VICTOIRE,** 10-14 Victoria Street
15. **GARRAHY'S FUDGE KITCHEN,** 30 High Street
16. **LE CHAMBERTIN,** 21 George Street
17. **NUMBER ONE,** 1 Princes Street
18. **COSMO RESTAURANT,** 58a North Castle Street
19. **36,** 36 Great King Street
20. **HADRIAN'S RESTAURANT,** 2 North Bridge
21. **CAFE ROUGE,** 43 Frederick Street
22. **TIPPON SAHIB INDIAN RESTAURANT,** 129a Rose Street
23. **DRUM AND MONKEY,** 80 Queen Street
24. **LA P'TITE FOLIE,** 61 Frederick Street
25. **HARD ROCK CAFE,** 20 George Street
26. **GOLDEN DRAGON RESTAURANT,** 21 Castle Street
27. **BEWLEY'S RESTAURANT,** 2/4 Charlotte Street
28. **PRESTONFIELD RESTAURANT,** Prestonfield Road
29. **THE ATRIUM,** 10 Cambridge Street
30. **THE GRILL ROOM,** 1 Festival Square
31. **THE TERRACE RESTAURANT,** 1 Festival Square
32. **THE DUNGEON RESTAURANT,** Dalhousie Castle, Bonnierigg

EDINBURGH'S TOP RESTAURANTS

The following restaurants are listed from most to least expensive. You can get more information on each selection in the reviews that follow.

16. LE CHAMBERTIN, *21 George Street, Edinburgh. Tel. 0131/225-1251, 0131/240-7178, Fax 0131/220-1417. £20-40. Open Monday through Friday from 12:30pm to 2:00pm, and Monday through Saturday from 7:00pm to 10:00pm. All major credit cards accepted. If you are looking for grace and elegance, look no further than Le Chambertin. This fine restaurant is truly world-class.*

1. WITCHERY BY THE CASTLE, *Castlehill, Edinburgh. Tel. 0131/225-5613, Fax 0131/220-4392. £20-35. Open daily from noon to 4:00pm and from 5:30pm to 11:30pm. All major credit cards accepted. An eerie setting and delicious meal await you at the Witchery by the Castle.*

2. THE SECRET GARDEN, *Castlehill, Edinburgh. Tel. 0131/225-5613, Fax 0131/220-4392. £20-35. Open daily from noon to 4:00pm and from 5:30pm to 11:30pm. All major credit cards accepted. This is the sister restaurant to the Witchery by the Castle Restaurant, and gets my vote for the most romantic restaurant in Edinburgh.*

9. THE GRAIN STORE RESTAURANT, *30 Victoria Street, Edinburgh. Tel. 0131/225-7635, 0131/225-7125. £10-15 lunch, £15-20 dinner. Open daily from noon to 2:00pm and 6:00pm to 11:00pm (until midnight on Saturday). Amex, MasterCard and Visa accepted. This is my favorite restaurant in Edinburgh. It has the look and feel of an old stone wine cellar, except that it is now warm and inviting. The food is pretty good too!*

5. JACKSON'S RESTAURANT, *209-213 High Street, Edinburgh. £20-30. Tel. 0131/225-1793, Fax 0131/220-0620. Open daily from noon to 2:30pm and 6:00pm to midnight. Amex, MasterCard and Visa accepted.*

Don't walk past this marvelous restaurant – Jackson's has an understated presence on the sidewalk level of High Street, but that's about all that is understated. Descend the stairs from street level (under the rack of red stag antlers) right next to Jackson's Close on High Street. As you descend the stairs, you may notice the sign that says, "Please mind y'er head." Please do.

Jackson's really packs them in. Once you've negotiated the stairs and entered the restaurant, you'll encounter flagstone walls, subdued lighting with candles all around and lots of happy people. It is a very chatty and convivial atmosphere here. Unbeknownst to many diners, there is also an upstairs dining room. Wend your way to the back of the restaurant and up a narrow stairway and you'll find another room that seats about 45. It has a similar ambience to the main dining room but offers a different décor: subdued lighting through a tented ceiling, flickering candles and green leafy wallpaper. Although the setting is a little different, the diners here are just as happy and friendly.

Maybe the reason for their joy is the food served here. Jackson's is *A Taste of Scotland* award winner, and you'll find traditional Scottish fare, including fresh fish, Aberdeen beef and vegetarian dishes, all prepared with the freshest ingredients. Try the ragout of monkfish tail, marinated in Ruby wine with seasoned vegetables and roasted with garlic pearls. I was personally delighted with the breast of spiced chicken baked in a chestnut and pistachio confit drizzled with a Ruby wine jus. There are a number of desserts available that will tempt the most faithful dieter. Try the decadent chocolate mousse cake set in a pool of white chocolate. Delicious. The dress is casual to nice casual. The lunch menu is a scaled down version of the dinner menu and offers two- and three-course meals from £7 to £12.

6. CARUBBER'S, *80 High Street, Edinburgh. Tel. 0131/557-9797. £15-26. Open daily from 6:30am to 10:30am (until 11:30am on Saturday and Sunday), noon to 2:00pm and 5:30pm to 10:30pm. All major credit cards accepted.*

Carruber's is the restaurant for the Crowne Plaza Hotel. It takes its name from a nearby close (alley) of the same name. It has the look and feel of a medieval village square. The walls sport murals that help create the feeling that you are dining in the midst of a French marketplace. The menu offers a surprising number of selections, and the food is good and filling. Try the seafood feuillette: flaky pastry filled with mussels, clams, prawns, and salmon in a parsley and garlic cream sauce. If that doesn't suit your fancy, you might try the supreme of chicken with Armagnac mousse, braised celery and red wine sauce. There is also a nice vegetarian menu to whet the appetite of even the fussiest diner. The wine list is a bit limited, with only a dozen selections from which to choose.

7. ROUND TABLE RESTAURANT, *31 Jeffrey Street, Edinburgh. Tel. 0131/557-3032. £6-15 lunch and £18-25 dinner. Open Tuesday through Saturday from 10:00am to 10:00pm. All major credit cards accepted.*

The Round Table Restaurant is located just a short distance off the Royal Mile on Jeffrey Street. Through the years it has been a tremendously successful restaurant, and has garnered a number of culinary awards, including recognition by *A Taste of Scotland*. Anne and Robert Winter are your hosts, and Robert doubles as your chef.

A large sign in the restaurant announces that the Round Table Restaurant serves "Classic Scottish Cuisine," but one look at the menu will tell you the same thing. Their award-winning meals are pretty simple and straight forward. In other words, they taste great and are good value for the money. Try the howtowdie chicken, smoked salmon or Aberdeen beef dishes. Vegetarian dishes are also available, and all are cooked using the freshest ingredients from the surrounding Scottish countryside.

Like the food, the atmosphere is simple and unassuming. Before you eat, check out the marvelous furniture: elm and oak fashioned to approximate what tables and chairs may have looked like in days of yore (and of course, the tables are round). This setting is enhanced by the strains of soft dining music playing in the background, including opera, New Age and other soft listening melodies. Dress is casual, and you'll find a comfortable, relaxed dining experience here. Reservations are recommended on the weekends and for every evening during the tourist season.

8. THE REFORM RESTAURANT, *267 Canongate, Edinburgh. Tel. 0131/558-9992. £15-25. Open daily from noon to 2:00pm and 6:00pm to 11:00pm (until midnight on Saturday). MasterCard and Visa accepted.*

Near the bottom o the Royal Mile, you'll find the Reform Restaurant. You'll also find fine dining and a wonderful ambience. The Reform has lately gained an avid following, and if you dine here, I suspect you will become one of its fans. You'll find a splendid blend of fresh Scottish ingredients with some wonderful continental influences, and a presentation of the food that is positively artistic. Rich maple tables, delicate candlesticks, silver and china accent the fine food you'll encounter here. Try the herb crusted salmon filet with light lemon and caper bisque, or a more traditional offering of tender filet of Aberdeen beef. Either way, you'll be pleased with your meal. Dress is nice casual, although you wouldn't be out of line with a suit and tie.

9. THE GRAIN STORE RESTAURANT, *30 Victoria Street, Edinburgh. Tel. 0131/225-7635, 0131/225-7125. £10-15 lunch, £15-20 dinner. Open daily from noon to 2:00pm and 6:00pm to 11:00pm (until midnight on Saturday). Amex, MasterCard and Visa accepted.*

All things considered, this is my favorite restaurant in Edinburgh. I was alerted to it by Maggie Urquhart, owner of Kildonan Lodge Guest House as one of her favorites. I can see why. From the moment you enter the restaurant, you're swept up by the atmosphere; stick around a bit and your meal will create another pleasant memory. (The judges for *A Taste of Scotland* must have agreed, as they have recognized The Grain Store Restaurant for their excellence also.)

The restaurant is on the second story above street level, and you ascend a wide avant-garde staircase (blue stairs amid pink walls) to reach the entrance to the restaurant. The moment you walk in, you will be enchanted by the surroundings: rough-hewn stone walls, plank floors that match the plank tables, and flickering candles that cast a warmth on your dining experience. Large floral arrangements strategically situated throughout the restaurant add an additional touch of class and beauty to the setting. The moment you walk in the door look to your right; at the far end of the restaurant you'll see an enormous old oak clock, with a ponderous pendulum swaying slowly and methodically.

The manager described their cuisine as "imaginative modern Scottish," and it is truly exceptional. The menu changes seasonally, but you might find such delicacies as roasted saddle of hare in juniper jus or a more traditional offering of filet of Aberdeen beef, cured pork and button mushrooms. Vegetarian dishes are also available for those so inclined. A fine wine list with about five dozen selections provides a wide range of choices and prices.

You'll have a pleasant, quiet dining experience at the Grain Store, and you'll find everything from very casual dress to very formal. The restaurant has a broad appeal. You'll see university students to folks who probably graduated from the university 50 years ago. But they all have one thing in common – they enjoy the excellent food and atmosphere immensely. And I believe you will too.

Selected as one of my picks for Scotland's Best Restaurants – see Chapter 11.

10. DEACON BRODIE'S, *435 Lawnmarket Street, Edinburgh. Tel. 0131/225-6531. £10-15. Open Monday through Saturday from noon to 10:00pm and Sunday from 12:30pm to 10:00pm. MasterCard and Visa accepted.*

Deacon William Brodie was the infamous soul that Robert Louis Stevenson used as a pattern for his principal character(s) in *The Strange Case of Dr. Jekyll and Mr. Hyde*. The building the restaurant occupies was built in 1703, and stands near the alley (Brodie's Close) where Deacon Brodie used to live. The side of the building, which is at the corner of Lawnmarket and Bank Streets, features a large mural that tells the sad tale of the mysterious Deacon.

You'll find mostly pub grub (primarily soups and sandwiches) here, although a tourist from Seattle swore to me that the beef stack he had ordered was the best beef he had eaten while in Scotland. The downstairs offers a pub atmosphere, while the restaurant is located upstairs. The upstairs restaurant has low ceilings and tartan carpets, and softly lit glow globes give it a pleasant, although unexceptional, atmosphere. Clearly the main draw to Deacon Brodie's is the character after which it is named, although the food is good and filling at a reasonable price. Dress is very casual.

11. THE FILLING STATION RESTAURANT AND BAR, *235 High Street, Edinburgh. Tel. 0131/226-2488. £10-15. Open daily from noon to 11:30pm. All major credit cards accepted.*

Have you ever eaten in a gas station? Well step right in and fill 'er up! The Filling Station Restaurant and Bar is decorated like an old gas station, with a wide range of automotive knick-knacks vying for your attention.

You'll be so busy gawking and exploring that you may forget to order (although helpful members of the wait staff will help you remember). You'll find spoked wheels, old glass gas pumps, old gas station signs (how many do you recognize? How many bring back memories?), and other assorted items.

This is all fine and good, but you might rightfully ask, "How's the food?" Well, it is of the fast-food variety, stuff like sandwiches, burritos and fajitas. You can order a steak if you like, but if you are a serious steak eater, you'll probably want to buy that someplace else. This is a nice place to stop in, if only for a beer. This is one of those restaurants that needs to be experienced (it really *is* a lot of fun). Dress is casual.

12. LE SEPT, *7 Old Fishmarket Close, Edinburgh. Tel. 0131/225-5428. £4-15. Open Monday through Thursday from noon to 2:15pm and 6:00pm to 10:30pm, Friday and Saturday from noon to 11:30pm (11:00pm on Saturday), Sunday from 12:30pm to 10:00pm. Amex, MasterCard and Visa accepted.*

Just below Edinburgh Castle, watch for Le Sept's sign at the top of Fishmarket Close on High Street. There is nothing particularly spectacular about Le Sept other than good food and a convivial atmosphere. You'll find a simple intimate setting with cane chairs and dark wood tables, and people enjoying themselves in quiet and pleasant conversation. This is one of those places the locals frequent for the easy ambience. French/Scottish food is the fare, although it seemed more French than Scottish to me. Crepes are the specialty of the house, but you'll find a pretty good range of entrées to interest you. If you're interested in seafood, try the greenshell mussels served in a curry and cream sauce; if you're a little adventurous, you might try the leek, mushroom and feta cheese crepe, topped with cheese.

PS – Be sure and check out the collection of black and white photographs that enhance the walls – they are phenomenal. The owner collects them, and there are some extraordinary shots. The photographs alone are worth the short walk off High Street to see them.

13. BELLA PASTA, *54-56 North Bridge, Edinburgh. Tel. 0131/225-2044. £7-12. Open daily from 10:30am to 11:00pm. All major credit cards accepted.*

This restaurant is part of a national chain of pasta restaurants in the UK. There are 75 restaurants (and growing), so they must be doing something right. All kinds of wonderful pastas and other Italian dishes are available at Bella Pasta. The restaurant features large windows, lots of plants and flowers. You'll find an atmosphere that is quite cheery and chatty, as people here obviously enjoy the food as well as the friendly scene.

You'll be able to choose from a mind-boggling list of pasta choices. One of the more popular choices at this location is pollo alla cacciatora: pan-fried chicken in a rich white wine, mushroom, bacon, onion garlic and tomato sauce (are you hungry yet?). Another popular dish is a twist on the more traditional linguine al pesto Genovese made with basil, chopped pine kernels, garlic, olive oil and parmesan cheese. *Magnifico!* This is a nice option if you like Italian food. The prices are reasonable and the environment is very cheery. The lunch menu is about half the cost of dinner menu, in the £4 to £7 range. Dress is casual.

14. PIERRE VICTOIRE, *10-14 Victoria Street, Edinburgh. Tel. 0131/ 225-1721. £5-10 for lunch, £15-20 for dinner. Open daily from noon to 2:30pm and from 6:00pm to midnight. MasterCard and Visa accepted.*

You'll find wonderful French cuisine and a pleasant and convivial dining experience at Pierre Victoire's. It just fits my mental image of a French café or bistro: tall white-washed stone walls, unvarnished wood floors, checkered tablecloths and candles in the wine bottles help create the image. This edition of the popular chain of French restaurants continues their theme: quality French food and wine at a reasonable price. You'll have a suspicion that something is truly special about this restaurant when you see the numbers of people who flock here to enjoy the food and ambience.

The food is great too. Try the roasted pigeon breast with red currants, ginger, coriander and orange butter. Or if you prefer seafood, you can't go wrong with the baked salmon served with a seafood mousse. Dress is casual.

15. GARRAHY'S FUDGE KITCHEN, *30 High Street, Edinburgh. £1.79 per square, buy three, get one free. Open Monday through Saturday from 10:00am to 6:00pm. MasterCard and Visa accepted.*

Okay, so this isn't a real restaurant with real food, unless you are one of those horrible children who ruin their dinner by eating sweets before supper. But if you are one of those unruly souls, then this is *the* "restaurant" for you! You'll find up to 20 different flavors of fudge here that will tempt even the most strident dieter.

Go ahead, try the whipping cream, vanilla or ginger fudge. Or perhaps you'd like to try the maple walnut or strawberry fudge. You could even get a plain ol' piece of traditional fudge. If you just can't make up your mind, you can even have a free sample of the "Flavor of the Day" (sorry – free samples are of the "Flavor of the Day" only – no grazing through 20 different samples). Fudge-making demonstrations are also available several times a day, and you'll be able to see how Garrahy's makes their fudge. So go ahead, stop by and indulge yourself: remember – you're on holiday. Dress is casual of course.

Princes Street

16. LE CHAMBERTIN, *21 George Street, Edinburgh. Tel. 0131/225-1251, 0131/240-7178, Fax 0131/220-1417. £20-40. Open Monday through Friday from 12:30pm to 2:00pm, and Monday through Saturday from 7:00pm to 10:00pm. All major credit cards accepted.*

This is the restaurant for the George Intercontinental Hotel, and it is in great demand by tourists and locals alike. You'll find quiet elegance here: soft lights, quiet conversations, and outstanding food. *A Taste of Scotland* award winner, Le Chambertin provides one of the most elegant and gracious dining experiences in Edinburgh.

Barnaby Hawkes is the manger who oversees the restaurant, and he and his staff have been successful in creating a wonderful dining experience. You'll be impressed with everything you find here, from the luxurious blue décor to the fine wine list to the sumptuous meals and everything in between. The service is also exceptional, as it is attentive yet not overbearing or intrusive.

The menu offers both modern and traditional Scottish fare, enhanced by continental influences. One of the reasons for this is their chef, Klaus Knust, who is a member of the *Confrerie de Chaine des Rotisseurs*, a prestigious world-renowned organization for chefs. His meals are truly wonderful creations. Try the ballotine of chicken stuffed with haggis in a pool of whisky sauce or the baked haunch of roe deer on braised savoy cabbage with a balsamic bacon broth. Vegetarian dishes are also available. Dress for Le Chambertin is suit and tie, and reservations are recommended on the weekends year-around, and always during the peak tourist seasons. Le Chambertin is located at the east end of George Street between Hanover Street and St. Andrew Square on the north side of the street.

17. NUMBER ONE, *1 Princes Street, Edinburgh. Tel. 0131/556-2414, Fax 0131/557-8740. £16-33. Open Monday through Friday from noon to 3:00pm and 7:00pm to 11:00pm, Saturday and Sunday from 7:00pm to 11:00pm. All major credit cards accepted.*

Number One is the formal restaurant for the Balmoral Hotel. Number One had kind of an oriental nightclub feel to me, with its lacquered walls and buoyant atmosphere. It also happens to serve some of the best food in Scotland. Annually, the Automobile Association in Scotland reviews restaurants throughout the country and awards them rosettes according to the quality and presentation of their fare. It is one of the most prized and coveted culinary recognition programs in Scotland. Number One has been awarded 3 Rosettes, a level that has been attained by only a handful of restaurants in Scotland.

You'll find traditional Scottish fare at Number One, and chef Jeff Bland and his team does a remarkable job of preparing and presenting your dinner with a bit of an elegant flair. Try the braised osso bucco with foie gras and woodland mushrooms in a port wine sauce or try the roast filet of sea bass and lobster pomme puree with lobster jus.

The entrance to the restaurant is at street level, just to the right of the main entrance to the Balmoral Hotel. There is also an inside entrance if you are staying at the Balmoral. You'll want to dress in nice casual at a minimum here, and you'll want to make reservations on the weekends.

18. COSMO RESTAURANT, *58a North Castle Street, Edinburgh. Tel. 0131/226-6743. £10-18 lunch and £20-31 for dinner. Open Monday through Friday from 12:30pm to 2:15pm and Monday through Saturday from 7:00pm to 10:45pm. Closed Sunday. Amex, MasterCard and Visa accepted.*

If you are looking for delicious Italian food in a marvelous setting, look no further. Cosmo Restaurant is china and crystal and silver and linen, all enhanced by elegant arched mirrors, subdued lighting and soft classical music playing in the background. You'll find a wide range of traditional and neo-traditional Italian dishes such as sautéed escalope of veal, mozzarella cheese, parma ham and mushrooms in a white wine and cream sauce. Dress is nice casual to suit and tie, especially in the evenings. Reservations are recommended on the weekends during the main tourist seasons. There are only about a dozen tables, and they do fill up fast.

19. 36, *36 Great King Street, Edinburgh. Tel. 0131/556-3636. £20-30. Open Monday through Friday from noon to 2:00pm, and from 7:00pm to 10:00pm, Saturday from 7:00pm to 10:00pm, and Sunday from noon to 2:00pm and from 7:00pm to 9:30pm. All major credit cards accepted.*

36 is the restaurant in the basement of The Howard Hotel. In recent years, it has gained quite a reputation for excellent meals and outstanding service. The fare might be described as traditional Scottish with a modern continental twist. An impressive menu awaits your choice, although it may be harder to choose than you expect. If you are having a hard time deciding, try the braised halibut filet with celeraic and truffle champagne sauce, or perhaps you'd be interested in the baked filo pastry parcels of haggis in a sweet plum sauce. If you are a vegetarian, there are always a few choices for you too. The dessert menu is outrageous, and will defy even the most hardened dieter. Try the hot banana and toffee soufflé with lime ice cream or the gratin of ginger, mango and papaya, doused in sugar and fresh berries. Dress is suit and tie, and reservations are highly recommended, especially during weekends and the summer months. 36 is a non-smoking restaurant.

20. HADRIAN'S RESTAURANT, *2 North Bridge, Edinburgh. Tel. 0131/557-5000. £11-18. Open 7:00pm to 11:00pm daily. All major credit cards accepted.*

Hadrian's Restaurant is the brasserie-style restaurant associated with the Balmoral Hotel. It is not at all like the rest of the hotel: it is very modern and features a European feel with subdued lighting and light jazz music playing. You'll find traditional Scottish fare here, enhanced with European influences. Try the Isle of Skye shellfish risotto with lobster oil or the gateau of artichokes and tomato confit with marinated olives and coriander sauce. Dress is casual to go along with the easy atmosphere you'll find here.

21. CAFÉ ROUGE, *43 Frederick Street, Edinburgh. Tel. 0131/225-4515. £5-10 for lunch, £15-20 for dinner. Open Monday through Saturday from 10:00am to 11:00pm, and Sunday from 10:00am to 11:30pm. MasterCard and Visa accepted.*

Just off George Street, this faux French café feels like the real thing. You'll find cane chairs surrounding small round marble-and-wood tables, and the subdued lighting and light jazz music playing in the background give the restaurant a pleasant and convivial ambience. Hardwood floors, mustard-colored walls and pillars round out the experience. In addition to the recorded jazz music, jazz bands also play here. Check the blackboard inside to see when the next live band will be. The fare is of course French, and it is quite good. Try the gigot d'agneau, cassoulet de haricots blancs (for you non-French speakers out there, that is marinated chargrilled lamb steak with a cassoulet of white beans, pimentos and red onions). Dress for Café Rouge is casual.

22. TIPPON SAHIB INDIAN RESTAURANT, *129a Rose Street, Edinburgh. Tel. 0131/226-2862. £6-8 for lunch, £12-18 for dinner. Open daily from noon to 2:00pm and 5:00pm to 11:30pm. All major credit cards accepted.*

The moment you enter Tippon Sahib Indian Restaurant, you'll know that you have arrived at an Indian restaurant. As with all other Indian restaurants I have been in, you'll be greeted by the strong aroma of curry and a myriad of other seasonings. If you like Indian food, it will be a welcome greeting. You'll descend a set of stairs to get to the smallish restaurant. Once you arrive, you'll find rose-colored wallpaper over dark borders. One wall has a hand-painted scene reflecting British occupation of India, French allies, etc. It is really quite interesting to study and held my attention for some time. You'll find traditional Indian cuisine here, including nahani chicken, chicken tikka kabob and curry lamb. Dress is casual. Tippon Sahib has been here for 20 years, always a good sign for restaurants! While Indian food isn't for everyone, if you like Indian food, you'll find a pleasant atmosphere, great food, and a central location. What more could you want?

23. DRUM AND MONKEY, *80 Queen Street, Edinburgh. Tel. 0131/538-8111, Fax 0131/226-9932. £10-15. Open daily from 11:30am to 7:00pm. All major credit cards accepted.*

The Drum and Monkey is a contemporary bistro that has somewhat of a cult following among the business as well as tourist communities.

Located at the corner of Charlotte and Queens Streets in New Town, this smallish café/pub has won recognition by *A Taste of Scotland*. The main floor features a pleasant and lively bar atmosphere that is enjoyed by business people and tourists alike. The main restaurant is downstairs and a bit more formal, with plenty of dark wood, gothic arches and snug alcoves to enhance your dining experience. The Drum and Monkey features contemporary Scottish fare, and in the main restaurant you'll find such delicacies as spinach tortellini with red peppers in a smoked salmon sauce. There are a few vegetarian selections for those who prefer that choice. Upstairs in the pub area you'll find great sandwiches and soups, perfect should the day be a bit damp. Dress is casual.

24. LA P'TITE FOLIE, *61 Frederick Street, Edinburgh. Tel. 0131/225-7983. £6-15. Open daily from noon to 3:00pm and 6:00pm to 11:00pm. MasterCard and Visa accepted.*

Formerly called Chez Jules, this pleasant French café will meet your casual dining needs. It's a small place, and judging by my few experiences with it, it will also be a busy place when you come. In this case, its smallness makes it that much more endearing, and allows the wait staff to provide personal attention to you and your dining needs. The fare is of course French, and you'll have a wide variety of offerings to choose from. Try the salmon, hake and mussels with choucoute, lemon and herb beurre blanc, or the coquilles Saint-Jacques (King scallops and prawns baked in cheese). Dress is casual.

25. HARD ROCK CAFÉ, *20 George Street, Edinburgh. Tel. 0131/260-3000, Fax 0131/225-4530. £5-8. Open daily from 11:30am to 1:00am. All major credit cards accepted.*

They're all over the world, so why not in Edinburgh? If you are a Hard Rock Café fan, you'll of course want to stop in for a few minutes to buy a shirt, check out the décor, and maybe even sample their food. You'll find Edinburgh's edition of this hot restaurant chain across the street from the George Intercontinental Hotel at the east end of George Street. The Edinburgh Hard Rock Café has a very similar feel and style to its cousin restaurants around the world, although the layout here is a bit different. You'll find lots of wood, brass and music memorabilia. The fare is essentially the same: burgers and sandwiches, soups and salads. Dress is of course casual. Children under 14 cannot be here after 8:00pm. If you are interested in purchasing one of those Hard Rock Café shirts or caps, the shop that sells these is only open from 9:00am to 1:00pm.

26. GOLDEN DRAGON RESTAURANT, *21 Castle Street, Edinburgh. Tel. 0131/225-7327. £4-8. Open daily from 12:30pm to 2:30pm and 6:00pm to 10:00pm. Amex, MasterCard and Visa accepted.*

If you have a craving for Chinese food while in Edinburgh, then stop by the Golden Dragon Restaurant. When you do, you'll enter a small dining area with white walls and black trim, presided over by a large aquarium in the middle of the room. The tartan carpet seems slightly out of place, but what the heck – the food is good. You'll find a pretty traditional menu of Chinese dishes – no surprises here. The food is good and tasty, if not spectacularly presented. Dress is casual.

27. BEWLEY'S RESTAURANT, *2/4 Charlotte Street, Edinburgh. Tel. 0131/220-1969. £5-7. Open Monday through Friday 8:00am to 5:00pm and Saturday from 9:00am to 6:00pm. Closed Sunday. MasterCard and Visa accepted.*

Like her Irish cousins, this location of the Bewley's chain offers a nice place to stop and grab a quick bite to eat as a break during your sightseeing. Located near the corner of Princes and Charlotte Streets, you'll find a cafeteria-style restaurant with a wide selection of soups, salads and sandwiches. Nothing fancy here, just lots of tables, a busy, congenial pace, and good, filling food for a reasonable price.

Just South of The Royal Mile
The following restaurants are located just south of the Royal Mile:

28. PRESTONFIELD RESTAURANT, *Prestonfield Road, Edinburgh. Tel. 0131/668-3346. £20-30. Open daily from noon to 2:30pm and from 7:00pm to 9:30pm. All major credit cards accepted.*

What a wonderful dining experience you'll have at the Prestonfield Restaurant. Set in a lovely mansion, you'll be dining in a section of the house that was built in 1827, and you will experience elegant dining in superb surroundings. The oval dining room where you will dine is presided over by the portraits of some of the former lords and ladies of Prestonfield House. Crystal and candlelight, linen and silver will enhance the meals, and the antique tables you will be dining at add an additional touch of class to the overall experience.

As you might expect, the meals are exceptional, having been prepared with the freshest Scottish ingredients. The fare has been described as Scottish with French influences. Try the magret de canard aux marron et purée de celery (breast of duck with chestnuts and a celery purée). Or if you'd prefer, try the filet of beef in a brioche with a goose liver and truffle sauce. This is a very nice dining experience, and you'll want to dress nicely (suit and tie) for your meal here. Reservations are a must during the tourist season.

29. THE ATRIUM, *10 Cambridge Street, Edinburgh. Tel. 0131/28-4438. £18-30. Open Monday through Friday from noon to 2:30pm and 6:00pm to 10:30pm, and Saturday from noon to 2:00pm and 6:00pm to 10:30pm. All major credit cards accepted.*

The Atrium is one of Edinburgh's most interesting restaurants. In addition to wonderful meals, you'll find an intriguing décor: look for a fabric ceiling and wrought-iron candlesticks to set the mood. Scottish fare is the word here, although it is prepared in most imaginative (and delicious) ways. The menu changes daily, so there's always reason to come back. The selections are wide ranging, and vegetarians are always taken care of here. You might find something as simple as pan-fried sea bass with rosti or something more elaborate like the breast of duck with orange, ginger and spring onion sauce. The Atrium has garnered a bit of a cult following with locals as well as returning tourists; reservations are suggested on weekends and during the tourist season.

30. THE GRILL ROOM, *1 Festival Square, Edinburgh. Tel. 0131/229-6422. £25-35. Open daily from noon to 2:30pm and from 6:00pm to 11:00pm. All major credit cards accepted.*

The Grill Room is the luxury dining room at the Sheraton Grand hotel. You'll be delighted with the elegance you encounter here. You'll also be impressed with the ample menu and the entrées from which to choose. Whether you are looking for beef, lamb, seafood or a vegetarian choice, you will be pleased with what you find. Try the mallard duck with winter truffle paté in Madeira jus, or the shellfish nage with saffron. The Grill Room also offers a fine wine list to complement the meal. Dress is suit and tie, and reservations are advised on weekends and during the tourist season.

31. THE TERRACE RESTAURANT, *1 Festival Square, Edinburgh. Tel. 0131/229-6422. £12-20. Open daily from 7:00am to 11:00am, noon to 2:30pm and from 6:00pm to 11:00pm. All major credit cards accepted.*

The Terrace is the brasserie-style restaurant at the Sheraton Grand. It provides great food and some of the best views of the city from a restaurant. As you dine you'll be treated to splendid views of Edinburgh Castle, a great sight by day and a stunning spectacle by night. There is always a broad selection of entrées from which to choose at the mouth-watering buffet. The buffet is perhaps one of the best around, complete with a wide selection of soups, salads and assorted delicacies. As an added attraction, chefs are on hand to whip up a stir fry meal right before your eyes if that's your dinner choice. Dress is nice casual.

South Suburbs

32. THE DUNGEON RESTAURANT, *Dalhousie Castle, Bonnierigg. Tel. 01875/820-153. Lunch from £8-12, dinner from £20-30. Open Monday through Thursday from 7:00pm to 9:00pm, and Friday through Sunday from 7:00pm to 9:30pm. All major credit cards accepted.*

Wow! The rest of Dalhousie Castle Hotel is spectacular, and the sensation continues as you enter their restaurant. You'll descend a series of steps into The Dungeon, passing swords, battle axes, and armor along the way. The restaurant is divided into three rooms, all featuring original rough-hewn stone walls of the castle. Each room is guarded by a suit of armor, standing stoically within one of the hand-hewn portals of each room. The setting is delightful, and the food is delicious.

But don't take my word alone for it – the meals here have been recognized by *A Taste of Scotland*, and that's always a good sign. The cuisine has been described as traditional Scottish with heavy French influences. The chefs at The Dungeon insist on only the finest and freshest produce and ingredients for the meals they prepare, and you benefit from that insistence. Maybe it's the fresh air of the country setting for the hotel, or perhaps it is these fresh ingredients, but it seems the flavor of the meals here is a notch above that which you sample in the city restaurants. Try the beetroot gravalax with fennel salad or the filet of Aberdeen beef. If you prefer that your meal come from the sea, then you can't go wrong with the filet of sea bass with dill mustard mash and French beans and bacon. Dress is nice casual, but most of the patrons dress up.

SEEING THE SIGHTS

There are plenty of things to see an do in Edinburgh, as it probably offers the most sights to see in the most compact area of any Scottish city. Most of the sights are clustered around two areas in downtown Edinburgh: the Royal Mile and Princes Street. Both are easily covered on foot, so either park your car or take a bus from your hotel or B&B.

The Royal Mile

The term **Royal Mile** describes the distance between Edinburgh Castle and the Palace of Holyroodhouse. It also refers to the fact that this road was traversed by generations of royal families who lived in both the castle and the palace, hence the name. Today, the Royal Mile possesses four street names. Beginning at the castle and descending downhill, it is named Castlehill, Lawnmarket, High and Canongate Streets. Along the journey, you'll encounter some of Edinburgh's best sights, hotels and restaurants (not to mention more than a few distracting tartan and souvenir shops!).

Let's start your tour of Edinburgh at **Edinburgh Castle**, *Castlehill, Tel. 0131/225-1012; open April through September daily from 9:30am to 6:00pm, and from October through March daily from 9:30am to 5:00pm (last admission is 45 minutes before closing); admission is £6 adults, £4.50 for seniors, and £1.50 for children.* Professional tourists have told me that Edinburgh Castle is one of the finest castle tours they have ever taken. Perhaps you will agree. The earliest history of the castle is a bit sketchy, but most historians agree that a fortress of some sort has been here atop the cone of an ancient volcano for at least 800 years. At that time, Malcolm Canmore and his wife

Queen Margaret had a castle built here. During an uprising two centuries later, that structure was entirely destroyed, with the exception of the small 12th-century chapel known as **St. Margaret's Chapel**. The castle is entered on the eastern side by proceeding through a large **Esplanade**, or parade ground. The Esplanade is the site of the fabulous Edinburgh Military Tattoo each evening of the Edinburgh Festival.

You'll have an opportunity to visit the **State Apartments**, including the small paneled bedroom where Mary Queen of Scots gave birth to James VI of Scotland, who eventually united the crowns of England and Scotland. One of my favorite rooms is the magnificent **Great Hall**, which was built in the 15th century and expanded extensively in the 16th century. Early Scottish parliaments convened here. Today it is a cavernous room that features rich oak paneling, armor and weaponry from various periods of Scotland's history. The most impressive aspect of the Great Hall is spectacular hammer-beam ceiling that soars about 30 feet above the room.

But certainly the crowning glory of Edinburgh Castle is (appropriately) called the **Crown Chamber**. You'll be able to see a number of artifacts important to Scotland: the royal crown, the scepter and sword (together, they are called the *Honors of Scotland*). The crown is spectacular: red velvet and white ermine covered with gold and bedecked with nearly 100 pearls, 10 diamonds, and 30 other semi-precious stones. (If it were costume jewelry, it would appear to be a bit overdone!) The sword and scepter were presented to James VI by Pope Alexander VI and Pope Julius II, respectively.

You'll also see the **Stone of Destiny**, also known as the **Stone of Scone**. It has the appearance of a common-looking stone, but it is reported to have supernatural powers which are transferred to any king crowned thereon. Over the course of 400 years, 34 Scottish kings were crowned on the Stone of Destiny, until it was captured and taken to England by Edward I in the early 14th century. It has only recently been returned to Edinburgh Castle. (Actually, the Scots may have pulled a fast one on Edward I: legend has it that an official-looking but rather ordinary stone was substituted for the Stone of Destiny just before its kidnap! If that is the case, then you will get a good look at that rather ordinary stone!)

While at Edinburgh Castle, you'll have the opportunity to look at a monster of a cannon called **Mons Meg**. Built in the 15th century (probably at Mons in Belgium), it was used in a number of Scottish skirmishes with the English. It could reportedly fire a 500-pound stone over two miles with reasonable accuracy. You'll find Mons Meg in one of the rooms of the cavernous **Vaults** that once served as a prison for foreign prisoners.

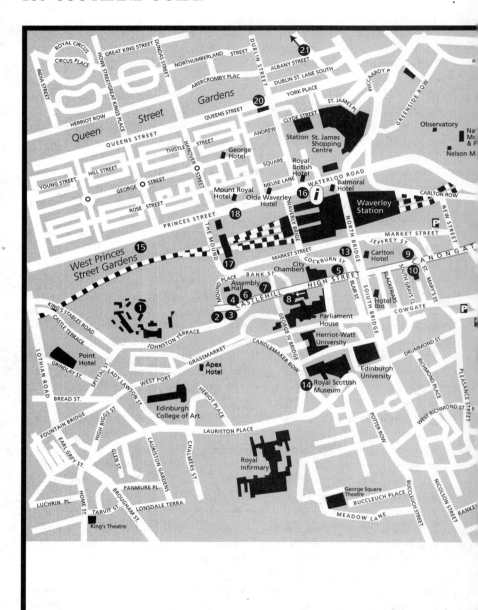

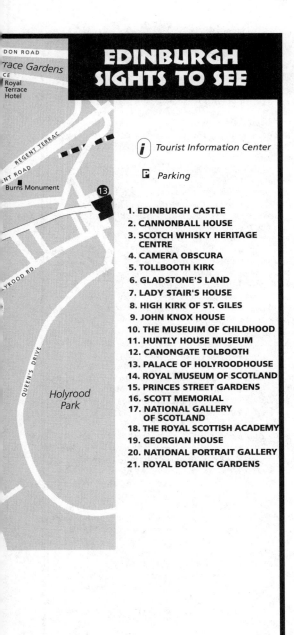

EDINBURGH SIGHTS TO SEE

DON ROAD

race Gardens

C E

Royal Terrace Hotel

REGENT TERRAC

REGENT

NT ROAD

Burns Monument

13

YROOD RD.

QUEEN'S DRIVE

Holyrood Park

i Tourist Information Center

Parking

1. EDINBURGH CASTLE
2. CANNONBALL HOUSE
3. SCOTCH WHISKY HERITAGE CENTRE
4. CAMERA OBSCURA
5. TOLLBOOTH KIRK
6. GLADSTONE'S LAND
7. LADY STAIR'S HOUSE
8. HIGH KIRK OF ST. GILES
9. JOHN KNOX HOUSE
10. THE MUSEUIM OF CHILDHOOD
11. HUNTLY HOUSE MUSEUM
12. CANONGATE TOLBOOTH
13. PALACE OF HOLYROODHOUSE
14. ROYAL MUSEUM OF SCOTLAND
15. PRINCES STREET GARDENS
16. SCOTT MEMORIAL
17. NATIONAL GALLERY OF SCOTLAND
18. THE ROYAL SCOTTISH ACADEMY
19. GEORGIAN HOUSE
20. NATIONAL PORTRAIT GALLERY
21. ROYAL BOTANIC GARDENS

THE EDINBURGH FESTIVAL - PARTY TIME!

The **Edinburgh Festival** was started after World War II as something to perk up the Scottish economy, and to chase the doldrums and dreariness that accompanied the years immediately following the end of the war. Little did its early organizers dream that it would become as profitable and world-renowned as it has become. The Festival officially runs for three weeks in August, although in reality almost all of August is packed with performances and Festival-related things to see and do. There is a flurry of impressive activity that occurs during this time. The locals simply refer to this series of events as The Festival, but it is in reality a series of six distinct festivals going on at more or less the same time.

The first is the **Edinburgh International Festival**. It runs from mid-August through the first day or two of September. It is a collection of music, drama and artistry presented at various venues around the city. Artists and actors, musicians and extroverts descend on Edinburgh to display their talents. There is no set program, although you are usually assured of a selection of opera, symphonies, and a wide variety of high-end theatrical performances. A brochure with the planned participants, dates and times is printed in April, and is available from the International Festival Society, 21 Market Street, Edinburgh, Tel. 0131/473-2001.

The **Edinburgh Film Festival** runs the last 15 days of August. It is of course viewed in the movie theaters in and around Edinburgh, although the main venue is The Filmhouse, 88 Lothian Road, Edinburgh, Tel. 0131/229-2550. The Film Festival features two solid weeks of film screenings. There is generally a plethora of European films, particularly English, as well as a Hollywood blockbuster or two receiving their introduction to European audiences.

The **Edinburgh Military Tattoo** is arguably the most popular and best-attended of all The Festival events. Set on the Edinburgh Castle Esplanade with the castle as its very impressive backdrop, the Military Tattoo is a nationalistic display of kilts and bagpipes. It is flash and bravado, pomp and circumstance. Over 200,000 individuals crowd onto temporary viewing stands to witness this flashy display of pipers, drummers and bagpipers. It is impressive and a memory not to miss if you are in Edinburgh during the festival. Tickets and information are available from the Military Tattoo Office, 22 Market Place, Edinburgh, Tel. 0131/225-1188.

The **Book Festival** is a bit more of a pedestrian activity compared to some of the other events, but it nonetheless draws authors from all over the world. The Book Festival runs the last two weeks of August. The authors participate in readings, panel discussions, and a variety of other activities. All this takes place in a series of large tents pitched in Charlotte Square. For information, contact the Scottish Book Centre, 137 Dundee Street, Edinburgh, Tel. 0131/228-5444.

The **Jazz and Blues Festival** usually begins the last day or two of July and runs through the first week or so of August. It is aptly named, and you can expect a rich assortment of high-quality jazz and blues music during this 10-day affair. Information on the Jazz and Blues Festival can be obtained from the Jazz and Blues Festival Office, 116 Canongate, Edinburgh, Tel. 0131/557-1642.

Finally, the last event is actually the longest running of the festival events: **The Fringe Festival**. Originally an eclectic collection of artists and troubadours who weren't invited to the more upscale International Festival, they sort of made their own festival wherever and whenever they could find an audience. All a person or group has to do is sign up and they are in. You'll experience everything from raw, undiscovered talent to raw, undiscovered wannabe's. The Fringe Festival begins a week or so prior to the Edinburgh International Festival (usually around August 8 or 9), and runs through the end of the month. It's a real treat, and you'll see every sort of talent imaginable, sort of like a Street Performers Rendezvous. For more information, contact the Fringe Festival Office, 180 High Street, Edinburgh. Tel. 0131/226-5257.

As you leave Edinburgh Castle headed downhill toward the Royal Mile, take a moment to notice the **Cannonball House** on your right as you leave the Esplanade. You'll note a large cannonball embedded in the west gable of the building – the result of a poorly aimed shot at Bonnie Prince Charlie's armies, so the legends say. (Most, however, agree it marks the height of the city's first piped-water system.)

Next door to the Cannonball House is the **Scotch Whisky Heritage Centre**, *354 Castlehill, Tel. 0131/220-0441; open daily from April through September from 9:30am to 6:00pm, and November through March from 10:00am to 5:30pm; admission is £4.20 for adults, £3.50 for students, £3 for seniors, £2 for children, and a family ticket for £11.40.* You'll take a Disneyesque ride in a whisky barrel as you receive an audiovisual presentation on the whisky-making process and history. While it is interesting, if you think you might visit a distillery or two while on holiday, I'd skip this presentation in favor of the guided tour most distilleries provide. They do have a nice shop with a wide selection of Scotch whiskies for sale.

Across the street and slightly downhill from the Scotch Whisky Heritage Centre is **Camera Obscura**, *Castlehill, Tel.0131/226-3709; open daily April through October from 9:30am to 6:00pm, and from November through March from 10:00am to 5:00pm; admission is £3.85 for adults, £3.10 for students, £2.50 for seniors, £1.95 for children, and a family ticket for £11.50.* This will probably be one of the more unique things you do while in Scotland. You'll be entertained by a unique and innovative tour of Edinburgh from inside a giant Victorian camera. A system of camera lenses projects images of the city onto a tabletop, where a guide gives you a running dialogue about the city. There is also a balcony that provides outstanding views of the city. A number of exhibits are also available, including one on holography, pinhole photography, and a fine collection of old photographs from the mid- to late 1800s.

Across the street you come to a large and impressive Gothic church known as the **Tolbooth Kirk** (kirk is the Scottish name for church). The kirk's 240-foot spire towers high and proud above Edinburgh and can be seen from all over the city. Built in the mid-1800s as the house of worship for the Church of Scotland, it now serves as the offices for the Edinburgh Festival.

As Castlehill Street gives way to Lawnmarket Street, you come to **Gladstone's Land**, *477b Lawnmarket, Tel. 0131/226-5856; open April through October Monday through Saturday from 10:00am to 5:00pm, and Sunday from 2:00pm to 5:00pm, last admission 30 minutes before close; admission is £3 for adults and £2 for seniors and children, family tickets available for £8.* In 1620, a wealthy merchant named Thomas Gledstone purchased this six-story home. It has withstood the winds of time, and in recent years has been renovated and furnished to give you the look and feel of what life was like for the well-to-do nearly 400 years ago. There are a number of interesting items to catch your eye. I was most impressed with the **Painted Chamber**, a room featuring interesting decorations on the ceilings and walls.

Similar to Gladstone's Land is **Lady Stair's House**, *Lady Stair's Close, Tel. 0131/225-2425; open Monday through Saturday from 10:00am to 5:00pm, until 6:00pm from June to September; admission is free.* Thomas Gledstone and his family were neighbors of Lady Stair during the first part of the 17th century. As with his home, Lady Stair's has been refurbished and features a nice collection of ancient portraits and artifacts. It also houses an interesting exhibit about three of Scotland's greatest literary sons: Robert Burns, Robert Louis Stevenson and Sir Walter Scott. Personal belongings and original manuscripts of the writers are on display.

Across from Gladstone's Land and Lady Stair's House is Brodie's Close, the close (alley) named after one of its most famous resident, Deacon William Brodie. Pause for a moment and consider the strange case of the good Deacon, a city councilman by day and a burglar by night. He served as the role model for Robert Louis Stevenson's *The Strange Case of Dr. Jekyll and Mr. Hyde* (see sidebar on the next page).

About a half-block further downhill you'll come to the **High Kirk of St. Giles**, *High Street, Tel. 0131/225-9442; open from April through September from 9:00am to 7:00pm, and October through March from 9:00am to 5:00pm, also open Sunday from 1:00pm to 5:00pm; admission to the kirk is free, admission to the Thistle Chapel is £1.* St. Giles was the home parish of the fiery reformer John Knox. As you enter the kirk, find a place among the pews and sit very still, listening carefully to see if you can imagine what it would have been like to be present when John Knox thundered his denunciations of Catholicism and Mary Queen of Scots from the pulpit.

Today the church is far more serene, and invites a visit. There has been a religious building on this site since the middle of the 9th century, although most of St. Giles was built years later. Most of the building you see today dates from the early 19th century, although the magnificent spire-topped tower was built three years after Columbus set forth on his epic voyage to America. In 1911, the lovely and elaborate **Thistle Chapel** was built by Sir Robert Lorimer. The workmanship is spectacular and it is worth the £1 to visit it. You'll find it in the southeast corner of St. Giles.

St. Giles is somewhat of a shrine to present-day Presbyterians, since John Knox was the minister here for the last dozen or so years of his life. It is still used for Sunday services, and you are more than welcome to join their worship services, which are at 8:00am, 10:00am and 11:30am on Sunday mornings. Attending services here was the spiritual highlight of their holiday for some Presbyterian friends of mine.

THE STRANGE CASE OF DEACON WILLIAM BRODIE

*Consider the strange case of **Deacon William Brodie**. He was an upstanding citizen, a member of the city council. When he was about town on his business, he got the layout of his associates' homes and offices. He even made wax imprints of their house keys when given the opportunity. His burglaries frightened the community: no one could figure out how the burglar had gotten into their homes. He was finally caught when his assistant, who had been convicted of another crime and was scheduled for deportation (to America), turned States' witness to have his sentence commuted.*

William Brodie was hung on October 1, 1788, ironically on the same gallows he had designed several years before. Following is the text from the Edinburgh Advertiser, dated March 14, 1788. It describes a pretty desperate character:

"Two-Hundred Pound Reward

Whereas William Brodie, a considerable house carpenter, and Burger of the City of Edinburgh has been charged with being concerned with breaking into the General Excise Office for Scotland, stealing from the cashier's office there a sum of money. And as the said William Brodie has either made his escape from Edinburgh, or is still concealed about that place, a reward of one hundred and fifty pounds sterling to secure him, and FIFTY pounds sterling more upon his conviction.

William Brodie is about 5 feet 4 inches; is about 48 years of age, but looks rather younger than he is. Broad at the shoulders and very small over the loins, has dark brown full eyes with large black eyebrows. Under the right eye is the scar of a cut;...and he has a fallow complexion. Black hair, twisted, turned up and tied behind, coming far down upon each cheek and the whiskers very fairly at the end. High smooth forehead, has a particular air in his walk, takes long steps, strides the ground first with his heel. Usually uses a walking stick under his hand and moves in a grand swaggering sort of way...Was dressed in a black coat, vest, breeches, and stockings, great coat and silver shoe buckles."

While you have John Knox on your mind, why not stop at the **John Knox House**, where he lived for a spell, at *43/45 High Street, Tel. 0131/556-9579; open Monday through Saturday from 9:00am to 5:00pm; admission is £1.75 for adults, £1.25 for students and seniors, and 75p for children over 7.* The house provides some interesting displays about the life and ministry of John Knox. The house was built in the middle of the 16th century.

The Museum of Childhood, *42 High Street, Tel. 0131/529-4142; open Monday through Saturday from 10:00am to 5:00pm; during the Edinburgh*

Festival, (mid-August to the first week of September) it is also open on Sunday from 2:00pm to 5:00pm; admission is free. You want to experience childhood memories? Then stop in at the Museum of Childhood. You'll find just about anything you could imagine here, both from your lifetime to the lifetimes of children through the ages. You'll find Teddy bears and toy trains, erector sets and costumes, educational updates and antique playthings, even the ever-popular castor oil that numerous generations of children endured! Stop by and see if it brings back childhood memories for you. It certainly did for me.

As you continue down the Royal Mile, you'll come to the **Huntly House Museum** on your right, *142 Canongate Street, Tel. 0131/529-4143; open Monday through Saturday from 10:00am to 5:00pm, and on Sunday during the Edinburgh Festival from 2:00pm to 5:00pm; admission is free.* This 16th-century mansion has been converted into a fine museum of (primarily) Edinburgh history. By now you should realize that I am a sucker for history of any kind, and really enjoy these kinds of places. Huntly House features period furnishings and art throughout. It's always intriguing to me to look at these rooms and imagine what life must have been like, for at least a portion of the population. There are also some splendid examples of Edinburgh silver and pottery on hand.

If you're wondering about that fine pointed structure across the street from Huntly House Museum, it is the **Canongate Tolbooth**, *163 Canongate.* It has been standing stoically since the end of the 16th century. Think of the people that passed beneath its shadow en route from the castle toward the Palace of Holyroodhouse, or vice versa. Watch for the tall, pointy-capped tower with the large clock extending out from it.

Inside the Canongate Tolbooth, you'll find a small but interesting exhibit called **The People's Story**, *Canongate Tolbooth, Tel. 0131/529-4057; open Monday through Saturday from 10:00am to 5:00pm, Sunday during the Edinburgh Festival only, from 2:00pm to 5:00pm; admission is free.* As you've ventured down the Royal Mile, you've experienced how the "other half" lived at Gladstone's Land and Lady Stair's House; now see how the *other* "other half" lived – this exhibit is dedicated to the ordinary people that were such a major part of Edinburgh's population. It covers many of the aspects of Edinburgh's "blue-collar" population.

At the bottom of Canongate Street you'll come to the ornate wrought-iron gates of the **Palace of Holyroodhouse**, *Canongate Street, Tel. 0131/556-1096; open daily April through October Monday through Sunday from 9:30am to 5:15pm, and daily November through March from 9:30am to 3:45pm; admission is £5 for adults, £3.50 for seniors, and £2.50 for children 15 and under; when the Queen is visiting, the palace is closed to visits (her visits are usually in late May and/or late June/early July, so call ahead during these times).* This is the Queen's weekend getaway, as well as one of Scotland's most-visited attractions. Much of the palace is off-limits to tourists, although there is enough open to make it worth visiting.

Most of the structure you see today was built in the 16th and 17th centuries. Famous names in Scottish history are associated with the palace, including Mary Queen of Scots, Sir William Bruce, King George IV and Queen Victoria and Prince Albert. William Bruce greatly expanded the palace in the 17th century for an upcoming visit by Charles II (a visit which never materialized!). Queen Victoria and Prince Albert often stayed here en route to Balmoral Castle, and Mary Queen of Scots lived here. One of the most grisly and infamous events associated with her life occurred within the walls of the palace. It seems her husband, Lord Darnley, became insanely jealous of a court-musician-turned-personal-secretary with whom Mary had become quite fond. Lord Darnley arranged to have the musician, one David Riccio, killed in front of Mary. As you take your tour of the palace, you'll see the room where the attack took place.

I am particularly impressed with the **Picture Gallery**. In this room you'll hear the story of Jacob De Witt, who was commissioned to paint the portraits of Scottish royalty. In the late 17th century he signed a contract to complete 110 paintings within two years (for you math majors out there, that's a little over two portraits per week). That he came anywhere close to completing the project is astounding. Today you can see most of those paintings on display in the 150-foot-long gallery. But don't get too excited; most of the portraits are from the painter's imagination, and may bear little or no resemblance to the actual personages they represent. You'll also be able to see the private bedrooms of Mary and Lord Darnley, as well as the **Throne Room**. The palace has been furnished throughout with a rich collection of period furnishings, tapestries, and *objets d' art*.

On the grounds of the Palace of Holyroodhouse are the impressive ruins of an ancient Augustinian abbey that predates the palace by some 500 years.

Back up near the middle of the Royal Mile and a block or two south on Chambers Street you'll find the **Royal Museum of Scotland**, *Chambers Street, Tel. 0131/225-7534; open Monday through Saturday 10:00am to 5:00pm, and Sunday from 2:00pm to 5:00pm; admission is £3 for adults, £2 for seniors and students, £1.50 for children, and a family ticket is available for £7.50.* This spectacular Victorian building is home to a wonderful museum full of interesting and intriguing things to see. The building itself is worth a visit, with its vaulted and ribbed ceiling.

The collection might be termed "a little of a lot of things," and you are sure to find something that will be of interest to you. Do you have Viking ancestors? Then you'll like the exhibit on Vikings. Or possibly you'll be drawn to the displays on the Roman Empire, and their impact on

Scotland. If these aren't enough to hold your attention, then ancient Greece, Egypt or maybe even Louis XIV's France will vie for your attention. You'll be impressed with the exhibit on China, and the costume section may be what draws you. Along with these, you'll find standard museum offerings of natural history, geology, fossils and taxidermy. Regardless of your interests, you'll be assured of finding something here that will hold your attention and interest.

Princes Street
The north side of Princes Street is lined with rather dull-looking modern storefronts. Fortunately you can walk across the street to the **Princes Street Gardens**, below the castle. This wide verdant area has been planted with beautiful flowers, trees, shrubs and grass punctuated periodically by statues. It provides some of the most pleasant walks in the city.

At the east end of Princes Street is arguably the most impressive building on the street: the **Balmoral Hotel**. Formerly the North British Hotel, it was built in 1902 as the principal railway hotel. Just west of the hotel is the imposing 200-foot-tall Scott Memorial. Built shortly after Sir Walter's death in 1832, it's Gothic spire rises impressively skyward in a tribute to one of Scotland's most famous writers. The memorial features a statue of Sir Scott with a favorite hunting dog, as well as sculptures of characters from his *Waverley* novels.

At the west end of the Princes Street Gardens you'll find the area known simply as **The Mound**. This area came about when late 18th-century Edinburghers got tired of sloshing through the swampy grounds to traverse between New Town and Old Town. Someone decided it was a wonderful place to put all the dirt that was being displaced by the rapidly expanding New Town. It is estimated that over two million cart loads were dumped to make The Mound. (What they would have given for a modern front-end loader.)

To start your tour of New Town's museums and art galleries, let's start at The Mound with the **National Gallery of Scotland**, *The Mound, Tel. 0131/624-6200; open Monday through Saturday 10:00am to 5:00pm, and Sunday from 2:00pm to 5:00pm; admission is free, except a nominal charge for special attractions.* I was a little surprised that the gallery is as small as it is, but it offers an exceptional collection of masterpieces spanning the range of artworks from the Renaissance through the post-Impressionism periods. As you marvel at the fine collection, please bear in mind that you have the duke of Sutherland's benevolence to thank – a number of the paintings are from his private collection, on extended loan to the gallery. One of the finest is Nicolas Poussin's *Seven Sacraments*. You'll find a number of masters and impressionists well-represented here, including works by El Greco (*Savior* and *Fabula*), Monet (*Shipping Scene – Night*

Effects), Raphael (*Madonna*), Rembrandt (*Woman in Bed*), Reynolds (*The Ladies Waldegrave*), and Rubens (*The Feast of Herod* and *The Reconciliation of Isaac and Esau*). Other works by such notables as Degas, Raphael, Romano, Titian, Turner, Van Dyke and Van Gogh are also on display. The lower level features a collection of Scottish and British artists. You'll find works by Raeburn, Ramsay, MacTaggart, and Wilkie.

The gallery is decorated lavishly and warmly, and you'll feel almost as though you've walked into the home of a very wealthy friend rather than an art gallery (except for all the paintings, of course!). The building is impressive in and of itself. It was designed and built in 1848 by famed Edinburgh architect William Playfair. Its classical, colonnaded design makes it one of the most impressive buildings in Edinburgh.

Take the short walk from the National Gallery to its neighbor, the **Royal Scottish Academy**, *The Mound, Tel. 0131/225-6671; open Monday through Saturday 10:00am to 5:00pm, and Sunday from 2:00pm to 5:00pm; admission varies depending on the exhibit.* The RSA features a host of exhibits throughout the year. It's an eclectic assortment that is presented here. You might see displays of art by local artists one week, and a fine collection of Old Masters displayed the following week.

Nearly as impressive is the area between the Royal Scottish Academy and the National Gallery of Scotland. It is used throughout the year for various ad hoc engagements: bagpipers, street preaching, political rallies, etc. It always seems to have something going, especially during the summer months.

George Street runs parallel to Princes Street and lies one block north thereof. From the Royal Scottish Academy, walk west on Princes Street a couple of blocks to South Charlotte Street. Head north for two blocks to the **Georgian House**, *7 Charlotte Square, Tel. 0131/225-2160; open April through October Monday through Saturday from 10:00am to 5:00pm, and Sunday from 2:00pm to 5:00pm, last admission is at 4:30pm; admission is £4.20 for adults, £2.80 for seniors, students and children, and a family ticket is available for £11.20.* This is one of the better examples of a Georgian house that has been refurbished and furnished to look as it might have in the late 18th century. This was the former home of wealthy Edinburgh business-man John Lamont. Three floors and a number of rooms have been renovated, and it is a pleasant and interesting visit, well worth the walk to get here. Guides in each room help you understand what you are seeing.

The Georgian House is across the street from **Charlotte Square**, at the west end of George Street. It was named after Queen Charlotte, George III's wife. It presents an outstanding example of a classic Georgian neighborhood, as elegant Georgian townhouses line the square. The memorial in the center of the grassy area of the square is of Prince Albert,

Queen Victoria's sweetheart. Alexander Graham Bell probably played in this lovely square as a child – he was born at 16 South Charlotte Street. From Charlotte Square, walk east along George Street until you get to St. Andrew Square. Turn left on St. Davis Street to Queen Street, where you'll find the **Scottish National Portrait Gallery**, *1 Queen Street, Tel. 0131/624-620; open Monday through Saturday 10:00am to 5:00pm, and Sunday from 2:00pm to 5:00pm; admission is free, except for special exhibits.* Take a pictorial stroll through Scotland's history as you view the portraits of famous Scots, from the ever-popular Robbie Burns and Sir Walter Scott to current heroes like **Sean Connery** and soccer star **Danny McGrain**. How many paintings do you recognize? I guarantee there are a number with which you will be familiar (especially if you purchased a postcard of Robert Burns or Sir Walter Scott, for example). You'll see the movers and shakers in Scottish history here: Bonnie Prince Charlie, Mary Queen of Scots, even the Queen Mother.

About a mile north of Princes Street, you'll find serenity plus at the **Royal Botanic Gardens**, *Inverleith Road, Tel. 0131/552-7171; open daily from April through August, from 9:30am to 7:00pm, September and March from 9:30pm to 6:00pm, October and February from 9:30am to 5:00pm, and November through January from 9:30am to 4:00pm; admission is free.* Seventy-two acres of splendid and spectacular gardens offer a quiet place to stop and smell the roses (literally as well as figuratively!) and the rhododendrons. You'll find over 2,000 different kinds of trees and shrubs, along with some wonderful rock gardens. Three greenhouses (called the **Glasshouse Experience**) bring a little of the tropics to Edinburgh, and a staggering variety of fabulous plants are found here. You'll be amazed at the sheer variety of orchids, lilies and other plants here. There is a small gift shop and snack bar, as well as the Terrace Café, which offers some of the most memorable views of Edinburgh.

To get to the gardens, take Hanover Street (Hanover / Queen Street Gardens / Dundas / Brandon Terrace) north from The Mound until you get to Inverleith Row. Turn left, and the gardens will be a couple of hundred yards' down on your left.

Suburbs

There are a number of sights to see on the outskirts of Edinburgh. Following are a few:

Edinburgh Zoo, *Corstorphine Road, Murrayfield, Edinburgh, Tel. 0131/334-9171; open April to September on Monday through Saturday from 9:00am to 6:00pm, and Sunday from 9:30am to 6:00pm, October to March Monday through Saturday from 9:00am to 4:30pm, and Sunday from 9:30am to 4:30pm; admission is £5.80 for adults, £3.60 for seniors and £3 for children, and a family ticket is available for £15.80.* If your kids are all museum-ed out, you might venture out to the Edinburgh Zoo. Zoos are always winners with children, and Edinburgh's offering is no exception. The zoo occupies 80 acres on the slopes of the Corstorphine Hills, and features all the zoo animals you expect to see at a zoo: lions and tigers and bears, and elephants, hippos, monkeys, rhinos, etc. You and your kids will especially enjoy the Penguin Parade, which takes place daily during the summer months at 2:00pm. The zoo reportedly has the largest population of penguins in Europe, and features four different species.

Another popular attraction for kids is **Deep Sea World**, *North Queensferry, Fife, Tel. 01383/411-411; open April through June and September daily from 10:00am to 6:00pm, July and August daily from 10:00am to 6:30pm, and November through March daily from 11:00am to 5:00pm; admission is £6.15 for adults, £4.25 for seniors and students, and £3.75 for children.* Scotland's award-winning national aquarium is a lot of fun, and interesting too. You'll be on a moving walkway that takes you through an acrylic tunnel among the fishy subjects of your viewing pleasure. The section that takes you among the sharks particularly mesmerized me. It brings you right up close and personal with them. You'll also see scads of other aquatic life, from eels and piranhas to stingrays and varieties of fish in about every conceivable color. The trip also gives the fish a "birds-eye" view of you. You kind of have the feeling *you* are on display for *them*.

NIGHTLIFE & ENTERTAINMENT
Pubs

The pub scene in Edinburgh is quite active, and there are many pubs to choose from. Here are a few of the best:

THE ABBOTSFORD PUB, *3 Rose Street, Edinburgh. Tel. 0131/225-5276. Open daily from 11:00am to 11:00pm. Food served from 11:00am to 2:15pm, and from 6:00pm to 10:00pm.*

If you are looking for a pub with a Victorian feel, then this is the place for you to go. Located on Rose Street in New Town, the Abbotsford features a circular bar and a fine Victorian décor that will make you feel you've walked back in time 100 years or so. The restaurant upstairs serves good pub grub, and an enjoyable atmosphere downstairs, where you'll mingle with tourists and local business men and women.

THE ANTIQUARY, *72-78 Stephen Street, Edinburgh. Tel. 0131/225-2858. Open Monday through Wednesday from 11:30am to 12:30am, Thursday through Saturday from 11:30am to 1:30am, and on Sunday from 11:30am to midnight.*

The Antiquary is highly popular with a wide range of clientele, from students to locals to tourists and businessmen and businesswomen. It has been described as possessing a bohemian and avant-garde feel, and I have to agree with that. The Antiquary has also earned a good reputation for their pub grub, which is served daily from 11:30am to 2:00pm (until 2:30pm on Sunday).

BANNERMAN'S PUB, *212 Cowgate, Edinburgh. Tel. 0131/556-3254. Open Monday through Saturday from noon to 1:00am, and Sunday from 11:00am to midnight.*

You'll find a vibrant and boisterous crowd at Bannerman's, especially on the weekends. Bannerman's is a large, vaulted bar that has been able to maintain a close and friendly atmosphere. You'll meet everything from rugby-playing college students to businessmen to tourists to an occasional travel guide writer here. On Wednesday and Saturday evenings you'll have the opportunity to sample the musical fare of some of the "local lads" who have come to make their mark in the musical world. You'll hear jazz and rhythm and blues on Wednesday, and rock music on Saturday.

CAFÉ ROYAL CIRCLE BAR, *17 West Register Street, Edinburgh. Tel. 0131/556-1884. Open Monday through Thursday from 11:00am to midnight, Friday and Saturday from 11:00am to 1:00am, and Sunday from 11:00am to 11:00pm.*

This is one of the most pleasant and well-known of Edinburgh's pubs. You'll get a distinct Victorian feel here, with lots (lots) of people, especially on the weekends and during the summer months. During the rugby and soccer seasons, it takes on the feel of a sports bar, with the large screen TV garnering lots of attention. The bar is well stocked with a wide variety of malt whiskies and international beers.

DEACON BRODIE'S, *435 Lawnmarket Street, Edinburgh. Tel. 0131/225-6531. Open daily from 11:00am to 11:00pm.*

Deacon Brodie's is a small bar honoring one of Edinburgh's most infamous sons: William Brodie. Deacon Brodie was an upstanding citizen by day and a burglar by night, often stealing from the homes of friends and associates. The good Deacon was eventually caught and hanged on gallows that he had several years before perfected. The main draw to the pub is the name (and its close proximity to Brodie's Close, where Brodie lived). Otherwise it's just a bar that serves drinks and pub grub. I'm not overly impressed with the ambience, although it always seems to be busy, so it would probably allow you to meet a few locals if that is your aim.

DRUM AND MONKEY, *80 Queen Street, Edinburgh. Tel. 0131/538-8111, Fax 0131/226-9932. Open Monday through Wednesday from 11:00am to midnight, Friday through Saturday from 11:00am to 1:00am.*

The Drum and Monkey is a popular bar with businessmen and women at the end of a hard day's work. It is more of an upscale bar than many of the others in the city, and its patrons seem to generally be more of the middle-aged crowd. There is a restaurant downstairs that is quite popular, so you may begin your evening in the bar, retire to the restaurant for dinner, and then close the evening out with a nightcap back upstairs.

A local jazz band plays on Saturday afternoons and the place can be pretty crowded.

FINNEGAN'S WAKE, *9B Victoria Street, Edinburgh. Tel. 0131/226-3816. Open Monday through Saturday from noon to 1:00am, and Sunday from 12:30pm to 1:00am.*

Here's your honest-to-goodness Irish pub. Once you walk in, you'll recognize the knick-knacks on the walls to be Irish. The atmosphere here is always lively, especially in the evenings when the live band plays traditional Irish music beginning around 10:00pm. And yes, you can certainly get Guinness and Bushmills here, along with a wide variety of other whiskies and beers.

Theaters

THE STAND COMEDY CLUB, *5 York Place, Edinburgh. Tel. 0131/558-7272. £1-5. Open nightly.*

The Stand Comedy Club is *the* place to go for comedy in Edinburgh. Nightly shows feature everything from beginning comedians (Sunday and Monday nights), to Connoisseur Evenings featuring established comedians (most Tuesday evenings), to a night set aside specifically for gays (the middle Tuesday of every month, it's called *Out on Tuesday*).

THE FESTIVAL THEATRE, *13-29 Nicholson Street, Edinburgh. Tel. 0131/662-1112. Open Monday through Saturday from 11:00am to 8:00pm, and Sunday from 4:00pm to 8:00pm. Admission ranges from £10 to £50, depending on the opera.*

If you attended an opera in Edinburgh in years gone by, then you probably attended it at the Empire Theatre. The Empire has been renovated and has changed its name to The Festival Theatre. It is the venue for all major operas that tour in Edinburgh. The Festival Theatre is a busy place during the Edinburgh Festival, as it is a major venue for productions. The **Royal Scottish National Orchestra** also calls the Festival Theatre home.

THE PLAYHOUSE THEATRE, *Leith Walk, Edinburgh. Tel. 0131/557-2590. Admission ranges from £10 to £100.*

The Playhouse Theatre is the place to go if you want to see touring Broadway (or London) plays. It holds 3,000 guests, and serves as a marvelous venue for these top-quality performances. In addition to these fine shows, you'll be able to sample ballet, rock concerts, and special screening of films.

QUEEN'S HALL, *Clerk Street, Edinburgh. Tel. 0131/668-2019. The box office is open 10:00am to 5:00pm Monday through Saturday, and Sunday from 6:00pm to 8:00pm. Admission ranges from £2 to £25.*

Queen's Hall is the venue for the **Scottish Chamber Orchestra**, and it also hosts a wide range of musical performers, mostly of the chamber orchestra or choral variety. Queen's Hall is a converted church, and offers comfortable seating for upwards of 800 spectators. The hall is also used for a number of school musical performances.

THE ROYAL LYCEUM, *Grindlay Street, Edinburgh. Tel. 0131/248-2848. Box office is open 10:00am to 7:00pm Monday through Friday. Admission ranges from £1 to £16.*

This smallish theater features many of the local plays and performances. It books a pretty full schedule, so there is usually something to see, no matter what time of year you are here.

THE TRAVERSE THEATRE, *10 Cambridge Street, Edinburgh. Tel. 0131/228-1404. Box Office open Monday from 10:00pm to 6:00pm, and Tuesday through Sunday from 10:00am to 11:00pm. Admission ranges from £4 to £8.*

The Traverse Theatre has gained a reputation for excellence in recent years for the wonderful fresh new talent they have introduced on their stage. Whether it is dance, music, comedy or drama, the theater has been aggressive in seeking and showcasing top new talent, particularly those who call Edinburgh or Scotland home.

SPORTS & RECREATION
Angling
If you'd like to do a little angling (fishing) while in Edinburgh, head out to **Markle Fisheries**, *Markle, East Linton, East Lothian, Tel. 01620/861-213.* While a little contrived, it gives you the opportunity to try your luck at fly fishing at any of three lochs.

Cycling
You can rent (hire) bicycles in the following shops in Edinburgh:
• **Central Cycle Hire**, *11 Lochrin Place, Edinburgh. Tel. 0131/228-6333*
• **Edinburgh Cycle Hire**, *Blackfriar Street, Edinburgh. Tel. 0131/556-5560*
• **Sandy Gilchrist Cycles**, *1 Cadzow Place, Abbeyhill, Edinburgh. Tel. 0131/ 652-1760*

Football
American football in Scotland? Absolutely! The Scottish Claymores are a professional football team in the NFL Europe league. They play their games in Edinburgh and at Hampden Park in Glasgow. For more information, call *0131/478-7200.*

Go Karts
If you'd like to try your hand at go karts, here are a few places where you can try your skill:

• **Capital Karts Limited**, *Middle Pier, Granton Square, Edinburgh. Tel. 0131/551-5511*
• **Racing Karts**, *Arrol Square, Deans Industrial Estate, Livingston. Tel. 01506/410-123*

Golf

There are about two dozen golf courses within about a thirty-minute drive of downtown Edinburgh, many more if you're willing to drive a little further. Here are a few:
• **Bathgate Golf Club**, *Edinburgh Road, Bathgate, West Lothian. Tel. 01506/630-505*
• **Deer Park Golf and Country Club**, *Golf Course Road, Livingston, West Lothian. Tel. 01506/431-037*
• **Gifford Golf Club**, *Edinburgh Road, Gifford, East Lothian. Tel. 01620/810-267*
• **Greenburn Golf Club**, *6 Greenburn Road, Fauldhouse. Tel. 01501/770-292*
• **Gullane Golf Club**, *West Links Road, Gullane. Tel. 01620/842-255*
• **Kings Acre Golf Course**, *Lasswade, Midlothian. Tel. 0131/663-3456*
• **Lothianburn Golf Club**, *106A Biggar Road, Edinburgh. Tel. 0131/445-5067*

Horseback Riding

If you'd like to do a little horseback riding while in the Edinburgh area, try **Pentland Hills Icelandics**, *Windy Fowl Farm, Carlops, East Linton, Tel. 01968/661-095.*

Horse Racing

If you've got horse racing in your blood, stop by **Musselburgh Racecourse**, *Linkfield Road, Musselburgh, East Lothian. Tel. 0131/665-2859.*

Sailing and Windsurfing

If you'd like to try a little sailing or canoeing, stop by **Port Edgar Sailing School**, *Shore Road, South Queensferry, Tel. 0131/331-3330.*

EXCURSIONS & DAY TRIPS

Edinburgh's relatively central location in the country allows you to use it as a base for a lot of touring. Access into and out of the city is generally pretty straight forward, and so using it as a base makes sense. Following are a few day trips that might be worth your time.

ST. ANDREWS

If you are a golfer, you are of course familiar with **St. Andrews**. Located about an hour's drive northeast of Edinburgh, this golf Mecca beckons golfers from all over the world. Golf has been played here for nearly 600 years, and it appears that it is well on its way to being played here for the next 600 years. The courses of St. Andrews have hosted some of the most famous people in the world through the centuries, including Mary Queen of Scots, Ben Crenshaw, Tom Watson, Sam Snead, Jack Nicklaus, Bobby Jones, Seve Ballesteros, and others.

But St. Andrews is not just about golf. It is a pretty seaside town that offers a few ruins to prowl through and a number of shops to spend the day in. You'll be able to stop in at the **University of St. Andrews**, an institution with nearly 600 years of history. The ruins of **St. Andrews Cathedral** and the **Castle of St. Andrews** make for an interesting visit.

ARRIVALS & DEPARTURES

By Bus

Buses arrive at **St. Andrews Bus Station**, *off City Road, St. Andrews, Tel. 01334/474-238.*

By Car

There are several ways to get to St. Andrews from Edinburgh and each wends through the beautiful Scottish countryside. I prefer to take the one that hugs the shoreline of the Firth of Forth for awhile. To take that route, follow the A90 north to the A921, then proceed to the A915 and head northeast to St. Andrews. There are plenty of signposts to point the way.

By Train

There is no train service directly to St. Andrews, but the train does go to Leuchars, eight miles from St. Andrews. Buses leave every half hour throughout the day for St. Andrews. It will cost you about £6 for the one-hour train ride.

ORIENTATION

For its huge reputation, St. Andrews is not a large town, measuring roughly one mile by one-half mile. It is laid out in a roughly north-south, east-west plan. The Old Course is at the west end of town, St. Andrews University is in the middle of town, and the ruins of St. Andrews Castle and Cathedral are at the east end of town.

Tourist Information
• **St. Andrews Tourist Information Centre,** *Market Street, St. Andrews. Tel. 01334/472-021*

GETTING AROUND TOWN

By Bicycle
The streets are narrow in St. Andrews, and the traffic is heavy, especially during the summer months. If you do choose to bicycle, be careful.

By Car
I think it best to park your car and walk most places in town. The traffic can be bad, and it's a pretty compact town.

By Foot
This is the best way to see St. Andrews and get a feel for the town. Its pleasant shop-lined streets make for a nice stroll. Even if you decide to go from the Old Course at the west end of town to the ruins of the castle and cathedral at the east end, the walk should take you no more than 20 or 25 minutes (depending on how often you stop along the way).

WHERE TO STAY

OLD COURSE HOTEL, *Old Station Road, St. Andrews. Tel. 01334/ 474-371, Fax 01334/477-668; E-mail: reservations@oldcoursehotel.co.uk; Website: www.oldcoursehotel.co.uk. 125 Rooms. Rates: £215-240 single; £215-240 per room double; £295-600 suite. Children under 11 stay free in their parents' room. Amex, MasterCard and Visa are accepted.*

If you are a golfer, St. Andrews is Mecca, and the Old Course hotel is the hotel for Mecca. This is a classically elegant hotel, and offers many amenities you would expect from a five-star hotel.

First of all, the public rooms in the Old Course Hotel are luxurious, bordering on opulent. There are several resident lounges to choose from; my favorite is the Library, where you can sink into a comfortable overstuffed leather chair or couch and contemplate your surroundings, discuss your latest round of golf, or strategize for your next round. Many of the pieces of furniture in the public rooms are antiques, and add a certain air of elegance to the atmosphere. I was particularly impressed with a number of old oil paintings of the Old Course, Scottish landscapes and various golf scenes. It is quite enjoyable to pull up a chair in the lobby and measure the excitement of newly arriving guests – it is electrifying. All are excited and anxious. Be sure and listen for accents and languages. I sat for 15 minutes, and heard American (we really do have a bit of a twang), Australian, English, German, Italian, Japanese, French, and several languages I couldn't identify.

The bedrooms are quite nice, as you might imagine. They are not extremely large, but they do feature top-quality furnishings. The rooms at the back of the hotel are the best, as they overlook the 17th fairway (the famous "Road Hole") on the Old Course. The bathrooms are also elegant, with upgraded fixtures and marble flooring and tubs.

There are several bars and restaurants on site (see the *Where to Eat* section), that will provide everything from light informal snacks to full-course meals. In addition, the Old Course Hotel offers a number of amenities, including a health spa, massage room, steam room, swimming pool, a beauty salon, and a pro shop. For all its loveliness and close proximity to the courses, I found the staff at the Old Course Hotel to be a bit impressed with their press clippings. They were supremely efficient but had a tendency toward snootiness. For the price, I'd suggest any of the other hotels or B&Bs I have listed here.

RUFFLETS COUNTRY HOUSE HOTEL, *Strathkinness Low Road, St. Andrews. Tel. 01334/472-594, Fax 01334/478-703; E-mail: rufflets@standrews.co.uk; Website: www.standrews.co.uk/hotels/rufflets. 25 Rooms. Rates: £70-90 single; £60-95 per person double; £85-90 per person for the Rose Cottages. All major credit cards accepted.*

Well, I fell in love with Rufflets Country House Hotel. This 1920s-era country house is a delightful and pleasant place to stay. It is one of those hotels that stands out in your memory because of the facility, the staff and the grounds. Elegance is the one word that comes to mind when I consider Rufflets. Whether you are nestled into the depths of a comfy leather chair in the drawing room or sitting on the patio taking in the lovely gardens, you'll feel a touch of class. You'll enjoy resting for a spell in the Old Library, a quirky room for visiting, card playing, or golf review sessions. It is really a disservice to call the gardener's handiwork here mere *gardens*. The gardens here are breathtaking, awe-inspiring works of art! And set amidst the 10 acres of the estate, they are beautiful indeed.

The bedrooms are wonderful. Large and well lit, each room is individually decorated and features antiques and designer wallpaper. The rooms are decorated in spring-time colors: lilacs, greens, yellows and roses. The rooms at the back of the property are the best, as they get the full effect of the gardens and grounds. Each room has a nice large tile bathroom with the latest fixtures. There are other rooms separate from the main house called the Rose Cottages. The rooms in these apartments are not quite as large as those in the main house, but the additional privacy is nice. There are no elevators in the main house, but there is wheelchair access in the one-story Rose Cottages. There is one restaurant and one bar on site. The restaurant is renowned for its fine cuisine (see the *Where to*

Eat section). The bar features over 100 varieties of malt whisky and a bartender who will be delighted to pick just the right one for you.

Rufflets Country House is not in downtown St. Andrews, but rather a 15-minute or so drive out into the country. Be sure and call for directions, as it is a bit difficult to find without them. All but two of the bedrooms are non-smoking, although smoking is allowed in certain parts of the public rooms.

Selected as one of my Best Places to Stay – see Chapter 12.

SHANDON HOUSE B&B, *10 Murray Place, St Andrews. Tel. 01334/ 472-412, Fax 01334/478-126; E-mail: paulterris@yahoo.com. 6 Rooms. Rates: £20-27 single; £20-27 per person double. Breakfast is included in the rate. MasterCard and Visa accepted.*

Sheila Terris is a delightful and conscientious hostess, and Shandon House B&B is a turn-of-the-century Victorian townhouse that has been updated and renovated for your staying pleasure. All the bedrooms are large, and the tall ceilings with their original ornate plasterwork gives each room an expansive and roomy feeling. The furnishings are all new and comfortable. Breakfast is served in the dining room, and Sheila shows she is a talented cook as well as a pleasant hostess.

Shandon House B&B is located in a small alcove off the main drag in St. Andrews. If you have come to St. Andrews to golf (a few do), then you'll be glad to know you are quite close to the courses. Parking is available for guests. Mrs. Terris requests that guests observe their no-smoking rule in the house. Shandon House B&B is incredibly popular with golfers due to its rate as well as its close proximity to all the St. Andrews golf courses.

WHERE TO EAT

THE ROAD HOLE GRILL, *Old Station Road, St. Andrews. Tel. 01334/ 474-371, Fax 01334/477-668. £30-40. Open daily from 7:00pm to 10:00pm. Amex, MasterCard and Visa are accepted.*

The Road Hole Grill is the elegant dining restaurant associated with the Old Course Hotel. Linen tablecloths, crystal and china and a softly lit room overlooking the Old Course all add to the fine meals you'll experience here. The restaurant has won numerous awards, including two AA rosettes and *A Taste of Scotland* recognition. Try the shellfish bisque with dill aiolis or any of the exceptional beef or lamb dishes. I find this restaurant a bit pricey, especially when compared to its competitors in the area. But the views are nice, especially if you are a golfer.

RUFFLETS COUNTRY HOUSE RESTAURANT, *Strathkinness Low Road, St. Andrews. Tel. 01334/472-594, Fax 01334/478-703. £25-30 for two-courses, £29-35 for 3 courses. Open daily from 7:00pm to 9:00pm, and for Sunday lunch from 12:30pm to 2:00pm. Lighter, "bar lunches" are available daily from 12:30pm to 2:00pm. All major credit cards accepted.*

As you'd expect in a country-house hotel, you'll find traditional Scottish fare served in the Rufflets Country House Restaurant. According to the dining room manager, the restaurant features a "modern, contemporary decorating motif in traditional style." Bold burgundy and gold colors are accented by candlelight and crystal, and provide an elegant setting for the exquisite meals that are served here.

But don't just take my word for it – this is an award-winning restaurant, with its most notable awards being two AA rosettes and recognition by *A Taste of Scotland*. The menu is extensive and changes frequently, but you might find such delightful offerings as chargrilled collop of monkfish served in spinach leaves and saffron potatoes glazed with crab hollandaise. If you're not into seafood, try the breast of chicken with asparagus spears, haggis and sweet peppers with straw potatoes and cream. For dessert, hot sticky toffee pudding with coddled cream is a favorite.

If you begin your meal before it gets dark (you probably will), you'll be gazing out on the marvelous gardens and landscaped grounds. Smart casual is the preferred attire for the Rufflets Country House Restaurant.

THE SANDS, *Old Station Road, St. Andrews. Tel. 01334/474-371, Fax 01334/477-668. £10-20. Open daily from 10:00am to 11:00pm. Amex, MasterCard and Visa are accepted.*

The new brasserie-style restaurant at the Old Course Hotel provides all-day dining in a pleasant and relaxed atmosphere. You'll be able to feast on an array of sandwiches, soups and salads. Like the fine-dining restaurant at the Old Course Hotel (The Road-Hole Grill) it's a little pricey, although the food is good and filling and the ambience is nice.

TUDOR INN, *129 North Street, St. Andrews. Tel. 01334/474-322. £7-12. Open daily from noon to 9:30pm. Amex, MasterCard and Visa accepted.*

You'll find wholesome Scottish fare throughout the day at the Tudor Inn in St. Andrews. You'll also find s simple pub atmosphere here. The menu offers a range of selections from roast beef to grilled salmon. The surroundings aren't great, but the food is filling and good.

SEEING THE SIGHTS

Golf has been played seriously in St. Andrews since the 1400s, and kings and queens (of kingdoms *and* the golf world) have tried their hand on the courses at St. Andrews. There are seven courses at St. Andrews, the most famous of which is the venerable **Old Course**, which has been challenging (and frustrating) many generations of golfers. The course has been described as deceitful and capricious, vile and villainous. With such anomalies on the course as the **Valley of Sin**, you can understand why it is such an invitation to so many. Bunkers (there are *only* 112) and hollows, swales and depressions, fairways that seem to delight in scattering well-placed shots, bunkers with names like **Coffin**, **Grave**, and **Hell** and undulating greens all conspire to make this one of the most intriguing and beguiling courses in the world. It has hosted the British Open 25 times, and the Walker Cup eight times.

All the courses in St. Andrews are owned by the city, and tee-times are available on a ballot basis. Ballots are drawn the day before you wish to play. If you're lucky you'll draw out on the Old Course. But if not, there are six other gems in the tiara of St. Andrews golf crown: the **New Course** (opened in 1896), **Jubilee** (1897), **Eden** (1914), **Strathtyrum** (1993) and **Balgrove** (opened in 1972 as a children's training course). The **Dukes** course, two miles away in Craigtoun Park, is also considered part of St. Andrews golf complex. If you wish to play the Old Course, you'll need a current handicap card or a letter of introduction from a golf club.

University of St. Andrews, *North Street, St. Andrews, Tel. 01334/462-000*, is the oldest university in Scotland, and the third oldest in the United Kingdom. Established in 1411, St. Andrews has been a place of learning for over half a millennium. You may either wander about the campus on your own self-guided tour, or guided tours run twice daily at 11:00am and 2:30pm (£3 per person), and leave from the International Office on Butts Wynd.

St. Andrews Cathedral and Priory, *Off Pends Road, St. Andrews, Tel. 01334/472-563; Visitor Centre open April through September Monday through Saturday from 9:30am to 6:00pm, Sunday from noon to 6:00pm, October through March Monday through Saturday from 9:30am to 4:30pm, and Sunday from 2:00pm to 4:00pm; admission is £1.50 for adults, £1 for seniors and 75p for children.* Your first impression of St. Andrews Cathedral will be of its size. And indeed, it is large – at one time the largest cathedral in Scotland. It was officially founded in 1160, but the building whose ruins you see today wasn't completed and consecrated until 1318, under the watchful eye of none other than Robert the Bruce. It had nearly 250 glorious years before it became the target of the Reformation and of John Knox's followers, who ransacked the cathedral and began its decline. The cathedral overlooks the harbor and certainly must have been a grand place in its heyday.

Near the cathedral is a tall stone structure known as **St. Rule's Tower**. St. Rule's Tower was part of the abbey that formerly inhabited this site. You can climb the 150-ish stairs (I kept losing count!) to fabulous views. It is a great place to really see the T-shaped layout of the cathedral and appreciate how large the cathedral once was. The tower is of ancient origin, and has stood the winds of time, political and religious turmoil for over 850 years.

St. Andrews Castle, *corner of The Scores and North Castle Streets, St. Andrews; open April through September Monday through Saturday from 9:30am* *to 6:00pm, Sunday from noon to 6:00pm, October through March Monday through Saturday from 9:30am to 4:30pm, and Sunday from 2:00pm to 4:00pm; admission is £2.30 for adults, 1.80 for seniors and £1.50 for children.* There isn't much left of St. Andrews Castle these days. Sitting on a small outcropping jutting into the North Sea, the castle must have once been a well-protected fortress. Three sides of the castle were protected by drop-offs into the sea, and the fourth side had a moat running in front of it. The castle has been here in one form or another since the beginning of the 13th century, although the scant remains you see today are from the 16th century.

Sinister and dastardly goings-on occurred in and around St. Andrews Castle. In 1546, Cardinal David Beaton decreed that Reformer George Wishart be burnt at the stake for heresy. The edict was carried out in front of the castle. A few months later, some of Wishart's friends and fellow Reformers dressed as stonemasons and got into the castle, where they stabbed the cardinal to death. His body was suspended from a window of the castle by an arm and a leg for a spell, after which he was cast into the bottle dungeon.

SPORTS & RECREATION
Golf
Of course you came to play golf at St. Andrews. Here's a little information about the St. Andrews courses:
• **The Old Course**, greens fees are £55. Par 72, 6,566 yards, handicap certificate required. Tee times are by ballot the day before.
• **Balgove**, par 30, 9-hole course for beginners and youth.
• **Eden**, green fees £20, par 70, 6,112 yards.
• **Jubilee**, green fees £25, par 72, 6,805 yards.
• **New Course**, green fees £25, par 71, 6,604 yards.
• **Strathtyrum**, green fees £15, par 69, 5,094 yards.
• **Dukes Course**, *Craigtoun Park, Fife. Tel. 01334/474-371.* Par 72, 7,110 yards. Considered part of St. Andrews, it is about two miles from the rest of the courses.

DUNDEE
Dundee is a busy city 60 miles northwest of Edinburgh. It is Scotland's third largest city, with a population that exceeds 190,000. Almost from its inception, Dundee has been a city that focused primarily on industry. From the whaling industry to jute and flax production to ship building, the citizens of Dundee always seemed to know how to make a buck (pound).

ARRIVALS & DEPARTURES

By Bus
Buses arrive at the **Dundee Bus Station**, *Seagate Street, Dundee, Tel. 01382/228-345*. Buses arrive here from Aberdeen, Edinburgh and Glasgow.

By Car
Dundee is located about 60 miles northwest of Edinburgh on the A90/M90 and 70 miles south of Aberdeen on the A90.

By Train
Trains arrive from Edinburgh, Glasgow and Aberdeen at the **Dundee Train Station**, *South Union Street, Dundee, Tel. 01382/228-046*.

SEEING THE SIGHTS

There are several maritime sights that might interest you while in Dundee. Let's begin with **HMS Unicorn**, *Victoria Dock, Dundee, Tel. 01382/200-900; open daily from Easter through September from 10:00am to 5:00pm; admission is £3 for adults, £2 for seniors and children*. When you visit the *HMS Unicorn*, you'll have the opportunity to walk aboard the oldest British ship still afloat. Built in 1824, the *HMS Unicorn* is in remarkably good shape considering it is over 175 years old. All four decks of the *Unicorn* are open to the public, and you'll enjoy seeing the various displays which share the history of the ship and a bit about the lives of the men who sailed on her. The ship bristles with 46 18-pound cannon, but they were never fired in anger. Check out the ornately carved unicorn masthead. If you've brought the kids along, this is a great place to stop.

About a half mile west of the *Unicorn* and on the other side of the Tay Bridge is another bit of Dundee maritime history. Alongside the banks of the Firth of Tay is **Discovery Point**, *Tayside, Dundee, Tel. 01382/201-245; open April through October Monday through Saturday from 10:00am to 5:00pm and Sunday from 11:00am to 5:00pm, November through March Monday through Saturday from 10:00am to 4:00pm and Sunday from 11:00am to 4:00pm; admission is £5 for adults, £3.75 for seniors and £3.25 for children, and a family ticket is available for £15*. Discovery Point is a flashy visitor center that focuses on the *Royal Research Ship Discovery*, which carried Captain Robert Falcon Scott and his crew to history in the Antarctica. The three-masted ship was built in 1901 in Dundee's shipyards, and has been restored to its former glory. But as you view the various exhibits, you'll understand very well that despite its gleaming brass and polished wood, great hardships, trials and tribulations were faced by its captain and crew.

You'll have an opportunity to walk on the ship that braved massive ice floes and bone-chilling conditions, but brought its crew back safely. Guides tell the story of the ship and her crew. Their tales are lively and will keep you entertained for quite awhile. The **Polarama** exhibit has a number of interactive activities for you and your children to participate in. Since I didn't know a lot about the Antarctica, it was a great learning opportunity for me. The stop here at Discovery Point is definitely worth the price of admission.

About one mile north of Discovery Point on Albert Square is the **McManus Art Galleries and Museum**, *Albert Square, Dundee, Tel. 01382/ 434-000; open Monday from 11:00am to 5:00pm and Tuesday through Saturday from 10:00am to 5:00pm; admission is free*. The massive Victorian building that houses the McManus Art Galleries and Museum is impressive in and of itself. A fine curved staircase and Gothic influences all work together to create a pleasant sight. But if you like either art galleries or museums, then you'll be very glad you stopped by.

The museum traces Scottish history from the earliest days through the Picts, Scoti, Britons and Romans, bringing you up to the present day. Along the way, you'll see ancient Pictish stones and various and sundry artifacts from each of the civilizations that once called Scotland home. Upstairs in the Albert Room, you'll even have the opportunity to view a number of ancient musical instruments. The art gallery features a number of fine paintings by some of Scotland's top artists, including MacTaggart, Raeburn and Raansay.

McManus Art Galleries and Museum is a very active participant in children's exhibits, and they change constantly. If you've brought your children along, be sure and call to see what special activity is being held for children. In the past, children have been delighted with such activities as puppet shows, fantasy castles, interactive Tam O' Shanter tales, etc. There is certain to be something scheduled that will be of interest to your young ones.

NEAR DUNDEE

Four miles east of Dundee is the village of Broughty Ferry. In the 15th century, a castle was built here to protect the Firth of Tay. That castle still stands straight and tall, and is worth a look. **Broughty Castle**, *Broughty Ferry, Tel. 01382/776-121; open Monday through Thursday and Saturday from 10:00am to 1:00pm and from 2:00pm to 5:00pm, from July through September it is also open Sunday from 2:00pm to 5:00pm; admission is free*. The castle is a stout four-story monolith that stares silently at all who pass. Inside, you'll find a fine collection of exhibits on the history of the area. It also has a small but nice collection of weapons and armor. Take a moment and walk to the top of the ramparts, where you'll be treated to wonderful views over the Firth of Tay.

While you're in this part of the country, you might as well stop by one of the most impressive castles in the country. Leave Dundee going north on the A90 toward for Aberdeen. After about five miles, head northwest on the A928 to **Glamis Castle**, *Glamis, Tel. 01307/840-242; open April through October 10:30am to 4:45pm daily; admission is £5.20 for adults, £4 for seniors and £3.50 for children.* First of all, a pronunciation lesson is in order: the name of the castle is pronounced *Gloms*. Glamis Castle is the childhood home of the Queen Mother (Queen Elizabeth), and the birthplace of Princess Margaret. The castle looks like a fairytale dream castle on steroids: turrets and flags and cupolas and towers are everywhere! Most of the castle you see today was built in the latter half of the 15th century, although it is said that there are parts that have been here since the 11th century. Unlike the royal getaway in Royal Deeside (Balmoral Castle), you are allowed in to a number of the rooms at Glamis.

A guided tour takes you through the castle, and the first stop is the dining room. Here you'll see a massive silver ship, wedding present of the 13th Earl of Strathmore. (The current owner of the castle is the 18th Earl of Strathmore, a direct descendant of the first Earl of Strathmore. He is also the Queen Mother's grand-nephew.) Other rooms on the tour include the crypt whose 12-foot walls supposedly house a "lost" room. It is said that there are more windows on the outside of the castle than can be accounted for on the inside. Legend has it that one of the former owners of the castle dared to play cards with Satan on the Sabbath. It cost him his life: he was supposedly sealed up in the room, doomed to forever play cards with the devil.

The drawing room was particularly interesting to me. The plasterwork is original to the room, and has been here since the early 1600s. Around the rooms you'll see the portraits of a number of those who lived in Glamis. Other rooms you can tour include the Billiard Room, Family Chapel, King Malcolm's Room and the Royal Apartments. The Royal Apartments contain several interesting items, including a magnificent gilded four-poster bed that was a wedding gift from Queen Elizabeth's mother.

While here, you might also have the opportunity to see one of the many ghosts that are thought to live here. One is the *Gray Lady*, who was burned to death for witchcraft in 1540 at the insistence of James V. Another is the 4th Earl of Crawford, known as Beardie Crawford. He was unfortunately playing in the same card game with the devil and the Earl of Strathmore, and has been doomed to wander the halls forever. Other assorted and sundry ghosts appear from time to time, including the *White Lady of the Clock Tower*. Her story is unknown, although it must be quite the story.

If you want more tourist information in this area, contact **Angus and Dundee Tourist Information Centre**, *4 City Square, Dundee, Tel. 01382/ 227-723.* And if you'd like to hit the links in these parts, your choice is **Carnoustie Golf Links**, *Carnoustie, Angus. Tel. 01241/853-789.*

LINLITHGOW

Just down the road from Edinburgh is the market town of **Linlithgow**. Linlithgow's main claim to fame is that the palace that Mary Queen of Scots was born in is within their city limits. For tourist information, contact **Linlithgow Tourist Information Centre**, *Burgh Halls, The Cross, Linlithgow, Tel. 01560/844-600.*

ARRIVALS & DEPARTURES

By Bus

Buses leave for Stirling daily from Glasgow's **Buchanan Street Station**, *North Hanover Street, Glasgow, Tel. 0141/332-7133, Fax 0141/332-9191* and Edinburgh's **St. Andrew Square Bus Station**, *St. Andrew Square, Edinburgh, Tel. 0990/050-5050.* Buses arrive at **Linlithgow Bus Station**, *The Cross, Linlithgow, Tel. 01506/844-600.*

By Car

Linlithgow is just off the M9 18 miles west of Edinburgh. Watch for the signposts on the M9.

By Train

The **Linlithgow Train Station**, *Tel. 01560/842-575,* is located on the south side of town, and is on the main line between Glasgow and Edinburgh.

SEEING THE SIGHTS

Linlithgow Castle, *Linlithgow, Tel. 01506/842-896; open April through September daily from 9:30am to 6:30pm, and from October through March Monday through Saturday from 9:30am to 4:30pm, and Sunday from 2:00pm to 4:30pm; admission is £2.50 for adults, £1.90 for seniors and £1 for children.* In its heyday, Linlithgow Castle was one of the finest castles in not only Scotland but also in the United Kingdom. In 1542 when it was about 100 years old, it served as the birthplace for the babe that was to become Mary Queen of Scots. After her return to Scotland, Mary visited Linlithgow Castle numerous times, always finding it a peaceful and pleasant place.

Not much has been done to renovate the castle, but with a little imagination, you can easily see what a stunning palace it must have been.

You can almost imagine the lovely fountain in the inner courtyard as it flowed with wine for the wedding of James V and Mary of Guise, parents of Mary Queen of Scots. A small museum on the second floor has some interesting objects, including some old wine bottles that have survived more or less intact for three hundred years.

The castle is quite extensive, and has lots of interesting nooks and intriguing crannies to explore. Placards placed throughout the castle give you the history, architectural information, etc. One of my favorite things to do is to ascend a spiral staircase (121 steps) to get gorgeous views of Linlithgow Loch and the surrounding countryside.

It is said that at least two ghosts haunt Linlithgow Castle. The first is Mary of Guise, who is said to still be waiting patiently for the return of her husband, James V. The other is identified only as the *Blue Lady*. It seems she appeared to James IV a few yards away at St. Michael's and warned him not to engage the English in battle. He ignored the warning, and rode to his death at Flodden Field in 1513. She has been seen occasionally since then, wandering the halls at Linlithgow.

St. Michael's Parish Church, *Linlithgow, Tel. 01560/842-188; open daily from 10:00am to noon and from 1:30pm to 3:30pm; admission is free.* As you walk up to Linlithgow Castle, you can't help but pass – and notice – St. Michael's. It has been standing strong and tall as a place of worship for Scotsmen since the mid-13th century. It has lasted through sieges and armies, including a short stint as a stable for Oliver Cromwell's horses (a favorite insult of his). Its greatest insult, however, may be the unfortunate aluminum spire that graces it. Incongruous at best, it really ruins the effect of this marvelous old church.

PRACTICAL INFORMATION FOR EDINBURGH

Automobile Association – AA

The **Automobile Association**, *Fanum House, 18/22 Melville Street, Edinburgh, Tel. 0990/444-444 (for information), and 0800/887-7666 (if you need assistance),* can help out if you run into problems getting your car to start, or if you need to be towed. If you are not a member and need assistance, call the first number and you can become a member immediately for £90.

Banks

Most banks in Edinburgh have an ATM machine either outside their main doorways or just inside the bank. The ATMs are part of the Cirrus and Plus international networks. Be sure to check with your bank to see if your personal identification number (PIN) will work on international ATMs. Most international ATMs only accept four-digit PINs.

Business Hours

Businesses are generally open from 9:00am to 5:30pm or 6:00pm in Scotland, although from a practical standpoint, most stores open at 9:30am or 10:00am. The exceptions to this rule are bakeries and Newsagents – they are usually open at 7:00am. On Friday evenings, many stores stay open until 7:00pm.

Embassies & Consulates

- **American Consulate**, *3 Regent Terrace, Edinburgh. Tel. 0131/344-3250*
- **Canadian Embassy**, *3 George Street, Edinburgh EH2 2HT. Tel. 0131/220-4333*

Emergencies

Remember this: dialing **999** in Scotland = dialing 911 in the States. Use it in the event of any emergency where you need assistance from the police, fire department, or the medical community.

Exchanging Money

You can exchange money at banks, most post offices, larger hotels, and at change booths at the Edinburgh Airport.

Laundry Service

As you might suspect in a city Edinburgh's size, there are a number of laundromats and dry cleaners around the city. Here are a few laundromats:

- **Capital Launderette**, *208 Dalkeith Road, Edinburgh. Tel. 0131/667-0825*
- **Clean Gear Laundry Service**, *15 Mayfield Road, Edinburgh. Tel. 0131/660-6670*
- **The Launderette**, *13 Radcliffe Terrace, Edinburgh. Tel. 0131/667-0248*
- **Luxury Speed Wash**, *85 Easter Road, Edinburgh. Tel. 0131/661-7146*
- **Park View Laundry**, *6 Peffer Road, Edinburgh. Tel. 0131/621-7090*
- **Suds-R-US**, *20 Polworth Gardens, Edinburgh. Tel. 0131/229-5131*
- **Swiss Wash**, *12 Telford Road, Edinburgh. Tel. 0131/332-8817*

Here are a few dry cleaners:

- **Capital Launderette**, *208 Dalkeith Road, Edinburgh. Tel. 0131/667-0825*
- **Care Clean**, *16 Roseburn Terrace, Edinburgh. Tel. 0131/313-3205*
- **Chinese Laundry**, *24 Grange Loan, Edinburgh. Tel. 0131/667-0433*
- **Dalkeith Dry Cleaning**, *25 Eskbank Road, Edinburgh. Tel. 0131/663-5707*
- **Deluxe Cleaning Services**, *75 Haymarket Terrace, Edinburgh. Tel. 0131/313-3166*

• **Edinburgh Dry Cleaning**, *17 East Norton Place, Edinburgh. Tel. 0131/661-8683*
• **Johnson Cleaners**, *402 Morningside, Edinburgh. Tel. 0131/447-1836*

Lost Credit Cards
• **American Express Card**, *Tel. 01273/696-933*
• **Diners Club**, *Tel. 01252/513-500, 0800/460-800*
• **MasterCard**, *Tel. 0800/964-767*
• **Visa**, *Tel. 0800/895-082*

Pharmacies
In Scotland, pharmacies are called "Chemists," and can be located through any of the Tourist Offices, or in the "Yellow Pages." Here is onr late-night pharmacy: **Boots the Chemist**, *48 Shandwick Place, Edinburgh, Tel. 0131/225-6757.*

Post Offices
In addition to the regular post offices, most *Newsagents* serve as post office outlets. Most post offices in Edinburgh are open Monday through Friday from 9:00am to 5:30pm, and Saturday from 9:00am to 12:30pm. Here are a few of the post offices in Edinburgh:
• **Frederick Street Post Office**, *40 Frederick Street, Edinburgh. Tel. 0131/ 226-6937*
• **Holyrood Office**, *110 Cannongate, The Royal Mile, Edinburgh. Tel. 0131/ 556-5361*
• **Hope Street Post Office**, *7 Hope Street, Edinburgh. Tel. 0131/226-6823*
• **St. James Post Office**, *10 Kings Mall, St. James Centre, Edinburgh. Tel. 0131/556-0478*

Tourist Information
There are a number of tourist offices in Edinburgh and its surrounding suburbs. Here are a few:
• **Dunbar Tourist Information Centre**, *143 High Street, Dunbar. Tel. 01368/863-353*
• **Edinburgh Airport Information Centre**, *Edinburgh Airport. Tel. 0131/ 333-2167*
• **Edinburgh and Scotland Tourism Information Centre**, *Princes Street, next to Balmoral Hotel, Edinburgh. Tel. 0131/473-3800*
• **Linlithgow Tourist Information Centre**, *Burgh Halls, High Street, Linlithgow. Tel. 01506/844-600*

14. GLASGOW

Glasgow was once proud to be called the "Second City of the Empire," but today it is battling being called the "Second City of Scotland." Indeed, Glaswegians (as those from Glasgow are called), are fiercely loyal to and proud of their city and are in constant competition with their metropolitan neighbor to the east – Edinburgh. Population statistics from the Scottish Tourism board show Edinburgh with a slight lead in that category: 725,000 to 700,000 (although other publications pronounce Glasgow as the leader in population). Regardless, both are tremendous cities and each has a plethora of art, cultural, athletic and historical sights to offer visitors to Scotland.

First off, let's set the pronunciation record straight: the last syllable of Glasgow rhymes with *moe*, not *cow*. Now that we have that simple yet important lesson learned, let me share a few more interesting tidbits with you about Glasgow.

There is some debate as to the origin and meaning of the name Glasgow, but most favor the appellation "dear green place." And Glasgow is that: it will endear itself to you in no time, and there is an abundance of parks, trees and vegetation to testify of its right to be called a "green place."

Glasgow began nearly 1,000 years ago as a small market town along the Clyde River. It remained a relatively small town until the end of the 18th century, when trade with the American colonies burgeoned, and money and people began pouring into Glasgow. The growth continued as the Industrial Revolution swept the western world, and Glasgow tried her hand – quite successfully – in that revolution. Ships built in Glasgow during this time were renowned for their quality and seamanship. At one point, the demand for more and more labor pushed Glasgow's population over the one million mark; today it has settled back to around 700,000.

Architecturally, Glasgow is considered one of the finest cities in Europe. In 1999, Glasgow was named the *United Kingdom City of Architecture and Design*, and as you visit this fair city, you will immediately see why.

Victorian architecture is enhanced by a blend of more modern designs. Seemingly everywhere you venture in Glasgow, you are either nostalgically reminded of the great Victorian age, or aesthetically pleased with the modern days we live in.

GLASGOW'S MUST-SEE SIGHTS

Burns Cottage & Museum – *You'll find the birthplace of Scottish National Poet Robert Burns on the southwest coast of Scotland, a short drive from Glasgow.*

Burrell Collection – *Don't miss this wonderful museum on the outskirts of Glasgow! It is one of the finest collections in the world.*

Glasgow Cathedral – *Scotland's only complete medieval cathedral, Glasgow Cathedral dates from the 12th century. Also called St. Mungo's Cathedral or the Cathedral of St. Kentigern.*

Hunterian Art Gallery – *This art gallery displays an impressive collection of world masterpieces by renowned artists such as Reubens, Rembrandt and Whistler.*

Kelvingrove Art Gallery & Museum – *A wide range of exhibits covers Scotland's history from medieval times to the present.*

Loch Lomond – *A short drive from the city, ;Loch Lomond is famed in poem and song. It is as splendid as it is well known.*

ARRIVALS & DEPARTURES

BY AIR FROM THE UNITED STATES

If you are flying to Glasgow from the United States or Canada, you'll land at **Glasgow International Airport** *in Abbotsinch, Tel. 0141/887-1111.* Once there, you are within about 15 or 20 minutes from downtown Glasgow, a mere eight miles down the road.

At the time of this writing, the only consistent direct flights to Glasgow from North America are offered by Continental Airlines. Continental flies to Glasgow through their hub in Newark, New Jersey. Other airlines (American, British Airways, Northwest and United) occasionally offer international flights from the US to Glasgow. Check with each airline to see if they are flying direct when you are planning your trip.

BY AIR FROM ENGLAND

There are a number of airlines that fly to Glasgow from London, and the route is extremely competitive, which works to your advantage. Watch for price wars, and you may be able to find fares as low as £55 to £70; normal fares run between £100 and £150.

The following airlines fly to Glasgow from the indicated London airports:

From Heathrow
• **British Airways**, *Tel. 0181/754-7321*
• **British Midland**, *Tel. 0345/554-554*

From Gatwick
• **British Airways**, *Tel. 0181/754-7321*

From London Luton
• **Easyjet Airlines**, *Tel. 0870/600-0000*

From London Stansted
• **KLM UK**, *Tel. 0181/750-9820*

Getting to Town by Taxi
Taxi service from Glasgow Airport to downtown is only slightly faster than other means, and will run you about £13. The trip should take about 20 minutes.

Getting to Town by Bus
If you wish to take the bus, Scottish Citylink bus lines run every 15 minutes (every 30 minutes in the evenings) from the airport to **Buchanan Street Bus Station**, *North Hanover Street, Tel. 0141/332-9191*, in the center of downtown Glasgow. Catch the 900 or 901 bus outside the Arrivals Hall. The fare for this short ride is £2.

Renting a Car at the Airport
After you retrieve your luggage, walk out the main doors and turn left. About 75 yards down on the left, you'll find a small building that houses several rental car counters, including Alamo, Avis, Budget, Hertz, National and Europcar. Sample trip lengths from Glasgow around the country (on the main roads without stopping to take pictures, visit sights or take detours):
• Aberdeen: 4 hours
• Edinburgh: 1 hour
• Inverness: 4 hours
• Fort William: 3 hours
• London: 7 hours
• Oban: 2 hours

BY BUS

Bus service reaches Glasgow from all points in Scotland and many in England. If you started your holiday in London and wish to come to Glasgow via bus, expect about 8 hours to traverse the 400 miles between the two cities. The fare is £27.

Scottish Citylink is the bus line that serves Scotland, and it has 190 locations throughout the country. If you are coming via bus from elsewhere in Scotland, you'll arrive at **Buchanan Street Station**, *North Hanover Street, Tel. 0141/332-7133, Fax 0141/332-9191*. The station is just northeast of George Square in downtown Glasgow.

BY CAR

As you might expect, many main arteries run into and out of Glasgow, and access is quite easy via auto. If you are coming from the southeast or from England, you'll be coming north on the M74 (which is the M6/A74 coming from England). If you are coming from Edinburgh or other points east, the main road into Glasgow is the M8. From the Highlands in the northwest, you'll take the A82, and if you're coming up from Prestwick or Ayr you'll use the A77.

BY TRAIN

Trains arrive in and depart from Glasgow in one of two stations: **Central Station**, *7 Shandwick Street, Tel. 0141/287-1266*, and at **Queen Street Station**, *Tel. 0141/204-2844*. Trains arriving from the north and east of Scotland use Queen Street Station, and trains coming from southern Scotland and England arrive at Central Station.

ORIENTATION

The center of Glasgow is laid out in a (nearly) north-south, east-west system, so it is relatively easy to keep your bearings during your explorations. The central part of the downtown area is pretty flat, so walking or bike riding is definitely an option if you have the desire. Most of the sights to see in the downtown area are clustered at the northwest side of downtown and in the north-central part of downtown. Downtown Glasgow is a maze of one-way streets, so if you have a rental car, I would suggest you find a car park and tackle the downtown areas on foot. Otherwise, expect to spend a lot of time circling blocks looking for parking places.

GETTING AROUND TOWN

By Bicycle

Much of downtown Glasgow is easily negotiated by bicycle as it is relatively flat. There are any number of bicycle shops in Glasgow where you can rent a bike. As you get out from the city center a bit, the going gets a little rougher, but bicycles are fine for the downtown area. Be advised, however, that traffic in Glasgow is pretty heavy.

If you do choose to ride a bicycle, here are a few shops you might consider if you are looking to "hire" a bicycle:

- **Argyle Cycles**, *Unit 1, Langbank Street, Glasgow. Tel. 0141/429-7577*
- **Alpine Bikes**, *116 Great Western Road, Glasgow. Tel. 0141/353-2226*
- **The Bicycle Chain**, *1417 Dumbarton Road, Glasgow. Tel. 0141/958-1055*
- **The Bicycle Chain**, *193 Clarkston Road, Glasgow. Tel. 0141/637-2439*
- **Bike Wise**, *25 Townhead, Glasgow. Tel. 0141/775-3722*
- **City Cycles**, *261 High Street, Glasgow. Tel. 0141/552-0961*
- **Clarkston Cycle Centre**, *681 Clarkston Road, Glasgow. Tel. 0141/633-1152*
- **Lomond Activities**, *64 Main Street, Drymen. Tel. 01360/660-066*

By Bus

City buses run all day throughout Glasgow, so if you have always wanted to see Glasgow via bus, you will have no problems. The main bus station is the **Buchanan Street Bus Station**, *North Hanover Street, Tel. 0141/332-9191*, but trains crisscross the city at regular intervals. Keep your eyes open for buses of the Kelvin Central Coach Company (either blue and yellow or red) or the Strathclyde Transport line. Either will be able to take you wherever you want to go.

By Car

My advice for driving in Glasgow is to drive until you find a car park, and then park your car. Many of the major sights are in the central downtown area and can be easily walked or bused to. Parking in this busy city is not particularly plentiful, and traffic can be bad. Add to that the maze of one-way streets, bicyclists, motorcyclists and tourists, and I think you'd be a tad daft to attempt sightseeing from a car in Glasgow. The **Buchanan Street Car Park**, *Buchanan Street*, is a centrally located car park which offers refuge for your car.

By Foot

Many of the sights to see in Glasgow are centered in the downtown area, so Glasgow is an ideal place to see while afoot. However, some of the major attractions such as the **Burrell Collection** are in the suburbs, so you may need a car or public transportation to get to them. Remember to look to the right instead of the left when crossing streets – cars will be coming from that direction since the Scots drive on the left.

By Taxi

Taxi service in Glasgow is efficient and relatively inexpensive. Unless you are going outside of the immediate downtown area, you're just as well off walking, taking any of the many buses that run all the time, or taking the underground. However, in the event you do decide to take a cab, here are the numbers of several taxi companies in Glasgow:

• **A1 Taxis**, *Tel. 0141/942-1414*
• **Arthurlie Taxis**, *Tel. 0141/881-6565*
• **Premier Taxis**, *Tel. 0141/644-5588*
• **Prime Cabs**, *Tel. 0141/641-0505*
• **Rank Taxis**, *Tel. 0141/762-0066*
• **Reid Taxis**, *Tel. 0141/550-3387*
• **Station Taxis**, *Tel. 0141/942-4555*
• **TOA Taxis**, *Tel. 0141/332-7070*

By Underground

Central Glasgow is circled by an underground train system referred to by Glaswegians as *Clockwork Orange* – a tribute to its circular route and distinctive orange trains. Constructed in the 1890s (but updated many times since), it is an efficient, rapid and inexpensive way to get from point-to-point in downtown Glasgow. There are two circular routes – the **Inner Circle** and the **Outer Circle** – that encircle the city.

The underground operates Monday through Saturday from 6:30am to 10:30pm, and on Sundays from 11:30am to 3:45pm. The fare is 65p, or you can purchase an underground pass for £2 which allows unlimited travel all day.

WHERE TO STAY

You'll have your pick of accommodations in Glasgow, from economy youth hostels to luxury hotels and everything in between. The rates I have listed are "rack" rates. Many hotels run mid-week or weekend specials that may be lower than the rates I have listed (especially during the off-season). Be sure and ask if the hotel has any special rates available when you make your reservations.

You will want to clarify whether the price you are quoted is per *person* or per *room*. For B&Bs and guest houses it will certainly be per person, but some hotels use per person pricing, while others use per room pricing. In the hotel listings, "All major credit cards accepted," means American Express, Diner's Club, MasterCard and Visa. If any one of these cards is not accepted, I have specifically listed those credit cards that are accepted. I have listed a range of rates if the rates vary throughout the year. The lower rates are typically only valid during the off or low seasons, and the higher rates are valid from about June through September.

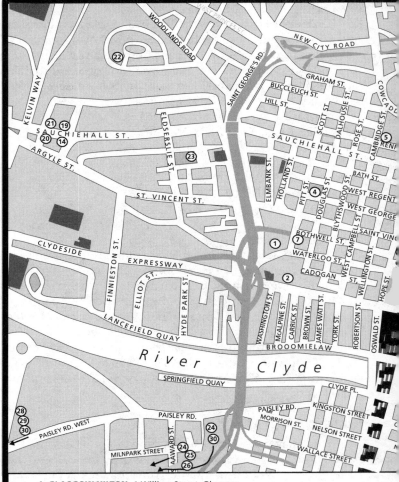

1. **GLASGOW HILTON,** *1 William Street, Glasgow*
2. **GLASGOW MARRIOTT,** *300 Argyle Street*
3. **COPTHORNE GLASGOW HOTEL,** *George Square*
4. **MALMAISON GLASGOW,** *278 West George Street*
5. **GLASGOW THISTLE,** *36 Cambridge Street*
6. **GLASGOW HOLIDAY INN,** *161 West Nile Street*
7. **FORTE POSTHOUSE GLASGOW,** *Bothwell Street*
8. **STAKIS GLASGOW HOTEL,** *201 Ingram Street*
9. **EWINGTON HOTEL,** *132 Queens Drive*
10. **CENTRAL HOTEL,** *99 Gordon Street*
11. **BABBITY BOWSER,** *16-18 Blackfriar Street*
12. **ONE DEVONSHIRE GARDENS,** *One Devonshire Gardens*
13. **DEVONSHIRE HOTEL,** *3 Devonshire Gardens*
14. **KELVIN PARK LORNE HOTEL,** *923 Sauchiehall Street*
15. **STAKIS GROSVENOR HOTEL,** *10 Grosvenor Terrace, Great Western Road*

GLASGOW HOTELS

(i) Tourist Information Center

(U) Underground Station

P Parking

16. **JURY'S GLASGOW HOTEL,** *Great Western Road*
17. **TOWN HOUSE GUEST HOUSE,** *4 Hughenden Terrace*
18. **WICKET'S HOTEL,** *52 Fortrose Street*
19. **SANDYFORD HOTEL,** *904 Sauchiehall Street*
20. **ARGYLL HOTEL,** *973 Sauchiehall Street*
21. **ARGUS HOTEL,** *970 Sauchiehall Street*
22. **GLASGOW SCOTTISH YOUTH HOSTEL,** *7/8 Park Terrace*
23. **BERKELY GLOBETROTTERS INDEPENDENT HOSTEL,** *63 Berkeley, St.Charing Cross*
24. **THE PEEL PARK HOTEL,** *Eaglesham Road, East Kilbride*
25. **EAST LOCHHEAD COUNTRY HOUSE,** *Larg's Road, Loch Winnoch*
26. **EAST LOCHHEAD SELF-CATERING LODGES,** *Larg's Road, Loch Winnoch*
27. **FORTE POSTHOUSE HOTEL,** *Glasgow Airport, Abbotsinch, Paisley*
28. **GLYNNHILL LEISURE HOTEL,** *169 Paisley Road, Renfrew*
29. **BOWFIELD HOTEL AND COUNTRY CLUB,** *Howwood, Renfrewshire*
30. **HOLLY HOUSE B&B,** *54 Ibrox Terrace*

City Center
1. **GLASGOW HILTON**, *1 William Street, Glasgow. Tel. 0141/203-5555, Fax 0141/204-5004; E-mail: glahiltwgm@hilton.com; Website: hilton.com. 319 Rooms. Rates: £180-215 single; £180-215 double; £350-455 suite. All major credit cards accepted.*

'As you come into Glasgow on the M8 from the airport, follow the signs for the City Centre and one of the first hotels you'll see is the Glasgow Hilton. This particular hotel, which was built in 1992, is first class and worthy of the Hilton name. The lobby is spacious and elegant, with mauves and marble greeting you. Traditional Scottish music playing at just the right level sets the atmosphere for your stay here. The tartan-trousered bellman at the door also reminds you that you have arrived in Scotland.

There are over 300 rooms in this 20-story hotel. Each is fair sized (although not exceptionally large) and comfortably and tastefully appointed. Each room has a mini-bar, two phones, hairdryer, TV and trouser press. You'll find a light blue color scheme throughout the hotel bedrooms. The executive floors are exceptionally nice, with a little higher quality furnishings and extras such as fluffy bathrobes to pamper those who stay on these floors. The hotel has two restaurants, and a pub that features a stock of over 150 malt whiskies. It also offers guests a pool, sauna, fitness room, spa and solarium. If you choose to stay at the Glasgow Hilton, you will receive the level and degree of service you associate with the Hilton chain of hotels. It is truly first class, and your accommodation experience here will also be first class.

2. **GLASGOW MARRIOTT**, *500 Argyle Street, Glasgow. Tel. 0141/226-5577, Fax 0141/221-9292. US toll-free reservations 800/228-9290. 300 Rooms. Rates: £80-125 single; £80-125 double; £185-275 suite. All major credit cards accepted.*

The Glasgow Marriott is located just a stone's throw off the M8 as you enter Glasgow from the airport. It is the rather plain 13-story, brown-brick building on your right as you get to the city. The entryway is a polished slab of black marble, and typical Marriott personnel staff the dark wood reception desk – people who make you feel welcome and help put you at ease after a long flight.

The bedrooms are fine, although not particularly memorable. They are fair sized and offer some nice amenities, such as free in-room movies. As with most hotels in Scotland, they offer a TV, phone, hairdryer, ironing board and trouser press. There is a nice gym associated with this Marriott, as well as squash courts, a pool, sauna and whirlpool. There are three restaurants and a pub for your dining and drinking pleasure.

3. COPTHORNE GLASGOW HOTEL, *George Square, Glasgow. Tel. 0141/332-6711, Fax 0141/332-4264. US toll-free reservations 800/465-6486. Website: mill-cop.com. 113 Rooms. Rates: £123-138 single; £133-148 double; £160-300 suite. All major credit cards accepted.*

The Copthorne Glasgow Hotel is located across the street from George Square and right next to the Queen Street train station, so you are pretty much right in the middle of all that is happening in Glasgow if you stay here. The Copthorne has a small but nicely appointed lobby, with marble floors and a rich mahogany reception desk. The tall ceilings betray its origin as a series of converted townhouses. It has a nice but smallish resident's lounge which provides a pleasant place to quench your thirst, read a paper or just relax after the rigors of the day's sightseeing.

Most of the rooms are nice and large, and all are furnished with high-quality furniture and tasteful artwork. They offer TV, free in-room movies, phone, hairdryer, tea- and coffee-making facilities and a trouser press. The best rooms are at the front of the hotel, where they overlook George Square and all that is going on there. Called "Antique Rooms," each room has either a four-poster bed or an extraordinary sleigh bed. The hotel boasts a formal dining room called *Window on the Square* and a more informal eatery called *Le Mirage*, which is immensely popular with Glaswegians (especially around 5:00pm to 6:00pm). (See the *Where to Eat* section.)

The Copthorne is part of the Millenium Hotels and Resorts chain. It boasts a 4-star rating, although I found it to be getting a little oldlooking and feeling. Nothing that a little fresh paint and wallpaper wouldn't fix. The management is anxiously awaiting an upcoming renovation project which should really enhance the hotel. Stay tuned! In the meantime, it's not a bad place to stay from a location standpoint, albeit a little pricey compared to other offerings in Glasgow. Once they have completed their anticipated renovation, I believe they'll be worth every pence you spend here.

4. MALMAISON GLASGOW, *278 West George Street, Glasgow. Tel. 0141/ 572-1000, Fax 0141/572-1002; E-mail: glasgow@malmaison.com; Website: www.malmaison.com. 72 Rooms. Rates: £90-120 single; £90-120 per person double; £130-150 suite. All major credit cards accepted.*

The Malmaison has an art deco design, with bold colors and furnishings. Each room is individually decorated in a swirl of geometric shapes and an eclectic collection of prints. The colors are an awesome blend of red and cream, blue and cream, green and cream, or beige and cream. Fluffy down comforters grace the beds and the prints in each room are intriguing (to say the least). The bedrooms are not particularly large, but you're so busy taking it all in that this seems secondary to the experience. Each room offers TV, CD players (bring your own CDs unless you are staying in a suite), robes and tea- and coffee-making facilities. There are two restaurants associated with the Malmaison: a Mediterranean café and a French brasserie-style restaurant. Both are unique and provide a wonderful dining experience (see the *Where to Eat* section for both). There is also a small exercise room for those who need that to relax after a hard day's sightseeing.

5. GLASGOW THISTLE, *36 Cambridge Street, Glasgow. Tel. 0141/332-3311, Fax 0141/332-3534. 320 Rooms. Rates: £70-110 single; £70-110 per person double; £150-190 suite. Rates include breakfast. All major credit cards accepted.*

Located about four blocks northwest of George Square, the Glasgow Thistle is an upscale hotel close to all that is happening in Glasgow. It is located just around the corner from the Cow Caddens underground station. The bedrooms here are some of the nicest in Glasgow. They are large and each has been decorated tastefully with soft lighting, nice wallpaper and gathered curtains at the windows. The furniture is top quality, and rounds out the pleasant rooms. Each room offers TV, phone, tea- and coffee-making facilities and a trouser press. The suites also offer mini-bars. Each floor has six family rooms, which are furnished with two double beds and a sleeper couch. They are ideal rooms for families. The restaurant is pleasant, newly renovated and also provides good value for the money. Each day they offer a carvery (buffet) that is well stocked and rather inexpensive.

6. GLASGOW HOLIDAY INN, *161 West Nile Street, Glasgow. Tel. 0141/332-0110, Fax 0141/332-7447. 113 Rooms. Rates: £80-100 single; £40-50 per person double; £70-90 suite. Rates include breakfast. All major credit cards accepted.*

If you stayed in the old ugly Holiday Inn in years past, you may want to check out this new rendition. Built in 1996, this latest Holiday Inn offers nice, clean furnishings in a centralized downtown location. While you won't find designer lodging here, you'll find relatively large rooms, quality furnishings, telephone, television, hairdryer and tea- and coffee-making facilities. If you have to work the kinks out, there is a fitness room. There is also a restaurant on site.

7. FORTE POSTHOUSE GLASGOW, *Bothwell Street, Glasgow. Tel. 0141/248-2656, Fax 0141/221-8986, US toll-free reservations 800/225-5843; Website: www.forte-hotels.com. 247 Rooms. Rates: £69-95 single; £69-95 double. All major credit cards accepted.*

As you enter the city on the M8 from the airport, you'll find the Forte Posthouse Hotel in the same area as the Hilton and Marriott. Although the exterior looks rather severe and uninviting, this lovely hotel is quite clean and comfortable. The bedrooms at the Forte Posthouse are a little on the smallish side, but they are all comfortably furnished with new furniture, and have been recently repainted and wallpapered. Take the time to notice the artwork that graces the walls in the hallways. You'll see wonderful ink etchings of castles, battles, and life in Scotland during earlier times. As interesting as the art is, it's a shame that the hallways are a little dark. There is a bar and restaurant on site.

8. STAKIS GLASGOW HOTEL, *201 Ingram Street, Glasgow. 0141/ 248-4401, Fax 0141/226-5149, US toll-free reservations 800/782-5471; E-mail: reservations@stakis.co.uk; Website: www.stakis.co.uk. 90 Rooms. Rates: £60-95 single; £60-95 double. All major credit cards accepted.*

Located about a block away from George Square, the Stakis Glasgow Hotel capitalizes on its location to draw guests. While the hotel is getting a bit old, it is not run down, and the staff seems genuinely interested in seeing that you have a pleasant stay. The rooms are a bit smallish and

---

GLASGOW'S BEST PLACES TO STAY

The following hotels, guest houses and B&Bs are listed from most expensive to least expensive. You can get more information on each selection in reviews that follow. I've left the numbers at the front of each selection for easy reference in the reviews and on the hotel map.

__ONE DEVONSHIRE GARDENS__, One Devonshire Gardens, Glasgow. Tel. 0141/339-2001, Fax 0141/337-1663; Website: www.one-devonshire-gardens.com. 27 rooms. Rates: £140-170 single; £155-190 double; £185-225 suite. All major credit cards accepted. One of the top hotels in the country. You'll find Victorian elegance and splendid furnishings.

__DEVONSHIRE HOTEL__, 5 Devonshire Gardens, Glasgow. Tel. 0141/339-7878, Fax 0141/339-3980; E-mail:devonshirs@aol.com; Website: www.the˜devonshire.co.uk. 14 Rooms. Rates: £115-145 single; £130-190 double; £190 suite. All major credit cards accepted. Another Victorian beauty on Glasgow's west side. Lavish and opulent, comfortable and relaxing.

__MALMAISON GLASGOW__, 278 West George Street, Glasgow. Tel.0141/572-1000, Fax 0141/572-1002; E-mail: glasgow@malmaison.com; Website: www.malmaison.com. 72 Rooms. Rates: £90-120 single; £90-120 double; £130-150 suite. All major credit cards accepted. Modern art and furnishings are all the rage at this ultra-contemporary hotel.

__EAST LOCHHEAD COUNTRY HOUSE__, Larg's Road, Loch Winnoch. Tel. 01505/842-610, Fax 01505/842-610; E-mail: winnoch@aol.com; Website: www.smoothhound.co.uk/hotels/eastloch. 2 Rooms. Rates: £33 single; £33 per person double. MasterCard and Visa accepted. In the country outside of Glasgow, this is one of the best B&Bs in Scotland. You'll find country elegance and a gracious hostess.

definitely older, but they are clean, well cared for and pleasantly decorated with a floral motif. The rooms facing Ingram Street can be a little noisy since they do not have double-glazed windows, so if you stay here, you'll have to decide if you want the view from the windows (mostly people watching) or the quiet of the rooms away from the street. The Stakis Glasgow has a nice location and is not too bad a price to pay to be within steps of George Square.

9. EWINGTON HOTEL, *132 Queens Drive, Glasgow. Tel. 0141/423-1152, Fax 0141/422-2030. 45 Rooms. Rates: £50-65 single; £45-50 per person double. All major credit cards accepted.*

The Ewington is another of Scotland's many converted Victorian mansions, and as such it makes for a wonderful place to stay. The owners have worked hard to provide a lovely, pleasant home-away-from-home. Each of the bedrooms is large and features those characteristic tall ceilings so pleasing in these Victorian mansions. Each is individually decorated with quality furnishings and a tasteful selection of wallpaper and paint. The Ewington's location on Queens Street also guarantees you a central Glasgow location and a safe place to stay.

10. CENTRAL HOTEL, *99 Gordon Street, Glasgow. Tel. 0141/226-3948, Fax 0141/226-3948. 222 Rooms. Rates: £67 single; £80-100 per room double; £100-120 suite. Rates include breakfast. Amex, MasterCard and Visa accepted.*

In former years, the Central Hotel was *the* hotel in Glasgow. This Victorian-era hotel is located near the railway station, and in its heyday it was the hotel of the stars and glitteratti. Today, it's getting a little tired, but with just a little imagination, you can see the beauty that was once hers. The bedrooms vary in size and quality, and are generally functional more than anything. They offer comfortable, clean furnishings and pleasant if not memorable surroundings. Many of the rooms have upgraded plumbing fixtures, and many do not. There is a small restaurant on site as well as a bar. The leisure facility includes a swimming pool, Jacuzzi, spa, sauna and two fitness rooms.

11. BABBITY BOWSER, *16-18 Blackfriar Street, Glasgow. Tel. 0141/552-5055, Fax 0141/552-7774. 6 Rooms. Rates: £35-50 single; £30-35 per person double. Rates include breakfast. Amex, MasterCard and Visa accepted.*

Babbity Bowser's is a marvelous old 18th-century hotel located on the east side of the downtown area, about a block north of Glasgow Green. The hotel is was formerly a townhouse designed by Robert Adam. Each of the six bedrooms has been individually decorated with antique reproductions, and feature white lace bedspreads and floral accents in the rooms. Each room has a television and tea- and coffee-making facilities.

West Side
12. ONE DEVONSHIRE GARDENS, *One Devonshire Gardens, Glasgow.*
Tel. 0141/339-2001, Fax 0141/337-1663; Website: one-devonshire-gardens.com.
27 rooms. Rates: £140-170 single; £155-190 double; £185-225 suite. All major
credit cards accepted.

One Devonshire Gardens is an elegant and choice place to stay in Glasgow, one of the best. From the moment you enter these three converted Victorian mansions, you sense that you have entered a world of splendor, elegance and grandeur. As you walk through the hotel, it's hard not to get whiplash as you look left and right, up and down to take in all the effects of the hotel. You'll find wonderful antiques, old oil paintings, extraordinary woodwork and tall stately ceilings graced with exquisite plasterwork.

My favorite room is the Resident's Lounge. It oozes elegance and Old World grace. This exceptional room features as its centerpiece a large marble fireplace, warm and welcoming. Overstuffed furniture, lovely old paintings and fresh flowers in vases throughout the room make this a wonderful room to sit and read, chat or just relax with a cup of coffee or tea after a hard day of sightseeing.

The bedrooms are as exceptional as the public areas of the house. Each is large and individually (and expensively!) decorated. A handwritten welcome card greets you and makes you feel like an honored guest. Add to that the fresh fruit, fluffy robes and complimentary Belgian chocolates and you'll truly feel comfortable here. Many of the rooms have lovely four-poster beds (be sure to specify this preference when you make your reservations). All but three of the bedrooms have large marble baths. Each room has a mini-bar, TV, stereo system, phone, trouser press and tea- and coffee-making facilities. There are a number of Executive/Presidential/Honeymoon suites (depending on the occasion!). Each is exquisite and has hosted a list of guests that reads like the *Who's Who* of entertainers and politicians that have visited Scotland. Just think, you can stay in one of the rooms that welcomed such luminaries as John Majors, Pierce Brosnan, Michael Keaton, Neil Diamond, Elton John and Eric Clapton. The Spice Girls also chose One Devonshire Gardens as their home-away-from-home when they were in Glasgow.

There is a wonderful dining room on the first floor that is considered one of the best restaurants in Glasgow (see *Where to Eat* section). I cannot stress enough how highly I regard One Devonshire Gardens. I believe it is one of the finest hotels in the United Kingdom, and I think you will agree.

Selected as one of my picks for Scotland's Best Restaurants – see Chapter 11.

13. DEVONSHIRE HOTEL, 5 *Devonshire Gardens, Glasgow. Tel. 0141/339-7878, Fax 0141/339-3980; E-mail:devonshirs@aol.com; Website: www.the~devonshire.co.uk. 14 Rooms. Rates: £115-145 single; £130-190 double; £190 suite. All major credit cards accepted.*

Your first impression of the Devonshire Hotel will be positive and that positive impression will continue throughout your stay here. You'll be welcomed at the front door by a woman dressed in a French maid's uniform, who will invite you into the impressive entry hall. The two-story entrance hall along with its softly playing classical music and crackling fire welcomes you warmly and pleasantly.

The Devonshire Hotel was formerly the home of one of Glasgow's wealthiest tobacco merchants from the 1860s. The owners have done all they could to help you experience what life was like for the former owner. A plethora of antiques, posh furnishings, exquisite woodwork, and tasteful decorating all combine to make their efforts highly successful. As you ascend the stairway to your room, take time to notice the original stained glass windows featuring a variety of scenes.

Once you arrive at your bedroom, you will continue to be impressed. Each room is large, and most have the characteristic tall ceilings that accompany these Victorian beauties. Each room is tastefully and impeccably decorated in mauve and pink, and is furnished with top-quality furnishings. Most of the rooms feature large bay windows. The suites are graced with the same quality furnishings and wonderful decorations, but they also feature lovely four-poster beds. If you choose to stay here, I predict it will be one of your most memorable nights in Scotland.

14. KELVIN PARK LORNE HOTEL, *923 Sauchiehall Street, Glasgow. Tel. 0141/314-9955, Fax 0141/337-1659. 100 Rooms. Rates: £85 single; £105 double; £135 suite. All major credit cards accepted.*

The Kelvin Park Lorne Hotel is located about 10 minutes from downtown Glasgow in the Victorian residential area near Kelvin Park. The hotel has been here for a number of years (the original part was built over 150 years ago) and it is beginning to show its age. But over the years it has been a popular hotel with Americans, so I have included it here.

While the rooms at the hotel are a bit on the small side, they are tastefully decorated with yellow or green wallpaper. The bathrooms are quality, feature upgraded plumbing and are fully tiled. Each room has a TV, hairdryer, phone and tea- and coffee-making facilities. As I said, the Kelvin Park Lorne Hotel has been very popular in previous years, but it is beginning to show its age. For my money, there are nicer, less expensive hotels in the area. However, it is clean, comfortable and close to downtown.

15. STAKIS GROSVENOR HOTEL, *10 Grosvenor Terrace, Great Western Road, Glasgow. Tel. 0141/339-8811, Fax 0141/334-0710. 99 Rooms. Rates: £65-80 single; £80-105 double; £115-175 suite. All major credit cards accepted.*

Several years ago the Stakis Hotel Group razed the inside of their building and replaced it with a modern, brass-and-chandelier look. The results are marvelous, and the hotel has been a popular place to stay ever since. They didn't skimp when it came to room sizes, although the rooms are all essentially the same from a decorating standpoint. (I suppose that's okay, since you'll probably only be staying in one room at a time.) Each room offers light colors, large windows, quality furnishings and satellite television, telephone, trouser press and tea- and coffee-making facilities. A restaurant and small bar are available on site.

16. JURY'S GLASGOW HOTEL, *Great Western Road, Glasgow. Tel. 0141/334-8161, US toll-free reservations 800/843-3322; Website: www.jurys.com. 137 Rooms. Rates: £55-105 single; £55-105 double. All major credit cards accepted.*

This Jury's hotel is located in Glasgow's Victorian west end about 10 minutes from downtown. I am on record as saying I like Jury's hotels – I feel they are generally pretty good value for the money. However, I'd put this Jury's in the lower tier of the Jury's hotels I have been to. It has the feel of a 60's vintage hotel, and is badly in need of new carpeting, upgraded lights, new paint and wallpaper. Couple that with a bit of a high price tag and it's a little disappointing.

Having said that, the bedrooms here are nice sized, and although they are all essentially the same, they do have quality blonde-wood furnishings. Each room has a TV, hairdryer, phone, trouser press, tea- and coffee-making facilities and 24-hour room service. Functional is the word that comes to mind when I consider their sleeping facilities. The hotel offers its guests a leisure club, a restaurant and two pubs. One of the pubs is only open to guests, and the other is open to the public as well as to the residents. Neither is exceptional, but the one does provide a place to meet a few local citizens. All in all, there are better places to stay in Glasgow, whether you are looking for a B&B experience, or prefer a hotel.

17. TOWN HOUSE GUEST HOUSE, *4 Hughenden Terrace, Glasgow. Tel. 0141/357-0862, Fax 0141/339-9605; E-mail: michael.ferguson1@virgin.net. 10 Rooms. Rates: £58-65 single; £34-50 per person double. Rates include breakfast. All major credit cards accepted.*

You'll like the Town House Guest House. Located on a cul-de-sac in one of Glasgow's most prestigious Victorian neighborhoods, the Town House has been converted into a wonderful three-star guest house. Formerly a Gentleman's Club, you'll enjoy the ambience whether or not you are a gentleman. You'll find 10 spacious bedrooms, each with those tall ceilings so characteristic of these old Victorian homes. Each room is individually decorated, and features top-quality furniture, television, telephone, hairdryer and tea- and coffee-making facilities. There are three twin rooms, five doubles and two family rooms. A small hotel on site serves delectable meals, and you will enjoy them. There are several hotels or guest houses in Glasgow named Town House; this is the one you want to say in.

18. WICKETS HOTEL, *52 Fortrose Street, Glasgow. Tel. 0141/334-9334, Fax 0141/334-9334. 10 Rooms. Rates: £60-75 single; £35-43 per person double. Rates include breakfast. All major credit cards accepted.*

Wickets is fast becoming a popular place to stay in Glasgow. This two-story Victorian mansion has been tastefully converted into a wonderful hotel oozing character. Each of the bedrooms is decorated in bright colors and presents a cheerful, pleasant demeanor. Comfortable, quality and complementary furniture adds to the feeling of the room. Each features a television, phone, trouser press, hairdryer and tea- and coffee-making facilities.

Wickets is probably better known for its bars and restaurant than it is for its rooms. You'll find two well-stocked bars and a fine restaurant here. The restaurant looks out onto the hotel's impressive garden. The hotel takes its name from those vertical sticks used in cricket games. Why is that? Because the hotel sits across from the cricket grounds of the West of Scotland Cricket Club. If you've never had the opportunity to watch a cricket game, this might be just the right time to do so.

19. SANDYFORD HOTEL, *904 Sauchiehall Street, Glasgow. Tel. 0141/334-0000, Fax 0141/337-1812. 65 Rooms. Rates: £29-35 single; £48 double; £60 triple/family room. Diner's Club, MasterCard and Visa accepted.*

The brochure for the Sandyford Hotel claims they are "interestingly different," and that they are. If you like bold red paint and carpet, then this is the place for you. If not, then the Sandyford will give you nightmares. Deep red carpet and wall coverings are the word here at Sandyford, and they haven't spared a drop of paint. The Sandyford is located in the heart of the west-end residential section of Glasgow, about a half mile from the Kelvin Hall underground station.

The bedrooms are fair sized and comfortably if not exquisitely furnished. There is a new section to the hotel, and some of the rooms have pine flooring and are nicer than most of the other rooms. Each room offers a TV and tea- and coffee-making facilities. If you are feeling wrinkled, an iron and ironing board are available at the front desk. If you are sensitive to cigarette smoke, you might steer clear of the Sandyford, as smoking is allowed in all of the rooms and the aroma is quite strong in some of them. Most of the rooms are located upstairs, and since there is no elevator that might also be a consideration for you.

20. ARGYLL HOTEL, *973 Sauchiehall Street, Glasgow. Tel. 0141/337-3313, Fax 0141/337-3283; E-mail: argyll_angus.hotel@virgin.net. 38 Rooms. Rates: £44 single; £59 per person double; £29 per person family room. Amex, MasterCard and Visa accepted.*

The Argyll Hotel is another of the hotels I am recommending in the west-end residential area. In a former life, it was two Victorian townhouses. These former townhouses make wonderful hotels and guest houses, and the Argyll is no exception. The bedrooms at the Argyll have those characteristic tall ceilings and spacious dimensions. Many of the rooms have retained their original plasterwork. They are bright and cheery, and feature rose or sand and cream colors and lovely lace curtains at the windows. Each bedroom also has a TV, hairdryer, phone and tea- and coffee-making facilities. An ironing board and iron are available at the front desk. There is a small restaurant and pub available to residents of the Argyll (see the *Where to Eat* section).

21. ANGUS HOTEL, *970 Sauchiehall Street, Glasgow. Tel. 0141/357-5155, Fax 0141/339-9469; E-mail: argyll_angus.hotel@virgin.net. 18 Rooms. Rates: £42 single; £26 per person double; £23 per person triple/family room. Amex, MasterCard and Visa accepted.*

The Angus is the sister hotel to the Argyll, and the two are across the street from one another. Two converted townhouses, it features those wonderful tall ceilings, large rooms and interesting plasterwork on the ceilings. Each of the bedrooms is furnished with soft colors, wallpaper and borders. The rooms offer a TV, phone, hairdryer and tea- and coffee-making facilities. The rooms facing Sauchiehall Street are a bit noisy, so you should ask for a room at the back of the hotel. The single and double rooms are not as large as the triple or family rooms, but they are not cramped either. While there is no restaurant at the hotel, there is one across the street at the Argyll, and a number of restaurants in the surrounding neighborhood.

22. GLASGOW SCOTTISH YOUTH HOSTEL, *7/8 Park Terrace, Glasgow. Tel. 0141/332-3004. 32 rooms. Rates: £9.95-10.95 youth, 11.50-£12.50 adults. Continental breakfast included in the rate. MasterCard and Visa accepted.*

You'll find the Glasgow Scottish Youth Hostel near Glasgow University in the western part of downtown Glasgow. As soon as you enter the building you'll know you are still in Scotland – the blue and green plaid tartan carpet fairly trumpets it! You'll also like the looks and feel of this old Victorian townhouse that has been converted into a youth hostel. Check out the hand-carved oak banisters – not your typical adornment in youth hostels around the world.

The hostel offers 144 beds spread across 32 rooms. Most of the dormitory rooms have four to six beds in them. The bedrooms are large and comfortable, and the facilities are clean. While the furnishings aren't top quality, they are clean, durable and comfortable. The common rooms are all large, well lit and quite comfortably furnished. There is a TV room, dining room and a small library. The self-catering kitchen has the necessary utensils to cook your own meals. However, if you wish, an inexpensive continental breakfast is available each day. This hostel is well known and well liked, and used pretty heavily during the summer months. Be sure and call ahead for reservations.

23. BERKELEY GLOBETROTTERS INDEPENDENT HOSTEL, *63 Berkeley Street, Charing Cross, Glasgow. Tel. 0141/204-5470. 8 Rooms, 60 beds. Rates: £7.50-12. Continental breakfast included in the rate. MasterCard and Visa accepted.*

This hostel opened in the mid-90s and has been a badly needed addition to the hostel market in Glasgow. Pretty Spartan, it provides a clean, safe and inexpensive place to spend the night. It has the added bonus of being close to the downtown area. There are six dormitory rooms and two private rooms. The dormitory rooms have bunk beds, and you'll find a bunk and twin bed in either of the two private rooms. One point of clarification: most hostels segregate males and females. The Berkeley Hostel does not. It has one dormitory room for women, and the others do not separate men from women. If you're a bit squeamish about that, be sure and specify your preference. The public rooms include satellite TV (a nice plus!) and a pleasant place to visit and meet new folks. There is also a laundry and drying room available on site, as well as a small store for supplies.

Suburbs
24. THE PEEL PARK HOTEL, *Eaglesham Road, East Kilbride, Glasgow. Tel. 01355/222-747, Fax 01355/234-346. 60 Rooms. Rates: £39 single; £39 per room double. MasterCard and Visa accepted.*

The Peel Park Hotel is the first entry into the Scottish lodging market for Lodge Inns, an immensely popular lodging chain in England. Why is it so popular? Because Lodge Inns have established the reputation for providing clean, safe and efficient lodging for a reasonable price. The Peel Park Hotel continues this tradition and reputation. The Peel Park is situated at the junction of the A726 (Paisley to Strathaven Road) and the B764 (Eaglesham Road) in the suburbs of western Glasgow. All the bedrooms are priced at £39 per room, and you can have up to five people share a room as long as three are children (in other words – only two adults per room). The rooms are large and comfortably if not elegantly furnished. Most of the rooms have a sofa bed, and cots are also available. If you've stayed in one room at the Peel Park, you've stayed in them all – each room is identical to its siblings. While it is true that you lose the individual attention and personality of a B&B or guest house, the Peel Park is great for economy lodging.

25. EAST LOCHHEAD COUNTRY HOUSE, *Larg's Road, Loch Winnoch. Tel. 01505/842-610, Fax 01505/842-610; E-mail: winnoch@aol.com; Website: www.selfcatering-accommodation.co.uk. 2 Rooms. Rates: £33 single; £33 per person double. MasterCard and Visa accepted.*

East Lochhead Country House is undoubtedly one of my favorite places to stay in Scotland. It combines a wonderful home, gracious hosts, and an idyllic setting to create one of the most memorable accommodation experiences you are likely to have in Scotland. This four-star Bed and Breakfast is located about 30 minutes outside Glasgow and sits in the rolling countryside east (and a little south) of Glasgow. It is also about 15 minutes from the Glasgow airport, so you might consider this for your last night's stay in Scotland.

Mrs. Janet Anderson is your hostess, and you will be hard-pressed to find a more gracious and elegant hostess in all of Scotland. She adds a touch of elegance to this oasis of hospitality. You will feel truly welcomed into her home when you arrive. The Andersons have lovingly and beautifully renovated this 100-year-old stone farmhouse. To put their efforts in perspective, their daughter Heather says the house was "horrific" prior to the renovations! You'd never know it now.

You'll take your breakfast (and dinner if you have arranged it previously) in an alcove off the sitting room. Enclosed by floor-to-ceiling windows, the alcove looks out onto the well-landscaped lawn and stunning gardens. A nearby bird feeder attracts scores of songbirds to complement your meal. Lift your eyes a little higher and you can see tranquil Barr Loch and beyond that the dappled hills of Renfrewshire. Not only is the dining experience wonderful because of the setting, but the meal itself is marvelous. Mrs. Anderson is an award-winning chef recognized for her expertise by *A Taste of Scotland*. The breakfast she prepares will be filling and delicious, and includes eggs, bacon, sausage and porridge. If you prefer a lighter meal, cereal, yogurt and fresh fruit are also available. Be sure and sample the honey – it's from Mrs. Anderson's own beehives.

After breakfast or dinner, stroll among the amazing variety of flowers and plants in the Anderson's gardens. Just a stone's throw (but please don't!) from the gardens you'll see several Highland cattle and Jacob's sheep gazing nearby. It is truly a peaceful setting.

There are two bedrooms in the main house at East Lochhead. Both are large and spacious, and feature tasteful decorations and exceptionally comfortable furniture. One room is ensuite, and while the other isn't ensuite, it has its own private bath in the hallway. (Check out the view from the private bathroom. It has been said that it is the best in Scotland.) In addition to the rooms in the main house, there are four self-catering apartments adjacent to the house (see the following entry). I'm telling you East Lochhead is wonderful, but don't just take my word for it. Following are some comments from the guest book: "A superb place in all aspects – a little jewel." "I count myself lucky to have found you." Perhaps the most telling is "We found you be accident, but next time we'll come by design." With that said, I think your designs for Scotland should include at least one night at East Lochhead. (The Andersons request that their guests not smoke at East Lochhead.)

Selected as one of my Best Places to Stay – see Chapter 12.

26. EAST LOCHHEAD SELF-CATERING LODGES, *Larg's Road, Loch Winnoch. Tel. 01505/842-610, Fax 01505/842-610; E-mail: winnoch@aol.com; Website: www.selfcatering-accommodation.co.uk. 4 apartments. Rates: £200-450 per week for 6-8 individuals; £175-350 per week for 2-4 individuals; £100-300 per week for 2-4 individuals. MasterCard and Visa accepted.*

Adjacent to East Lochhead Country House are a series of apartments converted from a barn and other old stone outbuildings that were formerly part of the farm. These lodgings provide a degree of autonomy – you prepare your own meals – in a wonderful setting. Each lodge has been professionally decorated and tastefully furnished in a modern country motif. Knotty pine is the predominant decor in the lodges.

Eat your breakfast in a breakfast nook that either overlooks the gardens and rolling fields and meadows, or better yet, several of the nooks look out onto the meadows where the spring lambs gambol about with one another. Either way, it is a wonderful, restful place to dine. The bedrooms are smartly efficient and very comfortable. The furnishings are new and high quality and will provide a pleasant place to spend the night. These kinds of self-catering cottages are beginning to catch on in Scotland and are ideal for families. And the self-catering accommodations at East Lochhead are among the best around. As with the country house, the Andersons request that their guests honor their no-smoking policy.

27. FORTE POSTHOUSE HOTEL, *Glasgow Airport, Abbotsinch, Paisley. Tel. 0870/400-9031, Fax 0141/840-4049. 299 Rooms. Rates: £55-89 single; £55-89 per room double. Rates include breakfast. All major credit cards accepted.*

The Forte Posthouse is a massive complex adjacent to the Glasgow airport, and if you're a traveler who worries about making flights on time, this is a nice option for you. The hotel has the feel of a large Holiday Inn in the US – everything is nice and clean, if not especially memorable. Each room is decent sized, and offers television, telephone, hairdryer and tea- and coffee-making facilities. The rooms have double-glazed windows, so the airport noise is minimal. While it's nothing special, you'll find safe, clean accommodations close to the airport.

28. GLYNHILL LEISURE HOTEL, *169 Paisley Road, Renfrew. Tel. 0141/886-5555, Fax 0141/885-2838, US toll-free fax 800/4262513; E-mail: glynhillleisurehotel@msn.com. 125 Rooms. Rates: £65-76 single; £75-86 double. Rates include breakfast. All major credit cards accepted.*

If you are a nervous traveler and always fret about making it to the airport on time, then the Glynhill Leisure Hotel may just be the perfect place for you to stay on your last night in Scotland. Glynhill is just a roundabout or two away from the Glasgow airport – literally about a five-minute drive. But even though you are only one mile from the airport, I wasn't bothered in the least with "airport noise."

The hotel itself isn't bad either. While it is an older hotel, it has been well maintained and you'll find it quite clean and comfortable. The bedrooms are all nice sized, and the furnishings are simple but comfortable. Each room has satellite TV, phone, hairdryer and tea- and coffee-making facilities. Fresh fruit in your room welcomes you on your first night's stay. A recent addition to the hotel added 50 new rooms, and these rooms are the nicest. If you'd like to swim or work out prior to your departure, then once again the Glynhill Leisure Hotel will meet your needs. You'll find a nice pool and exercise room here to help you get (or keep) the kinks out. You'll also enjoy the sauna and spa that are part of the leisure facilities.

There are two fine restaurants at Glynhill Leisure Hotel. The Palm Court Carvery is an informal buffet-style restaurant, and Le Gourmet provides a more formal dining experience. (See the *Where to Eat* section for more on Le Gourmet.)

29. BOWFIELD HOTEL AND COUNTRY CLUB, *Howwood, Renfrewshire. Tel. 01505/705-225, Fax 01505/705-230. 23 Rooms. Rates: £50-65 single; £35-43 per person double. Rates include breakfast. All major credit cards accepted.*

The Bowfield Hotel and Country Club sits on the outskirts of Glasgow, convenient to the sights to see and things to do in Glasgow, but also within about 10 minutes of the airport. So it makes an ideal place to stay on your last night in Scotland. You'll find the rooms to be average size, but tastefully decorated. The manager described the décor to me as sort of a country-cottage style. Regardless of what it's called, it works. Each of the rooms is furnished with comfortable furnishings, and features a television, telephone, hairdryer and tea- and coffee-making facilities. You may have noticed that the name includes the words "country club." The Bowfield features a number of nice amenities, including an indoor swimming pool, sauna, fitness room, squash courts and a snooker room.

30. HOLLY HOUSE B&B, *54 Ibrox Terrace, Glasgow. Tel. 0141/427-5609. 4 Rooms. Rates: £18 single; £18 per person double. No credit cards accepted.*

Holly House B&B is located in a quiet neighborhood in southwest Glasgow. In fact, it is a stone's throw from the Ibrox soccer stadium, so would serve as a great place to stay if you are interested in seeing a game. An older Victorian townhouse, it features tall ceilings and nice sized rooms. The furnishings are simple but pleasant and comfortable. There is no dining room, so guests take their continental breakfast in their bedrooms.

WHERE TO EAT

There are quite a few fine restaurants in Glasgow, and I have listed a number of them here. For each restaurant, I've included samples of what's on the menu and their price. Remember, however, that prices are subject to change, and restaurants tend to change their menus daily or seasonally. Unless specifically noted, all the prices listed here are for dinner (salad, entree, dessert and coffee). Often the lunch menus are merely scaled-down versions of the dinner menus, at about half to two-thirds the cost of dinner.

"All major credit cards accepted," means Access, American Express, EuroCard, MasterCard and Visa. If any one of these is not accepted, I have specifically listed those that are. As in the hotel section, I have Americanized the telephone numbers.

Most activities in Scotland are very casual, and dining is no exception. Every restaurant I've listed for Glasgow says casual dress is fine, although a number of the more upscale restaurants request no blue jeans or grubbies. In practice, however, most of the clientele in the nicer restaurants wear suit and tie and dresses. Restaurants in Glasgow automatically tack a 10% to 15% gratuity onto your bill. If you feel the service was exceptional beyond that level, feel free to leave an additional tip. Most waiters and waitresses expect an additional 3% to 5% from their guests. The legal drinking age is 18, although many restaurants (especially) and some pubs enforce a house minimum of 21 years.

City Center

1. CAMERON'S RESTAURANT, *1 William Street, Glasgow. Tel. 0141/204-5511, Fax 0141/204-5554. £19-24 for lunch and £45 for dinner. Open daily from noon to 2:00pm, and 7:00pm to 10:00pm. All major credit cards accepted.*

Cameron's restaurant is the formal restaurant for the Hilton Hotel. It creates a quiet dining experience for those who venture in. Cameron's strives to recreate the feeling and atmosphere of a Scottish hunting lodge.

(Be sure and check out their gun room. It has a nice collection of...walking sticks.) Tall ceilings and exquisite furnishings provide a regal feel to the restaurant, as do the crystal and china. My favorite area of the restaurant is the library. It is set aside from the rest of the dining area and allows for a little more intimate dining experience.

But a wonderful ambience is not the only thing Cameron's is known for. They are proud of the two AA rosettes they have garnered for the preparation and presentation of the French-Scottish fare you'll find here. The menu changes frequently, but you are likely to encounter such delicacies as seared smoked salmon set on gingered tomatoes or pan-fried filet of beef served with bengkulu sauce. A wide variety of desserts will also tempt you to set aside your diet for the evening. Management prefers that their guests wear a suit and tie or dress, although it not required. Reservations are generally necessary during the summer tourist season.

2. MINSKY'S BRASSERIE, *1 William Street, Glasgow. Tel. 0141/203-5555, Fax 0141/204-5004. £14-22. Open daily from 6:30am to 10:30am and from noon to 11:00pm. All major credit cards accepted.*

Minsky's is the casual-dining restaurant at the Hilton Hotel. It is really a very pleasant place with a friendly and vivacious atmosphere. It is modeled after a turn-of-the-century bar and grill called Mama Minsky's, named after a Russian immigrant to New York City who first started serving guests in her dining room, then she expanded beyond the dining room into the conservatory, until finally the volume became so great that she opened her own restaurant.

This Mama Minsky's features tile floors, ceiling fans, and lots of interesting and eye-catching knick-knacks scattered about. They offer a well-stocked buffet that ranges from appetizers to main courses. You'll find everything from pizza to burgers, steak, chicken and fish. The food is excellent, if not a little pricey (this *is* the Hilton, after all) You will feel very comfortable here in casual dress.

3. GHENGIS RESTAURANT, *36 Cambridge Street, Glasgow. Tel. 0141/332-3311, Fax 0141/332-3534. £7-20. Open daily from 5:00pm to 9:00pm. Amex, MasterCard and visa accepted.*

The Ghengis Restaurant is the main restaurant for the Glasgow Thistle Hotel. Recently redecorated, it features lots of chrome and glass, and is very bright and modern. They are striving for a Mediterranean theme, and you'll find a number of seafood entrées, in addition to soups, salads and pasta dishes. For those who prefer, several vegetarian dishes are also available. Dress is nice casual in this pleasant dining room.

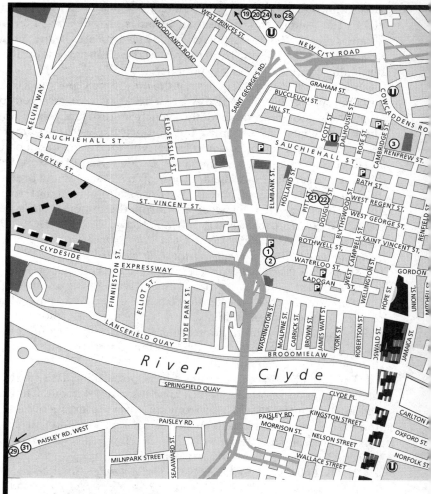

1. **CAMERON'S RESTAURANT**, *1 William Street, Glasgow*
2. **MINSKY'S BRASSERIE**, *1 William Street*
3. **GHENGIS RESTAURANT**, *36 Cambridge Street*
4. **CORINTHIAN BAR & GRILL**, *191 Ingram Street*
5. **LE COLONNE ITALIAN RESTAURANT**, *6a John Street*
6. **BELLA PASTA**, *St. Vincent Street*
7. **CAFE ROUGE**, *15 John Street*
8. **MILLER'S RESTAURANT** *201 Ingram Street*
9. **THE COUNTING HOUSE** *Corner of Queen and St. Vincent Streets*
10. **LE MIRAGE CAFE**, *Copthorne Hotel, Geurge Square*
11. **PIZZA HUT**, *Queen Street*
12. **THE ARK**, *44 Frederick Street*
13. **COSTA L'AMORE POR IL CAFFE**, *Royal Exchange Square, Queens Street*
14. **PIZZA EXPRESS**, *Queen Street*

GLASGOW RESTAURANTS

i Tourist Information Center

U Underground Station

P Parking

29. LE GOURMET RESTAURANT, *169 Paisley Road, Renfrew*

30. HOMESPREADS COCKET HAT RESTAURANT, *Eaglesham Road, East Kilbride, Glasgow*

31. THE PALM COURT *169 Paisley Road, Renfrew*

5. THE JENNY TEA ROOM, *Royal Exchange Square, Queen Street*
6. THE CELLAR BAR, *207 Ingram*
7. THE OLD PRINT SHOP, *36 North Frederick Street*
8. THE UPPER CRUST SANDWICH BAR, *Royal Exchang Square, Queen Street*
9. ONE DEVONSHIRE GARDENS RESTAURANT, *One Devonshire Garden,*
0. UBIQUITOUS CHIP, *12 Ashland Lane*
1. CAFE MALMAISON, *278 West George Street*
2. MALMAISON BRASSERIE, *278 West George Street*
3. SUTHERLAND'S RESTAURANT, *973 Sauchiehall Street*
4. THE CUL-DE-SAC RESTAURANT, *40 Ashland Lane*
5. ASHOKA RESTAURANT, *Ashton Lane, Glasgow*
6. JINTY MCINTY'S BAR AND RESTAURANT, *11 Ashland Lane*
7. O'BRIEN'S IRISH SANDWICHES, *229 Sauchiehall Street,*
8. STARBUCKS, *27 Sauchiehall Street*

4. CORINTHIAN BAR AND GRILL, *191 Ingram Street, Glasgow. Tel. 0141/552-1101, Fax 0141/559-6826. £6-14. Open Monday through Saturday from noon to midnight and Sunday from 12:30pm to midnight. All major credit cards accepted.*

The Corinthian Bar and Grill is a great place to slip in for a cool drink and meal while you are out and about on your sightseeing jaunts, and is probably unlike any other bar and grill you are likely to encounter. It is housed in a gorgeous old Georgian building with vaulted ceilings (and I mean vaulted – perhaps 60 feet high) and a magnificent glass dome. The effect is one of opulence and refinement. Of course, the marble and Italian renaissance décor also add to the effect. The building was built in the early 1800s for the Union Bank.

A number of booths for four to six guests are set amid other soft-upholstered chairs and love seats. The atmosphere is very pleasant, bordering on genteel. Relaxing soft rock and occasional jazz music is played continually to set the tone. The manger told me they are definitely not into the club scene, and in fact try to steer far clear of that. The clientele is in the mid- to late 20s on up. The food is restaurant quality, and you'll find such treats as hallumi cheese with baby leeks and asparagus with tabouleh, or peppered loin of tuna with salsa verde. (I didn't try the hallumi cheese, but the tuna is excellent.) Dress for the Corinithian Bar and Grill is definitely casual, although when I was there many of the diners were wearing suits and ties. There is also a piano and cocktail bar associated with the grill that is much more casual.

5. LE COLONNE ITALIAN RESTAURANT, *6a John Street, Glasgow. Tel. 0141/553-1950. £8-14. Open Monday through Saturday from noon to 2:30pm, Monday through Wednesday from 6:00pm to 11:00pm, and Thursday through Saturday from 6:00pm to 11:30pm. MasterCard and Visa accepted.*

This is my favorite Italian restaurant in Glasgow. Mario and Lynn DiPinto hail from Italy and are the owners and managers of this great restaurant. If you like Italian food, you are really going to like this restaurant. To get to Le Colonne, you'll descend a set of stairs that will bring you into the main dining room. You'll find mirrors, arches, statues, red linen tablecloths and soft Italian music playing in the background. All of which sets the stage perfectly for the meal you'll receive once you are here.

Leonardo DiPinto is the chef, and he takes great pride in creating new dishes to excite (and fill) his guests. In fact, a section of the menu is devoted to *La Pasta Nostre Creazioni* (Our Special Creations). The menu may prove a challenge for you, there are so many excellent choices from which to choose. If you get stuck, try the filetto al gorgonzola – beef filet with lombard soft cheese. If you prefer a little more traditional Italian meal, then try the fetuccine alfredo.

As you are waiting to be seated, (or as you leave), take a look at the DiPinto's "Wall of Fame." You'll see a number of rave reviews from previous customers who took the time to write after returning home from their vacations. (When was the last time *you* were so delighted with a restaurant that you wrote to them after returning home?) Mario told me that one of the reasons for the success of the restaurant was their insistence on having fresh ingredients delivered daily – fresh vegetables, herbs, meat, etc. Even though the restaurant seats about 60, you'll probably want to make reservations during the summer months and on the weekends throughout the year. Dress is nice casual, although casual will be acceptable.

GLASGOW'S TOP RESTAURANTS

The following restaurants are listed from most to least expensive. You can get more information on each selection in the reviews that follow.

20. UBIQUITOUS CHIP, *12 Ashland Lane, Glasgow. Tel. 0141/334-5007. £16-32. Open Monday through Saturday from noon to 2:30pm, and 5:30pm to 11:00pm, and Sunday from 12:30pm to 2:30pm, and from 6:30pm to 11:00pm. MasterCard and Visa accepted. This has been one of the most popular restaurants in Glasgow for the past 30 years. It will probably still be thirty years from now!*

24. THE CUL-DE-SAC RESTAURANT, *40 Ashland Lane, Glasgow. Tel. 0141/334-4749. £5-16. Open daily from noon to 11:00pm (sometimes until midnight depending on the demand). Amex, MasterCard and Visa accepted. This restaurant is very trendy and very popular, and they have great food, too!*

5. LE COLONNE ITALIAN RESTAURANT, *6a John Street, Glasgow. Tel. 0141/553-1950. £8-14. Open Monday through Saturday from noon to 2:30pm, Monday through Wednesday from 6:00pm to 11:00pm, and Thursday through Saturday from 6:00pm to 11:30pm. MasterCard and Visa accepted. This is my favorite Italian restaurant in Glasgow, and it may be yours too!*

7. CAFÉ ROUGE, *15 John Street, Glasgow. Tel. 0141/552-4433. £7-12. Open daily from 10:00am to midnight. Amex, MasterCard and Visa accepted. This French coffee house is definitely worth stopping by for a bite to eat.*

6. BELLA PASTA, *St. Vincent Street, 0141/221-5059. £7-12. Open daily from noon to 11:00pm. All major credit cards accepted.*

This restaurant is part of a national chain of pasta restaurants in the UK. There are 75 restaurants (and growing), so they must be doing something right. All kinds of wonderful pasta and other Italian dishes are available at Bella Pasta. The restaurant features large windows, lots of plants and flowers. Bright floral tablecloths, wicker and wood chairs add to the light, pleasant dining experience. The atmosphere is quite cheery and chatty, as people here obviously enjoy the food as well as the friendly scene.

You'll be able to choose from a mind-boggling list of pasta choices. One of the more popular choices is pollo di graziella – filet of chicken breast cooked over a selection of roasted vegetables in a leek, bacon and double cream sauce. Another popular dish is the more traditional linguine al pesto Genovese made with basil, chopped pine kernels, garlic, olive oil and parmesan cheese. This is a nice option if you like Italian food. The prices are reasonable and the environment is very cheery. The lunch menu is about half the cost of the dinner menu, in the £4 to £7 range. Dress is casual.

7. CAFÉ ROUGE, *15 John Street, Glasgow. Tel. 0141/552-4433. £7-12. Open daily from 10:00am to midnight. Amex, MasterCard and Visa accepted.*

This is a delightful and vibrant French coffee house/café located in the courtyard of the Italian Centre shopping area. As you walk in, mustard-colored walls, wood-plank floors, small tables and tall ceilings will greet you. You may also notice the interesting collection of items on the walls, from landscape paintings to sketches of fish to paintings of young ladies.

But the food is great, and is actually quite reasonably priced. Try the poulet fermier Normand et haricots verts (for those non-French speakers out there, that translates to corn-fed breast of chicken from Normandy). If that doesn't sound good, then you might try the confit de canard aux champignons des bois (confit of duck with wild mushrooms). There is a small wine list – about a dozen choices – should you feel the need to accompany your French meal with a glass of wine. This is a nice restaurant with a cheery and chatty atmosphere and really good food. I liked it, and I think you will too. Dress is casual.

8. MILLER'S RESTAURANT, *201 Ingram Street, Glasgow. Tel. 0141/ 314-1063. £7-12. Open daily from noon to 10:00pm. All major credit cards accepted.*

Miller's Restaurant is the dining room for the Stakis Glasgow Hotel. It is located just a block south of George Square. Miller's Restaurant is kind of a cross between pub grub and trendy restaurant. You'll find pleasant surroundings here – dark wood, functional table settings and lots of friendly chatting going on among diners. You'll find the inexpensive menu offers a variety of choices, from sandwiches to steaks. They cater to vegetarian needs with several vegetarian offerings, including vegetarian fajitas. Miller's isn't necessarily grand dining, but the food is good and filling in a pleasant atmosphere within minutes of a number of sights you might be visiting. Dress is casual.

9. THE COUNTING HOUSE, *corner of Queen and St. Vincent Streets, Glasgow. Tel. 0141/248-9568. £6-12. Open daily from 11:00am to 10:00pm. Amex, MasterCard and Visa accepted.*

The Counting House Restaurant is housed in an old Scottish bank building at the corner of Queen and St. Vincent Streets. Central to the restaurant is the bar (of course), but there are a number of small rooms off the center section of the restaurant. Dark oak tables clutter the rooms, along with the constant chatter of diners. These old bank buildings make such great restaurants. The owners have retained the frosted glass, ornate plaster work, dark wood and domed ceiling that were part of the bank, and they make a nice contribution to the feel of the dining environment. Black and white photos of Glasgow in the late 1800s and early 1900s grace the walls, along with a number of paintings of famous Scottish folk like Bonnie Prince Charlie and Flora MacDonald.

The food served here is mostly a cross between pub grub and a sandwich shop, but it is good and reasonably priced. You'll find fish and chips and sandwiches along with vegetarian offerings like mushroom stroganoff and vegetable burgers. The lunch menu is a little less expensive than the dinner menu, with entrées ranging between £4 and £5. Dress is casual, and grubbies are fine.

10. LE MIRAGE CAFÉ, *Copthorne Hotel, George Square, Glasgow. Tel. 0141/332-6711, Fax 0141/332-4264. £5-10. Open daily from 4:30pm to midnight. All major credit cards accepted.*

Le Mirage Café is an immensely popular café associated with the Copthorne Hotel across from George Square. If you visit in the middle of the day you might not believe it is all that popular, but look out as Happy Hour approaches! The décor isn't particularly memorable, in fact it is rather understated, but the place really packs 'em in between 5:00pm and 7:00pm. The favored seats are those in the conservatory – tables set in glass-enclosed boxes at the front of the café. It puts you right out with the pedestrian traffic looking across to all the tourists and street performers on George Square. Inside are a series of raised booths. Le Mirage is gaining a reputation for excellent pub grub, and you'll find a number of sandwiches, soups and fish and chips here. Dress is casual.

11. PIZZA HUT, *Queen Street, Glasgow. Tel. 0141/248-5682. £4-10. Open daily from 11:00am to 11:00pm. Amex, MasterCard and Visa accepted.*

I wasn't going to put this in – in my mind it's not a very Scottish dining experience. But as I walked by the restaurant, I noticed the place was packed and almost every table had children at it. So, in case you are traveling with a child and they are tired of haggis, porridge and skirlie, you might want to stop in here. The sign may say Pizza Hut, and the pizza may taste like Pizza Hut's, but this restaurant doesn't look like any Pizza Hut I've ever been in. It's more of a café-style, has tasteful bright wallpaper, is well lit and has jazz music playing in the background. The menu is about the same: pizza, pizza, pizza, soup and salads (and more pizza). As with Pizza Huts in the US, dress is casual and grubbies are okay.

12. THE ARK, *44 Frederick Street, Glasgow. Tel. 0141/559-4411. £3-9. Open daily from 11:00am to midnight. MasterCard and Visa accepted.*

The Ark is a lively modern pub frequented predominantly by the university crowd. Loud music (usually heavy metal), pinball machines and video games all combine to provide a vibrant atmosphere. I have been here several times and it has always been quite busy. It is just up the street from George Square, so a few tourists and backpackers do venture in to join the students who are taking a break from their classes or studies. Plank floors and light pine picnic tables round out the décor. The Ark specializes in pub grub, and you'll be able to get a burger or sandwich here after 3:00pm. The Ark isn't for everyone, but it certainly does have a bouncy atmosphere and is very popular with the younger crowd. You'll feel quite comfortable here with anything you are likely to be wearing while sightseeing – the more casual the better.

13. COSTA L'AMORE POR IL CAFFE, *Royal Exchange Square, Queen Street, Glasgow. Tel. 0141/221-9305. £5-8. Open Monday through Saturday from 8:00am to 8:00pm, Sunday from 10:00am to 5:00pm. MasterCard and Visa accepted.*

This is a marvelous little Italian coffee and sandwich shop located right next to the Museum of Modern Art. You'll pick it out quickly by its chrome tables and chrome-and-wicker chairs on the patio outside the shop. Inside you'll find wrought iron and oak tables (and generally, lots of happy people). The walls inside are mustard colored. You'll sit close to your neighbor – they have over a dozen tables packed pretty tightly together. The aroma is a delicious blend of the coffees they brew and serve. In addition to coffee, they sell a number of soups, salads and sandwiches as well. Dress is casual.

14. PIZZA EXPRESS, *Queen Street. Tel. 0141/559-3732. £4-7. Open Monday through Saturday from noon to 11:00pm. MasterCard and Visa accepted.*

White tile floors, black marble tables and purple plastic chairs are what you'll find at Pizza Express. Oh, and pizza too. Pretty good pizza; in fact, very good pizza. This place is usually very busy during lunch and dinner times, an indication of the quality of their fare. Pizza Express has been recognized as having some of the best pizza in Glasgow. If you are an adventurous pizza consumer, try the Neopolitana – it comes with capers, anchovies, olives, mozzarella and tomatoes. Or you might like the Giardiniera, which features sliced mushrooms, olives, pepperoni, leeks, parmesan, petit pois, and mozzarella. For the less adventurous, you can still get a plain ol' cheese pizza. As you would expect, dress is casual.

15. THE JENNY TEA ROOM, *Royal Exchange Square, Queen Street, Glasgow. Tel. 0141/204-4988. £3-7. Open Monday through Saturday from 8:00am to 6:30pm and Sunday from 10:00am to 5:00pm. MasterCard and Visa accepted.*

You'll find the Jenny Tea Room in the Royal Exchange Square right next to the Museum of Modern Art. It bills itself as a traditional Scottish restaurant, tea room and bistro. Their specialty is warm, delicious scones with honey or marmalade. That's not all you can have of course, but it is what brings most folks in (and what keeps them coming back). They also serve breakfast in the mornings from £3 to £7, as well as soups and sandwiches for lunch and dinner from £4 to £10. There are about 10 tables upstairs, but my favorite dining area is downstairs, where there are about 20 tables. The room is a wonderful old cellar with white-washed walls and warm, tasteful decorations. Wood paneling, old photos and lithographs round out the décor. It provides a quiet and pleasant dining experience. Dress is casual.

16. THE CELLAR BAR, *207 Ingram, Glasgow. Tel. 0141/248-4401. £3-7. Open daily from 11:00am to midnight. Amex, MasterCard and Visa accepted.*

The Cellar bar is the pub for the Stakis Glasgow Hotel. It is located in the cellar below the hotel, hence the name. It is a big draw to the many university students in the city. Low ceilings amid massive orange pillars give it kind of an art-deco feel. It's smoky, crowded, and very loud once things get rocking. It is one of those dark, dungeon-like places that some (many) people are drawn to like bugs to a light. So why is it listed here under the *Where to Eat* section? It is here because it offers outstanding pub grub – soup, sandwiches, chips, etc. Dress is definitely casual, and grubbies are okay.

17. THE OLD PRINT SHOP, *36 North Frederick Street, Glasgow. Tel. 0141/552-8160. £4-6. Open Monday through Thursday from noon to 9:00pm, Friday and Saturday from noon to 8:00pm, and Sunday from 12:30pm to 3:00pm. MasterCard and Visa accepted.*

The Old Print Shop is just up the street from George Square. As you might suspect, it takes its name from its original purpose. Patrons include university students and businessmen, blue-collar workers and tourists. Its location near the business district and several tourist attractions helps pull in a variety of people from all walks of life – although the inexpensive menu and decent food also probably have something to do with it.

The Old Print Shop has gained a reputation for good pub grub, sandwiches, fish and chips, etc. Plank floors are divided into five or six different areas so groups can be together – or not! There is a wide variety of art on the walls, and covers as wide a range as the clientele who frequent the Old Print Shop. You'll see pictures of ships, former MPs (Members of Parliament), reformers and old photographs of Glasgow. This is casual dining to be sure. The food is good and filling, the atmosphere generally quite busy, especially around meal times, and the patrons as well as the employees are friendly folks.

18. THE UPPER CRUST SANDWICH BAR, *Royal Exchange Square, Queen Street, Glasgow. £2-4. Open Monday through Saturday from 6:00am to 5:00pm. MasterCard and Visa accepted.*

This little café in the square next to the Museum of Modern Art opens quite early to serve breakfast to those early-rising businessmen and businesswomen (and a few tourists) who are out and about Glasgow at the crack of dawn. It stays open throughout the day, dispensing sandwiches of all varieties for their guests. As the name implies, their specialty is sandwiches, although they do offer a variety of other items, including soups, salads and baked potatoes.

There are six tables inside and four or five outside. Each is draped with green, blue and yellow checkered tablecloths. Inside, you'll find tile floors and yellow walls with blue trim. If you sit at the outside tables, you'll be able to study the architecture of the Museum of Modern Art while watching skateboarders try their skills on the stairs leading up to the museum. Dress is of course casual, and grubbies are fine. The Upper Crust provides great sandwiches at great prices, so you may have to stand in line around lunch and dinner times. But the wait is worth it.

West Side

19. ONE DEVONSHIRE GARDENS RESTAURANT, *One Devonshire Gardens, Glasgow. Tel. 0141/339-2001. £35-50. Open daily from noon to 1:45pm, and from 7:15pm to 9:45pm. All major credit cards accepted.*

This is the restaurant for One Devonshire Gardens Hotel, and it is as exquisite as you would expect it to be. This award-winning restaurant achieves excellence in food, wine and ambience. The dining room itself is exquisite: 14' ceilings, rich oak trim along the walls and modern art on the walls. Crystal and china, linen and silver are also part of the setting. A smaller overflow dining room with half a dozen tables is available for small dinner parties if you wish. Prior to your meal, you'll have the luxury of relaxing with a glass of wine in the marvelous Drawing Room in front of a crackling fire.

The menu changes frequently, but you'll find such offerings as herb-roasted chicken, fondant potatoes and Caesar salad, or you might also like to try the pavé of potato, roasted peppers and goat's cheese with parmesan. Whatever your choice of entrée, you'll be delighted with your selection. The meals prepared here are wonderful, and the presentation is nothing short of masterful. Dress ranges from nice casual to pretty formal. Personally, I would err on the side of dressing more formally for this restaurant. Reservations are a must during the summer months.

20. UBIQUITOUS CHIP, *12 Ashland Lane, Glasgow. Tel. 0141/334-5007. £16-32. Open Monday through Saturday from noon to 2:30pm, and 5:30pm to 11:00pm, and Sunday from 12:30pm to 2:30pm, and from 6:30pm to 11:00pm. MasterCard and Visa accepted.*

The Ubiquitous Chip is a little tough to find as it is tucked back in an L-shaped alley behind Byre Street, but it is well worth the effort to locate it. This little place has been going strong since its establishment in the early 1970s, and in fact has a bit of a cult following. Ronnie Clydesdale is the owner, and he has been highly successful in providing excellent food in a wonderful setting.

You'll find plain pine tables, flickering candles and white-painted brick walls. But the thing that will leave the greatest impression is the profusion of plants in the restaurant – they are everywhere! You will feel as though you are dining in the middle of a rain forest. There are so many that they threaten to block the massive skylight (actually, the ceiling is simply a series of windows). The atmosphere is one of pleasant chatter all around the room, from college-age kids to silver-haired businessmen to talkative tourists. The menu changes frequently, but you might find howtowdie breast of free-range chicken, skirlie, glazed shallots and quail's egg, Scottish salmon smoked in darjeeling tea, cured cabbage washed in riesling and potatoes in truffle oil. The Ubiquitous Chip has earned recognition by *A Taste of Scotland*. A set two-course meal and coffee runs £27, and a three-course meal is £32.

Selected as one of my picks for Scotland's Best Restaurants – see Chapter 11.

21. CAFÉ MALMAISON, *278 West George Street, Glasgow. Tel. 0141/572-1001. £15-20. Open daily from 6:00pm to midnight. All major credit cards accepted.*

The Café Malmaison strives to recreate the atmosphere and dining experience of a Mediterranean café. The restaurant provides a pleasant, chatty atmosphere in an unhurried setting. There are lots of young college-age people frequenting the place. A number of dishes are available, mostly a lot of salads, soups, pizza and pasta. A wide variety of wines is also available to help create the atmosphere. Dress is casual, and you'll probably need reservations during the summer months and on the weekends.

22. MALMAISON BRASSERIE, *278 West George Street, Glasgow. Tel. 0141/572-1001. £15-20. Open daily from 7:00pm to midnight. All major credit cards accepted.*

Originally, the Malmaison was known for its restaurant, and the accommodations were merely a sidelight. Today the hotel gets most of the publicity, but the Malmaison Brasserie still pulls in diners from all over the city. The Brasserie is designed to emulate a turn-of-the-century French brasserie. The menu claims that they provide "a collection of the simple things well done: the food, the wine, the service..." They succeed in all areas.

Subdued lighting and strategic positioning of tables and booths makes for an ideal setting to savor your meals. The menu provides such options as navarin of lamb with turnip fondant, or if you'd prefer something a little different, you might try the char-grilled chicken with buttered spinach. The food is complemented by a fine wine list, with over 65 selections to choose from. Small private dining rooms are available if you wish a private meal for groups of eight to ten. This is a great restaurant and one where you will enjoy the ambience, the food and the wine. Dress is casual, and you will probably need reservations, especially on the weekends.

23. SUTHERLAND'S RESTAURANT, *973 Sauchiehall Street, Glasgow. Tel. 0141/357-4711. £12-16. Open Monday through Thursday from noon to 2:00pm and 5:30pm to 9:30pm, Friday and Saturday from 5:30pm to 9:30pm and Sunday from 6:30pm to 9:00pm. Amex, MasterCard and Visa accepted.*

Sutherland's Restaurant is on the garden level below the Argyll Hotel. You'll smile at the green and gold tartan carpet (I did, anyway) and the dark green tartan wallpaper. I'm pretty used to tartan being everywhere in Scotland, but this was a little much even for me. However, several folks pointed me to Sutherland's because of the quality of their food, and I believe you will agree it's a good choice. It is a nice place and you'll find plenty of traditional Scottish menu items here. Sutherland's offers an a la carte menu or a table d'hôte option for £14 for a three-course meal or £10 for two courses. Either way you'll receive good food at pretty good prices. You might try the sirloin of Aberdeen beef in a light mustard and whisky sauce, or the poached haddock filet in a prawn and lobster sauce. If you're looking for more of a vegetarian option, you're in luck, as Sutherland's offers several good choices, including lightly curried sweet potato and braised leek strudel. No matter which menu item you select, you are sure to enjoy your feast at Sutherland's. Dress is casual.

24. THE CUL-DE-SAC RESTAURANT, *40 Ashland Lane, Glasgow. Tel. 0141/334-4749. £5-16. Open daily from noon to 11:00pm (sometimes until midnight depending on the demand). Amex, MasterCard and Visa accepted.*

At the end of Ashland Lane off Byre's Street is the appropriately named Cul-de-Sac Restaurant. This is a very popular, very trendy restaurant with an energetic Bohemian feel. Inside you'll find lots of people, yellow brick walls, plain pine tables with black-and-white checkered tablecloths and cane-style chairs. Large candles on the tables and subdued lighting are enhanced by light jazz music playing quietly in the background. Many of the patrons are college-age, but there is a wide range of folks who enjoy the Cul-de-Sac Restaurant. The menu reflects the Scottish-French cuisine prepared and presented here. Just reading the menu will stimulate your hunger: linguine with mussels, clams, sole, cod and prawns in a dill cream sauce is one of the house specialties. Other options include breast of chicken stuffed with gingered pak choi and shitake mushrooms and a good selection of vegetarian dishes.

25. ASHOKA RESTAURANT, *Ashton Lane, Glasgow. Tel. 800/454-817. £8-15. Open Monday through Thursday noon to midnight, Friday and Saturday noon to 12:30am, Sunday from 5:00pm to midnight. Amex, MasterCard and Visa accepted.*

Welcome to one of the busiest and best Indian restaurants in Glasgow. As you walk into the restaurant, a large colorful mural of a street scene in India will greet you – as will the unmistakable smell of curry. Indian sitar music adds appropriately to the atmosphere. The restaurant is smallish, with room for only 30 to 40 diners at a time. If you are a connoisseur of Indian food, you will be delighted with the range of dishes available. You'll also appreciate the excellence of the fare. Try the karahi Bhoona, a host of spices in a rich tarka base with an abundance of capsicums and onions simmered in karahi (an Indian wok). Or you might wish to try the Balti with a variety of tandoori spices, achari, kabli chana and a flourish of fresh yogurt.

The Ahsoka chain of restaurants is reputed to be one of the finest for Indian cuisine in the United Kingdom. There are six such restaurants in Glasgow. Even if you've never tried Indian food before, this is an excellent place to try it for the first time. The waiters are very helpful and will be happy to assist you in your selections. Whether or not you have eaten much Indian food in the past, you can rest assured that you will be sampling some of the best around at Ashoka restaurant. Dress is casual, and you will probably need reservations during the summer tourist months.

26. JINTY MCINTY'S BAR AND RESTAURANT, *11 Ashland Lane, Glasgow. Tel. 0141/337-3636. Open Monday through Saturday from 11:30am to 11:00pm, closed Sunday. MasterCard and Visa accepted.*

If you are looking for a loud, smoky, trendy sort of place packed to overflowing with university students, this is the place for you. Jinty McInty's is wonderful old bar that has a lot of character and oozes personality from its wooden plank floors to its smoky beamed ceiling. In addition to a wide variety of whiskies, beers and ales, you'll find some fine old traditional Irish/Scottish fare here – Irish stew, Highland lamb, fish and chips, and sandwiches. Jinty's serves true pub grub, and their guests seem to devour it. Casual dress is of course the dress code here.

27. O'BRIEN'S IRISH SANDWICHES, *229 Sauchiehall Street, Glasgow. Tel. 0141/333-9355. £2-4. Open Monday through Friday 7:00am to 6:00pm, Saturday from 8:00am to 6:00pm, and Sunday from 11:00am to 5:00pm. No credit cards accepted.*

While you are shopping on the pedestrianized Sauchiehall Street, stop in at O'Brien's for a sandwich. There are a couple of tables inside the sandwich shop, but if it's nice you'll enjoy sitting outside at the tables on the sidewalk. That way you can eat and people watch at the same time. There's nothing particularly spectacular about the sandwiches you'll get here, other than the fact they are good and reasonably priced.

28. STARBUCKS, *27 Sauchiehall Street, Glasgow. Tel. 0141/353-3149. £3-5. Open daily Monday through Friday from 7:30am to 7:00pm, Saturday from 7:30am to 8:00pm, and Sunday from 10:00am to 6:00pm. MasterCard and Visa accepted.*

Can't live without your Starbucks coffee in the morning? Are you longing for a latte, expiring for an espresso, or meditating about a muffin? Then never fear – your favorite chain for coffee and muffins has found its way to Glasgow. Located on Glasgow's stylish Sauchiehall Street, this Starbucks will be able to settle your jangled nerves and give you a boost to start the day. You'll enjoy the pleasant surroundings, the comfy sofas and low tables, and the constant buzz of coffee aficionados getting their morning "cup-a-joe." Dress is of course casual. Don't show up here before the sun comes up looking for your morning fix – you'll find the hours a little more leisurely here (that's okay – you're on holiday, remember?).

Suburbs

29. LE GOURMET RESTAURANT, *169 Paisley Road, Renfrew. Tel. 0141/886-5555, Fax 0141/885-2838. £10-22. Open daily for lunch Monday through Friday from noon until 2:30pm, and for dinner Monday through Saturday from 6:00pm to 10:30pm. All major credit cards accepted.*

Le Gourmet is the formal dining room for the Glynhill Leisure Hotel. As such, it provides a little more formal setting than the hotel's other restaurant, The Palm Court. You'll find a pleasant and cheerful atmosphere here, and many people enjoying themselves. Friday and Saturday evenings are especially nice, when candlelit dinner dances are offered from 6:00pm to 12:30am. The menu offers a surprising number of selections, including such delights as chicken Kiev, pork filet burgundy, pan-fried filet of Aberdeen beef, or grilled trout almondine. Le Gourmet has a surprisingly nice wine list, although the selections aren't extensive. The management has carefully selected those wines that seem to complement the tastes (and pocketbooks) of their clientele.

30. HOMESPREADS COCKET HAT RESTAURANT, *Eaglesham Road, East Kilbride, Glasgow. Tel. 01355/222-747. £5-15. Open Monday through Saturday from 11:00am to 11:00pm, and Sunday from 12:30am to 11:00pm. MasterCard and Visa accepted.*

This is a bright and casual family-dining restaurant serving everything from soups and salads to small inexpensive steaks. It represents economy dining, and provides good and filling meals. These are relatively new restaurants on the Scottish dining scene, and are associated with the Lodge Inns chain of hotels. They are extremely popular in England, and I believe that in the coming years that popularity will be duplicated in Scotland. While there will probably be no awards for fine cuisine anytime soon, the food is fine, and the environment is clean and very family-centered. Dress is very casual.

31. THE PALM COURT, *169 Paisley Road, Renfrew. Tel. 0141/886-5555, Fax 0141/885-2838. £5-12. Open for breakfast Monday to Saturday from 7:00am to 10:00am, and Sunday from 7:30am to 10:30am. Open for lunch Tuesday through Sunday from noon until 2:30pm, and open daily for dinner from 6:00pm to 10:30pm. All major credit cards accepted.*

The Palm Court is the buffet-style restaurant the serves guests of the Glynhill Leisure Hotel, as well as others who venture in. The atmosphere here is relaxed and comfortable, so you don't need to feel intimidated should you wish to bring your less-than-quiet-as-a-church-mouse children here to dine.

I like breakfast here, and am particularly impressed with the variety of offerings available. You'll be able to choose from all the elements of a traditional Scottish breakfast, such as eggs, bacon, sausage, black pudding, haggis, porridge and toast. In addition, there are a number of continental breakfast types of things to eat, like rolls, fruit, cereal and yogurt. Dinner is also a winner, with a wide selection of salads and appetizers, accompanied by various meats. My favorite part of buffets is the dessert section, and you won't be disappointed with the selection you have here. All in all, this is a nice dining experience, with good hearty food.

SEEING THE SIGHTS

There are a number of sights and activities in Glasgow that might be of interest to you. Cathedrals and art galleries, museums and pubs all vie for your attention. I would suggest that if you have a car, find a place to park it, since most of the sights to see in Glasgow are in the downtown area. As with the *Where to Stay* and *Where to Eat* sections, I have divided the *Seeing the Sights* section into three categories: **City Center**, **West Side** and **Suburbs**.

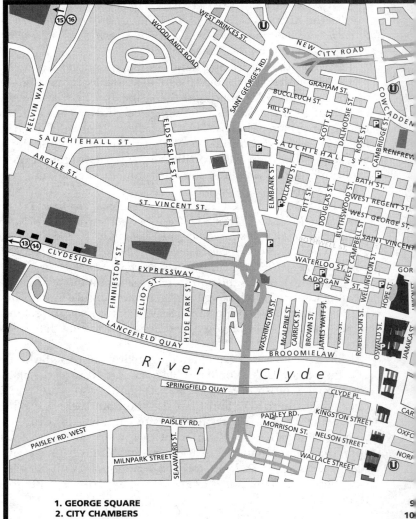

1. GEORGE SQUARE
2. CITY CHAMBERS
3. GLASGOW GALLERY OF MODERN ART
4. GLASGOW CATHEDRAL
5. NECROPOLIS
6. SAINT MUNGO'S MUSEUM OF RELIGIOUS LIFE AND ART
7. PROVAND'S LORDSHIP
8. TOLLBOOTH STEEPLE

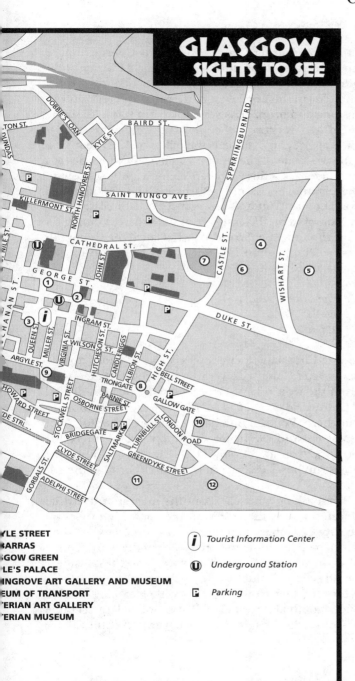

GLASGOW
SIGHTS TO SEE

YLE STREET
ARRAS
GOW GREEN
LE'S PALACE
NGROVE ART GALLERY AND MUSEUM
EUM OF TRANSPORT
ERIAN ART GALLERY
ERIAN MUSEUM

i   *Tourist Information Center*

Ⓤ   *Underground Station*

🅿   *Parking*

City Center

A good place to begin touring Glasgow's sights is **George Square**. George Square is in the center of the downtown business district, and is a concrete plaza with statues commemorating some of Scotland's greatest figures. There is an index in the northwest corner that will tell you who is memorialized in stone and bronze. As you walk from statue to statue, you'll get a *Reader's Digest* version of people who were important to Scottish history. Sir Walter Scott's statue is the tallest and in the middle of the square. On the west side of the square you'll find the statues of a woman and man on horseback – this is Queen Victoria and her husband Albert. Two poets have statues here, Robert Burns and Thomas Campbell, as does the inventor Thomas Watt and economist William Gladstone.

There is a War Memorial on the east side of the square, saluting the 200,000 Glaswegians who fought in World War II. Called the **Cenotaph**, it is guarded by two solemn, sphinx-like lions. The memorial has the following words emblazoned on it:

These died in war
That we at peace might live;
They gave their best,
So we our best should give.

If you are interested in taking a city tour via one of those double-decker buses you see all over Glasgow, several companies start their tours across the street from the west side of George Square. **ScotGuide**, *Tel. 0141/204-444*, and **Guide Friday**, *Tel. 0141/248/7644*, are two companies that begin their tours here. You can purchase an all-day ticket for £6.50 that will take you past most of the major sights that are of interest to tourists. The ticket allows you to get on and off the bus as you please. These tour companies run buses daily from late March through the end of October.

You may have been asking yourself about the magnificent official-looking building located across the street on the east side of George Square. That is the **City Chambers** building. It was completed in 1888, and it truly is a Victorian-era building in every sense of the word: Queen Victoria dedicated it on August 22, 1888. If you think the outside is impressive, you should see the inside!

As you enter the building, you'll be met with gleaming marble, polished granite and smooth alabaster. You'll also note a large ceramic mosaic on the floor – this is the Glasgow City coat of arms (see the sidebar below).

THE GLASGOW COAT OF ARMS

Wherever you go in Glasgow, you'll notice the coat of arms for Glasgow city. It features a shield with an oak tree in the center, a bird atop the tree, and a bell hanging from one of the limbs of the tree. On either side of the tree is a large fish, seemingly standing on its tail, and with a gold ring in its mouth. On top of it all is a clergyman standing with hand uplifted as if to bless those who come to him. The city motto underscores the entire coat of arms. Each element is of course symbolic of some event in Glasgow's past. Since you will see all or parts of the coat of arms throughout the city, I thought I'd share the significance of its major elements:

• The bird represents a wild robin that was accidentally killed. St. Mungo was blamed for the death. Legend has it that he took the bird in his hand and prayed over it, bringing it back to life.

• The tree represents another legend from St. Mungo's life. As a boy, St. Mungo was left to tend the holy fire in the rectory. He fell asleep and some naughty boys extinguished the fire, hoping to get St. Mungo in trouble. Young St. Mungo took some frozen branches and, after praying over them, they burst into flame.

• The bell represents a bell given to St. Mungo by the Pope.

• The fish with the gold ring is a salmon. It seems that the king at the time of St. Mungo gave a gold ring to his queen. She in turn gave the ring to a handsome knight. The king saw the knight with the ring and suspected some hanky-panky, so he stole it from him as he slept. He tossed the ring in the River Clyde, then demanded that his queen produce the ring or suffer death. She went to the knight, who in turn went and confessed his misdeeds to St. Mungo and explained the fix he was in. St. Mungo instructed a fellow priest to go fish in the River Clyde and bring him the first fish he caught. The priest obeyed, and upon delivering the fish, St. Mungo extracted the ring from the mouth of the fish, thus saving both the queen and her knight.

• The city motto reads "Let Glasgow flourish." It is a truncated version of the original motto: "Let Glasgow flourish through the preaching of thy word and praising thy name."

• Any guesses as to whom the clergyman at the top of the coat of arms is? That's right – it is St. Mungo, the patron saint of Glasgow.

If council meetings are not in session, you are able to take a tour of the rest of the building, and it is as stunningly splendid as the entry hall. My favorite room is the Council Chamber. It features exquisite gold-leafed ornamentation and Venetian stained glass in the windows and the domed ceiling. The Banqueting Hall is as lavish as the rest of the building. Huge murals depicting scenes from Glasgow history line the walls. The massive arched ceiling is hand-carved and gold-leafed. The three chandeliers are original to the room, and date to 1885. They were among the earliest electric lights in Scotland.

Tours are free, and run each weekday from 9:00am to around 4:00pm. Certain areas are not available for perusal, depending on the city council's schedule that day.

South of George Square on Queen Street, you'll find the wonderfully eclectic **Glasgow Gallery of Modern Art**, *Queen Street, Tel. 0141/229-1996, Fax 0141/204-5315; open Monday through Saturday from 10:00am to 5:00pm, Sunday from 11:00am to 5:00pm; admission free.* From the Palladian columns out front to the fractured mirrors in the entryway and all throughout the gallery, you'll discover that this gallery is a study in contrasts as the new and old and the impressionistic and realistic all vie for your attention. Lots to look at here, all housed on multiple floors.

There are three main sections or galleries, all named after the elements: Earth, Air, Wind and Fire. Don't miss the Fire Gallery in the downstairs area – it is really fascinating, and a bonus for those of you traveling with children. Particularly impressive is the display of a large human head with synapses firing, as well as a life-size version of the toy where you push the pins in to make an imprint (of your hand, nose, whatever), except this one is the size of your entire body. The gallery is located about a half block south of George Square on the Royal Exchange Square. Head back to George Square, then a couple of blocks east along George Street until you get to High Street.

Go up hill to the left, and you'll soon come to **Glasgow Cathedral**, *Cathedral Street, Tel. 0141/552-8198; open April through September Monday through Saturday from 9:30am to 6:00pm, Sunday from 2:00pm to 5:00pm, and from October through March on Monday through Saturday from 9:30am to 4:00pm, and Sunday from 2:00pm to 4:00pm; admission is free.* Also known as the Cathedral of St. Kentigern or St. Mungo's Cathedral, Glasgow Cathedral is a marvelous example of 12th-century craftsmanship. Sit in one of the pews and just gaze in awe at the incredible workmanship, and wonder at the immense effort this must have been with the tools that were available in the 1100s. Glasgow Cathedral is the only intact medieval cathedral in Scotland, and how she survived when the rest of her sisters were razed (many times) is a quirk of history. (See Jedburgh, Dryburgh, Kelso and Melrose Abbeys, for instance). The cathedral has some wonderful ancient stone carvings that are worth taking the time to see. Foremost among them is the depiction of the seven deadly sins on the stone screen in the nave.

Glasgow Cathedral gained literary notoriety as the place where the legendary revolutionary Rob Roy makes contact with Francis Osbaldistone in Sir Walter Scott's epic novel *Rob Roy*. The brief encounter takes place in the vaulted crypt of the Cathedral, below the main floor at the north end of the building. The crypts are worth more than a cursory glance: there is interesting and intriguing tombs to examine. In fact, don't miss the tomb of St. Mungo, the patron saint of Glasgow. It was St. Mungo who founded a church on the present site of Glasgow Cathedral. It is a wonderful place to spend a little time, just looking at the many things that will catch your interest. I am always intrigued by many of the tombstone memorials to important Glasgow citizens of former days.

From the Cathedral, cross the **Bridge of Sighs** into the adjacent **Necropolis**. This Glasgow city cemetery is packed with the remains and tombstones of the city's citizens of the past 170 years. Take a few minutes and walk through it, as you will be amazed at the sheer variety of tombstones and remembrances that you'll find here. It is a good example of the excesses of the Victorian age. The cemetery is modeled on the famed Pére la Chaise cemetery in Paris. The soaring Doric column with John Knox atop presides over the Necropolis.

On the same grounds as Glasgow Cathedral, you'll find **St. Mungo's Museum of Religious Life and Art**, *2 Castle Street, Tel. 0141/553-2557, Fax 0141/552-4744; open Monday, through Saturday from 10:00am to 5:00pm, and Sunday from 11:00am to 5:00pm; admission is free.* This modern museum offers a look at major religions of the world. Its three galleries focus on religious art, religious life and religion in Scotland. St. Mungo's Museum boasts Salvadore Dali's *Christ of St. John of the Cross*, and the museum is worth visiting if just for that. If you've ever wondered what a Japanese Zen Garden is like, the museum has recreated one for your information and enlightenment. The Religion of Scotland Gallery gives you a good overview of the religious history of Scotland, from its earliest days to the present.

While you are in the vicinity, you might like to pop in at the **Provand's Lordship**, *3 Castle Street, Tel. 0141/552-8819; open Monday through Saturday from 10:00am to 5:00pm, and Sunday from 11:00am to 5:00pm; admission is free.* This is Glasgow's oldest home, and Bishop Andrew Muirhead built it in 1471. After years of neglect, the city has renovated it into a museum decked out with period furnishings. It is said that Mary Queen of Scots stayed here (sort of like George Washington slept here).

Head south along High Street and you'll come to a broad intersection where five streets converge. Presiding over the convergence is the tall and proud **Glasgow Tolbooth Steeple**. The Tolbooth is a large medieval structure that once served as the jail and courthouse. Visitors to Glasgow were required to pay a toll here. The Tolbooth was immortalized in Sir Walter Scott's classic novel *Rob Roy*. It was here that Francis Osbaldistone visited his friend under the escort of a mysterious stranger (Rob Roy).

Next to the Tolbooth Steeple is the striking **Tron Steeple**. The steeple is all that remains of Tron Church, a 16th century church that burned to the ground several hundred years ago. The steeple is all that remains of what must have been a grand structure.

From Tron and Tolbooth Steeples, head west along Trongate Street to **Argyle Street**. Argyle Street is one of Glasgow's most popular shopping districts, and is a plethora of people and street entertainers during the summer months. Just a half block off Argyle Street you'll find the ultra-new shopping center called St. Enoch Centre, as nice and modern a mall as you have probably ever visited. Many shops, a food court and ice rink await your perusal.

After you've visited Argyle Street and St. Enochs, head back to Tolbooth Steeple and go east for a short distance on Gallowgate Street (care to guess where this street got its name?). Near the corner of Gallowgate and Ross Streets, you'll see the large wrought-iron gate for **The Barras**, a large indoor flea market. Open only on the weekends, this is one of the fun places to go and shop and kibitz.

A few hundred yards down High/Saltmarket Street you'll come to **Glasgow Green**, a large expanse of verdant green lawn running alongside the River Clyde. Set aside as a park for the residents of Glasgow over 300 years ago (1662), the park is a nice place to relax, people-watch, or throw a frisbee or two. The park is site to many activities, including marathons, political rallys and concerts.

While you're on Glasgow Green, stop by the **People's Palace**, *Glasgow Green, Tel. 0141/554-223, Fax 0141/550-0892; open Monday through Saturday from 10:00am to 5:00pm, and Sunday from 11:00am to 5:00pm; admission is free*. Housed in a late Victorian-era red sandstone building, the People's Palace is a museum devoted to the social, industrial and political lives of Glaswegians throughout the past 250 years. You'll see campaign posters from days gone by, the battle for women's suffrage, exhibits celebrating Glasgow's efforts during the previous two world wars, and furnishings and relics from the Tobacco Kings of Glasgow's earlier days. There is a lot to see here, and it is a nice place to stop for awhile.

West Side

The west side of Glasgow offers a number of fun and interesting museums and art galleries. If you do not have a car, the best way to get to these sights is to hop on one of the Glasgow City tour buses (see the entry on George Square to find out more about these). With your all-day ticket, you can get off at each stop, visit the sight, then jump back on any of the ensuing buses to go to the next sight.

Start your visit of the west side sights by stopping in at the **Kelvingrove Art Gallery and Museum**, *Kelvingrove, Argyle Street, Tel. 0141/221-9600;*

open Monday through Saturday from 10:00am to 5:00pm, Sunday from 11:00am to 5:00pm; admission free. The building itself is a work of art: it is a red sandstone structure built at the turn of the century. This is a marvelous museum that houses a splendid collection of fine old paintings from a number of Dutch, French and Italian masters. You'll find paintings by Rembrandt, Dali, Giorgine, Millet, Whistler and others. The museum doesn't have an extensive collection, but that which they have is well displayed. In addition to the art, there is broad variety of exhibits ranging from prehistory to Egyptian up to modern day. I particularly like the armor section, with a life-size replica of the armor worn by Imperial Storm Troopers from the epic movie *Star Wars.* I also admire the marble statue at the north entrance to the museum depicting Jacob administering to Esau.

Just down the street and around the corner from the Kelvingrove Art Gallery and Museum you'll find the **Museum of Transport,** *Kelvingrove, 1 Burnhouse Road, Tel. 0141/287-2720, Fax 0141/287-2692; open Monday through Saturday from 10:00am to 5:00pm, and Sunday from 11:00am to 5:00pm; admission is free.* This museum houses an impressive display of transportation, from horse-drawn buggies to steam engines, trolleys, jets, motorcycles and bicycles. There is an interesting display called *Shipbuilding on the River Clyde* portraying the incredible work that occurred in this important business that made Glasgow world-famous. You'll also enjoy the depiction of a late 1930's Glasgow street scene. On your left just as you enter the museum, you'll find an old car or two, and about a dozen shop windows. It's fun to stroll along the cobblestone street and peer into the windows at items that looked for all the world like they came from my grandmother's attic.

The Hunterian Art Gallery, *University of Glasgow, 82 Hillhead Street, Tel. 0141/330-5431, Fax 0141/330-3618; open Monday through Saturday from 9:30am to 5:00pm, (closed from 12:30pm to 1:30pm), closed Sunday; admission free.* You'll find this impressive art gallery on the campus of the University of Glasgow. The museum has been around since 1807 and is Glasgow's oldest museum. One of the world's most-recognized artists is **James Abbott McNeill Whistler.** We are all familiar with him because of the famous portrait he painted of his mother. But to be honest, until I visited this museum I don't believe I had ever seen anything else he painted. The museum displays a number of his paintings, and it is clear that he wasn't just a "one-hit sensation." In addition, the museum has recreated parts of the home of Glasgow-born avant-garde architect **Charles Rennie MacKintosh.** Truly a man ahead of his time, you'll find the combination of geometric designs, bold colors and modern art to be quite interesting and inspiring.

Across the street from the Hunterian Art Gallery is the **Hunterian Museum**, *University of Glasgow, University Avenue, Tel. 0141/330-4221, Fax 0141/330-3617; open Monday through Saturday from 9:30am to 5:00pm, closed Sunday*; *admission free*. This is an interesting and fun museum, one that would be of particular interest and enjoyment if you have the kids along. Not a large museum, it nonetheless has a number of interesting exhibits. Many of the exhibits change quarterly. There are various exhibits on Egypt and Africa, with a wonderful collection of fossils. There is a particularly interesting display on human evolution, and it includes a piece on the evolutionary hoax of the Piltdown man: a Neanderthal man who supposedly lived in Europe. The skull was really that of an ape that had been altered by the archaeologist who was apparently more interested in instant fame than long-lasting respect.

On the west end of town, you'll find a wonderful, peaceful and tranquil setting at the **Botanic Gardens**, *730 Great Western Road, Tel. 0141/334-2422; the gardens are open daily from 7:00am to sundown, and the greenhouses are open weekdays from 10:00am to 4:45pm, Saturday from 1:00pm to 4:45pm and Sunday from noon to 4:45pm; admission free*. The gardens are lushly extravagant and have a wonderful collection of exotic plants such as begonias, orchids, tropical plants and ferns. Established in 1817 by Thomas Kirkpatrick, it makes for a pleasant diversion from your rapid pace of sightseeing. You'll have a choice of walking through a series of greenhouses filled with tropical offerings or you may walk among more traditional gardens outside on the grounds.

Suburbs

About three miles southwest of downtown Glasgow, you'll find Scotland's number one tourist attraction: the **Burrell Collection**, *2060 Pollokshaws Road, Tel. 0141/649-7151; open Monday through Saturday from 10:00am to 5:00pm, and Sunday from 11:00am to 5:00pm; admission free*. Sir William Burrell was a wealthy Glaswegian who delighted in spending his children's inheritances on fabulous pieces of art and sculpture. Born in 1861, Sir Burrell spent the majority of his life collecting *objets d'art* from all over the world. During a lifetime of extensive museum-going, the Burrell Collection is one of my all-time favorites. You have a wide range of things to see, all tastefully displayed. You'll go from ancient Chinese dynasties to displays on Egyptian civilization to wood carvings, ancient city gates, tapestries, stained glass, and (it seems) just about everything in between.

Interested in Ming vases? Well, you can see them here. There are even objects from Chinese dynasties nearly 1,000 years older than the Ming dynasty, including items from the Qing dynasty (ca. 664 AD). You'd like to see paintings by Cezanne, Millet, Boudin and Degas? You say you've always wanted to see authentic bronze statues by famed sculptor Rodin? This is the place for all of these and much more.

In 1916, Sir Burrell purchased a castle in the Borders region of Scotland at Berwick-on-Tweed. He spent huge sums of money renovating and modernizing it, and much of his collection was housed there for years. Three of the rooms from that house have been reproduced here: the dining room, master hallway and drawing room. Each has been decorated with objects from Burrell's collection. In 1944, Sir Burrell donated his entire collection of 8,000 items to the city of Glasgow with the stipulation that they be shown in a rural setting, and not in Glasgow, which was already experiencing significant pollution when he made this caveat. At the time of his death in 1958, the city still had not found an appropriate site for his collection (bureaucracy at work!). However, in 1967 the Maxwell family donated acreage from their estate to enable a permanent home for the collection to be built. It was (in 1983), and you are the happy beneficiary of Sir Burrell's eccentricity and magnanimity. While admission is free to the Burrell Collection, there is a £1.50 charge for parking.

While you're here, don't overlook **Pollok House**, *2060 Pollokshaws Road, Tel. 0141/616-6410; open June to September on Monday through Saturday from 10:00am to 5:00pm, April through October it is open Monday through Saturday from 10:00am to 5:00pm and Sunday from 11:00am to 5:00pm, from November to March it is open daily from 11:00am to 4:00pm; admission is charged from April through November: £3 for adults, £2 for children, and an £8 family ticket is available; admission is free from November through March.* Pollok House is an elegant country house where you can see where the "other half" lived during the 18th and 19th centuries. The ancestral home of the Maxwell family, the family donated the house and 360 acres to the city of Glasgow in 1967.

You'll find a spectacularly elegant and lavish home in Pollok House. In addition, you will find one of the finest collections of European art in Scotland, the fruits of Sir William Maxwell's hobby of collecting art. Watch for paintings by such renowned masters as El Greco, Goya, Murillo, Signorelli and others. In addition to the paintings, you'll be astounded by the fine furnishings, silver and ceramic displays – all from the Maxwell family's daily life.

NIGHTLIFE & ENTERTAINMENT
Pubs
Sure, and you're anxious to have a drink and meet a few folks of an evening. Well, Glasgow has a number of pubs that can meet both these needs, and following are a few of the more popular ones.

THE ATTIC, *44 Ashland Lane, Glasgow. Tel. 0141/334-6688. Open Monday through Thursday from 8:00am to 11:00pm, and Friday and Saturday from 8:00am until midnight.*

The Attic is a an upscale pub occupying the "attic" above the Cul-de-Sac Restaurant at the end of Ashland Lane. It is a pleasant enough place, with open rafters (it *is* an attic, after all), and lots of college-age folks and tourists enjoying one another's company.

BAR BOOSHKA, *41 Dumbarton Road, Glasgow. Tel. 0141/357-1830. Open Sunday through Friday from noon until 11:00pm, and Friday and Saturday from noon until midnight.*

Bar Booshka (don't you love that name?) is the only self-proclaimed "vodka bar" in Glasgow. And when it comes to vodka, they know their stuff; at last count they were serving nearly 60 varieties of vodka. Don't worry – they serve other sorts of liquor too. You'll get a definite old Soviet feel here from the décor, and you'll encounter a wide range of patrons, from college-age students to middle-age businessmen to curious tourists.

BARGO, *80 Albion Street, Glasgow. Tel. 0141/553-4771. Open Monday through Saturday from 11:00am until midnight, and Sunday from 10:00am until midnight.*

Bargo is one of the trendiest bars in the city, and therefore in all of Scotland. This large bar affords plenty of room for the considerable crowds that pass through its doors, especially on the weekends. There's a good mix of people, especially a lot of young college-age students.

BAR 91, *91 Candleriggs, Glasgow. Tel. 0141/221-8353. Open daily from 11:00am until midnight.*

Bar 91 is one of the top hang-outs for Generation X-ers, and is a trendy (but not *too* trendy) place to chill or quaff a few beers. You'll find lots of people here, especially on the weekends.

BON ACCORD, *153 North Street, Glasgow. Tel. 0141/248-4427. Open Monday through Saturday from 11:00am to 11:45pm, Sunday from 11:30am until 11:00pm.*

The Bon Accord is a pleasant and friendly place to sample a portion of the city's best selection of ales. Lots of friendly people, ranging from college-age students on up, will make you feel right at home here. In addition to the ales, you'll find a wide variety of international beers on tap.

JINTY McGINTY'S, *11 Ashland Lane, Glasgow. Tel. 0131/337-3636. Open Monday through Saturday from 11:30am to 11:00pm, closed Sunday.*

This is a genuine smoke-filled Irish pub, located along Ashland Lane off Byre Street. You'll find a rowdy and robust crowd here most nights, especially during the tourist season. But have no fear – most of the patrons are indigenous to Scotland. The atmosphere is reminiscent of many of the pubs that are so prevalent across the Irish Sea from Scotland. And yes, in case you're wondering, they do have Guinness.

L'ATTACHÉ, *27 Waterloo Street, Glasgow. Tel. 0141/221-3210. Open Monday through Friday from 11:30am to 11:00pm, and Friday through Saturday from noon until midnight.*

If you are looking for a traditional Scottish pub experience, then L'Attaché is the place to go. You'll find stone floors and ale casks used to spice up the décor, and a lot of interesting folks. Live bands play on the weekends, with traditional Scottish music on Thursdays, disco on Fridays and a variety of local bands playing their gigs on Saturday evenings.

THE HORSESHOE BAR, *17 Drury Street, Glasgow. Tel. 0141/229-5711. Open daily from 11:00am until midnight.*

The Horseshoe Bar features the longest continuous bar in Britain, and so you might as well come for a look, if nothing else. However, you'll also find a chatty, convivial atmosphere here, and you should be able to strike up a conversation with more than one Scotsman/woman who has come to quench his (or her) thirst. You'll generally find a wide range of folks here, and it is especially busy on the weekends and during the tourist season.

Theaters

Theater is a popular diversion in Glasgow, and as a result there are quite a few theaters here. Many aspiring playwrights haunt Glasgow's streets, looking for their big break, and their works are often showcased at any number of Glasgow theaters. Tickets can be purchased at the box offices for each theater or at the **Ticket Centre**, *City Hall, Candleriggs, Tel. 0141/227-5511.*

CITIZEN'S THEATRE, *119 Gorbals Street, Glasgow. Tel. 0141/429-0022, Fax 0141/429-7374. Tickets are £2-6.*

The Citizen's Theatre is the most avant-garde theater in Glasgow, and productions by amateur and adventurous playwrights are featured here. Founded by James Bridie, one of Glasgow's foremost modern playwrights, the theater has provided some of Glasgow's most memorable albeit unconventional plays and sets in recent years.

CITY HALLS, *Candleriggs, Glasgow. Tel. 0141/287-5024, Fax 0141/287-5533.*

The Scottish Chamber Orchestra and the BBC Symphony Orchestra use this marvelous venue as their home theater. Considered one of Glasgow's top concert halls, the acoustics are exceptional.

KING'S THEATRE, *294 Bath Street, Glasgow. Tel. 0141/248-5153, Fax 0141/248-3361. Tickets are £6-25.*

This is the main theater in Glasgow for seeing the touring productions of London plays. Musicals, drama and everything in between finds its way onto the King's Theatre stage. A popular, enjoyable and different option is the pantomime performances that are presented during the winter. Aspiring playwrights fill in the gaps between major productions with their efforts. King's Theatre seats over 2,000 people, and has played host to such great thespians as Sir Lawrence Olivier, Fred Astaire and Katherine Hepburn.

THE MITCHELL THEATRE, *3 Granville Street, Glasgow. Tel. 0141/ 287-4855, Fax 0141/221-0695.* Tickets are £6-15.

The Mitchell Theatre provides a wide range of attractions, from amateur plays to conventions and large business meetings.

SCOTTISH MASK AND PUPPET THEATRE, *8-10 Balcarres Avenue, Kelvindale, Glasgow. Tel. 0141/339-6185, Fax 0141/357-4484.*

This is the home of the permanent exhibit entitled, "The Magical World of Puppets," a delightful exhibit. A small café on site serves up a limited menu.

THE THEATRE ROYAL, *Hope Street, Glasgow. Tel. 0141/332-9000, Fax 0141/332-4477. Tickets are £5-36.*

The Theatre Royal is the home of the Scottish Opera and the Scottish Ballet, and you'll find a variety of options available here, including ballet, opera, modern dance and children's theater. The theater is a performance in and of itself, with its Italian Renaissance décor and glittering chandeliers.

THE TRON THEATRE, *63 Trongate, Glasgow. Tel. 0141/552-4267, Fax 0141/552-6657. Tickets range from £3-7.* The Tron has the honor of being the theater that is housed in the oldest building of any theater. It makes its home in the 18th-century Tron Kirk (church). It features a wide range of performances, including primarily contemporary dramas, comedies and musicals by Scottish playwrights and others from the Continent.

SPORTS & RECREATION

Angling

Just a short drive from Glasgow are a number of lochs and streams where you can try your hand at angling. Here is a place to stop by that will help you plan your angling activities and purchase the necessary license and tackle: **The Glasgow Angling Centre**, *6 Claythorn Street, Gallowgate, Glasgow, Tel. 0141/552-4737; Website: www.dholt.demon.co.uk/gac.g.*

Football (American)

American football in Scotland? Absolutely! The **Scottish Claymores** are a professional football team in the NFL Europe league. They play their games in Edinburgh and at Hampden Park in Glasgow. For more information, call *0131/478-7200.*

Go Karts
• **Scotkart Indoor Kart Racing**, *Westburn Road, Glasgow. Tel. 0141/641-0222*

Horseback Riding
• **Bankfoot Farm Riding School**, *Bankfoot Farm, Renfrewshire. Tel. 01475/521-390*

Horse Racing
While not as popular as it is in Ireland, horse racing still has its loyal following in Scotland. If you wish to see a race, try the **Hamilton Park Racecourse**, *Bothwell Road, Hamilton, Tel. 01698/283-806.*

Scuba Diving
• Scottish Sub-Aqua Club, *The Cockburn Centre, 40 Bogmoor Place, Glasgow, G51 4TQ. Tel. 0141/425-1021, Fax 0141/445-6192; E-mail: m.maccallum@napier.ac.uk; Website: www.ssac.demon.co.uk/SSAChome*

Soccer
There are many soccer clubs in Glasgow. The two major clubs are the Rangers and the Celtics. The Rangers are the predominant Protestant team, and Catholics man the Celtics. The Rangers play at **Ibrox Stadium**, *150 Edmiston Drive, Glasgow, Tel. 0141/427-8500*, and the Celtics play at **Parkhead**, *Glasgow, Tel. 0141/556-2611.*

If you wish to learn a little more about the teams before arriving, both have official team websites, complete with schedules, information about upcoming opponents, the latest trades and injury reports, etc. Check them out: the Glasgow Rangers' website can be found at *www.rangers.co.uk*, and the Celtics' website is *www.celticfc.co.uk.*

SHOPPING

In recent years, Glasgow has emerged as a major shopping mecca for Scots and tourists. Here are some of my favorite places:

The Argyll Arcade, *30 Buchanan Stree.* In what may be one of the first shopping malls in the world, the Argyll Arcade is a collection of over 30 jewelers in one of the UK's oldest covered shopping areas. You'll find a wide variety of jewelry, from antique to traditional to modern.

The Barras, *Gallowgate and Ross Streets.* As mentioned earlier, this is a marvelous indoor flea market.

Buchanan Galleries, *Buchanan Street.* This modern new shopping center is at the north side of the downtown area and is hoping to rival St. Enoch's Shopping Centre for the hearts and pounds of Glasgow's shoppers.

Geoffrey Highland Crafts, Ltd., *309 Sauchiehall Street, Tel. 0141/331-2388*. If you'd like to take home a kilt made of your family tartan, you'll probably find it here. If you'd prefer taking tartan cloth home to make your own tartan clothing, you'll also find a wide selection of cloth here.

Marks and Spencer, *2-12 Argyle Street, Tel. 0141/552-4546*. This is one of the UK's top department stores. You'll find everything here from clothing to housewares and gifts.

Saratoga Trunk, *Unit 22, 57 West Regent Street, Tel. 0141/331-2707*. Stop by this classy store if you are interested in anything from antique Victorian clothing to antique jewelry.

St. Enoch Shopping Centre, *55 St. Enoch Square, Tel. 0141/204-3900*. The ultra-modern St. Enoch Shopping Centre is located in downtown Glasgow and is chock-full of interesting shops and stores. A large food court is also available if you get hungry during your shopping.

Tim Wright Antiques, *147 Bath Street, Tel. 0141/221-0364*. If you are an antique aficionado, this is the place for you to stop. This huge store is cram-packed with a wonderful assortment of antique furnishings and knick-knacks.

EXCURSIONS & DAY TRIPS

Within an easy drive from Glasgow are several places that you have probably heard of: **Loch Lomond** and **Stirling**. Both are marvelous places to visit, for different reasons. Loch Lomond is a lovely long loch that was immortalized in song and Stirling is famous for the military exploits of one **William Wallace**. There's also a pretty impressive castle there too.

The **Trossachs** are an area of such spectacular beauty that they are a favorite of locals as well as tourists. And if you are a **Robert Burns** fan, then you'll want to head southwest of Glasgow for **Ayr** and **Alloway**. Burns was born and lived a portion of his life in Alloway.

LOCH LOMOND AREA

Loch Lomond was immortalized in the melancholy folk song *Loch Lomond* written by one of Bonnie Prince Charlie's soldiers on the evening before his execution in Carlisle jail for his role in the Jacobite Rebellion. It romanticizes the prisoner's upcoming death and ensuing trip home to Loch Lomond via the underworld – the *low road* – and he theorizes that his trip will be quicker than that of his comrades-in-arms, who must take the normal or *high road*.

While the song may be a little sad, the views on Loch Lomond are anything but. They are beautiful. Loch Lomond is the largest fresh-water lake in Britain, and features 30 islands. It is nearly 24 miles long and five miles wide at its widest point. It sits at the foot of **Ben Lomond**, which at 3,192 feet rises in awesome majesty above the loch.

For tourist information, contact the **Loch Lomond Tourist Information Centre**, *The Marina, Balloch, Tel. 01389/753-533.*

ARRIVALS & DEPARTURES

Loch Lomond and the beautiful countryside around it is easily accessible after a one-hour drive from Glasgow. Buses also come here from Glasgow.

By Bus

One-day bus tours to Loch Lomond are available from **Buchanan Street Station**, *North Hanover Street, Glasgow, Tel. 0141/332-7133, Fax 0141/332-9191.*

By Car

This is the best way to get to Loch Lomond. Just take the A82 northwest out of Glasgow, and soon you'll be motoring along the lovely shores of the loch.

WHERE TO STAY

Helensburgh

THORNDEAN HOUSE, *64 Cloquhoun, Helensburgh. Tel. 01436/674-922, Fax 01436/679-913; E-mail: theurquharts@sol.co.uk; Website: sol.co.uk/t/the urquharts. 3 Rooms. Rates: £22-29 single; £22-26 per person double. Mastercard and Visa accepted.*

Thorndean House is a gem nestled above the Firth of Clyde in the village of Helensburgh. Your hosts are Anne and John Urquhart, and they are justifiably proud of this restored Victorian mansion. Anne has lent her hand to the interior decorating, and it will be immediately obvious that she is very talented. Lush green plants accentuate the mauves and creams that are the main theme for her decorating efforts.

There are three bedrooms, and each is large and spacious, and the rooms at the front of the house look out on the gardens. The rooms are tastefully decorated and feature first-class furnishings. As you walk through the house, take time to notice the paintings and pottery work that is around. The paintings are the handiwork of Anne and John's grandfathers, and their daughter crafted the pottery.

During the summers, the Urquharts fire up the barbecue for their guests, and you can either eat in the dining room our out in their lovely gardens. The sailboat is for sailing on the Firth of Clyde and if your schedule is flexible, John can usually be persuaded to take you out on a short sailing expedition. If you decide to take the Urquharts up on their hospitality, you won't be disappointed. Their home is lovely, and you will feel like an honored guest. The Urquharts would like their guests to know that Thorndean House is smoke-free.

Balloch

    GOWANLEA B&B, *Drymen Road, Balloch. Tel. 01389/752-456; E-mail: gowanlea@aol.com. 4 rooms. Rates: £25-30 single; £18-22 per person double. Mastercard and Visa accepted.*

    What a delightful find – Margaret and Austin Campbell have converted their lovely home into a first-class B&B, and we are truly fortunate. Gowanlea B&B sits in the pretty little town of Balloch at the southern reaches of Loch Lomond. Its Gaelic name reveals the history of the site upon which the B&B sits: *Gowanlea* means "field of daisies." As agreeable as that sounds, if you are looking for a place to stay around Balloch, you'd be hard-pressed to find a more pleasant place than Gowanlea.

    Margaret honed her B&B skills in her native Northern Ireland before coming to Scotland to raise her family. She has applied her decorating skills and tastes to all the rooms, and they fare very well. The bedrooms feature floral print wallpaper, which complement nicely the comfortable and quality furnishings you'll find here. In the morning, Margaret will show you that her talents are not limited to interior decorating. She'll impress you with her full Scottish breakfast, which consists of any or all of the following: porridge or cereal, sausage, bacon, an egg, black pudding, fried tomato, kipper fillet, cheese, fruit yogurt, tea, coffee and toast. (The porridge was incredible.) You'll take your breakfast in a dining room that will enable you to visit with other guests if you wish. When I last breakfasted there, I visited with a couple of English tourists who were well traveled in Scotland and England. They guaranteed me that Gowanlea was one of the best B&Bs they had stayed in and Margaret Campbell's breakfast was in the top tier of breakfasts across the United Kingdom. I agree with them, and I believe you will too.

    Mrs. Campbell proudly displays a number of industry awards for her B&B and her breakfasts on the walls of her dining room. Also included are stacks of *Thank You* cards from previous guests, all with glowing compliments. If you happen to be in the Loch Lomond area, Gowanlea would be an outstanding choice for your overnight lodging. I know I plan on staying here again.

    LOCH LOMOND YOUTH HOSTEL, *A8, Arden, Alexandria (west side of Loch Lomond). Tel. 01389/850-226; E-mail: lochlomondhostel<loch.lomond@syha.org.uk. 27 Rooms (160 beds). Rates: £11.75-12.75 adults, £10.25-11.25 children. MasterCard and Visa accepted.*

    If you are an *aficionado* of youth hostels, you'll swear you took a wrong turn when looking for the Loch Lomond Youth Hostel. It is located about

300 yards from Loch Lomond, and this youth hostel is one of the nicest in the country. It is also housed in a large old mansion which sits grandly amid exquisite grounds.

Take the time to walk through the public rooms of the hostel and admire the marvelous wood and plasterwork that is featured throughout the mansion. As you enter the hostel, a large sandstone mantle bears the inscription, "Welcome ever smiles, Farewell goes off sighing." There are 27 rooms, most of which have 3 to 5 bunkbeds arranged dormitory-style. Each room is large and spacious, and there is plenty of room. The beds are pretty basic, and come with linens and blankets. Most of the rooms have incredible views of either Loch Lomond or the lovely grounds.

The Scottish Youth Hostel Association has gone all-out on this location. In addition to the fine facilities, they provide a ghost for their guests. As the story goes, many years ago the Lord of the house disapproved of his daughter Veronica's love for the stable boy, and forbade her to see him. Distraught, she flung herself from the tower window (long fall). There are those who claim Veronica still roams the halls of the old mansion, forlorn without her love. This is a nice place, and if you do not mind the dormitory-style rooms and company, then this is a pretty good place to stay. Be sure and call ahead – the location and the quality of the facility keeps it booked well in advance, especially during the summer season.

Balmaha & Rowardennan

THE MONIACK B&B, *Balmaha, Loch Lomond. Tel. 01360/870-388 or 1360/870-357. 3 rooms. Rates: £27.50 per person. No credit cards accepted.*

Sandy and Lucy Fraser are the masterminds behind the only four-star B&B on the east side of Loch Lomond. Drive up the east side of Loch Lomond, and as you near the end watch for the Oak Tree Inn, and you'll find Moniack B&B. Each of the rooms is quite modern and very comfortable. They are tastefully decorated and have high quality comfortable furnishings. Breakfast is a treat – the owners of the B&B are also the owners of the excellent Oak Tree Inn Restaurant.

BEN LOMOND COTTAGE, *Rowardennan. Tel. 01360/870-411. 4 Rooms. Rates: £35 single; £22 per person double. No credit cards accepted.*

Ben Lomond Cottage is another of the B&Bs owned by Sandy and Lucy Fraser, and it is near the end of the road that skirts the east side of Loch Lomond. You'll find a pleasant B&B with quality furnishings throughout. Everything Sandy and Lucy do is top-notch, and you'll have a delightful and pleasant stay here at Ben Lomond Cottage. And as with the Moniack B&B, you'll not be disappointed in the breakfast served here.

WHERE TO EAT

THE OAK TREE INN, *Balmaha, Loch Lomond. Tel. 01360/870-357. £6-12. Open Monday through Thursday 8:00am to midnight, Friday through Sunday 8:00am to 1:00am. MasterCard and Visa accepted.*

Nestled snugly beneath the protective branches of a 500-year-old oak tree rests the Oak Tree Inn (wonder where they got the name!?). This lovely inn was constructed using 135-year-old beams and panels from a nearby home that was demolished. The slate you see on the outside, on the floors, and on the roof was quarried from a nearby quarry that had been closed for years. The owners, Sandy and Lucy Fraser, talked the owners of the quarry into opening up just so they could hand-quarry the tons of slate needed for their project.

The results are astounding. Although the Oak Tree Inn was built in 1997, the slate, beams and panels give it an "old world" feel, that is all that feels old here. The Oak Tree Inn provides a pleasant family-friendly dining experience. The walls are splashed with numerous newspaper articles about the restaurant and awards for their cooking expertise. But don't just take my word for it: try the roasted rack of lamb coated in a heather honey and mustard sauce, or for a non-traditional but delicious change, try the coconut chicken breast coated in a succulent sweet and sour sauce. A fine wine list accompanies the meal. For those vacationing with children, there is a children's menu available for £3.50.

SEEING THE SIGHTS

The A82 whizzes along the western shores of the loch, and there are frequent pull-outs for you to turn into for views and photographs of the loch. For a close-up look a the loch, stop in Balloch for a loch cruise with **Sweeney's Cruises**, *26 Balloch Road, Balloch, Tel. 01389/752-376; fare is £4 for adults, £3 for seniors and children.* The cruise lasts approximately an hour, and is well worth the time. You'll cruise on the *Silver Marlin*, and your trip will include a short stop at **Inchmurrin Island**. If the stop is too short for you, you can stay and explore for a bit, then hop on the next return of the ship to the island. The ship leaves from its pier in Balloch every hour on the half hour from 10:30am to 7:30pm. I most enjoy the evening rides. The loch is calm and serene, and the views are lovely in the evening light.

While you're in Balloch seeing Loch Lomond, you might like to stop in at the **Balloch Castle Country Park**, *Balloch, Tel. 01389/758-216; open daily from 8:00am to dusk; admission is free.* This gothic-style castle was built in the early 1800s on the site of a former castle. The gardens are fabulous, and have earned a reputation that draws Scots from all over the country. The azaleas and rhododendrons are spectacular, especially at the their height of beauty in late May.

TOUR THE TROSSACHS

*The **Trossachs** is an area of stunning natural beauty, and is one of the prettiest areas to drive and see the Scottish countryside. It is especially accessible from Glasgow, since it can be reached via automobile within one hour from downtown Glasgow. This area was home to **Rob Roy MacGregor**, the kilted-and-tartaned Robin Hood of the Scottish folk. Rob Roy was a real character, immortalized in Sir Walter Scott's novel of the same name. To some he was a vicious outlaw thumbing his nose at the authorities of the day. To others he was a folk hero, even during his lifetime, taking from the rich and giving to the poor (sort of). Regardless of how you feel about him, he certainly picked a lovely part of the country to tromp around in.*

*If you are coming from the Loch Lomond area, take the A811 east to the A81, which will take you to **Aberfoyle** (watch for the signposts to Aberfoyle about five miles east of Drymen). Aberfoyle is in the heart of the Trossachs, and from here you can branch out to see lovely **Loch Katrine**, the **Queen Elizabeth Forest Park**, and other areas of natural beauty. The drive from Aberfoyle over Duke's Pass to Brig o' Turk is a particularly pretty journey. The Queen Elizabeth Forest Park is a wonderful wilderness area with miles upon miles of marked hiking trails criss-crossing the 75,000 acres that makes up the park.*

STIRLING

About 30 miles north of Glasgow you'll find the small market town of **Stirling**. Stirling had been a fairly anonymous place outside of Scotland for many generations, until Hollywood and Mel Gibson introduced it as the sight of William Wallace's first major victory over an assembled English army. (Even though the location and circumstances in the movie bear little resemblance to the actual place or battle. Today Stirling is a busy town at the confluence of several major highways. Its medieval planners didn't anticipate the crush of automobiles that would descend upon and drive through Stirling at rush hour or during the height of the tourist season, and it can get quite (*quite!*) congested.

For tourist information, contact the **Stirling Tourist Information Centre**, *41 Dumbarton Road, Stirling, Tel. 01786/475-019.*

ARRIVALS & DEPARTURES

By Bus

Bus service reaches Stirling numerous times throughout the day. Scottish Citylink buses arrive in Stirling at the **Stirling Bus Station**,

Goosecroft Road, Stirling, Tel. 01786/613-777. The train station is about a mile or mile and a half from the main sites in Stirling.

By Car

You'll reach Stirling by any number of major highways. From Glasgow or Perth, you'll arrive via the A9. The A84 comes from the west, and the A91 will be your route if you are coming from the east.

By Train

Train service is frequent between Stirling and Scotland's two major cities, Glasgow and Edinburgh. Trains arrive at the **Stirling Train Station**, *Station Road, Stirling, Tel. 01786/484-950.* The train station is about a mile or mile and a half from the main sites in Stirling.

WHERE TO STAY

AUCHTERARDER HOUSE, *Auchterarder. Tel. 0764/636-646, Fax 0764/662-939; Website: www.wrensgroup.com. 15 Rooms. Rates: £120-140 single; £160-350 double. All major credit cards accepted. Auchterarder House is about 45 minutes north of Stirling on the M9/A9.*

There are many hotels in Scotland that strive to look and feel like an ancient Scottish hunting lodge, but few succeed. But some do, and one of the best is Auchterarder House in the Perthshire countryside. From the moment you enter Auchterarder House you will be enthralled (anyway, I was).

The home was originally built in 1832 for an army officer, but it wasn't until Mr. James Reid purchased it in 1882 that it became the lavish home you see today. Mr. Reid owned a company that manufactured steam engines, and you can see from the house that business was very, very good. Mr. Reid spent significant sums of money decorating this country getaway; many of the antiques and all of the tapestries and silk wallpaper in the house are those selected by Mr. Reid himself. Every public room has an ornate fireplace and most have exquisite Waterford crystal chandeliers. You'll marvel at the choice wood carvings that add to the elegance here.

Auchterarder House is run like the country home it was, and not merely as a hotel. For example, you'll not find a bar here, but rather a well-stocked cabinet with an array of fine malt whiskies and cognac – in the manner of a Victorian-era country house. Each room is exceptionally large and furnished with some of the finest bedroom furnishings in the country. All the rooms are generously endowed with antiques, most of which have been in the house for well over 100 years. Each room is named after an ancient Scottish clan. Each of the bathrooms in the house are stunning in and of themselves, and are nearly as large (or so it seems) as some entire hotel rooms and they are exquisitely furnished. As with most hotels and guest houses in Scotland, each room is equipped with a phone and TV. But taking their service a step beyond most, you'll enjoy complimentary malt whisky, along with an accompanying history of that particular brand. Fluffy bathrobes and a complimentary fruit tray help you feel at home. There are tea- and coffee-making facilities, but here you'll find them served with silver teapots.

The dining room is nothing less than exquisite. Again, superb silk wallpaper and ancient oil paintings grace the walls. Your meals will be served amid china, crystal and candlelight in a manner befitting the royal guests that have dined here through the years. (Be sure to see the *Where to Eat* section.) You'll either take your breakfast in the dining room or the conservatory (your choice). The conservatory is a former breezeway between the house and the family chapel. Encased in windows, the conservatory looks out onto the gorgeous grounds and gardens and a lovely Victorian fountain. Soft music provides just the right touch to your dining experience here.

The grounds are certainly worth more than a brief mention. They are, in a word, extraordinary. Seventeen acres of beautifully sculpted lawns punctuated with magnificent gardens. You'll find over 400 varieties of rhododendrons, firs, oaks and azaleas pleasantly placed for your viewing and strolling pleasure.

Selected as one of my Best Places to Stay – see Chapter 12.

STIRLING HIGHLAND HOTEL, *Spittal Street, Stirling. Tel. 01786/ 475-444, Fax 01786/462-929. 92 Rooms. Rates: £104 single; £140 double; £190 suite. All major credit cards accepted.*

The Stirling Highland Hotel is located just down the street from Stirling Castle. As such, it sits high on the hill above Stirling, and a number of the rooms have nice views of Stirling and the surrounding countryside. The rooms in the hotel are nice sized and comfortable. While not exquisite, they are clean, comfortable and have functional furnishings. All the rooms are decorated the same. Each bedroom features satellite TV, telephones, hairdryers, a trouser press and tea- and coffee-making facilities. There is also a 17-meter pool, spa and sauna, as well as an exercise room and a few squash courts to help you work off any extra energy you may have. The hotel was built in 1854 and has of course seen a number of renovations. In my opinion, it is due for another major one. The hotel has a bit of an old and tired feeling.

STIRLING YOUTH HOSTEL, *St. John's Street. Tel. 01786/473-442, Fax 01786/445-715. 129 beds. Rates: £12.25-13.25 single; £10.75-11.75 double and dormitory. MasterCard and Visa accepted.*

You'll find the Stirling Youth Hostel in the veritable shadow of Stirling Castle. This is another fine example of the quality lodging available throughout Scotland in youth hostels. From the front, you'll wonder if this could possibly be a youth hostel – it looks much like an ancient church. Well it is...sort of. The church was gutted and the youth hostel was built inside, but the outer walls of the church remain.

This hostel reminded me of some of the college dormitories I have spent time in over the years. It has many rooms, and all of them are furnished essentially the same. Each is clean and brightly painted. Nothing extremely impressive about the rooms; just a nice safe and comfortable place to stay. There is a large comfortable common room available for relaxing and watching TV. There is also a self-catering kitchen to fix your breakfast and dinner and a pleasant dining room in which to eat. The hostel is immensely busy because of its close proximity to Stirling Castle. You'll need to book a room months in advance if you wish to stay here during the summer tourist season.

WHERE TO EAT

AUCHTERARDER HOUSE RESTAURANT, *Auchterarder. Tel. 0764/ 636646, Fax 0764/662-939. £16.50 lunch, £39.50 dinner. Open daily from 7:00pm to 9:30pm. All major credit cards accepted. Auchterarder House Restaurant is about 45 minutes north of Stirling on the M9/A9.*

Well, if you want a taste treat as well as a dining experience, come to Auchterarder House Restaurant. The restaurant, which also serves the hotel of the same name, is housed in a lovely Victorian room with the original silk wall coverings and paintings. Both have been here since 1832, are original to the house, and are quite impressive. The menu changes daily; choices might include medallions of Scottish beef filet, tomatoes and herb compote, or grilled pink trout filet encrusted with walnuts with a red wine essence. The Auchterarder House Restaurant is proud of their two AA rosettes and recognition by *A Taste of Scotland.*

HERMAN'S RESTAURANT AND BRASSERIE, *St. John's Road, Stirling. Tel. 01786/473-402. £7.50-8.50 lunch and £11-20 dinner. Open daily from noon to 2:30pm and 7:00pm to 10:30pm. Amex, MasterCard and Visa accepted.*

You'll find Herman's Restaurant and Brasserie near the top of Castle Hill just before you get to Stirling Castle. The décor is reminiscent of Bavarian restaurants I spent time in. There are pine tables with candles, rough-hewn stone walls and simple table settings. You can expect to find both traditional Scottish fare as well as Austrian fare served here. Try the stuffed chicken breast with leeks and mushrooms or the wienerschnitzel (escalope of veal wrapped in bread crumbs and pan-fried).

SEEING THE SIGHTS

Stirling Castle, *Castle Hill, Stirling, Tel. 01786/450-000; open daily from April through October from 9:30am to 6:00pm, November through March from 9:30am to 5:00pm, last entrance 45 minutes before closing; admission is £5 for adults, £3.75 for seniors and £1.50 for children.* Stirling Castle may just be one of the most impressive castles in Scotland; it certainly ranks up there with Edinburgh and Eilean Donan castles. Stirling Castle sits regally atop the crag of an old extinct volcano with commanding views of the surrounding countryside. It was nearly impregnable, and served as the palace for many Scottish monarchs, including James IV, V, VI and Mary Queen of Scots. At night it is especially impressive, basking in floodlit majesty.

As you enter the castle grounds through the stout outer walls, you'll see **The Palace**, which dates to the mid-16th century. Straight ahead of you is the **Great Hall**, a banqueting hall that was completed in 1503. At press time it was in the process of renovation, and should soon be returned to its former elegance. Many of the rooms in the castle have been and are undergoing refurbishment with period furnishings. Once completed, these rooms will add more character and warmth to the inside of the castle, which today is somewhat sterile in most area of the castle.

There are a few rooms that have been decked out with old furnishings, and one room displays one of Mary Queen of Scots' dresses – it's in pretty good condition for being 450 years old. There is a fine regimental museum in one of the towers of the castle that features a plethora of old kilts, flags, bagpipes and weapons. As with so many royal castles, Stirling Castle was not immune from the plotting and intrigues that swirled around the royal folk in medieval times. Stirling Castle was the sight of a number of clandestine goings-on, including the murder of the powerful Earl of Douglas in 1452 (see the sidebar below). A small plot at the north end of the castle is called **Douglas Gardens**, and serves as a memorial to the murdered Earl of Douglas whose body was dumped unceremoniously to the ground from one of the castle windows.

Apparently there is more to be seen at Stirling Castle than that which meets the eye. For centuries, stories of ghostly apparitions have been told. One of them, the *Pink Lady*, has been seen slowly making her way through various parts of the castle. Although no one knows for sure, some have speculated that it is Mary Queen of Scots returning for a visit.

Stirling Town Jail, *St. John Street, Stirling, Tel. 01786/450-050; open daily from April through October from 9:30am to 6:00pm, November through March from 9:30am to 5:00pm; last entrance 45 minutes before closing; admission is £2.75 for adults, £2 for children and seniors, and a family ticket is available for £8.* You'll find the Stirling Town Jail just below Stirling Castle. The jail was built in 1847, and today the only captives held here are tourists who wander in and are captivated by what they see, hear and learn. The

TREASON & TREACHERY

James II was proclaimed the King of Scotland at the tender age of six years old. His mother tried to rule in his stead until he came of age, but she was no match for the headstrong Scottish nobility. Alliances and counter-alliances sprang up, all aimed at unseating the young monarch. Plots within plots multiplied, as powerful nobles sought to increase their power and influence. Some entered agreements of rebellion with England; others sought to increase their lands through subterfuge and murder at home.

For years, these cloak-and-dagger activities remained mainly behind closed doors. In 1451 the first serious challenge to James' rule raised its ugly head: **William Douglas,** *already considered the most formidable and powerful man in Scotland, formed a confederacy with several other powerful earls with the express purpose of wresting the kingdom from James. This confederacy, it was rumored, would soon move to set another on the throne of Scotland.*

But James II had inherited some of the Stewart mettle. Just barely 20 years old, James invited William Douglas to dinner. During the meal, James confronted William with his treasonous plans and insisted that he renounce his recent alliance. When Douglas refused, James reportedly replied, "If thou shalt not, this shall!" and plunged a knife into William's breast. James then cast Douglas' body from the two-story window into the garden below. Parliament refused to convict the king, claiming that William Douglas was guilty of treason and therefore responsible for his own death. Opposing earls claimed James was guilty of treachery, as he had invited Douglas to dinner under a promise of peace and hospitality.

Which was the greater sin: treason or treachery?

jail has been renovated to its former...splendor...and you'll enjoy the actors that play their parts as prisoners, wardens and reformers. You'll be escorted and entertained by the old town hangman himself, Jock Rankin. This is a fun and entertaining look at the seamier side of Stirling life.

National Wallace Monument, *Stirling, Tel. 01786/472-140; open March through May and October daily from 10:00am to 5:00pm, June and September daily from 10:00am to 6:00pm, and July and August from 9:30am to 6:30pm, during February and November it is open on Saturday and Sunday from 10:00am to 4:00pm; admission is free.* The Scots knew about and revered William Wallace long before US cinema audiences became aware of him through Mel Gibson and *Braveheart*, as is evidenced by this massive Victorian tower built completed in 1869. In 1297, Wallace and his armies trounced a far larger English force at nearby **Stirling Bridge**, and William Wallace earned the love and respect of most Scots. The ensuing years have merely made him larger than life. You can see the tower from the Stirling Castle esplanade, just beyond the statue of Robert the Bruce (clever photographers can take a picture of the statue of Bruce with the Wallace monument in the distance).

Argyll's Lodging, *St. John Street, Stirling, Tel. 01786/450-023; open daily from April through October from 9:30am to 6:00pm, November through March from 9:30am to 5:00pm, last entrance 45 minutes before closing; admission is free with admission to the castle.* Just below the castle on St. John Street is the restored Renaissance house known as Argyll's Lodging. Formerly the home of the Earl of Argyll, the home was built in the 1630s. It is representative of the splendor these nobles lived in. It has been faithfully restored in an effort to help us 21st-century tourists see what life was like for these nobles of days gone by. There are excellent displays covering the history of the times, the lives of the occupants, and various other aspects of medieval life.

Bannockburn Heritage Centre, *Glasgow Road, Tel. 01786/812-664; the battlefield is open all year, but the Heritage Centre is open daily from April through October from 10:00am to 5:30pm; admission is £3 for adults, £2 for seniors and children, and a family ticket is available for £6.50.* About two miles south of Stirling off the M80 (watch for the signposts) you'll find Bannockburn, the site of one of the most famous battles in Scottish history. In 1314, Robert the Bruce faced an army of nearly 20,000 men with a mere 6,000 Scots and won not only the battle, but the throne of Scotland. Heritage Centre has a nice audiovisual presentation that details these exciting events. Exhibits provide a linear look at the sometimes confusing history of Scotland and the so-called Union of the Crowns under James VI.

DOUNE

The small town of **Doune** is located about five miles west of Dunblane on the B820. A quiet, sleepy place, it is worth a side trip to see the castle which takes its name from the town – or is it the other way around?

Doune Castle, *Doune, Tel. 01786/841-742; open daily April through September from 9:30am to 6:30pm, and from October through March Monday through Saturday from 9:30am to 4:30pm and Sunday from 2:00pm to 4:30pm; admission is £2.30 for adults, £1.75 for seniors and £1 for children.* Doune Castle is a fine example of a massive fortification-style castle built in the late 14th century. Tall, thick walls typify this massive block of a building. The castle was built for the Duke of Albany, taken for a spell by the Stewarts, then given back to the Dukes of Albany.

A large grassy courtyard fills the interior and several spacious halls are under renovation. A large double fireplace in the Lord's Hall is most impressive, as are some exquisite oak carvings. It is a picturesque and photogenic castle, and the exterior was used by the BBC during filming of the classic *Ivanhoe* a few years ago. Today's castle is a quiet reminder of its former self. Daffodils now bloom where enemy archers formerly took aim at the castle. This is a nice place to visit, and including the foray off the main highway, could easily be toured in 30 to 45 minutes.

CALLANDER

Callander is a nice market town at the edge of the Trossachs. It hasn't fully developed its tourism potential, but it is worth a stop to stroll down its main street. Its location as a gateway to both the Trossachs and the Highlands, however, makes it a pretty busy place. There is a wide variety of shops to intrigue you, including antique stores, tartan shops, book stores, etc. It's definitely worth an hour or two of your time.

For tourist information, contact **Trossachs Tourist Information Centre**, *Ancaster Square, Tel. 01877/330-342.*

ARRIVALS & DEPARTURES

By Bus

Buses leave for Stirling daily from Glasgow's **Buchanan Street Station**, *North Hanover Street, Glasgow, Tel. 0141/332-7133, Fax 0141/332-9191* and Edinburgh's **St. Andrew Square Bus Station**, *St. Andrew Square, Edinburgh, Tel. 0990/050-5050.* All buses arrive at the **Stirling Bus Station**, *Goosecroft Road, Stirling, Tel. 01786/484-950.* After you arrive in Stirling, hop on a Bluebird Lines bus that will take you to Callander.

By Car

Take the A80 northeast out of Glasgow toward Stirling (follow the signposts to Stirling – you'll connect with the M80 and the M9). North of Stirling at Dunblane, watch for the signposts directing you to the A820 and A84 and Callander.

WHERE TO STAY

ROMAN CAMP COUNTRY HOUSE HOTEL, *Main Street, Callander. Tel. 01877/330-003, Fax 01877/301-533; E-mail: mail@roman-camp-hotel.co.uk. 14 Rooms. Rates: £70-85 single; £95-115 double per room; £140-165 superior double per room; £160-186 suite per room. All major credit cards accepted.*

Unbelievable – that's the only word I can think of to describe Roman Camp Country House Hotel. Well, maybe that and *elegant...and lavish.* And, well, *unbelievable.* In my humble opinion, this is one of the loveliest hotels in the United Kingdom. Eric and Marion Brown are your host and hostess, and they are rightfully proud of their hotel. They have accentuated your stay here with freshly cut flowers, welcoming fires in ancient fireplaces, and a staff that is attentive and friendly. The flowers are cut from those that grow throughout the 20-acre estate within which the hotel nestles.

Roman Camp was built in 1625 on the site of an old Roman army camp as a hunting lodge for the Dukes of Perth. It has attracted dukes and duchesses, kings and queens, and presidents and their first ladies ever since. Converted into a hotel in 1939, you may now enjoy what was once the domain of royalty. It has the grace of a French chateau, yet the comfort and welcome of a home in the country. Each bedroom is individually decorated with top-of-the-line furnishings, and complemented by a host of antique furniture and accoutrements (my room had an antique silver hand mirror, comb and brush). Most of the rooms are large and tastefully decorated, and each has views of the lovely gardens and grounds. Each room comes with complimentary sherry and bottles of mineral water. Each also offers hairdryers, tea- and coffee-making facilities, TV and a radio. Several rooms have been recently added, and though they are quite nice, they lack the antiquity of the others.

The public rooms are an absolute delight. Each is exquisitely adorned with fine and comfortable furniture, tasteful art and marvelous window coverings. Choose from the drawing room, library or conservatory to rest and relax, take afternoon tea or a wee dram in the evening. My favorite of the public rooms is the library. If you know where to look, you'll even find a small personal chapel behind those book-lined and paneled walls. Meals are served in the tapestry-lined round dining room. The room is painted in bright colors and provides elegant dining in a restful and alluring atmosphere. The meals are superb, having been prepared with only the freshest ingredients, including fresh herbs and seasonings from the walled garden on the estate (see *Where to Eat* below).

The hotel is in the middle of downtown Callander and can be a bit difficult to locate at first. The entrance is unobtrusively marked (on your left if you're coming from the south on the A84) between two cottages. But once you pass through the small entrance, the estate opens up before your eyes, and you will be delighted with all you find here. Flowerbeds and gardens, lush sculpted lawns and the meandering River Treith all invite your explorer's spirit. Roman Camp is definitely a place you'll want to asterisk for a stay.

Selected as one of my Best Places to Stay – see Chapter 12.

WHERE TO EAT

ROMAN CAMP RESTAURANT, *Main Street, Callander. Tel. 01877/ 330-003, Fax 01877/301-533. Breakfast £14.50, lunch £14-18, dinner £34. Open daily from 8:00am to 9:30am for breakfast, noon to 2:00pm for lunch, and 7:00pm to 9:00pm for dinner. All major credit cards accepted.*

The dining room for the Roman Camp Country House Hotel is a wonderful, elegant place to take your breakfast, lunch or dinner. Crystal and china, candlelight and silver accentuate the delicious meal that is prepared and artfully presented here. A dozen tapestries line the walls of the brightly painted dining room. The meals are superb, having been prepared with only the freshest ingredients, including fresh herbs and seasonings from the walled garden on the estate. The menu varies, but you might expect to enjoy such delicacies as pressed duck leg, quail and pigeon with proscuitto, or roast turbot with langoustine lasagna. There are also a number of vegetarian dishes available. Whether your favorite part of your dining experience is the meal, the ambiance, or the stroll around the 20-acre estate afterwards, the restaurant at the Roman Camp is sure to leave a lasting impression. I know it did with me.

SEEING THE SIGHTS

Rob Roy and Trossachs Visitor Centre, *Ancaster Square, Callander, Tel. 01877/330-342; open January and February on Saturday and Sunday from 10:00am to 4:00pm, March through May and October through December daily from 10:00am to 5:00pm, June and September from 9:30am to 6:00pm and July and August from 9:00am to 7:00pm; admission is £3 for adults, £2.50 for seniors and children.* Callander is the gateway to the Trossachs, and Rob Roy is after all this region's favored son. It is only right that there should be a place for folks to learn the truth about this humble, albeit dangerous, red-haired lad. Rob Roy goes high-tech here, and you'll learn a few things about the highwayman that you might not have known before.

KILLIN

In my humble opinion, one of the prettiest drives in Scotland is from Crieff (northeast of Stirling) along the A85/A821 to the tiny town of **Killin**. You'll drive through sheep-clad valleys and among towering peaks. You'll marvel at the lush green carpet that blankets these areas.

Killin is the town Scotland forgot. It was a popular resort town that many wealthy Edinburghers and Glaswegians flocked to a generation ago. Then a landslide in 1966 took out the train tracks, and people turned their holiday attention to other locales. However, Killin is the same beautiful town sitting at the eastern edge of **Loch Tay**, and the only difference is that there are fewer tourists today than a generation ago. Today there are lots of outdoor types of things to do, like fishing on Loch Tay, hillwalking on one of Scotland's tallest mountains (**Ben Lawers** – 3,984 feet), taking a boat ride on the lake, or just enjoying a peaceful walk or mountain bike ride.

ARRIVALS & DEPARTURES

By Car

You'll come to Killin via the A821 off the A85 if you are coming from the south or southeast. From Glasgow, take the A82 north to Crianlarich and then head east on the A85. Watch for signposts to the A821 and Killin.

WHERE TO STAY

DALL LODGE COUNTRY HOUSE HOTEL, *Main Street, Killin. Tel. 01567/820-217, Fax 01567/820-726; E-mail: wilson@dalllodgehotel.co.uk; Website: www.dalllodgehotel.co.uk. 10 Rooms. Rates: £43-49 single; £33-40 per person double; £40-50 per person four-poster bed suite; £85-100 family room. Breakfast is included in the rate. MasterCard and Visa accepted. Note: open only from March 1 through October 31.*

Owner David Wilson is the mastermind behind four-star Dall Lodge Country House Hotel. David spent 25 years in the Orient in the international hotel industry with several companies, and it is obvious that he has applied his many skills here at Dall Lodge. Check out the walls – they are adorned with mementos of David's travels in the Far East. Dall Lodge Country House Hotel was originally a Victorian mansion built in 1897. In the early 1950s it was converted into a hotel. In more recent years, David and Fatima purchased it and have spent significant sums of money and energy in its renovation, and they have been successful in restoring the Victorian elegance of the property. There are 10 bedrooms at Dall Lodge, and each is large, spacious and furnished with high-quality accessories. Each room features nice tile bathrooms. There are two rooms that provide wheelchair access, or provide a nice option for those whose legs are so tired from sightseeing that they would just as soon not climb the stairs.

Fatima oversees the cooking and you will appreciate her efforts and attention – the meals here are exceptional (see the *Where to Eat* section). The dining room is a pleasant room at the front of the hotel that looks out onto the River Lochay and the headwaters of fabulous Loch Tay. A conservatory lounge is located at the back of the hotel, and it is the place of some very pleasant memories for me. After the rigors of a full day of serving guests, David and Fatima can sometimes be convinced to relax for a few moments and share a few drams. They are delightful company and engaging conversationalists.

Several years ago, Dall Lodge became quite popular with the English soap opera set (actors and actresses, not just viewers) as a romantic getaway. So who knows what celebrities you might run into here? I highly recommend Dall Lodge if you venture into this part of the country (which you should do). The scenery here is phenomenal, and Dall Lodge provides accommodations that are just what you would expect them to be.

KILLIN YOUTH HOSTEL, *Main Street, Killin. Tel. 01567/820-546. 5 Rooms. Rates: £7.50-9 for juniors (under age 18) £8.50-10 seniors (over age 18). MasterCard and Visa accepted. Note: open daily from March 1 through October 31, and during weekends from November 1 through the end of February.*

On the north edge of Killin you'll find another of Scotland's youth hostels. Not as exquisite as some but nicer than many, the hostel is housed in a converted Victorian home. It is a no frills, nicely functional and clean place to spend the night. There are five dormitory rooms and 42 beds in the hostel. Two rooms have 12 beds, and there are rooms that have 4, 6 and 8 beds respectively. The rooms are all ample sized for the number of beds in them (they could, in fact, squeeze in a few more beds if they were of a mind to). In addition, tall ceilings add to the roomy feeling. Fresh light-colored paint throughout the hostel made it feel very clean and pleasant.

The hostel adds a nice touch by providing a drying room with a dehumidifier and heater for damp hiking gear. It is very effective and in no time at all will have you ready to go out exploring again in dry clothing. All in all, this is a nice, clean comfortable place to stay if you find yourself in Killin.

WHERE TO EAT

DALL LODGE COUNTRY HOUSE RESTAURANT, *Main Street, Killin. Tel. 01567/820-217, Fax 01567/820-726. MasterCard and Visa accepted.*

The restaurant for Dall Lodge Country House is a marvelous small restaurant that caters to local residents as well as the public. They have earned a reputation for fine meals by using absolutely the freshest ingredients available, and it will be obvious the moment you taste your meal. The dining room is lovely. Note the intriguing antique clock on the fireplace mantle. Wonderful paintings of Scottish landscapes and castles grace the walls, and soft dinner music serenades your meal. In addition to all this, you get large windows that look out onto the peaceful River Lochay as it flows from Loch Tay.

Fatima Wilson is the mastermind behind the restaurant, and her expertise and attention to detail is obvious. Grilled sirloin in black pepper sauce is stunningly delicious. The steak is as tender as any I've ever had, and the sauce is perfect. If red meat isn't for you, perhaps you'll enjoy the

A RECIPE WORTH TRYING

David and Fatima Wilson gave me the recipe for one of their specialty dishes at Dall Lodge Country House Restaurant, and here it is:

GUINEA FOWL SUPREME WITH SKIRLIE

Ingredients:
4 Guinea fowl supremes (6 – 7 ounces each)
4 ounces smoked bacon, fried and chopped into pieces
3 tablespoons vegetable oil
black pepper

Marinade:
1 pint of red wine
2 small onions, peeled and chopped
1 bay leaf
1 sprig of thyme
1 clove of garlic, crushed

Sauce:
1 tablespoon of plain flour
1.5 pints of chicken or game stock
6 tablespoons of double cream

Skirlie:
3 handfuls of oatmeal
2 chopped onions
seasoning
2 ounces of butter (optional)

Brown the oatmeal in the oven on a baking sheet. Put vegetable oil in frying pan and gently fry the onion, approximately five minutes. Add the browned oatmeal and seasoning and finally add butter and fry all ingredients until well browned and cooked. Keep warm.

Remove guinea fowl from marinade, save the liquid. Heat oil in frying pan, add onion and garlic, fry for a few minutes then add supremes and brown on both sides, stir in bacon pieces. Remove guinea fowl, pour in marinade liquid, scrape up the juices from bottom of pan, add thyme and bay leaf and stock, bring to boil, return guinea fowl to pan, cover and cook gently for 20 minutes. Put a portion of skirlie on warm plate, remove guinea fowl and put on top of skirlie then simmer the sauce and reduce it by half and add cream to finish the sauce. Check for seasoning and pour over supreme. Serve hot with new baby potato.

west coast scallops with basil taglitelli or any number of other gourmet offerings. After dinner, you may wish to move into the lounge behind the dining room to enjoy a nightcap and, depending on how busy it is, David and Fatima may come out and visit with you. The evening I stayed there, an English couple joined the Wilsons and me, and we visited and laughed until the wee hours of the morning.

SEEING THE SIGHTS

Breadalbane Folklore Center, *Breadalbane, Tel. 01567/820-254; open March through June and September and October daily from 10:00am to 5:00pm, July and August daily from 9:00am to 6:00pm, November to December and February Monday through Friday from 10:00am to 4:00pm, closed in January; admission is £1 for adults, 75p for seniors and children.* Calling all members of the MacGregor Clan – this is a small sight that covers some of the intriguing aspects of life in and around the Killin area in days of yore. If you're a MacGregor, you'll especially want to stop in and learn of the tribulations, triumphs and tragedies associated with our clan. Along the way, you'll enjoy some well-done exhibits, dioramas and audiovisual presentations on a wide variety of subjects, including fairy tales, giants and scoundrels.

Scottish Crannog Centre, *Kenmore, Loch Tay, Tel. 01887/830-583; open April through October daily from 10:00am to 5:00pm; admission is £3 for adults, £2 for seniors and children, and a family ticket is available for £9.* From Killin, take the A827 along the northern shore of Loch Tay. At the eastern end of the loch you'll find a small village called Kenmore. Just as you cross over the end of the loch, watch for signposts directing you to the Scottish Crannog Centre. This is an excellent place to learn more about *crannogs* – ancient homes built on small islands to afford protection from invaders. Lots of archaeological effort and research has gone into learning the whys and hows of the construction of these homes.

A short video gives you a good understanding of all that has been learned about these structures. You'll learn what it is like to live here, cook your food over a fire, spin your own cloth, etc. You'll be regaled by Scottish folk tales and maybe even hear some Scottish music. It won't take long, but this is a pleasant place to stop and learn.

SPORTS & RECREATION
Angling
• **Croft-na-Caber**, *Kenmore. Tel. 01887/830-588*
• **JR News**, *Main Street, Killin. Tel. 01887/820-632*

Cycling
• **Killin Outdoor Center**, *Main Street, Killin. Tel. 01567/820-652*

Golf
• **Killin Golf Club**, *Killin. Tel. 01567/820-312*

Horseback Riding
• **Milton Morenish Riding Centre**, *Killin. Tel. 01567/820-323*

Sailing and Windsurfing
• **Croft-na-Caber**, *Kenmore. Tel. 01887/830-588*
• **Killin Outdoor Center**, *Main Street, Killin. Tel. 01567/820-652*
• **Loch Tay Boating Centre**, *Pier Road, Kenmore. Tel. 01887/830-291*

AYR & ALLOWAY

Ayr is a very popular resort town about two hours' drive south west of Glasgow. It sits along the shores of the **Firth of Clyde**, and the Isle of Arran is just offshore from it. Many come here to walk along its nearly three miles of beaches or the accompanying esplanade. It also offers visitors golfing, fishing, and horse racing.

Ayr is not a small village, but rather a small city, with a population of just over 50,000. It has been a popular holiday spot since Victorian times, and is still a destination many Scots head for when they try to escape the daily grind. As much as these relaxing things to do, Ayr draws visitors because of its association with **Robert Burns**, the Scottish National Poet. Burns was born in the nearby village of Alloway and spent much of his time in and around Ayr. But he endeared himself to all who call Ayr home by referring to its citizens as "honest men and bonnie lasses."

Alloway is the village that proudly claims as its native son Robert Burns, National Poet of Scotland. A small village two miles south of Ayr on the B7024, it is besieged annually by those who are on Robert Burns' trail.

ARRIVALS & DEPARTURES

By Bus

Buses arrive at the **Ayr Bust Station**, *Sandgate, Ayr*. Buses make the two-hour jaunt from Glasgow numerous times daily.

By Car

Ayr lies 81 miles southwest of Glasgow. Take the M77/A77 south from Glasgow to get here. If you are coming from Edinburgh, it's probably best just to come to Glasgow first on the M8, then take the M77/A77 south to Ayr.

By Train

Trains arrive in Ayr several times a day from Glasgow. The train station is located just off Smith Street.

ORIENTATION

There are two parts of Ayr. The city straddles the river Ayr as it empties into the Firth of Clyde. The city is laid out in roughly a north-south, east-west orientation. The south part of the city lies alongside the three-mile beach that begins at the River Ayr and extends south. The old medieval portion of the city is a bit inland from the River Ayr estuary, south of the river.

For tourist information, contact **Ayr Tourist Information Centre**, *Burns House, Burns Statue Square, Ayr, Tel. 01292/611-684.*

GETTING AROUND TOWN

By Bicycle

Bicycling in the city is fine, as it is predominantly flat, but traffic can be heavy during the summer months, so be careful.

By Car

I think this is the best way to get around Ayr. There is really no centralized place where all the sights in this part of the country are located.

By Foot

The few sights to see in Ayr, along with the size of the town, make it unrealistic to see the town on foot.

WHERE TO STAY

FAIRFIELD HOTEL, *12 Fairfield Road, Ayr. Tel. 01292/267-461, Fax 01292/261-456; E-mail: info@fairfield-hotel.demon.co.uk. 44 Rooms. Rates: £80-130 single; £95-180 per room double. Breakfast is included in the rate. All major credit cards accepted.*

I stumbled across the Fairfield when I was wandering the streets of Ayr trying to get to the ocean, and what a find. The Fairfield is located at the end of a street (Fairfield Road) that takes you to within about 200 yards of the ocean. There is a large green expanse of grass right next to the hotel that gives way to the Firth of Clyde, an estuary of the North Channel.

As you walk into the front lounge area, you'll encounter comfortable leather furnishings and a lovely fireplace. The greeting you receive at the reception desk will be warm and cordial, and will set the tone for your entire stay here. The rooms are large, brightly and impeccably decorated, and furnished with the highest quality furnishings. Some of the rooms at the end of the hotel look out onto the Firth of Clyde and across to the Isle of Arran. These are the best rooms, of course. Most of the rooms are large and spacious, with tall ceilings and ornate plasterwork. Each bedroom features a top-quality tile bathroom. Whether you are here on honeymoon or not, ask to see the Honeymoon Suite. The room is impressive enough, but the huge and hand-carved four-poster bed is one of the finest I saw in Scotland. A new wing added 15 rooms to the hotel in 1999. The Victorian charm isn't there, but each room is still furnished with fine high-quality furnishings. I prefer the original part of the house, but these rooms are certainly nice too.

There are two restaurants on site at the hotel, and both offer delicious meals in a wonderful setting (see the *Where to Eat* section). The Fairfield Hotel features a marvelous pool and leisure facility. So if it is rainy or dreary outside and you would prefer to stay in for a little recreation, this is a nice option. All in all, the Fairfield Hotel is a very nice option if you venture into this corner of Scotland.

CALEDONIAN HOTEL, *Dalblair Road, Ayr. Tel. 01292/269-331, Fax 01292/610-722. 114 Rooms. Rates: £65 single; £49-60 per person double. All major credit cards accepted.*

The Caledonian Hotel is a 1970s vintage hotel near the train station, and it feels like it is about 30 years old. Each of the bedrooms are decorated essentially the same, and the furnishings are for the most part functional. The rooms have been softened a bit with pastels and floral accents, but the feeling is still a bit tired. But it is clean and would be an acceptable place to stay.

SAVOY PARK HOTEL, *16 Racecourse Road, Ayr. Tel. 01292/266-112, Fax 01292/611-488; E-mail: savoy@ayrcoll.ac.uk; Website: www.2.ayrcoll.ac.uk/ index. 15 Rooms. Rates: £65-70 single; £40-50 per person double. Amex, MasterCard and Visa accepted.*

This pretty Ayr hotel is a great place to stay and explore the southwest coast of Scotland with all of its nooks and crannies. A converted Victorian mansion, its red sandstone walls are distinctive and attractive. The Henderson family has run it for the last generation or so.

The Savoy Park Hotel is comfortable and relaxing. It offers you the look and feel of a traditional Scottish hunting lodge. Just off the reception area is the pleasant and roomy Monarch Room. You can relax here after a hard day's sightseeing, sip a wee dram of whisky to warm your heart and soul on a cold, damp day, or you can take your meal here (or all three!). The rich oak walls are preside over by a regal set of red stag antlers above the welcoming fireplace. The rooms are of varying sizes and shapes –

typical of these converted Victorian mansions. But in each you'll find tall ceilings, tasteful decorating and comfortable furnishings.

Roddie Henderson is the Managing Director for this family-run hotel. In addition to being a delightful conversationalist, Roddie is a wealth of information about things to do in and around Ayr. He gave me several tips on country walks that were pleasant and enjoyable. The ocean is a mere two-minute walk from the hotel, and Roddie offers you the use of his Wellies (rubber boots) and border collie Dougall to enhance your strolling experience. (You know of course, that collies were first bred in Scotland for sheep herding; border collies were bred here in the *Borders* region of Scotland.) The Henderson family is particularly proud of their Scottish Tourism Board designation as a Silver Award winner for their environmental efforts.

AYR SCOTTISH YOUTH HOSTEL, *5 Craigwell Road, Ayr. Tel. 01292/262-322, centralized reservations: 0541/553-255. 9 Rooms, 60 total beds. Rates: £6.50 juniors (under age 18); £7.75 seniors (over age 18). MasterCard and Visa accepted.*

This is another of Scotland's nice youth hostels. Housed in an old Victorian mansion, the hostel offers three 4-bed rooms, three rooms with seven beds, and three rooms with nine beds. The hostel is about a 10- or 15-minute walk from both the bus and train stations. Clean and comfortable, there are laundry facilities and a self-catering kitchen for you to prepare your own meals. A continental breakfast is available for £2.

WHERE TO EAT

THE OAK ROOM, *16 Racecourse Road, Ayr. Tel. 01292/266-112, Fax 01292/611-488. £15-20. Open daily noon to 2:30pm and 5:00pm to 9:00pm. Amex, MasterCard and Visa accepted.*

The Oak Room is the dining room for the Savoy Park Hotel, but they cater to the public also. Its rich oak paneling is a perfect complement to the candlelit dinner you'll enjoy here. Large bay windows at one end of the room keep the room well lit and allow you to look out onto the hotel's impressive gardens and landscaped grounds. One look and you'll understand why it is a popular venue for weddings. The menu provides a variety of selections, from fish to beef, lamb and chicken. Try the Scottish smoked salmon served with seasonal salad and drizzled with lemon and dill oil. I had the roast sirloin of beef served with green peppercorn and brandy cream. It was outstanding. Dress for the Oak Room is casual to nice casual.

FLEUR-DE-LYS RESTAURANT, *12 Fairfield Road, Ayr. Tel. 01292/267-461, Fax 01292/261-456. £15-20. Open daily from 7:00pm to 9:00pm. All major credit cards accepted.*

The Fleur-de-Lys Restaurant is the very popular restaurant that serves the guests of the Fairfield Hotel (they serve the public also). This award-winning restaurant (two AA rosettes) offers deep blue carpet enhanced by gold fleur-de-lys to accentuate the marvelous dining experience you'll have here. You'll experience candlelight and china, crystal and silver as you savor the meals that are prepared here. Try the marinated duck supreme served with bok choi with pimento coulis or the roast rack of Ayrshire lamb with herb crust on braised red cabbage and thyme jus. Dress for the Fleur-de-Lys Restaurant is suit and tie.

FOUTER'S BISTRO, *2a Academy Street, Ayr. Tel. 01292/261-291. £5-8 for lunch and £9-15 for dinner. Open Tuesday through Sunday from noon to 2:00pm and from 6:30pm to 7:30pm. All major credit cards accepted.*

I'll wager that you never ate so well in a bank. Fouter's Bistro has taken up residence in the cellar of the former British Linen Bank. The building was constructed in the 18th century, and despite renovations to make the cellar acceptable as a restaurant, much of the character has been retained. Fouter's has been in business here since the early 1970s, always a good sign for a restaurant. They have proven very popular with locals, tourists, and judges from *A Taste of Scotland* and the Automobile Association (which has awarded Fouter's two AA rosettes). Sandstone floors and stark white walls softened by stencils are what you'll find here, along with lots of cheerful diners, enjoying both the company and the food that is prepared and served here.

You'll find modern Scottish/British fare here, and you'll be delighted. Fish is of course one of their specialties, so you might try the lobster and monkfish thermidor or the sautéed west coast langoustine with watermelon salsa and fresh lime dressing. If seafood isn't for you, there's always the medallions of Aberdeen beef. Fouter's is immensely popular with locals as well as returning tourists, so be sure and call ahead for reservations, especially during the summer.

SEEING THE SIGHTS

Ayr

Burns Museum, *High Street, Ayr, Tel. 01292/611-684; open April through September, Monday through Saturday from 9:30am to 5:30pm; admission is £1 for adults, 50p for children.* The Burns Museum is housed in the Tam O'Shanter Inn in Ayr. The Inn was a brewhouse in Robert Burns' day. Today it serves up a number of artifacts and information from Burns' life.

The Auld Kirk, *Kirk Port, Ayr, Tel. 01292/262-580; open July and August on Tuesday and Thursday only.* Besides its antiquity, the main draw to the Auld Kirk is that it was the place where poet Robert Burns was baptized. Built in 1654, the original pulpit is still in the church, and several of Burns' buddies are buried outside in the cemetery.

After you've seen the old kirk, you may wish to stroll over and take a look at the 15th-century bridge that fords the River Ayr. The **Auld Brig**, as it is called, was scheduled to be replaced when preservationists saved it at the turn of the 20th century. They reportedly used one of Robert Burns' poems to save the old bridge. It was the main them of his whimsical poem *Twa Brigs* (Two Bridges).

Alloway

   Burns Cottage and Museum, *Alloway, Tel. 01292/441-215; open daily April through October from 9:00am to 6:00pm, November through March Monday through Saturday from 10:00am to 4:00pm and Sunday noon to 4:00pm; admission is £2.50 for adults, £1.25 for seniors and children.* Robert Burns was born in Burns Cottage on January 25, 1759. It was home his father has built, and today it houses a small museum to the great poet. Thatch-roofed and whitewashed, it is also a good example of the type of home 18th-century working-class Scots lived in. You'll be able to see a plenitude of Burns memorabilia here, including the family Bible, letters and msnuscripts. Some of the furnishings are said to have been original to the home, including the bed in which Burns was born.

   Tam O'Shanter Experience, *Murdoch Lane, Alloway, Tel. 01292/443-700; open daily April through October from 9:00am to 6:00pm, November through March daily from 10:00am to 4:00pm; admission is £2.50 for adults, £1.25 for seniors and children.* This is an informative and enjoyable experience. You'll begin with a short video on the life of Robert Burns. Following that, a multi-media presentation acquaints you with one of Burn's best-known works, *Tam O'Shanter*. The poem spins the tale of one Tam O'Shanter, who was coming home very late one night from drinking with his buddies (against his wife's wishes, of course). As he rode along on his gray mare Meg, he happened upon a strange gathering in the Auld Kirk of Alloway (see below). To his astonishment, he sees a coven of witches and warlocks, along with the master of all evil himself. Tam watches mesmerized for awhile but is eventually discovered.

   The ghouls immediately begin chasing Tam. He heads for the Brig O' Doon (the Bridge of Doon), since he knows well that witches and warlocks cannot cross running water. One of the witches nearly catches him, but is left instead holding the gray hairs of Meg's tail. An exciting ride, to say the least

   The Alloway Auld Kirk, *Alloway*. The Auld Kirk in Alloway was in ruins during Robert Burns' lifetime, and served as the setting in *Tam O'Shanter* where Tam comes upon the coven of witches and warlocks. In real life, it is also the very church where Burns' father is buried. Nearby is the **Brig O' Doon**, the very bridge over which Tam and his faithful mare Meg escaped from the clutches of their demonic pursuers. Today the bridge overlooks beautiful gardens as well as the tranquil River Doon.

SPORTS & RECREATION
Angling
• **Sea Angling Centre**, *Ayr. Tel. 01292/285-297*

Golf
• **Prestwick Golf Club**, *Prestwick, Ayrshire. Tel. 01292/774-044*
• **Turnberry Golf Club**, *Turnberry, Ayrshire. Tel. 01655/331-000*

MAYBOLE

Maybole is a small little place on the Ayrshire coast about 12 miles southwest of Ayr. Its main claim to fame is stately **Culzean Castle and Country Park**.

WHERE TO STAY

EISENHOWER APARTMENTS, *Culzean Castle, Maybole, Ayrshire. Tel. 01655/760-274, Fax 01655/760-615; Website: www.nts.org.uk. 6 Rooms. Rates: £140-265 single; £140-265 per room double; £200-375 suite. Rates include breakfast. MasterCard and Visa accepted.*

Would you like to stay at a place that combines Scottish history, a medieval castle, a World War II hero and the President of the United States? Well, if that is the case, then look no further, because the Eisenhower Apartments at Culzean Castle do all that. At the close of World War II, a grateful Scotland converted the top floor of Culzean Castle into a large apartment and offered it to General Dwight D. Eisenhower as a gift for his efforts on behalf of the Allies during the war.

There are six rooms that comprise the Eisenhower apartments. They are what I'd call "elegantly informal." The Eisenhower Room is of course the most expensive of the rooms because of its history and because of who slept here. There is a honeymoon suite, complete with a four-poster bed. There are four other rooms, one of which is called the Kennedy Room (although it has no relation to Ike's successor). Most of the rooms are furnished simply but pleasantly, and they have the feel of 1960s-era decorating. The apartments are chock-full of Eisenhower memorabilia – photos, paintings, etc. There's even a guest book with a cover page dedicated by President Eisenhower, which he presented to the owners of Culzean Castle in 1951. Take a moment and flip through its pages; you'll be surprised to learn who has stayed here through the years. Ike only visited and stayed here four times. He claimed it was a place where he could relax. He painted, walked the beaches and grounds, and just sort of unwound. And you can too.

SEEING THE SIGHTS

Culzean Castle and Country Park, *Maybole, Ayrshire, Tel. 01655/760-274, Fax 01655/760-615; Website: www.nts.org.uk; the castle and the park are open daily April through October from 10:30am to 5:30pm, and just the park is open from November through March from 9:30am to sunset; admission is £7 for adults and £5 for seniors and children; admission to just the park is £4 for adults, £3 for seniors and children, and a family ticket is available for £ 18.* About 12 miles southwest of Ayr is the impressive Culzean Castle (pronounced Cull'-ane). In 1790, renowned Scottish architect Robert Adam completed the castle for David Kennedy, the 10th Earl of the powerful Kennedy Clan. The castle remained in the Kennedy family until it was given to the National Trust for Scotland. Today it is a wonderful place to stop and spend at least a few hours, if not more.

Inside, you'll find many items to attract your attention. I was particularly impressed with the armory exhibit, which was displayed in a most interesting manner. Throughout the house you'll find many ancient oil paintings, period furnishings, and knick-knacks from days gone by. But the most impressive sight may well be the unique oval staircase designed by Robert Adam. It flows elegantly upwards, flanked by grand Corinthian and Ionic columns.

The red-carpeted stairway leads to an upper floor where you'll find a few more items of interest. A circular drawing room, called the *Saloon*, is furnished in period pieces and has large windows that look out to the sea and the Ailsa Craig, a lump of rock out in the Firth of Clyde. Around the corner is a small mini-museum dedicated to US President Dwight D. Eisenhower. It's pretty basic, with photographs of Ike shown in various military campaigns as well as during several visits to Culzean Castle. Other Eisenhower artifacts are present, including a field desk he used during the North African campaign.

In 1945, the top floor of Culzean Castle was given to Ike for his use, which he did use on several occasions after the war. Today, it is available to stay in (see below). The castle sits majestically at the edge of a cliff that drops off to the sea. Inland from the castle are 563 acres of woods and park-like grounds, much of which is crisscrossed with walking paths.

TROON

Troon lies seven miles north of Ayr. It is a small, relatively quiet town renowned for one thing: its fabulous golf course. In between rounds, the golfers can stroll along two miles of sandy beach. For tourist information, contact **Troon Tourist Information Centre**, *Municipal Building, South Beach, Troon, Tel. 01292/317-696.*

ARRIVALS & DEPARTURES
By Car
   From Ayr, take the A78 north a few miles and watch for the signposts to Troon. You'll be on the A759.
   Take the M77/A77 south from Glasgow to get here. After you get to Ayr, head north on the A78 until you see the signposts for Troon and the A759. If you are coming from Edinburgh, it's probably best just to come to Glasgow first on the M8, then take the M77/A77 south to Ayr and then north to Troon.

WHERE TO STAY
   PIERSLAND HOUSE HOTEL, *15 Craigend Road, Troon. Tel. 01292/ 314-747, Fax 01292/315-613. 31 Rooms. Rates: £70-90 single; £99-125 double; £99-135 suite. Rates include breakfast. All major credit cards accepted.*
   This popular hotel has served many guests who have ventured to Troon for golf or beach holidays. And whatever your motivation for coming, you'll be glad you chose Piersland House Hotel as your base. The Victorian house was built over 100 years ago for Sir Alexander Walker, grandson of the founder of Johnny Walker Whisky. Gabled and beamed, it looks like it belongs a few miles further to the south in England.
   Each of the bedrooms is large and exceptionally well furnished. They are tastefully decorated and offer satellite television, telephone, radio, hairdryer and tea- and coffee-making facilities. The hotel boasts four acres of gardens that are spectacular indeed. Tons of topsoil were brought in to reclaim a marshy wasteland, and the results are marvelous.

SPORTS & RECREATION
Golf
• **Royal Troon**, *Craigend Road, Troon, Ayrshire. Tel. 01292/311-555*

PRACTICAL INFORMATION FOR GLASGOW
Automobile Association – AA
   The **Automobile Association**, *Fanum House, 18/22 Melville Street, Edinburgh, Tel. 0990/444-444 (for information), and 0800/887-7666 (if you need assistance)*, can help out if you run into problems getting your car to start, or if you need to be towed. If you are not a member and need assistance, call the first number and you can become a member immediately for £90.

Banks

Most banks in Glasgow have an ATM machine either outside their main doorways or just inside the bank. The ATMs are part of the Cirrus and Plus international networks. Be sure to check with your bank to see if your personal identification number (PIN) will work on international ATMs. Most international ATMs only accept four-digit PINs.

Business Hours

Businesses are generally open from 9:00am to 5:30pm or 6:00pm in Scotland, although from a practical standpoint, most stores open at 9:30am or 10:00am. The exceptions to this rule are bakeries and Newsagents – they are usually open at 7:00am. On Friday evenings, many stores stay open until 7:00pm.

Emergencies

Remember this: dialing **999** in Scotland = dialing 911 in the States. Use it in the event of any emergency where you need assistance from the police, fire department, or the medical community.

Exchanging Money

You can exchange money at banks, most post offices, larger hotels and at change booths in the Glasgow Airport.

Laundry Service

As you might suspect in a city Glasgow's size, there are a number of laundromats around the city. Called launderettes, you can find one close to where you are by looking in the yellow pages. Here are a few:
- **Bendix Launderette**, *452 Cathcart Road, Glasgow. Tel. 0141/423-8493*
- **Majestic Launderette**, *1110 Argyle Street, Glasgow. Tel. 0141/339-6530*
- **The Laundromat**, *39 Bank Street, Glasgow. Tel. 0141/339-8953*
- **Shafton Launderette**, *14 Shafton Road, Glasgow. Tel. 0141/954-2860*
- **New Havelock Launderette**, *10 Havelock Road, Glasgow. Tel. 0141/339-1499*
- **Parade Launderette**, *492 Alexandra Parade, Glasgow. Tel. 0141/584-8700*
- **Park Launderette**, *14 Park Road, Glasgow. Tel. 0141/337-1285*

Lost Credit Cards
- **American Express Card**, *Tel. 01273/696-933*
- **Diners Club**, *Tel. 01252/513-500, 0800/460-800*
- **MasterCard**, *Tel. 0800/964-767*
- **Visa**, *Tel. 0800/895-082*

Pharmacies

In Scotland, pharmacies are called "Chemists," and can be located through any of the Tourist Offices, or in the "Yellow Pages." Here is a pharmacy that stays open late: **Boots the Chemist**, *200 Sauchiehall Street, Glasgow, Tel. 0141/332-1925.*

Post Offices

In addition to the regular post offices, most Newsagents serve as post office outlets. Most post offices in Glasgow are open Monday through Friday from 9:00am to 5:30pm, and Saturday from 9:00am to 12:30pm. If you have trouble finding a post office in Glasgow, you can call *0345/223-344* to find out where the closest post office is. There are many small branches of the post office throughout the city.

Here are a few:

- **Anniesland**, *900 Crow Road, Tel. 0141/954-8661*
- **Bothwell Street Office**, *85-89 Bothwell Street*
- **Hope Street Office**, *216 Hope Street*
- **Sauchiehall Street Office**, *533 Sauchiehall Street*

Tourist Information

There are two tourist offices in Glasgow:

- **Glasgow Tourist Information Centre**, *11 George Square, Glasgow. Tel. 0141/204-4400, Fax 0141/221-3524; E-mail: TourismGlasgow@ggcvtb.org.uk*
- **Glasgow Airport Tourist Information Centre**, *Tourist Information Desk, Glasgow Airport, Paisley. Tel. 0141/848-4440, Fax 0141/849-1444*

15. THE HIGHLANDS

Okay, admit it – when you think of Scotland, you think of the **Highlands**. Perhaps it's because of the moors and mountains or the many hues of heather. Or perhaps it is because of recent Hollywood movies about Scotland, like *The Highlander* or *Braveheart* (although you have to be careful with the latter movie – much of it was filmed in Ireland).

If you have come to Scotland for even a few days, you're probably going to try and come to the Highlands, as well you should. This area of Scotland is remarkable from a scenery as well as historical perspective. It includes one of Scotland's most beautiful cities (Inverness) and her most widely known character: **Nessie** of **Loch Ness**. It is home to lovely and lengthy lochs, lusty legends and hardy humans.

Let me clarify the areas I will cover in this chapter. There are many definitions of the Highlands, and I want to be sure we understand one another. In this chapter I will cover the area west of the **Great Glen**. If you look at a map of Scotland, you'll note that the northwestern third of the country almost looks like an island. It is held to the main landmass of Scotland by tentative land bridges between long narrow lochs. The lochs (Loch Ness, Loch Lochy and Loch Linnhe) run nearly north-south from Inverness in the north to Oban in the south. For the purposes of this guide, the area I will cover in this chapter on the Highlands is that which lies north and west of the Great Glen, beginning at **Fort William** in the south and extending north to **John O'Groats**. You'll find Fort William at the north end of Loch Linnhe.

You'll experience awesome **Ben Nevis**, the tallest mountain in Britain. We'll prowl around **Urquhart Castle** on the shores of Loch Ness and look for her famous resident. We'll check out the small villages of **Ullapool**, **Tongue**, **Durness** and **Inverness**, the capital of the Highlands. I'll introduce you to single-track roads, sandy beaches, and hidden caves. In other words, you're going to have a great time. Inverness is an excellent place to base your exploration of the Highlands, so we'll focus first on that lovely village.

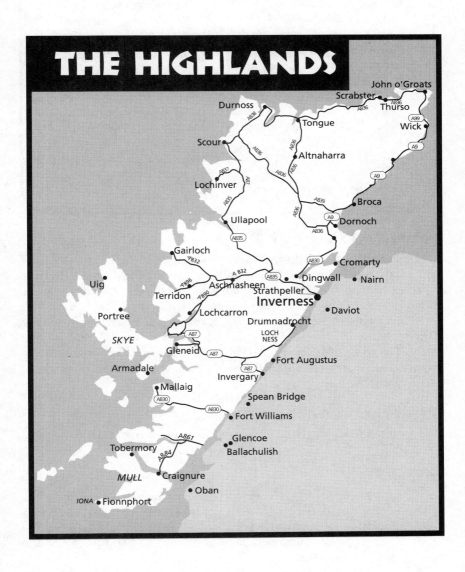

THE HIGHLAND'S MUST-SEE SIGHTS

Inverness – *The fair capital of and gateway to the Highlands. This is a pretty city, notwithstanding the tourists that descend upon it.*

Culloden Battlefield – *a battlefield that had the same magnitude on Scotland's history as Gettysburg did on America's history.*

Loch Ness – *You've come this far, you've got to go see this loch and peer into its gray depths in search of its most famous resident.*

Eilean Donan Castle – *sitting astride a small island in Loch Duich, Eilean Donan Castle is one of the most photographed castles in Scotland.*

Fort William – *The area around Fort William is a wonderful place to see the majesty of the Highland peaks soaring heavenward above beautiful lochs.*

Heather – *This seems like an incongruous entry, but if you are in Scotland from mid-August through mid-September, I guarantee you'll want to see the Highlands in heather.*

INVERNESS

Inverness is one of the prettiest towns in Scotland. It sits regally at the apex of the **Moray Firth**, with the Highland hills sloping down to it, paying homage to their historic capital. The **River Ness** (yes, it feeds the more famous loch of the same name) meanders quietly through the town, creating a sense of serenity and peacefulness. But beware – during the summer months, Inverness becomes a hotbed of tourists and is quite busy. The town of Inverness itself has little to offer from a sightseeing standpoint, but it's a fun place to knock about, visit shops and experience Scottish life.

ARRIVALS & DEPARTURES

You can reach the Highlands by air, bus, car and, to a limited extent, by train.

BY AIR

Flights land in Inverness from several of London's airports, Edinburgh, Glasgow and Aberdeen. Flights arrive at **Inverness Airport**, *Tel. 01463/232-471*. **British Regional Airways**, *Tel. 0345/222-111*, and **EasyJet**, *Tel. 0990/239292*, fly into Inverness from London. The flight from London takes a little over an hour.

The Inverness airport is quite small and compact. The four-mile drive from the airport into the city is marvelous – you drive through verdant green fields and forests, and past a picturesque castle (Castle Stewart).

Getting to Town from the Airport

You can catch a taxi at the airport. As you exit the terminal, just turn to your left and the taxi stand is about 50 yards down. You can also catch a bus into town by walking directly out of the terminal.

As mentioned above, the Inverness airport is quite small and compact. If you want to rent a car, you won't have a problem locating Avis or Hertz rental car booths – they are right there as you enter the Arrivals Hall (such as it is).

BY BUS

Buses from Edinburgh and Glasgow arrive numerous times throughout the day. These **Scottish Citylink** buses, *Tel. 0990/505-050*, arrive at the **Inveress Bus Station**, *Farraline Park, off Academy Street, Tel. 01463/233-371*. Fares from Edinburgh and Glasgow run £10 to £15 one way, and about £20 round-trip (called "return" tickets). **National Express**, *Tel. 0990/808-808*, buses also arrive from London after their 13-hour trip. Round-trip fares run around £40.

BY CAR

To get to Inverness from Edinburgh, take the M90 north to Perth, then the A9 north to Inverness. From Glasgow, take the A82 north past Loch Lomond and Fort William. Follow it along the banks of Lochs Linnhe, Lochy and Ness until you arrive in Inverness. If you're coming from Aberdeen, take the A96 northwest into Inverness.

Sample trip lengths from Inverness around the country (on the main roads without stopping to take pictures, visit sights or take detours):
• Aberdeen: 3 hours
• Fort William: 4 hours
• Glasgow: 4 hours
• John O'Groats: 4 hours
• London: 13 hours
• Oban: 5 hours
• Ullapool: 2 hours

BY TRAIN

About a half dozen trains arrive daily at the **Inverness Train Station**, *Academy Street, Tel. 01463/238-924,* from Edinburgh and Glasgow.

BEST PLACES TO STAY IN THE HIGHLANDS

There are a number of fine accommodations in the Highlands, from top-notch hotels and resorts to comfortable and enjoyable B&Bs. The following hotels, guest houses and B&Bs are listed from most expensive to least expensive. You can get more information on each selection in the reviews that follow.

MANSFIELD HOUSE HOTEL, Scotsburn Road, Tain. Tel. 01862/892-052, Fax 01862/892-260; E-mail: info@mansfield-house.co.uk; Website: www.mansfield-house.co.uk. 18 Rooms. Rates: £45-75 single; £70-130 per person double. Rates include breakfast. Amex, MasterCard and Visa accepted. This splendid and elegant Georgian house was built in 1875 as the landowner's home. Today it is a wonderful hotel that will delight you.

BOATH HOUSE, Aberdeen Road, Auldearn, Nairn. Tel. 01667/454-896, 01667/455-469; E-mail: wendy@boath-house.demon.co.uk; Website: boath-house.demon.co.uk. 7 Rooms. Rates: £80-100 single; £55-88 per person double. All major credit cards accepted. Boath House offers Georgian elegance and grace. You'll enjoy the splendor of Georgian life when you stay here.

GLENDRUIDH HOUSE, Old Edinburgh Road South, Inverness. Tel. 01463/226-499, Fax 01463/710-745; E-mail: michael@cozzee-nessie-bed.co.uk; Website: www.cozzee-nessie-bed.co.uk. 9 rooms. Rates: £25-45 single; £25-45 per person double; £45-59 per person suite; £19-33 per person villa. All major credit cards accepted. I fell in love with Glendruidh House the moment I drove onto their forest-like grounds, and I suspect you will too. This wonderful old home was built over 150 years ago, and it has been renovated in a splendid manner.

FELSTEAD GUEST HOUSE, 18 Ness Bank Road, Inverness. Tel. 01463/231-634, Fax 01463/231-634; E-mail: felstead@jafsoft.com; Website: www.jafsoft.com/felstead/felstead. 8 Rooms. Rates: £20-29 single; £26-34 per person double. Rates include breakfast. Amex, MasterCard and Visa accepted. This gorgeous Georgian guest house sits along the banks of the tree-lined Ness River about five minutes' walk from downtown Inverness.

ARDVRECK GUEST HOUSE, Morefield Brae, Ullapool. Tel. 08154/612-028, Fax 01854/613-000; E-mail: ardvreck.guesthouse@btinternet.com; Website: www.smoothhound.co.uk. 10 Rooms. Rates: £24-27 single; £24-27 per person double. Rates include breakfast. MasterCard and Visa accepted, although cash is preferred. Sitting high on the hill above Loch Broom, Ardvreck Guest House offers its guests spectacular views of the loch, the Highlands, and the nearby village of Ullapool.

CLACH MHUILINN, 7 Harris Road, Inverness. Tel. 01463/237-059, Fax 01463/242-092; E-mail: jacqi@ness.co.uk;Website: www.ness.co.uk. 2 Rooms. Rates: £35 single; £24-26 per person double. Rates include breakfast. MasterCard and Visa accepted. Iain and Jacqi Elmslie run this pleasant four-star B&B situated in a quiet residential neighborhood on the outskirts of Inverness.

ORIENTATION

The downtown area of Inverness is close and compact, and is only about three blocks long by three blocks wide. Next to the shops and restaurants, the castle is the main attraction in the downtown area. It sits at the south end of the downtown area, on a hill with commanding views. Several of the downtown streets have been closed to vehicles, but watch out for all the tourists. The River Ness meanders along quietly at the west edge of town.

GETTING AROUND TOWN

By Bicycle

A bicycle isn't a bad idea to get into downtown from the outlying areas, but once you're here, lock it up and walk around.

By Foot

This is the best way to see the downtown area. It's so compressed, that you should be able to see everything relatively easily on foot.

By Taxi

You don't need a taxi to get around town, unless it is to come in from your hotel, guest house or B&B. Here are a few of the taxi companies in Inverness:
- **Culloden Taxis**, *Tel. 01463/790-000*
- **Clubbies Cabs**, *Tel. 01463/719-777*
- **Inverness Taxis**, *Tel. 01463/221-111*
- **Rank Taxis**, *Tel. 01463/220-222*

WHERE TO STAY

In addition to some fine hotels, guest houses and B&Bs in Inverness, there are a number of outstanding facilities in the towns and bergs near Inverness. I have listed a few places in Inverness proper, as well as a number of others in the surrounding towns.

Inverness

CULLODEN HOUSE HOTEL, *off the Inverness–Aberdeen Road (A96), Inverness. Tel. 01463/790-461, Fax 01463/792-181; E-mail: 106237.663@compuserve.com; Website: www.cullodenhouse.co.uk. 28 Rooms. Rates: £135-150 single; £165-250 per room double; £230-270 per suite. Rates include breakfast. All major credit cards accepted.*

If you are looking for a historic place to stay, Culloden House Hotel should definitely be on your list of places. This gorgeous Georgian mansion is set amid acres of stunningly landscaped grounds, and was once used as headquarters by Bonnie Prince Charlie before his date with a fateful destiny on Culloden Battlefield. You'll find spacious rooms decorated individually in warm and inviting colors, and furnished with exceptionally high-quality furnishings. Many of the rooms are endowed with four-poster beds, and almost all have stunning views of the estate.

The service at Culloden House is quiet, efficient and quite friendly. You'll enjoy the luxury of the public rooms, and you'll revel in the meals prepared and served in the restaurant (see *Where to Eat* section). Many of the public rooms feature fireplaces and plasterwork designed by famed architect Robert Adam. You'll find a number of amenities available at Culloden House, including a croquet court, splendid gardens, a tennis court and a sauna. If you will be arriving by helicopter, you'll be glad to know there is a heliport available for you. If you are looking for a family hotel, however, this isn't the place for you: children under 12 years of age may not stay here.

The hotel can be a little tricky to find, so here are some easy directions. Take the A96 toward Aberdeen. After about one mile, watch for the signs directing you to Culloden Village, and turn right. One mile down you'll find a signpost directing you to Culloden House, and turn left there.

SWALLOW KINGSMILL HOTEL, *Culcabock Road, Inverness. Tel. 01463/237-166, Fax 01463/225-208. 82 Rooms. Rates: £110 single; £135-155 per room double; £195-220 suite. Rates include breakfast. Amex, MasterCard and Visa accepted.*

This is a beautiful old Scottish mansion house sitting just a little over a mile from the center of downtown Inverness. It was built in the late 18th century on the site of a former grist mill. As soon as you walk in, you'll get a feeling this is someplace special. Lots of dark oak, plaster cornices and quality artwork on the walls convey the feeling of elegance and luxury.

The bedrooms are all large and individually decorated. Designer drapes and wallpaper complement the top-quality furnishings. Each room is well lit, and many of the rooms feature marvelous views of the splendid gardens and grounds that surround this four-star hotel. Each room offers satellite TV, phone, trouser press, tea- and coffee-making facilities and hairdryers. There are also six two-bedroom lodges on-site, truly elegant and comfortable villas. They are large and furnished with the same high-quality furnishings you'll find throughout the hotel. The villas look out onto a new golf course, and the views are serene and peaceful.

I enjoyed just going up and down the hallways admiring the art on the walls. They held a treasure trove of Scottish scenes, including landscapes, castles, bagpipers and scenes from medieval Scottish life. There is a nice restaurant, as well as a spacious guest lounge, a small pub, and a nicely equipped exercise room, swimming pool, steam room, spa and solarium.

If you are traveling with children, you'll be interested in knowing that two children stay free when they share a room with their parents (one child per parent). This really is a first-class hotel in every respect, and you will enjoy staying here.

CALEDONIAN HOTEL, *Church Street, Inverness. Tel. 01463/235-181, Fax 01463/711-206. 85 Rooms. Rates: £85-150 single; £85-150 per room double. Amex, MasterCard and Visa accepted.*

The Caledonian Hotel in downtown Inverness is at the hub of the Inverness business district. The hotel is a 1960s-looking building on the outside, with the same look and feel on the inside. The bedrooms are all about average size, clean and functional. But beyond that, they are pretty basic. The rooms at the back of the hotel have pretty views of the city and the hills beyond Inverness. They also overlook the River Ness as it flows along. If you find yourself in a bind and can find no place else to stay, then I would consider the Caledonian. Otherwise, it's an awful lot to pay for this place. There are a lot nicer and more reasonable places to stay in and around Inverness.

GLENDRUIDH HOUSE, *Old Edinburgh Road South, Inverness. Tel. 01463/226-499, Fax 01463/710-745; E-mail: michael@cozzee-nessie-bed.co.uk; Website: www.cozzee-nessie-bed.co.uk. 9 rooms. Rates: £25-45 single; £25-45 per person double; £45-59 per person suite; £19-33 per person villa. All major credit cards accepted.*

I fell in love with Glendruidh House the moment I drove onto their forest-like grounds, and I suspect you will too. This wonderful old home was built over 150 years ago, and it has been renovated in a splendid manner. *Glen* comes from the Gaelic word for valley, and *Druidh* is named after the Druid temple found high on the hill above Glendruidh House. A short walk brings you to an ancient stone circle (all that is left of the ancient temple) within minutes from Glendruidh House. Your hosts at Glendruidh House are Michael and Christine Smith, and you will be as delighted with them as you are the reasonably priced accommodations.

Iron red is the predominant color theme throughout – but don't worry, it works. The bedrooms are more of a complementing salmon color. Each bedroom is very pleasant, comfortable and well furnished with quality furnishings. My favorite room in the house, though, is the resident lounge. It is a unique round room – including the windows and doors. It is used for guests to have a cup of coffee and chat a bit either before or after dinner, or both. The restaurant for Glendruidh House is as exceptional as the rest of the house. Christine Smith is the chef, and her efforts have earned recognition by *A Taste of Scotland*. They have a wine list that would be the envy of many of the restaurants in the country. You will definitely enjoy your meals here. The small bar is well stocked, and features about 50 malt whiskies representing every area of Scotland. It includes some very rare malt whiskies.

Behind the main house you'll find a modern villa with three large bedrooms and a large lounge with a fireplace. It does not have the personality of the old house, but it is really quite nice. Out front you'll notice a beautiful garden and a splendid croquet lawn. Try your hand at the game – but remember the winner gets to donate £1 to a local charity, a tradition the Smiths have been promoting for years. The house is non-smoking throughout.

FELSTEAD GUEST HOUSE, *18 Ness Bank Road, Inverness. Tel. 01463/231-634, Fax 01463/231-634; E-mail: felstead@jafsoft.com; Website: www.jafsoft.com/felstead/felstead. 8 Rooms. Rates: £20-29 single; £26-34 per person double. Rates include breakfast. Amex, MasterCard and Visa accepted.*

What a find – I stumbled across Felstead Guest House quite by accident, and my accident is your good fortune. This gorgeous Georgian guest house sits along the banks of the tree-lined Ness River about five minutes' walk from downtown Inverness. It has been spectacularly renovated by Anne and Diarmid Troup. But you needn't take my word for how exceptional this B&B is: the Scottish Tourist Board recently featured Felstead Guest House in a video promoting tourism in Scotland.

The residents' lounge is a lovely room that looks out onto Anne's beautiful flower-lined front yard and the Ness River flowing by just across the street. The tartans throughout the house are of the Drummond Clan. This comfortable and pleasant room is a great place to relax after a day's sightseeing. Built in 1835, this four-star guest house features those marvelous tall ceilings that make these old Georgian homes seem so spacious. The dining room is a smallish room, but it has a feel of quiet elegance. It also overlooks the River Ness and provides a pleasant dining atmosphere. Anne is an excellent cook, and you'll be delighted with the full Scottish breakfast she whips up for you.

The bedrooms are all large, and feature bright colors with floral borders and complementary bedspreads. The two rooms at the front of the house overlook the Ness River from large bay windows. The original plasterwork cornices are still very much in evidence in each of the rooms. Each room has a TV, hairdryer, radio and electric blankets. Anne also makes the rooms more welcoming by providing each with fresh flowers for your enjoyment. There are eight bedrooms, four of them are ensuite, one has a private bath in the hallway, and the three upstairs rooms share a hallway bathroom. The bathrooms are all nice size and offer showers but no bathtubs.

Anne and Diarmid cater to families, and you will appreciate their lower rates for children. Children ages 2-5 are 25% of the adult rate, ages 6 to 12 are half the adult rate, and ages 13 to 16 are 75% of the adult rate.

The Troups would like their guests to know that Felstead Guest house is non-smoking. Off-street parking is available behind the guest house. As icing on the cake, Felstead Guest House has an outstanding web page, one of the best in Scotland (*www.jafsoft.com/felstead/felstead*). It is full of information, and has many links that will be of immense interest to you, especially if you are planning a trip to Inverness or the surrounding areas. As wonderful as the guest house is, Anne is perhaps the best thing about Felstead Guest House. She is an elegant, gracious hostess who is sure to make your stay a memorable one.

CLACH MHUILINN, *7 Harris Road, Inverness. Tel. 01463/237-059, Fax 01463/242-092; E-mail: jacqi@ness.co.uk; Website: www.ness.co.uk. 2 Rooms. Rates: £35 single; £24-26 per person double. Rates include breakfast. MasterCard and Visa accepted.*

Iain and Jacqi Elmslie run this pleasant four-star B&B situated in a quiet residential neighborhood at the edge of Inverness. For those of you who do not speak Gaelic, Clach Mhuilinn is Gaelic for *Millstone*. Be sure and ask Jacqi to explain the true meaning of the name. I guarantee it will surprise and delight you.

Clach Mhuilinn has only two bedrooms, but they are both nice sized and very comfortable. Bright walls and good lighting make the rooms seem even larger than they are. Jacqi has thoughtfully provided electric blankets to help you chase the chill of a damp day. Each room has its own bathroom, and each bathroom is modern, clean, and pleasantly decorated. You will take your breakfast in the small family dining room. The meals Jacqi prepares are wonderful, and you will enjoy dining as you look out the windows at her spectacular gardens.

Jacqi organized a group known as *Scotland's Best B&Bs*, so you can imagine that she knows the B&B business well. She is also a great source for other B&Bs around the country should you want a recommendation for your upcoming travels. You can check out *Scotland's Best B&Bs* on their website at *www.b-and-b-scotland.co.uk*. Clach Mhuilinn is a pleasant and easy place to stay, and Iain and Jacqi are wonderful hosts. Their guest book contains more than a few comments that indicate the quality of the stay you will receive here. My favorite comment was, "Little things make wonderful holidays. This place is one of them." I agree, and you will too!

DAVIOT MAINS FARM, *Daviot. Tel. 01463/772-215, Fax 01463/772-099; E-mail: farmhols@globalnet.co.uk. 5 Rooms. Rates: £28-31 single; £21-25 per person sharing. Rates include breakfast. MasterCard and Visa included.*

About 10 miles south of Inverness on the A9, take the B851 toward Croy. You'll find Daviot Mains Farm at the first right. This is a wonderful old farmhouse built in 1820 in a square around a central courtyard, and there are only two other structures built like this in Scotland. The house is part of a 365-acre working farm, and you may encounter farm implements of all kinds, sheep, cattle, etc. Depending on the time of year you visit, you may be able to watch sheep shearing, help bottle-feed lambs, or participate in other agricultural-type activities. Mrs. Hutcheson is your hostess, and she is well qualified to meet your lodging needs. While she and her husband began hosting guests in 1982, she grew up in the business, and you benefit from her years of expertise.

None of the five bedrooms in this four-star facility is exceptionally large, but each is comfortable and tastefully decorated in attractive floral accents. One of the rooms, the Nairn Room, has an old Victorian bathtub, the likes of which you have probably never seen. Three of the rooms have their own bathrooms, and two have bathrooms in the hallway. Your breakfast will be nothing short of wonderful. Mrs. Hutcheson's efforts have been recognized by *A Taste of Scotland*. If you decide you'd like to see what she can do with dinner, you'll be equally as pleased (dinner is available for £13 per person).

Mrs. Hutcheson is a wonderful, gracious hostess. She has a way about her of making you feel immediately comfortable and at home. Perhaps that is why Daviot Mains Farm has hosted ambassadors, consulate generals and other dignitaries through the years. If you choose to stay here, I promise this will be one of your favorite memories.

HO HO HOSTEL, *23A High Street, Inverness. Tel. 01463/221-225; E-mail: mail@hohohostel.force9.net; Website: www.hohohostel.force9.co.uk. 10 Rooms. Rates: £8.50-10.50 per person. MasterCard and Visa accepted.*

You'll find this independent backpackers' hostel smack-dab in the middle of downtown Inverness, close to all that action. This former tartan warehouse has been converted into a rambling hostel with 81 beds. You have probably never stayed in a place quite like Ho Ho Hostel, and it is likely you never will again. It is an old Victorian-era building, with high ceilings and large rooms. The largest of these rooms is the residents' lounge, a large room with immensely tall ceilings, garish yellow paint and green trim. (okay – so it's not the Hilton). The walls throughout the complex boast...interesting...paintings. It is nothing if not eclectic.

You will find the rooms to be large and provided with a number of beds. It is a (relatively) clean, comfortable place to stay (although it has a bit of a cluttered feeling). But it is very different. You'll feel as though you should be wearing hip-huggers, flowers in your hair and sporting a peace symbol around your neck. It's definitely not for everyone, so you'll have to decide for yourself. It is open all year.

North of Inverness
MANSFIELD HOUSE HOTEL, *Scotsburn Road, Tain. Tel. 01862/ 892-052, Fax 01862/892-260; E-mail: info@mansfield-house.co.uk; Website:*

www.mansfield-house.co.uk. 18 Rooms. Rates: £45-75 single; £70-130 per person double. Rates include breakfast. Amex, MasterCard and Visa accepted.

My oh my – you are going to like Mansfield House Hotel. This splendid and elegant Georgian house was built in 1875 as the landowner's home. It was a private home until World War II, when it was converted into a hotel. In 1995 Norman and Norma Lauritsen purchased it and have renovated it to its former luxurious stature. Everywhere you look you see splendid pine paneling, ornate ceilings, quality furnishings and art. The tartan carpet on the stairs is that of the MacKenzie Clan. For years, Mr. Lauritsen was an international businessman used to seeing hotels from the traveler's point of view. He has brought that perspective to Mansfield House and the results are marvelous.

This stunning four-star country house sits in the midst of 3.5 acres of spectacular grounds. Among many other trees, there are two 140-year-old Canadian redwoods on the property. In addition, lots of well-manicured lawns give the grounds a park-like feeling. There are eight bedrooms in the main house, and another 10 are located in a new wing of the house that was completed in 1980. The rooms in the main house are spacious and most have large, well-appointed bathrooms. Four of the bathrooms include Jacuzzi baths. The best rooms in the main house are the Haakon, Ankerville, Rose, Ross and Croftmary rooms. The rooms in the new wing are generally a little smaller, but they are also furnished with top-quality furnishings and are very comfortable. These rooms feel more like traditional hotel rooms in a very nice hotel. Regardless of which room you stay in, you'll find a TV and radio, hairdryer, trouser press, tea- and coffee-making facilities and a complimentary decanter of sherry.

As you would expect, the dining room at the Mansfield House Hotel is marvelous. Keeping things in the family, the head chef is David Lauritsen. He has shown he earned this role by being more than merely the owners' son; he already has two AA rosettes to his credit, and I believe a third cannot be far behind (see the *Where to Eat* section). Mansfield House has recently added a Beauty Salon to the amenities they offer their guests. Why not try an aromatherapy treatment, or possibly a massage at the hands of a skilled masseuse?

As pleased as the Lauritsens are about their hotel and the food that is served here, there is another area of which they are especially proud. They and their staff have a focus on customer service that is truly above and beyond what most hotels expect. The Lauritsen's are experts in finding and retaining the best and the brightest individuals to serve their guests. A quick scan of their guest book will assure you that the service provided here is far more than lip service. It seems that a vast majority of the comments mention the staff (as well as the food). If you stay at Mansfield House, you will be joining politicians and movie stars that have called Mansfield House Hotel home, if only for a little while. I guarantee you will really enjoy it here.

Selected as one of my Best Places to Stay – see Chapter 12.

TULLOCH CASTLE HOTEL, *Tulloch Castle Road, Dingwall. Tel. 01349/861-325, Fax 01349/663-993. 19 Rooms. Rates: £42 single; £75 double; £85 four-poster suites. MasterCard and Visa accepted.*

This grand old castle sits high on the hillside above Dingwall and offers pretty views of the surrounding area. Originally built as a mansion, it has been converted into a hotel in recent years. The bedrooms are nice sized, and many have four-poster beds in them. The rooms at the front of the house look out over the valley and are the ones to ask for when you make your reservations. Take a moment to notice the wonderful woodwork throughout the hotel, and you can imagine what a magnificent place this must have once been.

There are more guests than meet the eye at Tulloch Castle hotel. At last count, there were 10 ghosts that regularly haunt the castle. Ken MacAuley, the owner, regales his guests with the stories of all the ghosts and their lives. The Green Lady, whose picture hangs in the Great Hall, has a particularly poignant story.

There is a restaurant and bar at the hotel. The restaurant is small, but the dining is elegant. Crystal and china will enhance the meals that are served here. This is a nice place, but it is showing signs of being old and tired. With a little bit of attention and a decorator's eye (and a bit of money), it could be so much more. The new owner, Mr. MacAuley, has started renovations. It will be interesting to see how well he succeeds.

Northeast of Inverness

BOATH HOUSE, *Aberdeen Road, Auldearn, Nairn. Tel. 01667/454-896, 01667/455-469; E-mail: wendy@boath-house.demon.co.uk; Website: boath-house.demon.co.uk. 7 Rooms. Rates: £80-100 single; £55-88 per person double. All major credit cards accepted.*

As you enter the spectacular grounds of Boath House, your anticipation will mount with each curve of the driveway. As you round the last bend, your anticipation will be rewarded with your first view of the palatial Georgian mansion you will be staying at. Built in 1820, the Boath House of today must look very much like it did 180 years ago. Your hosts at Boath House are Don and Wendy Matheson, and you will be hard pressed to find a more pleasant and congenial couple in Scotland. Don is charming and an exceptional conversationalist; Wendy is an elegant and gracious hostess and you will enjoy her attention as well as her home.

Don and Wendy have worked very hard to restore this splendid mansion to its former elegant and royal condition. In doing so, they have been painstakingly faithful to many details, including selecting paint from the "Georgian paint palate" that would have been in use during its construction. While Boath House is non-smoking, the Mathesons have provided a lounge especially for their guests who do wish to smoke. Another lounge and library are available for guests to relax, read, chat, or just enjoy the warmth of the open fire. Both the lounges and the library have been furnished with exquisite furniture and impressive artwork. The dining room is another delightful public room. It overlooks the Matheson's own private lake and part of the 20-acre estate. The meals here are superb, and they have been recognized with two AA rosettes (see the *Where to Eat* section.)

As you move from the public areas of the restaurant to the bedrooms, you won't be disappointed, as the richness of your experience will be continued. First of all, you'll likely ascend to your room via a magnificent spiral staircase. When you reach the rooms, you'll find spacious, comfortable and eye-catching places. Each bedroom has been individually and expensively decorated. You'll find antique French beds, claw-foot porcelain bathtubs and scads of antiques everywhere. My favorite bedrooms were Rooms 3 and 4. Each is huge, and they overlook the sumptuous grounds. Room 3 has a huge bathroom with a large porcelain tub in the center of the room; three other rooms have similar bathtubs.

Boath House also offers its residents an on-site beauty and well-being salon, including aromatherapy, massages and reflexology. A small exercise room, sauna and Jacuzzi are available to help you relax and unwind. The estate deserves a word or two. Boath House nestles serenely amid 20 acres of stunning scenery. The grounds were planned and laid out in the early 1700s, prior to the home being built. Many of the trees on the estate are over 400 years old, and include a wide variety of flora, including trees and shrubs from many countries. All things considered, Boath House is one of the best places to stay in Scotland. I guarantee that if you do stay here, you will thoroughly enjoy the experience.

Selected as one of my Best Places to Stay – see Chapter 12.

NEWTON HOTEL, *Inverness Road, Nairn. Tel. 01667/453-114, Fax 01667/454-026, US toll-free reservations 800/223-6510; E-mail: info@morton-hotels.com. 57 Rooms. Rates: £72-90 single; £97-152 per room double; £165-200 suite. The rate for children is £1 per year of age up to age 16. Rates include breakfast. Amex, MasterCard and Visa accepted.*

The Newton Hotel is a stately Georgian mansion nestled amid a lovely 21-acre green oasis. Located at the edge of Nairn, it is just minutes from Inverness. The four-star hotel is part of the Morton Hotel group, and a fine and elegant representative it is. In recent years, the Morton Hotel group has been very aggressive in renovating and refurbishing their properties to the highest degree possible, and they have been successful at the Newton Hotel.

The public rooms here are all quite elegant – kind of a modern rustic motif. Lots of fine wood is evident, as well as soft colors and effective lighting. Throughout the property you'll find tall ceilings and designer wallpaper that enhances your experience. The bedrooms are all quite large and have extraordinary furnishings. The rooms at the front of the hotel look out on emerald green lawns and the Moray Firth, an estuary of the North Sea. The bathrooms have all been recently refurbished and are completely re-tiled. Each room has offers a TV, phone, trouser press, hairdryer and tea- and coffee-making facilities.

The Newton offers its guests two restaurants and a bar. The main restaurant is considered one of the best restaurants in this part of Scotland. It provides a wonderful elegant atmosphere in which to partake of an array of award-winning meals (see the *Where to Eat* section). A recent addition added a number of bedrooms and a conference center. These rooms are all nice, but I felt the rooms with the most character are in the old part of the mansion. Non-smoking rooms are available upon request.

GOLF VIEW HOTEL, *Seabank Road, Nairn. Tel. 01667/452-301, Fax 01667/455-267, US toll-free reservations 800/223-6510; E-mail: info@morton-hotels.com. 48 Rooms. Rates: £80-98 single; £98-155 per room double; £160-190 suite. The rate for children is £1 per year of age up to age 16. Rates include breakfast. Amex, MasterCard and Visa accepted.*

This is the sister hotel to the Newton, and lies about 400 yards from the Newton. Both hotels are within about 20 minutes of 20 golf courses. In fact, the Golf View overlooks the Nairn Championship Golf Course, on of the major venues for professional golf in Scotland.

All the bedrooms are large and well appointed, and about half of them look out to the North Sea and the splendid sandy beach below. Light-colored designer wallpaper is in all the rooms, and adds a subtle elegance to your stay. Each room offers satellite TV, trouser press, phone, hairdryer and tea- and coffee-making facilities. There are two restaurants at the Golf View Hotel. One is a casual brasserie-style restaurant, and the other is an award-winning restaurant that provides a more elegant dining experience (see the *Where to Eat* section). Either restaurant should meet your needs most admirably. Unlike her sister hotel, the Golf View offers a nicely equipped exercise room, a marvelous swimming pool, sauna and tennis courts.

ROYAL GOLF HOTEL, *The First Tee, Dornoch. Tel. 01862/810-283, Fax 01862/810-923, US toll-free reservations 800/437-2687; E-mail: info@morton-hotels.com. 24 Rooms. Rates: £52-77 single; £90-125 per room double; £140-176 suite. Rates include breakfast. All major credit cards accepted. Note: The hotel takes a break during January and February, but reopens March 1.*

The Royal Golf Hotel is another member of the Morton Hotel group. It is billed as a golf hotel, but I am here to tell you that you it's not necessary to be a golfer to enjoy this marvelous three-star hotel. The hotel literally overlooks the first tee of the Royal Dornoch Golf course.

The bedrooms in the hotel are all nice sized, and have been furnished with comfortable, quality furnishings. Light pastel colors complement the rooms and furnishings. The suites are of course the nicest rooms at the hotel, and in addition to fine furnishings and creature comforts, each features splendid views of the golf course. The public rooms in the hotel are warm and inviting. You'll find comfortable furniture to sink into, blazing fires and plenty to chat with others about, whether you've just come off the 18th tee or reliving your day's sightseeing. The restaurant at the Royal Golf Hotel provides a quiet elegance to go along with your award-winning meal. The restaurant and its meals have been recognized by *A Taste of Scotland*.

CLAYMORE HOUSE HOTEL, *Seabank Road, Nairn. Tel. 01667/453-731, Fax 01667/455-290; E-mail: claymore@computerpages.co.uk; Website: claymorehousehotel.com. 16 Rooms. Rates: £45 single; £75 per room double; £105 suite. Rates include breakfast. All major credit cards accepted.*

The Claymore House Hotel is a lovely old Victorian mansion that has been renovated into a wonderful hotel oozing with personality. This four-star quality hotel features tall ceilings and the original cornice work that adds so much character to these old homes. Claymore House is located in a quiet residential area close to two championship golf courses, and just up the street from a broad sandy beach. What more could you ask for?

There are 16 bedrooms at Claymore House, and each is spacious. The furnishings are good quality, and each has a TV, phone, radio, hairdryer and tea- and coffee-making facilities. There are four non-smoking rooms available for guests upon request. The bar at the Claymore House serves residents as well as locals. It has created quite a reputation for itself with a well-stocked bar, extensive wine list and personable atmosphere enhanced by an open fire. The restaurant serves fine meals, and you'll enjoy them while gazing out to the hotel's well-cared-for gardens. This is a nice hotel that will provide a pleasant stay for you.

INVERAN HOUSE B&B, *Seabank Road, Nairn. Tel. 01667/453-731, Fax 01667/455-290; E-mail: claymore@computerpages.co.uk; Website: claymorehousehotel.com. 3 Rooms. Rates: £50 single; £50 per room double. Rates include breakfast. All major credit cards accepted. Note: Inveran House is open from Easter through the end of the year.*

When you stay at Inveran B&B, you will be sharing an old Victorian mansion with a local family. Chock-full of antiques, Inveran House oozes age and personality. Each of the three available bedrooms is quite large and very simply decorated. The bathrooms are all newly upgraded and modernized. There is no smoking allowed in the bedrooms, but you can participate in that activity in any of the public rooms.

The public rooms are a delight, and they'll be rooms you really enjoy. The upstairs drawing room serves as the residents' lounge, and you'll find a decanter of complimentary sherry to help you relax after the rigors of your day of sightseeing. You'll take your breakfast in the downstairs dining room, and it will be served on bone china. Be sure and take a moment to notice the artwork on the walls throughout the house. Most of the watercolors you see are the work of the owner's mother – a talented lady indeed. Inveran House is owned by Rosemary and Andrew Machen-Young, who also own the Claymore. When you make your reservations, you'll actually be calling Claymore House, and when you check in, you will do so at Claymore House, about 100 yards up the road from Inveran House.

Southeast of Inverness

DUNALLAN HOUSE, *Woodside Avenue, Grantown-on-Spey. Tel. 01479/ 872-140, Fax 01479/872-140; E-mail: dunallan@cwcom.net; Website: www.dunallan.mcmail.com. 7 Rooms. Rates: £34 single including breakfast or £49 including dinner and breakfast; £24 per person double including breakfast, or £45 per person including breakfast and dinner; £45 per person Honeymoon Suite including breakfast and dinner; £29 per person double including breakfast. MasterCard and Visa accepted. Note: Dunallan House is closed in December.*

This beautiful Victorian home was built in 1900 and has been lovingly and superbly renovated. Christine Gray, the owner of Dunallan House, has worked very hard to make it a comfortable and delightful place to stay, and she has succeeded. Light colors, dark pine doors and trim throughout the house give Dunallan House a comfortable, homey feel.

There are seven bedrooms, and all are large, light and furnished in outstanding manner. Each is decorated in soft colors (pink, cream and green), and is light and bright. There are two theme rooms: the Victorian Room and the Honeymoon Suite. The Victorian Room is exquisitely decorated with (surprise!) Victorian furnishings and accents. It is an elegant and memorable room. The Honeymoon Suite is a suite of two rooms and is designed to help its guests have a pleasant and memorable stay. The other bedrooms are also large, nicely furnished and pleasantly appointed. The public rooms are as welcoming and comfortable as the bedrooms. The resident lounge is a large, tall-ceilinged room presided over by a marvelous Victorian fireplace, and features extremely comfortable leather chairs and couch. Christine asks that her guests not smoke in any of the bedrooms.

The dining room is a delightful room, featuring natural sunlight and views of the landscaped yard. As incredible as the house is, Christine avers that the food served in that wonderful dining room may be the main reason her guests return again and again. It is truly first class, and you'll find meals here that rival those you'd find in Scotland's finer restaurants.

I cannot say enough positive things about Dunallan House. I guarantee you will like it – the home, the town, the Highlands, and the hostess. But don't just take my word for it; here are a few excerpts from the Dunallan House guest book: "Superb food and lodgings; I would recommend to anyone;" "Excellent hospitality, superb in every way;" and "Five-star food, welcoming and all-around excellent."

WHERE TO EAT

Inverness

CULLODEN HOUSE RESTAURANT, *just off the Inverness-Aberdeen Road (A96), Inverness. Tel. 01463/790-461. £10-20 for lunch, £30-40 for dinner. Open daily from noon to 2:30pm and from 7:00pm to 9:30pm. Amex, MasterCard and Visa accepted.*

The Culloden House Restaurant represents some of the finest of fine dining you'll find in Scotland. Housed in a gorgeous Georgian mansion that once served as Bonnie Prince Charlie's headquarters before his fateful engagement on Culloden Battlefield, the restaurant truly is something you might expect a bonnie prince to dine at.

Crystal and china, shiny silver and glistening chandeliers await you at Culloden House Restaurant. But that's not all – you'll find wonderful traditional Scottish cuisine served here, with just a touch of a Continental influence. Try the terrine of game made with pigeon, venison, rabbit, pheasant and mushrooms, served in a port wine sauce, or try the medallions of monkfish and lobster with asparagus and mushrooms in a splendid lobster sauce. Culloden House Restaurant has used these kinds of offerings to win a number of culinary awards, including two AA rosettes and recognition by *A Taste of Scotland*. Dress is suit and tie, and reservations are a must. No smoking is allowed in the dining room.

INGLIS RESTAURANT, *Culcabock Road, Inverness. Tel. 01463/237-166. £24-35. Open daily from noon to 2:00pm and from 7:00pm to 9:30pm. Amex, MasterCard and Visa accepted.*

The Inglis Restaurant is the formal restaurant for the Kings Mill Hotel, and it carries through the wonderful ambience the hotel creates. You'll find elegant dining in pleasant surroundings. The menu is pretty complete and changes monthly. You'll be able to select from a wide variety of fish, beef, lamb and wild game dishes. If you're a vegetarian, your needs will be met here, too. The restaurant serves an upscale pub grub in the beautiful conservatory. Enjoy a sandwich, salad or soup (or all three) while looking out to their lovely landscaped gardens and grounds. Nice casual is the dress.

CAFÉ 1, *75 Castle Street, Inverness. Tel. 01463/226-200. £15-30. Open daily from noon to 2:30pm and from 7:00pm to 9:30pm. Amex, MasterCard and Visa accepted.*

This is an intriguing, modern café located in the heart of Inverness. You'll find a nice, cheery dining atmosphere here, with lots of locals as well as tourists vying for the fine fare served here. The menu features a good variety of Scottish dishes prepared with a definite Continental flair and influence. If you prefer vegetarian dishes, you'll also find something here to please you. Café 1 has garnered numerous awards, including recognition by *A Taste of Scotland*. Menus change throughout the year, but you're guaranteed the freshest Scottish produce combined with some of the best that the waters off Scotland can provide. You might find such offerings as tender Dornoch lamb or Isle of Skye monkfish. Dessert is also a treat, including such delicious items as a caramelized apple tart. Dress is nice casual.

HEATHMOUNT PUB, *Kings Mill Road, Inverness. Tel. 01463/235-877, Fax 01463/715-749. £10-13. Open daily from 12:15pm to 2:15pm, and from 5:30pm to 9:30pm. Amex, MasterCard and Visa accepted.*

This pub for the Heathmount Hotel comes highly recommended by several locals I spoke with. It has made a name for itself serving a good selection of wholesome and tasty pub grub in a very Scottish-pub sort of atmosphere. The dining room is pretty simple and there is nothing special to recommend about it except the food that is served there. You'll find soups, salads, sandwiches and some standard offerings of beef, lamb and fish. Lunch will run you about £3 to £5 and a three-course dinner will run you about £10 to £13. Dress is casual.

THE MORAY, *Inglis Street, Inverness. Tel. 01463/701-131. £10-12. Open daily from 10:00am to 10:00pm. MasterCard and Visa accepted.*

You'll find the Moray Pub about a block from the train station in Inverness. They offer a quick bite to eat – nothing special, just some good pub grub: soup, salad and a sandwich. But the food is good, and tartan-clad booths will erase all question in your mind as to which country you are in. Dress is casual.

North of Inverness

FOWLER'S RESTAURANT, *Scotsburn Road, Tain. Tel. 01862/892-052, Fax 01862/892-260. £20-30. Open daily from noon to 2:00pm and from 7:00pm to 9:00pm. Amex, MasterCard and Visa accepted.*

Chef David Lauritsen is the proud owner of 2 AA rosettes, and in my opinion, a third cannot be far behind. Not only is the food marvelous, but David has mastered the *art* of presentation – the meals are almost too pretty to eat (almost). At my last visit here, the meal started with seared west coast scallops, with a tempura of squid with tomato and lemon dressing. That was polished off quickly to make room for the filet of Highland beef topped with langostine and coriander bake, served with a sloe gin glaze. Dessert was a mille feuille of meringue and fresh local berries, latticed with two chocolate sauces. It was delicious, and so pretty. If those dishes don't start your mouth watering, how about the breast of duck nestled in a bed of apricots and served with a cointreau sauce, topped with crispy leeks, or the wild Scottish salmon filled with hot smoked trout mousseline and a shellfish and lemongrass bouillabaise?

As good as your meal will be, the dining room adds a nice touch to the meal. It is a wonderful long room, with the original plasterwork around the ceiling. Large windows look out onto the sculpted lawns, and provide a wonderful setting in which to enjoy your meal. Dress is suit and tie, and reservations are a must on weekends and nightly during the tourist season.

Selected as one of my picks for Scotland's Best Restaurants – see Chapter 11.

TULLOCH CASTLE RESTAURANT, *Tulloch Castle Drive, Dingwall. Tel. 01349/861-325, Fax 01349/863-993. £15-20. Open Monday through Friday from 7:00pm to 9:30pm. MasterCard and Visa accepted.*

This is the restaurant for Tulloch Castle Hotel. It is smallish – it seats only about 35 or so. You'll experience a quiet, pleasant dining experience here, accented by candlelight, silver and crystal. The menu changes frequently, but you can expect to find a fine selection of fish, beef, venison and vegetarian dishes. The restaurant has been recognized but *A Taste of Scotland*, a sure sign of the quality and freshness of their meals. Dress is nice casual.

Northeast of Inverness

GOLF VIEW HOTEL RESTAURANT, *Seabank Road, Nairn. Tel. 01667/452-301. £25-30. Open daily 7:30am to 10:00am, and from 7:00pm to 9:00pm. All major credit cards accepted.*

This is the fine-dining restaurant for the Golf View Hotel, and you'll find quiet candlelit dining here. Crystal and china greet you, along with fine service and superb food. Like its sister restaurant at the hotel (The Conservatory), the Golf View Hotel is the proud owner of a AA rosette, as well as recognition from *A Taste of Scotland*. You'll find a small but well-represented menu with such items as char-grilled Dornoch lamb with a saffron ratataille and a basil pesto dressing. The dessert menu is also a winner, offering such delicacies as warm dark chocolate and malt whisky tart with a vanilla sauce.

The menu changes daily, so you could eat here each night and find new taste adventures to tempt your palate. If you are partial to vegetarian dishes, a fair selection is included each day. Dress is smart casual to suit and tie, and reservations are strongly recommended during the tourist season.

BOATH HOUSE RESTAURANT, *Aberdeen Road, Auldearn, Nairn. Tel. 01667/454-896, 01667/455-469. £21-32. Open Thursday through Sunday from 12:30pm to 2:00pm, and Wednesday through Sunday from 7:00pm to 9:00pm. All major credit cards accepted.*

The Boath House Restaurant is one of the finest restaurants in northern Scotland. Within their first 18 months of business they had garnered two AA rosettes, and during my last visit they had just been tested for a third rosette. Need I say more?

Charles Lochley is the gifted chef who has put Boath House Restaurant on the culinary map. The artful interpretation he brings to the traditional Scottish fare he prepares results in extraordinary meals. The menu changes frequently, but you might expect something along the lines of roast breast of pheasant with a confit of leg, celariac and Savoy cabbage topped with sautéed foie gras and Bayonne ham in a port wine and rosemary essence. As you'd imagine, the dessert offerings are also scrumptious, and you might find something like a banana toffee crumble or a nougat glace served with a dark chocolate sorbet and mascerated berries. Dress is definitely suit and tie, and reservations are required.

Selected as one of my picks for Scotland's Best Restaurants – see Chapter 11.

NEWTON HOTEL RESTAURANT, *Inverness Road, Nairn. Tel. 01667/ 453-114. £20-25. Open daily from 7:30am to 10:00am and from 7:15pm to 9:15pm. All major credit cards accepted.*

The restaurant at the Newton Hotel offers a marvelous setting: you'll enjoy the crystal and china, linen and silver. And you'll also be mightily impressed with what the chefs do with the menu selections. Apparently the AA judges were also, as they awarded the Newton Restaurant one AA rosette. There are a variety of menu items to choose from, and all sound delicious. Try the pan-seared breast of chicken, seasoned with star anise, carved over flash-fried vegetables with a roast plum sauce. Or perhaps you'd prefer the baked goats' cheese, sun-dried tomato and char-grilled pepper strudel, presented over a tossed seasonal salad with a sweet basil and garlic dressing. The wine list is exceptional also, with over six dozen selections. Dress is nice casual. Reservations are recommended on weekends and during the tourist season.

THE CONSERVATORY, *Seabank Road, Nairn. Tel. 01667/452-301. £20-25. Open daily from noon to 9:00pm. All major credit cards accepted.*

This is the brasserie-style restaurant that serves the Golf View Hotel, its guests and the public. The Conservatory is at the end of the hotel and has large floor-to-ceiling windows that provide brilliant views of the North Sea and the soft sandy beaches of Nairn. The dining room is very light and bright, with wicker chairs and glass-covered wicker tables. Large fans turn above, giving the restaurant a nice informal feel. Not only is it a perfect setting, but the restaurant has won many awards, including recognition by *A Taste of Scotland* and one AA rosette. You'll find such excellent fare as fettuccini with lobster, prawns and chorizo sausage in a roast tomato cream sauce and seared Isle of Skye monkfish and scallops with serrano ham and stir-fried vegetables and noodles. This is a pleasant place to take your meals, and the dress is casual.

SEEING THE SIGHTS

Inverness has been the sight of so many clan feuds, wars and skirmishes through the centuries, that little remains of the ancient fortifications that once graced the city. Looming on a knoll above town is **Inverness Castle**, *Castle Wynd; open mid-May through the end of September Monday through Saturday from 9:00am to 5:00pm*. This picturesque red sandstone castle was built in 1830 on the site where numerous predecessors had stood; each had been destroyed for one reason or another. Today, the castle serves as a city municipal building, namely the Sheriff's Court. During the summer months, the castle esplanade features a solitary kilted bagpiper playing melancholy and military tunes at 7:30pm each evening. You'll also find the bronze-and pigeon-splattered statue of one of Scotland's most famous women: Flora MacDonald.

When Bonnie Prince Charlie's bid for the crown received a crushing blow at Culloden, Flora housed and protected the would-be king and assisted in his escape. Her daring and compassion earned her status similar to that which is enjoyed by Betsy Ross, Florence Nightingale and Molly Brown in America. Flora stands facing south, arm uplifted to shade her eyes as she looks off into the distance, ever watchful for the return of her Bonnie Prince Charlie!

During the summer months, you'll be able to witness and/or participate in the **Castle Garrison Encounter**, *Castle Esplanade; £2.50 for adults, £1.90 for seniors, and £1 for children*, where you'll be able to dress up as a soldier from the mid-18th century. Even though no ancient edifice remains, plenty of intrigue and plotting was carried out below the ramparts of this hill. For example, Mary Queen of Scots ordered the hanging of the governor of the castle when he refused her entrance in 1562. Robert the Bruce razed one of the previous fortifications while besieging the occupying English army during Scotland's war for independence, and the Jacobites made a mess of things by destroying the fortifications found here in 1715 and then again in 1745.

Below the castle, you'll find the **Inverness Museum and Art Gallery**, *Castle Wynd; Tel. 01463/237-114; open Monday through Saturday from 9:00am to 5:00pm; admission is free*. You'll find a nice assortment of artifacts depicting the history of Inverness and the Highlands, and information covering the archeological, geographical and geological aspects of the Highlands. Upstairs is an eclectic collection of tartan, weaponry, bagpipes and fiddles, taxidermy and some silverwork. There is a reproduction of a silversmith's shop. I was particularly intrigued by Bonnie Prince Charlie's death mask (perhaps you will be too!). A small art gallery featuring the works of Scottish artists is also on site, as are a souvenir and coffee shop.

Near the corner of Bridge Street and Castle Wynd look for **Clach na Cuddain**, a stone on which wash women rested their wash tubs as they returned from the "laundromat" (the River Ness) in days gone by. It sits out front of the **Town House** *(High Street)*, whose claim to fame is that a meeting of the English cabinet took place here in 1921, the first ever held outside of London.

If you'll walk down Church Street a couple of blocks, you'll come to the **Old High Church**, *corner of Church Street and Friars Lane; open Friday from noon to 2:00pm, and during Sunday services*. This old church stands on the spot where St. Columba founded a church nearly 1,000 years ago. This structure, however, dates from the mid-16th century. While generations of Scots have worshiped here, this grand old church has seen its sad times too: captured Jacobite soldiers who survived the slaughter of Culloden were imprisoned in the church for a short time before being executed in the adjacent cemetery. If you take the tour Friday afternoon at 12:30pm, you'll be shown gravestones that still bear marks from the errant bullets of the firing squads. Near this end of Church Street you'll also find another of my favorite "attractions": **Leakey's Second-Hand Bookshop**, *Church Street, Tel. 01463/239-947; open Monday through Saturday from 10:00am to 5:30pm; MasterCard and Visa accepted*. If you're into used books, this is a great place to venture. You'll find many leather-bound tomes from days gone by. They boast over 100,000 books housed in a former church. So if you're into books, stop by for a treat.

Follow Friar's Lane toward the River Ness, and take the ornate footbridge that spans the river. Once across, walk along the river until you come to **St. Andrews Cathedral**, *15 Ardross Street, Tel. 01463/233-535; open daily from 9:00am to 6:00pm*. St. Andrews was built in the late 19th century, and if it looks a little unfinished, it is because the Episcopalian Church ran out of money before the great twin spires could be completed. Inside, the church isn't particularly memorable, although there is a set of gold icons given to Bishop Eden of St. Andrews by the Tsar of Russia that you should check out.

If you're still up for a stroll, continue along the peaceful banks of the River Ness for about 15 minutes, and you'll come to **Ness Islands**. This series of small islands has been connected to one another and to both banks of the River Ness via footbridges, and provide a serene public park for you to stroll through.

About five miles southeast of Inverness you'll find **Culloden Battlefield**, *Culloden Moor.* Culloden represents one of the most poignant chapters in Scottish history. Jacobites were those men and women who supported the return of a Stewart king to the throne. The ill-fated Jacobite Rebellion was a series of skirmishes between supporters of Bonnie Prince Charlie and the English army. On a cold day on April 16, 1746, the opposing armies met on Culloden Battlefield to do battle.

Unfortunately, the government troops held too many advantages: they were better equipped, better fed, and better generaled. Five thousand Jacobites marched through the cold rain and sleet to meet 9,000 English troops. When the battle concluded less than an hour later, one fourth of the Jacobites had been slain, compared to far fewer casualties among the government troops (estimates range from 50 to 300 casualties for the government). After the battle, eyewitnesses reported that government troops rushed forward bayoneting wounded Jacobite troops. Some have claimed the atrocities were at the command of the Duke of Cumberland; others claim it was merely over-zealous troops seeking revenge for slain companions. Whichever is the truth, the fact the many wounded Jacobites were dispatched cannot be denied.

The battlefield features markers indicating which clans fought in which part of the battle, as well as lonely headstones indicating the mass graves of clan members. A single stone marks the grave where the English were buried. Located on the battlefield is the small but effective **Culloden Battlefield Visitor Centre**, *Culloden Battlefield, Tel. 01463/790-607; open February, March and November and December daily from 9:00am to 4:00pm, and daily from April to October from 9:00am to 6:00pm; the visitor centre is closed in January, although the battlefield is open; admission is £2 for adults and £1 for seniors and children.*

About eight miles further east of Culloden Battlefield, you'll come upon **Cawdor Castle**, *Cawdor, Tel. 01667/404-615; open May to early October daily from 10:00am to 5:30pm; admission is £4.50 for adults, £3.50 for seniors and £2.50 for children.* When you see Cawdor Castle, you'll think you are seeing a fairy-tale castle. Turrets and battlements are at each end of the tower, and you'll expect a knight in shining armor to come out of the castle on a prancing steed. You may also think of the play Macbeth, for William Shakespeare presented the good king to us as the **Thane of Cawdor**, and the dastardly murder of Duncan took place in this very castle (in the play, at least). This was indeed the castle to which Shakespeare referred, but the real Macbeth ruled almost exactly 400 years before Cawdor Castle was built.

The castle is still the home of the Cawdor family, and they graciously open it for the public to peek inside. You'll be amazed at the luxury and medieval items you find here among the tapestries, ancient paintings, and furnishings. I particularly enjoyed the **Thorn Tree Room**. Deep inside the castle, you'll find the enigmatic remains of an ancient hawthorn tree. The story goes that 500 years ago the Thane of Cawdor had a dream in which he was instructed to build a castle on the very spot where his donkey laid down after its day's labors. The donkey laid next to a hawthorn tree – the very one now memorialized in the Thorn Tree Room. The ancient Thane began building immediately – right around the tree. It occurs to me that one of the most recent Thanes of Cawdor shared the twinkle in his ancient ancestor's eye. As you visit the castle, many of the items you see have placards explaining them. You'll note that several of them, written by the most recent Thane prior to his death, are written in a bit of a of tongue-in-cheek style.

The castle purports to have its own resident ghost. In a sad tale of teenage love gone wrong, the daughter of one of the lairds fell madly in love with the son of a rival landowner. The laird of Cawdor became so incensed with his daughter that he cut her hands off. She is said to have fallen to her death from the tower, and now she wanders the castle, a handless apparition. In addition to a wonderful visit in the castle, take a few minutes and walk around their beautiful walled garden or along the nature trails that have been laid out.

Once you've visited Cawdor Castle, why not head to nearby **Fort George**, *Ardesier, Tel. 01667/462-777; open April to September daily from 9:30am to 6:30pm, October through March Monday through Saturday from 9:30am to 4:30pm and Sunday from 2:00pm to 4:30pm; the last ticket is sold 45 minutes prior to closing; admission is £3.00 for adults, £2.30 for seniors and £1 for children.* Following the Jacobite Rebellion of 1745, the Hanoverian King George decided to flex his military muscle by building a massive fortification near Inverness. On a peninsula jutting into the Moray Firth, Fort George came to life. However, by the time it was completed in 1760, the Jacobite Rebellion was no more, and the fort never saw any action. Today it is still used as an army barracks. There are many parts of the fort open, and exhibits along the way give you a bit of a feel for military life in days gone by. Mannequins dressed in period English uniforms go about their daily tasks in barracks and offices. There is also an impressive display of military arms and equipment, from pikes and swords to muskets and cannon.

The Queen's Own Highlander's Regimental Museum is included in Fort George, and is a well-done museum that has exhibits on over 200 years of military units in the Highlands. The most fascinating things (for me anyway) were reading about the heroism of soldiers who won the

Victoria Cross. Walks along the ramparts impart spectacular views of the Moray Firth and provide an excellent viewing point to watch for dolphins.

EXCURSIONS & DAY TRIPS

When you come to Inverness, there are probably two things that are really on your mind: Loch Ness and The Highlands. I'll share a few tips on seeing both. The destinations in the remainder of this chapter can for the most part be done either as day trips from Inverness or as longer trips with overnights. You choose depending on your schedule.

First, we'll head north for a tour of some of my favorite Highland scenery. Then we'll head south to that great loch and see if we can't give you the opportunity to make headlines by being the first person in history to take a picture of Nessie that isn't out of focus and grainy. After that, we'll venture further south to some of the other places I'll recommend for your tour of the Highlands.

Beginning with a tour of the northern Highlands, I'd like to suggest a drive that will show you a wide variety of Highland scenery: barren hillsides, stunning seascapes, mysterious lochs, fabulous gorges and monumental mountains. The drive will take you from Inverness to Tongue, then southwest along the seashore to Ullapool and then back to Inverness. The drive will take the better part of one day, especially if you stop to see any of the scenery or explore some of the lovely sandy beaches you encounter. I think it is best to do this trip in a counter-clockwise fashion – the scenery and sights go from desolate to stunning, and they work toward a crescendo, slowly at first then ever-increasing as you reach Ullapool.

Within about an hour after you leave Inverness, you'll "enjoy" a new driving sensation: **single-track roads**. Single-track roads are narrow, single-lane, dual-direction roads. Every so often there is a pull-off – sort of a wide spot in the road, for you to pull into and allow on-coming traffic to pass by. This single-track road meanders through a desolate and undulating area of the Highlands. This single-track road is another reason I suggest making this drive in a counter-clockwise fashion, since you will be rather fresh and alert when you first encounter it.

To begin this trip, take the A9 north out of Inverness. Watch for the signposts directing you to the A836 just northwest of Tain, and take that road. Just outside Lairg you'll encounter your first single-track road. It will rise and fall through a barren and desolate part of the Highlands. Windswept hills and vast expanses will greet you, broken occasionally by long, slender lochs. These lochs have different moods, and depending on their mood, they'll be bright blue spots, mirroring the skies above them; other times they'll be gray and menacing.

PRACTICAL INFORMATION FOR INVERNESS

Laundry & Dry Cleaning Service

As you might suspect in a city the size of Inverness, there are a number of laundromats and dry cleaners around the city. Here are a few:
- **Alba Laundry Services**, *14 Grant Street, Inverness. Tel. 01463/239-205*
- **Dry Cleaning Factory**, *42B Thornbush Road, Inverness. Tel. 01463/853-368*
- **Johnson Cleaners**, *61 High Street, Inverness. Tel. 01463/862-102*
- **Munro Cleaners**, *34 Baron Taylors Street, Inverness. Tel. 01463/232-165*

Lost Credit Cards
- **American Express Card**, *Tel. 01273/696-933*
- **Diners Club**, *Tel. 01252/513-500, 0800/460-800*
- **MasterCard**, *Tel. 0800/964-767*
- **Visa**, *Tel. 0800/895-082*

Post Offices
- **Main Post Office**, *Queensgate, Inverness. Tel. 01463/234-111.*

Tourist Information
- **Inverness Tourist Information Centre**, *Castle Wynd, Inverness. Tel. 01463/234-353, Fax 01463/710-609*
- **Daviot Wood Tourist Information Centre**, *Picnic Area (A9), Daviot Wood. Tel. 01463/772-203, Fax 01463/772-022*

TONGUE

One hundred miles and several hours north of Inverness you'll find the small village of **Tongue**. Tongue is base to a number of natural phenomena, including the soaring **Ben Loyal**, which seems to leap from the barren landscape. At just over 2,500 feet, it is not as tall as nearby **Ben Hope**, which stands tall at 3,040 feet, but it is considered the more impressive of the two bens, and has earned the name *Queen of the Scottish Mountains*. Near Tongue, you'll also find such intriguing natural wonders as **Eas-Coul-Aulin**, the highest waterfall in the United Kingdom, and the **Falls of Shin**, famous for her leaping salmon.

As you approach Tongue from Inverness, you'll see a lonely ruin standing stoically on a rocky outcropping. **Varick Castle** has been standing as a silent sentinel over Tongue since the mid-1300s and is the ancestral home of the Mackay clan. Below you will see the **Kyle of Tongue**, a wide, flat estuary. It is hard to imagine that this lovely setting was the scene of a pitched naval battle during the Jacobite Rebellion. In 1746 the

Jacobite vessel *Hazard* traded fire with a much larger and better-equipped English ship, the *Sheerness*. Once the *Hazard* ran aground it was a veritable sitting duck as cannon from the English ship pounded it into submission. Its crew fled, carrying gold coins that had been sent from the king of France to finance the rebellion. They were later captured and the gold forfeited, thanks in part to members of the Mackay clan, who were not anxious to see Bonnie Prince Charlie ascend to the throne.

ARRIVALS & DEPARTURES

Take the A9 north out of Inverness. Watch for the signposts directing you to the A836 just northwest of Tain, and take that road.

WHERE TO STAY

TONGUE HOTEL, *Tongue. Tel. 01847/611-206, Fax 01847/611-345. 18 Rooms. Rates: £50-75 single; £50-70 per room standard double; £60-80 per room superior double. Rates include breakfast. MasterCard and Visa accepted.*

If you just made the three hour drive from Inverness to Tongue and want to relax a bit (or if you want to start fresh to tackle that looming 40 miles of single-track road), the Tongue Hotel is a good place to stop. The Tongue Hotel boasts a four-star rating from the Scottish Tourist Board, and sits high on the hill with commanding views of the Kyle of Tongue down below. It was formerly a hunting lodge for the Duke of Sutherland and was built in 1889.

The rooms are large and pleasantly decorated and the tall ceilings add to the feeling of spaciousness. Each room features nice, quality and relatively new furnishings. The best rooms are at the back of the hotel, as they have splendid views of the Kyle of Tongue. Each room offers a phone, TV, complimentary sherry and mineral water. The Tongue Hotel is very nice in a rustic sort of way, nicer than you might expect in this distant outpost of Scotland. The four-star rating seems a little generous when compared to many of the three-star and four-star properties elsewhere, but it is definitely worth three stars.

BEN LOYAL HOTEL, *Main Street, Tongue. Tel. 01847/611-216, Fax 01847/611-2112. 18 Rooms. £50-60 single; £50-65 per person double. Rates include breakfast. MasterCard and Visa accepted. Note: The Ben Loyal Hotel is only open from March 1 through October 31.*

The Ben Loyal Hotel is a pleasant place to stay if you decide to spend the night in Tongue. Eighteen rooms, including six in a detached building, are all decorated with rather plain but functional and comfortable furnishings. Several of the rooms have wonderful views of the Kyle of Tongue and others have the honor of looking out on Ben Loyal and Ben Hope. Half of the rooms offer ensuite facilities, and half merely have wash basins in them. The hotel restaurant has gained quite a reputation in this part of Scotland as a great place to eat. Apparently the judges from *A Taste of Scotland* agree, and the restaurant has earned one AA rosette for its fare (see the *Where to Eat* section).

TONGUE SCOTTISH YOUTH HOSTEL, *Tongue. Tel. 01847/611-301, centralized reservations: 0541/553-255. 5 Rooms. Rates: £7-9 juniors (under age 18); £8-10 seniors (over age 18). MasterCard and Visa accepted.*

After passing through Tongue en route to Durness (or just prior to arriving in Tongue when coming from Durness), is the Tongue Scottish Youth Hostel. Spartan and clean, it will provide you a safe and clean place to stay. A small guest lounge is available, as well as a self-catering kitchen. There are five rooms with four bunk beds in each room. Each bed comes with its own linens and blankets. There's not much more here, but it will provide a restful place to spend the night. Perhaps the most impressive thing about the Tongue Scottish Youth Hostel is its location. You'll be right next to the Kyle of Tongue, and it will provide a serene place to walk or just sit and meditate.

WHERE TO EAT

BEN LOYAL HOTEL RESTAURANT, *Main Street, Tongue. Tel. 01847/611-216, Fax 01847/611-2112. £10-20. Open daily from 7:00pm to 9:30pm. (Lunch is available if you are a guest and have made prior arrangements.) MasterCard and Visa accepted.*

It is hard to determine which is the best aspect of the Ben Loyal Hotel Restaurant: the food or the marvelous views. You may have to flip a coin to decide which is best, but either way you are a winner. The restaurant is proud of their menu offerings, and local produce, fish and beef are featured. Many of the vegetables come from the hotel's organic garden, and you are assured of a meal that combines the freshest ingredients. Seafood is a specialty, so you might try the smoked salmon and artichoke ravioli with a light balsamic cream.

DURNESS

Durness has been here for many years: it was originally settled by the Picts nearly 2400 years ago. This is a wonderful place to get away from it all. It is relatively quiet, and offers an abundance of natural sights to see. Soft sandy beaches and windswept grassy hillocks offer an attraction to walkers and thinkers. Nearby **Smoo Cave** (see below) is an impressive show. Today, Durness is mostly a fishing and *crofting* (farming) village, and those not associated with those industries in the traditional manner fish for tourists and harvest their holiday pounds.

The local **Tourist Information Centre**, *Durine, Durness, Tel. 01971/ 511-259, Fax 01971/511-368,* is renowned for its enthusiastic support for visitors.

ARRIVALS & DEPARTURES

From Tongue, you can either cross the Kyle of Tongue on the relatively new causeway bridge, or you can skirt the Kyle on a narrow road that meanders along the coastline around the Kyle. Either way, you will pick up the A838 into Durness.

WHERE TO STAY

SMOO FALLS B&B, *Durness. Tel. 01971/511-228. 4 rooms. Rates: £16-18 per person single; £16-18 per person double; £14 for the non-ensuite room. Rates include breakfast. No credit cards accepted.*

Mrs. Joy Conlon is your hostess at Smoo Falls B&B in the small hamlet of Durness. This delightful B&B sits right on the road, so it's easy to locate. A small resident's lounge provides comfortable overstuffed furniture to sink into for a few minutes of relaxation or for enjoying the fireplace on a chilly day. The bedrooms are all fair-sized – not huge, but certainly ample for your needs. Each is very clean and comfortably furnished. It definitely has the feel of staying in someone's home, and in fact, several of Mrs. Conlon's guests mentioned that point in their comments for her guest book. Each room has a TV and tea- and coffee-making facilities. The bathrooms are smallish and only offer showers, not tubs. Room 4 has the best views; as it is at the upstairs front of the house, you'll have nice views of the sea.

Mrs. Conlon is an outstanding cook, and delights her guests with her fine breakfasts, and with previous arrangement, the dinners she provides for £10 per person. For breakfast, you'll have a choice of a light continental meal or a full Scottish breakfast. On chilly days, this is a good place to try a bowl of piping-hot porridge. Mrs. Conlon is also adept at preparing delicious vegetarian meals if that is desired. Mrs. Conlon is rightfully proud of her guest book, which has signatures and comments of guests from all over the world. Here are a few examples of what previous guests have said about Smoo Falls B&B: "Warm, friendly hosts!" "Great breakfasts – I'll be back!" "Cozy, just like home." Smoo Falls B&B is a non-smoking facility, although the Conlons thoughtfully include a small smoker's lounge for their guests who need that.

Smoo Falls B&B is a short walk from Smoo Cave, a fascinating place to visit as you venture around this corner of Scotland. In addition, a short walk takes you to a lovely sandy beach and pleasant strolls along that seashore.

DURNESS SCOTTISH YOUTH HOSTEL, *Durness. Tel. 01971/511-244, centralized reservations: 0541/553-255. 4 Rooms. Rates: £7-9 juniors (under age 18); £8-10 seniors (over age 18). MasterCard and Visa accepted. Note: open from mid-March through the first weekend in October – usually!*

At the outskirts of Durness (on the road to Tongue), you'll find two low brown buildings that serve as the Durness Scottish Youth Hostel. As with the hostel in Tongue, this one is pretty Spartan, but it is clean and dry and will provide a place for you to stay and get out of the weather. Facilities here are limited, but right next door is a small café that serves full meals for a reasonable price (£2 to £5). This hostel can get busy during the summer months because of the number of hikers and backpackers that frequent this part of Scotland. Golden beaches and beautiful seascapes in this part of the country are a big draw, so be sure and call ahead for reservations.

WHERE TO EAT

WHITE HEATHER CAFÉ, *Durness. Tel. 01971/511-251. £4-13. Open Monday through Saturday from 10:00am to 7:00pm. MasterCard and Visa accepted.*

If you'd like a cup of coffee or a nice sandwich while you are out and about in Durness, this is a good place to stop. The Heather Café is located right on the main road next to the Durness Youth Hostel, Nothing particularly special here except good, filling food.

SEEING THE SIGHTS

There are several sights worth taking the time to see in and around Durness. The most popular offering near Durness is **Smoo Cave,** *open all day; admission is free, although the boat ride costs £2.50 for adults, £2 for children and seniors.* This massive limestone cavern was hollowed out by years of relentless pounding by the sea. A signpost at the edge of Durness directs you to the footpath that takes you to the cave. Smoo Cave is really three caves in one. The first is a large amphitheater that measures 200 feet long and is 120 feet wide. Ferns and lichen highlight the floodlit limestone walls and create quite a visual image. You'll take a footbridge from the main cavern into a second cave that features the tumbling waters of the Alt Smoo River as it cascades 75 feet into the cave from above, filling the cave with a fine mist. A third cave can only be reached by boat. The boat operates from April through October from 11:00am until 5:00pm. If you're wondering where the name Smoo originated, it comes from the Viking word *Smuga,* which means *cleft.*

Just west of Durness you'll find the lovely **Balnakiel Bay**, a wonderful area of grass and pristine white beaches. The views across the bay out to the North Sea are nothing short of magnificent. Nearby are the ruins of a 17th-century church which holds the remains of the infamous highwayman Donald McMurchow, a local boy gone bad. He was reportedly responsible for the deaths of 18 unfortunate individuals, many of whom were cast to their deaths in Smoo Cave. As you enter the ruins, look to your left and you'll find the skull and crossbones that mark his grave. Note: there was once quite a controversy as to whether Donald would be buried here due to his notorious nature. A healthy financial contribution to the local clergy assured Donald a resting place within the walls of the church.

You'll also find here the **Balnakiel Craft Village**, *Balnakiel; open daily from 10:00am to 6:00pm; admission free.* The village is a consortium of local crafters and artisans who have descended on a former Ministry of Defense early-warning station and developed a bit of a booming industry for themselves. You'll be able to see a number of workshops featuring potters, candle makers, wood carvers, knitters and others. Sort of a well-organized garage sale, many folks like it, although some aren't so sure. Personally, I enjoyed it.

If you have a few extra minutes to burn, it would be well worth your while to venture out to **Cape Wrath**. Cape Wrath is the site of a lonely lighthouse on this northwestern point of the Scottish mainland. To get here, you'll park your car in tiny **Keoldale** and take the **passenger ferry**, *Tel. 01971/511-376; May through September hourly from 9:30am to 4:30pm; fare is £3.50 for adults, £2 for children and seniors,* across the Kyle of Durness. It runs hourly from May through August from 9:30am to 4:00pm. It links up on the other side with a **mini-bus**, *Tel. 01971/511-287; fare is £6.50 for adults, £3.75 for children and seniors,* that will take you the 11 miles out to the lighthouse, which, by the way, was built by Robert Louis Stevenson's grandfather in 1828. The lighthouse is perched above **Clo Mor Cliffs**, the highest cliffs in Britain. As you can imagine, the views from this vantage point are nothing short of sensational. You'll have the opportunity to gaze seaward and you'll be able to see both Orkney and the Outer Hebrides. The trip out to Cape Wrath will take roughly two hours, depending on how long you linger at the lighthouse or along any of the walking paths that lead out from there.

After your visit to Cape Wrath, jump back on the A838 and head south toward Ullapool. This is a wonderful drive, and the scenery gets more impressive the further south you drive. This 100-mile trip will take you about two and a half hours, but the scenery makes it worth it. You'll pass no fewer than a dozen major bens (mountains) that leap heavenward from the marshy turf and rocky flats. These mountains vary anywhere from 519 meters (1,702 feet) to the tallest along this stretch of road at 908 meters (2,978 feet) (most along this stretch are between 2,500 and 2,700 feet). Take it from a Colorado boy – these may not be the Rocky Mountains, but they are impressive indeed. Generally speaking, the Rockies sort of "warm-up" to their height through a series of ever-increasing foothills and smaller pinnacles, and then finally give way to their lofty peaks. The thing that impresses me about these Highland bens is their abruptness. There are no foothills to speak of, just a sudden burst of rock and heather (not to mention a generous fringe of clouds that is seen frequently).

This is also a good time to follow your instincts – if something looks intriguing off on a side road, take the road and see what new kinds of scenery you can see. This is particularly true with the little roads that run off to the west. Many will meander through the countryside to small villages along the coast, and fabulous views await you. As you continue southward, keep following the signposts toward Scourie and Ullapool. At Laxford Bridge, take the right fork and the road is now the A894. About seven miles south of Ullapool you'll find yourself driving along the banks of Loch Assynt. Keep an eye out for **Ardvreck Castle**, sitting on a small island in the lake. Formerly a MacLeod stronghold, today it's lonely and forlorn, and obviously a shadow of its former self.

Continue south (the road has now merged with the A837) toward Ullapool. At Ledmore, again follow the right fork and now the road is the A835.

ULLAPOOL

Once upon a time, **Loch Broom** teemed with massive schools of herring. In the late 1700s, the British Fisheries Society decided this would be a great place for a fishing village, so they carefully planned a new community along the shores of the long and deep loch. Sort of an 18th-century *Field of Dreams* ("Build it and they will come"), **Ullapool** leaped into existence almost as abruptly as the Highland bens that are such an obvious feature of this part of the Highlands. Alas, the herring didn't cooperate, and the vast schools of fish didn't regenerate from the heavy fishing they were suddenly subjected to. After a generation or so the town began dying a slow death.

It revived somewhat when deep-sea trawlers discovered the sheltering safety of the deep loch. Today Ullapool is home to many who earn their living by commercial deep-sea fishing. It is also a jumping-off point to Stornoway on the Outer Hebrides for thousands of tourists each season. It is a pleasant village in which to stroll, popping into and out of the wide variety of shops and stores.

ARRIVALS & DEPARTURES

By Bus

Buses arrive in Ullapool from Durness and Inverness several times a day. They stop at the pier in the center of Ullapool.

By Car

You can reach Ullapool by taking the A9 northwest from Inverness and connecting with the A835 about seven miles out of Inverness. If you've followed my suggestion in the last few paragraphs above in the Durness section on *Seeing the Sights*, you've arrived here by car via the A838/A894/A837/A835 from Durness.

ORIENTATION

Ullapool is not a large town, and it is laid out on a grid-like plan. Most of the shops and things to see and do are centered around the pier at the western edge of town.

WHERE TO STAY

GLENFIELD HOTEL, *Ullapool. Tel. 01854/612-314, Fax 01854/612-158. 60 Rooms. Rates: £47-53 single; £32-48 per person double. Rates include breakfast. MasterCard and Visa accepted.*

This British Trust hotel sits at the edge of the village of Ullapool, and provides a relatively new, clean and comfortable place to spend the night. All of the bedrooms are decorated with light colors and complementary floral motif. They are average in size, but some of the rooms with twin beds are quite small. All the furnishings are new and mid-range quality. Each bathroom has new tile and fixtures. The dining room is a large room with tall windows looking out to Loch Broom. It is a nice place to take breakfast or dinner. Its not an upscale hotel, but you'll find the Glenfield Hotel to be a nice, safe place to stay.

ARDVRECK GUEST HOUSE, *Morefield Brae, Ullapool. Tel. 08154/612-028, Fax 01854/613-000; E-mail: ardvreck.guesthouse@btinternet.com; Website: www.smoothhound.co.uk. 10 Rooms. Rates: £24-27 single; £24-27 per person double. Rates include breakfast. MasterCard and Visa accepted, although cash is preferred. Note: open from March through the end of October.*

What a marvelous guest house. Sitting high on the hill above Loch Broom, Ardvreck Guest House offers its guests spectacular views of the loch, the Highlands, and the nearby village of Ullapool. Duncan and Evelyn Stockall are your host and hostess, although Evelyn is the one you'll probably see most often, since Duncan is a busy commercial fisherman. Ardvreck takes its name from an ancient castle, the picturesque ruins of which are nearby.

Ardvreck Guest House was built specifically as a guest house in 1992, and the Stockalls planned well. The guest house features large and roomy bedrooms, many of which have large windows overlooking the stunning scenery that is part and parcel of this part of Scotland. Even the rooms at the back of the house offer delightful garden views. The bedrooms are all decorated in light colors (white, cream and lemon) complemented by a floral motif on the borders and bedspreads.

The dining room and the guest lounge are on the first floor, and also face the loch. They are truly pleasant places to relax, eat, or just pass the time gazing out the windows. The dining room and lounge feature large windows to take maximum advantage of the views. Light pine furnishings add to the light and pleasant atmosphere you'll find here. Evelyn cooks up a great breakfast, and whether you prefer a light continental breakfast or a full Scottish breakfast, she can meet your needs. Eating in the dining room with its splendid views only enhances her efforts. Evelyn is a very gracious and friendly hostess who obviously enjoys the business she runs. She has a certain rustic elegance about her that I am sure you will appreciate. Ardvreck Guest House is a non-smoking facility.

GLENDHU B&B, *Garve Road, Ullapool. Tel. 01854/612-560, Fax 01854/612-814. 3 Rooms. Rates: £15 single; £14-16 per person double. Rates include breakfast. Credit cards not accepted.*

Iris Fraser is your hostess for this pleasant B&B that sits on a hill overlooking Loch Broom. Its location provides lovely views of the loch from several of the bedrooms, the dining room and the guest lounge. This pleasant and comfortable B&B features designer wallpaper and light colors in the bedrooms. Each room is good-sized and the beds are comfortable. The main drawback here is that none of the rooms offer bathrooms in the rooms – all three rooms share a bathroom in the hallway. If that is not an issue for you, you'll really enjoy this B&B and Mrs. Fraser's hospitality. Glendhu B&B is entirely non-smoking.

ULLAPOOL YOUTH HOSTEL, *Shore Street, Ullapool. Tel. 01854/612-254, centralized reservations: 0541/553-255. 9 Rooms. Rates: £7 junior (under age 18), £8 seniors (over age 18). MasterCard and Visa accepted. Note: closed from January 4 to January 28.*

The Ullapool Youth Hostel sits right on the docks of Ullapool at the edge of Loch Broom. From this perspective, it provides some of the prettiest views of Loch Broom and the mountains of the Highlands. There is a small guest lounge for relaxing, and a self-catering kitchen for whipping up something to eat. There are nine rooms in all: two have four beds, six have eight beds and one offers ten beds. The rooms are by no means spacious, but they are clean and safe, and the location is perfect.

WHERE TO EAT

LOCH BROOM RESTAURANT, *Ullapool. Tel. 01854/612-314, Fax 01854/612-158. £8-17. Open daily from noon to 2:00pm and from 6:30pm to 9:30pm. MasterCard and Visa accepted.*

The Loch Broom Restaurant serves the public as well as the residents of Glenfield Hotel in Ullapool. Perhaps the most impressive feature of the restaurant is the two-story, floor-to-ceiling windows that look out onto Loch Broom. The food isn't bad either. There is a surprisingly good menu, offering more than simply pub grub. You'll find a wide selection of seafood (this *is* a fishing village, after all), along with such sumptuous offerings as supreme of Grampian chicken, pork and filet of beef. Try the prawns or salmon – they may be some of the freshest around. There are also a number of vegetarian dishes available. The tall ceilings make the restaurant less than intimate, although the service is relaxed and friendly. Dress is informal.

MARINER'S RESTAURANT, *North Road, Ullapool. Tel. 01854/612-161. £5-10 for lunch and £10-20 for dinner. Open daily from noon to 2:00pm and from 6:30pm to 9:30pm. Amex, MasterCard and Visa accepted.*

Ullapool is a fishing village, and the word on the street is that Mariner's Restaurant is one of the best seafood restaurants in town. It is the restaurant that serves Morefield Motel, but they are more than willing to welcome the public. The Caulfields are the owners of the restaurant, and are proud of the fare they prepare and serve. Mr. Caulfield personally selects each evening's menu offerings from the Ullapool pier each day, so you can be sure that you have the freshest of seafood. Because the catch varies daily, so does the menu at the Mariner's Restaurant. But you might find such fare as fresh sea scallops pan-fried with garlic and parsley or smoked salmon and pine nut salad. Dress is nice casual.

SEEING THE SIGHTS

Frankly, there isn't much to see in Ullapool besides the town itself. For museum-goers, there is, however, the small **Ullapool Museum and Visitor Centre**, *West Argyle Street, Ullapool, Tel. 01854/612-987; open Monday through Saturday during January through March and November and December from noon to 4:00pm, and from April through October from 10:00am to 6:00pm; admission is free.* The museum is housed in an old church and features a number of displays on the history and people of Ullapool and the surrounding areas. There are a number of static displays as well as a few interactive displays. You'll learn of displaced crofters and the rise, fall and rise of the fishing industry in Ullapool.

For the most part, the sights to see around Ullapool are sponsored by Mother Nature. Drives any direction out of Ullapool offer stunning scenery. Particularly memorable is **Corrieshalloch Gorge**, an area of immense beauty about 12 miles southeast of Ullapool on the drive back to Inverness. The **Falls of Meashach** are the featured attraction here, and are phenomenal as they tumble over 150 feet into a narrow wooded gorge. A suspension bridge across the gorge isn't for the faint of heart, but the views are astounding! You'll be amazed at the variety and tenacity of the flora that clings precipitously to the nearly vertical sides of the ravine.

The drive from Ullapool to Inverness is spectacular, and reminded me of many drives in the Colorado Rockies. On the 63-mile drive from Ullapool to Inverness, you'll pass between two bens that soar more than 3,500 feet: Ben Dearg (3,556 feet) and Sgurr Mor (3,641 feet).

SPORTS & RECREATION
Scuba Diving
• **Atlantic Diving Services**, *Ullapool. Tel. 01854/622-261*

LOCH NESS
You must visit **Loch Ness** if you get anywhere near this part of Scotland! It is a huge magnet pulling tourists in from literally all over the world. During numerous visits, I have encountered visitors from the Pacific Rim, the United States, down under and the Continent. Fabled for the possibility of a huge monster living in its murky depths, the loch is a boon to the tourist industry in this part of the country. Scientists have of course pooh-poohed the possibility of the creature's existence. Extensive (and expensive) searches of the loch have proven unproductive. The loch's sheer size (21 miles long) and depth (800 feet) have made effective searches impossible. The presence of underwater caves also keeps the possibilities alive in the minds and imaginations of Nessie believers worldwide.

The loch is really quite intriguing. It is large enough to have significant wave action, and the rolling turbulence and frothy white-caps will make your heart leap on more than one occasion.

ARRIVALS & DEPARTURES
By Car
You'll reach Loch Ness by traveling south from Inverness on the A82. If you're coming from Edinburgh, take the M90 to Perth, and then go north on the A9. Near Dalwhinnie, take the smaller A889 to the A86 west toward Spean Bridge. At Spean Bridge, take the A82 north to Loch Ness.

From Glasgow, take the A82 north, always following the signposts for Inverness.

WHERE TO STAY

GLENMORISTON ARMS HOTEL, *Invermoriston. Tel. 01320/351-206, 01320/351-308; email: scott@glenmoriston.demon.co.uk; Website: nessie.co.uk/mori/mori. 8 Rooms. Rates: £55-70 single; £35-50 per person double; £42-55 per person suite. Rates include breakfast. MasterCard and Visa accepted.*

The Glenmoriston Arms Hotel sits at the convergence of the A82 and the A887 and Loch Ness. The hotel has been here since the end of the 18th century and you'll enjoy it immensely. Formerly the hunting lodge for one Lord Lovatt, it now serves tourists hunting for lodging.

There are seven bedrooms and one suite at the Glenmoriston Arms. Each is large and tastefully decorated in greens and reds with floral accents. The suite is popular with honeymooners, and features a four-poster bed. I especially like the bathrooms associated with each room – each is as large as some twin bedrooms in some hotels! The best rooms are at the front of the hotel, where they overlook the lovely verdant Glenmoriston Valley. Each room is equipped with a hairdryer, TV, telephone and tea- and coffee-making facilities.

The resident's lounge is a bit small, but very comfortable with couches and chairs gathered around a blazing fireplace. The prints and paintings in the lounge and throughout the hotel are traditional Scottish scenes: landscapes, historical events, castles and ruins, etc. The pub offers a wide variety of single malt whiskies – over one hundred at last count. The tartan carpet that graces the floors in this part of the hotel belongs to the Grant Clan. The award-winning restaurant is a pleasant and enjoyable place to dine. Rustic elegance and excellent meals are what you'll find here (see the *Where to Eat* section).

Due to its close proximity to Loch Ness, you'll want to book the Glenmoriston Arms months in advance, especially for the summer months. But if you are touring in January, the Glenmoriston isn't an option since it is closed during that month.

INCHNACARDOCH LODGE HOTEL, *Inverness Road, Fort Augustus. Tel. 01320/366-258, Fax 01320/366-248; E-mail: lochness97@aol.com. 18 Rooms. Rates: £40-50 single; £30-40 per person double. Rates include breakfast. MasterCard and Visa accepted.*

In my humble opinion, Inchnacardoch Lodge Hotel has one of the most memorable settings of any hotel in Scotland. The hotel sits on a lovely landscaped clearing above Loch Ness, and the views across that famous loch are spectacular. Formerly the hunting lodge for one Lord Lovatt, it now serves tourists who are hunting for lodging. (Lord Lovatt has the dubious honor of being the last Scottish rebel to be executed after the Battle of Culloden.) Inchnacardoch is a Gaelic word that means "Island of the Cherry Tree," and refers to a nearby island in Loch Ness.

If you decide to stop here, you will find a lovely old structure that has been (and is continuing to be) renovated and upgraded. You'll find rich dark wood and tartan carpets throughout the hotel, along with a warm welcome from the relatively new owners, Guy and Joan Coombes. The bedrooms are comfortably large, painted in white or light colors, and most have new high-quality furniture. The rooms at the front of the hotel are the best – they overlook Loch Ness and the surrounding countryside, and provide incredible views and marvelous memories.

There is a small pub at the hotel where you can chat with some of the local Scots who stop by for a dram and conversation. In addition, there is a wonderful restaurant that looks out onto Loch Ness that you shouldn't miss (see *Where to Eat* section). Guy and Joan are living out their very own dream come true by owning and operating Inchnacardoch Hotel. Several years ago they vacationed here from the US and fell in love with Scotland (most everybody does!). They decided they wanted to purchase a guest house or hotel, began checking into it, and the rest is, as they say, history. Ask them about it – they are delighted to share the particulars of their story.

COURT GREEN B&B, *Riverside, Invermoriston. Tel. 01320/351-287, Fax 01320/351-287; E-mail: jamesgray@graypics.u-net.com; Website: www.host.co.uk. 3 Rooms. Rates: £22 single; £20 per person double; £70 per room for the family room. Rates include breakfast. No credit cards accepted. Note: open from March 1 through October 31.*

Ulrike Green runs a beautiful new B&B at the edge of Invermoriston. It is very modern, quite comfortable and sparkling clean. In addition, it is located amidst expansive well-landscaped grounds and the effect is one of peace and tranquility.

There are three bedrooms: one twin, one double and one large family room. All the rooms are large, among the largest you'll encounter in a Scottish B&B. Each has been tastefully decorated in light pastels (lilac, peach and beige) highlighted with floral wallpaper borders and bed-spreads. The beige room is exceptionally large. Each room is well lit and has large windows that look out onto the extensive and lovely grounds. Ulrike is a talented and gifted chef, and you will enjoy the breakfast she prepares for you. You will be able to choose from a full Scottish breakfast, or if you prefer, you may have a light continental breakfast. You'll eat in a pleasant dining room that looks out onto the substantial front lawn. Alternatively, you could probably talk Ulrike into letting you eat on the back patio, where you'll enjoy another view of their pretty grounds.

Court Green B&B is close to famed Loch Ness, and the area is very popular for walking, mountain biking, fishing, riding and golf. The Greens are well versed in all there is to do in the area, and they are more than happy to assist you in planning your day's activities. Ulrike's guest book would be the envy of any B&B operator. Here are a few of her entries: "The ultimate and beautiful hostess, superb host!" "Beautiful room – kind hosts!" "Charming hostess, lovely rooms, great welcome," and finally "Terrific place – wonderful hostess."

SONAS B&B, *Inverness Road, Fort Augustus. Tel. 01320/366-291, Fax 01320/366-291. 3 Rooms. Rates: £20-36 single; £14-18 per person double. Rates include breakfast. Credit cards not accepted.*

The thing that first attracted me to Sonas B&B was the immaculate landscaped lawn and the multitude of gorgeous flowers planted and in bloom. I said to myself, "Now that's the kind of place I would like to stay." Upon further investigation, I found it was indeed a place I would like to stay, and you will too.

You'll get the very real sense of staying in someone's home at Sonas B&B. It just *feels* like you are in a home instead of a hotel. The bedrooms feature designer wallpaper, and are very large and exceptionally comfortable. The large windows and exceptional lighting assure you a bright and cheery room, and you will appreciate the new furnishings in each room. Each room has a TV, hairdryer and tea- and coffee-making facilities. While there is no smoking in the bedrooms, there is a resident's lounge where you may do so. The dining room is a pleasant room with large windows that look out onto a green hillside. The tartan carpets you encounter in the home are of the MacPherson Clan.

Perhaps the most impressive thing about Sonas B&B is your hostess, Lorna Service (what a great last name for a B&B owner). She is a delightfully gracious hostess and a genuine and sincere person. Her guest book had these one-word descriptors of the hostess of Sonas B&B: "Wonderful!" "Superb!" and "Warm!" I believe you will agree.

BACKPACKER'S LODGE, *Coltie Farm House, Drumnadrochit. Tel. 01456/450-807. 15 Rooms. Rates: £9-12 per person. Credit cards not accepted.*

At the edge of Drumnadrochit you'll find a small hostel for backpackers or Nessie watchers on a small lane off the A82 (watch for a sign on the east side of the road directing you to the Backpacker's Lodge; you'll travel down a narrow lane until you come to the hostel. You can't miss it – it is the last building on the left, and it has a huge mural depicting a large green monster with a backpack on – it looks a little like a large green Barney). There is one double room, and the dormitory rooms offer either three bunk beds or three bunk beds and a twin bed. It is a very clean and tidy place, and the price is right. A self-catering kitchen is available to cook your own meals, or a continental breakfast is available for £1.50.

LOCH NESS SCOTTISH YOUTH HOSTEL, *Inverness Road, Glenmoriston. Tel. 01320/351-274, centralized reservations: 0541/553-255. 11 Rooms. Rates: £5 juniors (under age 18); £7 seniors (over age 18). MasterCard and Visa accepted. Note: open from mid March through October 31.*

If you want to do your Nessie hunting right from your accommodations, here is the place to be. The Loch Ness Youth Hostel is literally on the banks of Loch Ness, between Fort Augustus and Drumnadrochit on the A82. As with other Scottish Youth Hostels, this one is clean and comfortable – but boy, what a location. There are 11 dormitory rooms at the hostel. Eight of them have four beds, and three of them have between five and eight beds. The rooms are a little on the small side. There is a small beach behind the hostel which affords a pleasant place to sit and contemplate the beautiful loch while searching for Nessie.

As you can imagine, it is immensely popular and you will need to call ahead for reservations. During the summer, you'll need to call several months ahead.

WHERE TO EAT

MORISTON RESTAURANT, *Invermoriston. Tel. 01320/351-206. £10-15 for lunch, £24-30 for dinner. Open daily from noon to 2:00pm and 6:00pm to 9:00pm. (Closed in January.) MasterCard and Visa accepted.*

The restaurant for the Glenmoriston Hotel is an award-winning place to eat, and you will truly enjoy it. The tartan-carpeted dining room (the Grant tartan) is complemented by comfortable chairs, linen tablecloths, silver, crystal and china. Subdued lighting and candlelight, coupled with soft Scottish tunes make for a pleasant dinning experience. The dinner menu offers a wide selection of seafood, beef and vegetarian dishes. Try the filet of west coast salmon with a lemon hollandaise sauce or the filet of Aberdeen beef. The tall ceiling is accentuated by open beams and around the top of the wall, rifles and muskets of by-gone days are displayed.

INCHNACARDOCH LODGE RESTAURANT, *Inverness Road (A82), Fort Augustus. Tel. 01320/366-258. £15-25. Open 6:30pm to 9:30pm. MasterCard and Visa accepted.*

The Inchnacardoch Lodge Restaurant is the restaurant that serves the hotel of the same name. Traditional Scottish fare is what you'll get, and it is simply outstanding. The menu changes frequently, but you might be treated to filet of Highland venison, Angus filet steak, or baked river salmon. Vegetarian dishes are also available. The dining room is a pleasant tall-ceilinged room with mauve paint, candlelit tables, and stunning views down onto Loch Ness. All in all, you'll enjoy this pleasant restaurant. Dress is casual to nice casual.

GLEN ROWAN HIGHLAND FAYRE RESTAURANT, *Invermoriston. Tel. 01320/351-352. £2-7 for lunch, £15-25 for dinner. Open daily from 9:00am to 9:00pm. MasterCard and Visa accepted.*

As you speed toward Loch Ness, slow down near the village of Invermoriston and stop at the Glen Rowan Highland Fayre Restaurant if you are hungry. This amiable little café also doubles as an antique shop, so you can eat and consider purchasing antiques at the same time (two of my favorite pastimes). Large windows in the restaurant look out on pretty green Glen Moriston. Flowers on the table and yellow tablecloths keep the atmosphere bright and cheery. You can expect soups and sandwiches, cakes and pastries as your fare here, and it is all good and quite reasonably priced.

SEEING THE SIGHTS

In addition to Loch Ness itself, there are a few sights in the area worth seeing. Caution: as you drive south from Inverness on the A82, please be careful. The road snakes along the western shore of Loch Ness, and if you're looking too hard for Nessie, you may end up getting a first-hand view of the loch – keep your eyes on the road, as it is narrow and twisty most of the way (I guarantee you that it will be difficult to keep your eyes from wandering).

The best place to view the loch is at **Castle Urquhart**, *A82, one mile south of Drumnadrochit, Tel. 01456/450-551; open daily April through September from 9:30am to 6:30pm and daily October through March from 9:30am to 4:30pm; the last ticket is sold 45 minutes before closing; admission is £3.80 for adults, £2.80 for seniors, and £1.80 for children, children under five are free; MasterCard and Visa are accepted.* Castle Urquhart is a marvelous old moss-covered ruin at the edge of Loch Ness. It is frankly a shame the castle gets over-shadowed by Loch Ness, since it really is a very impressive ruin and worth a visit in its own right. Plaques around the castle explain the various aspects and areas of the castle. It has lovely views up and down Loch Ness, which just add to the splendor of the ruins.

The castle was built in the 12th century, and has hosted many famous folks through the years. Edward I, Robert the Bruce, the Covenanters and Jacobites all held the castle at various intervals throughout its history. It was finally blown to pieces by government forces in 1692 to keep it from falling into the hands of the Jacobites. Most of the sightings of the Loch Ness monster have occurred from in or around Urquhart Castle. There are several hypotheses about the reason for this. The first is that the loch nears its deepest point just offshore from the castle, and the second is that there are always lots of people here, making it more likely that someone will see something on the loch. The third theory is that there is a cave hundreds of feet below the castle where Nessie makes her lair.

Drumnadrochit is the little village closest to Urquhart Castle, and arguably the village that has benefited most from its proximity. It is a sleepy little village with a few cheesy tourist attractions and gift shops centered on the Loch Ness monster. Vying for your heart and pocketbook are **The Official Loch Ness Monster Exhibition**, *Drumnadrochit, Tel. 01456/450-573, Fax 01456/450-770; open daily from Easter to May from 9:30am to 5:30pm, June and September from 9:30am to 6:30pm, July and August from 9:00am to 8:30pm, October from 9:30am to 6:00pm, and November to Easter from 10:00am to 4:00pm; admission is £6.50 for adults, £3.50 for seniors and children, children under five are free, and a family ticket is available for £14.50*, and **The Original Loch Ness Monster Visitor Centre**, *Drumnadrochit, Tel. 01456/450-342; open daily from Easter through October from 10:00am to 6:00pm; admission is £3.50 for adults, £3 for children, £2.50 for seniors, and a family ticket is available for £10.* Both offer short videos about the history of the loch and a series of grainy, out-of-focus prints and home movies of the alleged monster. No need to visit both (although I did, of course). Personally I liked *The Official* better than *The Original* exhibit, despite the fact that admission is more expensive than that of its competitor.

Another nice diversion is a cruise of Loch Ness. A number of cruise operators run out of Drumnadrochit, but my favorite is **Loch Ness Cruises**, *Drumnadrochit, Tel. 01456/450-395, Fax 01456/450-785; cruises run from Easter through the end of October at 9:30am, 10:30am, 11:30am, 1:00pm, 3:00pm, 4:00pm, 5:00pm and 6:00pm; costs are £8 for adults, £5 for seniors and children, and a family ticket available for £24.* George Edwards and Dick Raynor have been running cruises on Loch Ness since the early 1980s – the first commercial venture to do so on an ongoing basis. They have a 12-passenger boat called the *Nessie Hunter* that will take you out onto the loch for a one-hour tour. They'll provide commentary on the history of the loch, Urquhart Castle, and Nessie. Sign up for the tours right next to The Original Loch Ness Monster Visitor Centre.

The one sight that everyone comes to Loch Ness to see is seldom seen, and that's **Nessitera Rhombopteryx**, the scientific name of the Loch Ness Monster. Who visits this mysterious loch without craning their necks, and having their camera ready "just in case..."? If you do happen to see her, and better yet, if you do snap a photo or get a video of her, please drop me a line.

SPORTS & RECREATION
Windsurfing
• **Scottish Voyageurs: Travels with Paddles**, *Upper Wharf, Canal Bank, Fort Augustus. Tel. 01320/366-666, Fax 01320/366-636; E-mail: scotvoyg@netcomuk.co.uk*

JOHN O'GROATS

Four years after Columbus began his historic voyage, Dutchman Jan de Groot applied for and received the contract to run a ferry between this northeastern tip of Scotland's land mass and Orkney. Jan (John) allegedly built an eight-sided house with eight doors so that his quarrelsome children could each enter the house by the front door.

Unless you have lots of extra time in your itinerary, I'm not sure driving to John O'Groats is worth it. It takes between two and three hours to traverse the distance between Inverness and John O'Groats through largely unimpressive flat or undulating scenery. However, if you are one of those folks that likes to go to the furthest (inhabited) point of a land mass just to say you've been there, then so be it. If you fall into this category and decide to go to John O'Groats, then by all means take a few minutes and go just a little further to **Duncansby Head**. While not the northernmost point in Scotland (that's Dunnet Head, a few miles up the coast), it is the second-most northerly point. If you come here, you'll be treated to a stoic lighthouse and spectacular cliff views, as well as views out to Orkney.

Speaking of **Dunnet Head**, continue east around the John O'Groats peninsula until you come to the village of Dunnet. Take the B855 out to Dunnet Head for that northern-most spot of Scotland. You'll find sandy beaches, fine cliffs and a Victorian-era lighthouse.

ARRIVALS & DEPARTURES

By Bus

Buses stop in the carpark at John O'Groats, arriving from Wick. Three buses a day arrive in Wick from Inverness, where you can catch a local bus up to John O'Groats. One or two buses each day leave the Inverness bus station directly for John O'Groats.

By Car

From Inverness, just take the A9 north west and drive (and drive).

By Train

Train service from Inverness reaches as far as Wick, where you can hop on a bus to John O'Groats.

SOUTHERN HIGHLANDS

As you continue further south on the A82 into the southern extremities of the Highlands, the scenery continues to be an awesome draw. After you've had your fill of Loch Ness and Urquhart Castle, hop in the car and head south along the A82 until you come to Invermoriston. At the junction, take the right fork (A887) and head toward the Isle of Skye. Enjoy the scenery on this part of the drive, although during the summer months the traffic can be a bit much on this two-lane road.

You'll drive along the pretty shores of **Loch Cluanie** and **Loch Duich**. At the western end of Loch Duich, you'll come upon a marvelous sight: **Eilean Donan Castle**, *Dornie, near Kyle, Tel. 01599/555-202; open daily April 1 through October 31 from 10:00am to 6:00pm; last ticket sold at 5:30pm; admission is £3.75 for adults, £2.75 for seniors and children, and a family ticket is available for £9.* Eilean Donan Castle is a wonderful treat. Picturesque and romantic, it sits regally on a small island at the confluence of Loch Duich and Loch Alsh. The castle is reached via a stone bridge.

Due to its magnificent setting, it is probably one of the most photographed castles in Scotland. Hollywood likes it too, and it has been featured in several films, including *The Highlander*, and a cameo appearance as MI-6's Scottish headquarters in the 1999 James Bond movie *The World is not Enough*. The castle was built in the early 13th century, and has served as a stronghold for the MacKenzies for centuries. The castle was blasted to pieces by English warships for its role as a Jacobite stronghold and lay in ruins from the early 1700s until it was restored and rebuilt in the 1930s. (It is said that one of the soldiers killed in the English attack still wanders the ramparts, still protecting the castle.)

Today the castle is a memorial to the Jacobite cause, and there are a number of relics from that era. An exhibition hall tells the story of the castle's 600+ years of history, and features placards, paintings and models of the castle, all accompanied by an audio narrative. A number of rooms can be seen, and guides in each room point out items of interest and answer questions. A 30-minute guided tour is also available. Many of the furnishings date from the 1600s and 1700s, and there are some wonderful oil paintings around. I was particularly impressed with several swords and dirks (long knives) nearly 300 years old. There is a modern coffee shop and very complete gift shop associated with the castle.

This is a good point from which to venture onto the **Isle of Skye**, one of the islands included in the Inner Hebrides chain; for more about the Isle of Skye, turn to *The Islands* chapter.)

WHERE TO EAT

SEAGREEN RESTAURANT, *Plockton Road, Kyle of Lochalsh. Tel. 01599/534-388. £20-30. Open daily from 10:00am to 9:00pm. MasterCard and Visa accepted.*

In the Kyle of Lochalsh, just enroute to the Isle of Skye and not far from Eilean Donan Castle, you'll find this award-winning restaurant. The restaurant, along with a bookstore, is housed in an old renovated schoolhouse. The meals prepared and presented here by this *A Taste of Scotland* winner are simple, organic and very good. The menu ranges from soups and salads to full seafood, vegetarian and meat dishes. Much of their success comes from insistence on the use of only the freshest ingredients, which fortunately are available in abundance. As a special bonus, there is a terrace where you can take your meal, sip a glass of wine and read a book, or just gaze out over the stunning views of the Isles of Skye and Raasay.

JENNIE J'S, *Ardelve, Dornie. Tel. 01599/555-362. £8-18. Open daily March through October from 11:00am to 2:00pm and from 6:00pm to 9:00pm (open until 10:00pm July and August). MasterCard and Visa accepted.*

Jennie J's is a restaurant that sits on the banks of Loch Duich, just across the bridge from Eilean Donan Castle. They certainly know how to market their place: large windows assure diners marvelous views of the castle (especially at night, when it is bathed in floodlights). Light oak hardwood floors, pleasant tables, lacquered black cane chairs and flowers on the tables make for a nice dining environment. The fare is traditional Scottish, with an emphasis on seafood. Dress is casual.

EILEAN DONAN CASTLE COFFEE SHOP, *Dornie. Tel. 01599/555-202. £2-5. Open Easter through October daily from 10:00am to 5:00pm. MasterCard and Visa accepted.*

The coffee shop at Eilean Donan Castle is a large, modern and comfortable place to stop for a quick bite to eat before or after you tour the castle. Nothing fancy here, but you'll find a good selection of sandwiches, sodas, coffee, tea, yogurt and desserts.

FORT WILLIAM

As you travel farther south along the A82, you'll find the busy town of **Fort William**. Actually, it's not the town so much that is pretty, but rather its setting. Fort William (called *Fort Bill* by the many hillwalkers that descend on this region) is ringed by hills and valleys and nearby Loch Linnhe completes the pastoral setting. South of Fort William looms impressive Ben Nevis, the highest mountain in the United Kingdom at 4,406 feet.

As you head south of Fort William, you'll come to the beautiful and lonely **Glencoe**, site of one of the most infamous massacres in Scottish history. West of town is the solitary **Glenfinnan Monument**, a monument erected to commemorate the place where Bonnie Prince Charlie began the military campaign known as the Jacobite Rebellion.

ARRIVALS & DEPARTURES

By Bus

Four buses arrive daily from Glasgow at the **Fort William Bus Station**, *High Street, Fort William, Tel. 01397/703-791.* The three-hour trip from Glasgow costs £10. Buses also arrive here from Inverness after their two-hour jaunt.

By Car

You'll arrive in Fort William via the A82 whether you're coming from Inverness or Glasgow.

By Train

Trains arrive at the **Fort William Train Station**, *High Street, Fort William, Tel. 01397/703-791.*

WHERE TO STAY

ISLES OF GLENCOE HOTEL AND LEISURE CENTER, *Ballachulish, near Fort William. Tel. 01855/581-602, Fax 01855/581-602; E-mail: reservations @mysteryworld.com. 39 Rooms. Rates: £50 single; £50-60 per person sharing. Rates include breakfast. MasterCard and Visa accepted.*

Snug and secure at the edge of beautiful Loch Leven is the delightful Isles of Glencoe Hotel and Leisure Center. It is easy to tell this is a family-run hotel, because they are so attentive to family needs. Children's menus in the restaurant, a children's play area in the lobby and a set of playground equipment and toys on the front lawn give you the definite feeling that your children are welcome here.

The hotel was built in 1992, and the bedrooms are large and pleasantly decorated in peach, rose and other light colors. Because of the way the hotel is located along the loch, most of the rooms have views of that lovely loch. The few rooms that don't have that view have a panorama of the nearby mountains that would be considered premium views in other hotels. The Isles at Glencoe also features a nice large swimming pool – and a children's pool, of course! In addition, you'll find a nice sauna and steam room to help you unwind after a long drive or long day of sightseeing.

LODGE ON THE LOCH, *Onich, near Fort William. Tel. 01855/821-237, Fax 01855/821-463; E-mail: reservations@mysteryworld.com. 19 Rooms. Rates: £50 single; £45-60 per person double. Rates include breakfast. MasterCard and Visa accepted.*

The Lodge on the Loch Hotel is one of three hotels owned by the Norman Young family, and this is the most elegant of the three. Sitting just across the road from Loch Leven, the views of the loch and the mountains beyond are nothing short of spectacular.

There are four levels of bedrooms at this four-star hotel, and they are named after the familial leadership structure among Scottish clans: Chieftain, Lairds, Clansmen and Economy (probably sounded better than serf did!). The Chieftain rooms are spacious and have the premium views of the loch. The Lairds rooms are only slightly smaller (although they are still quite large), and have "side" views of the loch. The Clansmen and Economy rooms have views of the mountainside. Economy rooms (there are only two) are defined as such since they share a hallway bathroom. The restaurant at Lodge on the Loch Hotel is another nice feature. Pleasant and convivial, the chefs here pride themselves in preparing and presenting only the freshest Scottish fare to their guests. The dining room is smallish, but it too has lovely views of Loch Leven, which only serve to enhance your dining experience here.

The grounds are lovely and in the evenings you can sit on lawn furniture in front of the hotel and enjoy the views of the lake. It is very peaceful and tranquil. All in all, this is a very pleasant place to stay.

BALLACHULISH HOTEL, *Ballachulish, near Fort William. Tel. 01855/ 811-629, Fax 01855/811-629; E-mail: reservations@mysteryworld.com. 54 Rooms. Rates: £50 single; £40-55 per person double. Rates include breakfast. MasterCard and Visa accepted.*

The Ballachulish Hotel strives to maintain the feeling and tradition of a turn-of-the-century baronial mansion. Built in the 1880s, it features rich dark wood trim and banisters along with those wonderful tall ceilings that are such a notable trademark of these Victorian structures. Take a few moments to notice the artwork on the walls. It really enhances the feeling of the hotel, with its Scottish landscapes and scenes from medieval Scottish life. Most of the art is the work of a local artist, and is for sale if you are interested.

About half the bedrooms look out onto Loch Leven – a beautiful Scottish loch at the foot of the Highland Bens. Most of the rest of the rooms have exceptional views of the towering mountains. All the bed-rooms are large and comfortably furnished. Breakfast is taken in a restaurant that also looks out onto Loch Leven, and it presents a very pleasant panorama to consider during breakfast. This is a pleasant, comfortable place to stay should you find yourself in this part of the country.

HOME FARM, *Ballachulish, near Fort William. Tel. 01855/811-792. 3 Rooms. Rates: £30 single; £24-30 per person double. Rates include breakfast. No credit cards accepted.*

Let me tell you how I stumbled across the Home Farm. I saw this beautiful scene of a home snuggled at the foot of impressive Craig Mor in a small glen above Loch Leven, and decided to take a picture of it. After taking the picture and heading up the road, I saw the sign for Home Farm

B&B, and wondered, "Could it be the home I just took a picture of?" It was. You will really like the Home Farm – Joan and Ronnie McLauchlan run this four-star B&B, and they are rightfully proud of their home and setting.

Three ensuite rooms are available at Home Farm, and each is large and spacious. I complimented the McLauchlan's for not succumbing to the temptation to make the three rooms into five or even six rooms – they are that large. The rooms are known simply as the pink, green and blue rooms – giving you an idea of the predominant decorating theme in each room. Floral bedspreads and high-quality furnishings complete the picture. Each room has a large window that frames picturesque Loch Leven and the mountains which encircle it. All the rooms have electric blankets, TV, hairdryers, nice bathrooms and tea- and coffee-making facilities. The Home Farm is a non-smoking facility. An elegant and tasteful sitting room with comfortable furniture and a fireplace also features huge windows to present spectacular views, as does the dining room. Joan is an outstanding cook, and you will enjoy her culinary efforts in your behalf.

The land on which the Home Farm sits truly was the old home farm for the McLauchlans. Now they raise tourist's expectations and help them harvest wonderful memories and photographs. Don't be left out.

GLENMORVEN HOUSE, *Onich, near Fort William. Tel. 01855/821-247. 5 Rooms. Rates: £30 single; £24-30 per person double. Rates include breakfast. MasterCard and Visa accepted.*

You'll find a wonderful B&B perched along the banks of Loch Leven. This fine B&B is run by Andrew and Jean Coke, and they have worked very hard to provide a lovely B&B for your pleasure. Built in 1901 for the Pier Master, you'll enjoy the same views and tranquility that the Pier Master enjoyed during his lifetime. The Cokes have done a nice job of repainting and renovating this home. Each of the bedrooms are nice sized, and all but one have breathtaking views of Loch Leven and the surrounding bens (mountains). Each of the rooms is pleasantly and comfortably furnished, and each features an ensuite bathroom with a shower. Joan is remarkable cook, and you'll receive your breakfast in a large dining room with wide windows that allow you to drink in the marvelous views of the loch.

SPRINGBURN HOUSE, *Fort William-Invergary Road, Stronaba, Speanbridge. Tel. 01397/712-707. 8 Rooms. Rates: £18-23. Rates include breakfast. MasterCard and Visa accepted.*

Christine Fyfe runs a modern four-star B&B on the Fort William-Invergary road. It sits on a hill with commanding views of the Scottish Highland countryside, including a birds-eye view of Ben Nevis, the tallest mountain in Scotland (and in the UK, for that matter). Spacious is the word that best applies to the resident's lounge and all the bedrooms. Each room is decorated essentially the same, with pastel paint and floral-accent wallpaper and bedding. All the rooms have large windows that keep them feeling bright and airy, and that frame panoramic scenes of the Scottish countryside. Each room has a TV, trouser press, hairdryer and tea- and coffee-making facilities. Christine provides a full Scottish breakfast in the dining room that wisely continues the large windows found elsewhere in the house. Your breakfast will taste exceptionally delicious as you ponder the lovely scenes just beyond the windows.

Christine is a delightful and charming hostess, and you will enjoy her graceful hospitality. Springburn House is part of a working 50-acre croft (small family farm), and Christine assured me that any guests who wished to feed Highland cattle or help feed baby lambs would be accommodated. The setting for Springburn House is spectacular; the hostess is fabulous; the home is exceptional. What are you waiting for?

STRONCHREGGAN GUEST HOUSE, *Achintore Road, Fort William. Tel. 01397/704-644, Fax 01397/704-644; E-mail: pat@apmac.freeserve.co.uk; Website: host.co.uk. 7 Rooms. Rates: £29-34 single; £19-21 per person double. Rates include breakfast. No credit cards accepted.*

Pat and Archie McQueen run a very pleasant three-star guest house on the banks of Loch Linnhe. There are seven bedrooms in the guest house, and five of them are ensuite. Each room is large and tastefully decorated with light peach and cream colors. Floral accents and fresh flowers in the rooms add to the soft and comfortable feel you'll have here. All the rooms have been furnished with new top-quality furniture. The ensuite rooms all have showers, and the other two rooms have their own private hallway bathrooms. As a special bonus (at no extra charge) each of the rooms has marvelous views of the loch.

A resident lounge is comfortably furnished with leather furniture, so you'll be able to snuggle down most agreeably as you look out onto the loch and enjoy the beautiful scenes before you. The dining room also features the same lovely loch views. When I asked Pat what sort of cook she was, she smiled and said, "I enjoy cooking and I cook with love." With those qualities to her cooking, I don't believe you can go wrong here. You'll of course be treated to a full Scottish breakfast and if you wish, dinner is also available at £10 per person.

Stronchreggan Guest House takes its name from the valley in which it is located. It is a Gaelic name that means "the nose of the rocks." You'll love Stronchreggan Guest House in general and Pat in particular.

GLENSHIEL GUEST HOUSE, *Achintore Road, Fort William. Tel. 01397/702-271. 5 Rooms. Rates: £15-18 single; £15-18 per person double. Rates include breakfast. Credit cards not accepted.*

Alice and Bill Grant run this delightful B&B overlooking Loch Linnhe. There are four bedrooms at Glenshiel Guest House and all but one of them are ensuite. Three of the rooms look out on the loch through large, wide windows and the effect is almost like looking at a large picturesque mural. Each room is individually decorated and features floral accents and light-colored walls. Each ensuite room has a shower rather than a tub. The room at the back of the house has rather abrupt views of the lush hillside and terraced gardens that make up the back yard at Glenshiel Guest House. Each room has a TV and tea- and coffee-making facilities.

Alice describes herself (with a twinkle in her eye) as a "perfect" cook, since she has been doing this for over 50 years. You'll enjoy all the advantages of her years of expertise as you partake of traditional Scottish fare in the dining room. While here, you'll be able to gaze out another set of wide windows at the natural beauty of Loch Linnhe. A wonderful meal in a wonderful setting, served by a wonderful hostess.

You'll notice many of the rooms feature tartan carpets; if you are interested, the tartan is that of the William Wallace Clan (also known as the *Mel Gibson* tartan!). Glenshiel Guest House is non-smoking, immaculate and extremely comfortable and you will enjoy your hosts as much (or more!) than the facility itself. Bill in particular has a soft spot in his heart for Americans. He was a prisoner of war in Poland during World War II and it was Americans who liberated him and his friends. Glenshiel Guest House is open from Easter through the end of October.

WHERE TO EAT

ISLES OF GLENCOE RESTAURANT, *Ballachulish, near Fort William. Tel. 01855/581-602, Fax 01855/811-602. £5-8 for lunch, £10-20 for dinner. Open daily from 10:00am to 10:00pm. MasterCard and Visa accepted.*

The Isles of Glencoe Restaurant serves the hotel of the same name and is a very pleasant place to spend an hour or two. Especially nice is the glass-lined conservatory that looks out on Loch Leven and a small island offshore where dozens of headstones stand – lonely reminders of a grim day in Scottish history – the massacre of the MacDonald clan in Glencoe.

The food, however, is anything but grim and you will be delighted with your meal here. Try the deep-fried Mallaig haddock or the seared breast of duck. If you want seafood, then try the seafood croissant. Vegetarian dishes are also available. A children's menu offers pint-size dishes for £3.75 to £4.95. If you're traveling by and decide to stop in, the hotel reserves the 7:00pm to 9:00pm timeframes for their hotel guests. Dress is casual to nice casual and you'll want reservations during the summer months.

LODGE ON THE LOCH RESTAURANT, *Onich. Tel. 01855/821-237, Fax 01855/821-238. £20-30. Open daily from 7:00pm to 9:30pm. MasterCard and Visa accepted.*

The Lodge on the Loch Restaurant features elegant dining with stirring loch-side views. Candlelight and crystal, china and silver combine with excellent cuisine to provide a most memorable dining experience. In addition, out in the Resident's Lounge (during the summer months) soothing dinner music is provided by a local pianist or harpist.

The best tables in the dining room are along the front walls near the windows. Each has sensational views out over peaceful Loch Leven. However, if you don't get one of those tables, don't be disappointed, because your meal will be marvelous. You'll savor the traditional Scottish fare, with such offerings as Perthshire pheasant terrine studded with duck on garden leaves and home-baked sun-dried tomato bread. If you're hoping for seafood, then try the baked filet of Loch Leven trout resting on braised fennel and cream veloute. These and other meals are responsible for the restaurant's recognition by *A Taste of Scotland*.

SEEING THE SIGHTS

West Highland Museum, *Cameron Square, Fort William, Tel. 1397/ 702-169; open September through June Monday through Saturday from 10:00am to 1:00pm and 2:00pm to 5:00pm. July and August open daily from 10:00am to 1:00pm and from 2:00pm to 5:00pm; admission is £1.50 for adults, £1 for seniors and 40p for children.* This is a great museum that offers a lot of information on the Highlands and surrounding areas. There is a nice exhibit on the Jacobite Rebellion of 1745, as well as information about many of the main Highland clans and their tartans. Of particular interest is a rifle thought to have been used in the murder of government tax collector Colin Campbell in 1752. It was a well-publicized murder in Scotland and served as the inspiration for Robert Louis Stevenson's epic novel *Kidnapped*.

About two miles north of Fort William on the A82 are the ruins of **Inverlochy Castle**. This crumbling and lichen-covered ruin sits at a strategic point on the Lochy River. Built in the 13th century, the castle was the site of a fierce battle in 1645, where over 1,300 Covenanters were slain by the English army.

The tallest mountain in Britain soars majestically above Fort William. **Ben Nevis** tops 4,400 feet and has been popular with hillwalkers for centuries. A well-trodden trail begins about one mile southeast of town at Achintee Farm. The trail wends its way to the top, where you'll be treated to magnificent views over all of Scotland on a clear day.

About 17 miles west of Fort William on the A830 stands a solitary monument at **Glenfinnan** along the shores of lovely Loch Shiel. The monument memorializes the spot where Bonnie Prince Charlie hoisted his red-and-white flag and began rallying troops in an effort to regain the throne for the Stewart kings. It turned out to be the high point of the

Jacobite Rebellion of 1745, which seems to have been doomed from the beginning. You are probably familiar with Glenfinnan – its visage has been on many a postcard of Scotland. A small **Visitor Centre** nearby chronicles the ill-fated rebellion (*Glenfinnan, Tel. 01855/811-307; open April and May daily from 10:00am to 5:00pm and June through August daily from 9:30am to 6:00pm; admission is £1 for adults, 50p for seniors and children*).

Moving down the road a few miles, you come to beautiful and lonely Glencoe. Glencoe is the site of one of the most infamous pages in Scottish history: the **Massacre at Glencoe** (see the sidebar). The small **Glencoe Visitor Centre**, *Glencoe, Tel. 01855/811-307, Fax 01855/811-772; admission 50p for adults, 30p for seniors and children*, shows a short video (14 minutes) that gives a fine synopsis of the tragedy. It also has a number of exhibits highlighting the flora and fauna of the area. If you have a sharp eye, you might realize that Glencoe provided the backdrop for more than one Hollywood movie, including *Rob Roy* (1995, with Liam Neeson) and *The Highlander* (1986, with Sean Connery).

THE MASSACRE OF GLENCOE

As were most of his predecessors, **William of Orange** was convinced that the way to peace in Scotland was through a united religion. He insisted that all nobles and clan leaders sign an Oath of Loyalty to him. Under threats of clan annihilation, most of the clan chieftains signed the oath by the set date. One notable chieftain who did not sign in time was the head of **Clan MacDonald**. He did sign the oath, although a few days late. Some say it was because of procrastination, others say it was the weather and some claim it was confusion over the place of signing. Regardless, he was late signing the document.

It was excuse enough for William to set in motion a nefarious plan. An army consisting primarily of members of the Campbell clan was sent to Glencoe, the home of Clan MacDonald. Leaders of the army were told to board with the MacDonalds for several weeks and gain their confidence. Once their confidence was won, they were instructed to murder every MacDonald under the age of 70. The Campbells, hereditary enemies of the MacDonalds, were delighted to oblige their sovereign.

On a cold and snowy night in February 1692, the Campbells arose in the pre-dawn darkness and began to carry out their dastardly deed – but the cold, dark and confusion allowed many of the MacDonalds to escape and tell the tale. Even at that, more than three dozen MacDonalds were slain. Scotsmen nationwide were appalled. The killings were not so extraordinary – those happened frequently in Scotland. It was the breach of hospitality that infuriated them and has branded the Campbell clan forever.

SPORTS & RECREATION
Horseback Riding
• **Brenfield Estate and Farm**, *Brenfield. Tel. 01546/603-274*

Windsurfing
• **Brenfield Estate and Farm**, *Brenfield. Tel. 01546/603-274*
• **West Coast Outdoor Leisure Centre**, *102 High Street, Fort William. Tel. 01397/705-777*

PRACTICAL INFORMATION
Tourist Information
• **Fort William Tourist Information Centre**, *Cameron Square, Fort William. Tel. 01397/703-781*
• **Ballachulish Tourist Information Centre**, *Albert Road, Ballachulish. Tel. 01855/811-296*

OBAN
Oban is one of Scotland's busiest towns, although it seems that people mostly use Oban as a **jumping-off point** for several islands.

ARRIVALS & DEPARTURES
By Bus
Buses arrive throughout the day at the **Oban Bus Station**, *Station Square, Oban. Tel. 01631/563-083.*

By Car
To reach Oban from Glasgow, take the A82 north to Tyndrum, then head west on the A85.

By Train
Four trains per day arrive from Glasgow at the **Oban Train Station**, *Station Square, Oban, Tel. 01631/563-083.* Trains coming from Glasgow take 3 hours to make the trip.

SEEING THE SIGHTS/SHOPPING
There are many fine shops in the town, looking to capture a few pounds from tourists who have gotten to town enroute to the Isle of Mull and Iona. It is also a popular **dive center**, and many divers from all over the world descend on Oban to explore the waters around this part of Scotland.

SPORTS & RECREATION
Diving
- **Gaelic Rose**, *Lochaline, Oban, Argyll. Tel. 01967/421-654*
- **Nervous Wrecks**, *Oban. Tel. 01631/566-000*
- **Oban Dive Shop**, *Glenshellach Road, Oban. Tel. 01631/566-618*

Horseback Riding
- **Achnalarig Farm**, *Oban. Tel. 01631/562-745*

PRACTICAL INFORMATION
Tourist Information
- **Oban Tourist Information Centre**, *Boswell House, Argyll Square, Oban. Tel. 01631/563-122*

16. THE GRAMPIAN HIGHLANDS

The **Grampian Highlands** comprise a large geographic area in the northeastern portion of Scotland. The Grampian Highlands is that portion of Scotland that lies north of a line between Stonehaven (just south of Aberdeen) and Perth, and that which lies east of the A9 (which runs between Perth and Inverness).

This region gets largely overlooked by tourists and as such isn't as tuned so finely to tourism as the rest of the country. That can be good and bad, I suppose. You'll find fewer touristy attractions here, but you'll also find fewer crowds. Without the draw of Edinburgh or Stirling Castles, Loch Ness, or the spectacular abbeys (Jedburgh, Melrose, Kelso and Dryburgh) in the south, this area gets overlooked. But there are a few sights to see that may make this a place you'd like to venture. First of all, throughout this area you have beautiful scenery. Although not as dramatic as the Highlands, much of the area is still quite rugged and beautiful in its own right.

Aberdeen is the third largest city in Scotland, and is a good base for touring the surrounding areas. Known as the Granite City because so many of its buildings are constructed of that material, the city is large and sprawling and has a number of activities worth seeing.

There are two trails in the Grampian Highlands that you might like to check out. The first is the **Malt Whisky Trail**, and it consists of seven whisky distilleries and a cooperage. Along the trail, you'll find a few names you might be familiar with: **Glenlivet**, **Glenfarclas** and **Glenfiddich**. Each distillery offers a tour of their facilities, and as a reward for your patience shares a complimentary dram of their product with you at the close of the tour. The second trail is the **Castle Trail**. While tourists may not get to the Grampian Highlands as much as to other parts of Scotland, English armies didn't make it here often either. That means that there are many castles that are still in pretty good condition.

In addition to those castles included on the Castle Trail, there are several others that you may have heard of or seen. **Balmoral Castle** is the Queen of England's weekend home in the country, and **Braemar Castle** is just a few miles further down the road and is an interesting place to visit, especially if you are there for the **Braemar Highland Games**. A few miles south of Aberdeen is one of the most striking castle ruins in Scotland: **Dunnottar Castle**.

THE GRAMPIAN HIGHLAND'S MUST-SEE SIGHTS

Duff House – *Duff House is a spectacular example of early Georgian architecture, and is a satellite location for the National Gallery of Scotland. It contains many fine old oil paintings.*

Kildrummy Castle – *Once a great and nearly impregnable fortress, Kildrummy Castle is now an incredibly impressive set of ruins.*

Glenlivet Distillery – *The Distillery tour given at Glenlivet Distillery is one of the best in the country. You'll get a fascinating look at the process from beginning to end.*

Linn of Dee – *The Linn of Dee is one of the prettiest scenes in this part of the country.*

Elgin Cathedral – *This is one of the loveliest sets of ruins in Scotland. Elgin Cathedral was built in the early 13th century, and withstood (more or less – mostly less!) the ravages of war, pride and the Reformation. Today it is a photo-op waiting to happen.*

ABERDEEN

Aberdeen, the Granite City, is Scotland's third largest city with a population of 210,000. There has been a settlement here for many hundreds of years. In the early 1970s oil was discovered in the North Sea, and many companies chose Aberdeen as the headquarters for their North Sea oil operations. This pumped millions of pounds into the Aberdeen economy and thousands (some estimates as high as 75,000) of new residents.

Scots and tourists have a love-hate relationship with Aberdeen: they either love it or they hate it. Personally, I find it to be sprawling and a bit confusing to get around. There are a few interesting sights to see, and I have included them here. And so you ask, "What do you call a person who lives in Aberdeen?" The answer, of course, is an Aberdonian.

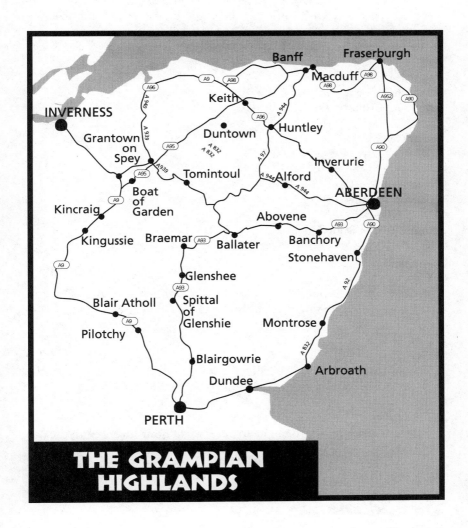

THE GRAMPIAN
HIGHLANDS

ARRIVALS & DEPARTURES

BY AIR

Due to the North Sea oil activity, the **Aberdeen Dyce Airport**, *Tel. 01224/722-331,* receives many flights from airports within Scotland as well as from London. Once you've landed, bus service leaves for downtown Aberdeen every 35 minutes throughout the day. After 6:00pm, buses run every 60 to 90 minutes. The buses will drop you off downtown at the bus station.

From Heathrow
• **British Airways**, *Tel. 0181/754-7321*
• **British Midland**, *Tel. 0345/554-554*

From Gatwick
• **British Airways**, *Tel. 0181/754-7321*

From London Luton
• **Easyjet Airlines**, *Tel. 0870/600-0000*

From London Stansted
• **KLM UK**, *Tel. 0181/750-9820*

BY BUS

Buses arrive at Aberdeen frequently from Dundee, Inverness, Glasgow and Edinburgh at the **Aberdeen Bus Station**, *Guild Street, Aberdeen, Tel. 01224/212-266.*

BY CAR

If you are coming to Aberdeen from the south you'll arrive on the A90. If you're coming from Inverness, the straightest route is the A96.

BY TRAIN

Trains arrive at Aberdeen nearly every half hour throughout the day from Glasgow and Edinburgh at the **Aberdeen Train Station**, *Guild Street, Aberdeen. Tel. 01224/594-222.* There are also four trains a day that arrive from London.

GETTING AROUND TOWN

By Bicycle

Due to the traffic, I'd be cautious about using a bicycle in the Granite City. If you wish to rent a bicycle, however, there are a few shops in and around town:

- **Aberdeen City Cycle Centre**, *188 King Street, Aberdeen. Tel. 01224/644-542*
- **Alpine Bikes**, *70 Holburn Street, Aberdeen. Tel. 1224/211-455*
- **Monster Bikes**, *Banchory. Tel. 1330/825-313*
- **Peterson's Bicycles**, *Kirkwall. Tel. 01330/873-097*

By Bus

There is good intra-city bus service in Aberdeen. Buses crisscross the city regularly.

BEST PLACES TO STAY
IN THE GRAMPIAN HIGHLANDS

STAKIS CRAIGENDARROCH, Braemar Road, Ballater. Tel. 01339/755-858, Fax 01339/755-447; Website: www.stakis.co.uk/craigendarroch. 44Rooms. Rates: £65 standard single, £90 club single, £140 suite; £65 per person standard double, £90 per person club double, £140 per person suite. In my opinion, this is one of the nicer Stakis properties in Scotland. This four-star hotel works very hard (and succeeds) at providing modern elegance.

MARCLIFFE AT PITFODELS, North Deeside Road, Aberdeen. Tel. 01224/861-000, Fax 01224/868-860; E-mail: reservations@marcliffe.com; Website: www.nettrak.co.uk/marcliffe. 42 Rooms. Rates: £105-155 single; £115-165 per room double. The Marcliffe is one of the most elegant and stately hotels in the country. This is where the politicians and actors head when they're in Aberdeen.

KILDRUMMY CASTLE HOTEL, Kildrummy, near Alford. Tel. 01975/571-288, Fax 01975/571-345, US toll-free 800/462-2748. 16 Rooms. Rates: £80-85 single; £130-160 double. Kildrummy Castle Hotel is a delicious old Scottish manor house set in the midst of spectacular gardens and overlooking the ruins of the original 13th-century Kildrummy Castle. This mansion was built during the 19th century, and has been renovated to echo the elegance and style that it once had.

CALLATER LODGE HOTEL, 9 Glenshee Road, Braemar. Tel. 01339/741-275, Fax 01339/741-345; E-mail: maria@hotel-braemar.co.uk; Website: www.hotel-braemar.co.uk. 7 Rooms. Rates: up to £30 single; £24-32 per person double. Callater Lodge is a lovely old Victorian home that has been renovated and provides a comfortable place to stay in the center of Braemar.

By Car
Traffic is generally heavy in Aberdeen, so I would advise finding a place to park your car and hop on the bus or see the city on foot.

By Foot
This is probably the best alternative for seeing the sights in Aberdeen. Traffic is bad, and parking is worse, so if you have a car, find a place to park it and walk around.

By Taxi
• **ABC Taxis**, *Tel. 01224/890-000*
• **Aberdeen Airport Taxis**, *Tel. 01224/725-728*
• **Cabbies**, *Tel. 01224/878-788*
• **Central Taxis**, *Tel. 01224/898-989*
• **Mairs Taxis**, *Tel. 01224/724-040*
• **Rainbow Taxis**, *Tel. 01224/878-787*

WHERE TO STAY

MARCLIFFE AT PITFODELS, *North Deeside Road, Aberdeen. Tel. 01224/861-000, Fax 01224/868-860; E-mail: reservations@marcliffe.com; Website: www.nettrak.co.uk/marcliffe. 42 Rooms. Rates: £105-155 single; £115-165 per room double. All major credit cards accepted.*

A host of world-renowned luminaries has stayed at the Marcliffe at Pitfodels, one of the nicest hotels in Scotland and also one of the best buys for the money. It is a grand hotel – a member of the *Small Luxury Hotels of the World*. And rightly so – it is truly a magnificent place to stay. Everything about the Marcliffe is first class, and a stay here will be one of your most pleasant memories.

Top-of-the-line furnishings, designer wallpaper and window coverings, and a vast array of antiques sprinkled liberally throughout the hotel assures you of a comfortable and delightful stay. And yet, the Marcliffe is anything but stuffy. It is a truly welcoming and warm reception you'll receive here. As you would expect, the bedrooms are all large and well-appointed. Top-quality furniture, bright colors and creature comforts like fluffy bathrobes, mini-bars, and fresh fruit are all standard offerings for those who stay here. The bathrooms are all ultra-modern and furnished nicely.

You'll take your breakfast in a cobblestoned, glass-enclosed Conservatory. Views onto an inviting patio (where you can also dine, weather-permitting) and the woods beyond enhance the delicious fare served in the Conservatory. For more formal dining, the Invery Restaurant also serves residents of the Marcliffe. This award-winning restaurant provides a marvelous atmosphere and delicious meals (see the *Where to Eat* section for both the Conservatory and the Invery Restaurant). The Marcliffe sits regally amid 20 acres of sculpted lawns, brilliant gardens and tremendous trees. You may choose to go for a walk among the verdant greenery, or perhaps you'll have a spot of tea on one of the many benches provided for your benefit. If your travels bring you to Aberdeen, then the Marcliffe should be at the top of your list of places to stay. I know it is at the top of mine.

Selected as one of my Best Places to Stay – see Chapter 12.

PALM COURT HOTEL, *81 Seafield Road, Aberdeen. Tel. 01224/310-351, Fax 01224/312-707, central reservations 01339/883-500. 24 Rooms. Rates: £40-50 single; £25-45 per person double. Rates include breakfast. MasterCard and Visa accepted*

Located in a quiet residential area just off the city center, the four-star Palm Court Hotel provides a pleasant place to stay in the busy city of Aberdeen. The hotel has been recently expanded and renovated from top to bottom and the results are marvelous. The bedrooms are all nice sized, and feature new furnishings, soft colors and floral accents. Each room has a telephone, tea- and coffee-making facilities and television. The Conservatory Restaurant at the hotel does a nice job for its guests, having earned a number of awards for their meals.

ATHOLL HOTEL, *54 King's Gate, Aberdeen. Tel. 01224/323-505, Fax 01224/321-555. 35 Rooms. Rates: £60-80 single, £30-45 per person double. Rates include breakfast. MasterCard and Visa accepted.*

This restored four-star Victorian mansion is in one of Aberdeen's tree-lined residential areas. Recently refurbished, Atholl House offers just the right balance of elegance and hominess. The granite exterior exudes grace and invites you to explore further. You can expect a warm welcome when you come to Atholl House. David Parkinson is the owner, and either he or his sociable staff will avail themselves of your every need. Each room has been individually decorated and furnished with exceptional furnishings. Each room is ensuite, and offers standard amenities such as telephone, television and tea- and coffee-making facilities.

THE COCKET HAT, *North Andrews Drive, Aberdeen. Tel. 01224/695-684, Fax 01224/692-438. 60 rooms. Rates: £39 per room single; £39 per room double; £39 per room up to 5 individuals. MasterCard and Visa accepted.*

B&B, guest house and small hotel owners across Scotland hope these Lodge Inns don't catch on. This is the second entry into the Scottish accommodations market by this immensely popular hotel chain that has nearly two dozen locations in England. The reason for their concern? Clean rooms, nice ensuite facilities, sleeping accommodations for up to five individuals, all for £39 per room. You can put up to five people in a room, as long as three are kids under 15 years of age (in other words, only two adults per room). True, you give up the personality and personal attention of a B&B or guest house, but it is good, safe and inexpensive lodging. All of the rooms are large, have a shower and bath and are clean and new with quality furnishings. While it is not for everyone, if you are traveling with your family around Scotland and are on a tight budget, this is a nice option.

ABERDEEN SCOTTISH YOUTH HOSTEL, *8 Queens Road, Aberdeen. Tel. 01224/646-988, centralized reservations: 0541/553-255. 23 Rooms. Rates: £10.75 (under age 18); £11.75 (over age 18). MasterCard and Visa accepted.*

Here is another low-cost alternative for travelers in Aberdeen. This youth hostel is like so many others in Scotland: it is in a nice neighborhood, clean, and offers affordable lodging if you don't mind sleeping in a room with a bunch of strangers. This particular hostel is an old renovated Georgian mansion in one of the (predominantly) business districts of Aberdeen. As is customary with these Georgian mansions, tall ceilings enhance the feeling of the rooms. There are 23 rooms here, offering anywhere from 2 to 16 beds. A self-catering kitchen is available for cooking your own meals, or for £2 you can have a continental breakfast. This hostel provides you with pretty nice accommodations close to downtown Aberdeen.

WHERE TO EAT

THE INVERY, *North Deeside Road, Aberdeen. Tel. 01224/861-000, Fax 01224/868-860. £25-45. Open daily from 8:00am to 10:00am, noon to 2:30pm, and 6:30pm to 10:00pm. All major credit cards accepted.*

The Invery is the immensely popular, award-winning formal dining room for the Marcliffe Hotel. Elegant but not at all intimidating, it provides a genteel dining adventure. Crystal and silver, china and candlelight help make this an intimate and memorable place to come. The restaurant has garnered significant praise for its culinary accomplishments, including two AA rosettes and high praise from *A Taste of Scotland*. The fare is traditional Scottish with French influences. The menu offers selections that range from shellfish to salmon, and from beef to venison and lamb. For a treat, try the salad of smoked haddock, salmon, crispy bacon and quail eggs, or the pan-fried venison filet with red currant and port sauce. Include a wine list of over 400 wines and a dessert menu that adds calories by just reading it, and you'll have a great dining extravaganza. Dress is suit and tie.

THE CONSERVATORY, *North Deeside Road, Aberdeen. Tel. 01224/861-000, Fax 01224/868-860. £8-12 for breakfast, £15-25 for lunch, £20-30 for dinner. Open daily from 8:00am to 10:00am, noon to 2:30pm, and 6:30pm to 10:00pm. All major credit cards accepted.*

The Conservatory is the informal dining room for the Marcliffe in Aberdeen. Pleasant sun-lit dining takes place in its glass-enclosed walls and on its cobble-stoned floor. It gives the feel (slightly) of an outdoor French café. If the weather cooperates, there is a small patio where you can take your meals. The Conservatory is open for breakfast, lunch and dinner, and you'll vie with locals for a seat during lunch and dinner. It is especially popular with business men and business women. The menu selections vary, but expect selections like traditional beef steak pie or roasted salmon steak. These and other dishes have earned numerous awards for the restaurant, including recognition by *A Taste of Scotland*. Dress is casual.

GERARD'S, *50 Chapel Street, Aberdeen. Tel. 01224/639-500, Fax 01224/ 630-688. £8-10 for lunch, £17-25 for dinner. Open Monday through Saturday from noon to 2:00pm and from 6:30pm to 9:30pm. MasterCard and Visa accepted.*

Gerard's has been serving tourists and Aberdonians alike since 1974, and once you come here, you will see why owner Gerard Flecher has stayed in business so long. He has combined bright and comfortable settings with outstanding food to delight his guests. You'll find plants and bright colors, intimate table settings and pleasant company here. You'll have a choice of a la carte or fixed-price menus that feature a good selection of meat, wild game and fish. Gerard has earned a reputation for his imaginative preparation of vegetarian dishes, so there is something for everyone. Prior to going to your table, stop in the Garden Room for a wee bit of pre-dinner refreshment, and enjoy the live fig tree and other plants. Dress is nice casual for Gerard's.

OWLIES BRASSERIE, *Littlejohn Street, Aberdeen. Tel. 01224/649-267, Fax 01224/590-342. £6-8 for lunch, £18-25 for dinner. Open Tuesday through Thursday from noon to 2:00pm and from 5:30pm to 11:00pm, Friday and Saturday from noon to 2:30pm and 5:30pm to 11:00pm. Closed Sunday and Monday. All major credit cards accepted.*

This avant-garde brasserie is just around the corner from Marischal College, and is in fact housed in what used to be the engineering building for the college. You'll ascend stairs from the street level and enter a tall-ceilinged, spacious room with light mustard walls, salmon-colored floors, plants everywhere and gadgets on the walls (large iron sprockets, chains and pulleys, flywheels, etc.) Light jazz music plays harmoniously in the background. The atmosphere is as light and bright as the surroundings, and the diners, especially on a weekend evening, are engaging. The menu is varied, from seafood to beef and everything in between. Try the traditional oak-smoked salmon – it's great. Vegetarian dishes are also available. The lunch menu is a little lighter, and features soups and salads.

While it's not your typical Scottish restaurant, I really like this place, and I think you will too. Dress is casual.

HOMESPREADS COCKET HAT RESTAURANT, *North Andrews Drive, Aberdeen. Tel. 01224/695-684, Fax 01224/692-438. £10-15. Open Monday through Saturday from 11:00am to 11:00pm, Sunday from 2:30pm to 11:00pm. MasterCard and Visa accepted.*

This is a light and casual family dining restaurant, serving everything from soups and salads to small inexpensive steaks. It's a relatively new restaurant, part of a chain that is extremely popular in England and is now trying the Scottish market. This is a fun place for children, very similar to those play places that some fast-food restaurants in the US have. The play place here is called "The Funky Forest," and it is decked out to look like a rain forest, with slides, jungle gyms, etc. The food is fine and the environment is clean. Dress is casual.

SEEING THE SIGHTS

Aberdeen Art Gallery, *Schoolhill, Tel. 01224/646-333; open Monday through Saturday from 10:00am to 5:00pm (Thursday until 8:00pm) and Sunday from 2:00pm to 5:00pm; admission is free.* The Aberdeen Art Gallery is an immensely popular gallery with locals as well as tourists. It offers a wide range of artists and artworks, from early 18th century to contemporary offerings. You'll be able to see works by such well-known artists as Monet, Pissarro and Bonnard, as well as works by lesser-known artists like Hogarth, Raeburn and Ramsay. There is also an interesting Decorative Arts Collection that features a nice assortment of jewelry, tapestries, ceramics and silver.

Aberdeen Maritime Museum, *Shiprow, Tel. 01224/585-788; open Monday through Saturday from 10:00am to 5:00pm; admission is free.* If you have a bit of salt air in your heart and spirit, then take a few minutes and stop in at the Aberdeen Maritime Museum. The museum is located in **Provost Ross's House**, one of the oldest houses in Aberdeen (1593), and the museum covers an intriguing side of Aberdeen's history: its development as a harbor town. Exhibits cover its beginnings as a harbor and continue from its days as a whaling capital up until today's extensive North Sea oil operations.

Throughout the museum you'll be greeted with many models that will vie for your attention. The most obvious is the large (27') model of an oil rig, but you'll also enjoy the finer work of models of all kinds of ships. There is also an interesting exhibit on shipwrecks that intrigued me. If all the wonderful things to see here aren't enough, the house overlooks the harbor and affords great views out the windows/

Provost Skene's House, *Flourmill Lane, Tel. 01224/641-086; open Monday through Saturday 10:00am to 5:00pm; admission free.* As you ap-

proach the towered-and-turreted stone house that once belonged to
Aberdeen mayor Sir George Skene, imagine what life must have been like
here when this home was built in 1545. If you have a hard time with that,
as luck would have it, you don't really have to use your imagination, since
the house has been furnished with period furnishing so that you can see
what life was like for a well-to-do Aberdonian in the 16th century.

Cruickshank Botanic Gardens, *St. Machar Drive, Tel. 01224/272-704;
open all year Monday through Friday from 9:30am to 4:30pm, and from May
through September they are also open on Saturday and Sunday from 2:00pm to
5:00pm; admission is free.* You'll find these lovely and peaceful gardens just
off St. Machar Drive. Walks wend their way through an impressive array
of plants, rock gardens and a wide assortment of shrubs and bushes.

St. Machar Cathedral, *Chanonry, Tel. 01224/485-988; open daily from
9:00am to 5:00pm; admission is free.* There has been a religious structure of
one type or another here since the end of the 6th century. Today, you'll
see the latest iteration of those structures in St. Machar Cathedral. Built
in the 15th and 16th centuries, the building is impressive in and of itself.
Once inside, however, you'll be doubly impressed. Most striking is the oak
ceiling that features the coats of arms for many of the leading families of
Scotland. Included are the shields from Pope Leo X, St. Margaret, the
Stewarts, and others.

Legend has it that the site for the original place of worship that graced
this spot was chosen after a difficult assignment was given. According to
legend, St. Columba sent St. Machar to find a site that was on a flat, grassy
promontory overlooking the sea and a river that flowed in the shape of
a bishop's crossier (shepherd's hook). St. Machar found it, and St.
Machar's Cathedral now graces that spot.

Satrosphere, *19 Justice Mill Lane, Tel. 01224/213-232; open daily
Monday through Saturday from 9:30am to 5:00pm and Sunday from 2:00pm to
5:00pm, closed on Tuesdays from November through March; admission is £4 for
adults, £3.50 for seniors and children.* The Satrosphere is billed as a place for
children, but I am here to tell you that it is a place that I found very
interesting and quite intriguing. This is a place where kids (and adults too)
can get some hands-on experience with many different exhibits. They can
pretend to be a TV newscaster, or whisper into a parabolic reflector that
amplifies their voice across the hallway. They can build a waterwheel or
look into ant farms and a cut-away cross-section of a beehive. This is
fascinating and educational for the whole family.

Aberdeen Esplanade, *Aberdeen Beach.* About a 10-minute walk from
the end of Union Street is the Aberdeen Esplanade and beach. This
esplanade runs the length of the two-mile beach, and is a local favorite:
lovers walk arm-in-arm, children gambol ahead of their sauntering
parents and poets muse on the singular beauty so close to the city.

EXCURSIONS & DAY TRIPS

Aberdeen is a good place to use as a base while exploring the Grampian Highlands. Within just an hour or so of Aberdeen, you can get to the **Malt Whisky Trail** and the **Castle Trail**. Or perhaps you'd like to spend a little time at the ruins of picturesque **Dunnottar Castle**. There is a lot of pretty country in this part of Scotland, so fasten your safety belt and head out to see what there is to see.

If you are a fan of the English royalty (or even if you're not), then you'd probably like to stop by **Balmoral Castle**, their home in the country. Just down the road is little Braemar, home of the **Braemar Highland Games** and **Braemar Castle**. You can visit these places as a day trip from Aberdeen, but I treat them as separate destinations later in this chapter.

THE CASTLE TRAIL

In the northeastern portion of the Grampian Highlands, you'll find the **Castle Trail**. This is a 150-mile circuitous route that takes in seven castles and medieval homes. Since much of the Grampian Highlands was ignored by English troops throughout the years, many (but not all) of the castles in this part of the country are still in good condition. Even though the Castle Trail wends through some lonely (and lovely!) backroads in this part of Scotland, the Trail itself is fairly well signposted, so you should have no problem finding each of these sites.

We'll start your tour of the Castle Trail about 15 miles northwest of Aberdeen. Take the A90 north out of Aberdeen. About 12 miles out of town, watch for signposts to Pitmedden and the A920. On the A920 just northwest of Pitmedden, follow the signposts and you'll find **Tolquhon Castle**, *near Pitmedden, Tel. 01651/851-286; open April through September Monday through Saturday from 9:30am to 6:00pm and Sunday from 2:00pm to 6:00pm, and October through March Saturday and Sunday from 9:30am to 4:00pm; admission is £1.50 for adults, £1 for seniors and children.* These lonely ruins speak of a time of elegance and finery. As you walk among the ruins, you can imagine what a grand castle this must have once been. Built in the 15th century by the Forbes family, the gatehouse façade is a fine example of medieval craftsmanship. A central tower was originally in place; that was followed by a large mansion that surrounded a grassy courtyard.

A mile or two up the B999 in the churchyard of tiny town of **Tarves**, you'll find the fine altar tomb of William Forbes, who built the mansion house at Tolquhon Castle.

From Tolquhon Castle, head four miles north (follow the Castle Trail signposts) to **Haddo House**, *Gordon, Tel. 01651/851-770; open May through September from 1:30pm to 4:45pm, and in October on Saturday and*

Sunday from 1:30pm to 4:45pm; admission is £4.50 for adults, £3.50 for seniors and children. Haddo House was designed in 1735 by William Adam for the second Earl of Aberdeen. On the outside the home looks a little like an old 1930s school to me (sorry, Mr. Adam!), but the interior is exquisitely elegant. Not all of the rooms in the house are open, but those that are open are furnished in fine style. A Gothic chapel was added in the late 1800s, and the stained-glass windows are impressive. Haddo House sits amid 180 acres of woods and parklands, lakes and streams. If you've a few minutes on your itinerary, stroll around and feel the serenity that abounds here. The house is now the venue for orchestral and dramatic performances, which are presented in the home's Victorian Hall.

From Haddo House, head over to Fyvie and **Fyvie Castle**, *Fyvie, Tel. 01651/891-266; open Easter through June and September daily from 1:30pm to 5:30pm, July through August daily from 11:00am to 5:30pm, October on Saturday and Sunday from 1:30pm to 5:30pm; last admission is 45 minutes before closing; admission is £4.50 for adults, £3.50 for seniors and children.* Fyvie Castle was begun in the 13th century, and traded hands numerous times. Each time, the new family felt compelled to add a bit to the castle, until you have the five towers that grace the tawny castle today. Each tower bears the name of each successive family: Seton, Meldrum, Preston, Gordon and Leith.

In 1889, Alexander Forbes-Leith, a local lad, became a very wealthy man in America. He used a portion of his earnings to purchase the castle and convert the interior to the Edwardian opulence you see today. Throughout the castle, you'll find extravagant and elegant furnishings, including medieval Flemish tapestries and a fine collection of oil paintings, including a dozen by Sir Henry Raeburn as well as many others. (Sir Raeburn is the one who painted the most famous portrait of Sir Walter Scott – you've seen it on postcards, most likely. It is a painting of him sitting, with a castle – The Hermitage – seen dimly in the distance.)

The castle features a wide staircase featuring the coats of arms of 22 families who have ties to the castle. Look very closely at that stairway, for it is where the ghost of Lillias Drummond-Seton, a former lady of the castle, has been seen. It seems that Lady Drummond, known as the *Green Lady*, died mysteriously in May 1601. Shortly after, her husband remarried. It is said that the broken-hearted first lady wanders the castle at night.

From Fyvie, press on toward Banff, where you'll find our next stop on the Castle Trail, **Duff House**, *Banff, Tel. 01261/818-181; open daily April through October from 11:00am to 5:00pm, November through March Thursday through Sunday from 10:00am to 5:00pm; admission is £3 for adults, £2 for seniors and children, and a family ticket is available for £7.* Duff House is a spectacular example of early Georgian architecture, and a favorite of architect William Adam. He designed the house for the Earl of Fife, and it was completed in 1730. In recent years, the house has undergone massive and expensive renovations to return it to its Georgian elegance, and the effects are marvelous. Today it serves as a satellite location for the **National Gallery of Scotland**. There is a breathtaking assortment of paintings here by a number of the 18th and 19th century's best painters, including works by Allen, El Greco (*St. Jerome in Penitence*), Ramsay (*Elizabeth*), Raeburn and Urquhart.

If you can drag yourself away from the splendor of Duff House, head southwest on the A97 toward Huntly and **Huntly Castle**, *Huntly, Tel. 01466/793-191; open April through September Monday through Saturday from 9:30am to 6:00pm and Sunday from 2:00pm to 6:00pm, October through March Monday through Wednesday and Saturday from 9:30am to 4:00pm, Thursday from 9:30am to noon, and Sunday from 2:00pm to 4:00pm; admission is £2.30 for adults, £1.80 for seniors, and £1 for children.* While Huntley Castle may not be an extensive ruin, it is nonetheless one you should stop by and see. Built in the mid-15th century, the castle sports a fine front doorway and heraldic coat of arms. The castle has a checkered history of pomp and promise, but in the end its owners came up short in a Scottish civil war, and the castle was sacked. It seems the Earl of Huntly had a son who was madly in love with Mary Queen of Scots (there were many who were). When he couldn't win her heart, the young earl-to-be and his father aligned against her. The result was the ruin of the family Gordon, the Earls of Huntly.

Notwithstanding the roofless nature of the ruin, you can still see some of the original plasterwork, now well over 400 years old. You can also see the castle's prison, a place that must have been uncomfortable for its occupants. Ancient graffiti still graces its walls.

Leith Hall is your next stop on the Castle Trail, *near Rhynie; open daily May through September from 1:30pm to 4:30pm, October on Saturday and Sunday from 1:30pm to 4:30pm; admission is £4 for adults, £3 for seniors and £2 for children.* Leith Hall sits regally in the midst of its nearly 300-acre estate. The estate is open for walks year around (from 9:30am to dusk), and there is much to see in the area. The house has been in the Leith or Leith-Hays family since 1650, and the rooms that are open to the public feature the military memorabilia of many members of the family.

Kildrummy Castle is the next stop on the Castle Trail. *10 miles southwest of Alford on the A97; Tel. 01975/571-331; open daily April through September from 9:30am to 6:30pm, October through November on Monday through Saturday from 9:30am to 4:30pm, Sunday from 2:00pm to 4:30pm; last admission 30 minutes before closing, closed December through April; admission is £1.80 for adults, £1.30 for seniors, and 75p for children.* Once a great and nearly impregnable fortress, Kildrummy Castle is now mostly ruins. Robert the Bruce's wife was from Kildrummy Castle, and when Robert came out in open rebellion against England, he sent his family here for safety. The English besieged the castle and would probably not have prevailed had it not been for one **Osbourne the Blacksmith**. Seems the traitorous Osbourne made a pact with the English to betray the family in exchange for gold. His treachery carried the day, and when it came time to pay him, the story goes that he was paid – by pouring the molten gold down his throat! Robert the Bruce's family and supporters didn't fare much better. His brother Nigel was executed on the spot, and the soldiers that supported him were hung, drawn and quartered. Bruce's wife and daughter were taken prisoner.

Today, you can tell what an extensive castle this must have been. There is very little left but the partial remains of four round towers, the hall, the chapel, a gatehouse and some sundry walls. The castle stood for another 400 years, when it was finally razed by government troops during the first Jacobite Rebellion in 1715.

Southwest of Kildrummy Castle you'll find **Corgarff Castle**, *near Cock Bridge, A939/A944, Tel. 01975/651-460; open January through March and December on Saturday from 9:30am to 4:30pm and Sunday from 2:00pm to 4:00pm, April through September Monday through Saturday from 9:30am to 6:00pm and Sunday from 2:00pm to 6:00pm, and October through November Monday through Wednesday and Saturday from 9:30am to 4:00pm, Thursday from 9:30am to 2:00pm, and Sunday from 2:00pm to 4:00pm (got all that?); admission is £2.30 for adults, £1.80 for seniors and £1.50 for children.* Corgarff Castle is built after the Braemar Castle style, and features a unique star-shaped fortress wall. It was built in 1537, and seemed to attract a lot of military attention through the years. Whether from feuding neighbors or the English military, it is frankly lucky to still be standing. One sad episode in the castle's history was the time a neighboring rival set fire to the castle, killing the wife, children and servants of the owner (26 in all). It is said that if you listen intently, their anguished screams can still be heard some moonlit nights.

After the Battle of Culloden, Hanoverian troops displaced the family and used the castle for a headquarters and barracks. Their job? To police the district and stop the smuggling of whisky (sort of like medieval *revenuers* seeking to stamp out white lightning). Today, there's not much to see, although the interior has been renovated to look like the army barracks it was for so many years.

On to the last castle on Castle Trail, **Castle Fraser**, *off the A944 between Dunecht and Kemnay, Tel. 01330/833-463; open Easter, May, June and September daily from 2:00pm to 5:30pm, July through August daily from 9:30am to 5:30pm, October Saturday and Sunday from 2:00pm to 4:30pm; admission is £2.30 for adults, £1.80 for seniors and £1.50 for children.* Castle Fraser is a fine example of a 16th-century tower house, and is in wonderful condition. Set in the midst of lovely grounds, the turreted, gabled and towered castle just looks like an ancient medieval castle should. The castle was begun in 1575 for the laird (landowner) of the area, Michael Fraser. The castle has been in the Fraser family ever since.

Inside you'll find a few rooms open that have been furnished with period furnishings, tapestries and more than a few portraits of the former owners of Castle Fraser. The seven-story tower (**Michael Tower**, named after the original owner) has a viewing platform that allows you to get a birds-eye view of the park-like grounds.

WHERE TO STAY

KILDRUMMY CASTLE HOTEL, *Kildrummy, near Alford. Tel. 01975/ 571-288, Fax 01975/571-345, US toll-free 800/462-2748. 16 Rooms. Rates: £80-85 single; £130-160 double. Rates include breakfast. Closed January 4 through January 31. All major credit cards accepted.*

Kildrummy Castle Hotel is a delicious old Scottish manor house set in the midst of spectacular gardens and overlooking the ruins of the original 13th-century Kildrummy Castle. This mansion was built during the 19th century, and has been renovated to echo the elegance and style that it once had. During the restoration, care was taken to maintain the splendid oak paneling, wall tapestries and wonderful hand-carved oak staircase.

My favorite rooms are the Library and Drawing Room. Each is furnished magnificently, and each has wonderful unobstructed views of the ruins of Kildrummy Castle. Each of the bedrooms has been individually decorated, and each features high-quality furnishings. The views from the rooms are fabulous, and whether you look out onto the well-manicured grounds, gardens or the ruins of Kildrummy Castle, all are great. Each room has a telephone, television and tea- and coffee-making facilities. Fifteen of the sixteen bedroom have ensuite facilities, and the remaining room has its own private bath, although it is in the hall. This is a nice place to stay, especially if you are in the midst of your Castle Trail tour.

THE MALT WHISKY TRAIL

Over half of the 90-plus whisky distilleries in Scotland are in the Grampian Highlands and seven of them are on the **Malt Whisky Trail**. To be honest, once you've seen one distillery, you've pretty much seen them all. After sampling them, I'd say my favorite tour is the one offered by Glenlivet, so that is the one I will feature here. But depending on where you're coming from, that may be the farthest for you to drive to, so you may wish to visit one of the closer ones. Regardless, I have included the main information: name, address, telephone number, opening and closing hours and admission prices for all of the distilleries on the Malt Whisky Trail.

Glenlivet Distillery, *Glenlivet, Tel. 01542/783-220, 01542/783-220; open mid-March through June, September and October Monday through Saturday from 10:00am to 4:00pm and Sunday from 2:30pm to 4:00pm, and daily in July through August from 10:00am to 6:00pm; admission is £2.50 for adults and seniors, children under 18 are free (admission charge includes a £2 coupon toward purchase of a 70-centiliter bottle of whisky in the distillery's gift shop); children under 8 are not allowed in the production areas.* Glenlivet Distillery receives between 75,000 and 80,000 visitors each year, and they have this tour stuff down pat. You won't see brown-robed, balding monks bending over oak casks – you'll experience very modern and scientific processes on the tour.

You'll be amazed at the information you'll learn during the tour. I was astounded to hear that the distillery uses 400 tons of barley – not annually, not monthly, but every seven to ten days! Multiply that times 90-ish distilleries operating in Scotland, and that's a lot of barley! That amount of barley produces approximately 5.9 million liters of whisky. You'll learn oak casks are still used to age the whisky, and you'll learn about "angel's breath" and the "angel's share," two terms that go hand-in-hand with Scotland, their whisky and their legends. I learned that whisky must be aged at least three years to qualify as whisky; Glenlivet ages their product 12 years, and most other distilleries age theirs for 10, 15, or 16 years. At the end of the tour, you'll be treated to a wee dram of Glenlivet whisky (of course). Fruit juice is available for children and non-imbibers.

In addition to the tour, there is a small but well-done exhibit on the history of whisky in Scotland in general and Glenlivet Distillery in particular. Afterwards, there is a small snack bar and gift shop for you to visit. This is really a very fascinating experience, one I would suggest that you try for yourself.

Speyside Cooperage, *Dufftown Road, Craigellachie, Tel. 01340/871-108, Fax 01340/881-437; open January to mid-December Monday through Friday from 9:30am to 4:30pm, and June through September on Monday through Friday from 9:30am to 4:30pm and Saturday from 9:30am to 4:00pm; admission is £2.95 for adults, £2.45 for seniors, and £1.75 for children.* The Speyside Cooperage is not a distillery, but they are indispensable to the distilleries in the area: they make and repair the large oaken casks that are so important to the whisky-making process. Each year they repair or manufacture over 100,000 casks! So stop by and see these artisans practice their craft that dates back to medieval times.

HITTING THE MALT WHISKY TRAIL

In addition to the other distilleries discussed above, here are some other options for you"

Glenfiddich Distillery, *Dufftown. Tel. 01340/820-373, Fax 01340/ 820-805. Open January to Easter and mid-October through mid-December Monday through Friday from 9:30am to 4:30pm, and Easter through mid-October Monday through Saturday from 9:30am to 4:30pm, and Sunday from noon to 4:30pm. Admission is free.*

Strathisla Distillery, *Keith. Tel. 01542/783-044, Fax 01542/783/ 039. Open mid-March through November Monday through Saturday from 9:30am to 4:00pm and Sunday from 12:30pm to 4:00pm; from February to mid-March Monday through Friday from 9:30am to 4:00pm. Admission is £4 for adults and seniors. Children under 18 are free. (Admission charge includes a £2 coupon toward purchase of a 70-centiliter bottle of whisky in the distillery's gift shop.) Children under 8 are not allowed in the production areas.*

Dallas Dhu Distillery, *Mannachie Road, Forres. Tel. 01309/676-548. Open April though September daily from 9:30am to 6:30pm, and October through March Monday through Friday from 9:30am to 4:30pm, Saturday from 9:30am to 12:30pm, and Sunday from 2:00pm to 4:30pm. Admission is £2.50 for adults, £1.90 for seniors and £1 for children.*

Glen Grant Distillery, *Rothes. Tel. 01542/783-318, Fax 01542/783-304. Open March through October Monday through Saturday from 10:00am to 4:00pm and Sunday from 11:30am to 4:00pm, and June through September daily from 10:00am to 5:00pm. Admission is £2.50 for adults and seniors. Children under 18 are free. (Admission charge includes a £2 coupon toward purchase of a 70-centiliter bottle of whisky in the distillery's gift shop.) Children under 8 are not allowed in the production areas.*

Cardhu Distillery, *Knockando. Tel. 01340/872-555, Fax 01340/872-556. Open March through June and October Monday through Friday from 9:30am to 4:30pm, July through September Monday through Saturday from 9:30am to 4:30pm and Sunday from 11:00am to 4:00pm, and December through February from 10:00am to 4:00pm. Admission is £2 for adults and seniors. Children under 18 are free. (Admission charge includes a coupon toward purchase of a 70-centiliter bottle of whisky in the distillery's gift shop.)*

Glenfarclas Distillery, *Ballindalloch. Tel. 01807/500-245, Fax 01807/ 500-234. Open April and May Monday through Friday from 9:30am to 5:00pm, June through September Monday through Friday from 9:30am to 5:00pm, Saturday from 10:00am to 4:00pm and Sunday from 12:30pm to 4:30pm, October through March Monday through Friday from 10:00am to 4:00pm. Admission is £3.50 for adults.*

WHERE TO STAY

MINMORE HOUSE HOTEL, *Glenlevit. Tel. 01807/590-378, Fax 01807/590-472. 10 Rooms. Rates: £50-65 single including breakfast, or £75-90 including breakfast, dinner and high tea; £50 per person sharing including breakfast, or £75 per person double including breakfast, dinner and high tea. MasterCard and Visa accepted.*

You'll find Minmore House Hotel in the shadow of Glenlevit Distillery. This exceptional four-star hotel was once the residence of George Smith, the founder of Glenlevit Distillery. It was built in the early 1800s and has been tastefully renovated by the current owners. There are a number of pleasant public rooms, including the Drawing Room, Dining Room and Guest Lounge. Each offers rich oak paneling, a fireplace and comfortable furniture for your relaxing pleasure. The Guest Lounge features a well-stocked bar that boasts nearly 100 single malt whiskies from which to choose. The Drawing Room is my favorite of the public rooms. It has large windows that allow you to look out onto the lovely grounds. High tea is served in the Drawing Room each afternoon.

Most of the bedrooms are large, although there are a few that are a bit on the small side. Each is nicely decorated and features comfortable quality furnishings. The rooms all have tall ceilings and are painted in bright colors. Each room has a phone, alarm clock and tea- and coffee-making facilities. There are no TVs in the rooms at Minmore House Hotel, so you'll be forced to enjoy the scenery outside the windows. Most of the rooms have lovely views – some overlook the marvelous terraced garden, and others look out across the scenic Scottish countryside. The Glenlevit Room has a four-poster bed artfully draped with lace and views of the rolling Scottish countryside and, of course, Glenlevit Distillery. Minmore House Hotel is open from April 1 through mid-October.

WHERE TO EAT

MINMORE HOUSE RESTAURANT, *Glenlivet. Tel. 01807/590-378, Fax 01807/590-472. £4-12 for lunch, £20-30 dinner. Open daily noon to 2:30pm and 7:30pm to 8:00pm. MasterCard and Visa accepted.*

This little restaurant in the Minmore House Hotel has really made an outstanding culinary reputation for itself. It has won a number of awards, and among others, can boast one from *A Taste of Scotland*. The dining room is simple – large windows look out onto the Speyside countryside. But you probably won't be doing a lot of looking – you'll probably be paying attention to the fine meal you'll get here.

The menu varies, and each evening only two main courses are offered – so be certain you like at least one of them when you make your reservations. My last meal there they offered a choice of seared filet of wild Scottish salmon with an avocado salsa and oriental sauce, and the other entrée was pan-fried mallard with stir-fried greens and a whisky, soy, honey and lemon sauce. Be sure and make reservations ahead of time if you hope to dine here. Dress is nice casual.

GLENLIVET CAFÉ, *Glenlivet Distillery, Glenlivet. Tel. 01542/783-220. £2-5. Open mid-March through June, September and October Monday through Saturday from 10:00am to 4:00pm and Sunday from 2:30pm to 4:00pm, and daily in July through August from 10:00am to 6:00pm.*

This is the café associated with the Glenlivet Distillery, and they offer surprisingly good café-style food. Grab a sandwich or bowl of soup for less than £2, or at the expensive end of the spectrum, order a shepherd's pie for £4.50. Nothing fancy here, just good filling food at very reasonable prices.

NEAR STONEHAVEN

Now that you've finished with the Malt Whisky and Castle Trails, let's get back to exploring the other sites to see in the Grampian Highlands. The first stop is along the coastline south of Aberdeen. Take the A90 south to Stonehaven, then take the A92 two miles further south. Watch for the signposts directing you to **Dunnottar Castle**, *two miles south of Stonehaven; open late March through October Monday through Saturday from 9:00am to 6:00pm, Sunday from 2:00pm to 5:00pm, November to late March Monday through Friday from 9:00am to dusk; admission is £2.50 for adults, £1.80 for seniors and £1 for children.* Dunnottar Castle is a remarkable example of a 14th-century castle. The castle ruins sit stoically on a three-sided cliff with sheer drops to the churning sea below. It has a similar feel to Dunluce Castle in Northern Ireland. Considered nearly impregnable due to its stunning position, it once withstood a Cromwellian siege for eight months before having to capitulate due to approaching starvation.

Once the most powerful and well-protected fortress in this part of Scotland, it drew its fair share of enemies who wished to subdue it. William Wallace and Oliver Cromwell were two of the more notable assailants. Today the ruins are a photo-op waiting to take place. Silent and moody on a cloudy day, their skeletal image stands stark against the backdrop of sea and clouds.

ROYAL DEESIDE

The River Dee flows from its headwaters in the Glen of Dee at the base of 4,295-foot Ben Macdui through a beautiful valley eastward until it empties into the North Sea at Aberdeen. That valley and the surrounding countryside is known as **Royal Deeside**, perhaps because the scenery along the way is so majestic, but probably because the queen's weekend home is at **Balmoral Castle**, between **Ballater** and **Braemar**. Along the way, there are a number of things to see and do, like stopping in at **Crathes** and **Craigievar castles** (see below).

BANCHORY

Banchory is a pleasant little berg about 15 miles west of Aberdeen on the A93. It is the center for seeing some beautiful scenery, as well as having two prominent castles to visit, Crathes Castle and Craigievar Castle.

Crathes Castle And Gardens, *two miles east of Banchory, Tel. 01330/ 844-525; open April through October daily from 11:00am to dusk, closed November to March; admission is £4 for adults, £2 for seniors and children.* Crathes Castle is an impressive block-style castle, obviously built for fortification as well as for living. Built in the 16th century, there are turrets, towers and windows on the upper stories, while the lower stories are plain and menacing.

In 1323, Robert the Bruce gave the lands Crathes Castle now occupies to Alexander Burnett, and as a symbol of that gift, presented Alexander with an ivory horn (like a powder horn). That horn is on display in the main hall of the castle. While Crathes Castle is impressive from the outside, you should see the inside. Several of the rooms have exquisitely painted ceilings, including the Chamber of the Muses and the Chamber of the Nine Nobles. Beware – you'll strain your neck trying to take it all in.

The castle has a local ghost that has appeared many times in the Green Lady's Room. I am told that when seen, she walks across the room with a small baby in her arms toward the fireplace, where she then disappears. The story is that she was the daughter of one of the lords of Crathes Castle and became pregnant out of wedlock. To hide the pregnancy, the maiden was killed. Workmen reportedly once found the skeletal remains of a young woman and a baby while working around the house. Eerie goings-on, indeed.

The castle also features wonderful gardens and walking paths through those gardens. The yew hedges there are said to be nearly three hundred years old. In 1951, Sir James Burnett, descendant of Alexander Burnett, gave the castle to the National Trust for Scotland, whose care it is now in.

Craigievar Castle, *A980, six miles south of Alford, Tel. 01339/883-635; open May through September daily from 1:30pm to 4:30pm. Closed October through April; admission is £5 for adults, £2.50 for seniors and children.* Craigievar Castle is about 14 miles north of Banchory on the A980, and is an excellent example of a 17th-century Scottish baronial mansion. It was originally built for William Forbes in 1626 and remained in the family until it was given to the National Trust for Scotland in the early 1960s.

Today the pink exterior is studded with turrets, arches and gables, and cuts quite the impressive figure. Inside, you'll be delighted with the period furnishings and the ornate plasterwork throughout the castle. Most impressive is the Great Hall, with its arched ceiling covered with ornate plasterwork and a large coat of arms above the fireplace also in plaster.

PRACTICAL INFORMATION FOR ABERDEEN

Tourist Information
• **Aberdeen Tourist Information Centre**, *St. Nicholas House, Broad Street, Aberdeen, Tel. 01224/632-727*

Laundry Service
• **A1 Launderette**, *555 George Street, Tel. 01224/621-211; Holburn Street, Aberdeen, Tel. 01224/573-003*
• **Culter Cleaning Co.**, *270 George Street, Tel. 01224/644-259; 11 Back Wynd, Tel. 01224/627-293; 161 Royal Deeside Road, Tel. 01224/734-217; 5 Rose Street, Tel. 01224/646-994; 158 King Street, Tel. 01224/627-389*

Post Offices
• **Bieldside Post Office**, *45 North Deeside Road, Aberdeen. Tel. 01223/867-139*
• **Berryden Post Office**, *Berryden Road, Aberdeen. Tel. 01224/649-588*
• **Bankhead Post Office**, *Bankhead Road, Aberdeen. Tel. 01224/712-627*

BALLATER & BALMORAL CASTLE

Ballater is a popular resort town 40 miles west of Aberdeen in the Dee Valley. The spectacular **Grampian Mountains** and nearby **Balmoral Castle** draw large numbers of folks to this area.

ARRIVALS & DEPARTURES

By Bus
Buses make the short trip to Ballater from Aberdeen several times a day, and arrive at the **Ballater Bus Station**.

By Car
Take the A93 west from Aberdeen and you can't miss Ballater.

WHERE TO STAY

STAKIS CRAIGENDARROCH, *Braemar Road, Ballater. Tel. 01339/ 755-858, Fax 01339/755-447; Website: www.stakis.co.uk/craigendarroch. 44 Rooms. Rates: £65 standard single, £90 club single, £140 suite; £65 per person standard double, £90 per person club double, £140 per person suite. Breakfast is included in the rate. All major credit cards accepted.*

This is one of the nicer Stakis properties in Scotland. It sits atop a hill at the western edge of Ballater on the Ballater-Braemar Road (A93). This four-star hotel works very hard (and succeeds!) at providing modern elegance – lots of oak and high-quality furnishings are prevalent throughout the facility.

Each bedroom is nice and large with top-quality furniture. Each room is smartly decorated, and you'll enjoy the nightly turn-down service with chocolates on your pillow. The suites are of course larger and more exquisitely decorated. Each suite features a complimentary decanter of sherry and fluffy bathrobes to make your stay that much more pleasant. This Stakis includes an impressive leisure center, and features an extensive array of quality leisure activities. You'll find a large swimming pool (and a smaller children's pool), steam room, spa, exercise room, squash courts, tennis courts, a game room and a snooker table. You'll even find a dry slope out back to practice your skiing technique!

There always seems to be a lot going on here. It would be a very comfortable base from which to explore the surrounding countryside, including nearby Balmoral Castle, Braemar and a score of castle ruins in the vicinity.

BALGONIE COUNTRY HOUSE, *Braemar Place, Ballater. Tel. 01339/ 755-482, Fax 01339/755-482. 9 Rooms. Rates: £70-90 single; £52-65 per person double. Breakfast is included in the rate. Closed from early January to mid-February. Amex, MasterCard and Visa accepted.*

Edwardian splendor and graceful service are what you'll find at Balgonie Country House. Set amid four acres of splendid gardens with views of the spectacular Scottish countryside, Balgonie Country House also has the added benefit of being just a few minutes' walk from downtown Ballater. Each of the bedrooms is individually decorated with pastels in a tasteful manner, and one that will put you immediately at ease. The best rooms are at the front of the house, as they overlook Ballater Golf Course and the beautiful Scottish countryside. Each room is equipped with a television and telephone.

Your breakfast will be a treat, and if you wish, you can stay for dinner. Balgonie Country House has earned recognition from *A Taste of Scotland*, as well as being the recipient of two AA rosettes. (See the *Where to Eat* section.) The hotel is a member of the prestigious *Scotland's Hotels of*

Distinction, and has won multiple awards throughout the years. If you stay here, I predict it will be one of your most pleasant lodging memories.

DARROCH LEARG, *Braemar Road, Ballater. Tel. 01339/755-443, Fax 01339/755-252. 18 Rooms. Rates: £40-60 single; £38-58 per person double. Breakfast is included in the rate. All major credit cards accepted.*

Prepare to be impressed. This Victorian mansion house was built in the late 1800s (1888 to be precise) and has been restored to its former Victorian elegance. Nestled snugly into the hillside and enjoying some of the finest views in Scotland, this small hotel will enchant and delight you. Two drawing rooms – one for smokers and one for non-smokers – are an especially nice touch.

Each of the bedrooms has been individually decorated using top-quality furnishings. They are large, pleasant rooms, some of which have outstanding views out across the Scottish countryside. Thirteen of the rooms are in the main house, and five others are in the separate Oakhall, a separate turreted mansion that will not disappoint you. Breakfast will be memorable, as Darroch Learg has won multiple awards for their meals here, including *A Taste of Scotland* and three AA rosettes. Breakfast (and dinner if you wish) is in the Conservatory, which has views that most restaurants would die to have (see the *Where to Eat* section).

AULD KIRK HOTEL, *Braemar Road, Ballater. Tel. 01339/755-762, Fax 01339/755-707; E-mail: auld-kirkhotel@compuserve.com. 7 Rooms. Rates: £30 single; £25 per person double. Breakfast is included in the rate. MasterCard and Visa accepted.*

If you've been sleeping in church for years and feeling guilty about that, here's your chance to do it with a clear conscience. On the western edge of Ballater on the road from Ballater to Braemar (the A93), you'll find the Auld Kirk Hotel (kirk is Scottish for church). You can't miss it – just look for the tall steeple. The church was built in the 19th century, and has since been converted into a nice guest house.

All the rooms are large with nice, comfortable furnishings. Each has its own upgraded bathroom, and each is individually decorated. The hotel sits right next to the road, but the double-glazed windows are very effective in keeping the noise out, so you shouldn't have to worry about that at all. A pretty impressive restaurant is also on-site. There are plenty of knick-knacks and bric-a-brac all throughout the hotel to look at, including a stained glass depiction of the "Burning Bush" that was originally part of the church. It has been moved to the main stairway for your viewing pleasure.

WHERE TO EAT

DARROCH LEARG, *Braemar Road, Ballater. Tel. 01339/755-443, Fax 01339/755-252. £21-30 for lunch, £30-45 for dinner. Open daily from noon to 2:30pm and 6:30pm to 9:00pm. All major credit cards accepted.*

With three AA rosettes, Darroch Learg Restaurant is in the upper echelon of dining establishments in Scotland, as there are only a handful of restaurants that have earned this honor. I'm sure the dining room had nothing to do with the level of their award (well, maybe just a little). Before you even sample any of their excellent cuisine, you'll be delighted with the wonderful verdant views that appear before your eyes. It really is a treat. Called "modern Scottish cuisine with an imaginative flair," you'll love it. The menu changes frequently, but you might encounter something like breast of Gressingham duck with homemade boudin, asparagus, truffle cream and plum chutney. Dress for Darroch Learg Restaurant is suit and tie.

THE OAKS RESTAURANT, *Braemar Road, Ballater. Tel. 01339/755-447. £30-45. Open daily from 6:30pm to 9:45pm. All major credit cards accepted.*

This is generally recognized as one of the best restaurants in this part of Scotland. The food is outstanding and the atmosphere is upscale and elegant. As you would expect, the predominant decorating motif is oak. Enhance that with Scottish crystal and china, and subdued lighting and you have set the stage for an excellent evening. The menu changes daily, but a typical offering might be breast of mallard duck with a celeriac rave on a bed of humus with smoked bacon and port wine jus, or a roulade of Scottish salmon on a squid pasta with cucumbers, olives, cherry tomato coulis, saffron potatoes and asparagus spears. Dress for The Oaks is suit and tie.

BALGONIE COUNTRY HOUSE RESTAURANT, *Braemar Place, Ballater. Tel. 01339/755-482, Fax 01339/755-482. £10-20 for lunch, £20-30 for dinner. Closed from early January to mid-February. Amex, MasterCard and Visa accepted.*

Balgonie Country House is a wonderful place to stay, and whether you stay here or not, their restaurant is a wonderful place to eat. Winners of numerous industry awards for their cooking (*A Taste of Scotland* and two AA rosettes, to name two), the restaurant is truly one of the top places to eat in this part of the country.

Their cooking has been referred to as inventive and innovative, and that combination does wonders for the traditional Scottish fare you'll find here. Try the Aberdeen angus beef flambéed in cognac and finished with black peppercorn sauce, it's delicious. Vegetarians are welcome, although you need to let them know when you make reservations that you will be ordering a vegetarian meal. One of the secrets to their success is the insistence on only the freshest ingredients, either from their own garden or from the farms and gardens around the area.

SEEING THE SIGHTS

Balmoral Castle, *between Braemar and Ballater on the A93, Tel. 01339/ 741-219; open mid-April through July daily from 10:00am to 5:00pm (except Sundays in April). Last recommended entry at 4:00pm; admission is £4 for adults, £3 for seniors and £1 for children.* Sometimes it's hard to imagine how the "other half" lives. As you approach Balmoral Castle, your imagination will run rampant and you will get excited about seeing the inside of this fabulous castle to really see how that other half lives. Unfortunately, your imagine won't get any help...only the Grand Ballroom at the castle is open to the public, and that is pretty sterile, with a few sparse exhibits.

In 1855, Prince Albert expanded the castle from a previous building for his sweetheart, Queen Victoria. The castle serves as the Queen's home-away-from-home, and with the pressures of public life, you can see how this would be a favorite of getaway for the royal family. Since you cannot experience the castle, it's a good thing that much of the estate is available for walks, and there are a few souvenir shops, along with pony trekking available.

SPORTS & RECREATION

Cycling
• **Making Treks**, *Tullich Road, Ballater. Tel. 01339/755-865*
• **Wheels and Reels**, *Braemar Road, Ballater. Tel. 01339/755-864*

Hang Gliding
• **Fishnaller's Hang Gliding**, *Cairnwell, Glenshee. Tel. 01338/741-331*

Hillwalking
There are a number of fine Highland walks that originate from the **Balmoral Rangers Visitors' Centre**, *Ballater, Tel. 01339/755-059.* They have maps, directions and suggestions available here.

Horseback Riding
• **Balmoral Pony Trekking**, *Balmoral Castle Estates, Ballater. Tel. 01339/ 742-334*
• **Glen Tanar Equestrian Centre**, *Aboyne. Tel. 01339/886-448*

PRACTICAL INFORMATION

Tourist Information
• **Ballater Tourist Information Centre**, *Station Square, Ballater. Tel. 01339/ 755-306*

BRAEMAR

Braemar is most famous for hosting the granddaddy of all Highland Games, the **Braemar Highland Games**. They are the culmination of all Highland Games in the country. But Braemar has a few other things to offer visitors during other times of the year, including scenic walks, **Braemar Castle**, and a little slower pace than you find elsewhere.

ARRIVALS & DEPARTURES

By Bus

Buses run several times a day from Aberdeen to Braemar.

By Car

Take the A93 west from Aberdeen through Banchory and Ballater.

WHERE TO STAY

INVERCAULD ARMS HOTEL, *Ballater Road, Braemar. Tel. 01339/ 741-605, Fax 01339/741-428. 68 Rooms. Rates: £55-109 single; £55-109 double. All major credit cards accepted.*

The Invercauld Arms Hotel is a member of the *Thistle Country House Hotel Group*. It was built in 1645 and has been expanded to its current size and state through the intervening years. In 1870, it became a roadside inn, and has served travelers in this part of Scotland ever since. As you'd expect in a hotel this old, there is a lot of rich dark oak used in the public areas. Most of the bedrooms are large and quite comfortably furnished. Keeping with the tradition of the times, most of the rooms have those wonderful tall ceilings that make every room seem so large and spacious.

The artwork on the walls throughout the hotel is very complementary, as it showcases personalities, castles and scenes depicting Scottish history. The hallways are nice and wide and decorated with cream and beige wallpaper, thus avoiding the dank darkness of so many hotels of this vintage. Non-smoking rooms are available upon request.

CALLATER LODGE HOTEL, *9 Glenshee Road, Braemar. Tel. 01339/ 741-275, Fax 01339/741-345; E-mail: maria@hotel-braemar.co.uk; Website: www.hotel-braemar.co.uk. 7 Rooms. Rates: up to £30 single; £24-32 per person double. Rates include breakfast and all taxes. MasterCard and Visa accepted.*

Callater Lodge is a lovely old Victorian home that has been renovated and provides a comfortable place to stay in the center of Braemar. Callater Lodge was built in 1861 as a hunting lodge. It rests on a little over and acre, and the area wildlife think they are the owners here, so you may be fortunate to encounter deer, rabbits, red squirrels and/or ducks as you explore the grounds. Michael and Maria Franklin work hard to make sure that you have a pleasant and enjoyable stay while you're here. Michael is a wealth of knowledge about things to see and do in the area, including hillwalks, lovely drives and castles to see.

The bedrooms are all very comfortable, and include electric blankets to help chase the chill away if you've encountered a damp Scottish day. The guest lounge is a pleasant room to relax or chat with other guests, or to just sit and enjoy the fireplace. If you have been hillwalking and return with damp clothing (a definite possibility), the Franklins have thoughtfully provided a drying room for your clothing. Maria is the chef, and guests at Callater Lodge enjoy the fruits of her labors. She insists on only the freshest of local produce to prepare a full Scottish breakfast in the mornings, or a fine meal in the evenings (by prior arrangement please). The menu changes daily, but she is quite adept at her craft and you'll be delighted with whatever she serves up. The hotel has a liquor license, so you'll be able to enjoy a wee dram (or two) of malt whisky or a glass of wine should you so desire.

Be sure and check out Callater Lodge's website (see above). It is quite good, and includes information on things to do in Braemar and Royal Deeside. There are two self-catering cottages on the premises if your plans call for you to stay in Braemar for more than a few days – see below.

CALLATER LODGE SELF-CATERING COTTAGES, *9 Glenshee Road, Braemar, Aberdeenshire. Tel.01339/741-275, Fax 01339/741-345; E-mail: maria@hotel-braemar.co.uk; Website: www.hotel-braemar.co.uk. 2 facilities. Rates: £270/week for the Chalet, and £320/week for the Cottage. (Reductions are available during the off-season.) MasterCard and Visa accepted.*

At the back of the Callater Lodge property are two self-catering facilities, the Cottage and the Chalet. If you find that you'll be here for more than a few days, either of these would make an excellent base from which to explore the surrounding area.

The Cottage is a renovated coachman's house, and provides accommodations for up to four people. Two nice-sized bedrooms, a full kitchen, and a wood-paneled, traditional living room with a fireplace provide comfortable surroundings. The Chalet is a newer building that is designed for two people. Twin beds in the bedroom can be connected to make a double bed, or they can be kept separate, depending on your needs (such is the case in the cottage as well). There is a full kitchen complete with microwave oven, refrigerator and dishwasher to help meet all your culinary needs. The Chalet features knotty-pine paneling and quality furnishings throughout. Large patio doors allow you to sit in the living room and watch an occasional deer gambol on the lawn, or you can just study the lovely Scottish countryside through them. If you are here on a biking holiday, your bicycles (and motorcycle, for that matter) can be stored in the garage.

WHERE TO EAT

BRAEMAR LODGE RESTAURANT, *Glenshee Road, Braemar. Tel. 01339/741-627. £15-18. Open daily from 5:00pm to 9:30pm. MasterCard and Visa accepted.*

This is the best restaurant in Braemar, and also serves as the restaurant for the Braemar Lodge. The dining room is housed in two renovated rooms of an old Victorian mansion. The plasterwork has been retained, and the atmosphere is quite pleasant. It is advisable to get reservations if you wish to eat here. There are often an equal number of tourists and locals vying for the few available tables. The reason? Great food at great prices. Try the baked Orkney salmon with herb crust and lemon grass butter, or the chicken filet with a creamy tarragon sauce. For dessert, try the butterscotch tart with raspberry sauce. Dress is casual.

INVERCAULD ARMS COCKTAIL LOUNGE, *Ballater Road, Ballater. Tel. 01339/741-605, Fax 01339/741-428. £8-10. Open daily from noon to 2:30pm and from 6:30pm to 9:30pm. MasterCard and Visa accepted.*

The Cocktail Lounge for the Invercauld Arms Hotel serves the best pub grub in town. Located at the Ballater end of town (the east side), the smallish bar serves a menu that provides not only burgers but such delicacies as chicken paprika and ham Balti. This isn't much more than a pub atmosphere, but you can get pretty good, filling food here. Dress is casual.

SEEING THE SIGHTS

Braemar Castle, *Ballater Road, Braemar, Tel. 01339/741-219, 01339/741-224; open from Easter through October, Saturday through Thursday from 10:00am to 6:00pm; admission is £2.50 for adults, £2 for seniors and £1 for children.* Braemar is the historic seat of the powerful Farquharson clan, and at the outskirts of Braemar you'll find their ancestral home, Braemar Castle. If you'll take a few minutes to stop by, I think you'll be pleasantly surprised at all this compact castle has to offer.

The castle was built in 1628, and many of the furnishings in the castle date from the intervening years. A number of the rooms have been renovated to look as they did at various periods throughout history. The dining room is particularly impressive, as it features a number of very impressive artifacts from days gone by. The grandfather clock, for example, is over 200 years old (1794), and the two globes are also over 200 years old. The Farquharson clan has held Braemar Castle for the past 300 years. But just before taking it, one Colonel John Farquharson attacked it and burned it. The Black Colonel, as he came to be called, does penance for his misdeed by haunting the castle. You'll note his presence by the smell of smoke, kind of a cross between cigar and a pipe. (There is no smoking in the castle, except for Colonel John.) This is a very real and pungent smell that is in the castle at times, and at times it is not. I have smelled it, and it is quite distinctive.

Note the spiral staircase – it is said to be one of only two in the country that circles counter-clockwise. Some say it was built that way because most of the Farquharson's were left-handed.

Linn of Dee, *west of Braemar*. Watch for a small blue sign in the center of town directing you to the Linn of Dee, then head that way. About six miles down the road you'll come to the Linn of Dee (*Linn* is the Scottish word for ravine or gorge). Cross the bridge, go about 100 yards further along then park on the left and walk back to the stream. This will be a great *Kodak moment,* as the photos of the stream and old stone bridge will be some of your favorites from your trip. Tumbling waters, tranquil pools and green foliage all combine to make this a memorable and serene setting.

Linn of Quioch, *west of Braemar*. After you've visited the Linn of Dee, continue driving on the road you just came on for another three miles or so. It narrows and becomes a single-track road; just follow it until it ends. Park your car and walk about 500 yards along the trail that runs parallel to the stream, enjoying the beauty of the Linn of Quioch. Shortly after you come to a footbridge that spans the stream, you'll see a large rock with a hole in it called the **Devil's Punchbowl**. During days of yore, there was a bottom to this rock. Legend has it that during the 1745 Jacobite Uprising, a clan chieftain brought his army to this rock, poured a drink into the hollow of the rock (what do you want to bet it was whisky!?), and bade his entire army to drink from it. The walk to the Devil's Punchbowl is slightly uphill and not very arduous.

Braemar Highland Games, *Princess Royal and Duke of Fife Memorial Park, Braemar; admission prices are £5 and £8 for general admission seats, and £20 for covered stand seating*. These are Braemar's own Highland Games, and they are considered the culminating games in Scotland. Held the first Saturday of September (make your reservations early), the games include Highland dancing, bagpipe competition, caber toss, putting the stone, hammer toss, sprinting, long jump, tug-of-war and relay races. Winners of the various events from all the Highland Games around Scotland are invited to come to Braemar and compete against the "local lads" for all the marbles. For advanced ticket sales, send a stamped, self-addressed envelope to **Braemar Games Booking Secretary**, *Collaoriech, Ballater, Scotland*. For covered stand tickets, you should probably order by December of the previous year.

DUFFTOWN

You'll find Dufftown between Glenlivet and the Castle Trail – specifically Huntley Castle. Mostly, this small crossroads town is a fun place to stop and peruse the shops. Whisky shops, old bookstores, tartan shops and several restaurants await your visit. All roads converge on the town's Clocktower, which houses the town tourist information center.

ARRIVALS & DEPARTURES

By Bus

Buses arrive at the **Dufftown Town Square** from Aberdeen several times a day.

By Car

Dufftown is located 60 miles west of Aberdeen. Take the A96 northwest from Aberdeen and just beyond Huntley take the A920 due west into Dufftown. It is about the same distance from Inverness. From Inverness, take the A96 east to Elgin, then the A941 southeast to Dufftown.

ORIENTATION

Four main roads converge on Dufftown, and all meet at the town's clocktower-dominated **Town Square**.

WHERE TO EAT

A TASTE OF SPEYSIDE, *10 Balvenie Street, Dufftown. Tel. 01340/820-860. £2-7 for lunch, £12-15 for dinner. Open daily from March through October from 11:00am to 4:30pm and from 6:00pm until 9:00pm. Closed November through February.*

This agreeable little restaurant has been serving Dufftown residents and tourists for more than a decade, and they seem to be pretty good at what they do – good enough to gain recognition from *A Taste of Scotland*. The tartan carpet assures you that you are in Scotland (it's the William Wallace/Mel Gibson tartan).

The dining room is simple and uncomplicated, but the food is wonderful. In addition to their Taste of Scotland Award, this small café boasts one AA rosette. The reason for their success is their insistence on only the freshest ingredients from the surrounding countryside. The lunch menu is mostly soups, sandwiches and salads, but each evening you'll find such delicacies as haddock baked in a cream and cheese sauce, or a large smoked salmon with salad. Raymond MacLean is the chef, and he and his partner Peter Thompson are rightfully proud of their pleasant restaurant.

SEEING THE SIGHTS

Dufftown proclaims itself **The Malt Whisky Capital of the World**, and there is more to their title than mere boasting. Little Dufftown exports whisky in a big way – more than any other town in the United Kingdom.

The Whisky Shop, *1 Fife Street, Tel. 01340/821-097, Website: whiskyshop@dufftown.co.uk; open 10:00am to 5:00pm Monday through Saturday.* Peter Crews is your host and whisky is his game. This mildly eccentric and delightful man can provide you a great experience in his whisky shop. Peter has over 300 varieties of whiskies to choose from, including some very old and expensive whiskies. What's more important is that Peter is willing to let you have a wee sample of any of the whiskies he has in his store. Lest you think Peter is uni-dimensional, his store features a wide variety of other liquors, including Scottish fruit wines, vintage port, beers and ales.

If you happen to be in Dufftown at 7:00pm on Wednesday evenings during July or August, you might enjoy attending a meeting of the *Taste and Talk* group. This is a get-together where a variety of topics relating to the whisky industry are discussed, and visitors are welcome. The Whisky Shop is located at the confluence of the main roads that hit town, in the shadow of the town clocktower.

You can also visit Dufftown's very own distillery: **Glenfiddich Distillery**, *Tel. 01340/820-373.* For more information, see above under The Malt Whisky Trail excursion under Aberdeen.

Dufftown Bookshop, *5 Balvenie Street, Tel. 01340/820-027; open 8:00am to 5:00pm Monday through Saturday.* Okay, this is a tough one for me to put in the book, since it is my favorite bookshop in Scotland and I don't want to spoil it. However, it's so delightful that I just can't leave it out. You'll find everything here from old paperbacks to old leather-bound volumes from the 1700s and 1800s. Just downhill from the clock tower, this small bookstore has a nice collection of old (very old) books, but doesn't charge big-city prices.

PRACTICAL INFORMATION

Tourist Information
• **Tourist Information Centre**, *Clock Tower, Dufftown. Tel. 01340/820-501.*

ELGIN

If you're in this neck of the woods, Elgin is worth a stop just to see the **Elgin Cathedral**, or more specifically, the ruins of Elgin Cathedral. The town itself has a buoyant feeling that is contagious.

ARRIVALS & DEPARTURES

By Bus

Buses arrive at the **Elgin Bus Station**, *Alexandra Road*, from Scotland's major cities throughout the day.

By Car

Elgin is located 40 miles east of Inverness on the A96. To get here from Aberdeen, which is 65 miles southeast of Elgin, take the A96 northwest from Aberdeen for the direct route. A longer, more circuitous route follows the coast north out of Aberdeen on the A90, then east on the B9031/A98/A96.

By Train

Trains arrive from Aberdeen and Inverness at the **Elgin Train Station**, *Station Road*, several times each day.

ORIENTATION

Elgin is centered around a medieval cobblestoned town square, and along the pretty **River Lossie**.

SEEING THE SIGHTS

Elgin Cathedral, *King Street, Tel. 01343/547-171; open April through September Monday through Saturday from 9:30am to 6:00pm, and Sunday from 2:00pm to 6:00pm, and October through March Monday through Thursday from 9:30am to 4:00pm, and Sunday from 2:00pm to 4:00pm; admission is £1.50 for adults and £1 for seniors and children.* This is one of the loveliest sets of ruins in Scotland. Elgin Cathedral was built in the early 13th century, and withstood (more or less – mostly less) the ravages of war, pride and the Reformation. In its heyday, Elgin rivaled St. Andrews as the religious capital of Scotland. It caught fire in the late 13th century, was rebuilt only to be razed in 1390 by the Wolf of Badenoch, the Earl of Buchan. It seems the Wolf took offense at being excommunicated for leaving his wife, and burned Elgin Cathedral and the town to the ground. It was rebuilt once again, but the ravages of time, wind and weather once again humbled it. In 1711, the main bell tower collapsed, taking the majority of the roof and parts of the walls with it.

Today the cathedral's serene grounds, tranquil setting and ruined condition all combine to make a great place to visit and an even better place to capture a few memories through your camera lens.

PERTH

Pretty **Perth** sits along the meandering banks of the River Tay. Formerly the *capital* of Scotland, it now plays an important role with the *capital* of Scotland – it has evolved into an important Scottish financial center. Perth is the fourth largest city in Scotland, and it is a busy, bustling city.

In years gone by, Perth took center stage in both the religious as well as political wars that raged across Scotland. Many have cited a fiery sermon delivered by Reformer **John Knox** in Perth as the catalyst that began the Reformation. Preaching in St. John's Kirk in Perth in 1559, Knox so inflamed his followers against Catholicism that they stormed out of the church and razed four nearby monasteries. And in 1437, King James I was slain in a Perth monastery by a traitor.

ARRIVALS & DEPARTURES

By Bus

Buses arrive at the **Perth Bus Station**, *Leonard Street,* from Scotland's major cities throughout the day.

By Car

Perth is located 45 miles north of Edinburgh on the A90/M90 and 85 miles south of Aberdeen on the A90.

By Train

Trains arrive from Edinburgh, Glasgow and Aberdeen at the **Perth Train Station**, *Kings Place.*

ORIENTATION

Perth straddles the **River Tay** as it wends its way through town, although most of the sights to see are on the west side of town.

WHERE TO STAY

PARK LANE GUEST HOUSE, *17 Marshall Place, Perth. Tel. 01738/ 637-218, Fax 01738/643-519; E-mail: parkland@sol.co.uk; Website: www.sol.co.uk/p/parklane. 6 Rooms. Rates: £24-30 single; £24-30 per person double. Rates include breakfast. MasterCard and Visa accepted.*

Built in 1807, this old Georgian home has been lovingly and carefully renovated and the results are marvelous. And as great as the facility is, your host, Michael Davison, is even better. You'll be delighted with his attentiveness and his wry sense of humor. Park Lane is located across the street from a park, convenient to the center of the city and all the things to do there. The public rooms are quite memorable, with their tall ceilings and fine plasterwork. Antique furnishings complement these wonderful rooms. The dining room is particularly memorable, presided over as it is by a striking marble fireplace. Each bedroom is individually and tastefully decorated with quality furnishings. There are six rooms, including one single, two doubles, two with twin beds, and one family room. Each has a television, hairdryer and tea- and coffee-making facilities.

TOPHEAD B&B, *Stanley, Perth. Tel. 01738/828-259. 3 Rooms. Rates: £22 single; £18-22 per person double. Rates include breakfast. Credit cards not accepted.*

Located about five miles north of Perth, this old stone farmhouse is part of a working farm. Mrs. Dorothy Dow is your hostess, and she is rightfully proud of her four-star B&B, which is a member of the prestigious *Scotland's Best B&Bs* organization. Each of the bedrooms is large and most comfortably furnished with king-size beds. One of the rooms is ensuite, one has a private bath in the hallway, and one shares a bath. Be sure and specify your preference when you call. Mrs. Dow asks that her guests not smoke while at Tophead B&B.

PARKLAND'S HOTEL, *2 St. Leonards Bank, Perth. Tel. 01738/622-451, Fax 01738/622-046. 14 Rooms. Rates: £55-60 single; £40-60 per person double. Rates include breakfast. All major credit cards accepted.*

If you want to stay in a lovely Georgian townhouse when you come to Perth, then look no further. The grounds are lovely and feature serene views of nearby Inch Park, one of Perth's prettiest parks. When Allen Deeson opened Parkland's in the early 1990s, he was striving for a country house feeling in the city, and he has accomplished his goal. You'll find each room inviting and comfortable, with rich wood paneling and top-quality furnishings. Each room is large, bordering on spacious, and offers telephone, television, hair dryers and tea- and coffee-making facilities. Dining here is is a treat you won't want to miss, and the restaurant here is one of the most notable in Perth. The breakfast alone is worth the stay - the quality is exceptional, and the selections are fabulous (see the *Where to Eat* section).

HUNTING TOWER HOTEL, *Crieff Road, Perth. Tel. 01738/583-771, Fax 01738/583-777. 27 Rooms. Rates: £75-85 single; £100-130 per room double. Rates include breakfast. All major credit cards accepted.*

It may take a few extra minutes to get to Hunting Tower Hotel (it is about 10 minutes from the city center), but once you arrive you'll be glad you made the short jaunt. This most impressive Victorian mansion sits regally amid acres of stunning gardens and greenery, and offers a pleasant place to relax after a hard day's sightseeing.

Most of the rooms are quite large, although some are a bit on the small side. There are 15 rooms in the main house and three suites adjacent to the property in a small cottage. In addition, there are nine lodge suites located in cabins on the grounds. The rooms in the main house and the cottage are all decorated smartly and with an eye for comfort. The lodge suites have more of a Scandanavian feel, and are exceptionally comfortable. The rooms in the cabins have a small efficiency kitchen, and all the rooms (in the main house, the cottages, and the cabins) feature telephone, television, hair dryer, radio and tea- and coffee-making facilities. Like the Parkland's Hotel, the Hunting Tower hotel boasts a fine restaurant which serves breakfast, lunch and dinner to its guests as well as the public (see the *Where to Eat section*).

WHERE TO EAT

PARKLAND'S RESTAURANT, *2 St. Leonards Bank, Perth. Tel. 01738/ 622-451, Fax 01738/622-046. £14-16 for lunch, £20-26 for dinner. Open 7:00am to 9:00am for breakfast, noon to 2:15pm for lunch, and 7:00pm to 9:30pm for dinner. All major credit cards accepted.*

The Parkland's Restaurant is the main dining room for the hotel of the same name, and it carries the casual elegance you find in the hotel into the dining room. Renowned as one of Perth's finest restaurants, Parkland's provides a meal fit for a king. You'll find marvelous Scottish fare here, including a host of seafood, beef and vegetarian dishes. Try the filet of sole lightly steamed and mashed with mushroom and parsley cream. If you'd like a little more traditional offering, try the roast sirloin of Scottish beef with a rich red wine and shallot essence. The meals are exquisite, the atmosphere perfect and the experience delightful.

HUNTING TOWER RESTAURANT, *Crieff Road, Perth. Tel. 01738/ 583-771, Fax 01738/583-777. £15-22. Open daily from 7:00pm to 9:30pm. All major credit cards accepted.*

The restaurant for the Hunting Tower Hotel is a wonderful, elegant place to stop and savor a bit of Scottish fare. If you are looking for continental cuisine, that is also available here. You'll find a nice selection of seafood, beef and vegetarian dishes, and each will be cooked with delectable precision and presented in a marvelous manner. There are a number of pricing options, including table d'hote (set menu) menu selections for two-, three-, or four-course meals.

SEEING THE SIGHTS

St. John's Kirk, *St. John Street, Tel. 01738/638-353; open daily 10:00am to noon and 2:00pm to 4:00pm; admission is free.* St. John's is famed as the place where the glowing embers of the Reformation were fanned into a full-fledged fire. On May 11, 1559, irritable Reformer **John Knox** preached a fiery sermon against Catholicism that so infuriated his adherents that they stormed from the church and laid waste to four nearby monasteries.

There has been a place of worship on the spot where St. John's now stands from the earliest history of Scotland, perhaps as early as 300 AD. A church was founded here by David I in 1126, and the structure you see today was built in the 15th century. Look for the tombstone of **King James I** of Scotland, who was murdered nearby by Sir Robert Graham (see sidebar below).

THE MURDER OF A KING

*In May 1424, **James I** was crowned King of Scotland at the age of thirty. James was the second great-grandson of Walter Stewart, the first of the Stewart kings of Scotland. The Scots found in him a man worthy of the Kingdom. Strong and handsome, fiery tempered, high-spirited and energetic, James immediately set out to establish law and order in Scotland. But doing so required an iron fist in a velvet glove. He had both.*

*He began by rounding up dissident nobles and imprisoning or executing them (although far more were imprisoned than executed). But James' reign came to an abrupt and ignominious end in 1437 when the grandson of one of the nobles that he had slain 10 years earlier betrayed him. After a short chase, James was found hiding in the closet of a monastery and stabbed to death. His attackers claimed they had removed a tyrant from the throne, but public sentiment was against them. The people vilified **Sir Robert Graham**, the leader of the attack, and his deeds were proclaimed in the ditty, "Sir Robert Graham that slew our king, God give him shame."*

The Fair Maid's House, *North Port Street, not open to the public*. If you are an aficionado of Sir Walter Scott's romantic novel *The Fair Maid of Perth*, then you'll at least want to stop by and see the outside of this house. In Scott's novel, this was the home to which hopeful suitors came, vying for the hand of the Fair Maid of Perth, Catherine Glover.

Perth Art Gallery and Museum, *George Street, Tel. 01738/632-488; open Monday through Saturday from 10:00am to 5:00pm; admission is free*. This small gallery and museum has a number of exhibits on the history of Perth through the years. Exhibits focus on archaeology and natural history, with a particular look at the development of the whisky industry in Scotland.

Balhousie Castle, *Hay Street, Tel. 01738/441-944; open May through September Monday through Saturday from 10:00am to 4:30pm, October through April Monday through Friday from 10:00am to 4:30pm; admission is free*. At the north edge of town across from North Inch Park you'll find Balhousie Castle, a restored 15th-century castle. This castle has been restored in the

Scottish baronial style. The most impressive thing about the castle is that it is home to the **Museum of the Black Watch**, sort of a memorial to a historic 18th-century regiment, recognized by the color of their tartans. Exhibits include articles of clothing (tartan, of course), weaponry and miscellaneous items associated with the regiment.

Scone Palace, *A93 north of Perth, Tel. 01738/552-308; open Easter through October from 9:30am to 5:00pm; admission is £5 for adults, £3.50 for seniors and children.* If you'd like to take a quick peek at the way "the other half" lives, stop by Scone Palace for an hour or so. Scone palace has been in the Mansfield family for the last 400 years, and it is now owned by the current Earl of Mansfield. He and his wife have graciously opened it to the public (for an admission charge, of course), and it is definitely worth your while to stop by.

What will you see? For starters, you'll see a number of rooms full of antique furniture, a fine collection of porcelain, stunning oil paintings and tapestries of ancient date. You'll feel like a privileged guest as you move through the palace, and you'll revel at the elegance and opulence you'll see. Scone Palace was built in the 16th century, although most of the furnishings you see date from the 19th century. On the grounds stands **Moot Hill**, where the **Stone of Destiny** once stood. It was upon this stone that over 40 of Scotland's kings were crowned from the earliest ages up until the beginning of the 14th century. At that point, the stone was confiscated as part of the spoils of war and taken back to England. The Scots may have pulled a fast one here, though: legend has it that an official-looking but rather ordinary stone was substituted for the Stone of Destiny just before its kidnap.

SPORTS & RECREATION
Golf

Gleneagles is one of Scotland's premier golf courses, and is located about 15 miles southwest of Perth. It's a short drive, and if you are a golfer, you should definitely plan to swing by: **Gleneagles Golf Course**, *Auchterarder, Perthshire, Tel. 01764/663-543.* Monarch Course: par 72, 7,100 yards. King's Course: par 70, 6,471 yards. Queen's Course: par 68, 5,965 yards.

PRACTICAL INFORMATION
Tourist Information
• **Perth Tourist Information Centre**, *45 High Street, Perth. Tel. 01738/638-353*

PITLOCHRY

Pitlochry finds itself in the midst of beautiful country, situated in a pretty green valley along the banks of the Tummel River and at the foot of 2,730-foot **Ben Vrackie**. Pitlochry is a favorite holiday spot, especially with hillwalkers who come from all over Scotland (and elsewhere) to experience the beauty of Ben Vrackie.

ARRIVALS & DEPARTURES

By Bus

Buses pull into **Pitlochry Bus Station**, *Station Road*. Pitlochry is on the main bus line from Perth to Inverness, so there are many buses that stop daily in Pitlochry. The bus station is at the north end of town, about a half mile from the downtown area, an easy 10–minute walk.

By Car

Pitlochry is on the A9 30 miles north of Perth. From Edinburgh, take the A90/M90 north to Perth and then on to Pitlochry via the A9. From Glasgow, take the A80/M80 northeast to Stirling then on to Perth, where you'll pick up the A9 for Pitlochry.

By Train

Trains pull into **Pitlochry Train Station**, *Station Street*. Pitlochry is on the main train line from Perth to Inverness, so there are many buses that stop daily in Pitlochry. The train station is at the north end of town, about a half mile from the downtown area, an easy 10–minute walk.

WHERE TO STAY

SCOTLAND'S HOTEL, *40 Bonnethill Road, Pitlochry. Tel. 01796/472-292. 60 Rooms. Rates: £65-70 single; £55-80 per person double. Breakfast is included in the rate. Children under 13 stay free in their parents' room. MasterCard and Visa accepted.*

This 3-star hotel sits just above Main Street in Pitlochry. As you walk in off the street, you enter a comfortable guest lounge, where you can relax, have a drink, or pass a few moments before or after your exploration of Pitlochry. The hotel is a little on the older side, but provides safe, clean and comfortable lodging. The bedrooms are for the most part nice sized, although some are a little on the small side. While some of the furnishings could use upgrading, all are clean and comfortable. Each comes with a hairdryer, TV, and tea- and coffee-making facilities. There is a leisure center on site with a nice 12-meter pool, spa, sauna, solarium and exercise room to help you work the kinks out. There is also a pleasant though basic restaurant in the hotel.

TIGH-NA-CLOICH HOTEL, *Larchwood Road, Pitlochry. Tel. 01796/ 472-216, Fax 01796/472-216; E-mail: tnchotel@lineone.net. 12 Rooms. Rates: £18-25 single; £18-26 per person double. Rates include breakfast. No credit cards accepted.*

This pleasant hotel sits on a hill above the main street in Pitlochry. From its perch above the village, it keeps you close to all that's happening, but also allows you to get out of the hustle and bustle fairly quickly. This old Victorian mansion still has its traditional tall ceilings, and much of the original plasterwork has been maintained. The bedrooms are all nice sized (but not huge), and each is tastefully decorated. The bathrooms all have a shower, but no bathtub. The two rooms at the front of the house are the best, as they offer sweeping views of Ben Vrackie and the mountainous Scottish countryside. All rooms also have electric blankets should you need to chase the chill of a damp Scottish day. Two of the rooms do not have bathrooms in them, but share a bathroom in the hall. These rooms are a pound or two cheaper, but if in-room bathroom facilities are of concern to you, be sure and specify your preference when calling for reservations.

The dining room is a very pleasant room to take breakfast in. The most outstanding features of the dining room are the large windows that look out on the beautiful countryside. You may choose from a continental breakfast or a full Scottish breakfast.

WHERE TO EAT

GARDEN ROOM RESTAURANT, *160 Atholl Road, Pitlochry. Tel. 01796/472-266. £5-9 for lunch and £15-20 for dinner. Open daily from noon to 2:00pm and from 6:15pm to 9:30pm. MasterCard and Visa accepted.*

A good place to satisfy your hunger is the Garden Room Restaurant, the main dining room for the Westlands of Pitlochry Hotel. This award-winning restaurant focuses on the freshest produce and provides sumptuous, yet very affordable meals. Children are also welcome and a special menu for them helps them feel included. The fare here is traditional Scottish, and the meals prepared here have won acclaim from *A Taste of Scotland*. Try the fresh salmon with dill soup or the medallions of Perthshire beef. You'll enjoy your meal immensely, and have wonderful views of the Scottish countryside to feast on at the same time.

PITLOCHRY FESTIVAL THEATER RESTAURANT, *banks of the River Tummel, Pitlochry. Tel. 01796/473-054. £5-10 for lunch, £10-20 for dinner. Open from May through the end of September from noon to 10:00pm. Amex, MasterCard and Visa accepted.*

This restaurant and coffee bar serve the patrons of the Pitlochry Theater, and they have earned a reputation for excellence. A buffet is served at lunchtime, and a more formal dinner is prepared for the evening meal. The evening meal is served as early as 6:30pm to accommodate the theater performances (which begin at 8:00pm). Seafood is one of their specialties, whether from the nearby stream or from the sea. Try the fresh trout in a cream sauce. Vegetarian dishes are also available.

THE PLAICE TO BE, *8 West Moulin Road, Pitlochry. Tel. 01796/473-737. £7-10. Open daily in July and August from noon to 10:30pm, and from noon to 2:00pm and from 4:00pm to 10:00pm the rest of the year. MasterCard and Visa accepted.*

You've probably caught the pun in the title of this restaurant, so you know right off that this is a fish-and-chips restaurant. The Plaice to Be has won several awards for their fare and is a great place to stop if you have a hankering for fish and chips. Nothing fancy in the ambience, but really good food. You can get pizza here also (surely with anchovies).

SEEING THE SIGHTS

Pitlochry Power Station and Dam, *Tel. 01796/473-152.* So you came all the way to Scotland and stopped to see a power station? That makes for an exciting holiday. However, the interesting thing about this hydroelectric power plant is the salmon ladder that provides a way around the plant for spawning salmon. A portion of the ladder has been enclosed in glass, giving onlookers a marvelous view of one of nature's greatest phenomena. Pretty impressive.

Pitlochry Festival Theater, *Tel. 01796/472-680; open Easter through early October; evening performances begin at 8:00pm, with 2:00pm matinees on Wednesday and Saturday; admission ranges from £10 to £15.* This is Scotland's "Theater in the Hills," and Scots flock here during the theater season. The festival was founded in 1951, and the performances seem to get better and better each year. The performances have gained such international acclaim that actors from all over the world vie for roles in the plays.

Blair Antiques, *414 Bonnethill Road, Tel. 01796/472-624; open 9:30am to 5:00pm Monday through Saturday.* For a change of pace, stop in at Blair Antiques just off Main Street to see if there are any old knick-knacks you're interested in. If nothing suits your fancy, just step a few feet further uphill to **Moulin Antiques** and see if they have anything of interest.

17. THE BORDERS & THE SOUTHWEST

The Borders region is the area of southern Scotland that borders England (hence the name). It is an area rich in tradition and lore, and one where many of Scotland's ballads found their source. Due to its close proximity to England, the Borders region saw hundreds of years of violence as opposing armies criss-crossed this area in search of fame, fortune and one another. While they were at it, homes, towns, castles and monasteries were attacked and burnt. After the departure of the armies, these same homes, towns, castles and monasteries were rebuilt, and so the cycle went time and again.

It is the region where you will find some of the most splendid ruins in Scotland. From the sister abbeys of **Jedburgh**, **Kelso**, **Dryburgh** and **Melrose** to **Threave Castle** and **Caerlaverock Castle** and countless others, you'll marvel at the architectural masterpieces and sheer antiquity of the structures.

This region is also the home of two of Scotland's greatest literary figures: **Sir Walter Scott** and **Robert Burns**. Scott is renowned for his historical novels, including *Rob Roy*, *Ivanhoe* and *Waverly*. Robert Burns has been called Scotland's National Poet, and a prolific poet he was. Volumes of work poured from his pen, but his best-known work is *Auld Lang Syne*. While born in Ayr, Burns spent the last years of his life in **Dumfries**.

Today this area boasts a booming woolens industry, and some of the world's finest cashmere comes from here. As you drive through the rolling hills you'll see the omnipresent sheep that donate their winter's coats to the industry that keeps this part of Scotland thriving. Many of the main sights to see in the Borders and the Southwest could probably be seen as day trips from either Edinburgh or Glasgow. However, I have made it its own chapter since I felt the region had already suffered so many

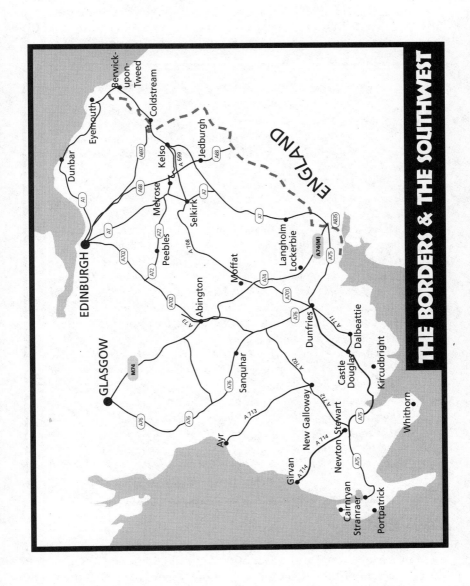

indignities from its English neighbors, and I didn't want to be responsible for heaping yet another indignity on this lovely part of the country.

Don't overlook this quiet corner of Scotland. Many tourists coming to Scotland from England whisk through the Borders region on their way to Glasgow and Edinburgh, giving scant notice to this interesting area. It's a great place to visit, with many memorable sights to see.

THE BORDERS & THE SOUTHWEST'S MUST-SEE SIGHTS

Abbotsford House – *Sir Walter Scott lived at Abbotsford from 1812 until his death in 1832. Not only did he call Abbotsford home, but he also used it to display a wide variety of interesting and intriguing items that he collected throughout his life.*

Jedburgh Abbey – *Jedburgh Abbey is one of the most complete and picturesque ruins in Scotland. Built in the 12th century, it is a monument to the faith and devotion of those who have gone before us.*

Melrose Abbey – *Melrose is one of the sister abbeys of Jedburgh, and although it is architecturally different, it is every bit as beautiful. It was a favorite of Sir Walter Scott's, who memorialized it in a poem.*

Floors Castle – *Floors Castle is home to the Duke and Duchess of Roxburghe, and they have graciously allowed significant portions of their home to be opened to the public. It feels like you are wandering through someone's own private museum, and you'll love the ancient tapestries, oil paintings and period furnishings.*

Sweetheart Abbey – *The story of Sweetheart Abbey is the story of devotion and love, with perhaps a little obsessive-compulsive disorder thrown in. The ruins of this 13th-century abbey are spectacular, but the story behind them is even better.*

Caerlaverock Castle – *This is a great ruin! The castle is a massive three-sided affair with a huge and impressive gatehouse at one corner and towers at the other corners.*

Scott's View – *This is one of the most beautiful vistas in Scotland, one which you have probably seen on brochures touting the beauty of Scotland.*

MELROSE

Begin your tour of the Borders region in the picturesque market town of **Melrose**. Sheltered at the foot of the tri-peaked Eildon Hills and built along the banks of the River Tweed, it saw its share of grief at the hands of English armies. Time and again the armies destroyed lovely Melrose Abbey, the centerpiece of the town of Melrose. And time and again the church and townspeople rebuilt it.

Today Melrose is a quiet market town that does a booming business centered around the tourism industry.

ARRIVALS & DEPARTURES

By Bus

Catch the bus for Galashiels at Edinburgh's **St. Andrew Square Bus Station**, *St. Andrew Square, Edinburgh, Tel. 0990/050-5050,* or at Glasgow's **Buchanan Street Station**, *North Hanover Street, Glasgow, Tel. 0141/332-7133, Fax 0141/332-9191.* From Galashiels, transfer to one of the many buses that run to Melrose.

By Car

You'll reach Melrose by taking the A68 south from Edinburgh. As you near Melrose, watch for signposts directing you there. From Glasgow, it is probably quickest to go to Edinburgh on the M8, then east on the A720 and then south on the A68.

By Train

The nearest train service reaches Berwick-upon-Tweed from Edinburgh's **Waverley Station**, *Princes Street, Edinburgh, Tel. 0131/556-2451.* From there you can switch to bus service for Melrose. Numerous buses run between Berwick-upon-Tweed and Melrose throughout the day; call **National Express**, *Tel. 0131/452-8777,* for schedule information.

ORIENTATION

Melrose is a small town, nestled against and built on the foothills in the area. There are a number of interesting shops, and everything is in a pretty compact area.

GETTING AROUND TOWN

By Bicycle

Melrose is a tiny town built on a hillside, so you can either park your bicycle and walk, or just coast along to the sights you would like to see. However, during the height of the summer season the town is pretty busy, with lots of cars and narrow streets. So you might be safest to just put your bicycle aside and walk.

By Car

Park it.

By Foot

This is the best way to see Melrose. It is not a very large place, so you should be able see it nicely on foot.

BEST PLACES TO STAY IN THE BORDERS & THE SOUTHWEST

ROXBURGHE HOTEL AND GOLF COURSE, *Heiton, Kelso. Tel. 01573/450-331, Fax 01573/450-611; E-mail: sunlaws.roxgc@virgin.net; Website: www.roxburghe.bordernet.co.uk. 22 Rooms. Rates: £105-115 single; £115-205 per room double; £250-255 suite. MasterCard and Visa accepted.*

It was love at first sight when I saw Roxburghe Hotel. And like so many of these love-at-first-sight romances, it just got better the more I got to know the object of my affections!

PHILIPBURN COUNTRY HOUSE, *Selkirk. Tel. 01750/720-747, Fax 01750/721-690; E-mail: centuryhousehotels@compuserve.com. 14 Rooms. Rates: £79-85 single; £99-135 double; £135-180 suite; £99.50 family room per room (kids £10 extra). This is my personal favorite in the Borders region, and one of the best country house hotels in Scotland. This splendid old home predates the Revolutionary War (it was built in 1751) and has recently been renovated and refurbished top-to-bottom, with marvelous results.*

TRAQUAIR HOUSE, *Traquair, Innerleithen, near Peebles. Tel. 01896/830-323, Fax 01896/830-639; E-mail: enquiries@traquair.co.uk; Website: www.traquair.co.uk/accom. 2 Rooms. Rates: £80 single; £65 per person double. With Traquair House, you have the opportunity to stay in the oldest inhabited house in Scotland. Traquair House was built over 1,000 years ago (don't worry – it has been renovated many times since then!). You'll be staying where kings and queens have stayed, and you'll love every minute of it.*

WHERE TO STAY

TORWOOD LODGE, *High Cross Avenue, Melrose. Tel. 01896/822-220. 3 Rooms. Rates: £23 per person single, £23 per person double. No credit cards accepted.*

Spend a little time in this lovely old Victorian mansion, and you'll enjoy every minute you're here. Mrs. Schofield is your hostess, and she works hard to see that you have a wonderful stay. Each of the bedrooms is large and furnished with quality furnishings. Each has those marvelous tall ceilings that make these Victorian homes perfect for B&Bs. The rooms are individually decorated in soft colors and feature televisions and tea- and coffee-making facilities. You also get a special bonus with views of the River Tweed and the Scottish Borders countryside. You're also just a few minutes' walk from Melrose Abbey and the other sights to see in Melrose.

BURT'S HOTEL, *Market Square, Melrose. Tel. 01896/822-285, Fax 01896/822-870. 20 Rooms. Rates: £40-60 per person single, £40-45 per person double. All major credit cards accepted.*

Burt's Hotel is one of those "old-world-feel" hotels that has been updated with modern amenities. And no wonder it has an older feel – the hotel was built four years before the American Revolution began. Each of the rooms in this converted 3-story townhouse has been comfortably and expertly decorated with reproduction antiques and quality furnishings. Each room features a television, telephone, hair dryer and tea- and coffee-making facilities. The hotel is located in the center of town, and is close to all there is to see and do in town, including Melrose Abbey and the Teddy Bear Museum. This part of town can get a little congested, so it is nice to know there is ample parking available.

MELROSE SCOTTISH YOUTH HOSTEL, *Priorwood, Melrose. Tel. 01896/822-521, centralized reservations: 0541/553-255. 76 beds, 13 Rooms. Rates: £10.75-11.25 for seniors (over 18) and £10.50-11 juniors (under 18). Open Easter through the end of September. MasterCard and Visa accepted.*

The Melrose Youth Hostel is centrally located in Melrose, and overlooks Melrose Abbey (not a bad view). It offers 10 four-bed rooms and several very large dormitory rooms. This is a pleasant hostel with lots of things to do nearby. The rates include continental breakfast. The hostel is clean and provides a nice option for budget accommodations while in Melrose.

WHERE TO EAT

BURT'S HOTEL RESTAURANT, *Market Square, Melrose. Tel. 01896/822-285, Fax 01896/822-870. £12-18 for lunch and £20-25 for dinner. Open 11:45am to 2:00pm for lunch and 6:30pm to 9:00pm for dinner. All major credit cards accepted.*

The elegant dining room for Burt's Hotel guests is also open to the public and provides a pleasant, elegant dining experience. You'll find traditional Scottish fare here amid the crystal and linen, and entrées that range from seafood to beef to wild game (they do wonders with venison), with even a vegetarian choice or two. Dress here is nice casual, and if you want to eat here during the tourist season, reservations are a must.

MARMION'S BRASSERIE, *Buccleuch Street, Melrose. Tel. 01896/822-245. £10-18. Open 11:00am to 2:30pm and 6:00pm to 9:30pm. MasterCard and Visa accepted.*

Marmion's is a comfortable little restaurant that has earned a reputation for fine traditional Scottish fare. It makes an ideal choice for dining either at lunch or dinner, as a break during or after your sightseeing in the area. The menu has been described as innovative, and you'll find a nice selection of local produce and delicious meals here. It provides a friendly, busy bistro feel, and is a pleasant place to stop. You'll find vegetarian, beef, lamb, poultry and seafood options here, all prepared imaginatively with the freshest ingredients from the surrounding countryside. Dress at Marmion's is casual.

SEEING THE SIGHTS

Melrose Abbey, *Abbey Street, Tel. 01896/822-562; open April to September daily from 9:30am to 6:30pm, and from October through March Monday through Saturday from 9:30am to 4:30pm and Sunday from 2:00pm to 4:30pm; admission is £3 for adults, £2.30 for seniors and £1 for children.* Melrose Abbey is such a peaceful and picturesque place, it is hard to imagine that it was formerly a favorite target of invading armies. The ruins are quite complete, and seem to invite exploration and meditation. Built in 1136 by a Cisterian order of monks, it must have been a Gothic beauty in its day. Alongside the abbey is a lovely and ancient cemetery that bears a few minutes' exploration.

One of the most popular Borders legends avers that the heart of Robert the Bruce was buried at Melrose Abbey, and for centuries its location was thought to be the long-lost secret of some nameless and long-departed monk. However, a few years ago a small casket was discovered, and authorities determined it was the casket in which the former king's heart was buried. The casket was reburied in 1998, and a stone marker in the cemetery marks the spot.

You will be entranced by the abbey's splendor, as was famed novelist Sir Walter Scott. He was so taken with Melrose Abbey that he led a movement to repair it. In addition, he memorialized the Abbey in his epic poem *The Lay of the Last Minstrel* (see sidebar). While Sir Scott recommends a visit "...by the pale moonlight...," take notice of the hours the abbey is actually open.

If you are traveling with your children, then you might like to stop in at **Teddy Bear Museum**, *The Wynd, Tel. 01896/823-854; open daily June through August from 10:00am to 5:00pm, the rest of the year Friday through Sunday from 11:00am to 4:00pm' admission is £1.50 for adults and 50p for children.* Teddies here, teddies there, teddies, teddies everywhere – tiny teddies, tartan teddies, tremendous teddies. If you like teddy bears, this is a great place to come. It's not a large collection, so it shouldn't take you long to visit. You'll enjoy the short history lesson on teddy bears in Britain. There is of course a small gift shop, should you be in the mood to purchase your own teddy bear (you can even have one made-to-order).

MELROSE ABBEY IN POEM

Sir Walter Scott had a soft spot in his heart for the solemn and silent beauty of Melrose Abbey. You can almost imagine Sir Scott walking the silent grounds of Melrose Abbey in the pale moonlight, and drawing inspiration from its peaceful repose. Following are a few lines penned by the great writer regarding this poetic beauty:

If thou wouldst view fair Melrose aright,
Go visit it by the pale moonlight;
For the gay beams of lightsome day,
Gild, but to flout, the ruins grey.
When the broken arches are black in night,
And each shafted oriel glimmers white;
When the cold light's uncertain shower
Streams on the ruined central tower;
When buttress and buttress alternately,
Seem framed of ebon and ivory;
When silver edges the imagery,
And the scrolls that teach thee to live and die;
When distant Tweed is heard to rave,
And the owlet to hoot o'er the dead man's grave,
Then go – but go alone the while –
Then view St. David's ruin'd pile;
And, home returning, soothly swear,
Was never scene so sad and fair.

*(From **The Lay of the Last Minstrel**, contained in The Poetical Works of Sir Walter Scott, Adam and Charles Black Publishers, Edinburgh, 1883. Cited with permission from the Scott family.)*

After you've had your fill of the things to see and do in Melrose, head west on the A6091 out of Melrose towards Galashiels to the home of **Sir Walter Scott**. He purchased the house and made extensive renovations, including changing the name to **Abbotsford House**, *near Melrose on Road B6360, Tel. 01896/752-043; open from late March to the end of October Monday through Saturday from 10:00am to 5:00pm, on Sunday June to September from 10:00am to 5:00pm, and from March to May and during October on Sunday from 2:00pm to 5:00pm; admission is £3.50 adults and £1.80 for children.* Sir Walter lived at Abbotsford from 1812 until his death in 1832. Not only did he call Abbotsford home, but he also used it to display a wide variety of interesting and intriguing items that he collected throughout his life. The house was built over the span of a number of years, and Sir Walter added a little here and a little there as it suited his fancy. It eventually ended up as a gray stone structure, very proper and handsome.

Inside, you'll be allowed to see a number of the rooms, including his library with its 9,000+ volumes, the drawing room with period furnishings, the entrance hall (a replica of the entry hall at Linlithgow Palace), and armory. The armory includes battlefield souvenirs from the Battle of Waterloo (Sir Walter may have had a keen interest in Napoleon – they were born on the same day and the same year). Another item that invokes keen interest among visitors is the broadsword reportedly owned by the outlaw Rob Roy. In addition, you'll be able to see his study where much of his writing took place – speaking as a writer, this was a very inspirational room. Finally, you'll see the dining room with its lovely views of the River Tweed. This was one of Sir Walter Scott's favorite rooms, and the room where he died. In addition to all there is to see in the home, you'll find the walled garden to be a pleasant, tranquil place. A small gift shop and tearoom are available at Abbotsford.

PRACTICAL INFORMATION
Tourist Information
• **Melrose Tourist Information Centre**, *Abbey House, Abbey Road, Melrose. Tel. 01896/822-555*

DRYBURGH
There isn't much in Dryburgh except the ruins of an ancient abbey, a hotel and a few homes. Both the abbey and the hotel share the name of the town.

ARRIVALS & DEPARTURES
You'll find Dryburgh on the B6356 a few miles south of Melrose and about four miles outside St. Boswells. It is well signposted (the road number is not), so keep your eyes peeled for signs directing you to the abbey.

WHERE TO STAY
DRYBURGH ABBEY HOTEL, *St. Boswell's. Tel. 01835/822-261, Fax 01835/823-945; E-mail: enquiries@dryburgh.co.uk. 37 Rooms. Rates: £49-75 single; £49-75 per person sharing double. Amex, MasterCard and Visa accepted.*

If you've ventured into the Borders region to see the scenery or the ruins, what better place to stay than Dryburgh Abbey Hotel? This lovely old hotel is full of character and personality, and stands overlooking its namesake. The management team at Dryburgh has worked very hard to see that their four-star hotel is pleasant and comfortable, and that your stay here will be memorable. The rooms at the Dryburgh are all large and tastefully decorated in light-colored designer wallpaper. The tall ceilings accentuate the room sizes, and each room is furnished with top-quality furnishings. All the bathrooms are tiled, large and feature upgraded plumbing and fixtures.

As wonderful as the rooms are, the views from them are the best part about them. About half of the rooms overlook Dryburgh Abbey, which is just a stone's throw from the hotel. Those rooms that do not overlook the Abbey do look out on the mellow and meandering River Tweed – premium rooms at most other hotels. Breakfast and dinner are taken in the elegant dining room called the Tweed Room, and it is sumptuous indeed. The meals in this pretty dining room are also enhanced by views of the River Tweed flowing along its merry way. Oh yes – the food is pretty good too – see the *Where to Eat* section.

WHERE TO EAT

THE TWEED RESTAURANT, *Dryburgh Abbey, near St. Boswells. Tel. 01835/822-261. £20-30. Open daily from 7:00pm to 9:15pm. Amex, MasterCard and Visa accepted.*

This is the fine-dining restaurant for the Dryburgh Abbey Hotel. It is a cunningly elegant dining room, featuring tall ceilings, attractive window coverings and large windows that look out onto the Scottish countryside. Candlelight, crystal, silver and linen add just the right touch to the meals, which have been recognized for their quality by *A Taste of Scotland*. You'll find traditional Scottish fare here. Try the filet of sole lightly steamed and mashed with mushroom and parsley cream. If you'd like a little more traditional offering, try the roast sirloin of Scottish beef with a rich red wine and shallot essence. Dress is suit and tie, and the management asks that you not smoke in the restaurant.

SEEING THE SIGHTS

Dryburgh Abbey, *Tel. 01835/822381; open April to September daily from 9:30am to 6:30pm, and October to March on Monday through Saturday from 9:30am to 4:30pm and Sunday from 2:00pm to 4:30pm; admission is £2.50 for adults, £1.90 for seniors, and £1 for children.* This graceful Gothic ruin is the sister abbey to those at Melrose, Jedburgh and Kelso. Built in 1150 and razed numerous times throughout its traumatic history, Dryburgh Abbey is one of the prettiest ruins in Scotland. It was built in a crook of the River Tweed, and today it sits serenely amid a cluster of yew trees and beautiful landscaping. The most famous resident of the abbey is Sir Walter Scott, whose modest marble memorial is found inside the Gothic tower. The cemetery that surrounds most of the abbey is filled with interesting, intriguing and ancient tombstones and memorials. The peace and tranquility that pervades the grounds is worth the price of admission. There is also a small gift shop as you enter the grounds.

As you leave Dryburgh Abbey and head back north on the B6356, watch for signs directing you off the road to **Scott's View** and the **Wallace Memorial**. The first you will come to is the Wallace Memorial. Actually, you first come to a small car park with a trailhead that takes you to a mammoth statue of William Wallace. Erected in 1814 by (no doubt) an admirer of Sir William the Guardian of Scotland, the statue is huge – about 22' tall. William is standing tall and strong and overlooking the River Tweed and the lush Borders region. Look at his eyes – they are wide open, scanning the countryside for approaching English armies. Either that, or they are registering shock that tourists would labor up the 473-yard path to see him! Actually, it isn't a bad walk, and is only slightly uphill for the first 100 yards or so. But the views are phenomenal from this vantage point.

Speaking of phenomenal views, after you finish with the Wallace Memorial, follow the road up to **Scott's View**. Sir Walter Scott traveled this road often and on each trip stopped at this point to admire the views. And admirable views they are! This is perhaps one of the most frequently photographed images of Scotland. The panoramic views out across the Borders countryside over the River Tweed to the Eildon Hills is simply stunning, especially in spring and summer when the land is in full bloom. A plaque at the sight bears these words penned by Sir Walter Scott:

> *Breathes there the man with soul so dead,*
> *Who never to himself hath said,*
> *This is my own native land!*

As Scott's body was being carried past this point to his final resting place at Dryburgh Abbey just a few miles below, the horses stopped of their own accord. Some say it was because they were so used to stopping here when Scott traveled the road; others feel it was to give their master one last glimpse of the countryside he loved so well.

JEDBURGH

As with several other towns in this part of Scotland, **Jedburgh** grew up around an abbey that had been established here in the mid-12th century. Unfortunately, at the same time there was a castle in the town, and Jedburgh's close proximity to their hostile English neighbors made them a favorite target. The citizens got so tired of cleaning up after invading armies that they prevailed upon the Scottish parliament to raze the fort and allow the citizens of Jedburgh a little peace and quiet.

Today Jedburgh is a small but busy market town. As in days gone by, hordes of English still descend mercilessly upon the town, accompanied by other tourists of all sizes and nationalities.

ARRIVALS & DEPARTURES
By Bus
Catch the bus for Jedburgh at Edinburgh's **St. Andrew Square Bus Station**, *St. Andrew Square, Edinburgh, Tel. 0990/050-5050*, or at Glasgow's **Buchanan Street Station**, *North Hanover Street, Glasgow, Tel. 0141/332-7133, Fax 0141/332-9191*. The trip takes about two hours.

By Car
You'll find the Borders village of Jedburgh about 50 miles southeast of Edinburgh. Take the A68 south out of Edinburgh and you're sure to find it.

By Train
As with all the towns in this part of the Borders, there is no train service. The nearest train service reaches Berwick-upon-Tweed from Edinburgh's **Waverley Station**, *Princes Street, Edinburgh, Tel. 0131/556-2451*. From there you can switch to bus service for Jedburgh. Numerous buses run between Berwick-upon-Tweed and Jedburgh throughout the day; call **Scottish Citylink**, *Tel. 0990/050-5050*, for schedule information.

ORIENTATION
Jedburgh is a small town located on the A68, and most of the activity and shops are located near the abbey.

GETTING AROUND TOWN
By Bicycle
During the summer months, it's probably advisable to just lock your bicycle up and walk around Jedburgh. The traffic is heavy and a bit dangerous for bicyclists on the narrow town roads.

By Car
Chances are you arrived here by car; I'd suggest you park it and walk to the few sights and shops that are in Jedburgh.

By Foot
This is undoubtedly the best way to see Jedburgh.

WHERE TO STAY

GLENFRIAR'S HOTEL, *The Friars, Jedburgh. Tel. 01835/862-000. 6 Rooms. Rates: £40-60 per person single, £40-45 per person double. Rates include breakfast. MasterCard and Visa accepted.*

The Glenfriar's Hotel is a small hotel housed in a wonderful old Georgian house near the north end of High Street. You'll be pleased with the warm greeting you receive from Jenny Bywater, your hostess during your stay here. Jenny is a careful hostess, careful to see that your needs are met and that you have a memorable and pleasant stay while at Glenfriar's. The rooms are comfortable and large, and two of them feature four-poster beds. You'll find wonderful antique furnishings throughout the house, and your stay here should be a most pleasant one.

THE SPINNEY GUEST HOUSE AND LODGES, *Langlee, Jedburgh. Tel. 01835/863-525, Fax 01835/864-883; E-mail: TheSpinney@btinternet.com. 4 Rooms. Rates: £25 per person single, £20 per person double. MasterCard and Visa accepted.*

Spinney Guest House is located within a hop, skip and a jump (that is – within about two miles) of Jedburgh. It features several comfortable rooms, as well as two log cabins that are offered on a self-catering or a B&B basis, whichever best meets your needs. The guest house is clean and comfortable, and is a favorite of those who are exploring the sights to see in this part of Scotland. Each room is nice sized, pleasantly decorated in light colors with floral accents, and offers a television, hair dryer and tea- and coffee-making facilities.

The guest house is set amid lovely landscaping and mature gardens, and is surrounded by woods, all of which guarantee a pleasant atmosphere for your stay. Spinney Guest House is run by Mr. and Mrs. Fry, and they are rightfully proud of their 4-star rating from the Scottish Tourism Board. The Frys would like to remind their guests that Spinney Guest House and Lodges is a non-smoking facility.

WHERE TO EAT

SIMPLY SCOTTISH, *High Street, Jedburgh. Tel. 01835/864-696. £5-9 for lunch and £10-15 for dinner. Open 10:00am to 9:00pm. MasterCard and Visa accepted.*

With a name like Simply Scottish, any question about the type of fare you'll experience here? In addition to modern as well as traditional Scottish fare, you will find that fare in this bistro-style restaurant to be affordable and prepared with the freshest ingredients and produce from the local countryside. Your hosts are Linda Ferguson and Charles Masraff, and their expertise has earned them a Taste of Scotland award. You'll enjoy stopping by and dining as you visit the sights in Jedburgh. You'll be able to select from a menu that features beef, lamb, seafood, wild game and vegetarian dishes. Dress at Simply Scottish is casual.

SEEING THE SIGHTS

Jedburgh Abbey, *Highway A68, Tel. 01835/863-279; open April to September daily from 9:30am to 6:00pm, October to March Monday through Saturday from 9:30am to 4:00pm, and Sunday from 2:00pm to 4:00pm; admission is £3 for adults, 2.50 for seniors, and £1 for children.* Scottish King David I built Jedburgh for an order of French Augustinian monks in 1138. Like so many of her sister abbeys, Jedburgh Abbey fared poorly at the hands of well-armed and mischievous soldiers for centuries. Time and again it was ransacked, and time and again it was rebuilt. It was finally abandoned in 1546 after a particularly thorough job was done by English forces as part of Henry VIII's "rough wooing" of Mary Queen of Scots.

Today, Jedburgh Abbey is a fairly substantial and extremely impressive ruin. It must have been one of the finest buildings of its kind in its day. As you approach the abbey, look up at the Gothic windows and try and imagine how they must have looked with stained glass windows depicting scores of Biblical scenes. It must have once been an awesome and inspiring sight. It is truly a monument to the faith and dedication of these early clerics. Around the sides of the abbey are stone memorials – take a moment and read a few. Some tell their story and are quite poignant, like the one for Frances Fair Barnett, who lost her 21-year-old son (James Fair Barnett) at sea. There is a small museum in the visitor center that gives the history of abbeys in general and Jedburgh Abbey in particular. The museum is not extensive, but it is well done.

Mary Queen of Scots House, *Queen Street, Tel. 01835/863-331; open March through November, closed December through February. Open March and November Monday through Saturday from 10:30am to 3:45pm, and Sunday from 1:00pm to 4:00pm, in April and October Monday through Saturday from 10:00am to 4:45pm, and Sunday from noon to 4:30pm, from June through August Monday through Saturday from 10:00am to 4:30pm and Sunday from 11:00am to 4:00pm; admission is £2 for adults and £1 for seniors and children.* Mary Queen of Scots was reportedly one of the most beautiful women in Scottish history, and anything she did or anywhere she went was big news. In 1566 she visited Jedburgh and became violently ill. During her illness she was sequestered for four weeks in this house that now bears her name. Years later when her quality of life was not as she would like, she wrote of her time here, "Would that I had died in Jedburgh."

The house is an excellent example of a fortified house of that period, and has been converted into an excellent museum about Mary. The small but nicely done museum contains facts and information about Mary and her life, as well as curios from the time that she lived.

Among the items that interested me most were copies of several letters that Mary had written. The first is a letter that she wrote while staying at this house. Her penmanship was remarkable, even for those days. The other letter on display was one written the evening before her death (actually, it was written at 2:00am, just six hours before her death). Take a few moments and read through it – she seemed amazingly calm and clear headed. Her greatest concern seemed to be that her brother-in-law (to whom the letter was written) would see to it that her servants were paid. She also made it clear that she was dying as a martyr for Catholicism.

PRACTICAL INFORMATION
Tourist Information
•**Jedburgh Tourist Information Centre**, *Murray's Green, Jedburgh. Tel.*
01835/863-435

SELKIRK
Selkirk is a busy market town in the central Borders area, and a town which employed Sir Walter Scott as its sheriff for the last three decades of his life. As a Border town, Selkirk saw its fair share of activity in the border wars with England through the centuries. But one particularly painful engagement that nearly broke her spirit was the **Battle at Flodden Field** (see the sidebar below).

Today it is a lot quieter in Selkirk. The town is laid out amid the hilly country that typifies this part of Scotland.

ARRIVALS & DEPARTURES
Selkirk is about five miles south of Melrose on the A7.

WHERE TO STAY
PHILIPBURN COUNTRY HOUSE, *Selkirk. Tel. 01750/720-747, Fax 01750/721-690; E-mail: centuryhousehotels@compuserve.com. 14 Rooms. Rates: £79-85 single; £99-135 double; £135-180 suite; £99.50 family room per room (kids £10 extra). Amex, MasterCard and Visa accepted.*

This is my personal favorite in the Borders region, and you wouldn't go wrong if you used it as a base for your touring in this part of Scotland. This splendid old home predates the Revolutionary War (it was built in

1751) and has recently been renovated and refurbished top-to-bottom, with marvelous results.

Each of the bedrooms at Philipburn are large, and have the latest in quality furnishings and creature comforts. Each room has been individually decorated with attractive designer wallpaper and light colors. The decorating motif might best be described as contemporary traditional, with soft colors, lots of light pine furnishings and accenting woodwork throughout. Several of the suites are huge, and feature split-level accommodations and Jacuzzis. The hotel offers both a bar and restaurant (see *Where to Eat* section), and both are pleasant places to pass a few hours. Each generally offers a nice blend of tourists and local folk.

The grounds are gorgeous. Philipburn House sits amid trees and the lovely Scottish countryside. There is a large and luxurious croquet court out back, along with a heated outdoor swimming pool. You might enjoy sitting in the lawn furniture and enjoying the pleasant surroundings, or you might like to stroll among the beautiful gardens. Either way, you'll feel a pleasant tranquility here. Here are a few entries from their guest book: "...a very friendly, happy, relaxing weekend," "Fantastic! Great staff, great team!" "Faultless! Well – we did find only one fault – we had to go home!" and finally, "Excellent in every respect."

WHERE TO EAT

RESTAURANT 1745, *Selkirk. Tel. 01750/720-747. £20-30. Open daily from 6:00pm to 11:00pm. Amex, MasterCard and Visa accepted.*

Restaurant 1745 takes its name from the year of the failed Jacobite Rebellion that attempted to reclaim the crown for the Stewarts. It is also the restaurant for the Philipburn House. You'll find a pleasant crystal and candlelight ambience here, although you would never call it stuffy; perhaps casual elegance is a better way to describe it.

The restaurant features large windows that look out on the hotel's croquet lawn and fabulous gardens. The food is pretty good too. The menu changes daily, and while it doesn't offer a broad selection, it does offer a little for most any taste. (The restaurant manager told me, "We strive for quality, not quantity.") I've had the filet of plaice and sole lightly poached in white wine partnered with a tomato parsnip and vermouth sauce, which was very good. For you beef lovers out there, there might be gateau of beef filet layered with grilled aubergines complemented with a green berry and Dijon mustard and brandy sauce. Nice casual dress is fine.

PHILIPBURN BISTRO, *Selkirk. Tel. 01750/720-747. £5-12. Open daily from 6:00pm to 11:00pm. Amex, MasterCard and Visa accepted.*

This is the informal dining room at the Philipburn Country House. It is a pleasant dining room, featuring light pine furnishings with views out onto the carefully sculpted croquet lawns and beautiful gardens. The fare here is primarily soups, salads and sandwiches. There are also some light entrees available. The food is good and filling, and the atmosphere is light and pleasant. Dress is casual.

SEEING THE SIGHTS

Sir Walter Scott's Courtroom, *Market Place, Tel. 01750/720-096; open April through October Monday through Saturday from 10:00am to 4:00pm and Sunday from 2:00pm to 4:00pm; admission is free.* Sir Walter served as the town's sheriff for the last three decades of his life. The courtroom where he conducted much of his business is open to the public, and you can see a small but informative exhibit that features Scott's life, writings, and particularly his time as judge/sheriff. Sir Scott's statue graces the center of the market place.

Flodden Memorial. Little Selkirk lost 79 of 80 of her sons who went to fight with James IV at the Battle of Flodden Field. One lone soldier, a man named Fletcher, returned to the town, a weary – but surviving – member of the routed army. It is his image that tops the memorial to these fallen sons just east of the market place.

FLODDEN FIELD

*On September 9, 1513, the acrimonious relationship between London and Edinburgh resulted in a sad episode in Selkirk history. When **Henry VIII** came to power in England, he asserted his claim to both the English and Scottish thrones. This did not sit well with the Scots, particularly Scottish king **James IV**. He renewed a centuries-old alliance with France, hoping the power of France would quiet Henry's claims. It did not. Skirmishes with England erupted into battles, and James gathered an army of 20,000 men and invaded England. After some initial successes, he met an army equal in numbers to his at Flodden Field in northern England. The battle was a rout, and James IV was killed, along with his eldest son. Patriotic Selkirk sent 80 young men to the battlefront. They were shocked and dismayed when only one lonely Selkirk soldier returned from the battle. Today, a statue stands in Selkirk in memorial to those who gave their lives that autumn day so long ago.*

Selkirk Glass, *Galashiels Road, Tel. 01750/720-954; open daily Monday through Friday 9:00am to 4:30pm, Saturday 10:00am to 4:30pm, and Sunday noon to 4:00pm; admission is free.* If you have never seen glass blown and then worked into wonderful glassware, then this is a good time to stop and see it being done. The Selkirk Glass factory runs a short but fascinating tour that gets you up close and personal to this incredible art. The glass-blowing tours are only offered during weekdays. There is also a small café and showroom for you to visit.

Bowhill House and Country Park, *three miles west of Selkirk, Tel. 01750/722-204; house only open daily in July from 1:00pm to 4:30pm, grounds and playground open May through September Saturday through Thursday noon to 5:00pm; open daily in July from noon to 5:00pm; admission to the house and grounds is £4.50 for adults, £4 for seniors and £2 for children, admission to just the grounds is £2.* Bowhill House is another of those stately mansions that grace this part of the Borders. It was built in the early 19th century, and belongs to the Duke of Buccleuch. The Georgian mansion is filled with antiques and paintings, and is more like a museum than a residence. You'll find glorious paintings by such world-renowned painters as Bassano, Canaletto, Gainsborough, Lorraine, Raeburn and Van Dyck. Antiques adorn every room, and much of the period furniture is original to the house. The grounds also draw a lot of visitors. The woods are chock full of walking and biking paths, and it makes for a pleasant diversion. This is such a grand house to visit that it is a little frustrating that the house is only open during July. But if you are here in July, then I would heartily recommend a visit.

PRACTICAL INFORMATION
Tourist Information
• **Selkirk Tourist Information Centre**, *Halliwell's House, Selkirk. Tel. 01750/720-054*

KELSO

Kelso is a busy, bustling village at the confluence of the Tweed and Teviot rivers. Considered an important strategic point in military days gone by, the town has settled down to deal with charging tourists rather than charging armies. It is home to the lovely ruins of **Kelso Abbey** and the incredible home of the Duke and Duchess of Roxburghe, **Floors Castle**.

ARRIVALS & DEPARTURES
By Bus
Catch the bus for Galashiels at Edinburgh's **St. Andrew Square Bus Station**, *St. Andrew Square, Edinburgh, Tel. 0990/050-5050*, or at Glasgow's **Buchanan Street Station**, *North Hanover Street, Glasgow, Tel. 0141/332-7133, Fax 0141/332-9191*. From Galashiels, transfer to one of the many buses that run to Kelso.

By Car
From Edinburgh, take the A68 south to St. Boswells. Watch for signposts directing you to Kelso, and take the road indicated (it is the A699 on your map).

By Train
The nearest train service reaches Berwick-upon-Tweed from Edinburgh's **Waverley Station**, *Princes Street, Edinburgh, Tel. 0131/556-2451.* From there you can switch to bus service for Kelso. Numerous buses run between Berwick-upon-Tweed and Kelso throughout the day; call **National Express**, *Tel. 0131/452-8777,* for schedule information.

ORIENTATION
Kelso is a busy market town centered around a picturesque town square. Surrounding the square are a bevy of shops and residential areas.

GETTING AROUND TOWN
By Bicycle
You'll probably want to find a place and lock your bicycle and tackle the center of town on foot. The roads are very busy, especially during the summer months.

By Car
Find a parking place and enjoy the town on foot. You'll probably want to drive your car to Floors Castle from the center of town, although it wouldn't be entirely necessary.

By Foot
This is the best way to get around the downtown area of Kelso.

WHERE TO STAY
ROXBURGHE HOTEL AND GOLF COURSE, *Heiton, Kelso. Tel. 01573/450-331, Fax 01573/450-611; E-mail: sunlaws.roxgc@virgin.net; Website: www.roxburghe.bordernet.co.uk. 22 Rooms. Rates: £105-115 single; £115-205 per room double; £250-255 suite. MasterCard and Visa accepted.*
It was love at first sight when I saw Roxburghe Hotel. And like so many of these love-at-first-sight romances, it just got better the more I got to know the object of my affections. (Don't tell the current owners, the Duke and Duchess of Roxburghe – they might get jealous.)
The Roxburghe is a first-class country house set amid 200 acres of stunning greenery. An 18-hole golf course adds to the beauty and attractiveness of the facility. Built in 1853, the entire facility is warm and

delightful. The public rooms are all furnished with comfortable furniture and feature large fireplaces with welcoming fires. Old oil paintings, divine hand-crafted woodwork and tasteful decorating complement the atmosphere that is here.

Each of the bedrooms is individually decorated, and the results are marvelous. The large rooms feature soft colors, warm furnishings, and quality everything! Some of the rooms have light floral accents, and all are well lit and give you a sense of being home. All the rooms have lovely views of the vast estate; some of the views are of landscaped lawns and others are of wooded parklands. The suites are of course a cut above the rest of the rooms. Not so much in quality perhaps, but in size and ambience. There are two dining rooms, and both provide simple dining elegance. Both are crystal-and-china, linen-and-silver kinds of environments. If you happen to catch a salmon during the day in the nearby River Teviot or River Tweed, you'll be pleased to know that the chefs will be delighted to cook it up for you (see the *Where to Eat* section). All in all, I'd say you will have a wonderful time if you choose to stay here.

EDNAM HOUSE HOTEL, *Bridge Street, Kelso. Tel. 01573/224-168, Fax 01573/226-319. 32 Rooms. Rates: £43 single; £38-58 per person double. Dinner, bed and breakfast is available from £56-76 per person. Rates include breakfast. MasterCard and Visa accepted.*

This gorgeous Georgian mansion has been magnificently converted into a hotel, and the results are marvelous. Ralph Brooks is the owner and he is devoted to seeing that his guests have a wonderful stay. Set in three fabulous acres of gardens, Ednam House also boasts some of the best views in Scotland for their guests. Each of the bedrooms is individually decorated and features quality and comfortable furnishings. Breakfast is a treat, as Ralph is *A Taste of Scotland* award winner. You'll enjoy a full Scottish breakfast that is the rival of any that you'll have in Scotland. If you choose to stay for dinner, you'll again enjoy a marvelous repast (see the *Where to Eat* section) as well as the views of the River Tweed from the dining room.

WHERE TO EAT

ROXBURGHE HOTEL RESTAURANT, *Heiton, Kelso. Tel. 01573/ 450-331, Fax 01573/450-611. £30-40. Open daily 11:30am to 2:00pm, and 6:30pm to 10:00pm. All major credit cards accepted.*

This is fine dining at its best. The restaurant for the Roxburghe Hotel and Golf Course is one of those fine elegant dining settings. Crystal and china, linen and silver, and top-notch service all await you and your appetite. The restaurant is proud of their recognition by *A Taste of Scotland*, and once you dine here, you'll know their selection was no accident. Using only the freshest ingredients from the local countryside, the chef and his staff do a magnificent job of preparing and presenting a wide range of dishes that will be certain to pique your interest. If you've been fortunate enough to catch a salmon during the day, the chefs will be happy to prepare it for your meal. Specialties of the house include fresh Scottish beef, salmon and a good selection of vegetarian dishes. Dress is smart casual to suit and tie. Most of the diners were dressed in the latter the evening I dropped by.

EDNAM HOUSE RESTAURANT, *Bridge Street, Kelso. Tel. 01573/ 224-168, Fax 01573/226-319. £20-27. Open daily from noon to 2:30pm and 6:00pm to 9:00pm. MasterCard and Visa accepted.*

Some say the meals here are what keeps bringing people back; others say it is the wonderful views of the River Tweed. I say it's both – how's that for sitting on the fence? If you are in the Kelso area at lunch or dinner time, you won't go wrong by stopping at Ednam House Restaurant. The view truly is tremendous, and chef Ralph Brooks didn't earn his reputation and *A Taste of Scotland* recognition by serving anything but the best meals possible. The menu isn't extensive, but does provide you with a good selection of entrées, from fish to chicken to wild game. Vegetarian meals are also available, but you need to call ahead and let them know. The menu changes frequently, but you might expect something along the lines of Highland venison served with lentil and cider pudding and apple vinaigrette, or you might try a roulade of Guinea fowl with wild mushrooms. Dress is nice casual, although I don't think you'd feel out of place in a suit and tie.

SEEING THE SIGHTS

Floors Castle, *just north of Kelso, Tel. 01573/223-333; open daily April 2 through October from 10:00am to 4:30pm; admission is £5 for adults, £4.50 for seniors, £3 for children ages 5-15, and a family ticket is available for £14; admission to the gardens only is £3.* Floors Castle is home to the Duke and Duchess of Roxburghe, and they have graciously allowed significant portions of their home to be opened to the public. You'll enjoy the drive into the estate – it is gorgeous. After you park and approach the castle, you will be struck by its fairytale appearance.

The castle was designed by famed Scottish architect William Adam in 1721, and then the exterior was modified by William Playfair in a Tudor style in the 1840s. As impressive as the exterior is, the interior is even more impressive. It feels like you are wandering through someone's own private museum. Huge oil paintings hundreds of years old, tapestries of equal vintage and original Louis XVI furniture are everywhere. Most of the furnishings you see are original to the castle, and guides in each room relate the history of the room and its furnishings (some of the guides looked like *they* are original to the castle).

One of my favorite items is a splendid tapestry in the ante-room, the first room you enter on the tour. It is over the mantle and entitled *The Day of Pentecost*. It was woven in a Belgium abbey in 1490 using gold and silk threads. It is stunning. Other tapestries in the castle date primarily from the 1600s, and are equally as impressive, as are the hand-woven carpets that you see throughout the castle. The ballroom features some handsome carpets and 10 incredible chairs that are embroidered in Italian velvet. The chairs in the room are from the William and Mary period (late 1600s), are beautiful and in great condition.

The castle was featured in the Tarzan movie *Greystoke*. It was also the setting of Prince Andrew's proposal to Sarah Ferguson.

During the 15th century, a previous castle stood on the spot where Floors now stands. On August 3, 1460, Stewart King James II was leading an assault on the castle, which was held by an English army at the time. One of the cannons used in the siege exploded, taking the 29-year-old king with it. A holly tree on the grounds marks the spot where James was killed. As you would expect, the grounds are immaculately kept, and the castle gardens are worth a visit in and of themselves.

PRACTICAL INFORMATION
Tourist Information
• **Kelso Tourist Information Centre**, *Town House, The Square, Kelso. Tel. 01573/223-464*

PEEBLES
Peebles is a quiet little market town of about 7,000 folks known for its fine shops and friendly people. It was once a place where Scottish kings came to play, and today it is a pleasant place for tourists to gather. Situated at the foot of wooded rolling hills along the gently flowing River Tweed, the town just has a nice feel to it.

ARRIVALS & DEPARTURES
By Bus
Buses arrive in Peebles across from the post office. Buses come here from Edinburgh and Galashiels.

By Car
You'll arrive in Peebles by taking the A703 south from Edinburgh. If you are coming from Selkirk, take the A72 west.

GETTING AROUND TOWN

By Bicycle
The town is small enough to enjoy on bicycle or on foot.

By Car
Park your car and experience the town by foot.

By Foot
This is the best way to see Peebles.

WHERE TO STAY

CRINGLETIE HOUSE, *Eddleston, near Peebles. Tel. 01721/730-233, Fax 01721/730-244. 13 Rooms. Rates: £55-70 single; £49-55 per person double. Rates include breakfast. Amex, MasterCard and Visa accepted.*

This marvelous old Scottish mansion with its turrets, towers and gables sits regally amid 28 acres of lush Borders countryside. Surrounded by a walled garden, you'll fall in love with Cringletie House before you set foot inside it. The public rooms are elegantly furnished and one of them, the Drawing Room, has lovely views of the surrounding countryside. Each bedroom is large and individually decorated. The furnishings are not extravagant, but they are comfortable and pleasant. A fine restaurant is on site and will provide you a nice meal in a warm and pleasant setting (see the *Where to Eat* section).

TRAQUAIR HOUSE, *Traquair, Innerleithen, near Peebles. Tel. 01896/830-323, Fax 01896/830-639; E-mail: enquiries@traquair.co.uk; Website: www.traquair.co.uk/accom. 2 Rooms. Rates: £80 single; £65 per person double. Rates include breakfast. MasterCard and Visa accepted.*

Do you want to stay in the oldest inhabited house in Scotland? Traquair House was built over 1,000 years ago (don't worry – it has been renovated many times since then). You'll be staying where kings and queens have stayed, and you'll love every minute of it. The rest of Traquair House is also a bit of a museum, but you can really experience it first hand by spending the night. There are two rooms, the Pink Room and the Blue Room. Each room is large, chock-full of antiques and features comfortable furnishings and exquisite décor. Breakfast is taken in the pleasant Still Room, where you'll enjoy a wide variety of menu items to choose from. Be sure and take a minute to look at their collection of porcelain dishes in the room. Some are quite exquisite.

VENLAW FARM B&B, *Peebles. Tel. 01721/722-040. 4 Rooms. Rates: £20 single; £17-18 per person double. Rates include breakfast. Credit cards not accepted.*

If you are looking for B&B accommodations in the Peebles area, this is one of the best around. Sheila Goldstraw is your hostess, and she is rightfully proud of her four-star B&B. You'll find two ensuite rooms, one ensuite room with a private bath and one standard room here at Venlaw Farm. All are pleasantly decorated and comfortably furnished. The B&B is part of a working farm, so you will be able to experience that atmosphere while you are here. Venlaw Farm B&B is a totally non-smoking establishment.

WHERE TO EAT

CRINGLETIE HOUSE RESTAURANT, *Tel. 01721/730-233, Fax 01721/730-244. £11-18 for lunch, and £20-35 for dinner. Open daily from noon to 2:00pm and from 6:30pm to 9:00pm. Amex, MasterCard and Visa accepted.*

Remember that garden you saw on your way into Cringletie House? Well, that's where many of the vegetables and herbs came from that grace your meal here at Cringletie House Restaurant. Perhaps their freshness is one of the reasons for Cringletie's recent recognition by *A Taste of Scotland*. You'll enjoy a wonderful meal here, both from an ambiance as well as from a culinary standpoint. If you are here with your sweetheart, then you will find the dining room the perfect mix of attentive service and romantic setting.

The food isn't bad either. The menus change frequently, depending on what is in season, but you can expect something along the lines of roast rack of lamb with a mint-scented gnocchi, tomato and caper jus, or smoked venison with avocado fan and cranberry parfait. Vegetarian dishes are of course available and in fact are a specialty. Dress for the restaurant is either formal or nice casual.

BIG EB'S CHIPPY, *12-16 Northgate, Peebles. Tel. 01721/721-497. £4-10. Open daily from 11:45am to 11:00pm. MasterCard and Visa accepted.*

At the other end of the dining spectrum from Cringletie House Restaurant, you'll find Big Eb's Chippy. But that's okay, because you probably won't find fish and chips at Cringletie. Big Eb's is a fish-and-chips place that also offers fried chicken, baked potatoes, and assorted desserts. The food is good, it is filling and the atmosphere is busy. There are children's menus and vegetarian dishes are also available.

SEEING THE SIGHTS

Traquair House, *Traquair, Innerleithen, Tel. 01896/830-323, Fax 01896/830-639; open late April, May, September and October from 12:30pm to 5:30pm and June through August from 10:30am to 5:30pm; admission is £4 for adults, £3 for seniors and £2 for children; last admission is 30 minutes prior to closing.* Traquair House is the oldest inhabited house in Scotland. Built over 1,000 years ago, the house has been among the most important in this part of the country for centuries. Twenty-seven kings have passed through its doors, and many of them have spent the night here. Mary Queen of Scots was fond of the owners (the Maxwell-Stuarts), who were also Catholic. It is said she spent quite a bit of time here, and you can see the room she stayed in and the bed she slept in. Across the bed is a hand-made quilt said to have been sewn by her ladies-in-waiting, the *Four Marys*. The cradle at the foot of the bed held her infant son James, who later became James I of England.

Traquair House is jam-packed with antiquities including ancient oil paintings, embroideries, manuscripts and maps. The Old Library is stunningly splendid, with over 3,000 old volumes lining its walls. Bonnie Prince Charlie once visited here, and according to legend has visited here many times since. When he visited Traquair House the first time, he apparently entered the grounds through the Bear Gates. After his departure, the 7th Earl of Traquair, a confirmed Jacobite, reportedly locked the gates and gave strict instructions that the gates not be unlocked until a Stewart king once again graced the throne. That was over 250 years ago, and since no Stewart king has been crowned, the gates are still locked to this day. Many have reported seeing the ghost of Bonnie Prince Charlie, wandering aimlessly in the area of the gates. If you have come to this part of the Borders, be sure and stop by Traquair House.

SPORTS & RECREATION

Angling
• **Tweeddale Tackle Centre**, *1 Bridgegate, Peebles. Tel. 01721/720-979.*

Cycling
• **George Pennel Cycles**, *3 High Street, Peebles. Tel. 01721/720-844.*
• **Scottish Border Trails**, *Glentress Forest, A72 near Peebles. Tel. 01721/722-934.*

PRACTICAL INFORMATION

Tourist Information
• **Peebles Tourist Information Centre**, *High Street. Tel. 01721/720-138, Fax 01721/724-401*

DUMFRIES

Dumfries is in the southwestern region of Scotland in an area known as Galloway. Dumfries is most noted for the fact that Scottish national poet Robert Burns spent the last six years of his life here, and you'll encounter many references to him should you visit. In fact, it was here that Robbie Burns penned the immortal words to *Auld Lang Syne*.

Dumfries is not a sleepy little market town – it is a busy, bustling city of 30,000 folks that swells to many times more that size during the peak tourist season. The city is built in the crook of the River Nith as it makes a hard left turn and heads toward Solway Firth.

ARRIVALS & DEPARTURES

By Bus

Buses stop in downtown Dumfries at the **Dumfries Bus Station**, *Whitesands, Tel. 01387/253-496.* It is located just two blocks from the city center.

By Car

If you are coming from Glasgow, take the M74 south to the A701 and then head southwest. From Edinburgh, take the A702 south until it intersects the M74, then head south to the A701 and then southwest to Dumfries. It is well signposted along the way.

By Train

Trains arrive in Dumfries at the **Dumfries Train Station**, *Lovers Walk.* Seven trains per day arrive from Glasgow following the two-hour ride.

WHERE TO STAY

CAIRNDALE HOTEL AND LEISURE CLUB, *132 English Street, Dumfries. Tel. 01387/254-111, US toll-free reservations 800/468-3750, Fax 01387/250-555. 76 Rooms. Rates: £65-85 single; £45-55 per person double; £65-80 suite. Rates include breakfast. All major credit cards accepted.*

The Cairndale Hotel and Leisure Club is housed in a fine old turn-of-the-century building, and a number of renovations have kept it fresh and ready for guests. The hotel has 76 bedrooms and each is large and quite comfortable, pleasantly decorated with quality furnishings. Each room has radio, hairdryer, and tea- and coffee-making facilities. The suites are a step above the regular rooms, and also offer trouser press, mini-bar and whirlpool baths. The public rooms are attractive and comfortable. There are three bars to choose from, as well as a wonderful restaurant and a more informal café. An on-site leisure center includes a steam room, spa, solarium, gym and beauty salon.

ORCHARD HOUSE B&B, *298 Annan Road, Dumfries. Tel. 01387/ 255-099. 3 Rooms. Rates: £25 single; £20 per person double. Credit cards not accepted.*

The Orchard House B&B is a little under two miles from the downtown area of Dumfries, and is one of the best B&Bs you'll find in the Dumfries area. Mrs. Murphy is your hostess, and she is very proud of her four-star B&B. Once you arrive, you'll see why Mrs. Murphy's B&B was awarded four stars by the Scottish Tourist Board. First of all, you'll find an exceptionally clean, pleasant B&B. Next, each of the rooms has been individually and tastefully decorated. Each features comfortable, top-quality furnishings, television, hairdryer and tea- and coffee-making facilities. You'll take your breakfast in the dining room where Mrs. Murphy will continue to amaze you. She offers a wide variety of wonderful breakfast items, and you'll not be disappointed in your meal.

WHERE TO EAT

BENVENUTO PIZZERIA TRATTORIA, *42 Eastfield Road, Dumfries. Tel. 01387/259-890. £5-12. Open daily from 5:00pm to 11:00pm. MasterCard and Visa accepted.*

This is a pleasant family restaurant that serves up a smorgasbord of Italian and Scottish dishes, from pizza and pasta to seafood and beef. The atmosphere is lively, and the food is pretty good too. On nice, sunny days, feel free to take your meal on their patio, where you can enjoy the nice weather. Dress is casual.

GLOBE INN, *56 High Street, Dumfries. Tel. 01387/252-335. £3-6. Open Monday through Friday from 11:00am to 11:00pm, Saturday 11:00am to midnight, and Sunday from 12:30pm to 11:00pm. No credit cards accepted.*

If it is near lunchtime and you are hungry, why not combine your meal with your sightseeing and stop in at the Globe Inn? The Globe was one of Robert Burns' favorite hang-outs, whether for the food or a particular barmaid it is hard to tell. (He did have a child with Anna Park, who worked here as a barmaid.) Today you'll find Burns memorabilia around the pub, as well as a small museum devoted to their most famous son. The pub has been here since the early 1600s, and is still going strong. You'll only be able to get a meal here from noon to 3:00pm Monday through Saturday, as food is not served any other time.

SEEING THE SIGHTS

St. Michael's Church, St. Michael's has been serving the people of Dumfries and the surrounding area for nearly 300 years, and it sits on a site that has been used for worship for many more centuries than that. The most interesting thing about St. Michael's is the **Burns Mausoleum**, a large white-columned building where the great poet was re-interred from his original resting place next to the church. Along with Burns, his wife and five children are buried here.

Burns' House, *Burns Street, Tel. 01387/255-297; open April through September Monday through Saturday from 10:00am to 1:00pm and 2:00pm to 5:00pm, Sunday from 2:00pm to 5:00pm, October through March Tuesday through Saturday from 10:00am to 1:00pm and 2:00pm to 5:00pm; admission is £1 for adults and 50p for seniors and children.* This simple two-story sandstone house is the home where Robert Burns lived out the last few years of his life, and in fact died here in 1796, a casualty of rheumatic fever. The house has been turned into a small but informative museum with a number of items from Burns' life, including manuscripts, letters, some clothing and other items. Upstairs, Burns scratched his initials into one of the windows with his diamond ring. Apparently this was a hobby of his, as you'll find some similarly etched panes in his favorite hang-out, the Globe Inn. He waxed a bit more poetic at the pub, however; the panes there have lines of poetry scratched into them.

Robert Burns Centre, *Mill Road, Tel. 01387/264-808; open April through September Monday through Saturday from 10:00am to 8:00pm, Sunday from 2:00pm to 5:00pm, October through March Tuesday through Saturday from 10:00am to 1:00pm and from 2:00pm to 5:00pm; admission is £1.20 for adults, 60p for seniors and children.* By now, you know that Robert Burns, National Poet of Scotland, lived the last six years of his life in Dumfries. This museum is jam-packed with Burns memorabilia, including original manuscripts, personal belongings and information on his life. A short audio-visual program acquaints you with the poet and his life.

Dumfries Museum and Camera Obscura, *Church Street, Tel. 01387/253-374; open April through September Monday through Saturday from 10:00am to 5:00pm, Sunday from 2:00pm to 5:00pm, and October through March from 10:00am to 1:00pm and from 2:00pm to 5:00pm; admission to the museum is free, admission to Camera Obscura is £1.50.* The Dumfries Museum has informative and interesting exhibits on the history of this region of Scotland. Remember, this area was right in the path of invading English armies, and a lot of history occurred here. The exhibits trace the history of this area from prehistoric times to present. From dinosaur footprints to stone carvings, you'll enjoy the various exhibits. Displays also address the flora and fauna of the region. The top floor is devoted to the Camera Obscura, an astronomical device that also allows you to look at the city and surrounding countryside.

SPORTS & RECREATION
Cycling
• **Ace Cycles**, *Church Street, Castle Douglas. Tel. 01556/504-542*
• **Drumlanrig Castle Cycle Rental**, *Drumlanrig Castle, north of Thornhill. Tel. 01848/330-248*
• **Galloway Sailing Centre**, *Loch Ken, Castle Douglas. Tel. 01644/420-626*
• **Greirson and Graham Cycles**, *10 Academy Street, Dumfries. Tel. 01387/259-483*
• **Rik's Bike Shed**, *Mabie (three miles south of Dumfries). Tel. 01387/270-275*

Golf
• **Dumfries and Galloway Golf Club**, *Dumfries. Tel. 01387/253-582*

Horseback Riding
• **Barend Riding Centre**, *Sandyhills, near Dalbeattie. Tel. 01387/780-663*

Windsurfing
• **Galloway Sailing Centre**, *Loch Ken, Castle Douglas. Tel. 01644/420-626*

EXCURSIONS & DAY TRIPS

There are a number of fine sights to see in the countryside around Dumfries. Here are a few of the better ones:

Sweetheart Abbey, *New Abbey, Tel. 0131/668-8800; open April through September daily from 9:30am to 6:30pm, October through March Monday through Wednesday and Saturday from 9:30am to 4:30pm, Thursday from 9:30am to 1:00pm and Sunday from 2:00pm to 4:30pm; admission is £1.20 for adults, 90p for seniors and 50p for children.* The story of Sweetheart Abbey is the story of devotion and love, with perhaps a little obsessive-compulsive disorder thrown in. Sweetheart Abbey was founded in 1273 by a group of Cisterian monks. Their benefactress was Devorgilla Balliol, wife of John Balliol. Upon her husband's death, Devorgilla became one of the wealthiest women in Europe and by extension, in the world. She showed her love by founding this abbey, as well as Balliol College, Oxford.

But her commitment to and adoration of her husband didn't stop there. Devorgilla had her husband's heart embalmed and placed in an ivory-and-silver casket, which she kept at her side the remainder of her life. At her death 20 years after her beloved, she was laid to rest in front of the abbey altar, along with her beloved's heart. The fame of her love and devotion spread, and soon the abbey was dubbed *Dulce Cor*, Latin for *Sweetheart*. Sweetheart Abbey is eight miles south of Dumfries on the A710.

If you are a sailor or an American Civil War buff, while you're in this part of the country you should drive about seven miles further south on the A710 to the tiny village of **Kirkbean**. Why is that, you ask? Well, because it is the birthplace of Paul Jones. If that name doesn't ring a bell, then add the name that Paul added to the front of his name. That's right, Kirkbean is the birthplace of **John Paul Jones**, Father of the American Navy. There is a small museum called the **John Paul Jones Cottage**, *Kirkbean; open April through June and September Tuesday through Sunday from 10:00am to 5:00pm, July and August daily from 10:00am to 5:00pm; admission is £2 for adults, £1 for seniors and children.* There are a few interesting exhibits here, and you might learn a thing or two about the Scottish seaman-turned-American-naval-hero (like the fact that after the civil war he accepted a commission from Catherine the Great as a Rear Admiral in the Russian navy). A short video is shown in the replica of Jones' ship cabin on the *Bonhomme Richard*.

Caerlaverock Castle, *south of Dumfries, near Bankend, Tel. 01387/770-244; open April through September on Monday through Saturday from 9:30am to 6:30pm, and Sunday from 2:00pm to 6:30pm, October through March on Monday through Saturday from 9:30am to 4:30pm and Sunday from 2:00pm to 4:30pm; admission is £2.30 for adults, £1.75 for seniors and £1 for children.* Caerlaverock Castle is located about seven miles southeast of Dumfries on the B725 (watch for signposts to Bankend). This is a great ruin! Completed in 1280, the castle was the focal point for many a military campaign. In 1300, Edward I ("The Hammer of Scotland") was the first to besiege and capture the castle. Its final capture was in 1640 by the Covenanters after a 13-week siege. They dismantled much of the castle, guaranteeing that it was never used as a stronghold again. The castle is a massive three-sided affair with a huge and impressive gatehouse at one corner and towers at the other corners. A moat completely surrounds the castle, and you can see why it might have taken attacking armies quite a bit of effort to capture it.

Caerlaverock Wildfowl and Wetlands Centre, *south of Dumfries, near Bankend, Tel, 01387/770-200; open daily from 10:00am to 5:00pm; admission is £3 for adults, £2 for seniors and £1.30 for children.* If you've journeyed to see Caerlaverock Castle, then you might as well drive three more miles and see the Caerlaverock Wildfowl and Wetlands Centre. Located in salt mashes, 1,350 acres of wetlands are home to an amazing number of birds year-round.

Drumlanrig Castle, *Thornhill, Tel. 01848/330-248; open May 2 through August 23 daily from noon to 4:00pm; admission is £6 for adults, £4 for seniors, £2 for children, and a family ticket is available for £14.* Thornhill is about 15 miles north of Dumfries, and about three miles north of Thornhill is stately Drumlanrig Castle. The first thing that will occur to you is that the castle is pink, gaining its blush from the locally quarried pink sandstone. The next thing you'll realize is that this a very stately and elegant home. But for all its turrets, towers and cupolas, it is really more of a country mansion than a castle. An inner courtyard is encircled by the surrounding structure, and the effect is marvelous.

Drumlanrig Castle was built in the 17th century by Robert Mylne, the king's master mason. It was the home of William Douglas, the Duke of Queensberry. The home has remained in the family's possession these many years, as attested by the many family heirlooms scattered throughout the house. It is currently owned by the Duke of Buccleuch and Queensberry. Apparently William didn't care much for Drumlanrig, and only spent one night here, choosing instead to live in another castle he had purchased. His son, however, was not so picky, and over 300 years' worth of Douglases have lived here since. Most of their portraits grace the walls of Drumlanrig Castle. You'll find exquisite furniture inside, most of it original to the house. One exception is a beautiful cabinet that Louis XIV gave to Charles II. Charles later gave it to his son, the Duke of Buccleuch. Add that to the other antique French furniture in the house, and you have the makings of a fine museum.

But that's not all. Would you like to see oil paintings by da Vinci, Holbein, or Reynolds? How about works by Kneller, Ramsay or Gainsborough? If so, you needn't travel to Glasgow or Edinburgh; just look around at Drumlanrig Castle. There is a small visitor center, gift shop, cycle museum, adventure playground for the children, and a tearoom on the grounds of the castle. There are also daily demonstrations of birds of prey at 1:00pm and 3:00pm. This is a wonderful place to visit, even if you just stayed outside and enjoyed the gardens and grounds. The setting is splendid, the scenery spectacular.

Threave Castle, *west of Castle Douglas, open April through September Monday through Saturday from 9:00am to 6:30pm, and Sunday from 2:00pm to 6:30pm; admission is £1.80 for adults, £1.80 for seniors and 75p for children.* If you are in this part of Scotland, make the effort to come to Threave Castle. It sits on a small island in the middle of the River Dee about two miles from Castle Douglas. A half-mile walk along a well-worn footpath brings you to the river, where you'll ring a brass bell to summon a boatsman to take you across to the castle.

The castle is a large square keep that was built for Archibald the Grim (doesn't he sound like a neighbor you'd like to have?) in 1360. Archibald was a member of the Black Douglas clan. It is obvious that the castle was built for defensive purposes: its massive five-story tower, tiny windows and island location would have made it difficult to attack. If you recall the history of the border wars with England that were prevalent in this part of the country for centuries, you'll know that Archibald the Grim was a pretty wise man when it came to site selection for his castle.

In 1451, William Douglas, the eight Earl of Douglas, was invited to dine with Scottish King James II at Stirling Castle. William was a bit of a malcontent when it came to the Stewart kings, and he had been plotting the overthrow of James. James confronted the Earl with his treason and demanded that he renounce his plans. When the Earl refused, James murdered him. He then besieged Threave Castle, peppering it with cannon fire until the occupants surrendered. It is said that gold coins, not iron cannonballs, caused the fall of Threave Castle. When the cannon did not budge the troops holding the castle, James reportedly offered them money if they yielded the castle. The defenders opted for the more peaceable – and profitable – solution. In 1640, the castle was once again besieged, this time by the Covenanters, and they did a pretty thorough job of wrecking it. Today you can go inside the castle and get a good feel for what it must have been like in its glory days.

Threave Gardens, *west of Castle Douglas, Tel. 0345/090-510; oOpen daily from 9:30am to sunset; admission is £3.70 for adults, £2 for seniors and for children.* You'll find Threave Gardens a mile west of Castle Douglas just off the A75. Sixty-four acres of gardens are featured here, with a seemingly countless number of varieties of flowering plants. April is the time to come and see the daffodils, and if you do come, you'll be treated to nearly 200 varieties of that lovely flower. Rhododendrons steal the show in May, and it seems that there is always something abloom here. Threave Gardens is sponsored by the National Trust for Scotland as a teaching garden for horticulture students. It is a nice place to stop and smell the roses (and daffodils, rhododendrons, daisies, bluebells, etc.).

PRACTICAL INFORMATION
Tourist Information
- **Castle Douglas Tourist Information Centre**, *Markethill Car Park, Castle Douglas. Tel. 01556/502-611*
- **Dumfries Tourist Information Centre**, *64 Whitesands, Dumfries. Tel. 01387/253-862, Fax 01387/245-555*

KIRKCUDBRIGHT

Kirkcudbright (pronounced Ker-koo'-bree) is a wonderful little village that sits at the head of Kircudbright Bay, an inlet of the Solway Firth. It is a handsome town with a splendid harbor, ruins of ancient origin and attractive houses. It has become the arts capital of the southwest, and artists of all kinds flock here (painters, potters, travel guide writers, etc.) to seek inspiration.

ARRIVALS & DEPARTURES
By Car
Take the A75 west from Dumfries and branch off to the south on the A711 to get to Kirkcudbright.

WHERE TO STAY
SELKIRK ARMS HOTEL, *Old High Street, Kirkcudbright. Tel. 01557/330-402, Fax 01557/331-639. 15 Rooms. Rates: £50 per person single, £40 per person double. All major credit cards accepted.*
Like so many other pubs, hotels and places in this part of Scotland,

the Selkirk Arms Hotel has ties to Robert Burns. It was while Robert Burns was staying here that he penned the famous Selkirk Grace. The Selkirk Arms has been here since 1770, and has been serving travelers to this part of Scotland ever since.

You'll find a regal Georgian home with large, comfortable rooms that were renovated in the mid-1990s. Each room offers television, telephone and tea- and coffee-making facilities. While there is nothing special about the decorating or furnishings, this is still a nice place to stay if you find yourself in Kirkcudbright of an evening. A small bistro on site offers a good choice for meals if you don't want to go out in the evening.

WHERE TO EAT

THE AULD ALLIANCE RESTAURANT, *5 Castle Street, Kirkcudbright. Tel. 01557/330-569. £8-15. Open daily from 6:30pm to 9:00pm. Open from Easter through the end of October. Credit cards not accepted.*

If you know anything about what the Auld Alliance is (historically speaking), then you might have an idea that the fare in this small restaurant is French with Scottish influences. The reason you might know that is because the Auld Alliance refers to a political agreement that was struck between Scotland and France hundreds of years ago.

The restaurant is housed in a small stone cottage across from Kirkcudbright Castle, and offers a pleasant place to get a good meal. Not only is the restaurant across from the castle, but stones from the castle were used in its construction. The Alistair Crawford family is proud of their *Taste of Scotland* recognition, and once you dine here, you'll know immediately why they earned this award. You'll find a wide variety of foods here, but the specialty of the house is seafood, and you'll have to look hard to find fresher cuisine. Try any of the scallops dishes that are offered, or if you really want to be pampered, try the fresh salmon. The Auld Alliance is one of the top restaurants in this part of the country, and you may wish to make reservations to ensure a table, especially during the tourist season.

SEEING THE SIGHTS

In Kirkcudbright, you'll find the foreboding ruins of **MacLellan's Castle**, *Tel. 01557/331-886; open April through September Monday through Saturday from 9:30am to 6:00pm, and Sunday from 2:00pm to 6:30pm, October through March Monday through Saturday from 9:30am to 4:30pm, and Sunday from 2:00pm to 4:30pm; admission is £1.20 for adults, 90p for seniors, and 50p for children.* Built in 1577 for Sir Thomas MacLellan, the castle has been abandoned since the mid-18th century. It is interesting to walk around in and see if you can recreate in your mind what it used to look like.

Broughton House, *High Street, Tel. 01557/330-437; open daily from April through mid-October from 1:00pm to 5:30pm; admission is £2.40 for adults and £1.60 for seniors and children.* Broughton House was the Georgian mansion owned by local artist Edward Hornel. At his death, Edward donated the house and its belongings to Scotland. Hornel was the catalyst behind the formation of an art colony in Kirkcudbright. There are a number of impressionist oil paintings in the house, painted by Mr. Hornel and some of his friends and fellow members of the art colony. A pretty Japanese garden is also associated with the house. Apparently, Mr. Hornel liked all kinds of beauty, as he was also the designer of the gardens. He was a frequent visitor to Japan, and brought back ideas for this garden from there.

Stewartry Museum, *St. Mary Street, Tel. 01557/331-643; open March, April and October to February Monday through Saturday from 11:00am to 4:00pm, May and June Monday through Saturday from 11:00am to 5:00pm and Sunday from 2:00pm to 5:00pm, and July and August from 10:00am to 5:00pm and Sunday from 2:00pm to 5:00pm; admission is £1.50 for adults, 75p for seniors, and children are free.* This is one of the better-stocked museums in this part of the country. Venture in and you'll find a host of interesting items that represent the every-day life of southern Scots through the years. Tri-corner hats worn by city officials (just like in the movies) are on display, along with such artifacts as old bottles, pipes, watches and other mundane things from long ago. The museum also looks at the natural history of the area.

SPORTS & RECREATION

Art Schools

Kirkcudbright Painting Holidays, *Tel. 01557/330-274,* offers courses in painting and drawing over a three-day weekend. Courses are offered for beginners as well as advanced students. Classes are conducted May through September at a cost of £77.

Beach

Just outside of Kirkcudbright, you'll find **Brighouse Bay Beach**, a nice safe beach to relax and, if you have kids along, for them to play.

Golf

• **Brighouse Bay Golf and Leisure Club**, *Borgue, near Kirkcudbright. Tel. 01557/870-267*
• **Kirkcudbright Golf Club**, *Kirkcudbright. Tel. 01557/330-314*

Horseback Riding
• **Brighouse Bay Leisure Club**, *Borgue, near Kirkcudbright. Tel. 01557/870-409*
• **Brighouse Bay Trekking Ponies**, *Borgue, near Kirkcudbright. Tel. 01557/870-222*

PRACTICAL INFORMATION
Tourist Information
• **Kirkcudbright Tourist Information Centre**, *Town Harbor, Kirkcudbright. Tel. 01557/330-494*

WIGTOWN

Wigtown is a small village found along Wigtown Bay, an inlet of the Solway Firth. The village has a nice wide main street and pleasant houses. But the thing most people come here for is something Wigtonians would probably just as soon forget. In 1685, the tidal flats below Wigtown were the scene of the murder of two young women who would not deny their Covenanting faith (see the sidebar on the next page). A plain stone marker near the flats identifies the sight where Margaret MacLachlan and Margaret Wilson voluntarily gave their lives rather than renounce their faith.

ARRIVALS & DEPARTURES
By Car
To reach Wigtown, take the A75 southwest out of Dumfries until you get to Newton Stewart. At that point, take the A714 south out of Newton Stewart (watch for the signposts directing you to Wigtown).

WHERE TO STAY
If you come to Wigtown, you'll probably just want to stay at one of the other towns in the region, like Kirkcudbright or Dumfries.

WHERE TO EAT
You'll also want to dine in one of the nearby towns, like Kirkcudbright or Dumfries.

THE KILLING TIMES

Scotland in the 1680s was a time of religious intolerance. Charles II was convinced that the only way to truly unite the kingdoms of Scotland and England was to unite their religions. The Scots rebelled and Charles' armies invaded Scotland. As with so many religious wars, fanaticism and intolerance fanned the flames of men's souls. Martyrs for the true religion were made at seemingly every turn. Common folk became legends for their suffering for Christ's sake.

*Two such martyrs were **Margaret MacLachlan** (63 years old) and **Margaret Wilson** (18 years old). In May 1685, both were caught and tried for attending outlawed religious meetings called Conventicles. Both were sentenced to die, and they were taken to the seashore and tied to stakes. They watched in horror as the tide came slowly in, climbing inexorably up the stakes to which they were tied. Margaret Wilson was tied to a stake on higher ground than Margaret MacLachlan. She watched as her friend and fellow worshiper drowned. As the waters slowly enveloped her after the death of her friend, Miss Wilson was offered her freedom if she would recant her religious beliefs. She chose to die a martyr.*

18. THE ISLANDS

There are 800 islands peeking stonily out of the waters that surround Scotland, and 130 of them are inhabited. The best-known islands are the **Inner** and **Outer Hebrides**, **Orkney** and the **Shetland Islands**. All are a throwback to an earlier day, and thus far they all provide a visit relatively unsullied by touristy sites. Rather, ancient dwellings, abandoned religious sites and marvelous seascapes await visitors.

The Hebrides lay off the west coast of Scotland. The three best-known islands that make-up the Inner Hebrides are the **Isle of Mull**, **Iona** and the **Isle of Skye**. Mull is accessible via ferry from Oban, and boasts rugged and romantic scenery, including impressive Ben More that juts suddenly out of the island's core to over 3,100 feet. It is accompanied by about a dozen smaller peaks that range from 1,000 to 2,500 feet above the island. In addition, a number of fine ruins are available to visit, including Aros, Duart and Moy Castles.

A short ferry ride from the Isle of Mull is the pretty little island of Iona. Known primarily for the monastic settlement founded here in the 13th century, it is also the site of a 6th century monastery founded by St. Columba, and it was from here that he launched his missionary efforts into Scotland. Don't miss the **Graves of the Kings** – the burial place for dozens of ancient Scottish kings, including **Macbeth** and his predecessor and victim, **Duncan**.

Further north you come to the Isle of Skye. This beautiful island provides visitors a plethora of seascapes and fascinating flora and fauna. Popular with hillwalkers, the Isle of Skye is easily reached either by bridge at the Kyle of Lochalsh or via ferry from Mallaig.

Further west from the Isle of Skye are the remote and rocky **Outer Hebrides**, a chain of islands that stretches over 130 miles along the northwest coast of Scotland. They are for the most part barren and windswept, and the main draws to these islands are the craggy seascapes and remote reaches. Walkers and bird watchers seem to be the most prevalent tourists to these rugged places.

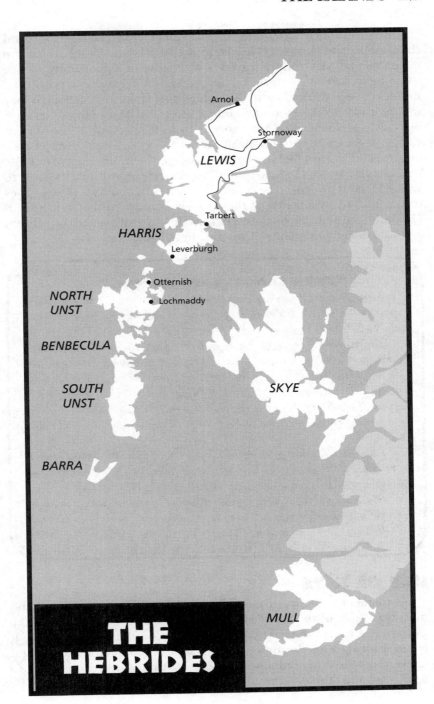

Arnol

Stornoway

LEWIS

Tarbert

HARRIS

Leverburgh

Otternish

Lochmaddy

NORTH UNST

BENBECULA

SOUTH UNST

SKYE

BARRA

MULL

THE HEBRIDES

About six miles north of the Scottish mainland you'll find the island chain known as Orkney. This large set of islands, 29 of which are inhabited, (at last count) provides a wonderful opportunity to see stunning scenery, do some serious fishing and even do some wreck diving. Besides these activities, one of the highlights of your Scottish holiday may well be a visit to the Stone Age burial site called **Maes Howe**. Another incredible archaeological find not far from Maes Howe is the ancient village of **Skara Brae**. This small Stone Age village was covered by a massive sandstorm 4,500 years ago. Uncovered by another storm in 1850, it presented archaeologists with a nearly perfect and intact village to study. Today it provides 21st century tourists with a glimpse into the lives of the ancient inhabitants of these lonely islands. Further north from Orkney you'll find the Shetland Islands. Rocky and rugged, windswept and wild, you'll find plenty of solitude in the Shetlands.

THE ISLANDS' MUST-SEE SIGHTS

Maes Howe – *When you walk into Maes Howe, you are walking where people walked nearly 5,000 years ago. Maes Howe is a Stone Age tomb that dates to 2700 BC.*

Skara Brae – *In 1850, local residents weathered a fierce windstorm that blew in off the Atlantic. The storm uncovered a small fishing village that had been covered by sand and grass for literally centuries. Archaeologists quickly discovered that this was a village that had been covered up in a massive sandstorm, and with its reappearance they were able to study an intact village built sometime between 3000 BC and 2500 BC. And today, so can you.*

Callanish Standing Stones – *These massive stones are silent relics of a religion that has long been forgotten from men's memories. Like Stonehenge, these stoic stones show an astronomical orientation.*

Old Man of Hoy – *This massive 450-foot sandstone tower stands on a finger of rock extending out into the sea. If you can make it to Hoy and its Old Man, you'll have some phenomenal photos.*

ISLE OF SKYE

A member of the Inner Hebrides, the **Isle of Skye** is the largest and most accessible of the Inner Hebrides. It lies off the west coast of the western Highlands, and has become a popular location for hillwalking. It features the dark and brooding Cuillin range of mountains. Ragged and uneven, they feature a number of peaks that range from 1,600 feet to 3,200 feet, and they are a haven for hillwalkers. Some of the walks can be quite tricky and require a pretty good level of ability, while other trails simply meander through the Skye countryside.

The Isle of Skye is 48 miles long, 25 miles wide at its widest point and 3 miles wide at its narrowest. Lonely and windswept, like most of the Scottish isles, it is nonetheless beautiful. As you drive through its immense loneliness, try and fathom how Bonnie Prince Charlie felt as Flora MacDonald brought him to this out-of-the-way place after the fiasco at Culloden.

ARRIVALS & DEPARTURES
By Car
From Glasgow, take the A82 north to Invergary to the A87, then west to Skye. From Inverness, take the A82 south to Invermoriston, then head west on the A887 until it merges with the A87, then to Skye. The island is reached via the **Skye Bridge** over the Sound of Sleat at the Kyle of Lochalsh. The toll is £5.20.

By Ferry
Ferry service runs between Mallaig on the mainland and Armadale on the Sleat Peninsula. The 30-minute ferry ride costs £2 per person and £12.60 per vehicle each way. There is no charge for bicycles. The service runs three times per day, so call ahead for reservations, especially in the summer. Contact **Caledonian MacBrayne Ferries** for schedule information, *Tel. 01471/844-248 or 01687/462-403.*

BEST PLACES TO STAY IN THE ISLANDS
AUCHRANNIE COUNTRY HOUSE, Brodick, Isle of Arran. Tel. 01770/302-234, Fax 01770/302-812. 28 Rooms. Rates: £40-60 single, £40-60 per person double. If you stay at Auchrannie Country House you may just have one of the finest accommodation experiences of your Scottish holiday.

ROSKHILL GUEST HOUSE, Roskhill, near Dunvegan, Isle of Skye. Tel. 01470/521-317, Fax 01470/521-761; E-mail: stay@roskhill.demon.co.uk; Website: www.roskhill.demon.co.uk. 5 Rooms. Rates: £32-40 single; £27-35 per person double. What a delightful find! Roskhill House is an exceptional B&B just outside of Dunvegan on the Isle of Skye. Your hostess here is Gillian Griffith, and her hostessing philosophy is, "The whole idea of Roskhill is home, not hotel," and she has successfully implemented her philosophy at Roskhill House.

WHERE TO STAY

SLIGACHAN HOTEL, *Sligachan, Isle of Skye. Tel. 01478/650-204, Fax 01478/650-207; E-mail: reservations @sligachan.demon.co.uk; Website: www.sligachan.demon.co.uk. 22 Rooms. Rates: £35 single; £35-40 per person double; £105 per family room. Rates include breakfast. MasterCard and Visa accepted.*

This hotel sits at the crossroads between the east and west coasts of the Isle of Skye. It is incredibly popular with hillwalkers since it puts them right in the middle of fabulous hillwalking country. The bedrooms in this hotel are all quite large. Each is comfortable and decorated with light yellow or cream wallpaper. Most have views of either the nearby loch or any of the many surrounding mountains. Each room is equipped with a TV, hairdryer and tea- and coffee-making facilities.

There are two restaurants and a bar associated with the hotel. Since the Isle of Skye is, well, an island, you might expect the restaurant here to be a seafood restaurant. You will not be disappointed in that expectation. You will indeed enjoy excellent seafood here, along with a wonderful full Scottish breakfast to begin your day. The bar is quite famous in the area (partly because it is one of the few bars on this part of the island!), and you'll enjoy the wide selection of malt whiskies they have. Sligachan Hotel is open all year. It is an older hotel and could probably use a few fresh coats of paint. But other than that, it is comfortable, clean and safe. It is also exceptionally convenient if you are looking to do some serious hillwalking on the Isle of Skye.

ROSKHILL GUEST HOUSE, *Roskhill, near Dunvegan, Isle of Skye. Tel. 01470/521-317, Fax 01470/521-761; E-mail: stay@roskhill.demon.co.uk; Website: www.roskhill.demon.co.uk. 5 Rooms. Rates: £32-40 single; £27-35 per person double. Rates include breakfast. Amex, MasterCard and Visa accepted.*

Roskhill House is an exceptional B&B sitting just off the A863 as you come into (or as you are leaving) Dunvegan. Your hostess here is Gillian Griffith, and she will provide you a warm welcome, a warm meal, and marvelous memories of a great place to stay. The home was built in 1890, and it has been renovated tastefully, resulting in a warm, comfortable B&B. Gillian's hostessing philosophy is summed up in these words, "The whole idea of Roskhill is home, not hotel," and she has successfully implemented her philosophy at Roskhill House.

There are five bedrooms, and all of them are good sized and decorated with light paint and floral accents. The furnishings are new and very comfortable. Four of the rooms are ensuite, and the fifth has its own private bath in the hallway. The bathrooms have showers that I would suggest might be among the best in Scotland, if not all of Europe. They are exceptionally powerful, an unusual find in a Scottish B&B.

In addition to her significant abilities as a hostess, Gillian is a fabulous cook. Her efforts have gained her recognition by *A Taste of Scotland*, an unusual feat for a B&B owner. You'll of course have breakfast here, and that will be a treat. Just let Gillian know before noon what you wish to have for dinner, and she will procure the necessary ingredients – all fresh from the local countryside or sea. Nothing frozen here. On my last visit, she made chicken in a sage sauce that was nothing short of exquisite. It was followed by a delectable banana mousse that was spectacular. Both were of the quality and presentation you would expect to find in some of the finest restaurants in the country. Dinner is a reasonable £14.50 per person for two courses and £17.50 per person for three courses. Gillian also tends a small bar that offers about 20 malt whiskies, wines from all over the world, and a fine selection of beers and ales.

When you arrive, in addition to Gillian, you will probably be greeted by Minnie the Mouser, the feline part-owner of the B&B. She makes her home in the lounge area. If you are allergic to cats, Gillian and Minnie will vote on whether Minnie will leave. So far, all votes have been ties, so Minnie stays.

Roskhill House takes its name from Gaelic words meaning "white water," and in this case, those Gaelic words refer to a nearby waterfall. Before you come, you might wish to check out Gillian's website: it is excellent, listing not only information about Roskhill House, but also about the things to see and do around the Isle of Skye. It is an impressive website, and doubly so once you learn that Gillian developed it herself. If you venture to the Isle of Skye, I strongly suggest that you stay and dine with Gillian. Both experiences may be some of your finest while touring Scotland.

Selected as one of my Best Places to Stay – see Chapter 12.

SILVERDALE B&B, *14 Skinidin, near Dunvegan, Isle of Skye. Tel. 01470/521-251. 3 Rooms. Rates: £25 single; £19-22 per person double. Rates include breakfast. No credit cards accepted.*

Just a few miles outside of Dunvegan is four-star Silverdale B&B, run by Anne Gracie. Sitting on a small hill, it has commanding views of the Skye countryside and an inlet of the Sea of Hebrides. It is a quiet, peaceful and idyllic place. One of the best seascapes I photographed on a recent trip was shot within several hundred yards of Silverdale B&B. The B&B itself is warm and comfortable, and Anne lends just the right touch to enhance it. Each of the three bedrooms is nice sized and decorated tastefully. You'll find comfortable new furnishings along with pleasant views of Skye. Each room has a TV, hairdryer and tea- and coffee-making facilities. Anne is a Gaelic speaker, so perhaps you could get a short Gaelic lesson over your full Scottish breakfast. Silverdale B&B is open all year and is a non-smoking facility.

SHILOH HOUSE B&B, *Breakish, Isle of Skye. Tel. 01471/822-346. 3 Rooms. Rates: £25 single; £18-20 per person double. Rates include breakfast. Credit cards not accepted. Note: open from Easter through the end of October.*

Mrs. Mary MacInnes runs this pleasant B&B in the tiny village of Breakish. It was redecorated in 1995 and the MacInnes' have done a fine job in making it a pleasant and comfortable place to stay. There are three bedrooms available for guests, and all have spectacular views of the sea and a number of offshore islands. The best views, however, are from the upstairs bedroom. It is a former attic room so you have to deal with a slanting ceiling, but the marvelous unobstructed views of the islands are worth it. Each of the rooms is average in size, and furnished functionally and comfortably. Each also offers a TV and tea- and coffee-making facilities. A hairdryer is available for use if you have that need. Each room is ensuite, although all of the bathrooms offer showers and not bathtubs.

Breakfast is served in the dining room, which also features views of the landscaped lawns of Shiloh House and the islands beyond. This is a comfortable place to stay, and you'll enjoy Mrs. MacInnes' hospitality while you are here.

WHERE TO EAT

THREE CHIMNEYS RESTAURANT, *Highway B884, Colbost, near Dunvegan. Tel. 01470/511-258. £8-13 lunch and £22-35 dinner. Open Monday through Saturday from noon to 2:00pm and from 7:00pm to 9:30pm. Closed November through February. MasterCard and Visa accepted.*

The Three Chimneys Restaurant is arguably the best restaurant on the Isle of Skye, and one you'll enjoy should you decide to dine here. It is about four miles west of Dunvegan on the B884. This small whitewashed stone building is home to a fine restaurant. Inside, you'll find a wonderful dining experience and outstanding food – outstanding enough to not only be *A Taste of Scotland* award winner, but also outstanding enough to be named *1999 Restaurant of the Year* by *A Taste of Scotland*. Renowned in these parts for their outstanding seafood, you'll find out soon enough that they have earned their reputation for excellence. Only the freshest ingredients and staples from the land and sea of Skye are used here.

Inside you'll find either white-washed or natural stone walls, rough-hewn dark wood accents, subdued lighting and low, open-beam ceilings. The effect is one of intimacy and closeness. And yes, there are three fireplaces. The menu changes monthly, but if you like seafood, you'll find such delicacies as west coast halibut filet with leek and fennel with red pepper sauce and rosti, or scallops and monkfish brochette, spiced couscous and saffron cream. For non-seafood eaters, you'll be able to try such items as red deer collops-in-the-pan, skirlie mash, savoy cabbage and rich game gravy. Seating is limited at the Three Chimneys Restaurant, so do call ahead for reservations. Reservations are required for dinner, and suggested for lunch, especially during the summer months.

CAIRIDH RESTAURANT, *Sligachan, Isle of Skye. Tel. 01599/650-204. £20-35. Open daily from 6:30pm to 11:00pm (last dinner order at 9:30pm). MasterCard and Visa accepted.*

The Cairidh Restaurant serves the Sligachan Hotel, and is a very good restaurant specializing in seafood. Large windows overlook Sligachan, so you get marvelous views as well as great food. The menu changes often, but you might find such treats as collops of monkfish and mussels pan-fried in pernod and tomato sauce, served on a bed of jeweled couscous, or filet of wild salmon filled with prawn mousse wrapped in Parma ham and served with a white wine and fennel sauce. Lamb, duck, beef and vegetarian dishes are also available.

AN CRAN FIGE TEA ROOM AND RESTAURANT, *Broadford, Isle of Skye. Tel. 01471/822-616. £3-7 for lunch, £10-18 for dinner. Open daily from 10:30am to 8:00pm. MasterCard and Visa accepted.*

An Cran Fige (Gaelic for *The Fig Tree*) Tea Room and Restaurant is a great place to stop for a bite to eat on the Isle of Skye. Pleasant surroundings coupled with good food always makes for a good dining experience. The Fig Tree provides leisurely dining amid lots of natural light from the large windows. Vaulted ceilings and light pine slats on the walls and ceilings keep it light and bright. The lunch menu includes sandwiches and soup. Evening meals are a little more substantial, with a good selection of fish, beef, vegetarian and poultry offerings.

SEAMUS' BAR, *Sligachan, Isle of Skye. Tel. 01478/650-204. £2-6. Open daily from 9:00am to 9:00pm (serving food), until 11:30pm on Saturday and 12:30am on Sunday. MasterCard and Visa accepted.*

This is a very popular pub, located at the crossroads of the main roads between the east and west of the Isle of Skye. They serve a variety of pub grub throughout the day and evening, and it is a great place for hillwalkers to put their feet up and relax after a hard day's hike. Saturday evenings are especially festive and this rather large pub is packed with local clientele listening to one of the local bands, or one from the mainland. Over 100 malt whiskies are available, as well as a variety of soups, salads, baked potatoes and sandwiches.

SEEING THE SIGHTS

The Isle of Skye in and of itself is a great sightseeing trip. Sandy beaches, precipitous cliffs, jagged peaks and lots of lonely countryside are great. But there are a few other things worth visiting.

Clan Donald Visitor Centre, *Armadale, Tel. 01471/844-305; open from March through October daily from 9:30am to 5:30pm; admission is £3.40 for adults, £2.60 for seniors and £2 for children.* Clan Donald Visitor Centre is housed in the ruins of the neo-Gothic Armadale Castle. The visitor center provides a historic look at the MacDonald Clan through the centuries, including their reign as *Lords of the Islands*. A fine audio-visual presentation takes you through the history. The gardens are remarkable evidence that Skye is not as inhospitable to plants as you might think. A vast variety of flora can be seen here, including the rhododendrons that flower so beautifully.

Luib Croft Museum, *Luib, Tel. 01471/822-427; open daily from 10:00am to 5:00pm; admission is £1*. This small folk museum features the Isle of Skye through the centuries. Several exhibits cover the period of time known as the *Clearances*, when wealthy landowners cleared massive tracts of land of the sharecropping peasants. Newspaper articles from the time help you understand the indignation that the Clearances caused in this part of the country.

Skye Heritage Centre, *Portree, Tel. 01478/613-649; open daily from 11:00am to 5:30pm; admission is £2.50*. The Skye Heritage Centre tells the story of the Isle of Skye for the last 300 years. Fine audiovisual presentations. Exhibits and videos focus your attention on some of the more difficult times faced by islanders through the years, including information on the Clearances and the Jacobite Rebellion.

Dunvegan Castle, *north of Dunvegan, Tel. 01470/521-206, Fax 01470/ 521-205; open Easter through the end of October daily from 10:00am to 5:00pm; admission is £5.20 for adults, £4.60 for seniors and £2.60 for children*. Dunvegan Castle is the ancestral home for Clan MacLeod, and has been for the past 750-plus years. The castle commands a prominent position on a rocky outlook, and once upon a time could only be reached by boat. Today, the moat has been covered to allow a little easier access.

A number of the rooms are open to the public, and they have been furnished with pieces that are hundreds of years old, and all of them are original to the castle. Of particular interest is the faded and raggedy *Fairy Flag*, a flag reportedly given to one of the MacLeod chieftains by a fairy, with the promise that it would bring the MacLeods victory in battle whenever displayed at the forefront of the battle. There was only one small catch: it could only be used three times, and two of its times have been used (it worked both previous times). Fact or fiction? You be the judge. The castle grounds are also a sight to see, and are carefully cared for, for your viewing pleasure and enjoyment.

At the castle jetty you can catch a boat ride out into Loch Dunvegan on a **seal-watching** expedition (*the cost is £4 for adults, £3.60 for seniors, and £2.50 for children*). It's a nice diversion, and the playful seals seem to enjoy the company. From Portree, take the A855 north for about six miles. Watch for the carpark for the **Old Man of Storr**. This 165-foot stack of rock is an interesting geographic feature of this part of the island.

Flora MacDonald Gravesite, *Kilmuir Church, Kilmuir.* At the north end of the Trotternish Peninsula, you'll find Kilmuir Church and a tall monument to the impressive and daring Flora MacDonald. By now you understand that Flora is one of Scotland's greatest heroines, a position earned for helping Bonnie Prince Charlie escape from his enemies after the failed 1745 Jacobite Rebellion.

SPORTS & RECREATION

Cycling
- **Fairwinds Bicycle Hire**, *Fairwinds, Broadford, Isle of Skye. Tel. 01471/822-270*
- **Island Cycles**, *The Green, Portree, Isle of Skye. Tel. 01478/613-121*
- **Skye Bikes**, *Kyleakin, Isle of Skye. Tel. 01599/534-795*

Diving
- **Hebridean Diving Services**, *Lochbay, Isle of Skye. Tel. 01478/592-219*

Hillwalking
Some of the Cuillin Mountains require advanced hiking skills, and rapidly changing weather patterns just add to the danger. If you're a little unsure about striking out on your own to do some hillwalking, here are a few guide services available on the Isle of Skye:
- **Guiding on Skye**, *4 Gedintailor Road, Portree, Isle of Skye. Tel. 01478/650-380*
- **Island Horizons**, *5 Kirkton Road, Lochcarron, Isle of Skye. Tel. 01520/722-238*
- **Mike Lates Hillwalking Guide**, *3 Luib, Broadford, Isle of Skye. Tel. 01471/822-116*

Horseback Riding
- **Portree Riding Stables**, *Garalapin, Portree, Isle of Skye. Tel. 01478/612-945*
- **Skye Riding Centre**, *Borve, near Portree, Isle of Skye. Tel. 01470/532-233*
- **Skye Riding Stables**, *Portree, Isle of Skye. Tel. 01470/582-419*
- **Uig Hotel Pony Trekking**, *Uig, Isle of Skye. Tel. 01470/542-205*

Windsurfing
- **Whitewater Activities**, *Number 19 Lincro, Kilmuir, Isle of Skye. Tel. 01470/542-414*

PRACTICAL INFORMATION

Tourist Information
• **Broadford Tourist Information Centre**, *Broadford, Isle of Skye. Tel.* 01471/822-361
• **Portree Tourist Information Centre**, *Mealle House, Portree, Isle of Skye. Tel.* 01478/612-137

ISLE OF MULL

The **Isle of Mull** lies off the west mainland of Scotland across from Oban. Part of the Inner Hebrides, the Isle of Mull is the second largest of those islands. It is also a popular tourist destination, receiving up to 500,000 visitors per year. The island measures roughly 25 miles square, and is a green, green place. Between 90 and 100 inches of rain fall here each year, making it one of the rainiest places in Scotland. If you are a fan of Robert Louis Stevenson, you are probably familiar with the Isle of Mull through his novel *Kidnapped*. Many of David Balfour's adventures were featured here. Mr. Stevenson is thought to have used the island for inspiration, as he stayed in a cottage on an island just south of Fionnphort while he wrote the novel.

Hillwalking is a favorite pastime of visitors to the Isle of Mull, and it is also the departure point for two other popular Scottish Isles, Iona and Staffa.

ARRIVALS & DEPARTURES

By Bus
Buses reach Oban numerous times per day from Glasgow, where you can catch a ferry across to the Isle of Mull.

By Car
Cars arrive on the Isle of Mull via the ferry from Oban (see below).

By Ferry
Ferry service reaches the Isle of Mull from Oban several times a day. A less commonly used ferry operates between Lochaline and Fishnish. Round-trip fare for the 45-minute ferry ride from Oban to Craignure costs £5.75 per person; if you have a car, it will cost an additional £40 per vehicle. Bicycles cost £1 each direction, in addition to the per-person charge. Contact **Caledonian MacBrayne Ferries** for schedule information, *Tel. 01631/566-688 or 01680/812-343.*

WHERE TO STAY

WESTERN ISLES HOTEL, *Tobermory, Isle of Mull. Tel. 01688/302-012. 25 Rooms. Rates: £38-45 single; £38-150 per person double. Rates include breakfast. Amex, MasterCard and Visa accepted.*

The Western Isles Hotel sits majestically on a promontory overlooking the Mull town of Tobermory and its harbor. It is a handsome gray stone Victorian hotel, built in 1888. It was formerly used as a hunting lodge for a whisky company's top executives and their top clients. Today, you get to enjoy the Victorian elegance. Each bedroom is large and individually decorated in a variety of design schemes, all with pleasant floral and/or tartan accents. Canopied beds are featured in several of the rooms. All rooms have a television, hairdryer and tea- and coffee-making facilities.

About half the rooms look out onto Tobermory Bay, and are of course the most desirable, although you'll pay a few more pounds for the sea views. But they really are magnificent views. The Conservatory Restaurant looks out onto the harbor and provides great views as well as wonderful food (see the *Where to Eat* section).

THE TOBERMORY HOTEL, *53 Main Street, Tobermory, Isle of Mull. Tel. 01688/302-091, Fax 01688/302-254. 16 Rooms. Rates: £35-45 single; £35-45 per person double. Rates include breakfast. MasterCard and Visa accepted.*

Three homes across from Tobermory Bay were combined and converted into this wonderful hotel. Of the 16 rooms, almost all of them have views of the tranquil harbor; those that don't have a close-up view of the cliff behind the hotel. If you had your heart set on a view of the harbor, be sure and specify that when you make your reservations. About half of the rooms are ensuite, but that means that the other half are not, so that is another thing to specify when you make your reservation. Most of the rooms without ensuite baths, however, do have bathrooms in the hallway dedicated to them. Each bedroom has been renovated within the past few years, and you are assured of a pleasant stay. Each room is furnished with quality furnishings and tastefully decorated.

ACHNACRAIG HOUSE, *Dervaig, Isle of Mull. Tel. 01688/400-309. 3 Rooms. Rates: £23-28 single; £17-23 per person double. Rates include breakfast. Credit cards not accepted.*

You'll find the Achnacraig House at the northern end of the Isle of Mull at the head of a deep sea loch. This traditional old stone cottage has been modernized throughout, and you'll have a pleasant stay here. Old oak beams, a nice large resident lounge and a warm greeting from Mrs. Smith await your arrival. The bedrooms are not particularly large, but they are comfortably furnished.

RED BAY COTTAGE, *Deargphort, Fionnphort, Isle of Mull. Tel. 01681/ 700-396. 3 Rooms. Rates: £20-22 single; £16-20 per person double. Rates include breakfast. Credit cards not accepted.*

Red Bay Cottage is a wonderful place to stay on the northwestern tip of the Isle of Mull. This modern new house features three comfortable bedrooms, stunning views of the Isle of Iona, and a wonderful host and hostess in John and Eleanor Wagstaff. The cottage is located a mere 70 feet from the sea, and you'll enjoy the sea views you'll have here. If you have a few extra minutes on your hands, Eleanor runs a silversmithing school that might be of interest to you.

WHERE TO EAT

CONSERVATORY RESTAURANT, *Tobermory, Isle of Mull. Tel. 01688/302-012. £20-30. Open noon to 2:30pm and 6:30pm to 9:30pm. Amex, MasterCard and Visa accepted.*

The Conservatory Restaurant is the restaurant associated with the Western Isles Hotel. The hotel, a converted Victorian mansion, sits high above Tobermory Bay, and the restaurant faces out onto the bay. It is difficult to say which is better: the views of the bay or the meals on your plate. The Conservatory has gained quite a reputation for fine seafood. But their menu isn't limited to seafood, and you'll find a good selection of beef, lamb and vegetarian dishes. Dress is nice casual.

WATERSEDGE SEAFOOD RESTAURANT, *53 Main Street, Tobermory. Tel. 01688/302-091. £20-30. Open daily from 6:30pm to 9:30pm. MasterCard and Visa accepted.*

The Watersedge Seafood Restaurant is the formal dining room for the Tobermory Hotel, and is considered one of the best places to eat on the Isle of Mull. The menu changes fairly regularly, but you can expect dishes like grilled brochette of prawns with whole fresh garlic roasted in olive oil, or grilled sea bass with saffron noodles. Dress is nice casual.

GANNET'S RESTAURANT, *25 Main Street, Tobermory, Isle of Mull. Tel. 01688/302-203. £4-12. Open Daily 9:30am to 10:00pm. Closed November through Easter. MasterCard and Visa accepted.*

If you're looking for fine seafood in a wonderful setting, try Gannet's Restaurant in Tobermory. The building the restaurant is housed in is over 200 years old, and it has a wonderful feel to it. The menu changes every so often, but you can expect a number of fine dishes from the sea as well as venison, lamb and beef dishes. If you prefer, there are also a number of vegetarian entrees. The food is plentiful and simply prepared, and you'll enjoy it. Dress is casual.

SEEING THE SIGHTS

Upon your arrival on the Isle of Mull, the first thing to see is **Torosay Castle and Gardens**, *Craignure, Tel. 01680/812-421; open Easter to mid-October daily from 10:30am to 5:30pm; admission is £4.50 for adults, £3.50 for seniors, £1.50 for children, and a family ticket is also available for £10*. You can either take the half-hour walk to the castle from Craignure, or you can hop on the *Lady of the Isles*, a narrow-gauge railroad that operates between the town and the castle. It's a pretty ride that features picturesque vistas of mountains and sea. Contact **Mull Railway**, *Old Pier, Craignure, Tel. 01680/812-494; the train operates from mid-April through mid-October; fare is £2.50 or adults and £1.10 for seniors and children.*

The castle is not really a castle, but rather a 19th-century Victorian mansion that has been restored to its former elegance. A number of rooms are open to the public, and feature period furnishings and old paintings of the family and the wildlife that abounds on Mull. It is currently owned by the Guthrie family, and many of the items you see are from their family. However, the highlight of Torosay Castle is its famous gardens. You'll find 12 acres of terraced and perfectly sculpted gardens that are spectacular and well worth a few minutes of your time. Venetian statues are located at strategic points in the garden.

About three miles beyond Torosay on a side road off the A849 is **Duart Castle**, *off the A849, Tel. 01680/812-309; open May through mid-October from 10:30am to 6:00pm; admission is £3.50 for adults, £2.50 for seniors and £2 for children.* You probably saw Duart Castle looming above the Sound of Mull as you came across on the ferry. The ancestral home of the powerful MacLean clan, this 13th-century castle was restored in the early part of this century. Duart Castle just looks like a castle is supposed to look: strongly fortified, turreted and perched on a rocky crag with commanding views all around it.

The MacLean clan was one of the most powerful Scottish families in this part of Scotland for many generations, and their war-like demeanor is renowned. A number of rooms of the castle are open, and exhibits help you understand the role the MacLean clan played in Scottish history. You can see both ends of the social spectrum at Duart Castle, with stops by the Banqueting Hall and a visit to the dungeon. You can also climb out on the ramparts for splendid views (bring your camera).

From Duart Castle, get back on the A849 and head south. At Strathcoil, take the signpost directing you to Lochbuie. This is a pretty drive, and at the end of it you'll find Lochbuie, and in Lochbuie, you'll find the crumbling ruins of **Moy Castle**, a former stronghold of the MacLean clan. Nearby is an ancient **stone circle**, dating from around 200 BC. It features eight standing stones. The beach at Lochbuie is sandy and invites a stroll along the seashore.

Head back to Strathcoil, and then left on the A849 toward Fionnphort. This small town's main claim to fame is its ferry out to **Iona** (see the next destination below). There is, however, a relatively new museum that focuses on St. Columba, the cleric responsible for firmly planting Christianity in Scotland. It is called **The St. Columba Centre**, *Fionnphort; open daily, Monday through Saturday from 10:00am to 6:00pm, and Sunday from 11:00am to 6:00pm; admission is £3.50 for adults and £2 for children.* A number of fine displays trace St. Columba's life, from his beginnings as an Irish monk, to his ill-fated battle over broken copyright laws, to his eventual founding of a monastic community on Iona.

After Fionnphort (and your probable trip to Iona), the next place to see is Tobermory. You'll enjoy the drive from Fionnphort to Tobermory, as it skirts Mull's tallest mountain, Ben More (3,169 feet), and snakes along the coastline most of the way. Tobermory is a most pleasant seaside village, and its multi-colored houses and store fronts make it look for all the world like a basket of Easter eggs.

While here, you might wish to stop by the **Mull Museum**, *Main Street, Tobermory; open from Easter through mid-October Monday through Friday from 10:30am to 4:30pm and Saturday from 10:30am to 1:30pm; admission is £1 for adults and 50p for children.* The museum offers a look at the Isle of Mull and her history, and has a few interesting exhibits, including one on the *Florencia*, a ship of the ill-fated 1588 Spanish Armada that stopped in Tobermory Harbor for repairs and replenishing of stores. It seems she sunk in the harbor, some say for trying to leave without paying her bill. Regardless of the reason, the ship did sink, and there is rumored to be vast amounts of unrecovered gold that went down with her still resting at the bottom of the harbor.

IONA & STAFFA

Iona is an island oasis that rests about a five-minute ferry ride off the west coast of the Isle of Mull, across from Fionnphort. Iona is famous for the monastic community that was founded here in the 6th century by St. Columba.

Staffa is a tiny dot that lies northeast of Iona and is accessible from a ferry from Iona. Staffa is famous for **Fingal's Cave**, a natural amphitheater of impressive proportions.

ARRIVALS & DEPARTURES
By Ferry
You can reach Iona via ferry from the Mull port town of Fionnphort. Ferries run frequently throughout the day. The round-trip fare for the

five-minute ferry ride costs £3.10 per person (no cars are allowed on Iona). Bicyclists can bring bicycles over for free.

Staffa is reached via ferry that runs between Iona and Staffa. The ferry leaves Iona, stops briefly in Fionnphort to pick up more passengers and then heads to Staffa. The cost is £8 for adults and £4 for children.

WHERE TO STAY

ST. COLUMBA HOTEL, *Isle of Iona. Tel. 01681/700-304. 23 Rooms. Rates: £55-60 per person single, £48-50 per person double. MasterCard and Visa accepted.*

The St. Columba hotel began its life over 150 years ago as a mansion for the local Presbyterian minister. Not long after its construction, however, it was converted into a hotel and has been serving that purpose ever since. Today, you'll find a comfortable but basic place to stay. It is located just a few hundred yards from the docks, and has outstanding views of the sea (ask for a sea-facing room; you'll be glad you did).

ARGYLL HOTEL, *Isle of Iona. Tel. 01681/700-334, Fax 01681/700-510. 17 Rooms. Rates: £50-60 per person single, £40-50 per person double. The hotel is open from Easter through the beginning of October. MasterCard and Visa accepted.*

Mrs. Fionna Menzies runs the Argyll Hotel, which is within about two minutes' walk from the ferry dock on Iona. The hotel is a converted Victorian mansion, and is a pleasant place to stay if you come to Iona for a visit. The home was built in 1868, and has been renovated several times in the ensuing years. There are 17 rooms, and 15 of them are ensuite, while two share a bathroom in the hall. The Argyll Hotel fills up quickly in the summer months, so if you feel like you want to stay here, be certain and make reservations ahead of time.

WHERE TO EAT

For dining, I would suggest finding a place to eat while you are on the Isle of Mull.

SEEING THE SIGHTS

Iona

The island of Iona rests just off the west coastline of the Isle of Mull. It is a mere one mile wide by three miles long. Small it may be, but its fame is huge. For it is on Iona that **St. Columba** and a dozen fellow monks landed to begin the ministry in Scotland. St. Columba was not the first to bring Christianity to Scotland; that honor is reserved for St. Ninian, who started the work some 150 years before St. Columba ventured here in 563 AD. But St. Columba is the one who finally got Christianity to get a foothold in Scotland. Fiery and passionate, St. Columba began his ministry in Scotland in a most unorthodox manner (see the sidebar).

QUARRELING SAINTS

*Prior to his arrival in Scotland in 563 AD, **St. Columba** had been a bishop in Ireland. As the story goes, his teacher **St. Finian** lent a book to St. Columba, who copied it secretly (by hand, of course). St. Finian found out, and claimed not only the original, but also the copy that had been made. The two could come to no agreeable solution, so the case was presented to the king of Ireland, who judged in favor of St. Finian. He said, "To every cow its calf, and to every book its copy." (Early copyright law?). Rather than return the copy, St. Columba decided to fight (not very saintly); over 3,000 men lost their lives in the ensuing battle. St. Columba was reportedly so distraught over the results of his squabble with St. Finian that he vowed to bring as many souls to Christ as were slain in the battle. The records state that he was successful in his penance – more than 3,000 additional souls embraced Christ before the end of his life. Unfortunately for the Irish, but fortunate for the Scottish, St. Columba was banished from Ireland for his part in the war. He had to find another vineyard to labor in, and Scotland was a short boat ride away.*

Once he landed on Iona, St. Columba established a monastic community that sent missionaries throughout Scotland. The community flourished for centuries, despite the ravages of less-than-friendly neighbors like the Vikings. The Vikings repeatedly plundered Iona, their most infamous raid coming in 806, when they murdered 68 clerics.

The main sight to see on Iona is the **Abbey of Iona**, *open daily; admission is free, although a donation of £2 is requested.* The abbey lay in ruins for centuries until the Iona Community, a religious group that also conducts religious workshops in and around the abbey, restored the abbey in the 1930s. Of particular interest is the peaceful cloister. Note the sandstone columns – they are reproductions of those that were originally here. Fortunately one of the originals remained, and architects were able to copy it and reproduce the many columns you now see.

In addition to the abbey, the **Reilig Oran** (*Graves of the Kings*) is also a popular place to visit. It is about 100 yards from the abbey and is the final resting place of 48 Scottish kings, and several others from Ireland and Norway. (Its most famous residents are Macbeth and his victim, Duncan.)

During the summer months, the abbey is besieged by tourists, and it can get a little hectic. If you'd like to take a walk to get away from the hubbub, there is a small hill on the north side of the abbey with a path to the top. From there you can look down on the religious community, as well as have other splendid views. You can almost feel the presence of St. Columba, and you know he must have spent time on this hill, meditating about his mission to the Scots.

Staffa
At the pier in Baile Mor on Iona, you can catch a ferry for the tiny dot of an island called Staffa. Here you'll find **Fingal's Cave**, a cathedral-like orifice that features intriguing basalt columns similar to those found at Giant's Causeway in Northern Ireland. You can visit the cave by foot by walking along a platform, or you can go via boat. Through the years, the cave has received a number of noted tourists, including Queen Victoria and her husband Albert, and the composer Mendelssohn, who was reportedly so inspired by the cave that he composed the *Hebrides Overture* after his visit. Other notable individuals to visit the cave include poets Burns, Keats, Tennyson and Wordsworth, as well as writers Robert Louis Stevenson, Sir Walter Scott and Dan McQuillan (you may know this last writer as the author of Open Road's *Scotland Guide*).

SPORTS & RECREATION
Cycling
• **Mull Bicycle Hire**, *Craignure, Isle of Mull. Tel. 01680/812-487*
• **On Yer Bike**, *Salen, Isle of Mull. Tel. 01680/300-501*
• **Tom Mhuillin Bike Hire**, *Tobermory, Isle of Mull. Tel. 01688/302-164*

PRACTICAL INFORMATION
Tourist Information
• **Craignure Tourist Information Centre**, *Craignure Pier, Craignure, Isle of Mull. Tel. 01680/812-377*
• **Tobermory Tourist Information Centre**, *Main Street, Tobermory, Isle of Skye. Tel. 01688/302-182*

ISLE OF ARRAN
Arran Island lies about 20 miles off the southwest coast of Scotland. It is an island of immense geographic diversity. Indeed, it has been called *Scotland in Miniature* because it seems to possess many of the geographic characteristics found throughout Scotland, including moors and lochs, glens and beaches and rocky sea cliffs. The northeastern section of the island boasts a number of mounts that soar over 2,000 feet, including **Goat Fell**, which tops out at 2,866 feet. As you can imagine, this is a very popular destination for rock climbers and hillwalkers.

The southern part of the island draws hikers also, although you'll find a little gentler terrain to cope with here. Forests and moorlands punctuated with occasional standing stones and rocky ruins invite you to consider what this must have been like for those who lived here so many hundreds of years ago. The island is about 25 miles long and 10 miles wide, but for all its compactness there is a wide variety of natural sights to see.

ARRIVALS & DEPARTURES

By Car
You can take a vehicle over to Arran on the car ferry that leaves from Ardrossan. The A841 is the one main road that encircles the island, so you'll be able to see the island that way.

By Ferry
Ferry service runs between Ardrossan to Brodick four times a day (three times on Sunday) from April through October, four times a day Monday through Friday and three times Saturday and Sunday from November through March. The fare is £5.75 per passenger in addition to £34.50 per vehicle.

WHERE TO STAY

AUCHRANNIE COUNTRY HOUSE, *Brodick, Isle of Arran. Tel. 01770/302-234, Fax 01770/302-812. 28 Rooms. Rates: £40-60 single, £40-60 per person double. Amex, MasterCard and Visa accepted.*

If you stay at Auchrannie Country House you may just have one of the finest accommodation experiences of your Scottish holiday. Not only has this gorgeous pink sandstone Victorian mansion been restored with taste and elegance, but its staff is regarded as one of the friendliest around. Top that off with a setting amid six acres of gardens and wooded countryside and you've got all the ingredients necessary for a great memory.

Each of the bedrooms has been comfortably and expensively decorated using designer fabrics and furnishings. All the rooms are full of creature comforts, such as television, telephone, hairdryer and tea- and coffee-making facilities. There are two restaurants associated with Auchrannie Country House, the Garden Restaurant and Brambles Bistro and both provide a great dining experience (see the *Where to Eat* section). Auchrannie features a host of wonderful activities to participate in while you are here. They have a 20-meter swimming pool, sauna and steam room, a fitness center and an aromatherapy room. Pound for pound, Auchrannie Country House may well be one of the best accommodation buys in Scotland.

TIGH-NA-ACHAIDH, *Corrie, Isle of Arran. Tel. 01770/810-208. 3 Rooms. Rates: £26 single, £23-27 per person double. Rates include breakfast. Credit cards not accepted.*

You'll like this small B&B that sits serenely at the edge of the northeastern Arran village of Corrie. The B&B is nestled on a little over an acre of land with outstanding views across the Firth of Clyde. Ken and Helen Thornburn are your hosts, and they are a gracious and pleasant couple to spend time with. They are proud of their four-star B&B, and they are members of *Scotland's Best B&Bs*. All three bedrooms are nice sized and comfortably furnished. Each is equipped with a television, hairdryer and tea- and coffee-making facilities.

LOCHRANZA SCOTTISH YOUTH HOSTEL, *Lochranza, Isle of Arran. Tel. 01770/830-631, centralized reservations: 0541/553-255. 14 Rooms, 68 total beds. Rates: £7.75 for seniors (over 18) and £6.50 juniors (under 18). MasterCard and Visa accepted.*

In the northern Isle of Arran town of Lochranza, right on the A841, you'll find the Lochranza Scottish Youth Hostel. Lochranza has long been a haven for artists and hikers, so this hostel housed in a white frame house should meet your needs just fine, especially if you are looking for budget accommodations. There are eight 4-bed rooms, and six larger dormitory-style rooms. The rooms are large but not spacious, but they are clean and comfortable.

WHERE TO EAT

THE GARDEN RESTAURANT, *Brodick, Isle of Arran. Tel. 01770/302-234, Fax 01770/302-812. £20-30. Open daily from noon to 2:00pm and from 6:30pm to 9:30pm. Amex, MasterCard and Visa accepted.*

The Garden Restaurant is the formal dining room for Auchrannie Country House. It is housed in the original dining room, although a conservatory has expanded the room to take advantage of the beautiful setting visible outside those windows. You'll find a delicious meal here, no matter what you order. Recognized by the judges from *A Taste of Scotland*, the restaurant prepares their meals with only the freshest ingredients. Seafood is their specialty, so you can expect such dishes as sea bass roasted on fennel fronds with stuffed baby artichokes, or if you'd prefer something a little more beefy, try the prime beef filet with hazelnuts brazed with a rosemary essence. Vegetarian dishes are also available for those with that preference. Dress is nice casual.

BRODICK CASTLE RESTAURANT, *Brodick Castle, Brodick, Isle of Arran. Tel. 01770/302-202, Fax 01770/302-312. £5-10. Open daily from 11:30am to 9:00pm. MasterCard and Visa accepted.*

The Brodick Castle restaurant is located, interestingly enough, in Brodick Castle. To be precise, it is located in the former servants' quarters. The menu is filled with tasty treats and light snacks, such as soup, salads and sandwiches. It is open all day, so you can satisfy your hunger at whatever time it comes calling. In the evening you can sample more substantial meals such as goujons of salmon with a crispy crust of pine nuts, herbs and sugar served with Scottish berries. This dish and others like it helped earn the restaurant *A Taste of Scotland* awards. Dress is casual.

BRAMBLES BISTRO, *Brodick, Isle of Arran. Tel. 01770/302-234, Fax 01770/302-812. £5-10. Open daily from noon to 11:00pm. Amex, MasterCard and Visa accepted.*

Brambles Bistro is the informal dining restaurant for Auchrannie Country House. It is a great place to stop in for snacks or light meals, and features a light and vibrant atmosphere. The fare here is primarily traditional Scottish, and you'll find soup, salads and sandwiches here.

SEEING THE SIGHTS

As you depart the ferry in Brodick, that large mountain just to the northwest of you is **Goat Fell**, the tallest mountain on the Isle of Arran. It soars 2,866 feet above sea level (and you *are* at sea level). The mountain draws hillwalkers from all over Scotland and elsewhere to its jagged slopes.

While in Brodick, you should definitely visit **Brodick Castle**, *Brodick, Tel. 01770/302-202; open daily Easter through October from 11:30am to 5:00pm; admission is £4.50 for adults and £3 for seniors and children.* There has been a castle here for centuries, although most of the one you see before you dates from the 19th century. There are parts, however, that have been here since the 15th century. The castle is the ancestral home of the Hamilton Clan. Inside you'll find a delightful assortment of exquisite period furniture, original oil paintings, and collections of porcelain and silver that have been in the Hamilton family for generations. A walled garden outside the castle has been restored to its Victorian glory. It features award-winning beds of rhododendrons, daffodils and a dozen other varieties of flowers.

If you're lucky, you might catch a glimpse of one of the two ghosts that call Brodick Castle home. The Gray Lady is an apparition that has been seen numerous times through the years wandering the halls of the older parts of the castle. And a ghostly gentleman has been reported sitting in the Library at various and sundry times.

After you've explored Brodick Castle, stop in for a brief visit at the **Arran Heritage Museum**, *Brodick, Tel. 01770/302-636; open April through October Monday through Saturday from 11:00am to 5:00pm; admission is £1.50 for adults and £1 for children.* The museum is housed in neighboring croft buildings, and features an assortment of furniture and farm implements that represent life through the years in a crofting community on Arran.

From Brodick, head out on the A841 and just follow your nose. The rest of the island is pretty well undeveloped from a tourism standpoint, but provides a wide breadth of scenery to see and explore.

SPORTS & RECREATION
Cycling
- **Brodick Boat and Cycle Centre**, *The Beach, Brodick, Isle of Arran. Tel. 01770/302-009*
- **Brodick Cycles**, *Main Street, Brodick, Isle of Arran. Tel. 01770/302-460*
- **Spinning Wheels**, *Corrie, Isle of Arran. Tel. 01770/810-640*
- **Whiting Bay Cycle Hire**, *Elim, Whiting Bay, Isle of Arran. Tel. 01770/700-382*

Horseback Riding
- **Cairnhouse Riding Centre**, *Blackwaterfoot, Isle of Arran. Tel. 01770/860-466*
- **Cloyburn Equestrian Centre**, *Brodrick, Isle of Arran. Tel. 01770/302-800*

PRACTICAL INFORMATION
Tourist Information
- **Isle of Arran Tourist Information Centre**, *The Pier, Brodick, Isle of Arran. Tel. 01770/302-140*

THE OUTER HEBRIDES - LEWIS & HARRIS
Windswept and barren, the **Outer Hebrides** lay about 40 miles off the western coast of Scotland. There are a number of islands in this chain, although the main ones that draw attention from tourists are the islands of **Lewis and Harris**. Actually, it is just one large island, but it has two names. The island is a study in contrasts – some parts are lunar-like, others are mountainous, and still others consist of lochs and moorland. The Outer Hebrides are also called the Western Isles.

There are not a lot of typical tourist sorts of things to do in the Outer Hebrides. It is a quieter pace here, with few people and even fewer tourist attractions. Unless you like hillwalking, bird watching, or are into seascapes, then there is not much to recommend. But if you like solitude and a place to get away from it all, then you might consider these islands. The Outer Hebrides draw artists to their lonely and tranquil existence: writers, poets, sculptors and others who want to be alone with their thoughts and creativity.

LEWIS

Lewis is at the northern two-thirds of the single island called Lewis and Harris. It has a population of around 20,000 souls, nearly half of which live in the only town of any size – **Stornoway**. The most notable tourist attraction on Lewis is the **Callanish Standing Stones**, which are only rivaled by Stonehenge in their megalithic presence.

Gaelic is the official language of the Western Isles, and you will definitely hear it spoken if you journey to Lewis or Harris. Many of the signposts will be in Gaelic, and most will be in English also (but not always). It's not a bad idea to have a good map of the area, obtained from the Western Isles Tourist Information Centre in Stornoway.

ARRIVALS & DEPARTURES

Lewis is reached via a three-hour ferry ride from Ullapool. Ferries dock in Stornoway's sheltered harbor several times a day, Monday through Saturday.

By Air

A small airport north of Stornoway receives flights from Glasgow and Inverness. From there you can take a £6 taxi ride into Stornoway.

By Ferry

Ullapool is the point of departure for ferries coming from the Scottish mainland. The three-hour voyage costs £21.15 per person, as well as £95 per vehicle. Motorcycles cost £48, and bicycles are £2. Two or three ferries a day make the trip between Ullapool and Stornoway. There is no ferry service on Sundays. Contact **Caledonian MacBrayne Ferries** for schedule information, *Tel. 01851/702-361 or 01854/612-358.*

WHERE TO STAY

SEAFORTH HOTEL, *9 James Street, Stornoway. Tel. 01851/702-740, Fax 01851/703-900. 70 rooms. Rates: £35-45 single; £35-45 per person double. Rates include breakfast. Amex, MasterCard and Visa accepted.*

The Seaforth is one of the newest hotels on the Isle of Lewis, and they have some of the amenities you have come to expect from hotels in Scotland. There are 70 rooms, and each is pretty much like the other. Each room is tastefully decorated and the furnishings are new and comfortable, if not exquisite. Each room features telephones, hairdryers and tea- and coffee-making facilities. There is a restaurant (see *Where to Eat* section) and a pub.

ESCHOL GUEST HOUSE, *Callanish, Isle of Lewis. Tel. 01851/621-357, Fax 01851/621-357. 3 Rooms. Rates: £29-33 single; £29-33 per person double. Open March through October. No credit cards accepted.*

If you have ventured over to west Lewis to take a look at the Callanish Standing Stones, then you may wish to stop at Eschol Guest House for your night's lodging. Eschol Guest House is a nice modern home that features three double rooms. Each bedroom is nice sized and pleasantly and comfortably furnished. There is no extra charge for the outstanding views you'll get here across a deep sea loch. Breakfast here deserves your fullest attention, as Eschol Guest House has earned a reputation for fine dining.

WHERE TO EAT

LA TERRAZZA RESTAURANT, *9 James Street, Stornoway. Tel. 01851/702-740, Fax 01851/703-900. £15-25. Open noon to 2:30pm and from 6:30 to 9:30pm. Amex, MasterCard and Visa accepted.*

La Terrazza Restaurant is the dining room for the Seaforth Hotel. They feature Scottish and Italian fare, and the meals are quite delicious. Expect pasta cooked with a Scottish flair, and lamb, beef and seafood with an Italian influence!

SEEING THE SIGHTS

Once you arrive in Stornoway, get on the A858 and head for the west coast of Lewis. As you near the coast, watch for signs directing you to the **Callanish Standing Stones** (the Gaelic spelling may be used: *Calanais*). These massive stones are silent relics of a religion that has long been forgotten from men's memories. As with Stonehenge, archaeologists, religionists and others are left to speculate about their meaning and significance. Like Stonehenge, these stoic stones show an astronomical orientation. A circle of 13 stones encircles a small chambered tomb; 19 massive stones lead northward from the circle, with spokes branching off in the direction of the other compass points at regular intervals. It is estimated that these stones have stood their ground for the past 3,500 to 5,000 years.

What were they used for, and who put them there? And how on earth did they do it? Answers to those questions at this point are merely speculative, since these people kept no records to assist our learning of their ways. Information plaques near the stones share some of the theories and facts that are known (or thought to be known!).

If you haven't brought your rental car with you, bus tours to Callanish can be arranged in Stornoway by stopping at the Tourist Information Centre (see below for address and telephone number).

While you're in the neighborhood, you might also want to check out **Carloway Broch**. Brochs are fortified towers that were built thousands of years ago as protective houses, forerunners to fortified castles. In one sense, they are similar to the round towers used in Ireland for centuries to protect against the depredations of the Vikings. Perched atop a rocky outcropping with magnificent views of the sea, Carloway Broch is one of the finest remaining examples of brochs that litter the Scottish coasts. Nearly 30 feet tall at certain points, this broch gives you some idea of what it looked like when it was intact. The broch is located about a quarter of a mile off the A858 just before you reach the turn-off for Dun Carloway (*Dun Charlabhagh*). A small interpretive center nearby tells a little more about what we know about these ancient brochs.

Continuing on the A858, head for Shawbost (*Slabost*). You'll find a small, no-frills museum called the **Shawbost School Museum**, *Shawbost, Tel. 01851/710-213; admission is free, but a small donation is requested.* About 30 years ago, Lewis school children competed to put together a museum that had items representative of life on Lewis. This small museum might be called precious in its child-like look at Lewis. The museum is in an old church, and features items donated by local townsfolk.

Back on the A858 heading north, you'll come to the small village of Arnol and the **Arnol Black House**, *Arnol, Tel. 01851//710-395; open May through September Monday through Friday from 10:00am to 1:00pm and from 2:00pm to 5:00pm, and on Saturday from 11:00am to 1:00pm and from 2:00pm to 5:00pm; admission is £1.50.* By now, you have experienced a bit of the weather on Lewis. Perhaps you encountered bright sunshine and warm temperatures (perhaps). Whether or not that is true, you certainly experienced a little wind. As you can imagine, the weather on this western coast can be tough – cold and windy at times. Keep that thought in mind as you explore the Arnol Black House, a home that is representative of the way people on Lewis lived for many generations.

The home was built with stones using no mortar, and the roof was a thatched affair. The name (Black House) is taken from the dark sootiness that seems to permeate the home. For generations, it was believed that rising smoke from peat fires helped keep the thatched roof water-tight, so these habitations were built without chimneys, and featured an open peat fire in the middle of the room. The furnishings you see and many of the utensils are original to the house.

Head north out of Arnol on the A857 toward the **Butt of Lewis Lighthouse**. This lighthouse was built in 1862 by the father of Robert Lewis Stevenson. Watch for signposts to *Rubha Robhanais*.

HARRIS

The **Isle of Harris** is really the southern end of the island that shares two names: Lewis and Harris. **North Harris**, which lies north of a narrow finger of land between East and West Loch Tarbert, is quite mountainous and rocky, while **South Harris** features more of a rolling landscape. The main town in Harris is **Tarbert**, which is either reached via car from Stornoway (on the A859) or by ferry from Uig on the Isle of Skye.

ARRIVALS & DEPARTURES

By Car

You can reach Harris by driving south out of Stornoway on the A859.

By Bus

Buses run frequently between Stornoway and Tarbert, the principal city of Harris. The trip takes 75 minutes.

By Ferry

Ferries run twice a day Monday through Friday from Uig on the Isle of Skye to Tarbert. The two-hour trip costs £13.80 per person plus £65 per vehicle. Motorcycles cost £33, and bicycles cost £4. Contact **Caledonian MacBrayne Ferries** for schedule information, *Tel. 01859/502-444.*

WHERE TO STAY

HARRIS HOTEL, *Tarbert. Tel. 01859/502-154, Fax 01859/502-281; E-mail: cameronharris@btinternet.com. 24 Rooms. Rates: £29-35 single; £29-35 per person double. Rates include breakfast. MasterCard and Visa accepted.*

The Harris Hotel has taken up residence in a former Victorian mansion built in the mid-19th century. There are 24 rooms, 18 of which are ensuite. The rooms vary in size, although most are large and all are comfortably, if not expensively, furnished. Several have views out to the fine garden that is kept here. You'll enjoy the cordial, relaxed atmosphere you'll find at this family-run hotel. All in all, this is a pleasant, comfortable place to stay if you venture to this outpost of the Western Isles.

HILL CREST GUEST HOUSE, *West Tarbert. Tel. 01859/502-119. 3 Rooms. Rates: £20-25 single; £18-23 per person double. Rates include breakfast. MasterCard and Visa accepted.*

Hill Crest Guest House sits on a hill with splendid views of West Tarbert Loch. They offer three rooms, including one family room. Each bedroom is pleasantly and comfortably furnished. Breakfast is of course included in the rate, but you'll also be able to have dinner here if you wish.

WHERE TO EAT

HARRIS HOTEL RESTAURANT, *Tarbert. Tel. 01859/502-154, Fax 01859/502-281. £15-22. Open 6:00pm to 9:30pm daily. MasterCard and Visa accepted.*

The restaurant for the Harris Hotel is one of the better places to eat on Harris. Seafood is a specialty, but you'll also be able to select from beef, lamb and wild game dishes. There are those who feel that lamb from Harris is the best in Scotland, and where better to savor this dish than in Harris itself?

SEEING THE SIGHTS

The sights to see in and around Harris are mostly natural, since there are few developed tourist sights here. But the natural sights make it worth your time. Single-track roads (primarily) take you around Harris, and you'll experience a diverse geographic land.

If you head north out of Tarbert, you'll wend your way amid conical peaks like **Sgaoth Aird** (1,890 feet) and **Clisham**, at 2,619 feet the tallest mountain in the Western Isles. The land here is quite barren and windswept, and the winds can howl through these canyons with little to stop their advance. You'll find few towns in North Harris. One of those few is **Scalpay** (*Caolas Scalpaigh*), resting along the northern shore of the East Loch Tarbert.

If you head west off the A859 you'll skirt the northern shore of West Loch Tarbert, again creeping along pretty barren landscapes with impressive mounts. The road ends at the small fishing village of **Hushinish** (*Husinis*). Here you'll find lovely seascapes and views out to sea, as well as fine sandy beaches. Heading south out of Tarbert, you drive through a rocky lunar landscape. When you reach the west coast village of **Luskentyre** (*Losgaintir*), you'll be treated to a wonderful view of Luskentyre's expansive sandy beaches.

Heading further south, you'll come to the village of **Rodel** (*Roghadal*). Here you'll find the 15th-century **St. Clement's Church**. This fine old church was built in the form of a crucifix. Inside there are a number of tombs, including that of Alexander MacLeod (also known as Alastair Crotach), Lord of Dunvegan Castle on the Isle of Skye. Take a few minutes and check out the sculpted panels around the inside of the church.

SPORTS & RECREATION
Angling
• **Lacasdale Loch Fishery**, *Old School House, Bunaconeader, Isle of Harris. Tel. 01859/502-189*
• **Scaliscro Lodge Hotel**, *Scaliscro, Uig, Isle of Lewis. Tel. 01851/672-325, Fax 01851/672-393*

• **Sea Trek**, *16 Uigen, Miavaig, Isle of Lewis. Tel. 01851/672-464, Fax 01851/ 672-464*
• **The Stornoway Trust**, *Leverhulme House, Stornoway, Isle of Lewis. Tel. 01851/702-002, Fax 01851/706-915*

Cycling
• **Alex Dan Cycle Centre**, *67 Kenneth Street, Stornoway. Tel. 01851/704-025*

Cruises
• **Hamish Taylor Scenic Cruises**, *Tigh an Tobair, Isle of Harris. Tel. 01859/ 530-310, Fax 01859/530-289; E-mail: hamtay@flodabay.corce9.co.uk*

Diving
• **Scalpay Diving Services**, *Scalpay. Tel. 01859/540-328*

Surfing
• **Hebridean Surf Holidays**, *17 Keith Street, Stornoway. Tel. 01851/705-862; E-mail: heb.surf@virgin.net*
• **Surf 'n' Sports**, *Stornoway. Tel. 01851/705-862*
• **The Surf Shop**, *26 Francis Street, Stornoway. Tel. 01851/705-862*

PRACTICAL INFORMATION
Tourist Information
• **Tarbert Tourist Information Centre**, *Tarbert. Tel. 01859/502-011*
• **Western Isles Tourist Information Centre**, *26 Cromwell Street, Stornoway. Tel. 01851/703-088*

ORKNEY

The term **Orkney** refers to a group of islands that are found off the northern coast of the Scottish mainland. Orkney is separated from the mainland by the **Pentland Firth**, a dangerous stretch of sea that is infamous for fast-moving tides, wicked whirlpools and towers of water taller than some ships. During half the day, the tide rushes from the Atlantic Ocean on the west to the North Sea on the east, then reverses itself for the other half of the day. The results can be quite dramatic – and perilous. It was an area that was avoided if at all possible by ancient mariners.

Orkney is a Norse word meaning *Seal Islands*. The *ey* at the end of the word means *islands* in Norse, so saying the 'Orkney Islands' is redundant, and would be like saying the 'Orkney Islands Islands.'

Spectacular sheer cliffs, shimmering sandy beaches and fertile farm-land typify Orkney. The rich farmland along the outer edges of the main island give way to rougher and more barren land in the interior. Visiting Orkney is an entirely different experience than visiting the rest of Scotland. It is like a journey into the past. One of the highlights of your Scottish holiday may well be a visit to the Stone Age burial site called **Maes Howe**. Another incredible archaeological find not far from Maes Howe is the ancient village of **Skara Brae**. This small Stone Age village was covered by a massive sandstorm 4,500 years ago. Uncovered by another storm in 1850, it presented archaeologists with a nearly perfect and intact village to study. Today it provides 21st century tourists with a glimpse into the lives of the ancient inhabitants of these lonely islands.

Divers, golfers, archaeologists, bird watchers, seal watchers and anglers are among those that are drawn to Orkney to savor her activities. Do you fall into any of those categories? If not, don't despair, read on, and perhaps you'll find something to hold your interest.

ARRIVALS & DEPARTURES

By Air

British Airways flies to the Orkney capital of Kirkwall from Aberdeen, Edinburgh, Glasgow and Inverness. They also operate flights from the English cities of Birmingham, London and Manchester to Kirkwall. See Chapter 6, *Planning Your Trip*, for British Airways contact information,

By Ferry

Ferry service to Orkney runs from either John O'Groats or Scrabster. **P&O Ferries**, *Scrabster, Tel. 01856/850-655,* runs a ferry for pedestrians or for passengers between Scrabster and Stromness two or three times a day during the summer. The fare is £18 per person and £50 per vehicle. If you are in John O'Groats, you can take a passenger-only ferry to Burwick that is operated by **John O'Groats Ferries**, *John O'Groats, Tel. 01955/611-353.*

GETTING AROUND ORKNEY

By Bicycle

Once you arrive on Orkney, there are a number of bicycle shops that will be glad to supply you with wheels. Or, you can bring your bicycle across on the ferry with you. The terrain on Orkney is mostly flat, so touring on bicycle shouldn't be too bad (but watch the narrow roads).

By Bus

Several bus lines operate on Orkney, and you should be able to get to many different places while letting someone else worry about the narrow roads:

- **Causeway Coaches**, *Kirkwall. Tel. 01856/831-444*
- **JD Peace Coaches**, *Kirkwall. Tel. 01856/872-866*
- **Rosie Coaches**, *Kirkwall. Tel. 01856/751-232*
- **Shalder Coaches**, *Stromness. Tel. 01856/850-809*

By Car

You can either bring your car across on the ferry, or you can rent one from one of the following agencies on Orkney:
- **Brass's Self-Drive Car Hire**, *Blue Star Garage, North End Road, Stromness. Tel. 01856/850-850, Fax 01856/850-985*
- **JD Peace Car Hire**, *Junction Road, Kirkwall. Tel. 01856/875-300*
- **Scarth Car Hire**, *Great Western Road, Kirkwall. Tel. 01856/872-125, Fax 01856/872-750*
- **Stromness Self Drive Cars**, *Castle Street, Kirkwall. Tel. 01856/850-973, Fax 01856/851-777*

WHERE TO STAY

WEST END HOTEL, *Main Street, Kirkwall. Tel. 01856/872-368, Fax 01856/876-181. 16 Rooms. Rates: £30-37 single; £30-35 per person double. Rates include breakfast. MasterCard and Visa accepted.*

You'll like this precise family-run hotel sitting in a quiet neighborhood a block or two from the downtown area. Jim and Isobel Currie are the proprietors, and they are anxious to see that you have a nice stay. This three-star hotel features comfortable bedrooms that are simply but pleasantly decorated. Each room has a telephone, television and tea- and coffee-making facilities. A pleasant pub/lounge allows you to stop by for some refreshment, pub grub, or company. Reduced rates for children are available.

WOODWICK HOUSE, *Tel. 01856/751-330, Fax 01856/751-383. 8 Rooms. Rates: £30-37 single; £28-43 per person double. Rates include breakfast. Credit cards not accepted.*

Located in Evie, about 20 to 25 minutes north of both Stromness and Kirkwall, not only will you have a wonderful place to stay, but you'll also be able to experience one of the best restaurants on Orkney (see *Where to Eat* below). But first, let's talk about Woodwick House, the accommodation. Woodwick House bills itself as a country house, and that it is. You'll drive through a few miles of fertile farmland and across a small bridge as you approach the house. The bedrooms here are soft and comfortable, and have been decorated simply but attractively. There are eight rooms, but only four of them are ensuite, so if that matters to you, be sure and specify that at the time you make your reservations. Woodwick House sits in 12 acres of pleasant Orkney countryside, with wonderful views, and a small stream that flows into the nearby bay.

ROYAL HOTEL, *Victoria Street, Kirkwall. Tel. 01856/873-477, Fax 01856/872-767. 25 Rooms. Rates: £25-50 single; £18-38 per person double. Rates include breakfast. MasterCard and Visa accepted.*

The Royal Hotel is conveniently located in central Kirkwall. Parts of the hotel were built in the 18th century (but don't worry – they have had one or two upgrades since that time). There are 25 bedrooms, and each is fair sized and comfortable. They are simply but tastefully decorated, and each has been recently refurbished. Each room has a television, radio and tea- and coffee-making facilities. Several of the rooms also feature four-poster beds. About one third of the rooms are not ensuite, so if that is an issue for you, mention it when you make your reservations. There are some pleasant gardens available for you to enjoy, as well as several pubs in which to sit back and relax.

INSKEYFT HOUSE, *Cannigall Road, St. Ola. Tel. 01856/876-515. 2 Rooms. Rates: £18-20 single; £15-17 per person double. Rates include breakfast. Credit cards not accepted.*

If you want to spend a little time in the home of a local family, then head for Mrs. Pratt's Inskeyft House. Just five minutes from Kirkwall, Inskeyft House is a modern, relatively new B&B. You'll be most pleased with your comfortable bedroom and the wonderful feeling you'll have when you stay here. You'll also enjoy gorgeous views out over Scapa Flow.

HOY SCOTTISH YOUTH HOSTEL, *Hoy. Tel. 01856/873-535. 6 Rooms, 26 beds. Rates: £6.10 per adult, £5 juniors. Credit cards not accepted.*

This basic youth hostel is on the island of Hoy, the second largest of the islands that are part of Orkney. You'll get pretty basic accommodations here, but for under £10, you can put up with a little less than extreme luxury. There are four four-room bedrooms, and two rooms with five beds. This is one of the few hostels in Scotland that doesn't include bed linens in the price. It is simple and basic, but it puts you in a great position to see fabulous cliffscapes and the Old Man of Hoy.

WHERE TO EAT

THE CREEL RESTAURANT, *Front Road, St. Margaret's Hope. Tel. 01856/831-311. £20-30. Open October to March on Saturday and Sunday from 6:30pm to 9:00pm, April to September daily from 6:30pm to 9:00pm (closed January). MasterCard and Visa accepted.*

If you're looking for fabulous dining on Orkney (or in Scotland for that matter), then stop at The Creel Restaurant. Sitting along the quay, this restaurant just seems to win one award after another, including two AA rosettes, *A Taste of Scotland* recognition, and several other industry awards. The menu changes daily, depending on what the catch of the day is, but you can expect such traditional delicacies as seared scallops sautéed in hazelnut oil, or North Ronaldsay lamb. Vegetarian dishes are also

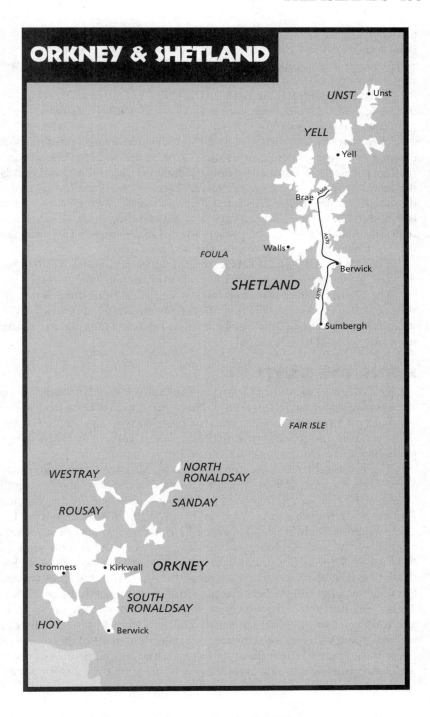

ORKNEY & SHETLAND

UNST • Unst

YELL

• Yell

A968

Brae

A970

Walls •

FOULA

Berwick

SHETLAND

A970

Sumbergh •

FAIR ISLE

WESTRAY

NORTH RONALDSAY

ROUSAY

SANDAY

Stromness •   • Kirkwall   ORKNEY

SOUTH RONALDSAY

HOY

• Berwick

provided for those who prefer that choice. Seating is limited, and the restaurant is one of the most popular and well known in this part of Scotland, so it is a good idea to call ahead for reservations during the summer months. Dress is nice casual.

WOODWICK HOUSE RESTAURANT, *Tel. 01856/751-330, Fax 01856/751-383. £20-30. Open noon to 2:00pm and 6:30pm to 9:00pm. Credit cards not accepted.*

Those in the know will tell you that Woodwick House is one of the best places to eat on Orkney. Part of the reason is the pleasant and cordial service, part is the insistence on only the freshest ingredients, and part is the talent of those preparing the meals. Woodwick House has earned a top-notch reputation (and *A Taste of Scotland* award) for their fare, which is traditional Scottish. You can expect an outstanding meal, whether it is seafood or lamb or beef. The presentation is marvelous, in fact you may feel your meal is too pretty to eat. Dress is nice casual.

THE MUSTARD SEED CAFÉ, *86 Victoria Street, Kirkwall. Tel. 01856/ 871-596. £4-9. Open 9:30am to 5:30pm. MasterCard and Visa accepted.*

The Mustard Seed is a combination Christian bookstore and craft shop that also has a small café that offers a nice selection of pastries, rolls, soup and sandwiches. Nothing exceptional, but just a nice place to pause for a bite to eat. Dress is casual.

SEEING THE SIGHTS

Let's begin your tour of Orkney in the capital city of **Kirkwall**. There are a few sights to see in this former Norse city that has been here at the head of a picturesque bay for at least the past 900 years. Its original Norse name was Kirkjuvagr, which meant *Church Bay,* signifying that the Vikings probably built a church here at this site.

The most impressive site in Kirkwall is **St. Magnus Cathedral**, *Broad Street, Kirkwall; open Monday through Saturday from 9:00am to 6:00pm and Sunday during services, which begin at 11:00am; admission is free.* St. Magnus Cathedral was founded in 1137 by Earl Rognvald Kolson in memory of his uncle Magnus Erlendson, who was killed at the demand of a jealous cousin. He became St. Magnus, and is considered the patron saint of Orkney. St. Magnus Cathedral is an interesting study in architecture for those who have that interest. Some of the original cathedral still survives, but much of what you see is as a result of additions through the centuries. Today the interior in particular is warm and inviting, despite the customary soaring ceilings. Pink sandstone columns give way to a splendid arched ceiling with exposed brick arches. As with so many of these ancient cathedrals, many of the walls are adorned with the tombstones of those who have gone before, and in this case you can see the tombstone for St. Magnus himself near the central arch.

Across from the cathedral, you'll find the ruins of the **Bishop's Palace**, *Broad Street, Kirkwall; open April through September Monday through Saturday from 9:30am to 6:00pm, Sunday from 2:00pm to 6:00pm; admission is £1.50 for adults and 75p for children.* This structure was built for Bishop William the Old. It was built in the middle of the 12th century, and rebuilt in the 15th and 16th centuries. A mortally wounded King Haakon of Norway died here after an unsuccessful military campaign further south in Scotland. The Bishop's Palace features an immense hall and a round central tower. The tower has a spiral staircase that takes you to the top of the tower and affords impressive views of St. Magnus Cathedral. Be sure and bring your camera – the views are great.

Not to be outdone, across the street from the Bishop's Palace is the **Earl's Palace**, *Watergate Street, Kirkwall; open April through September Monday through Saturday from 9:30am to 6:00pm, Sunday from 2:00pm to 6:00pm; admission is £1.50 for adults and 75p for children.* The Earl's Palace was built in 1600, for Earl Patrick Stewart, a (much despised) nephew of Mary Queen of Scots. Its French Renaissance architecture is much studied by artists and architects, as it is considered one of the finest examples of that particular architectural scheme in Scotland. It is a fine structure, and a real treat to visit, with a little something for everyone, from its fine fireplaces to its musty dungeons. The Earl's Palace is a more complete set of ruins than the Bishop's Palace, and there is still enough of the original structure standing to enable you to imagine what it must have been like once upon a time.

Across the street from both St. Magnus Cathedral and the Bishop's Palace is **The Orkney Museum**, **Tankerness House and Gardens**, *Broad Street; open October through March Monday through Saturday from 10:30am to 12:30pm and 1:30pm to 5:00pm, and April through September Monday through Saturday from 10:30am to 5:00pm and Sunday from 2:00pm to 5:00pm; admission is free from October through March, and from April through September it is £1.50 for adults and 75p for children.* This is a restored mansion/townhouse of one of the wealthier merchant's in 16th-century Kirkwall. Many fine displays in the mansion chronicle Orkney history from her earliest Stone Age inhabitants to present day. A nice variety of ancient artifacts is on display from the Stone and Iron Ages through the periods when the Picts and Vikings were the masters of Orkney.

One of the most intriguing displays is a set of *ba* balls, the object of a game played on Orkney. Each leather ball is filled with cork to help it withstand the rigors of the game, which can last upwards of seven hours and involve some 200 combatants. It is a sort of football game that is played every Christmas and New Year's Day in Kirkwall (they say rugby looks civilized compared to this game). Don't miss the marvelous gardens, which are a burst of color in the midst of the city. The gardens are open all year long.

Striking out from Kirkwall to the surrounding **Mainland** of Orkney, there are a number of things to see and do. Seemingly everywhere you drive there are signposts to this ancient ruin or that little museum. I'll list a few of my favorites, but by all means, if something looks interesting or intriguing, go see it.

First stop is south of Kirkwall on the A964 at **Orphir Church**, *Orphir*. You'll find here the ruins of the only circular medieval church in Scotland. Built in the early 12th century, I'm relatively certain it was a curiosity even then! Nearby are the remains of a 12th-century Viking Banquet Hall.

Head north on the A964 until you reach the A965, and follow the signposts for Kirkwall, **Maes Howe** and the **Ring of Brodgar**. Maes Howe may simply be one of the most stunning sites you visit on your Scottish holiday. **Maes Howe**, *Stenness, near Loch Harray; open April through September Monday through Saturday from 9:30am to 6:30pm and Sunday from 2:00pm to 6:00pm, October through March Monday through Saturday from 9:30am to 4:00pm and Sunday from 2:00pm to 4:00pm. Admission is £2.50 for adults and £1.50 for children.* When you walk into Maes Howe, you are walking where people walked nearly 5,000 years ago. Maes Howe is a Stone Age tomb that dates to 2700 BC. This type of burial chamber is known in archaeological parlance as a *passage grave*, owing to its long central passage.

You will pass down the long passage until you come to a central burial chamber, where persons of great importance – usually kings and queens – were buried. The chamber has a celestial alignment: it is aligned with the midwinter solstice and the sun shines through the narrow entrance brightly onto the far wall of the chamber on that one day of the year. You'll also shake your head when you consider the mischief of those naughty seafarers, the Vikings. At some point, a group of these intrepid mariners discovered Maes Howe for themselves, took anything of value that may have been here, and left their mark (literally) on many of the stones in the tomb in the form of Runic graffiti! Their handiwork is still easily discernible in the main chamber.

Less than two miles from Maes Howe you'll find the **Ring of Brodgar**, a wide circle of 27 standing stones. These stones stand impressively on a narrow strip of land between Lochs Harray and Stenness. A channel hewn out of solid rock circumscribes the stone circle. Archaeologists estimate these stones have been standing here since 1500 BC. As impressive as that is, consider the fact that when these stones were placed here, nearby Maes Howe was already 1,200 years old. As you consider this impressive and solemn sight, ask yourself, "Who put these stones here?" and "Why?" Many theories have been offered, and the one most agree on (although not all) is that they may have been used to track the celestial movements of the moon (perhaps to track or predict the tides).

Okay, once you've finished meditating on the cosmic significance of these flinty antiquities, head back toward **Stromness** on the A965. Stromness is considered the second town of the Mainland. Stromness is a memorable village which features narrow winding streets, cobblestones and old stone houses huddled tightly together for warmth and protection against the winds that pelt Orkney from off the Atlantic.

Despite those winds, Stromness sits at the head of a relatively sheltered bay, and it has served as a safe haven for many a mariner throughout the centuries. Vikings sailed their longboats into her harbor, and whale and herring fishermen rejoiced to be back home in Stromness once again. During the 18th and 19th centuries, the Hudson's Bay Company recruited Orcadians heavily to open North America to the fur trade, and in more recent times, soldiers, sailors and merchants used Stromness as their final port of call before heading across the Atlantic. And it is here that ferries from the *south* (Scotland) arrive on Orkney.

There isn't a lot to see or do in Stromness besides marvel at the delightful town. However, you might enjoy spending a while in the interesting **Stromness Museum**, *Alfred Street, Stromness, Tel. 01856/850-025; open daily from May through September from 10:00am to 5:00pm, October through April Monday through Saturday from 10:30am to 12:30pm and 1:30pm to 5:00pm; admission is £1.50 for adults and 75p for children.* The museum is at the south end of Victoria/Dundas/Alfred Street, and features a number of exhibits and artifacts that played a part in the history of Orkney. You'll learn about the Hudson's Bay Company's affinity to Orcadians in general, and to the citizens of Stromness in particular. You'll read about the scuttling of 74 German ships during World War I just outside of Stromness in Scapa Flow. A natural-history exhibit focuses on some of the flora and fauna you'll find on Orkney.

On the waterfront, you'll find the more contemporary **Pier Arts Centre**, *Victoria Street, Stromness, Tel. 01856/850-209; open Tuesday through Saturday from 10:30am to 12:30pm and 1:30pm to 5:00pm, and from June through August it is also open on Sunday from 2:00pm to 5:00pm; admission is free.* The Pier Arts Centre is an art gallery devoted to contemporary paintings and sculptures by local artists. It is housed in a building built in 1800, which was once inhabited by the recruiting agent for the Hudson's Bay Company. If you've been here before, come again; while there is a central core of displays, some exhibits change frequently.

When you've had your fill of Stromness, head north on the A967. About seven miles up the road, watch for signposts pointing you to **Skara Brae**, *open April through September Monday through Saturday from 9:30am to 6:30pm and Sunday from 2:00pm to 6:00pm, October through March Monday* *through Saturday from 9:30am to 4:30pm and Sunday from 2:00pm to 4:30pm; admission is £3 for adults and £1.50 for children.* In 1850, local residents weathered a fierce windstorm that blew in off the Atlantic. Now, this area of Orkney is used to terrible storms, but this particular one was worse than any ever experienced by any of these folks. Sometime after the storm passed, they made a startling discovery. At the head of the pretty Bay of Skaill, the storm had uncovered a small fishing village that had been covered by sand and grass for literally centuries. Archaeologists quickly discovered that this was a Stone Age village that had been covered up in a massive sandstorm, and with its reappearance they were able to study an intact village built sometime between 3000 BC and 2500 BC. And today, so can you.

You'll find 10 small sod-covered huts built from the native stones in the area. Each house is connected to the others via narrow passageways that were probably once covered with turf or wood and stone. You will marvel at the Stone Age ingenuity of the people who lived here as you consider beds hewn out of the stone walls, boxes and cabinets made from stone and even cupboards. As you pop out of one of the huts, step back a moment and consider the countryside around you. The barren and windswept land you see, the curving bay and the sheep and cattle grazing in the distance are probably about the same views the inhabitants of these huts had five millennia ago. What were their lives like? Where did they go when the sands claimed their homes? So many questions, so few answers.

Back on the road, you should still be heading north on the A967. As it loops around the northern end of the Mainland, the road becomes the A966. Near the village of Evie, you'll find the **Broch of Gurness**, *Evie; open April through September Monday through Saturday from 9:30am to 6:30pm and Sunday from 2:00pm to 6:30pm. Admission is £2.50 for adults and £1.50 for children.* Brochs are ancient fortifications used (probably) for defense against war-like neighbors, whether they were feuding clans or marauding Vikings. This particular broch is thought to have been built around 200 BC. A small village was gathered around the broch, and in times of trouble or tribulation, its residents took shelter within its thick protective walls. This broch even features its own spring – a must in times of siege. It is estimated that there are over 500 of these structures on Orkney, and this is considered one of the finest.

There are literally hundreds of other brochs, ruined churches and stones standing in fields, but those I have listed here are the best, in my estimation. But if you are driving about and see something that catches your eye, by all means, venture there.

SPORTS & RECREATION

Angling
• **Eric Kemp Water Sports**, *31-33 Bridge Street, Kirkwall. Tel. 01856/872-137*

Cycling
• **Orkney Cycle Centre**, *54 Dundas Street, Stromness. Tel. 01856/850-255*
• **Bobby's Cycle Centre**, *Tankerness Lane, Kirkwall. Tel. 01856/875-777*
• **Orkney Two Wheels**, *Tankerness Lane, Kirkwall. Tel. 01955/873-097*

Diving
There are a number of dive companies on Orkney:
• **The Diving Cellar**, *4 Victoria Street, Stromness, Orkney. Tel. 01856/850-055 Fax 01856/850-395; E-mail: leigh@divescapaflow.co.uk; Website: www.divescapaflow.co.uk*
• **Dolphin Scuba**, *Garisle, Burray, Orkney. Tel. 01856/731-269*
• **Eric Kemp Sports and Outdoor Centre**, *31-33 Bridge Street, Kirkwall. Tel. 01856/872-137, Fax 01856/874-750*
• **Houton Diving**, *Heatherlea, Houton, Orphir, Orkney. Tel. 01856/811-251*
• **Scapa Flow Charters**, *5 Church Road, Stromness, Orkney. Tel. 01856/850-879*
• **Scapa Flow Diving Centre**, *Burray, Orkney. Tel. 01856/731-225*
• **Scapa Flow Diving Holidays**, *Lerquoy, Outertown, Stromness, Orkney. Tel. 01856/851-110*
• **Scapa Flow Technical Diving**, *Polrudden, Pickaquay Road, Kirkwall, Orkney. Tel. 01856/874-761*
• **Stormdrift Charters**, *1 Sabiston Crescent, Weyland, Kirkwall, Orkney. Tel. 01856/873-475*
• **Stromness Diving Centre**, *Barkland, Cairston Road, Stromness, Orkney. Tel. 01856/850-624*

EXCURSIONS & DAY TRIPS

In addition to the Mainland, there are some fine sights to see on some of the other islands that can be reached via ferry from the Mainland. Those islands include Egilsay, Flotta, Graemsay, Hoy, Papa Westray, Rousay, Shapinsay, Westray and Wyre.

Arrivals & Departures By Air
The world's shortest commercial airline flight runs between Westray and Papa Westray, and you'll be in the air roughly one minute.

Arrivals & Departures By Ferry
Orkney Ferries, *Shore Street, Kirkwall, Tel. 01856/872-044, Fax 01856/872-921*, runs ferry service to these islands on a regular basis from April

through September, less frequently at other times. Fares vary slightly, but are about £5 per person and £15 per vehicle. Orkney Ferries run from Kirkwall, Houton and Tingwall on the Mainland; contact them for schedule information for the passenger-and-car ferries.

A passenger-only ferry also runs from Stromness to Hoy and Graemsay during the summer months. Call *01856/850-624* for schedule information.

Where to Stay

PIEROWALL HOTEL, *Pierowall Village, Westray. Tel. 01857/677-208, Fax 01857/677-707. 5 Rooms. Rates: £35 per person single, £30-38 per person double. Rates include breakfast. Credit cards not accepted.*

This Victorian-era home was originally built for the local Presbyterian minister, but has since been renovated to provide a comfortable place to stay if you venture to Westray. There are five rooms, but only two of them are ensuite, so if that matters to you, be sure and specify that you prefer an ensuite room when you call for reservations. The bedrooms are quite comfortably furnished, and they are pleasantly decorated.

NORTH RENDALL B&B, *North Rendall, Papa Westray. Tel. 01857/644-246, Fax 01857/644-246. 2 Rooms. Rates: £12 per person single, £12 per person double. Rates for dinner, bed and breakfast from £20 per person. Credit cards not accepted.*

If you are looking for stunning views, a working farm/ranch, wonderful hosts and a pleasant place to stay, they head for North Rendall B&B when you are on Papa Westray. Mrs. Alice Davidson runs North Rendall B&B while her rancher husband takes care of the Angus cattle on the ranch. Both are proud of their home, and anxious to share it with visitors to Papa Westray. If you decide you'd like to eat dinner with the Davidsons, that can also be arranged (Alice is very flexible). The Davidsons stress that their B&B is a non-smoking facility.

Where to Eat

PIEROWALL HOTEL RESTAURANT, *Pierowall Village, Westray. Tel. 01857/677-208, Fax 01857/677-707. £3-7. Open noon to 2:00pm for lunch and 7:00pm to 9:00pm for dinner. Rates include breakfast. Credit cards not accepted.*

The pub at the Pierowall Hotel is gaining quite a reputation for the quality of its pub grub, so if you are in Pierowall and need a bite to eat, be sure and stop by here for good, filling fare at a reasonable price. Nothing fancy, but you're sure to find something to satisfy you. If you enjoy seafood, then you'll be especially glad you came, since that is their specialty.

Visiting Orkney's Other Islands

Hoy is the second largest of the islands that belong to the group called Orkney, and it is found south of the Mainland. Its most famous site is the **Old Man of Hoy**, a massive 450-foot sandstone tower that stands on a finger of rock extending out into the sea. No roads lead here, just a four-mile-long footpath that you can pick up in the hamlet of Rathwick. The area around the Old Man of Hoy is noted for its striking cliffs, which provide ideal locations for nesting birds. Bird watchers can see a wide variety of their feathered friends here, including kittiwakes, puffins, razorbills and shags.

The eastern shore boasts a front-row seat to the **Scapa Flow**, a large natural harbor that is largely protected from the weather. For centuries, mariners have heaved a sigh of relief as they sailed safely into this relatively peaceful harbor. During both world wars of this century, Scapa Flow served an important role of harboring allied ships. One of the most dramatic events that occurred here was the scuttling of 74 captured German ships in the waters of Scapa Flow during World War I. While most have been removed, there are still a few that divers from all over the world come to check out. There is a small visitor center that features some fine photographs and exhibits focusing on the war.

Graemsay is a small island between Stromness and Hoy in the Scapa Flow. It is mostly noted for its fine views.

Flotta is located off the southeastern tip of Hoy. It is known as *The Island of the Flame*. No, it's not some mystical Celtic or Norse appellation, but rather refers to the (seemingly) eternal flame that burns from a tall oil terminal and can be seen for miles around. Flotta is also known primarily for the views it has, particularly from a point called Stanger Head.

The island of **Rousay** is located about one mile off the northeastern tip of the Mainland. It is an island of undulating terrain, and has become quite popular with trout fishermen and off-the-beaten-path hillwalkers, who head for the island's interior. There are not many roads on Rousay, but one does encircle the island, beginning and ending at the ferry slip.

Rousay has an incredible number of archaeological sites (over 200 by some estimates), and most of them are located at the southern end of the island. The most-visited site is **Midhowe Cairn**, a communal burial chamber located about five miles from the ferry. It is over 5,500 years old and nearly 100 feet long. The main passageway has small alcoves where 25 bodies were found by archaeologists. Just south of the cairn is the most impressive **Midhowe Broch**, another fine example of an ancient defensive tower.

Egilsay is just off Rousay's eastern shore, and features the fairly complete and impressive ruins of **St. Magnus Church**. Built in the 12th century in honor of the patron saint of Norway, the church has withstood years of weather and depredation. Roofless now, it sports a straight and tall round tower, one of the few left standing.

Wyre is a tiny dot of land off the southern tip of Rousay. But it is large enough to offer visitors the ruins of **Cubbie Roo's Castle**, a Viking stronghold built in 1150.

Shapinsay is the next island to consider investigating. It is a few miles northeast of Kirkwall. The most impressive sight on Shapinsay is **Balfour Castle**, home of the Balfour family. Built in 1847, the castle has an almost fairytale presence to it. Victorian architect David Bryce designed the castle. Family members conduct tours on Wednesday and Sunday afternoons. Make your reservations at the **Kirkwall Tourist Information Centre**, *6 Broad Street, Kirkwall, Tel. 01856/872-856.*

Westray is a fertile emerald isle north of Rousay. The most impressive thing to see here is **Noltland Castle**, *near Pierowall.* You'll look at the substantial ruins of this massive 16th-century castle with its square stone keeps, six dozen gun loops, tiny windows and massive walls, and you'll know immediately that it was built for protection. Mary Queen of Scots was so impressed with its builder that she invited him to become master of her household.

Papa Westray rests northeast of Westray, and is most famous for the **Knap of Howar**. This Stone Age house was built over 5,500 years ago and is billed as the oldest standing house in western Europe. It makes for some nice photos, and it's hard to imagine the lives of those who once called this home.

PRACTICAL INFORMATION FOR ORKNEY

Tourist Information
- **Kirkwall Tourist Information Centre**, *6 Broad Street, Kirkwall. Tel. 01856/872-856*
- **Stromness Tourist Information Centre**, *Stromness. Tel. 01856/850-716*

THE SHETLAND ISLANDS

The **Shetland Islands** are found 60 miles north of Orkney and 93 miles north of John O'Groats on the Scottish mainland. Over 100 islands make up this archipelago, 15 of which are inhabited (several just barely). Windswept and wild, the Shetlands provide a place to get away from the rest of the world and find some peace and solitude. The islands are typified by jagged edges, rough-hewn arches and astounding sea cliffs, all of which were chipped out of the solid rock by multiple millennia of gale-force winds and pounding surf. Sheltered all along the ragged coastline are countless oases: protected bays with sandy harbors that invite exploration.

I know it sounds a little inhospitable, but those who venture here are struck by its incredible beauty and splendid solitude. The ancient Romans ventured this far north in their seafaring, and promptly dubbed these islands *Thule*, signifying that they felt this surely must be the very edge of the world. The Shetland Islands are at the same latitude as Greenland, but thanks to the Gulf Stream, they enjoy a much milder climate than their neighbor to the west. Don't get me wrong – it can still get chilly here, especially so since the wind seems to be an ever-present partner when you are here. Lerwick is the capital, and is 200 miles from both Aberdeen and Bergen, Norway.

Shetlanders and their visitors enjoy the remarkable "simmer dim" associated with these parts – it seems perpetually light here during the summer months. Midnight golf tournaments are one of the peculiar products of this phenomenon. However, it averages out: during the winter months, there are only five hours of daylight to get your golf game or sightseeing in. During the transition months of September and October, you'll have a front-row seat to that natural light show called the *Aurora Borealis,* or *Northern Lights.*

Prehistoric ruins are scattered through the width and breadth of the Shetland Islands, mute testimony that ancient man was a pretty hardy fellow. You'll be able to visit ruins that date from the Stone and Iron Ages, as well as some of more modern construction.

There are approximately 24,000 souls that call the Shetlands home, but they are far outnumbered by the animals that live here. Estimates are that there are several million birds that nest or migrate through here, including 250,000 puffins, 300,000 gull-like fulmars, 140,000 guillemots and 30,000 gannets. If you are a bird watcher, you will be positively delighted with the numbers and varieties of birds that live in the Shetlands. Throw in another 330,000 sheep, 100,000 cattle and countless seals, and you can see that Shetlanders are far outnumbered by the fauna of the area.

Like their cousins to the south (the Orcadians of Orkney), when the Shetlanders refer to the Mainland, they speak of the largest of the Shetland Islands, not the mainland of Scotland. And yes, the Shetland Islands are the place where Shetland ponies come from. In the late 1800s they were bred for maximum strength and minimum size to enable them to work in coal mines in England. It is claimed that Shetland ponies can pull more weight per pound than Clydesdales. So, pull on your sweater, hold onto your hat, and come on up to the northern-most tip of the United Kingdom. It will be a different kind of tourism experience, but one I believe you will look back on with fondness.

UP HELLY AA FESTIVAL

Much of the culture you experience here is Norse, not Scottish. In the middle of the 15th century, a marriage was arranged between Scotland's James III and Margaret, the daughter of Christian I, the king of Denmark, Norway and Sweden. A sizable dowry was promised, with the Shetland Islands and Orkney pledged as surety. When the good King Christian couldn't come up with the dowry payment, these archipelagos became part of Scotland. Even though the Shetlands formally became part of Scotland, many of the traditions that exist on the island today are purely Norse, having been woven tightly into the fabric of Shetland life through the centuries. Take for example the **Up Helly Aa** *Festival.*

The last Tuesday of January, over 1,000 torch-bearing revelers dress in Viking costume and follow a full-size replica of a Viking longship through the streets of the city. The procession is led by the **Guizer Jarl**, *a Shetland citizen chosen for his civic accomplishments. The procession culminates at the King George V playing fields, where each of the marchers tosses their burning torches into the bowels of the longship, and the crowds watch as the ship is consumed in the flames. A fireworks display usually follows. The whole affair is reminiscent of the at-sea cremation of Viking warriors.*

ARRIVALS & DEPARTURES

By Air

British Airways, *Tel. 0345/222-111,* flies to the Shetland Islands from Aberdeen, Edinburgh, Glasgow, Inverness, Kirkwall and Wick. Flights arrive at **Sumburgh Airport** about half an hour south of Lerwick. Standard fares run about £248 for a round trip, but the airlines run specials that are sometimes as low as £122 to £200 from Aberdeen.

From the airport, you can catch a bus every hour that takes you into Lerwick. Taxis are also available, as are rental cars. A taxi ride into Lerwick will cost you about £25-30.

By Ferry

P&O Ferries, *Jamieson's Quay, Aberdeen, Tel. 01224/572-615.* P&O Ferries operates a car ferry that makes the 14-hour jaunt to the Shetlands four or five evenings per week, depending on the time of year. Twice a week there are ferries that leave in the afternoon, make a short stop in Stromness, Orkney, and then head on up to the Shetlands.

There are a number of fares available for this service. If you want to go economy, then the cost is £49-55 per person, and you get a reclining chair to sleep in (remember – this is a 14-hour, overnight ferry trip). Cabins cost from £53 per person for a six-berth economy cabin, to £93 per person for a two-berth cabin with views. Seniors get a 10% discount, and children ages 4 to 13 are half the adult rate. Children under 4 are free. These are all one-way fares; double them for a round trip.

In addition to the per-person fare, if you have a vehicle, it will cost you from £110 to £141 one way, and from £155 to £179 round trip. The price varies depending on the time of year and the size of your car. The cost for bicycles is £10 round trip.

WHERE TO STAY

Since most of the sights to see on Shetland are within easy driving distance from **Lerwick**, I have listed all the places to stay and eat in the same section.

BUSTA HOUSE HOTEL, *Brae, Shetland. Tel. 01806/522-506, Fax 01806/522-588. 20 Rooms. Rates: £55-70 single; £42-58 per person double. Rates include breakfast. MasterCard and Visa accepted.*

When your explorations take you to the northern reaches of the Mainland of Shetland, you will really enjoy staying at Busta House Hotel outside the village of Brae. Busta House Hotel is a fine three-star hotel that understands the meaning of providing first-class service to their guests. Peter and Judith Jones are your host and hostess, and they take their roles seriously.

The hotel occupies the former home of a 16th-century laird (land-owner) of Shetland. Views from the rooms are splendid, whether they look out to the Atlantic and the Jones' personal harbor, or whether they overlook the hotel's fine walled garden. The bedrooms are all comfort-able and decorated tastefully in vibrant colors. Each has a radio, televi-sion, telephone, hairdryer and tea- and coffee-making facilities. Legends of ghosts and the premature deaths of former residents and visitors to Busta House abound, and the Joneses will be more than happy to share a few of the more salty stories with you.

GRAND HOTEL, *Commercial Street, Lerwick, Shetland. Tel. 01595/692-826, Fax 01595/694-048. 22 Rooms. Rates: £62 single; £44 per person double. Rates include breakfast. MasterCard and Visa accepted.*

The Grand Hotel is located in the center of the Mainland's principal town, Lerwick. It is a handsome building with weather vane-tipped turrets, gray stonework and a stately presence. It is also one of the few four-star hotels on Shetland, and once you arrive, you'll realize they have earned every one of those stars. Each bedroom is large and quite comfortably furnished with good quality furnishings, light paint and soft floral accents. Each room is equipped with a telephone, radio, satellite television, hairdryer and tea- and coffee-making facilities. If you are going to be staying in Lerwick, this would be a great choice for accommodations.

LERWICK HOTEL, *15 South Road, Lerwick, Shetland. Tel. 01595/692-166, Fax 01595/694-419. 35 Rooms. Rates: £72 single; £44 per person double. Rates include breakfast. MasterCard and Visa accepted.*

The Lerwick Hotel is one of the largest hotels in Lerwick and the Shetlands. Located about a half mile from the downtown area of Lerwick, it sits on a hill overlooking Breiwick Bay. Most of the rooms are large, and those at the front of the hotel offer outstanding views of the shore and bay. The bedrooms are decorated with quality furnishings and attractive designer wallpaper, and are exceptionally comfortable. Each bedroom is equipped with telephone, satellite television, hairdryer and tea- and coffee-making facilities. The public rooms of the hotel are bright and cheery, and like the bedrooms, tastefully decorated. The restaurant offers stunning views as well as excellent cuisine (see the *Where to Eat* section). This is a comfortable hotel out of the hubbub of the city, but still close enough to get there quickly.

QUEEN'S HOTEL, *24 Commercial Street, Lerwick, Shetland. Tel. 01595/692-826, Fax 01595/694-048. 24 Rooms. Rates: £62; £44 per person double. Rates include breakfast. MasterCard and Visa accepted.*

Queen's Hotel is located in the center of Lerwick and right on the harbor. As you can imagine, the rooms that overlook the harbor have exquisite views (and they really do overlook the harbor – just stick your head out the window and look down, and there it is). The Queen's Hotel is housed in an old stone mansion built at the turn of this century, and its owners have turned it into a very nice place to stay. The bedrooms are simply decorated and furnished, with a variety of the usual hotel amenities, including telephone, television, hairdryer and tea- and coffee-making facilities.

WHINRIG HOUSE B&B, *12 Burgh Road, Lerwick, Shetland. Tel. 01595/693-554. 3 Rooms. Rates: £19-20 single; £17-19 per person double. Rates include breakfast. MasterCard and Visa accepted.*

Whinrig House B&B is one of the nicest B&Bs in the Shetland Islands. This four-star B&B sits in a quiet residential area in Lerwick that is still close to all that's going on downtown. There are three bedrooms, and all are decorated simply but tastefully. Only one is ensuite, so if you have that preference, be sure and specify that at the time of your reservation. Whinrig House B&B is a totally non-smoking establishment.

WESTAYRE B&B, *Muckle Roe, Brae. Tel. 01806/522-368. 2 Rooms. Rates: £16-18 single; £16-18 per person double. Dinner, Bed and Breakfast available for £25-30 per person. Rates include breakfast. MasterCard and Visa accepted.*

If you have come to the northern Mainland to see the sights and are looking for a quality B&B where you'll experience top-notch Shetland hospitality, then look no further. Westayre will satisfy all your accommodation needs. This tidy home is located on a working croft (small farm) outside of the town of Brae. Mrs. Wood is your hostess, and she will give you a warm and pleasant welcome. There are only two rooms, but both are quite comfortable and pleasantly furnished. Each room has a television and radio and tea- and coffee-making facilities. Your hostess is an expert on all to see and do in this part of the Shetlands, and she will help you plan your sightseeing if you wish.

LERWICK SCOTTISH YOUTH HOSTEL, *Islesburgh House, King Harald Street, Lerwick, Shetland. Tel. 01595/692-114, Fax 01595/696-470; E-mail: islesburgh@zetnet.co.uk. 11 Rooms, 64 beds. Rates: £7.75-9.60 adult (over 18) and £6.50-8.10 junior (under 18). Open from April through September. MasterCard and Visa accepted.*

This old Victorian mansion has recently been refurbished and the results are outstanding. If you are trying to do the Shetland Islands on a budget, this would be a good option for you. There are 11 rooms, ranging from four to nine beds. There is also a fine café on site, one of the better ones you'll find in youth hostels. The hostel is located in a nice neighborhood just a few blocks from the pier, so it is close to all that is going on while you are in Lerwick.

WHERE TO EAT

BREIWICK RESTAURANT, *15 South Street, Lerwick, Shetland. Tel. 01595/692-166, Fax 01595/694-419. £20-30. Open daily from 6:30pm to 9:00pm. MasterCard and Visa accepted.*

The Breiwick Restaurant is the main dining room for the Lerwick Hotel. Next to the food, the best thing about this restaurant is the splendid views you'll have out across Breiwick Bay. You'll find tall ceilings and large windows to complement the intimate dining experience you'll have here. Seafood is the specialty in this fine restaurant, and the chefs here have gained a well-deserved reputation for their cuisine. The menu changes frequently, but you might find such treats as stuffed filet of salmon with haddock and mustard rarebit, served with saffron jus, mussels and scallops, or the more traditional rack of Shetland lamb served in a bed of vegetables. Dress is nice casual.

BUSTA HOUSE RESTAURANT, *Brae, Shetland. Tel. 01806/522-506, Fax 01806/522-588. £10-15 for lunch and £20-30 for dinner. Open daily from 12:30pm to 2:00pm and from 6:30pm to 9:00pm. MasterCard and Visa accepted.*

The restaurant for Busta House is famed for its fine dining and wonderful atmosphere. It has earned recognition by *A Taste of Scotland* as one of the best restaurants in the Shetland Islands. Housed in a mansion that was built in 1588, you will find a pleasant and intimate dining experience when you choose to dine here. Candlelight and crystal enhance the fine traditional Scottish meals served here. While the menu changes occasionally, you can expect to find such delicious offerings as roast scallops wrapped in bacon with dill butter, or roast Shetland lamb with tarragon mousse and a madeira jus. So if you are on the northern half of the Mainland and it's getting close to dinner time, head over to the Busta House Restaurant for a great meal. It is advisable, however, to call ahead for reservations during the summer months, especially on the weekends. Dress is nice casual.

MONTY'S BISTRO, *Mounthooly Street, Lerwick, Shetland. Tel. 01595/ 696-555, Fax 01595/696-955. £5-10 for lunch and £10-20 for dinner. Open Monday through Saturday from 10:00am to 4:00pm and from 6:30pm to 9:00pm. MasterCard and Visa accepted.*

You'll find Monty's Bistro in downtown Lerwick just behind the Tourist Information Centre, and you'll be glad you did. Housed in a 100-year-old building, Monty's wowed *A Taste of Scotland* judges with their fine modern Scottish fare and intimate setting. Rough-hewn stone walls, unpretentious tables and table settings and wonderful food are what you'll find here. Raymond Smith is the proprietor and genius behind the fare. A seasoned (no pun intended) and world-renowned chef, Raymond has put Monty's on the map, and current chef Michael Skinner continues the tradition with innovative, delicious meals.

The menu changes with the seasons, but you might find such delicacies as warm smoked brown loch trout with gooseberry and horseradish chutney, or Halibut medallions with scallops and prawns in a cream sauce. Vegetarian dishes are popular here, and it is said that few prepare the Shetland lamb better than Monty's. The specialty of the house is a delicious rosemary bread that keeps locals coming back for more. If you are in the area for more than a day, it might just bring you back too. Dress is casual.

QUEEN'S HOTEL RESTAURANT, *24 Commercial Street, Lerwick, Shetland. Tel. 01595/692-826, Fax 01595/694-048. £5-10 for lunch and £10-18 for dinner. Open daily from noon to 2:00pm and from 6:00pm to 9:30pm. MasterCard and Visa accepted.*

The fine dining room for the Queens Hotel is the place to go for a satisfying and intimate dining experience. The dining room is a pleasant, quiet room with soft creams and blues, candlelight and crystal to enhance the meals served here. Fresh local produce from the land and sea are featured here, where you'll find modern Scottish fare and outstanding service. Dress is nice casual.

GOLDEN COACH CHINESE RESTAURANT, *17 Hillhead, Lerwick, Shetland. Tel. 01595/693-848, Fax 01595/695-923. £8-17. Open Monday through Friday from noon to 2:30pm and from 5:00pm to 11:30pm, and Saturday and Sunday from noon to 11:30pm. MasterCard and Visa accepted.*

If you want to try something a little different than the Scottish fare you have been eating since you arrived in Scotland, then perhaps you should try the Golden Coach Chinese Restaurant. If you do decide to stop by, you'll have a wonderful intimate dining experience here. Subdued lighting, linen and crystal enhance the feeling at this tastefully appointed restaurant. You can expect to find those dishes you would find in a Chinese food restaurant in the US: sesame chicken, cashew chicken, sweet-and-sour pork, etc. All are cooked and presented to perfection, and the service seems just a cut above most Chinese restaurants I have been in. In addition, you have a choice of several Korean, Japanese, Malaysian and Thai dishes. Dress is nice casual, and you should plan to make reservations if you decide you'd like to eat here on the weekends during the summer months.

HAVLY CENTRE, *Charlotte Street, Lerwick, Shetland. Tel. 01595/692-100. £4-12. Open Tuesday through Saturday from 10:00am to 4:45pm and Wednesday from 10:00am to 3:00pm. MasterCard and Visa accepted.*

This Norwegian café features a nice selection of homemade cakes, pizza and burgers, as well as soups and sandwiches. It's a good place to stop for a quick bite to eat and to warm yourself up a bit. The restaurant is a comfortable place to dine, especially if you have children. You'll see lots of children here, because the menu is affordable and because the restaurant caters to families. Dress is casual.

SEEING THE SIGHTS

Let's begin your visit to the Shetland Islands in **Lerwick**, its 16th-entury capital. It sits in a protected harbor along the eastern coast of the Mainland (remember, Shetlanders refer to the largest island of the 100-island chain as the Mainland). The city is a maritime city, and has been home to herring fleets and pirates for centuries, and since the 1970s, it has served as an important harbor for oil-related North Sea traffic.

Lerwick is the largest and most energetic town you'll find in the Shetland Islands. It is to Lerwick that most Shetlanders come to do their shopping and transact whatever business that needs to be transacted. The harbor is busy, with its daily traffic of fishing boats, ferries and pleasure craft. One of the first places to stop in Lerwick is the **Shetland Islands Tourism Centre**, *Market Cross, Tel. 01595/693-434, Fax 01595/695-807*. They are primed to see that you have a wonderful stay while in Shetland, and can help you plan itineraries, give you an idea of how long it will take to get from one place to another, etc. There are a number of tours available in and around the Shetland Islands, and all are registered at and advertise with the tourist office.

After visiting the tourist office, stroll to the nearby **Shetland Museum**, *Lower Hillhead Street, Tel. 01595/695-057, Fax 01595/696-729; open*

Monday, Wednesday and Friday from 10:00am to 7:00pm, and Tuesday, Thursday and Saturday from 10:00am to 5:00pm; aAdmission is free. The Shetland Islands have been inhabited for an estimated 5,000 years, and the Shetland Museum takes a look at most of that 5,000 years. Professional exhibits and interesting displays discuss topics that range from archaeology to folk tales to displays of contemporary art of local artists. As you would expect, the maritime history of the Shetlands gets quite a bit of coverage. The recent oil boom in the North Sea is given quite a bit of attention also.

I thought one of the most intriguing exhibits in the museum was that of *The Treasure of St. Ninian's Island.* St. Ninian's Island is a small island off the southwest coast of the Mainland, about four miles from Sandwick. On the island are foundations of a 12th-century chapel that Aberdeen University archaeology students began excavating in the late 1950s. While doing so, they unearthed a cache of silver – bowls, jewelry and various religious implements. It is thought that the treasure was hidden by monks who feared some thugs, probably Vikings. You can see the original treasures that were found at the site in the Royal Museum of Scotland in Edinburgh; there are a number of replicas of the find here in the Shetland Museum.

Worth a visit is **Fort Charlotte**, *open during the summer months from 9:00am to 10:00pm, and from October to December from 9:00am to 4:00pm; admission is free.* Fort Charlotte is a 17th-century fort built by Cromwellian armies to repel the Dutch, who took a disliking to it and razed it less than 10 years after it was built. The Shetlanders rebuilt it in the late 18th century. It has commanding views of the harbor, and some great photos can be taken from its ramparts.

Heading out of Lerwick (but not too far yet), you'll find **Clickhimin Broch**, dating from the beginning of the Iron Age (700 BC). It's worth a short visit, and the workmanship will absolutely amaze you. As you gaze at those stones laid precisely upon one another, it makes you wonder how long it took them to build this broch. What back-breaking work it must have been! From a distance, it actually looks as though the rocks have begun to grow together, they are so tightly knit.

Another impressive broch awaiting your visit rests south of Lerwick at **Mousa Broch**, *Mousa Island; open April through September Monday through Saturday from 9:30am to 6:00pm and Sunday from 2:00pm to 6:00pm.* Take the A970 south of Lerwick 10 miles until you come to the town of Sandwick. Take the 15-minute ferry ride over to Mousa Island. Contact Tom Jamieson, *Leebitton, Sandwick, Tel. 01950/431-367,* to schedule your trip.

You will be absolutely amazed at what you find here. Mousa Broch is thought to be the finest example of a broch anywhere in the world. When you visit, try and imagine what this broch meant to the folks that lived around it. At over 40 feet tall, with thick double walls, it must have been a massive defensive boon for those people. There are two round walls, one inside the other. In between the two walls is a staircase that ascends to sleeping and storage rooms. It is amazing that the broch has lasted in the kind of condition it is in for these many years. It is estimated that the broch has been here since about 100 BC. It is interesting to note the slight hourglass shape of the broch. That wasn't merely a nice architectural touch – it helped keep antagonists from scaling the walls.

After you've explored Mousa Broch long enough, head back over to the Mainland, and take the A970 south again, towards the airport. Watch for signs directing you to an unnumbered road and **St. Ninian's Island**. You can reach St. Ninian's Island by walking along a sandy causeway out to the island. In addition to many birds (puffins seem to love this island), you'll find the foundations of a 12th century church that was here. However, the most impressive thing about St. Ninian's Island and this small church is not what is here, but what is *not* here.

As you may have read in the Shetland Museum entry, archaeology students from Aberdeen University stumbled across ancient treasure when they began excavating this site in 1958. They discovered a horde of silver items that had probably been hidden by some monk to protect it from an impending attack. The attack apparently came, and he apparently didn't survive the attack, leaving the treasure hidden until its recovery. The originals are now in the Royal Museum of Scotland in Edinburgh, and replicas can be seen in the Shetland Museum in Lerwick. How many more of these undiscovered treasures are there, just waiting to be found?

Back to the A970 and heading south again, just before you get to the airport, watch for signs directing you to **Jarlshof**, *Sumburgh, Tel. 01950/ 460-112; the site is open all year, but the Visitor Centre is only open April through September from 9:30am to 6:30pm; admission is £2.50 for adults, £1.90 for children, and £1 for seniors.* Like Skara Brae on Orkney, Jarlshof was uncovered by gale-force winds that swept initial layers of grass, sand and dirt away from this buried village. Archaeologists had a field day uncovering the rest, and when they were completed, they had discovered evidence of no fewer than seven separate groups that had inhabited Jarlshof. From the Bronze Age to the relatively recent Viking civilization, the find was a treasure trove of archaeological information. A number of the artifacts unearthed since the windstorm are on display in the various huts.

Today it makes for an interesting and informative visit, especially if you have the handbook for the self-guided tour; it is available at the Visitors Center. As you go from one hut to another, think of what life must have been like here. What were the winters like? The scenery is breathtaking right here on the sea, but it must have been a very windy place, even three millennia ago.

Heading back towards Lerwick, watch for the signposts to Scalloway and turn off there. Scalloway is about 6 miles southwest of Lerwick, and was Shetland's capital until Lerwick's rise to prominence in the 16th and 17th centuries. Today it is still a fishing port, and also hosts traffic from the North Sea oil fields.

In Scalloway, you'll find the ruins of **Scalloway Castle**, a dark and foreboding fortress once owned by the Earl of Stewart, who also possessed much of the same spirit (dark and foreboding). The Earl was a nephew of Mary Queen of Scots, and was somewhat Machiavellian in his approach to ruling. His castle was built through forced labor, and there were few in Scalloway who mourned his execution in Edinburgh in 1615. *Admission is free, and the castle is open Monday through Saturday from 9:30am to 7:00pm and Sunday from 2:00pm to 7:00pm.*

Near the castle is the small but interesting **Scalloway Museum**, *Main Street, Scalloway,* The museum has a few interesting exhibits on the maritime history of the area; one of the most uplifting is the story of the **Shetland Bus**. During World War II, local fishermen ran arms and munitions from Shetland to hidden fjords in Norway to keep the Norwegian Freedom Fighters armed and in business. On the return trip, they brought refugees and anyone who wanted (or needed) to escape Norway. It is interesting to read of the heroism that prevailed on this far-flung rock.

Along the west coast of the Mainland is a large, peninsular-like patch of land that juts into the Atlantic Ocean. This area is known as the **West Mainland**, or more colloquially as the **Westside**. As with most of the Shetlands, various ruins of ancient origin are scattered about in this area. However, the real draw to this part of Shetland is for those who enjoy hillwalking. Undulating hills, stunning seascapes and purple heather all combine to make this an enchanting place to see afoot. Several peaks jut out of the island mantle, including the 750-foot **Sandness Hill**, which drops abruptly to the Atlantic.

Walls (pronounced *Waas*) lies on the southern portion of the West Mainland. About 2 miles outside of town on the A971 you'll find the ruins of **Staneydale Temple**. While the four-foot walls don't look much like a temple to me, I understand that someone thought the structure looked somewhat like a similar building in Malta that has also been called a temple. The thick walls made me think it might once have been a place of refuge rather than worship.

Heading onto the northern portion of the Mainland, you find a more rugged and cracked landscape, especially along the shoreline. You'll find fine seascapes, hidden coves with sandy beaches and cliffs with countless birds nesting and mating and doing what birds do. Some of the best scenery is along the western coast near **Esha Ness**.

SPORTS & RECREATION

Angling
- **Rod and Line**, *91 Harbour Street, Lerwick, Shetland. Tel. 01595/693-366*
- **Shetland Anglers Association**, *North Road, Lerwick, Shetland. Tel. 01595/ 695-903, Fax 01595/696-568; E-mail: alec.miller@zetnet.co.uk*
- **Shetland Islands Tourism Centre**, *Market Cross, Lerwick, Shetland. Tel. 01595/693-434, Fax 01595/695-807.* You can purchase fishing permits at the Tourist Information Centre.

Bird Watching Tours
- **Bressaboats and Shetland Wildlife Tours**, *Sundside, Bressay. Tel. 01595/ 693-434*
- **Delta Marine**, *5 Gladstone Terrace, Lerwick, Shetland. Tel. 01595/694-700, Fax 01595/692-685; Website: www.delta-marine.co.uk*

Cycling
- **Eric Brown's Raleigh Cycles**, *North Road, Lerwick, Shetland. Tel. 01595/ 692-709, Fax 01595/695-017*
- **Puffins Pedals**, *Mounthooly Street, Lerwick. Tel. 01595/695-065*

EXCURSIONS & DAY TRIPS

In addition to the Shetland Mainland, there are some fine sights to see on some of the other islands that can be reached via ferry from the Mainland. Those islands include Bressay, Fetlar, Foula, Noss, Papa Stour, Unst and Yell.

Arrivals & Departures By Ferry
Ferry service between the Mainland of Shetland and various of the isles found just off her shores can be arranged through the **Shetland Islands Tourism Centre**, *Market Cross, Lerwick, Shetland, Tel. 01595/693-434, Fax 01595/695-807*. There is an efficient and inexpensive ferry system that runs between the major islands in the Shetland Island chain. It is run by the **Shetland Island Council**.

Visiting Shetland's Other Islands
Foula lies 27 miles off the southwest coast of the Mainland. It is reached via a 2.5-hour ferry ride from Walls on Tuesdays, Saturdays and alternate Thursdays. Also, there is one sailing on the other Thursday from Scalloway. Foula is known as Bird Island, and as you near its cliffs, you'll

quickly understand why. Thousands upon thousands of these feathered creatures call Foula home, if only during migration and mating times. While the winged population of the island shows no hint of subsiding, the human population of the island has dwindled from a high of 400 souls a generation ago to fewer than 40 today. The western side of the island features some spectacular cliffs, one set of which plunge some 1,241 feet. These are the second highest cliffs in the United Kingdom.

Papa Stour lies just a mile or so off shore from the western Mainland of Shetland. It is reached via ferry from Burrafirth on Monday, Wednesday and Friday mornings, as well as Friday, Saturday and Sunday evenings. Papa Stour is known as the Great Island of the Priests, and it takes little imagination to envision this island as a place for ancient priests to come for solitude and serenity. Its most popular features are the sea caves and arches that have been carved by centuries of pounding surf. There are a number of ancient ruins on the island, and you can get self-guided tour pamphlets from the **Shetland Islands Tourism Centre**, *Market Cross, Lerwick, Shetland, Tel. 01595/693-434, Fax 01595/695-807.*

Yell Island is the large island due north of the Mainland, and flanked by Unst and Fetlar. Rolling hills and vast stretches of heather greet you on Yell. If you take a detour to any of its coastal areas, you are likely to see dolphins, seals and otters at play. Even the occasional whale ventures into sight every now and again. To get to Yell, drive your car to Toft and cross over to Ulsta; ferry service leaves about every 30 minutes throughout the day and early evening. The undulating countryside that typifies Yell draws walkers from all over.

Fetlar lies off the east coast of Yell, and can be reached via ferry from Gutcher in northeast Yell. The ferry departs every 30 minutes throughout the day. Fetlar has been called the Garden of Shetland, because of its rich fertile farmland (Yell and Unst must have protected it from being blown into the sea).

Unst, it is said, is the end of the British Empire. From here, the next landmass north is a long ways away. You can reach Unst by ferry from the ferryport in Gutcher on Yell. It leaves frequently throughout the day. Unst, like its two neighbors, sports some splendid seascapes, cliffs and protected harbors with nice sandy beaches.

Bressay is the large island that you see as you look across the harbor at Lerwick. It is accessible via a car and passenger ferry from Lerwick. Bressay gets overlooked by most visitors as they whisk to the eastern side of the island to head over to Noss. You can do a little walking here, and there are lighthouses at the northern and southern ends of the island to check out. But the real interest is in **Noss**, is a small island that lies due east of Bressay. It has been turned into a **National Nature Reserve** managed by the Scottish National Heritage Foundation. The island is reached via an inflatable boat, and the short ferry ride from Bressay takes about two minutes. The cost for the ride is £2.50 round trip. It runs daily from late May through the end of August. When the weather is bad, or when a red flag is flying on Noss, the ferry does not run. Check at the Tourist Information Centre in Lerwick to see if it is running.

The ragged coastline and dramatic cliffs of Noss have caused thousands of birds and tourists to flock to it. The most spectacular cliff site is the 500-foot **Noup**, and you can see countless birds hanging around it. See how many different varieties you can identify. Here's some help: some of the most prolific breeds you'll see include fulmars, gannets, guillemots, puffins, razorbills and shags. A small **visitor centre** at the ferry landing details a walk that will take you close to these nesting areas. But beware – if you get uncomfortably close, you are fair game for dive-bombing attacks by great skuas, a bird that inhabits these parts. By the way, the birds are the ones who decide if you are getting too close; your vote doesn't count.

PRACTICAL INFORMATION

Laundry Service
• **Lerwick Laundry and Dry Cleaning**, *36 Market Street, Lerwick, Shetland. Tel. 01595/693-043*

Pharmacies
• **Freefield Pharmacy**, *Lerwick, Shetland. Tel. 01595/693-502, Fax 01595/693-502. Open daily 9:00am to 5:00pm*

Post Offices
• **Lerwick Post Office**, *Commercial Street, Lerwick, Shetland.*
• **Toll Clock Post Office**, *Toll Clock Shopping Center, 26 North Road, Lerwick, Shetland*

Tourist Information
• **Shetland Islands Tourism Centre**, *Market Cross, Lerwick, Shetland. Tel. 01595/693-434, Fax 01595/695-807*

INDEX

Abbey of Iona, 440
Aberdeen, 20, 50, 101, 110, 111, 347, 348-368, 465
  Arrivals and Departures, 350
  Where to Stay, 352-354
  Where to Eat, 354-356
  Sights to See, 356-357
Aberdeen Art Gallery, 356
Aberdeen Esplanade, 357
Abbotsford House, 390
Alexander III, 47
Alloway, 19, 281
Andrew of Moray, 49
Ardvreck Castle, 324
Argyle Street, 254
Arnol Black House, 448
Aros Castle, 424
Arran Heritage Centre, 444
Art Galleries:
  Aberdeen Art Gallery, 356
  Burrell Collection, 14, 18, 27, 29, 31, 211, 256
  Glasgow Art Gallery and Museum, 18
  Hunterian Museum and Art Gallery, 18, 27, 29, 31, 44, 211, 255, 256
  Kelvingrove Art Gallery, 26, 28, 31 211, 254
  Inverness Museum and Art Gallery, 313
  McManus Art Galleries and Museum, 204
  National Gallery of Scotland, 16, 135, 188, 360
  Perth Art Gallery and Museum, 383
  Royal Scottish Academy, 25, 26, 28, 30, 33, 189

  Scottish National Portrait Gallery, 16, 25, 26, 28, 30, 33, 109, 135, 190
  Scottish National Gallery of Modern Art, 16, 25, 28, 30, 33, 135
  St. Mungo Museum, 34, 253
Arthur's Seat, 25, 28,33
Attila the Hun, 45
Aurora Borealis, 465
Ayr, 19, 93, 110, 281-287

Badenoch, Wolf of, 379
Balfour Castle, 464
Balhousie Castle, 383
Ballachulish, 29, 339
Ballater, 367, 368-372
Balliol, John, 48, 50, 51, 416
Balloch, 27, 29, 31, 263
Balloch Castle Country Park, 27, 29, 31, 263
Balmoral Castle, 20, 33, 187, 348, 358, 367
Balnakiel Bay, 322
Balnakiel Craft Village, 323
Banchory, 367
Bannockburn, 13, 27, 29, 32, 51, 273
Barras, The, 254
Bell, Alexander Graham, 36, 39, 87, 102, 187
Ben Lawer, 31, 277
Ben Lomond, 263
Ben Loyal, 318
Ben Macdui, 366
Ben More, 22, 424, 438
Ben Nevis, 38, 292, 337, 340, 343
Ben Vrackie, 385, 386
Bishop's Palace, 457
Blair Antiques, 387
Bonaparte, Napolean, 396

Bonnie Prince Charlie, 13, 16, 189, 36, 59, 60, 262, 309, 313, 314, 315, 337, 343, 412, 427
Book Festival, 182
Borders, The, 13, 14, 21, 26, 30, 34, 35, 388-423
Botanic Gardens, 34, 256
Bothwell, Lord, 57
Bowhill House and Country Park, 405
Braemar, 30, 33, 101, 367, 373-376
Braemar Castle, 14, 20, 33, 348, 358, 361, 373, 375-376
Breadalbane Folklore Centre, 280
Bressay Island, 476
Bridge of Sighs, 253
Broch of Gurness, 460
Brodick Castle, 443-444
Brodie, William, 16, 184, 185, 192
Broughton House, 421
Broughty Castle, 204
Bruce, Robert, 48
Bruce, Robert the, 13, 19, 37, 50, 51, 273, 313, 319, 333, 360, 361, 367, 394
Burns House, 414-415
Burrell Collection, 14, 18, 27, 29, 31, 211, 256
Butt of Lewis Lighthouse, 448

Caerlaverock Castle, 21, 110, 388, 390, 416
Caerlaverock Wildfowl and Wetlands Centre, 417
Callander, 27, 32, 274-276
Callanish Standing Stones, 426, 446-447
Calvin, John, 54
Camera Obscura, 25, 28, 30, 108, 183
Canmore, Malcom, 47, 178
Canongate Tolbooth, 186
Cannonball House, 183
Cape Wrath, 323
Cardhu Distillery, 364
Carloway Broch, 448
Carnoustie, 17, 93, 97
Castles:
    Ardvreck Castle, 324

Aros Castle, 424
Balfour Castle, 464
Balhousie Castle, 383
Balloch Castle, 27, 29, 31, 263
Balmoral Castle, 20, 33, 187, 348, 358, 367
Braemar Castle, 14, 20, 33, 348, 358, 361, 373, 375-376
Brodick Castle, 443-444
Broughty Castle, 204
Caerlaverock Castle, 21, 110, 388, 390, 416
Cawdor Castle, 14, 19, 30, 315
Corgarff Castle, 361
Craigievar Castle, 367-368
Crathes Castle, 367
Culzean Castle, 14, 287, 288
Doune Castle, 27, 29, 31, 273
Drumlanrig Castle, 417
Duart Castle, 424, 437
Dunluce Castle, 366
Dunnotar Castle, 110, 358, 366
Dunseverick Castle, 45
Dunvegan Castle, 32, 110, 292, 320
Edinburgh Castle, 13, 14, 16, 24-28, 30, 33, 108, 134, 138, 178, 271, 347
Eilean Donan Castle, 20, 32, 271, 294, 336
Floors Castle, 21, 26, 31, 34, 390, 408-409
Frasier Castle, 30, 33, 361-362
Fyvie Castle, 30, 33, 359
Glamis Castle, 205
Huntly Castle, 360, 377
Inverlochy Castle, 343
Inverness Castle, 313
Kildrummy Castle, 14, 20, 30, 33, 110, 348, 360-362
MacLellan's Castle, 420-421
Moy Castle, 22, 424, 437
Notland Castle, 464
St. Andrews Castle, 26, 27, 201
Scalloway Castle, 474
Stirling Castle, 14, 26, 27, 29, 31, 271, 347, 418
Threave Castle, 14, 21, 110, 388, 418-419
Tolquhon Castle, 358

Torosay Castle, 437
Urquhart Castle, 13, 29, 32, 292, 333, 334
Varick Castle, 318
Castle Douglas, 21, 418
Castle Garrison Encounter, 313
Castle Trail, 30, 33, 347, 358-362, 377
Cawdor Castle, 14, 19, 30, 315
Central Lowlands, 35, 37
Cezanne, 14, 256
Charles I, 57, 58
Charles II, 58, 59, 187, 423
Charles Rennie MacKintosh House, 27, 29, 31
Charlotte Square, 189
Clach na Cuddain, 314
Clan Donald Visitor Centre, 431-432
Clickhimin Broch, 472
Clo Mor Cliffs, 323
Connery, Sean, 102, 190
Corgarff Castle, 361
Corrieshalloch Gorge, 328
Covenanters, 58, 333, 343, 417, 419
Conventicles, 59, 423
Craigievar Castle, 367-368
Crathes Castle, 367
Cressingham, Hugh, 48-50
Cromwell, Oliver, 13, 58, 366, 472
Cromyn, Red John, 51
Cruikshank Botanic Garden, 357
Cubbie Roo's Castle, 464
Cuillin Mountains, 426
Culloden Battlefield, 13, 19, 30, 32, 36, 60, 294, 313-315, 361, 427
Culzean Castle, 14, 287, 288
Customs Regulations, 65-66

Dali, Salvadore 253, 255
Dallas Dhu Distillery, 364
Dalriada, 45
Da Vinci, Leonardo, 418
Darnley, Lord, 56, 57, 187
David II, 52, 53
Dean Gallery, 135
Declaration of Independence, 52
Deep Sea World, 17, 25, 28, 109, 191
Degas, Hilaire Germaine Edgar, 135, 189, 256

Devil's Punchbowl, 33, 376
Devolution, 60
Disbanding Act, 60
Discovery Point, 203
Diving, 103, 104, 261, 328, 346, 433, 451, 461
Dolphin watching, 109, 317
Douglas, William, 271, 272, 418
Doune, 27, 29, 31, 273-274
Doune Castle, 27, 29, 31, 273
Doyle, Sir Arthur Conan, 36, 39
Druids, 44, 46
Drumlanrig Castle, 417
Drumnadrochit, 29, 32, 334
Dryburgh Abbey, 21, 26, 30, 34, 252, 347, 388, 396-398
Duart Castle, 424, 437
Duff House, 348, 359-360
Dufftown, 377-378
Dufftown Bookshop, 378
Dumfries, 388, 412-416
Dumfries Museum and Camera Obscura, 415
Duncansby Head, 335
Dundee, 38, 202-204
Dunluce Castle, 366
Dunnet Head, 335
Dunnotar Castle, 110, 358, 366
Dunseverick Castle, 45
Dunvegan Castle, 32, 110, 292, 320
Durness, 32, 110, 292, 320

Earl of Douglas, 271, 272, 418
Earl of Hertford, 13, 53
Earl's Palace, 457
Edward I, 47, 48, 50, 51, 179, 333, 417
Edward II, 51, 52
Edward III, 52
Edinburgh, 13, 14-17, 33, 134-195
   Arrivals and Departures, 136-138
   Where to Stay, 140-161
   Where to Eat, 161-177
   Sights to See, 177-191
Edinburgh Castle, 13, 14, 16, 24-28, 30, 33, 108, 134, 138, 178, 271, 347
Edinburgh Festival, 61, 182
Edinburgh Film Festival, 182

Edinburgh Fringe Festival, 182
Edinburgh Jazz and Blues Festival, 182
Edinburgh Military Tattoo, 182
Edinburgh Zoo, 17, 25, 28, 109, 190
Egilsay, 463
Eilean Donan Castle, 20, 32, 271, 294, 336
Eisenhower, Dwight, 287, 288
El Greco, 188, 257
Elgin, 101, 377
Elgin Cathedral, 348, 378-379
Elizabeth, Queen, 37, 57, 205
Eric of Norway, 47, 48

Fair Maid's House, 353
Falls of Meashach, 328
Fergus Mor, 45
Fetlar Island, 476
Fionnphort, 438
Fort Charlotte, 472
Fingal's Cave, 438, 441
Flodden Field, 207, 402, 404
Flodden Memorial, 404
Floors Castle, 21, 26, 31, 34, 390, 408-409
Flotta, 463
Fort George, 316
Fort William, 98, 292, 294, 337-346
Foula, 475
Francois, King of France, 54
Frasier Castle, 30, 33, 361-362
Fringe Festival, 182
Fyvie Castle, 30, 33, 359

Gauguin, Paul, 135
George Square, 18, 27, 29, 31, 250
Georgian House, 189
Giant's Causeway, 441
Gladstone's Land, 108, 183
Glamis Castle, 205
Glasgow, 13, 14, 18, 19, 210-291
  Arrivals and Departures, 211-213
  Where to Stay, 215-232
  Where to Eat, 232-247
  Sights to See, 247-257
Glasgow Art Gallery and Museum, 18

Glasgow Cathedral, 18, 27, 29, 31, 211, 252
Glasgow City Chambers, 34, 250
Glasgow Green, 18, 34, 254
Glasgow Tolbooth Steeple, 252
Gleneagles, 17, 96, 97, 384
Glen Grant Distillery, 344
Glencoe, 29, 32, 337, 344
Glencoe Visitor Centre, 344
Glenfarclas Distillery, 347, 364
Glenfiddich Distillery, 347, 364, 377
Glenfinnan Monument, 337, 343
Glenlivet Distillery, 30, 33, 347, 348, 362, 363, 377
Goat Fell, 441
Goya, Francisco de, 135, 257
Graemsay, 463
Grampian Highlands, 14, 20-21, 347-387
Graves of the Kings, 22, 424, 440
Great Glen, 20, 29, 292
Greenland, 465
Guise, Mary, 53, 207

Haakon, King, 457
Haddo House, 358-359
Hadrian's Wall, 45
Haggis, 111
Hebrides, 22, 38, 323, 336, 424, 445
Henry II, 54
Henry VIII, 13, 53, 55, 401, 404
High Kirk of St. Giles, 184
Highland Games, 101, 348, 358, 373, 376
Highlands, 13, 14, 19, 20, 32, 35, 38, 292-347
Hillwalking, 93, 98, 109
Hitchhiking, 79
HMS Unicorn, 203
Holyroodhouse, Palace of, 13, 14, 16, 25-28, 30, 33, 108, 109, 123, 134, 135, 178, 186
Holy Trinity Church, 33
Home Rule, 60
Horseback riding, 99, 100, 101, 109, 195, 261, 281, 345, 346, 416, 422, 433

Horse racing, 195, 261
Hunterian Museum and Art Gallery, 18, 27, 29, 31, 44, 211, 255, 256
Huntly Castle, 360, 377
Huntly House Museum, 16, 25, 26, 28, 30, 33, 109, 186

Inchmurrin Island, 27, 29, 31, 266
Inverlochy Castle, 343
Inverness, 14, 20, 29, 32, 33, 101, 292-318
  Arrivals and Departures, 294-295
  Where to Stay, 297-309
  Where to Eat, 309-313
  Sights to See, 313-317
Inverness Castle, 313
Inverness Museum and Art Gallery, 313
Inverness Townhouse, 314
Iona, 22, 32, 345, 424, 434-438, 441
Island of Staffa, 32, 438, 441
Islands, The, 22-23, 424-477
Isle of Arran, 441-445
Isle of Mull, 22, 32, 345, 424, 434-438
Isle of Skye, 20, 22, 31, 119, 336, 424, 426-434

Jacobites, 19, 59, 262, 313-318, 336, 337, 343, 361, 376, 412
Jazz and Blues Festival, 182
James VI, 36, 56, 57, 179, 271, 412
Jedburgh, 21, 34, 252, 398-402
Jedburgh Abbey, 21, 26, 31, 34, 347, 388, 390, 401
John Knox House, 25, 27, 30, 33, 185
John O'Groats, 292, 335, 464
John Paul Jones Cottage, 416
Jones, John Paul, 36, 416

Kelso, 21, 26, 31, 34, 405-409
Kelso Abbey, 21, 26, 31, 34, 252, 347, 388, 405
Keoldale, 323
Kelvingrove Art Gallery, 26, 28, 31, 211, 254
Kildrummy Castle, 14, 20, 30, 33, 110, 348, 360-362
Killin, 32, 276-281

Kirchner, 16
Kirkcudbright, 419-422
Knap of Howar, 464
Knox, John, 25, 27, 30, 33, 36, 54, 55, 58, 134, 184, 185, 253
Kolson, Earl Reginald, 456
Koschka, 16
Kyle of Lochalsh, 22, 32, 336, 424

Lady Stair's House, 25, 28, 30, 33, 108, 184
Leith Hall, 360
Lerwick, 465, 471-472
Lewis, 445, 446
Lexington, 19
Liddell, Eric, 36
Linlithgow, 17, 26, 206, 211, 262-263, 396
Linlithgow Castle, 26, 53, 206
Linn of Dee, 33, 348, 375
Linn of Quioch, 376
Loch Assynt, 324
Loch Buie, 437
Loch Broom, 324
Loch Cluanie, 336
Loch Duich, 20, 336
Loch Katrine, 19
Loch Linnhe, 292
Loch Leven, 338, 339, 342
Loch Lomond, 19, 27, 29, 31, 38, 98, 110
Loch Morar, 38
Loch Ness, 13, 14, 20, 29, 32, 38, 102, 292, 294, 317, 328-334, 335, 347
Loch Ness Exhibit, 29, 32, 334
Loch Tay, 32, 276, 277, 280
Luib Croft Museum, 432
Luskentyre, 450

MacAlpin, Kenneth, 47
MacBeth, 22, 37, 47, 315, 424, 440
MacDonald, Flora, 16, 19, 36, 313, 427, 433
MacGregor, Rob Roy, 18, 252, 253, 276, 280, 388, 396
MacKintosh, Charles Rennie, 18, 255
MacLellan's Castle, 420-421
Maes Howe, 22, 44, 426, 452, 458

Mallaig, 22, 424
Malt Whiskey Trail, 20, 30, 33, 347, 358, 362-364
Mary Queen of Scots, 13, 16, 17, 26, 36, 37, 53-57, 1324, 179, 184, 187, 206, 207, 253, 271, 313, 360, 401, 412, 457, 464
Mary Queen of Scots House, 26, 31, 34, 401-402
Massacre of Glencoe, 29, 32, 337, 342, 344
Matisse, Henri, 16
Maybole, 287
McManus Art Galleries and Museum, 204
McMurchow, Donald, 323
Melrose, 21, 26, 30, 34, 390-396
Melrose Abbey, 21, 26, 30, 34, 252, 347, 388, 390, 394-395
Mendelssohn, Felix, 441
Mentieth, Sir John, 50, 51
Midhouse Cairn, 463
Midhowe Broch, 463
Ming Dynasty, 14, 18, 256
Monet, Claude, 135, 188, 356
Moscow, 38
Mound, The, 188
Mousa Broch, 472
Moy Castle, 22, 424, 437
Mull, Isle of, 22, 32, 345, 424, 434-438
Mull Museum, 438
Munros, 32, 93
Museum of the Black Watch, 384
Museum of Childhood, 17, 25, 27, 30, 33, 109, 185
Museum of Transport, 18, 27, 29, 31, 255

Napier, John, 39
National Covenant, 58
National Gallery of Scotland, 16, 135, 188, 360
Necropolis, 18, 253
Nessie Hunting, 102
Ness Islands, 314
New Town, 135

Noss Island, 476, 477
Noss Island National Nature Reserve, 476
Notland Castle, 464
Noup, 477

Oban, 22, 31, 101, 119, 345-346, 424
Old Course, 17, 97, 200, 202
Old High Church, 314
Old Town, 135
Orkney, 22, 23, 38, 44, 47, 323, 424, 426, 451-466
Orkney Museum, 457
Orphir Church, 458
Osbourne the Blacksmith, 361

Palace of Holyroodhouse, 13, 14, 16, 25-28, 30, 33, 108, 109, 123, 134, 135, 178, 186
Papa Stour, 476
Passage Graves, 44
Passport requirements, 64-65
Peebles, 409-412
Pentland Firth, 451
People's Palace, 254
People's Story, 186
Perth, 347, 380-384
Perth Art Gallery and Museum, 383
Phone cards, 88, 91
Picasso, Pablo, 16, 135
Picts, 45-46
Pissarro, Camille, 356
Pitlochry, 385-387
Pitlochry Festival Theatre, 387
Pitlochry Power Station and Dam, 387
Polarama, 203
Pollock House, 257
Pope Alexander VI, 179
Pope John XXII, 52
Pope Julius, 11, 179
Princes Street Gardens, 25, 26, 28, 33, 109, 138, 188
Provand's Lordship house, 34, 253
Provost Ross's House, 356
Provost Skene's House, 356-357

Queen Elizabeth Forest Park, 98
Queen's Own Highland Regimental
    Museum, 316

Radio stations, 86
Raphael, 135, 189
Reformation, 54
Reilig Oran, 22, 424, 440
Rembrandt Van Rijn, 135, 189, 255
Renoir, Pierre Auguste, 135
Rental cars, 75-78, 137
Riccio, David, 56, 187
Ring of Broadgar, 458
River Ness, 32, 294
Robert the Bruce, 13, 19, 37, 50, 51,
    273, 313, 319, 333, 360, 361, 367,
    394
Rodel, 450
Rodin, Auguste, 14, 18, 257
Round-abouts, 73
Roundheads, 58
Rowardennan, 27, 29, 31
Roy, Rob, 18, 252, 253, 276, 388, 396
Royal Botanic Gardens, 17, 25, 28,
    135, 190
Royal Deeside, 205, 366
Royal Dornoch, 93, 96, 97
Royal Mile, 16, 17, 24, 25, 27, 30, 33,
    108, 109, 134, 135, 138, 178
Royal Museum of Scotland, 16, 25,
    28, 30, 33, 108, 135, 187, 472
Royal Scottish Academy, 25, 26, 28,
    30, 33, 189
Royal Troon, 93, 96, 97, 289
Rubens, Peter Paul, 135, 189
Rugby, 92

Sailing, 102, 195, 281
St. Andrews, 17, 26, 27, 33, 93,
    196-202, 379
St. Andrews Castle, 26, 27, 201
St. Andrews Cathedral, 26, 27, 201,
    314
St. Andrews Golf Course, 96, 97
St. Clement's Church, 450
St. Columba, 22, 37, 39, 46, 314, 357,
    424

St. Columba Centre, 438
St. Finian, 440
St. John's Kirk, 380, 382
St. Kentigern Cathedral, (see Glasgow
    Cathedral)
St. Machar, 357
St. Machar's Cathedral, 357
St. Magnus, 456
St. Magnus Cathedral, 456, 457
St. Michael's Church, 416
St. Michael's Parish Church, 207
St. Mungo, 251-253
St. Mungo Museum, 34, 253
St. Ninian, 39, 46, 439
St. Ninian's Island, 473
St. Rule's Tower, 201
Satrosphere, 357
Scalloway Castle, 474
Scalloway Museum, 474
Scalpay, 450
Scapa Flow, 458, 463
Scone Palace, 384
Scotch Whisky Heritage Centre, 25,
    28, 30, 33, 183
Scoti, 45
Scotland's Best Restaurants, 113-117
Scotland's Best Places to Stay, 120-
    133
Scott, Robert Falcon, 203
Scott, Sir Walter, 18, 21, 26, 30, 34,
    39, 250, 252, 253, 359, 388, 390,
    394-397, 404, 441
Scott's Courtroom, 404
Scott's View, 390, 396
Scottish Crannog Centre, 280
Scottish National Portrait Gallery, 16,
    25, 26, 28, 30, 33, 109, 135, 190
Scottish National Gallery of Modern
    Art, 16, 25, 28, 30, 33, 135
Scottish Tourist Board, 79-80
Scuba Diving, 103, 104, 261, 328,
    346, 433, 451, 461
Selkirk, 402-405
Selkirk Glass, 405-406
Sgaoth Aird, 450
Shakespeare, William, 37, 315
Shawbost School Museum, 448

Shetland Bus, 474
Shetland Islands, 22, 23, 38, 46, 424, 426, 464-477
Shetland Museum, 471, 473
Shopping, 105
Silicon Glen, 61
Simmer Dim, 38, 91, 465
Skara Brae, 22, 44, 426, 452, 459-460, 473
Skye, Isle of, 20, 22, 31, 119, 336, 424, 426-434
Skye Heritage Centre, 432
Smith, Adam, 37, 39
Smoo Cave, 32, 320, 320-323
Soccer, 92, 93, 261
Speyside Cooperage, 363
Staneydale Temple, 474
Stevenson, Robert Louis, 16, 37, 39, 343, 434, 441, 448
Stewart, James, 52
Stewart, Patrick, 457
Stewart, Robert, 52
Stirling, 13, 19, 26, 29, 31, 93, 267-273
Stirling Bridge, 49, 50, 272
Stirling Castle, 14, 26, 27, 29, 31, 271, 347, 418
Stirling Town Jail, 271
Stonehaven, 366
Stonehenge, 44, 447
Stone of Destiny, 48, 49, 179, 384
Stone of Scone, 48, 49, 179, 384
Stornoway, 446
Strathisla Distillery, 364
Summer Time, 62, 91
Surfing, 104, 451
Sweetheart Abbey, 390-416

Tarbert, 449, 450
Teddy Bear Museum, 394
Telephones, 88-91
Television stations, 86
Tennyson, Alfred, 441
Threave Castle, 14, 21, 110, 388, 418-419
Threave Gardens, 419
Tipping, 87, 113
Titian, 189

Tobermory, 435-438
Tolbooth Kirk, 183
Tolquhon Castle, 358
Tongue, 32, 292, 317, 318
Torosay Castle and Gardens, 437
Tron Steeple, 254
Troon, 288-289
Trossachs, The, 18, 38, 267, 274, 276
Tsar of Russia, 314
Turnberry, 93, 98

Uig, 449
Ullapool, 20, 32, 292, 317, 323-328
Ullapool Museum and Visitor Centre, 327
Unst, 476
Up Helly AA Festival, 466
Urquhart Castle, 13, 29, 32, 292, 333, 334

Van Dyck, Sir Anthony, 135, 189, 405
Van Gogh, Vincent, 135, 189
Varick Castle, 318
Victoria, Queen, 187, 250, 441
Vikings, 46, 47, 187, 458, 460, 464, 466, 472, 473

Wallace, William, 13, 19, 26, 33, 37, 40, 49, 50, 272-273, 366, 377, 398
Warenne, John de, 48, 49
Watt, James, 37, 39, 250
West Highland Museum, 343West Highland Way, 98
Westray, 464
Whistler, James MacNeill, 18, 255
Wigtown, 422-423
William of Orange, 59, 344
William Wallace Monument, 26, 27, 29, 34, 272
William Wallace Statue, 26, 30, 398
Windsurfing, 102, 195, 281, 334, 345, 416, 433
Wordsworth, William, 441
Writer's Museum, 25, 28, 30, 33

Yell Island, 476

THINGS CHANGE!

Phone numbers, prices, addresses, quality of food, etc, all change. If you come across any new information, we'd appreciate hearing from you. No item is too small! Send us an e-mail note at: Jopenroad@aol.com, contact the author directly at danielmcq@juno.com – or write us at:

Scotland Guide
Open Road Publishing, P.O. Box 284
Cold Spring Harbor, NY 11724

TRAVEL NOTES

TRAVEL NOTES

TRAVEL NOTES

TRAVEL NOTES

TRAVEL NOTES

TRAVEL NOTES

TRAVEL NOTES

TRAVEL NOTES